Study Guide

for use with

Economics

Eighth Edition

David Colander
Middlebury College

Prepared by
David Colander
Jenifer Gamber

 McGraw-Hill Irwin

Boston   Burr Ridge, IL   Dubuque, IA   New York   San Francisco   St. Louis
Bangkok   Bogotá   Caracas   Kuala Lumpur   Lisbon   London   Madrid   Mexico City
Milan   Montreal   New Delhi   Santiago   Seoul   Singapore   Sydney   Taipei   Toronto

Study Guide for use with
ECONOMICS
David Colander

Published by McGraw-Hill/Irwin, an imprint of The McGraw-Hill Companies, Inc., 1221 Avenue of the
Americas, New York, NY 10020. Copyright © 2010, 2008 by The McGraw-Hill Companies, Inc. All rights reserved.

1 2 3 4 5 6 7 8 9 0 PAT/PAT 0 9

ISBN: 978-0-07-724721-8
MHID: 0-07-724721-3

www.mhhe.com

Contents

Preface

We wrote this study guide to help you do well in your economics course. We know that even using a great book such as the Colander textbook, studying is not all fun. The reality is: most studying is hard work and a study guide won't change that. Your text and lectures will give you the foundation for doing well. So the first advice we will give you is:

1. Read the textbook.
2. Attend class.

We cannot emphasize that enough. Working through the study guide will not replace the text or lectures; this study guide is designed to help you retain the knowledge from the text and classroom by practicing the tools of economics. It is not an alternative to the book and class; it is **in addition to them**.

Having said that, we should point out that buying this guide isn't enough. You have to *use* it. Really, if it sits on your desk, or even under your pillow, it won't do you any good. Osmosis only works with plants. This study guide should be well worn by the end of the semester—dog-eared pages, scribbles beneath questions, some pages even torn out. It should look used.

WHAT CAN YOU EXPECT FROM THIS BOOK?

This study guide concentrates on the terminology and models in your text. It does not expand upon the material in the textbook; it reinforces it. It primarily serves to give you a good foundation to understanding principles of economics. Your professor has chosen this study guide for you, suggesting that your economics exams are going to focus on this kind of foundational understanding. You should be sure of this: if your professor is going to give you mainly essay exams, or complex questions about applying the foundations (such as the more difficult end-of-chapter questions in your textbook) this study guide will not be enough to ace that exam.

To get an idea of what your exams will be like, ask your professor to take a look at these questions and tell the class whether they are representative of the type of questions that will be on the exam. And if they will differ, how.

HOW SHOULD YOU USE THIS STUDY GUIDE?

As we stated above, this book works best if you have attended class and read the book. Ideally, you were awake during class and took notes, you have read the textbook chapters more than once, and have worked through some of the questions at the end of the chapter. (So, we're optimists.)

Just in case the material in the book isn't fresh in your mind, before turning to this study guide it is a good idea to refresh your memory about the material in the text. To do so:

1. Read through the margin comments in the text; they highlight the main concepts in each chapter.
2. Turn to the last few pages of the chapter and reread the chapter summary.
3. Look through the key terms, making sure they are familiar. (O.K., we're not only optimists, we're wild optimists.)

Even if you do not do the above, working through the questions in the study guide will help to tell you whether you really do know the material in the textbook chapters.

STRUCTURE OF THE STUDY GUIDE

This study guide has two main components: (1) a chapter-by-chapter review and (2) pretests based upon groups of chapters.

Chapter-by-chapter review
Each chapter has eight elements:

1. A chapter at a glance: A brief exposition and discussion of the learning objectives for the chapter.
2. Short-answer questions keyed to the learning objectives.
3. A test of matching the terms to their definitions.

4.   Problems and applications.
5.   A brain teaser.
6.   Multiple choice questions.
7.   Potential essay questions
8.   Answers to all questions.

Each chapter presents the sections in the order that we believe is most beneficial to you. Here is how we suggest you use them:

Chapter at a Glance: These should jog your memory about the text and lecture. If you don't remember ever seeing the material before, you should go back and reread the textbook chapter. The numbers in parentheses following each learning objective refer to the page in the text that covers that objective. Remember, reading a chapter when you are thinking about a fantasy date is almost the same as not having read the chapter at all.

Short-Answer Questions: The short-answer questions will tell you if you are familiar with the learning objectives. Try to answer each within the space below each question. Don't just read the questions and assume you can write an answer. Actually writing an answer will reveal your weaknesses. If you can answer them all perfectly, great. But, quite honestly, we don't expect you to be able to answer them all perfectly. We only expect you to be able to sketch out an answer.

Of course, some other questions are important to know. For example, if there is a question about the economic decision rule and you don't remember that it excludes past costs and benefits, you need more studying. So the rule is: Know the central ideas of the chapter; be less concerned about the specific presentation of those central ideas.

After you have sketched out all your answers, check them with those at the end of the chapter and review those that you didn't get right. Since each question is based upon a specific learning objective in the text, for those you didn't get right, you may want to return to the textbook to review the material covering that learning objective.

Match the Terms and Concepts to Their Definitions: Since the definitions are listed, you should get most of these right. The best way to match these is to read the definition first, and then find the term on the left that it defines. If you are not sure of the matching term, circle that definition and move on to the next one. At the end, return to the remaining definitions and look at the remaining terms to complete the matches. After completing this part, check your answers with those in the back of the chapter and figure out what percent you got right. If that percent is below the grade you want to get on your exam, try to see why you missed the ones you did and review those terms and concepts in the textbook.

Problems and Applications: Now it's time to take on any problems in the chapter. These problems are generally more difficult than the short-answer questions. These problems focus on numerical and graphical aspects of the chapter.

Working through problems is perhaps one of the best ways to practice your understanding of economic principles. Even if you are expecting a multiple choice exam, working through these problems will give you a good handle on using the concepts in each chapter.

If you expect a multiple choice exam with no problems, you can work through these fairly quickly, making sure you understand the concepts being tested. If you will have a test with problems and exercises, make sure you can answer each of these questions accurately.

Work out the answers to all the problems in the space provided before checking them against the answers in the back of the chapter. Where our answers differ from yours, check to find out why. The answers refer to specific pages in the textbook so you can review the text again too.

Most of the problems are objective and have only one answer. A few are interpretative and have many answers. We recognize that some questions can be answered in different ways than we did. If you cannot reconcile your answer with ours, check with your professor. Once you are at this stage— worrying about different interpretations—you're ahead of most students and, most likely, prepared for the exam.

A Brain Teaser: This section consists of one problem that is generally one step up in the level of difficulty from the "Problems and Applications" exercises or is a critical–thought question. It is designed to provide a challenge to those students who have studied the way we have suggested.

Multiple Choice Questions: The next exercise in each chapter is the multiple choice test. It serves to test the breadth of your knowledge of the text material. Multiple choice questions are not the final arbiters of your understanding. They are, instead, a way of determining whether you have read the book and generally understood the material.

Take this test after having worked through the other questions. Give the answer that most closely corresponds to the answer presented in your text. If you can answer these questions you should be ready for the multiple choice part of your exam.

Work through all the questions in the test before grading yourself. Looking up the answer before you try to answer the questions is a poor way to study. For a multiple choice exam, the percent you answer correctly will be a good predictor of how well you will do on the test.

You can foul up on multiple choice questions in two ways—you can know too little and you can know too much. The answer to knowing too little is obvious: Study more—that is, read the chapters more carefully (and maybe more often). The answer to knowing too much is more complicated. Our suggestions for students who know too much is not to ask themselves "What is the answer?" but instead to ask "What is the answer the person writing the question wants?" Since, with these multiple choice questions, the writer of many of the questions is the textbook author, ask yourself: "What answer would the textbook author want me to give?" Answering the questions in this way will stop you from going too deeply into them and trying to see nuances that aren't supposed to be there.

For the most part questions in this study guide are meant to be straightforward. There may be deeper levels at which other answers could be relevant, but searching for those deeper answers will generally get you in trouble and not be worth the cost.

If you are having difficulty answering a multiple choice question, make your best guess. Once you are familiar with the material, even if you don't know the answer to a question you can generally make a reasonable guess. What point do you think the writer of the question wanted to make with the question? Figuring out that point and then thinking of incorrect answers may be a way for you to eliminate wrong answers and then choose among the remaining options.

Notice that the answers at the end of the chapter are not just the lettered answers. We have provided an explanation for each answer — why the right one is right and why some of the other choices are wrong. If you miss a question, read that rationale carefully. If you are not convinced, or do not follow the reasoning, go to the page in the text referred to in the answer and reread the material. If you are still not convinced, see the caveat on the next page.

Potential Essay Questions: These questions provide yet another opportunity to test your understanding of what you have learned. Answering these questions will be especially helpful if you expect these types of questions on the exams. We have only sketched the beginning of an answer to these. This beginning should give you a good sense of the direction to go in your answer, but be aware that on an exam a more complete answer will be required.

Questions on Appendixes: In the chapters we have included a number of questions on the text appendixes. To separate these questions from the others, the letter A precedes the question number. They are for students who have been assigned the appendixes. If you have not been assigned them (and you have not read them on your own out of your great interest in economics) you can skip these.

Answers to All Questions: The answers to all questions appear at the end of each chapter. They begin on a new page so that you can tear out the answers and more easily check your answers against ours. We cannot emphasize enough that the best way to study is to answer the questions yourself first, and then check out our answers. Just looking at the questions and our answers may tell you what the answers are but will not give you the chance to see where your knowledge of the material is weak.

Pretests

Most class exams cover more than one chapter. To prepare you for such an exam, we provide multiple choice pretests for groups of chapters. These pretests consist of 20-40 multiple choice questions from the selected group of chapters. These questions are identical to earlier questions so if you have done the work, you should do well on these. We suggest you complete the entire exam before grading yourself.

We also suggest taking these under test conditions. Specifically,

Use a set time period to complete the exam.
Sit at a hard chair at a desk with good lighting.

Each answer will tell you the chapter on which the question is based, so if you did not cover one of the chapters in the text for your class, don't worry if you get that question wrong. If you get a number of questions wrong from the chapters your class has covered, worry.

There is another way to use these pretests that we hesitate to mention, but we're realists so we will. That way is to forget doing the chapter-by-chapter work and simply take the pretests. Go back and review the material you get wrong.

However you use the pretests, if it turns out that you consistently miss questions from the same chapter, return to your notes from the lecture and reread your textbook chapters.

A FINAL WORD OF ADVICE

That's about it. If you use it, this study guide can help you do better on the exam by giving you the opportunity to use the terms and models of economics. However, we reiterate one last time: The best way to do well in a course is to attend every class and read every chapter in the text as well as work through the chapters in this study guide. Start early and work consistently. Do not do all your studying the night before the exam.

THANKS AND A CAVEAT

We and our friends went through this book more times than we want to remember. All the authors proofed the entire book, as did our good friends, Pam Bodenhorn and Helen Reiff. We also had some superb students, Andrew Chong, Eric Elderbrock, Samuel Carson Parnell, and Jing Zhuang go through it. (Our sincere thanks go to them for doing so.) Despite our best efforts, there is always a chance that there's a correct answer other than the one the book tells you is the correct answer, or even that the answer the book gives is wrong. If you find a mistake, and it is a small problem about a number or an obvious mistake, assume the error is typographical. If that is not the case, and you still think another answer is the correct one, write up an alternative rationale and e-mail Professor Colander the question and the alternative rationale. Professor Colander's e-mail is:

colander@middlebury.edu.

When he gets it he will send you a note either thanking you immensely for finding another example of his fallibility, or explaining why we disagree with you. If you're the first one to have pointed out an error he will also send you a copy of an honors companion for economics—just what you always wanted, right?

David Colander
Jenifer Gamber

ECONOMICS AND ECONOMIC REASONING

● CHAPTER AT A GLANCE

This review is based upon the learning objectives that open the chapter.

1a. Economics is the study of how human beings coordinate their wants and desires, given the decision-making mechanisms, social customs, and political realities of the society. (4)

1b. Three central coordination problems any economy must solve are: (5)
- What, and how much, to produce.
- How to produce it.
- For whom to produce it.

Most economic coordination problems involve scarcity.

2. If the marginal benefits of doing something exceed the marginal costs, do it. If the marginal costs of doing something exceed the marginal benefits, don't do it. This is known as the economic decision rule. (8)

You really need to think in terms of the marginal, or "extra" benefits (MB) and marginal, or "extra" costs (MC) of a course of action. Also, ignore sunk costs.

Economic decision rule:
If MB>MC →<u>Do more of it</u> because "it's worth it."

If MB<MC→<u>Do less of it</u> because "it's not worth it."

NOTE: The symbol "→" means "implies" or "logically follows."

3. Opportunity cost is the basis of cost/benefit reasoning; it is the benefit forgone, or the cost of the next-best alternative to the activity you've chosen. That cost should be less than the benefit of what you've chosen. (9)

Opportunity cost → "What must be given up in order to get something else." Opportunity costs are often "hidden." You need to take into consideration <u>all</u> opportunity costs when making a decision.

4. Economic reality is controlled by economic forces, social forces, and political forces. (10-12)

What happens in a society can be seen as the reaction and interaction of these 3 forces.

- *Economic forces: The market forces of demand, supply, prices, etc.*

- *Social and cultural forces: Social and cultural forces can prevent economic forces from becoming market forces.*

- *Political and legal forces: Political and legal forces affect decisions too.*

5. Microeconomics considers economic reasoning from the viewpoint of individuals and builds up; macroeconomics considers economic reasoning from the aggregate and builds down. (15)

Microeconomics (micro) → concerned with some particular segment of the economy. Macroeconomics (macro) → concerned with the entire economy.

6a. <u>Positive economics</u> is the study of what is, and how the economy works. (17)

Deals with "what is" (objective analysis).

6b. <u>Normative economics</u> is the study of what the goals of the economy should be. (18)

Deals with "what ought to be" (subjective).

6c. The _art of economics_ is the application of the knowledge learned in positive economics to the achievement of the goals determined in normative economics. (18)

The art of economics is sometimes referred to as "policy economics."

"Good" policy tries to be objective. It tries to weigh all the benefits and costs associated with all policy options and chooses that option in which the benefits outweigh the costs to the greatest degree.

● SHORT-ANSWER QUESTIONS

1. What are the three central problems that every economy must solve?

2. What is scarcity? What are two elements that comprise scarcity? How do they affect relative scarcity?

3. How does deduction differ from induction?

4. State the economic decision rule.

5. Define opportunity cost.

6. What is the importance of opportunity cost to economic reasoning?

7. What is an economic force? What are the forces that can keep an economic force from becoming a market force?

8. How does microeconomics differ from macro-economics? Give an example of a macroeconomic issue and a microeconomic issue.

9. Define positive economics, normative economics, and the art of economics. How do they relate to one another?

MATCHING THE TERMS
Match the terms to their definitions

____ **1.** abduction	**a.** Additional benefit above what you've already derived.
____ **2.** art of economics	**b.** Additional cost above what you've already incurred.
____ **3.** deduction	**c.** If benefits exceed costs, do it. If costs exceed benefits, don't.
____ **4.** economic decision rule	**d.** The study of individual choice, and how that choice is influenced by economic forces.
____ **5.** economic force	**e.** Necessary reactions to scarcity.
____ **6.** economic model	**f.** The benefit forgone, or the cost, of the next-best alternative to the activity you've chosen.
____ **7.** economic policy	**g.** The study of what is, and how the economy works.
____ **8.** economic principle	**h.** The insight that a market economy, through the price mechanism, will allocate resources efficiently.
____ **9.** economics	**i.** The study of the economy as a whole, which includes inflation, unemployment, business cycles, and growth.
____ **10.** efficiency	**j.** The study of how human beings coordinate their wants.
____ **11.** experimental economics	**k.** Goods available are too few to satisfy individuals' desires.
____ **12.** induction	**l.** The application of the knowledge learned in positive economics to the achievement of the goals determined in normative economics.
____ **13.** invisible hand	**m.** An economic force that is given relatively free rein by society to work through the market.
____ **14.** invisible hand theorem	**n.** The price mechanism.
____ **15.** macroeconomics	**o.** A framework that places the generalized insights of theory in a more specific contextual setting.
____ **16.** marginal benefit	**p.** A commonly-held economic insight stated as a law or general assumption.
____ **17.** marginal cost	**q.** Achieving a goal as cheaply as possible.
____ **18.** market force	**r.** Action taken by government to influence economic actions.
____ **19.** microeconomics	**s.** Study of what the goals of the economy should be.
____ **20.** natural experiment	**t.** Cost that has already been incurred and cannot be recovered.
____ **21.** normative economics	**u.** A combination of deduction and induction.
____ **22.** opportunity cost	**v.** Method of reasoning that begins with almost self-evident principles and develops models and conclusions based on those principles.
____ **23.** positive economics	**w.** Method of reasoning in which one develops general principles by looking for patterns in the data.
____ **24.** precepts	**x.** A naturally occuring event that approximates a controlled experiment.
____ **25.** scarcity	**y.** A branch of economics that studies the economy through controlled laboratory experiments.
____ **26.** sunk cost	**z.** Rules that conclude that a particular course of action is preferable.
____ **27.** theorems	**aa.** Propositions that are logically true based on the assumptions in a model.

● PROBLEMS AND APPLICATIONS

1. State what happens to scarcity for each good in the following situations:

    a. New storage technology allows college dining services to keep peaches from rotting for a longer time. (Good: peaches).

    b. More students desire to live in single-sex dormitories. No new single-sex dormitories are established. (Good: single-sex dormitory rooms).

2. State as best you can:
    a. The opportunity cost of going out on a date tonight that was scheduled last Wednesday.

    b. The opportunity cost of breaking the date for tonight you made last Wednesday.

    c. The opportunity cost of working through this study guide.

    d. The opportunity cost of buying this study guide.

3. Assume you have purchased a $15,000 car. The salesperson has offered you a maintenance contract covering all major repairs for the next 3 years, with some exclusions, for $750.

    a. What is the sunk cost of purchasing the maintenance contract? Should this sunk cost be considered when deciding to purchase a maintenance contract?

    b. What is the opportunity cost of purchasing that maintenance contract?

    c. What information would you need to make a decision based on the economic decision rule?

    d. Based upon that information how would you make your decision?

4. State for each of the following whether it is an example of political forces, social forces, or economic forces at work:

    a. Warm weather arrives and more people take Sunday afternoon drives. As a result, the price of gasoline rises.

    b. In some states, liquor cannot be sold before noon on Sunday.

    c. Minors cannot purchase cigarettes.

    d. Many parents will send money to their children in college without the expectation of being repaid.

● A BRAIN TEASER

1. Suppose you are a producer of hand-crafted picture frames. The going market price for your frames is $250 a piece. No matter how many frames you sell your revenue per unit (equal to the selling price per unit) is constant at $250 per frame. However, your per unit costs of producing each additional picture frame are not constant. Suppose the following table summarizes your costs of producing picture frames. Use cost/benefit analysis to determine the most economical (profit maximizing) number of frames to produce given the price per unit and the accompanying cost schedule shown. What are your total profits per week?

# of Frames	Price	Total Cost
0	$250	$0
1	$250	$25
2	$250	$75
3	$250	$150
4	$250	$300
5	$250	$560

● MULTIPLE CHOICE

Circle the one best answer for each of the following questions:

1. Economic reasoning:
    a. provides a framework with which to approach questions.
    b. provides correct answers to just about every question.
    c. is only used by economists.
    d. should only be applied to economic business matters.

2. Scarcity could be reduced if:
    a. individuals work less and want fewer consumption goods.
    b. individuals work more and want fewer consumption goods.
    c. world population grows and world production remains the same.
    d. innovation comes to a halt.

3. In the textbook, the author focuses on coordination rather than scarcity as the central point of the definition of economics because:
    a. economics is not really about scarcity.
    b. scarcity involves coercion, and the author doesn't like coercion.
    c. the author wants to emphasize that the quantity of goods and services depends upon human action and the ability to coordinate that human action.
    d. the concept "scarcity" does not fit within the institutional structure of the economy.

4. In the U.S. economy, who is in charge of organizing and coordinating overall economic activities?
    a. Government.
    b. Corporations.
    c. No one.
    d. Consumers.

5. You bought stock A for $10 and stock B for $50. The price of each is currently $20. Assuming no tax issues, which should you sell if you need money?
    a. Stock A.
    b. Stock B.
    c. There is not enough information to tell which to sell.
    d. You should sell an equal amount of both.

6. In deciding whether to go to lectures in the final weeks the semester, you should:
    a. include tuition as part of the cost of that decision.
    b. not include tuition as part of the cost of that decision.
    c. include a portion of tuition as part of the cost of that decision.
    d. only include tuition if you paid it rather than your parents.

7. In making economic decisions you should consider:
    a. marginal costs and marginal benefits.
    b. marginal costs and average benefits.
    c. average costs and average benefits.
    d. total costs and total benefits, including past costs and benefits.

8. According to the economic decision rule, if
   MB>MC, one should:
   a. do less.
   b. do more.
   c. do nothing
   d. exit the market.

9. In arriving at a decision, a good economist
   would say that:
   a. one should consider only total costs and
   total benefits.
   b. one should consider only marginal costs and
   marginal benefits.
   c. after one has considered marginal costs and
   benefits, one should integrate the social and
   moral implications and reconsider those
   costs and benefits.
   d. after considering the marginal costs and
   benefits, one should make the decision on
   social and moral grounds.

10. In making decisions economists primarily use:
    a. monetary costs.
    b. opportunity costs.
    c. benefit costs.
    d. dollar costs.

11. The opportunity cost of reading Chapter 1 of a
    38-chapter text:
    a. is about 1/38 of the price you paid for the
    book because the chapter is about 1/38 of
    the book.
    b. is zero since you have already paid for the
    book.
    c. has nothing to do with the price you paid for
    the book.
    d. is 1/38 the price of the book plus 1/38 the
    price of tuition for the course.

12. Rationing devices that our society uses
    include:
    a. the invisible hand only.
    b. the invisible hand and social forces only.
    c. the invisible hand and political forces only.
    d. the invisible hand, social forces, and political
    forces.

13. If at Female College there are significantly more
    females than males (and there are not a
    significant number of gays or off-campus
    dating opportunities), economic forces:

a. will likely be pushing for females to pay on
dates.
b. will likely be pushing for males to pay on
dates.
c. will likely be pushing for neither to pay on
dates.
d. are irrelevant to this issue. Everyone knows
that the males always should pay.

14. Individuals are prohibited from practicing
    medicine without a license. The legal
    prohibition is a direct example of:
    a. the invisible hand.
    b. social forces.
    c. political forces.
    d. market forces.

15. Which of the following is most likely an
    example of a microeconomic topic?
    a. The effect of a flood in the Midwest on the
    price of bottled water.
    b. How a government policy will affect infla-
    tion.
    c. The relationship between unemployment and
    inflation.
    d. Why an economy goes into a recession.

16. Which of the following is most strongly an
    example of a macroeconomic topic?
    a. The effect of a frost on the Florida orange
    crop.
    b. Wages of cross-country truckers.
    c. How the unemployment and inflation rates
    are related.
    d. How income is distributed in the United
    States.

17. The statement, "The distribution of income
    should be left to the market," is:
    a. a positive statement.
    b. a normative statement.
    c. an art-of-economics statement.
    d. an objective statement.

18. "Given certain conditions, the market achieves
    efficient results" is an example of:
    a. a positive statement.
    b. a normative statement.
    c. an art-of-economics statement.
    d. a subjective statement.

POTENTIAL ESSAY QUESTIONS

You may also see essay questions similar to the "Problems & Applications" and "A Brain Teaser" exercises.

1. Respond to the following statement: "Theories are of no use to me because they are not very practical. All I need are the facts because they speak for themselves."

2. The United States is one of the wealthiest nations on earth, yet our fundamental economic problem is scarcity. How can this be?

3. Does economics help teach us how to approach problems, or does it give us a set of answers to problems?

ANSWERS

SHORT-ANSWER QUESTIONS

1. The three central problems that every economy must solve are (1) what and how much to produce, (2) how to produce it, and (3) for whom to produce it. (5)

2. Scarcity occurs when there are not enough goods available to satisfy individuals' desires. Scarcity has two elements, our wants and our means of fulfilling those wants. Since each of these two elements can change, relative scarcity can also change. If we can reduce our wants, relative scarcity will be reduced. Likewise if we can increase our efforts to produce more goods or if technological changes allow people to produce more using the same resources, relative scarcity will be reduced. (5)

3. Deduction is a method of reasoning in which one deduces a theory based on a set of almost self-evident principles while induction develops theories based on patterns in the data. Induction is more data driven. (5)

4. If the marginal benefits of doing something exceed the marginal costs, do it. If the marginal costs of doing something exceed the marginal benefits, don't do it. (8)

5. Opportunity cost is the benefit forgone by undertaking an activity. Indeed, it is the benefit forgone of the next best alternative to the activity you have chosen. Otherwise stated, it is what must be given up in order to get something else. (9-10)

6. Opportunity cost is the basis of cost/benefit economic reasoning. It takes into account benefits of all other options, and converts these alternative benefits into costs of the decision you're now making. In economic reasoning, opportunity cost will be less than the benefit of what you have chosen. (9-10)

7. An economic force is the necessary reaction to scarcity. All scarce goods must be rationed in some way. If an economic force is allowed to work through the market, that economic force becomes a market force. The invisible hand is the price mechanism, the rise and fall of prices that affects our incentives and guides our actions in a market. Social and political forces can keep economic forces from becoming market forces. (10-12)

8. Microeconomics is the study of how individual choice is influenced by economic forces. Microeconomics focuses on a particular segment of the economy, like how a specific market price and quantity sold is determined. Macroeconomics is the study of the economy as a whole. It considers the problems of inflation, unemployment, business cycles, and growth. (15)

9. Positive economics is the study of what is and how the economy works. Normative economics is the study of what the goals of the economy should be. The art of economics is the application of the knowledge learned in positive economics to the achievement of the goals determined in normative economics. (17-18)

ANSWERS

MATCHING

1-u; 2-l; 3-v; 4-c; 5-e; 6-o; 7-r; 8-p; 9-j; 10-q; 11-y; 12-w; 13-n; 14-h; 15-i; 16-a; 17-b; 18-m; 19-d; 20-x; 21-s; 22-f; 23-g; 24-z; 25-k; 26-t; 27-aa.

ANSWERS

PROBLEMS AND APPLICATIONS

1. a. Scarcity will fall because fewer peaches will rot. (5)
   b. Scarcity of single-sex dorm rooms will rise since the number of students desiring single-sex dorm rooms has risen, but the number available has not. (5)

2. a. The opportunity cost of going out on a date tonight that was scheduled last Wednesday is the benefit forgone of the best alternative. If my best alternative was to study for an economics exam, it would be the increase in my exam grade that I would have otherwise gotten had I studied. Many answers are possible. (9-10)

b. The opportunity cost of breaking the date for tonight that I made last Wednesday is the benefit forgone of going out on that date. It would be all the fun I would have had on that date. Other answers are possible. (9-10)

c. The opportunity cost of working through this study guide is the benefit forgone of the next-best alternative to studying. It could be the increase in the grade I would have received by studying for another exam, or the money I could have earned if I were working at the library. Many answers are possible. (9-10)

d. The opportunity cost of buying this study guide is the benefit forgone of spending that money on the next-best alternative. Perhaps it is the enjoyment forgone of eating two pizzas. Other answers are possible. (9-10)

3. a. The sunk cost of purchasing the maintenance contract is the $15,000 cost of the car because it is a cost that has already been incurred and cannot be recovered. Sunk costs should always be ignored when making a current decision because only marginal costs are relevant to the current decision. (7)

b. The opportunity cost of purchasing the maintenance contract is the benefit I could receive by spending that $750 on something else, such as a moon roof. (9-10)

c. I would need to know the benefit of the maintenance contract to assess whether the cost of $750 is worthwhile. (7-8)

d. For me the benefit of the maintenance contract is the expected cost of future repairs that would be covered and the peace of mind of knowing that future repairs are covered by the contract. The cost is the opportunity cost of using the $750 in another way. Notice that the cost of a decision includes opportunity costs only; it does not include sunk costs because they are not relevant. If the benefit exceeds the cost, do it. If the cost exceeds the benefit, do not do it. (7-8)

4. a. This is an example of an economic force. (10)

b. This is an example of political forces. Some states have laws, called blue laws, against selling liquor on Sundays altogether or selling it before noon. (10-12)

c. This is an example of a political force. This is a federal law. (10-12)

d. This is an example of a social force. (10-12)

ANSWERS

A BRAIN TEASER

1. The most economical (profit-maximizing) quantity of frames to produce is 4 frames. This is because the marginal benefit of producing frames (the revenue per unit equal to the price per unit of $250) exceeds the marginal (extra) cost of producing frames through the first 4 frames produced. The 5th frame should not be produced because the marginal benefit (the price received) is less than the marginal (extra) cost of production. You would be adding more to your costs than to your revenues and thereby reducing your profits. Your profit would total $700 per week if you produce 4 frames. (6-7)

(Q)	Price = Marginal Benefit	Total Cost (TC)	Marginal Cost	Total Revenue (TR=PQ)	Profit TR−TC
0	$250	$0	—	$0	$0
1	$250	$25	$25	$250	$225
2	$250	$75	$50	$500	$425
3	$250	$150	$75	$750	$600
4	$250	$300	$150	$1000	$700
5	$250	$560	$260	$1250	$690

ANSWERS

MULTIPLE CHOICE

1. a As discussed on pages 5 and 6, the textbook author clearly believes that economic reasoning applies to just about everything. This eliminates c and d. He also carefully points out that it is not the only reasoning that can be used; hence b does not fit. So the correct answer must be a.

2. b   On page 5 of the textbook, the author states that the problem of scarcity depends upon our wants and our means of fulfilling those wants. An implication of this is that scarcity could be reduced if individuals worked more and wanted less.

3. c   On page 5 of the textbook the author emphasizes the human action reason for focusing on coordination. He explicitly points out that scarcity is important, but that the concept of coordination is broader.

4. c   As discussed on page 10, the invisible hand of the market coordinates the activities and is a composite of many individuals rather than just any one individual. If you were tempted to say b, corporations, your instincts are right, but the "overall" eliminated that as a possible answer.

5. c   As is discussed on page 7 of the book, in making economic decisions you consider that only costs from this point on are relevant; historical costs are sunk costs and therefore have no relevance. Since the prices of the stocks are currently the same, it doesn't matter which you sell.

6. b   As discussed on page 7, in economic decisions, you only look at costs from this point on; sunk costs are sunk costs, so tuition can be forgotten. Economic decisions focus on forward-looking marginal costs and marginal benefits.

7. a   The economic decision rule is "If marginal benefits exceed marginal costs, do it." As is discussed on pages 7 and 8 of the text, the relevant benefits and relevant costs to be considered are *marginal* (additional) costs and *marginal* benefits. The answer d is definitely ruled out by the qualifying phrase referring to past benefits and costs. Thus, only a is correct.

8. b   The economic decision rule is "If marginal benefits exceed marginal costs, do it." See page 8 of the text.

9. c   As the textbook points out on page 7, economists use a framework of costs and benefits initially, but then later they add the social and moral implications to their conclusions. Adding these can change the estimates of costs and benefits, and in doing so can change the result of economic analysis, so there is an integration between the two. (This was a hard question that required careful reading of the text to answer correctly.)

10. b   As discussed on page 9 of the text, opportunity costs include measures of nonmonetary costs. The other answers either do not include all the costs that an economist would consider, or are simply two words put together. The opportunity costs include the benefit forgone by undertaking an activity and should always be included in measuring marginal costs.

11. c   As discussed on pages 7 and 9-10, the correct answer is that it has nothing to do with the price you paid since that is a sunk cost that has already been paid, so a and d are wrong. The opportunity cost is not zero, however, since there are costs of reading the book. The primary opportunity cost of reading the book is the value of the time you're spending on it, which is determined by what you could be doing with that time otherwise.

12. d   As discussed on page 10 of the text, all of these are rationing devices. The invisible hand works through the market and thus is focused on in economics. However, the others also play a role in determining what people want, either through legal means or through social control.

13. a   As discussed on page 11 of the text, if there are significantly more of one gender than another, dates with that group must be rationed out among the other group. Economic forces will be pushing for the group in excess quantity supplied (in this case women) to pay. Economic forces may be pushing in that direction even though historical forces may push us in the opposite direction. Thus, even if males pay because of social forces, economic forces will be pushing for females to pay.

14. c As discussed on pages 11 and 12, laws are political forces.

15. a As discussed on page 15, macroeconomics is concerned with inflation, unemployment, business cycles and growth. Microeconomics is the study of individuals and individual markets.

16. c As discussed on page 15, macroeconomics is concerned with inflation, unemployment, business cycles, and growth. Microeconomics is the study of individuals and individual markets. The distribution of income is a micro topic because it is concerned with the distribution of income among individuals.

17. b As discussed on pages 17 and 18, this could be either a normative or an art-of-economics statement, depending on whether there is an explicit "given the way the real-world economy operates." This qualifier is not there, so "normative" is the preferable answer. After all, normative economics deals with what *should* be.

18. a As discussed on pages 17 and 18 this is a positive statement. It is a statement about *what is,* not about what should be.

━━━━━ ANSWERS ━━━━━

POTENTIAL ESSAY QUESTIONS

The following are annotated answers. They indicate the general idea behind the answer.

1. Theories are practical because they are generalizations based on real-world observations or facts. They enable us to predict and to explain real-world economic behavior. Because they are generalizations, they enable us to avoid unnecessary details or facts. The drawback, however, is that because they are generalizations, at times there will be exceptions to the prediction we would generally expect to observe.

Facts, on the other hand, do not always speak for themselves. One can often be overwhelmed by a large set of data or facts. Not until one systematically arranges, interprets, and generalizes upon facts, tying them together, and distilling out a theory (general statement) related to those facts, do they take on any real meaning. In short, theory and facts are inseparable in the scientific process because theory gives meaning to facts and facts check the validity of theory.

2. The United States is still faced with scarcity because we are unable to have as much as we would like to have. Our resources (as vast as they are) are still scarce relative to the amount of goods and services we would like to have (indeed, our wants appear to be unlimited).

3. Economics is a methodology, or an approach to how we think about the world. It does not come to us equipped with a whole set of solutions to complex real-world problems. However, it may help shed some light on the complexities of real-world issues and thus help us to find solutions.

THE PRODUCTION POSSIBILITY MODEL, TRADE, AND GLOBALIZATION

CHAPTER AT A GLANCE

This review is based upon the learning objectives that open the chapter.

1. The production possibilities curve shows the trade-off (or opportunity cost) between two things. (25-27)

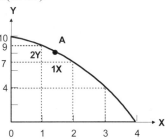

The slope tells you the opportunity cost of good X in terms of good Y. In this particular graph you have to give up 2 Y to get 1 X when you're around point A.

2. The principle of increasing marginal opportunity cost states that opportunity costs increase the more you concentrate on the activity. In order to get more of something, one must give up ever-increasing quantities of something else. (27-28)

    The following production possibility curve and table demonstrate the principle of increasing marginal opportunity cost.

    Production Possibility Curve

Production Possibility Table

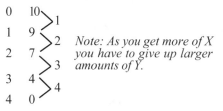

X	Y	Opportunity cost of X (amount of Y which must be forgone)
0	10	1
1	9	2
2	7	3
3	4	4
4	0	

Note: As you get more of X you have to give up larger amounts of Y.

3. In general, the production possibility curve is bowed outward, meaning that in order to get more and more of something, we must give up ever-increasing quantities of something else. The outward bow of the production possibility curve is the result of comparative advantage. (28-29)

    Some resources are better suited for the production of certain goods than they are for the production of other goods. The outward bow of the production possibility curve reflects that when more and more of a good is produced, we must use resources whose comparative advantage is in the production of the other good.

4. Countries can consume more if they specialize in those goods for which they have a comparative advantage and trade. (32-37)

    Country A can produce 30Y or 10X, or any combination thereof, while Country B can produce 20Y or 30X or any combination thereof. Since country A has a comparative advantage in Y, it should produce 30Y and Country B should produce 30X. If they divide the goods equally, each can consume 15 units of each good, or point C in the graph on the next page. Each can consume beyond its individual production possibilities.

Constructing a production possibility curve that shows the combination of goods these two countries can produce together is useful. You can draw this curve by connecting three points: if both produce good X, if both produce good Y, and if each specializes in the good in which it has a comparative advantage. This is done below.

5. Globalization and outsourcing is a response to the forces of the law of one price. (37-39)

The law of one price states that wages of workers in one country will equal the wages of equal workers in countries with similar institutions. If wages differ sufficiently, companies will relocate jobs to a low-wage country until parity is reestablished.

Remember: all jobs cannot be outsourced. Every country has, by definition, a comparative advantage in the production of some good if the other country has a comparative advantage in the production of another good.

See also, Appendix A: "Graphish: The Language of Graphs."

⬤ SHORT-ANSWER QUESTIONS

1. Design a grade production possibility curve for studying economics and English, and show how it demonstrates the concept of opportunity cost.

2. State the principle of increasing marginal opportunity cost.

3. What would the production possibility curve look like if opportunity cost were constant?

4. What happens to the production possibility curve when people specialize and trade? Why do specialization and trade make individuals better off?

5. What is the positive effect of globalization for firms? What is the negative effect?

6. State the law of one price. How is it related to globalization and outsourcing?

MATCHING THE TERMS
Match the terms to their definitions

____ 1. comparative advantage

____ 2. globalization

____ 3. laissez-faire

____ 4. law of one price

____ 5. outsourcing

____ 6. principle of increasing marginal opportunity cost

____ 7. productive efficiency

____ 8. production possibility curve

____ 9. production possibility table

a. A curve measuring the maximum combination of outputs that can be obtained from a given number of inputs.

b. Achieving as much output as possible from a given amount of inputs or resources.

c. An economic policy of leaving coordination of individuals' actions to the market.

d. In order to get more of something, one must give up ever-increasing quantities of something else.

e. Table that lists a choice's opportunity cost by summarizing alternative outputs that can be achieved with your inputs.

f. The advantage that attaches to a resource when that resource is better suited to the production of one good than to the production of another good.

g. The relocation to foreign countries of production once done in the United States.

h. Wages of (equal) workers in one country will not differ significantly from wages in another institutionally similar country.

i. The increasing integration of economies, cultures, and institutions across the world.

PROBLEMS AND APPLICATIONS

1. Suppose a restaurant has the following production possibility table:

Resources devoted to pizza in % of total	Output of pizza in pies per week	Resources devoted to spaghetti in % of total	Output of spaghetti in bowls per week
100	50	0	0
80	40	20	10
60	30	40	17
40	20	60	22
20	10	80	25
0	0	100	27

a. Plot the restaurant's production possibility curve. Put output of pizza in pies on the horizontal axis.

b. What happens to the opportunity cost of making spaghetti as the number of bowls of spaghetti made increases?

c. What would happen to the production possibility curve if the restaurant found a way to toss and cook pizzas faster?

b. What is the per unit opportunity cost of increasing the production of guns from 20 to 30? From 40 to 50?

c. What happens to the opportunity cost of producing guns as the production of guns increases?

d. What would happen to the production possibility curve if the restaurant bought new stoves and ovens that cooked both pizzas and spaghetti faster?

d. What is the per unit opportunity cost of increasing the production of butter from 10 to 15? From 20 to 25?

2. Suppose Ecoland has the following production possibility table:

% resources devoted to production of guns	Number of guns	% resources devoted to production of butter	Pounds of butter
100	50	0	0
80	40	20	5
60	30	40	10
40	20	60	15
20	10	80	20
0	0	100	25

a. Plot the production possibility curve for the production of guns and butter. Put the number of guns on the horizontal axis.

e. What happens to the opportunity cost of producing butter as the production of butter increases?

f. Given this production possibility curve, is producing 26 guns and 13 pounds of butter possible?

g. Is producing 34 guns and 7 pounds of butter possible? Is it efficient?

3. Using the following production possibility tables and using production possibility curves, show how the United States and Japan would be better off specializing in the production of either food or machinery and then trading rather than producing both food and machinery themselves and not trading.

United States Production per year		Japan Production per year	
Food (tons)	Machinery (1000 units)	Food (tons)	Machinery (1000 units)
10	0	12.5	0
8	5	10.0	1
6	10	7.5	2
4	15	5.0	3
2	20	2.5	4
0	25	0.0	5

4. Assume that France can produce wine for 25 euros per bottle and can produce butter for 5 euros per pound. Assume that Italy can produce wine for 16 euros per bottle and butter for 10 euros per pound.

   a. In terms of pounds of butter, what is the opportunity cost of producing wine in each country?

   b. Who has the comparative advantage in producing butter?

   c. To obtain the greatest combined production possibilities, which country should specialize in wine and which should specialize in butter?

d. What is likely to happen to each country's consumption possibilities if each specializes in the good for which it has a comparative advantage and then trades?

⬤ **A BRAIN TEASER**

1. Consider the production possibilities for an entire nation. Within any national economy there are only two general kinds of products that can be produced–consumer products and capital products. Consumer products (e.g., food, clothes, medical services, etc.) satisfy our wants directly when we use them and while we consume them. Capital products (e.g., machines and other plant and equipment) satisfy our wants indirectly and in the future because they increase our productivity and help us produce even more products over time. Answer the following questions based on the production possibilities of consumer and capital products for a national economy shown in the following graph.

   a. Does production possibility A or B provide the greatest amount of current consumption? Why?

   b. What is the opportunity cost of moving from point B to point A?

c. Consider the choice of currently producing a relatively large amount of consumer products shown at point B (which means, given limited resources, relatively few capital products can be produced), compared to producing a relatively large amount of capital products now, shown at point A (which means relatively few consumer products can be produced). Which of these two points (or combinations of consumer and capital goods production) do you think will increase the production possibilities (shift the curve to the right) the most over time, giving rise to the greatest rate of economic growth? Why? *(Hint: Whenever workers have more capital, such as factories and machinery, to work with, they become more productive.)*

● MULTIPLE CHOICE

Circle the one best answer for each of the following questions:

1. If the opportunity cost of good X in terms of good Y is 2Y, so you'll have to give up 2Y to get one X, the production possibility curve would look like:
a. a.
b. b.
c. c.
d. a, b and c.

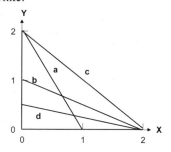

2. If the opportunity cost of good X in terms of good Y is 2Y, so you'll have to give up 2Y to get one X, the production possibility curve would look like:
a. a.
b. b.
c. c.
d. d.

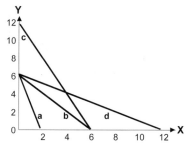

3. If the opportunity cost of good X in terms of good Y is 2Y, so you'll have to give up 2Y to get one X, the production possibility curve could look like:
a. A only.
b. B only.
c. C only.
d. A, B, or C.

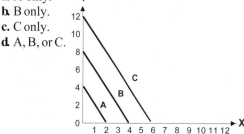

4. If the opportunity cost is constant for all combinations, the production possibility curve will look like:
a. a.
b. b.
c. c.
d. d.

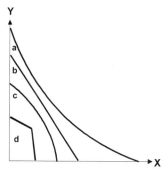

5. If the principle of increasing marginal opportunity cost applies at all points, using the graph for question 4, the production possibility curve looks like:
a. a.
b. b.
c. c.
d. d.

6. Given the accompanying production possibility curve, when you're moving from point C to point B the opportunity cost of butter in terms of guns is:
a. 1/3.
b. 1.
c. 2.
d. 3/2.

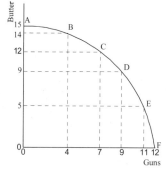

7. In the graph for question 6, in the range of points between A and B there is:
    a. a high opportunity cost of guns in terms of butter.
    b. a low opportunity cost of guns in terms of butter.
    c. no opportunity cost of guns in terms of butter.
    d. a high monetary cost of guns in terms of butter.

8. In the accompanying production possibility diagram, point A would be:

    a. an efficient point.
    b. a superefficient point.
    c. an inefficient point.
    d. a non-attainable point.

9. The efficiency of producing computers is increasing each year. Which of the four arrows would demonstrate the appropriate shifting of the production possibility curve?

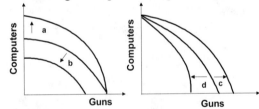

    a. a.
    b. b.
    c. c.
    d. d.

10. Say that methods of production are tied to particular income distributions, so that choosing one method will help some people but hurt others and that the society's income distribution is one of its goals. Say also that method A produces significantly more total output than method B. In this case:

    a. method A is more efficient than method B.
    b. method B is more efficient than method A.
    c. if method A produces more and gives more to the poor people, method A is more efficient.
    d. one can't say whether A or B is more efficient.

11. If the United States and Japan have production possibility curves as shown in the diagram below, at what point would their consumption possibilities most likely be after trade?
    a. A.
    b. B.
    c. C.
    d. D.

12. If countries A and B have production possibility curves A and B respectively, country A has a comparative advantage in the production of:
    a. no good.
    b. both goods.
    c. good X only.
    d. good Y only.

13. If countries X and Y have production possibility curves I and II respectively, which curve represents their combined production possibilities if they specialize and trade?
    a. I
    b. II
    c. III
    d. IV

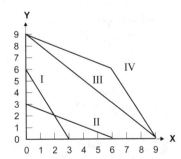

14. Suppose country A can produce either 100 cars or 50 tractors, or any combination thereof, while country B can produce either 200 cars or 50 tractors, or any combination thereof, and both countries consume both goods. Which of the following combination of goods can be produced only if the countries specialize and trade:
    a. 300 cars, 0 tractors.
    b. 0 cars, 100 tractors.
    c. 200 cars, 50 tractors.
    d. 300 cars, 100 tractors.

15. When trade is allowed between two countries, the slope of the combined production possibility curve is determined by the country with the:
    a. highest output.
    b. lowest output.
    c. highest opportunity cost.
    d. lowest opportunity cost.

16. Outsourcing in the United States is evidence that:
    a. the United States does not have any comparative advantages.
    b. the U.S. dollar is valued too low.
    c. the law of one price doesn't hold.
    d. the law of one price is affecting global production.

17. Globablization:
    a. is decreasing in importance.
    b. increases competition.
    c. reduces the need to specialize.
    d. reduces productivity.

18. According to the law of one price:
    a. wages will eventually be the same for every industry.
    b. wages will eventually be the same in every country.
    c. wage differences cannot continue unless they reflect differences in productivity.
    d. wage differences can continue as long as product prices can differ among countries.

19. Assuming productivity differentials diminish, the law of one price will likely result in:
    a. a decline in nominal U.S. wages.
    b. a rise in nominal U.S. wages.
    c. a decline in the value of the U.S. dollar.
    d. a rise in the value of the U.S. dollar.

20. Because of international competition and the ease with which technology is transferable among many nations with similar institutional structures, we can expect the wages for workers with similar skills to:
    a. increase in developing countries faster than they increase in developed nations.
    b. decrease in developing countries while they increase in developed nations.
    c. increase in developing countries while they decrease in developed nations.
    d. decrease in both developed and developing countries.

A1. In the graph below, point A represents:

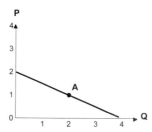

    a. a price of 1 and a quantity of 2.
    b. a price of 2 and a quantity of 2.
    c. a price of 2 and a quantity of 1.
    d. a price of 1 and a quantity of 1.

A2. The slope of the line in the graph below is
    a. 1/2.
    b. 2.
    c. minus 1/2.
    d. minus 2.

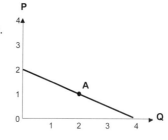

A3. At the maximum and minimum points of a nonlinear curve, the value of the slope is equal to
    a. 1.
    b. zero.
    c. minus 1.
    d. indeterminate.

A4. Which of the four lines in the graphs below has the largest slope?

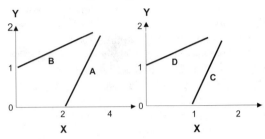

   a. A.
   b. B.
   c. C.
   d. A and C.

A5. Which of the following equations represents the line depicted in the graph to question A2?
   a. $P = 2 - .5Q$.
   b. $P = 2 - 2Q$.
   c. $Q = 4 - 2P$.
   d. $Q = 2 - .5P$.

A6. Suppose the demand curve is represented by $P = -2Q + 8$. Which of the following equations represents a *shift to the right* in that demand curve, with no change in slope?
   a. $P = -Q + 8$.
   b. $P = -2Q + 10$.
   c. $P = -2Q + 6$.
   d. $P = -4Q + 8$.

● POTENTIAL ESSAY QUESTIONS

You may also see essay questions similar to the "Problems & Applications" and "A Brain Teaser" exercises.

1.   What did Adam Smith mean when he said, "It is not from the benevolence of the butcher, the brewer, or the baker, that we expect our dinner, but from their regard to their own interest" (*Wealth of Nations*, Book 1, Chapter 2)? How does this quotation relate to specialization?

2.   Your study partner tells you that because wages are higher in the United States than in many other countries, eventually all U.S. jobs will be outsourced. How do you respond?

ANSWERS

SHORT-ANSWER QUESTIONS

1. The production possibility curve below shows the highest combination of grades you can get with 20 hours of studying economics and English. The grade received in economics is on the vertical axis and the grade received in English is on the horizontal axis. The graph tells us the opportunity cost of spending any combination of 20 hours on economics and English. For example, the opportunity cost of increasing your grade in economics by 6 points is decreasing your English grade by 4 points (a 2/3-point reduction in English grade for each one-point improvement in economics grade). (26-28)

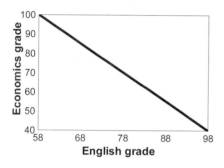

2. The principle of increasing marginal opportunity cost states that in order to get more of something, one must give up ever-increasing quantities of something else. (27-28)

3. Such a production possibility curve would be a straight line connecting the maximum number of units of each product that could be produced if all inputs were devoted to one or the other good. (26-27)

4. The production possibility curve shifts out with trade. By concentrating on those activities for which one has a comparative advantage and trading those goods for goods for which others have a comparative advantage, individuals can end up with a combination of goods to consume that would not be attainable without trade. (32-37)

5. The rewards for winning in a global market are bigger because the market is larger. The negative effect is that the firm faces more competitors, some of which may have lower costs. (37-40)

6. The law of one price is that wages of workers in one country will not differ significantly from the wages of equal workers in another institutionally similar country. Globalization means that firms will seek low-cost areas for production throughout the world. Outsourcing is the result of differing wages among countries. As the high-wage country outsources jobs to lower-wage countries, wages will tend to equalize. So, outsourcing is the result of the law of one price in action. (41)

ANSWERS

MATCHING

1-f; 2-i; 3-c; 4-h; 5-g; 6-d; 7-b; 8-a; 9-e.

ANSWERS

PROBLEMS AND APPLICATIONS

1. **a.** The restaurant's production possibility curve is shown below. (25-27)

    b. The opportunity cost of spaghetti increases because the number of pizza pies that must be given up to make an additional bowl of spaghetti increases as the number of bowls of spaghetti produced increases. (29-31)

    c. If the restaurant found a way to toss and cook pizzas faster, the production possibility curve would rotate out along the pizza axis as shown below. (29-31)

d. The production possibility curve would shift out to the right as shown in the figure below. (29-31)

2. a. The production possibility curve is a straight line as shown below. (28-31)

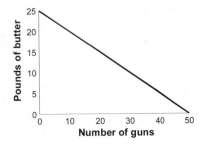

b. The opportunity cost of increasing the production of guns from 20 to 30 is 0.5 pounds of butter per gun. The opportunity cost of increasing the production of guns from 40 to 50 is also 0.5 pounds of butter per gun. (26-28)

c. The opportunity cost of producing guns stays the same as the production of guns increases. (26-28)

d. The opportunity cost of increasing the production of butter from 10 to 15 is 2 guns per pound of butter. The opportunity cost of increasing the production of butter from 20 to 25 is also 2 guns per pound of butter. (26-28)

e. The opportunity cost of producing butter stays the same as the production of butter increases. (26-28)

f. Producing 26 guns and 13 lbs of butter is not attainable given this production possibility curve. We can produce 20 guns and 15 lbs of butter. To produce six more guns, Ecoland must give up 3 lbs of butter. Ecoland can produce only 26 guns and 12 lbs of butter. (26-28)

g. Ecoland can produce 34 guns and 7 pounds of butter. To see this, begin at 30 guns and 10 pounds of butter. To produce 4 more guns, 2 pounds of butter must be given up. Ecoland can produce 34 guns and 8 pounds of butter, which is more than 34 guns and 7 pounds of butter. 34 guns and 7 pounds of butter is an inefficient point of production. (27-31)

3. The production possibility of producing food and machinery for both Japan and the United States is shown in the graph below. The United States has a comparative advantage in the production of machinery. It must give up only 0.4 tons of food for each additional thousand units of machinery produced. Japan must give up 2.5 tons of food for each additional thousand units of machinery produced. If they specialize and trade, they could attain the combined production possibility curve shown below.

To draw the combined production possibility curve, connect these three points: (1) a point along the food axis when both produce food (22.5 units), (2) a point along the machinery axis when both produce machines (30 units), (3) a point where each produces only that good for which it has a comparative advantage (food = 12.5, machinery = 25). If each country specializes in their comparative advantage and equally divides that production they will each consume 6.25 units of food and 12.5 units of machinery (point C in the graph)—more than either could have consumed if they produced just for themselves. (32-37)

4. a. In France, the opportunity cost of producing wine is 5 pounds of butter. In Italy, the opportunity cost of producing wine is 1.6 pounds of butter. Calculate this by finding how much butter must be forgone for each bottle of wine in each country. (26-28)

b. France has the comparative advantage in producing butter because it can produce butter at a lower opportunity cost. (28-29)

c. To obtain the greatest combined production possibilities Italy should specialize in producing only wine and France should specialize in producing only butter. (32-37)

d. Each country's consumption possibilities increase. (34-37)

ANSWERS

A BRAIN TEASER

1. a. Production possibility B. Why? Because consumer products provide for *current* satisfaction, and at B we are getting a relatively larger amount of consumer products. (26-31)

   b. 3 units of consumer products. (26-31)

   c. Point A. Producing a relatively larger amount of capital products now means workers will have more plant and equipment to work with in the future. This will increase workers' productivity and the nation's production possibilities over time. Producing more capital is an ingredient for economic growth (greater production possibilities over time). (26-31)

ANSWERS

MULTIPLE CHOICE

1. a   As discussed on pages 26-28, the production possibility curve tells how much of one good you must give up to get more of the other good; here you must give up 2Y to get one X, making a the correct answer.

2. c   As discussed on pages 26-28, the production possibility curve tells how much of one good you must give up to get more of another good. Opportunity cost is a ratio; it determines the slope, not the position, of the production possibility curve. Thus, the correct answer is c because the 12 to 6 trade-off reduces to a 2 to 1 trade-off.

3. d   As discussed on pages 26-28, the production possibility curve tells how much of one good you must give up to get more of

the other good. Opportunity cost is a ratio; it determines the slope, not the position, of the PPC curve. Since all have the same correct slope, all three are correct, so d is the right answer.

4. b   As discussed in the "Reminder" box on page 29 of the book, if the opportunity costs are constant, the PPC is a straight line, so b must be the answer.

5. c   As discussed on pages 27-28 of the book, with increasing marginal opportunity costs, as you produce more and more of a good, you will have to give up more and more of the other good to do so. This means that the slope of the PPC must be bowed outward, so c is the correct answer. See Figure 2-2, page 28 for an in-depth discussion.

6. d   As discussed on pages 27-28, the slope of the PPC measures the trade-off of one good for the other. Since moving from point C to B means giving up 3 guns for 2 pounds of butter, the correct answer is 3/2 (d).

7. b   As discussed on page 29, the flatter the slope, the higher the opportunity cost of the good measured on the vertical axis; alternatively, the flatter the slope the lower the opportunity cost of the good measured on the horizontal axis. In the AB range the slope is flat so guns have a low opportunity cost in terms of butter; one need give up only one pound of butter to get four guns.

8. c   As discussed on page 31 (See Figure 2-3), point A is an inefficient point because it is inside the PPC.

9. a   As discussed on page 31 (See Figure 2-3), technological change that improves the efficiency of producing a good shifts the PPC out for that good, but not for the other good. So a is the correct answer.

10. d   The answer is "You can't say," as discussed on page 31. The term "efficiency" involves *achieving a goal as cheaply as possible.* Without specifying one's goal, one cannot say what method is more efficient. The concept of efficiency

generally presumes that the goal includes preferring more to less, so if any method is more productive, it will be method A. But because there are distributional effects that involve making additional judgments, the correct answer is d. Some students may have been tempted to choose c because their goals involve more equity, but that is their particular judgment, and not all people may agree. Thus c would be incorrect, leaving d as the correct answer.

11. d As discussed in Figure 2-7 on page 35, with trade, both countries can attain consumption possibilities outside their production possibility curves. The only point not already attainable by either country is D.

12. d Country A must give up 2Y to produce an additional X while Country B must give up only 1/2 Y to produce an additional X. Therefore, Country A has a comparative advantage in good Y and Country B has a comparative advantage in good X. See pages 28-29.

13. d To construct the combined production possibilities with specialization and trade, sum the production if each country produced the same good (these are the axis intercepts). Connect these points with that point that represents the combination of goods if each country specialized in that good for which it has a comparative advantage. See pages 34-36, especially Figure 2-7 on page 35.

14. c The greatest gains are when each country specializes in the good for which it has the lowest opportunity cost. If Country A specializes in tractors, producing 50 tractors, and Country B specializes in cars and produces 200 cars, production of 200 cars and 50 tractors is possible. The combination of 300 cars and 100 tractors is unattainable even with specialization and trade. The other combinations are possible without trade. See pages 34-36, especially Figure 2-7.

15. d This is the principle of lowest cost rules. It is by producing where costs are lowest that countries can achieve gains from trade. See page 36.

16. d The law of one price is that workers in one country are paid the same as equal workers in other countries with similar institutional structures. If this isn't true, the forces of this law will lead to outsourcing. The United States continues to have comparative advantages. The U.S. dollar is likely too high to equalize wages across nations. See pages 37-39.

17. b Globalization is increasing in importance. It also increases specialization, productivity, and competition. See pages 37-39.

18. c According to the law of one price wages of workers in one country will not differ substantially from equal workers in another country with similar institutions. That is, there will be pressure for equally productive workers to receive similar wages. See page 41 for a discussion of the law of one price.

19. c The text suggests that it is unlikely that nominal wages will decline in the United States. It is more likely that the exchange value of the dollar will decline to offset wage differentials between the United States and other countries. See page 40.

20. a According to the law of one price, wages of (equal) workers in one country will not differ significantly from the wages of workers in another institutionally similar country. It is unlikely that wages will fall, but if the law of one price holds then wages in developing countries will rise faster than wages in developed nations rise. See pages 39-44.

A1. a As discussed in Appendix A, pages 46 and 47, a point represents the corresponding numbers on the horizontal and vertical number lines.

A2. c As discussed on page 48 of Appendix A, the slope of a line is defined as rise over run. Since the rise is −2 and the run is 4, the slope of the above line is minus 1/2.

A3. b As discussed on page 49 of Appendix A, at the maximum and minimum points of a nonlinear curve the slope is zero.

A4. c As discussed in Appendix A, pages 48 and 49, the slope is defined as rise over run. Line C has the largest rise for a given run so c is the answer. Even though, visually, line A seems to have the same slope as line C, it has a different coordinate system. Line A has a slope of 1 and line B has a slope of 1/4. Always be careful about checking coordinate systems when visually interpreting a graph.

A5. a   To construct the equation, use the form $y = mx + b$ where m is the slope and b is the y-axis intercept. The y-axis intercept is 2 and the slope is -rise/run $= -2/4 = -.5$. Plugging in these values we get $y = -.5x + 2$. Since P is on the y-axis and Q is on the x axis, this can also be written as $P = 2 - .5Q$. See page 50.

A6. b   A change in the intercept represents a shift in the curve. A higher intercept is a shift to the right. See page 50.

━━━━━ ANSWERS ━━━━━

POTENTIAL ESSAY QUESTIONS

The following are annotated answers. They indicate the general idea behind the answer.

1. Adam Smith was saying that it is not out of the kindness of producers that we are able to purchase what we want to consume, but the benefit that they will receive from selling their product. If each producer specializes in producing that good for which he receives the greatest benefit (produce at lowest cost) then the consumer will be able to consume the most goods at the lowest cost.

2. I would remind my study partner that the jobs that are being outsourced tend to be in the manufacturing industry. The U.S. does have a comparative advantage in creativity and innovation and jobs in industries such as advertising and marketing are being insourced to the United States. In addition, I would remind my partner that the very definition of comparative advantage means that if one country has a comparative advantage in one good, the other country has a comparative advantage in another good.

ECONOMIC INSTITUTIONS

● CHAPTER AT A GLANCE

This review is based upon the learning objectives that open the chapter.

1. A <u>market economy</u> is an economic system based on private property and the market. It gives private property rights to individuals, and relies on market forces to coordinate economic activity. (56)

   A market economy is characterized by:
   (I) mainly private ownership of resources
   (II) a market system that solves the What? How? and For whom? problems.

   A market economy's solutions to the central economic problems are:
   ● *What to produce: what businesses believe people want, and what is profitable.*
   ● *How to produce: businesses decide how to produce efficiently, guided by their desire to make a profit.*
   ● *For whom to produce: distribution according to individuals' ability and/or inherited wealth.*

2. <u>Capitalism</u> is an economic system based on the market in which the ownership of the means of production resides with a small group of individuals called capitalists. (57)

   <u>Socialism</u> is, in theory, an economic system that tries to organize society in the same way that most families are organized—all people should contribute what they can, and get what they need. (57)

   A command, or centrally planned socialist economy's solutions to the three central economic problems are:
   ● *What to produce: what central planners believe is socially beneficial.*

   ● *How to produce: central planners decide, based on what they think is good for the country.*
   ● *For whom to produce: central planners distribute goods based on what they determine are individuals' needs.*

   All economic systems are dynamic and evolve over time so the meaning of terms referring to economic systems is evolving. Ours has evolved from feudalism, mercantilism, and capitalism.

3. Businesses, households, and government interact in a market economy. (60)

   For a bird's-eye view of the U.S. economy, see Figure 3-1 (sometimes called the "circular flow of income model"). Be able to draw and explain it.

   Note: there are 3 basic economic institutions:

   ● *Businesses:*
   a. Supply goods in a goods market.
   b. Demand factors in a factor market.
   c. Pay taxes and receive benefits from government.

   ● *Households:*
   a. Supply factors.
   b. Demand goods.
   c. Pay taxes and receive benefits from government.

   ● *Government:*
   a. Demands goods.
   b. Demands factors.
   c. Collects taxes and provides services.

   It will be important to remember who does the demanding and the supplying in goods and factor (resource) markets.

4. The advantages and disadvantages of the three forms of business are shown in a table on page 63.

✔ *Know the advantages and disadvantages of the three forms of business:*
- *Sole Proprietorship*
- *Partnership*
- *Corporation*

E-commerce is changing the nature of trade relationships among businesses and consumers.

5. Although, in principle, ultimate power resides with the people and households (consumer sovereignty), in practice the representatives of the people–firms and government–are sometimes removed from the people and, in the short run, are only indirectly monitored by the people. (62, 65-66)

Also note: Economics focuses on households' role as the suppliers of labor.

- *Do we control business and government, or do they control us?*
- *The distribution of income (rich vs. poor) determines the "for whom" question. If you're rich you get more.*
- *Social forces affect what business and government do or don't do.*

6. Six roles of government in a market economy are: (66-71)

- Provide a stable set of institutions and rules.
  The government specifies "the rules of the game."

- Promote effective and workable competition.

✔ *Know the different consequences associated with competition vs. monopoly power.*

- Correct for externalities.
  Government attempts to restrict the production and consumption of negative externalities, while promoting the production and consumption of positive externalities.

- Ensure economic stability and growth.
  Government tries to ensure: full employment, low inflation, economic growth (which increases the standard of living)

- Provide for public goods.
  Government provides public goods by collecting taxes from everyone to try to eliminate the free-rider problem.

- Adjust for undesired market results.
  Sometimes the market result is not what society wants. For example, an unequal distribution of income may be undesirable. Government can adjust for these failures, but when correcting for these failures, it may make matters even worse. These are called "government failures."

7. There is no central world government. Governments enter into voluntary agreements that perform the role of regulating international markets. (72-74)

Countries have developed international institutions to oversee global business as well as promote economic relations among countries. These include the UN, the World Bank, the WTO, and the IMF. Regional trade organizations such as the EU and NAFTA work to reduce trade barriers among member countries.

See also, Appendix A: "The History of Economic Systems."

● **SHORT-ANSWER QUESTIONS**

1. What is a market economy? How does it solve the three central economic problems?

2. What is socialism? In practice, how have socialist economies addressed the three central economic problems?

3. Draw a diagram of the U.S. economy showing the three groups that comprise the U.S. economy. What is the role of each group in the economy?

4. Your friend wants to buy a coin-operated laundromat. Her brother has offered to be a partner in the operation and put up half the money to buy the business. They have come to you for advice about what form of business to create. Of course you oblige, letting them know the three possibilities and the advantages and disadvantages of each.

5. What is consumer sovereignty? Why is much of the economic decision-making done by business and government even though households have the ultimate power?

6. Briefly distinguish between the two general roles of government.

7. What are the six roles of government?

8. Should government always intervene when markets fail?

9. Why are trade agreements important in the international market?

A1. Why did feudalism evolve into mercantilism?

A2. Why did mercantilism evolve into capitalism?

A3. Explain what is meant by the statement that capitalism has evolved into welfare capitalism.

MATCHING THE TERMS
Match the terms to their definitions

___	**1.** consumer sovereignty	**a.**	A business with two or more owners.
___	**2.** corporation	**b.**	Principle that the consumer's wishes rule what's produced.
___	**3.** demerit good or activity	**c.**	Corporation with substantial operations on both production and sales in more than one country.
___	**4.** e-commerce	**d.**	A business that has only one owner.
___	**5.** entrepreneurship	**e.**	The stockholder's liability is limited to the amount that stockholder has invested in the company.
___	**6.** externality	**f.**	Buying and selling over the Internet.
___	**7.** free rider	**g.**	What's left over from total revenue after all appropriate costs have been subtracted.
___	**8.** global corporation	**h.**	The ability to organize and get something done.
___	**9.** government failure	**i.**	A business that is treated as a person, and is legally owned by its shareholders who are not liable for the actions of the corporate "person."
___	**10.** institutions	**j.**	An economic system based on individuals' goodwill toward others, not on their own self-interest, in which society decides what, how, and for whom to produce.
___	**11.** limited liability	**k.**	An economic system based on private property and the market, in which individuals decide how, what, and for whom to produce.
___	**12.** market economy	**l.**	Certificate of ownership of a corporation.
___	**13.** merit good or activity	**m.**	A good that if supplied to one person must be supplied to all and whose consumption by one individual does not prevent its consumption by another individual.
___	**14.** partnership	**n.**	A good or activity that government believes is good for you even though you may not choose to engage in the activity or consume the good.
___	**15.** profit	**o.**	A situation where the government intervenes and makes things worse.
___	**16.** public good	**p.**	A person who participates in something for free because others have paid for it.
___	**17.** socialism	**q.**	Good or activity that society believes is bad for people even though they choose to use the good or engage in the activity.
___	**18.** sole proprietorship	**r.**	The effect of a decision on a third party not taken into account by the decision maker.
___	**19.** stock	**s.**	The formal and informal rules that constrain human economic behavior.

● PROBLEMS AND APPLICATIONS

1. Fill in the blanks with the appropriate economic institution (households, businesses, or government).
    a. In the goods market, _____ and _____ buy goods and services from _____.
    b. In the goods market, _____ sell goods and services to _____ and _____.
    c. In the factor market, _____ and _____ buy (or employ) the resources owned by _____.
    d. In the factor market, _____ supply labor and other factors of production to _____ and _____.
    e. _____ redistributes income.
    f. _____ provides services to the public with tax revenue.

2. For each of the following, state for which form or forms of business it is an advantage: Sole proprietorships, partnerships, corporations.
    a. Minimum bureaucratic hassle.
    b. Ability to share work and risks.
    c. Direct control by owner.
    d. Relatively easy (but not the easiest) to form.
    e. Limited individual liability.

    f. Greatest ability to get funds.

3. For each of the following, state for which form or forms of business it is a disadvantage: Sole proprietorships, partnerships, corporations.
    a. Unlimited personal liability.
    b. Possible double taxation of income.
    c. Limited ability to get funds.
    d. Legal hassle to organize.

4. State some of the benefits global corporations offer countries. What is one problem that global corporations pose for governments?

● A BRAIN TEASER

1. Why do some politicians who wish to significantly reduce federal government spending find it difficult to achieve that reduction in practice?

● MULTIPLE CHOICE

Circle the one best answer for each of the following questions:

1. For a market to exist, you have to have:
   a. a capitalist economy.
   b. private property rights.
   c. no government intervention.
   d. externalities.

2. In theory, socialism is an economic system:
   a. that tries to organize society in the same ways as most families organize, striving to see that individuals get what they need.
   b. based on central planning and government ownership of the means of production.
   c. based on private property rights.
   d. based on markets.

3. In practice, a command or socialist economy is an economic system:
   a. that tries to organize society in the same ways as most families organize, striving to see that individuals get what they need.
   b. based on central planning and government ownership of the means of production.
   c. based on private property rights.
   d. based on markets.

4. In a market economy, the "what to produce" decision in practice is most often made directly by:
   a. consumers.
   b. the market.
   c. government.
   d. firms.

5. In practice, in command or socialist economies, the "what to produce" decision is most often made by:
   a. consumers.
   b. the market.
   c. government.
   d. firms.

6. In the factor market:
   a. businesses supply goods and services to households and government.
   b. government provides income support to households unable to supply factors of production to businesses.
   c. households supply labor and other factors of production to businesses.
   d. households purchase goods and services from businesses.

7. The ability to organize and get something done generally goes under the term:
   a. the corporate approach.
   b. entrepreneurship.
   c. efficiency.
   d. consumer sovereignty.

8. In terms of numbers, the largest percentage of businesses are:
   a. partnerships.
   b. sole proprietorships.
   c. corporations.
   d. nonprofit companies.

9. The largest percentage of business receipts are by:
   a. partnerships.
   b. sole proprietorships.
   c. corporations.
   d. nonprofit companies.

10. A sole proprietorship has the advantage of:
    a. raising funds by selling stocks or bonds.
    b. limited personal liability.
    c. minimum bureaucratic hassle.
    d. sharing work and risks.

11. All of the following are reasons why e-commerce and the Internet increase competition *except*:
    a. they increase the size of the marketplace in which goods are sold.
    b. they increase the value of companies who can establish brand name first.
    c. they reduce the cost of obtaining information.
    d. they reduce the importance of geographical location.

12. The largest percentage of federal government expenditures is on:
    a. education.
    b. health and medical care.
    c. infrastructure.
    d. income security.

13. The largest percentage of state and local expenditures is on:
    a. education.
    b. health and medical care.
    c. highways.
    d. income security.

14. All of the following are examples of government's role as referee *except*:
    a. setting limitations on when someone can be fired.
    b. collecting Social Security taxes from workers' paychecks.
    c. setting minimum safety regulations for the workplace.
    d. disallowing two competitors to meet to fix prices of their products.

15. When government attempts to adjust for the effect of decisions on third parties not taken into account by the decision makers, the government is attempting to:
    a. provide for a stable set of institutions and rules.
    b. promote effective and workable competition.
    c. provide for public goods and services.
    d. correct for externalities.

16. The ability of individuals or firms currently in business to prevent others from entering the same kind of business is:
    a. comparative advantage.
    b. market failure.
    c. monopoly power.
    d. externality.

17. A good whose consumption by one individual does not prevent its consumption by another individual has a characteristic of:
    a. a public good.
    b. a private good.
    c. a macroeconomic good.
    d. a demerit good.

18. If a firm automatically transfers 5 percent of an employee's salary to a pension program and offers the employee the option to opt out, behavioral economists predict that the employee will likely:
    a. choose to stay in the pension program.
    b. opt out of the pension program.
    c. request the amount be reduced to 3 percent.
    d. request the amount be doubled to 10 percent.

19. Global corporations:
    a. offer enormous benefits to countries but rarely any problems.
    b. are easy for governments to control.
    c. reduce competition in countries.
    d. have substantial operations on both the production and the sales sides in more than one country.

A1. In feudalism the most important force was:
    a. the price mechanism.
    b. cultural force.
    c. legal force.
    d. anarchy.

A2. In mercantilism, the guiding force is:
    a. the price mechanism.
    b. legal force.
    c. cultural force.
    d. anarchy.

A3. Mercantilism evolved into capitalism because:
    a. government investments did not pan out.
    b. the Industrial Revolution undermined the craft guilds' mercantilist method of production.
    c. the guilds wanted more freedom.
    d. serfs wanted more freedom.

A4. Marx saw the strongest tension between:
    a. rich capitalists and poor capitalists.
    b. capitalists and government.
    c. capitalists and the proletariat.
    d. government and the proletariat.

A5. State socialism is an economic system in which:
    a. business sees to it that people work for their own good until they can be relied upon to do that on their own.
    b. business sees to it that people work for the common good until they can be relied upon to do that on their own.
    c. government sees to it that people work for their own good until they can be relied upon to do so on their own.
    d. government sees to it that people work for the common good until they can be relied upon to do so on their own.

● POTENTIAL ESSAY QUESTIONS

You may also see essay questions similar to the "Problems & Applications" and "A Brain Teaser" exercises.

1. Contrast the market economy and the command economy in addressing the three fundamental economic problems.

2. Uglies is a brand of boxer shorts sold on the Internet. Their claim to fame is that the front of the shorts doesn't match the back. Their marketing ploy is the boxer-short-of-the-month club. Suppose you were the one who came up with the idea for Uglies and wanted to start the business. What form of business would you select and why? (Thinking about where the funds to start the business will come from, who will make the shorts, and how the shorts will be sold will help you answer this question.)

3. How are global economic issues different from national economic issues? How have governments attempted to grapple with global economic issues? What is a major drawback associated with these attempts?

■■■ ■■■ ANSWERS ■■■ ■■■

SHORT-ANSWER QUESTIONS

1. A market economy is an economic system based on private property and the market. It gives private property rights to individuals, and relies on market forces to coordinate economic activity. In a market economy businesses produce what they believe people want and think they can make a profit supplying. Businesses decide how to produce efficiently, guided by their desire to make a profit. Goods are distributed according to individuals' ability and/or inherited wealth. (56)

2. In theory, socialism is an economic system that tries to organize society in the same way as most families are organized—all people contribute what they can and get what they need. In practice, socialism is an economic system based on government ownership of the means of production, with economic activity governed by central planning. So, central planners (not market forces) decide *what* is produced, *how* it is produced, and *for whom* it is produced. (57-59)

3. As seen in the diagram below, the three groups that comprise the U.S. economy are households, businesses, and government. Households supply factors of production to businesses in exchange for money; businesses produce goods and services and sell them to households and government in exchange for money. The government taxes businesses and households, buys goods and services from businesses and labor services from households, and provides goods and services to each of them. (60)

4. I would advise each of them to think hard about their situation. There are three main possibilities: sole proprietorship, partnership and a corporation. Each form of business has its disadvantages and advantages. If your friend wants to minimize bureaucratic hassle and be her own boss, the best form of business would be a sole proprietorship. However, she would be personally liable for all losses and might have difficulty obtaining additional funds should that be necessary. If her brother has some skills to offer the new business and is willing to share in the cost of purchasing the company, she might want to form a partnership with him. Beware, though: Both partners are liable for any losses regardless of whose fault it is. I would ask her if she trusts her brother's decision-making abilities.

As a partnership they still might have problems getting additional funds. What about becoming a corporation? Her liability would be limited to her initial investment, her ability to get funds is greater, and she can shed personal income and gain added expenses to limit taxation. However, a corporation is a legal hassle to organize, may involve possible double taxation of income, and if she plans to hire many employees she may face difficulty monitoring the business once she becomes less involved. I would tell her she needs to weigh the costs and benefits of each option and choose the one that best suits her needs. (62-63)

5. Consumer sovereignty is the notion that the consumer's wishes rule what's produced. It means that if businesses wish to make a profit, they will need to produce what households want. That is not to say that businesses don't affect the desires of consumers through advertising. However, in practice, business and government do much of the economic decision-making even though households retain the ultimate power. This is because people have delegated much of that power to institutions and representatives–firms and the government–that are sometimes removed from the people. In the short run, households only indirectly control government and business. (62-66)

6. Two general roles of government are as actor and as referee. As an actor, government collects taxes and spends money. As a referee, government sets the rules governing relations between households and businesses. (66-68)

7. Six roles of government are (1) provide a stable set of institutions and rules, (2) promote effective and workable competition, (3) correct for externalities, (4) provide public goods, (5) ensure economic stability and growth, and (6) adjust for undesirable market results. (68)

8. The fact that a market has failed does not mean that government intervention will improve the situation; it may make things worse. (71)

9. Ongoing trade requires rules and methods of trade. The international market has no central government to set rules and methods for trade. Governments enter into voluntary trade agreements to fulfill some of these roles. (73)

A1. Feudalism evolved into mercantilism as the development of money allowed trade to grow, undermining the traditional base of feudalism. Politics rather than social forces came to control the central economic decisions. (79)

A2. Mercantilism evolved into capitalism because the Industrial Revolution shifted the economic power base away from craftsmen toward industrialists and toward an understanding that markets could coordinate the economy without the active involvement of the government. (79-80)

A3. Capitalism has evolved into welfare capitalism. That is, the human abuses marked by early capitalist developments led to a criticism of the market economic system. Political forces have changed government's role in the market, making government a key player in determining distribution and in making the what, how, and for whom decisions. This characterizes the U.S. economy today. (80-82)

ANSWERS

MATCHING

1-b; 2-i; 3-q; 4-f; 5-h; 6-r; 7-p; 8-c; 9-o; 10-s; 11-e; 12-k; 13-n; 14-a; 15-g; 16-m; 17-j; 18-d; 19-l.

ANSWERS

PROBLEMS AND APPLICATIONS

1. a. In the goods market, **households** and **government** buy goods and services from **businesses**. (60-61)
   b. In the goods market, **businesses** sell goods and services to **households** and **government**. (60-61)
   c. In the factor market, **businesses** and **government** buy (or employ) the resources owned by **households**. (60-61)
   d. In the factor market, **households** supply labor and other factors of production to **businesses** and **government**. (60-61)
   e. **Government** redistributes income. (60-61)
   f. **Government** provides services to the public with tax revenue. (60-61)

2. a. Sole proprietorship. No special bureaucratic forms are required to start one. (62-63)
   b. Partnership. The owners have another one to work with and risks are shared. (62-63)
   c. Sole proprietorship. This is a firm of one person who controls the business. (62-63)
   d. Partnership. This is easy to form relative to the easiest (sole proprietorship) and the hardest (corporation). (62-63)
   e. Corporation. The individual liability is limited by individual investment. (62-63)
   f. Corporation. Because it can issue stock and has limited liability, it has more access to financial capital. (62-63)

3. a. Sole proprietorship and partnership. (62-63)
   b. Corporation. (62-63)
   c. Sole proprietorship and partnership. (62-63)
   d. Corporation. (62-63)

4. Global corporations can benefit countries by creating jobs, by bringing new ideas and new technologies to a country, and by providing competition to domestic companies, keeping them on their toes. But, global corporations, because they exist in many countries and there is no world government, may be difficult to regulate or to control. If they don't like one government's taxes, regulation, or other policies, they can shift operations to another country with more favorable policies. (72-73)

■ **ANSWERS** ■

A BRAIN TEASER

1. A significant reduction in federal government spending would require cuts in income security (like social security), national defense, and other major components of federal government expenditures that are politically popular. Many people applaud attempts to reduce government spending as long as there are no cuts in programs they support. See Figure 3-4 on page 67.

■ **ANSWERS** ■

MULTIPLE CHOICE

1. b   As discussed on page 56, markets require private property rights because these give people the framework within which they can trade and markets rely on trading. Markets also require government, but government and private property rights are not the same thing, which rules out a and c. And d is a throwaway answer.

2. a   As discussed on page 57, a is the correct answer. If the question had said "In practice," b would have been an acceptable answer.

3. b   As discussed on page 56, b is the correct answer. If the question had said "In theory, a socialist economy..." a would have been an acceptable answer.

4. d   Under a market economy, firms decide what to produce based on what they think will sell. See pages 61-62.

5. c   As discussed on page 58, in command economies, central planners decide what to produce based upon what they believe society needs.

6. c.   In Figure 3-1 households supply labor and other factors of production while businesses demand these inputs used in the production process. See page 60.

7. b   Entrepreneurship is the ability to organize and get something done. See page 61.

8. b   Most businesses are sole proprietorships. See Figure 3-2 on page 62.

9. c   Corporations account for most business receipts (revenues). See Figure 3-2 on page 62.

10. c   Corporations have the advantages of options a and b. Partnerships have the advantage of option d. See page 63.

11. b   While it is true that e-commerce and the Internet can increase the value of companies that establish their brand names first, this characteristic decreases competition once that name brand is established. See pages 64-65.

12. d   The largest component of federal government spending is income security. See Figure 3-4 on page 67.

13. a   The largest state and local government spending is on education. See Figure 3-3 on page 67.

14. b   Collecting Social Security taxes to fund the Social Security system is government as an actor. Government as referee refers to laws regulating interaction between households and businesses. See pages 66-68.

15. d   Economists call the effect of a decision on a third party not taken into account by the decision maker an externality. Government sometimes attempts to adjust for these effects. See pages 67-70.

16. c   Monopoly power is the ability of individuals or firms currently in business to prevent others from entering their businesses. Monopoly power gives existing firms or individuals the ability to raise their prices. See page 69.

17. a   A public good is a good that if supplied to one person must be supplied to all and whose consumption by one individual does not prevent its consumption by another individual. See page 70.

18. a   The default option bias says that people tend to select the default option. So, choosing to stay in the default program will be most likely. See page 71.

19. d   Option d is the definition of global corporations. They often create problems. Governments often find it difficult to control them and they increase competition, not decrease it. See pages 71-73.

A1. b   As discussed on page 78, in feudalism tradition reigned.

A2. b   As discussed on page 79, in mercantilism government directed the economy.

A3. b   Mercantilism evolved into capitalism because of the changes brought about by the Industrial Revolution. See pages 79-80.

A4. c   To the degree that government was controlled by capitalists, d would be a correct answer, but it is not as good an answer as c, which represents the primary conflict. Remember, you are choosing the answer that best reflects the discussion in the text. See pages 80-81.

A5. d   The author defines state socialism as option d. Socialists saw state socialism as a transition stage to pure socialism. See page 81.

ANSWERS

POTENTIAL ESSAY QUESTIONS

The following are annotated answers. They indicate the general idea behind the answer.

1. Both economic systems have to address the three central economic problems. (1) What to produce? In a market economy, firms produce what they believe people want and what will make them a profit. In socialism, or a command economy, central planners decide what is produced. (2) How to produce? In a market economy, firms decide how to produce efficiently, guided by their desire to make a profit. In socialism, central planners decide how to produce. (3) For whom to produce? In a market economy, distribution is decided according to ability and inherited wealth. In socialism, distribution is according to individuals' needs (as determined by central planners).

2. The answer to this question will vary from person to person and will depend on personal finances, how much risk one is able and willing to undertake, how much responsibility one wants to take on, and whether or not you want to share in any profits. Given limited financial resources, I'd find a partner I can trust who has the funds needed to launch a web site, hire a firm to carry out transactions, and build inventory. With a partnership I can share the work and the risks of the venture. Since the liability associated with selling boxer shorts is not too great, unlimited liability with a partnership is not a problem. I would not choose a corporation because establishing one is a legal hassle requiring even more money. I would not choose a sole proprietorship because I don't have the funds to start the company on my own.

3. Global economic issues differ from national economic issues because national economies have governments to referee disputes among players in the economy; global economies do not; no international government exists. Governments, however, have developed a variety of international institutions to promote negotiations and coordinate economic relations among countries. These include the UN, the World Bank, the World Court and the International Monetary Fund. Countries also have developed global and regional organizations whose jobs are to coordinate trade among countries and reduce trade barriers. Some are the WTO, the EU, and NAFTA. In addition to these formal institutions, there are informal meetings of various countries like the Group of Five and the Group of Eight. A major drawback associated with governmental attempts to deal with global economic issues is that because government membership in international organizations is voluntary, then the power of international organizations is limited. An individual government may simply choose to ignore an international ruling with little impunity.

SUPPLY AND DEMAND

CHAPTER AT A GLANCE

This review is based upon the learning objectives that open the chapter.

1. The <u>law of demand</u> states that the quantity of a good demanded is <u>inversely related</u> to the good's price. When price goes up, quantity demanded goes down. When price goes down, quantity demanded goes up. (84)

   Law of Demand (Inverse Relationship):
   arrows move in $\uparrow P \rightarrow \downarrow Q_d$
   opposite directions $\downarrow P \rightarrow \uparrow Q_d$

   Law of Demand expressed as a <u>downward-sloping curve</u>:

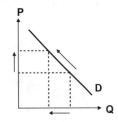

   To derive a demand curve from a demand table, plot each point on the demand table on a graph and connect the points.

P	Q
$10	5
7	9

2a. The law of demand is based on opportunity cost and individuals' ability to substitute. If the price of a good rises, the opportunity cost of purchasing that good will also rise and consumers will substitute a good with a lower opportunity cost. (84)

   As the P of beef ↑s, we buy less beef and more chicken.

2b. The law of supply, like the law of demand, is based on opportunity cost and the individual firm's ability to substitute. Suppliers will substitute toward goods for which they receive higher relative prices. (90-91)

   If the P of wheat ↑s, farmers grow more wheat and less corn.

3. Changes in quantity demanded are shown by movements along a demand curve. Shifts in demand are shown by a shift of the entire demand curve. (85) *(Note: "Δ" means "change.")*

   Don't get this confused on the exam!

   ΔQ_d is caused <u>only</u> by a Δ in the P of the good itself.

   $\Delta P \rightarrow \Delta Q_d \rightarrow$ movement along a given D curve.

   $\uparrow P \rightarrow \downarrow Q_d$: movement along a curve (e.g. from point A to point B).

   ΔD is caused only by Δs in the shift factors of D (<u>not</u> a Δ in the P of the good itself!) <u>Δ in shift factors of $D \rightarrow \Delta D \rightarrow$ shift of a D curve</u>

✔ *Know what can cause an increase and decrease in demand:*
   $\uparrow D \rightarrow$ <u>Rightward Shift</u>   *$\downarrow D \rightarrow$ <u>Leftward Shift</u>*

4. The <u>law of supply</u> states that the quantity of a good supplied is <u>directly related</u> to the good's price. When price goes up, quantity supplied goes up. When price goes down, quantity supplied goes down. (90-91)

Law of Supply (Direct Relationship):
arrows move in $\uparrow P \rightarrow \uparrow Q_s$
same direction $\downarrow P \rightarrow \downarrow Q_s$

Law of Supply expressed as an <u>upward-sloping curve</u>:

To derive a supply curve from a supply table, plot each point on the supply table on a graph and connect the points.

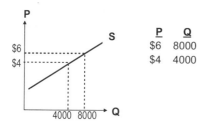

P	Q
$6	8000
$4	4000

5. Just as with demand, it is important to distinguish between a change in supply (due to a change in shift factors and reflected as a shift of the entire supply curve) and a change in the quantity supplied (due to a change in price and reflected as a movement along a supply curve). (91-92)

     Don't get this confused on the exam!

ΔQ_s *is caused <u>only</u> by a* Δ *in the P of the good itself.*

$\Delta P \rightarrow \Delta Q_s \rightarrow$ *movement along a given S curve.*

$\uparrow P \rightarrow \uparrow Q_s$: *movement along a curve (e.g. from point A to point B).*

ΔS *is caused only by* Δs *in the shift factors of S (<u>not</u> a* Δ *in the P of the good itself!)*

Δ *in shift factors of S* $\rightarrow \Delta S \rightarrow$ *shift of a S curve*

✔ *Know what can cause an increase and decrease in supply:*
$\uparrow S \rightarrow$ *<u>Rightward Shift</u>* $\downarrow S \rightarrow$ *<u>Leftward Shift</u>*

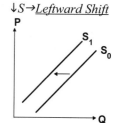

6. Equilibrium is where quantity supplied equals quantity demanded: (95-96)

- If quantity demanded is greater than quantity supplied (excess demand), prices tend to rise;
- If quantity supplied is greater than quantity demanded (excess supply), prices tend to fall.
- When quantity demanded equals quantity supplied, prices have no tendency to change.

✔ *<u>Know this!</u>*

- If $Q_d > Q_s \rightarrow$ Shortage $\rightarrow P$ will $\uparrow$.
- If $Q_s > Q_d \rightarrow$ Surplus $\rightarrow P$ will $\downarrow$.
- If $Q_s = Q_d \rightarrow$ Equilibrium $\rightarrow$ no tendency for P to change (because there is neither a surplus nor a shortage).

Shortage	**Surplus**	**Equilibrium**
$(Q_d > Q_s)$	$(Q_s > Q_d)$	$(Q_s = Q_d)$
P is below equilibrium	P is above equilibrium	

7. Demand and supply curves enable us to determine the equilibrium price and quantity. In addition, changes (shifts) in demand and supply curves enable us to predict the effect on the equilibrium price and quantity in a market. (98-99)

Anything other than price that affects demand or supply will shift the curves.

✔ *Know how a change in demand or supply affects the equilibrium price and quantity!*

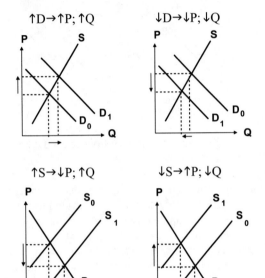

8. Simple supply and demand analysis holds other things constant. Sometimes supply and demand are interconnected, making it impossible to hold other things constant. When there is interdependence between supply and demand, a movement along one curve can cause the other curve to shift. This is especially prevalent when one analyzes goods that constitute a large percentage of the entire economy. Thus, supply and demand analysis used alone is not enough to determine where the equilibrium will be. (99-100)

When the "other things are constant" assumption is not realistic, feedback or ripple effects can become relevant. The degree of interdependence differs among various sets of issues. That is why there is a separate micro and macro analysis–microeconomics and macroeconomics.

The fallacy of composition is the false assumption that what is true for a part will also be true for the whole. This means that what is true in microeconomics may not be true in macroeconomics.

● SHORT-ANSWER QUESTIONS

1. What is the law of demand?

2. Draw a demand curve from the following demand table.

    Demand Table

Q	P
50	1
40	2
30	3
20	4

3. Demonstrate graphically a shift in demand and on another graph demonstrate movement along the demand curve.

4. State the law of supply.

5. What does the law of supply say that most individuals would do with the quantity of labor they supply employers if their wage increased? Explain the importance of substitution in this decision.

6. Draw a supply curve from the following supply table.

    Supply Table

Q	P
20	1
30	2
40	3
50	4

7. Demonstrate graphically the effect of a new technology that reduces the cost of producing Linkin Park CDs on the supply of Linkin Park CDs.

8. Demonstrate graphically the effect of a rise in the price of Linkin Park CDs on the quantity supplied.

9. What are three things to note about supply and demand that help to explain how they interact to bring about equilibrium in a market?

10. Demonstrate graphically what happens to the equilibrium price and quantity of M&Ms if they suddenly become more popular.

11. Demonstrate graphically what happens to the equilibrium price and quantity of oranges if a frost destroys 50 percent of the orange crop.

12. What is the fallacy of composition and how is it related to why economists separate micro from macro economics?

MATCHING THE TERMS
Match the terms to their definitions

____ **1.** demand

____ **2.** demand curve

____ **3.** equilibrium

____ **4.** equilibrium price

____ **5.** equilibrium quantity

____ **6.** excess demand

____ **7.** excess supply

____ **8.** fallacy of composition

____ **9.** law of demand

____ **10.** law of supply

____ **11.** market demand curve

____ **12.** movement along a demand curve

____ **13.** movement along a supply curve

____ **14.** quantity demanded

____ **15.** quantity supplied

____ **16.** shift in demand

____ **17.** shift in supply

____ **18.** supply

____ **19.** supply curve

a. A specific amount that will be demanded per unit of time at a specific price, other things constant.

b. Curve that tells how much of a good will be bought at various prices.

c. The effect of a change in a shift factor on the supply curve.

d. Curve that tells how much of a good will be offered for sale at various prices.

e. The graphic representation of the effect of a change in price on the quantity supplied.

f. Quantity demanded rises as price falls, other things constant.

g. Quantity supplied rises as price rises, other things constant.

h. A schedule of quantities of a good that will be bought per unit of time at various prices, other things constant.

i. Quantity supplied is greater than quantity demanded.

j. A concept in which opposing dynamic forces cancel each other out.

k. The effect of a change in a shift factor on the demand curve.

l. The price toward which the invisible hand (economic forces) drives the market.

m. The horizontal sum of all individual demand curves.

n. Amount bought and sold at the equilibrium price.

o. Quantity demanded is greater than quantity supplied.

p. The graphic representation of the effect of a change in price on the quantity demanded.

q. A specific amount that will be offered for sale per unit of time at a specific price.

r. A schedule of quantities a seller is willing to sell per unit of time at various prices, other things constant.

s. The false assumption that what is true for a part will also be true for the whole.

● PROBLEMS AND APPLICATIONS

1. Draw two linear curves on the same graph from the following table, one relating P with Q_1 and the other relating P with Q_2.

P	Q_1	Q_2
$30	60	100
35	70	90
40	80	80
45	90	70

    a. Label the curve that is most likely a demand curve. Explain your choice.

    b. Label the curve that is most likely a supply curve. Explain your choice.

    c. What is the equilibrium price and quantity? Choose points above and below that price and explain why each is not the equilibrium price.

2. Correct the following statements, if needed, so that the terms "demand," "quantity demanded," "supply," and "quantity supplied" are used correctly.

    a. As the price of pizza increases, consumers demand less pizza.

    b. Whenever the price of bicycles increases, the supply of bicycles increases.

    c. The price of electricity is cheaper in the northwestern part of the United States and therefore the demand for electricity is greater in the northwest.

    d. An increase in the incomes of car buyers will increase the quantity demanded for cars.

    e. An increase in the quantity demanded of lobsters means consumers are willing and able to buy more lobsters at any given price.

    f. A decrease in the supply of frog legs means suppliers will provide fewer frog legs at any given price.

3. You are given the following individual demand tables for compact discs.

Price	Juan	Philippe	Ramone
$7	3	20	50
$10	2	10	40
$13	1	7	32
$16	0	5	26
$19	0	3	20
$22	0	0	14

    a. Determine the market demand table.

b. Graph the individual and market demand curves.

c. If the current market price is $13, what is the total market quantity demanded? What happens to total market quantity demanded if the price rises to $19 a disc?

d. Say that a new popular Usher compact disc hits the market that increases demand for compact discs by 25%. Show with a demand table what happens to the individual and market demand curves. Demonstrate graphically what happens to market demand.

4. The following table depicts the market supply and demand for oranges in the United States (in thousands of bushels).

Price per bushel	Quantity supplied	Quantity demanded
$15	7000	2000
$14	5500	3000
$13	4000	4000
$12	2500	5000
$11	1000	6000

a. Graph the market supply and demand for oranges.

b. What is the equilibrium price and quantity of oranges in the market? Why?

c. Suppose the price is $14. Would we observe a surplus (excess supply) or a shortage (excess demand)? If so, by how much? What could be expected to happen to the price over time? Why?

d. Suppose the price is $12. Would we observe a surplus or a shortage? If so, by how much? What could be expected to happen to the price over time? Why?

5. Draw a hypothetical demand and supply curve for cyber cafes — coffee houses with computers hooked up to the Internet with access to daily newspapers (among other things) at each table. Show how demand or supply is affected by the following:

a. A technological breakthrough lowers the cost of computers.

b. Consumers' income rises.

c. A per-hour fee is charged to coffee houses to use the Internet.

d. The price of newspapers in print rises.

e. Possible suppliers expect cyber cafes to become more popular.

6. Use supply and demand curves to help you determine the impact that each of the following events has on the market for surfboards in Southern California.

a. Southern California experiences unusually high temperatures, sending an unusually large number of people to its beaches.

b. Large sharks are reported feeding near the beaches of Southern California.

c. Due to the large profits earned by surfboard producers there is a significant increase in the number of producers of surfboards.

d. There is a significant increase in the price of epoxy paint used to coat surfboards.

7. Use supply and demand curves to help you determine the impact that each of the following events has on the market for beef.

a. New genetic engineering technology enables ranchers to raise healthier, heavier cattle, significantly reducing costs.

b. The CBS program "60 Minutes" reports on the unsanitary conditions in poultry processing plants that may increase the chances of consumers getting sick by eating chicken.

c. In addition to developing new genetic engineering technology, highly credible new research results report that abundant consumption of fatty red meats actually prolongs average life expectancy.

d. Consumers expect the price of beef to fall in the near future.

⬤ A BRAIN TEASER

1. The invention of a self-milking cow machine allows cows to milk themselves. Not only does this reduce the need for higher-cost human assistance in milking, but it also allows the cow to milk herself three times a day instead of two, leading to both a healthier cow and increased milk production.

   a. Show the effect of this innovation on the equilibrium quantity and price of milk.

   b. Show the likely effect on equilibrium price and quantity of apple juice (a substitute for milk).

⬤ MULTIPLE CHOICE

Circle the one best answer for each of the following questions:

1. The law of demand states:
   a. quantity demanded increases as price falls, other things constant.
   b. more of a good will be demanded the higher its price, other things constant.
   c. people always want more.
   d. you can't always get what you want at the price you want.

2. There are many more substitutes for good A than for good B.
   a. The demand curve for good B will likely shift out further.
   b. The demand curve for good B will likely be flatter.
   c. You can't say anything about the likely relative flatness of the demand curves.
   d. The demand curve for good A will likely be flatter.

3. If the weather gets very hot, what will most likely happen?
   a. The supply of air conditioners will increase.
   b. Quantity of air conditioners demanded will increase.
   c. Demand for air conditioners will increase.
   d. The quality of air conditioners demanded will increase.

4. If the price of air conditioners falls, there will be:
   a. an increase in demand for air conditioners.
   b. an increase in the quantity of air conditioners demanded.
   c. an increase in the quantity of air conditioners supplied.
   d. a shift out of the supply for air conditioners.

5. An increase in demand:
   a. is reflected as a rightward (outward) shift of the demand curve.
   b. is caused by a decrease in price.
   c. means demanders are buying less at any price
   d. shifts the demand curve to the left (inward).

6. The demand curve will likely shift outward to the right if:
   a. society's income falls.
   b. the price of a substitute good falls.
   c. the price of the good is expected to rise in the near future.
   d. the good goes out of style.

7. The difference between the quantity demanded and demand is:
   a. the quantity demanded is associated with a whole set of prices, whereas demand is associated with a particular price.
   b. the quantity demanded is associated with a particular price, whereas demand is associated with a whole set of prices.
   c. the quantity demanded is the whole demand curve, whereas demand is a particular point along a demand curve.
   d. a change in the quantity demanded is reflected graphically as a shift of the demand curve, whereas a change in demand is reflected as movement along a given demand curve.

8. If there is a flood, what will most likely happen in the market for bottled water?
   a. Demand will increase.
   b. Demand will fall.
   c. Supply will increase.
   d. Supply will decrease.

9. The movement in the graph below from point A to point B represents:

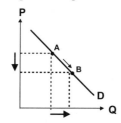

   a. an increase in demand.
   b. an increase in the quantity demanded.
   c. an increase in the quantity supplied.
   d. an increase in supply.

10. Using the standard axes, the demand curve associated with the following demand table is:

Demand Table

P	Q
7	5
9	4
11	3

   a. a
   b. b
   c. c
   d. d

11. To derive a market demand curve from two individual demand curves:
    a. one adds the two demand curves horizontally.
    b. one adds the two demand curves vertically.
    c. one subtracts one demand curve from the other demand curve.
    d. one adds the demand curves both horizontally and vertically.

12. The market demand curve will always:
    a. be unrelated to the individual demand curves and slope.
    b. be steeper than the individual demand curves that make it up.
    c. have the same slope as the individual demand curves that make it up.
    d. be flatter than the individual demand curves that make it up.

13. The law of supply states that:
    a. quantity supplied increases as price increases, other things constant.
    b. quantity supplied decreases as price increases, other things constant.
    c. more of a good will be supplied the higher its price, other things changing proportionately.
    d. less of a good will be supplied the higher its price, other things changing proportionately.

14. In the graph below, the arrow refers to:

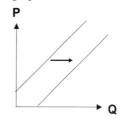

    a. a shift in demand.
    b. a shift in supply.
    c. a change in the quantity demanded.
    d. a change in the quantity supplied.

15. If there is an improvement in technology one would expect:
    a. a movement along the supply curve.
    b. a shift upward (or to the left) of the supply curve.
    c. a shift downward (or to the right) of the supply curve.
    d. a movement down along the supply curve.

16. You're the supplier of a good and suddenly a number of your long-lost friends call you to buy your product. Your good is most likely:
   a. in excess supply.
   b. in excess demand.
   c. in equilibrium.
   d. in both excess supply and demand.

17. At which point on the graph below will you expect the strongest downward pressure on prices?

   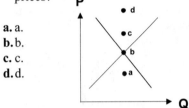

   a. a.
   b. b.
   c. c.
   d. d.

18. If at some price the quantity supplied exceeds the quantity demanded, then:
   a. a surplus (excess supply) exists and the price will fall over time as sellers competitively bid down the price.
   b. a shortage (excess demand) exists and the price will rise over time as buyers competitively bid up the price.
   c. the price is below equilibrium.
   d. equilibrium will be reestablished as the demand curve shifts to the left.

19. If the price of a good:
   a. rises, it is a response to a surplus (excess supply).
   b. falls, it is a response to a shortage (excess demand).
   c. is below equilibrium, then a shortage will be observed.
   d. is below equilibrium, then a surplus will be observed.

20. If the demand for a good increases, you will expect price to:
   a. fall and quantity to rise.
   b. rise and quantity to rise.
   c. fall and quantity to fall.
   d. rise and quantity to fall.

21. If the supply of a good decreases, you will expect price to:
   a. fall and quantity to rise.
   b. rise and quantity to rise.
   c. fall and quantity to fall.
   d. rise and quantity to fall.

22. Consider the market for bikinis. If bikinis suddenly become more fashionable, you will expect:
   a. a temporary shortage of bikinis that will be eliminated over time as the market price of bikinis rises and a greater quantity is bought and sold.
   b. a temporary shortage of bikinis that will be eliminated over time as the market price of bikinis rises and a smaller quantity is bought and sold.
   c. a temporary surplus of bikinis that will be eliminated over time as the market price of bikinis falls and a smaller quantity is bought and sold.
   d. a temporary surplus of bikinis that will be eliminated over time as the market price of bikinis rises and a greater quantity is bought and sold.

23. Compared to last year, fewer oranges are being purchased and the selling price has decreased. This could have been caused by:
   a. an increase in demand.
   b. an increase in supply.
   c. a decrease in demand.
   d. a decrease in supply.

24. If demand and supply both increase, this will cause:
   a. an increase in the equilibrium quantity, but an uncertain effect on the equilibrium price.
   b. an increase in the equilibrium price, but an uncertain effect on the equilibrium quantity.
   c. an increase in the equilibrium price and quantity.
   d. a decrease in the equilibrium price and quantity.

25. An increase in demand for a good will cause:
   a. excess demand (a shortage) until price changes.
   b. movement down along the demand curve as price changes.
   c. movement down along the supply curve as price changes.
   d. a higher price and a smaller quantity traded in the market.

26. The fallacy of composition is:
   a. the false assumption that what is false for a part will also be false for the whole.
   b. the false assumption that what is true for a part will also be true for the whole.

c. the false assumption that what is false for a whole will also be false for the part.

d the false assumption that what is true for a whole will also be true for the part.

⬤ POTENTIAL ESSAY QUESTIONS

You may also see essay questions similar to the "Problems & Applications" and "A Brain Teaser" exercises.

1. Many university campuses sell parking permits to their students allowing them to park on campus in designated areas. Although most students complain about the relatively high cost of these parking permits, what annoys many students even more is that after having paid for their permits, vacant parking spaces in the designated lots are very difficult to find during much of the day. Many end up having to park off campus anyway, where permits are not required. Assuming the university is unable to build new parking facilities on campus due to insufficient funds, what recommendation might you make to remedy the problem of students with permits being unable to find places to park on campus?

2. Discuss how changes in demand or supply impact a market equilibrium price and quantity.

■■■ **ANSWERS** ■■■

SHORT-ANSWER QUESTIONS

1. The law of demand states that the quantity of a good demanded is inversely related to the good's price, other things constant. (84)

2. To derive a demand curve from a demand table, plot each point of the demand table on a graph and connect the points. This is shown on the graph below. (88)

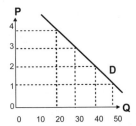

3. A shift in demand is shown by a shift of the entire demand curve resulting from a change in a shift factor of demand as shown in the graph below on the left (which illustrates an increase in demand because it is a rightward shift). A movement along a demand curve is shown on the right as a movement from point A to point B due to a price decrease. (85 and Figure 4-2 on page 87)

4. The law of supply states that the quantity supplied rises as price rises, other things constant. Or alternatively: quantity supplied falls as price falls. (90)

5. The law of supply states that quantity supplied rises as price rises; quantity supplied falls as price falls. According to this law, most individuals would choose to supply a greater quantity of labor hours if their wage increased. They will substitute work for leisure. (Figure 4-5 on page 91)

6. To derive a supply curve from a supply table, you plot each point on the supply table on a graph and connect the points. This is shown on the graph in the next column. (93)

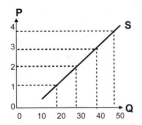

7. A new technology that reduces the cost of producing Linkin Park CDs will shift the entire supply curve to the right from S_0 to S_1, as shown in the graph below. (92)

8. A rise in the price of Linkin Park CDs from P_0 to P_1 results in a movement up along a supply curve and the quantity of Linkin Park CDs supplied will rise from Q_0 to Q_1 as shown in the graph below. (91-92)

9. The first thing to note is that when quantity demanded is greater than quantity supplied, prices tend to rise and when quantity supplied is greater than quantity demanded, prices tend to fall. Each case is demonstrated in the graph below. Price tends away from P_1 and P_2 and toward P_0.

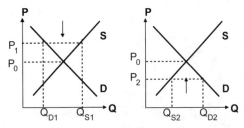

The second thing to note is that the larger the difference between quantity supplied and quantity demanded, the greater the pressure on prices to rise (if there is excess demand; a shortage) or fall (if there is excess supply; a surplus). This is demonstrated in the graph below. At P_2, the pressure for prices to fall toward P_0 is greater than the pressure at P_1 because excess supply (surplus) is greater at P_2 compared to excess supply at P_1.

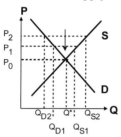

The third thing to note is that when quantity demanded equals quantity supplied, the market is in equilibrium. This is shown graphically at the point of intersection between the demand and supply curves. (95-96)

10. Increasing popularity of M&Ms means that at every price, more M&Ms are demanded. The demand curve shifts out to the right from D_0 to D_1, and both equilibrium price and quantity rise to P_1 and Q_1 respectively. (98-99)

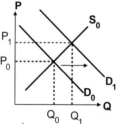

11. A frost damaging oranges means that at every price, suppliers will supply fewer oranges. The supply curve shifts in to the left from S_0 to S_1, and equilibrium price rises to P_1, and quantity traded falls to Q_1. (98-99)

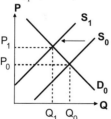

12. The fallacy of composition is the false assumption that what is true for a part will also be true for the whole. In micro, economists isolate an individual person's or firm's behavior and consider its effects, while the many side effects are kept in the background. In macro, those

side effects become too large and can no longer be held constant. These side effects are what account for the interdependence of supply and demand. Macro, thus, is not simply a summation of all micro results; it would be a fallacy of composition to take the sum of each individual's (micro) actions and say that this will be the aggregate (macro) result. (100)

◼◼◼◼ ANSWERS ◼◼◼◼

MATCHING

1-h; 2-b; 3-j; 4-l; 5-n; 6-o; 7-i; 8-s; 9-f; 10-g; 11-m; 12-p; 13-e; 14-a; 15-q; 16-k; 17-c; 18-r; 19-d.

◼◼◼◼ ANSWERS ◼◼◼◼

PROBLEMS AND APPLICATIONS

1. The linear curves are shown on the right. See Figure 4-8 on page 97.

   a. As shown in the graph, the downward sloping curve is a demand curve. We deduce this from the law of demand: quantity demanded rises (falls) as the price decreases (increases). (84)

   b. As shown in the graph, the upward sloping curve is a supply curve. We deduce this from the law of supply: quantity supplied rises (falls) as the price rises (falls). (91)

   c. The equilibrium price and quantity are where the demand and supply curves intersect. This is at $P = \$40$, $Q = 80$. At a price above $40, such as $45, quantity supplied exceeds quantity demanded and there is pressure for price to fall. At a price below $40, such as $35, quantity demanded exceeds quantity supplied and there is pressure for price to rise. (95-96)

2. a. As the price of pizza increases, the *quantity demanded* of pizza decreases. (85)

Note that a change in the price of an item will cause a change in the quantity demanded; not a change in demand! A change in something else other than the price may cause a change in demand– such as a change in one of the shift factors of demand discussed in the textbook.

b. Whenever the price of bicycles increases, the *quantity of bicycles supplied* also increases. (92)

   Note that a change in the price will cause a change in the quantity supplied; not supply! A change in something else other than the price–such as a change in one of the shift factors of supply discussed in the textbook–may cause a change in supply.

c. The price of electricity is cheaper in the NW part of the U. S. and therefore the *quantity demanded* of electricity is greater in the NW. (85)

d. An increase in incomes of car buyers will increase the *demand* for cars. (85-86)

   Notice that a change in a shift factor of demand, such as income, will change demand; not the quantity demanded!

e. An increase in the *demand* for lobsters means consumers are willing and able to buy more lobsters at any given price (whatever the current price is). (85-86)

   In order for there to be an increase in the quantity demanded there would have to be a decrease in the price. Moreover, recall that an increase in demand is reflected as a rightward shift of the demand curve. Upon viewing a graph where the demand curve has shifted to the right you will see that more will be purchased at any given price.

f. This is a correct use of the term "supply." Notice that a decrease in supply is reflected graphically as a leftward shift of the curve and less will be provided in the market at any given price. (92)

3. a. The market demand table is the summa-tion of individual quantities demanded at each price as follows (88-89):

P	Q
$7	73
10	52
13	40
16	31
19	23
22	14

b. The individual and market demand curves are shown to the right of the demand table. (88-89)

c. At $13 a disc, total market quantity demanded is 40 discs. Total market quantity demanded falls to 23 when the price of discs rises to $19 per disc. (88-89)

d. Quantity demanded at each price rises by 25% for each individual and for the market as a whole. The new demand table is shown below. Graphically, both the individual and market demand curves shift to the right. The graph below shows the rightward shift in market demand. (88-89)

Price	Juan	Philippe	Ramone	Market
$7	3.75	25	62.50	91.25
$10	2.50	12.5	50	65
$13	1.25	8.75	40	50
$16	0	6.25	32.5	38.75
$19	0	3.75	25	28.75
$21	0	0	17.5	17.5

4. a. See the graph below. (See Figure 4-8 on page 97.)

b. The equilibrium price is $13, the equilib-rium quantity is 4000. This is an equilib-rium because the quantity supplied equals the quantity demanded at this price. That is, there is neither a surplus (excess supply) nor a shortage (excess demand) and hence no tendency for the price to change. (95-96)

c. Because the quantity supplied exceeds the quantity demanded when the price is $14 per bushel, we would observe a surplus of 2,500 bushels (in thousands of bushels). We can expect the price of oranges per bushel to fall as sellers scramble to rid themselves of their excess supplies. (95-96)

d. Because the quantity demanded exceeds the quantity supplied at $12 per bushel, we would observe a shortage of 2,500 bushels (in thousands of bushels). We can expect the price of oranges per bushel to rise as some buyers competitively bid up the price just to get some oranges. (95-96)

5. A hypothetical market for cyber cafes shows an upward sloping supply curve, a downward sloping demand curve and an equilibrium price and quantity where the two curves intersect.

   a. A technological breakthrough that lowers the cost of computers will shift the supply of cyber cafes to the right as shown in the graph below. (92)

   b. A rise in consumers' income will shift the demand for cyber cafes to the right as shown in the graph below. (86)

   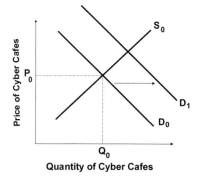

   c. If a fee is charged to coffee houses to use the Internet, the supply of cyber cafes will shift to the left as shown in the accompanying graph. (92)

   d. If the price of newspapers in print rises, the demand for cyber cafes will shift to the right as shown in the graph for answer (b). (92)

   e. If possible suppliers expect cyber cafes to become more popular, the supply of cyber cafes will shift to the right as shown in the graph for answer (a). (92)

6. **a.** This will increase the demand for surfboards shifting the demand curve to the right. At the original price a temporary shortage would be observed putting upward pressure on price. We end up with a higher equilibrium price and a greater equilibrium quantity as illustrated in the graph below. (*When dealing with a change in D or S curves, just remember to go from the initial point of intersection to the new point of intersection. The initial point of intersection will give you the initial equilibrium P and Q and the new point of intersection the new equilibrium P and Q. Then recall that if the price went up in the market, it was a response to a temporary shortage (excess demand). If the equilibrium price went down, then it was a response to a temporary surplus (excess supply).* (98-99)

   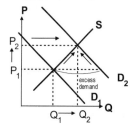

   b. This would cause a decrease in the demand for surfboards shifting the demand curve to the left. At the original price a temporary surplus would be observed putting downward pressure on price. We end up with a lower equilibrium price and a lower equilibrium quantity, as illustrated in the graph below. (98-99)

c. This would cause an increase in the supply of surfboards, shifting the supply curve to the right. At the original price a temporary surplus would be observed, putting downward pressure on price. We end up with a lower equilibrium price and a higher equilibrium quantity, as illustrated in the graph below. (98-99)

d. This would cause a decrease in the supply of surfboards, shifting the supply curve to the left. At the original price a temporary shortage would be observed, putting upward pressure on price. We end up with a higher equilibrium price and a lower equilibrium quantity, as illustrated in the graph below. (98-99)

7. a. An increase in production technology will increase the supply of beef. The temporary surplus (excess supply) of beef at the original price will cause the market price to fall. Eventually we get a lower equilibrium price of beef and a greater amount bought and sold in the market. (98-99)

b. Chicken and beef are substitute goods–they can be used instead of each other. Therefore, this "60 Minutes" report will likely increase the demand for beef. The temporary shortage (excess demand) at the original price will cause the price to be competitively bid up. Eventually we observe a higher equilibrium price and a greater equilibrium quantity. (98-99)

c. The new development would increase the supply of beef while the reports of the health benefits of beef would increase the demand for beef. Quantity of beef sold would definitely rise. The impact on equilibrium price, however, depends upon the relative sizes of the shifts. (98-99)

d. Because people will postpone their purchases of beef until the price decreases, the demand for beef will fall today. A decrease in demand is reflected as a leftward shift of the demand curve. The temporary excess supply (surplus) that is created at the original price puts downward pressure on the market price of beef. Eventually we get a lower equilibrium price and quantity. (98-99)

ANSWERS

A BRAIN TEASER

1. a. This innovation will shift the supply curve to the right as shown in the graph on the left below. As a result, this creates excess supply and the equilibrium price falls while the equilibrium quantity rises. (98-99)

b. The market demand and supply for apple juice is shown below on the right. As a result of the fall in milk prices (assuming milk and apple juice are substitutes), the demand for apple juice shifts to the left. This creates excess supply of apple juice. The equilibrium price will fall. The equilibrium quantity will also fall. (98-99)

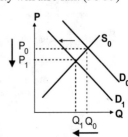

ANSWERS

MULTIPLE CHOICE

1. a As discussed on page 84, the correct answer is a. A possible answer is d, which is a restatement of the law of demand, but since the actual law was among the choices, and is more precise, a is the correct answer.

2. d An equal rise in price will cause individuals to switch more to other goods when there are more substitutes. See page 84.

3. c As discussed on pages 85-86, it is important to distinguish between a change in the quantity demanded and a change in demand. Weather is a shift factor of demand, so demand, not quantity demanded, will increase. Supply will not increase; the quantity supplied will, however. Who knows what will happen to the quality demanded? We don't.

4. b As discussed on page 85, when the price falls there is a movement along the demand curve which is expressed by saying the quantity demanded increased. Moreover, as the price falls, the quantity supplied falls.

5. a As discussed on pages 85-86, an increase in demand is expressed as an outward (or rightward) shift of the demand curve. It is caused by something other than the price. It means people will buy more at any price or pay a higher price for a given quantity demanded.

6. c All of these are shift factors of demand. However, only c will increase demand and shift the demand curve to the right. See pages 85-86.

7. b As is discussed on page 85, b is the only correct response.

8. a A flood will likely bring about a significant increase in the demand for bottled water since a flood makes most other water undrinkable. A flood would be a shift factor of demand for bottled water. See pages 85-86.

9. b The curve slopes downward, so we can surmise that it is a demand curve; and the two points are on the demand curve, so the movement represents an increase in the quantity demanded, not an increase in demand. Moreover, as price falls, the quantity demanded rises. A shift in demand would be a shift of the entire curve. See the figures on page 87.

10. b This demand curve is the only demand curve that goes through all the points in the table. See page 88.

11. a As discussed in the text on page 89 (Figure 4-4), market demand curves are determined by adding individuals' demand curves horizontally. That is, you add the quantities demanded at each price.

12. d Since the market demand curve is derived by adding the individual demand curves horizontally, it will always be flatter. See pages 88-90 and Figure 4-4.

13. a As discussed on pages 90-91, the law of supply is stated in a. The others either have the movement in the wrong direction or are not holding all other things constant.

14. b It is a shift in supply because the curve is upward sloping; and it's a shift of the entire curve, so it is not a movement along. See pages 91-92 and Figure 4-6.

15. c As discussed on page 92, technology is a shift factor of supply so it must be a shift of the supply curve. Since it is an improvement, it must be a shift rightward (or downward). See also Figure 4-6 on page 91.

16. b When there is excess demand, demanders start searching for new suppliers, as discussed on pages 95-96.

17. d The greater the extent to which the quantity supplied exceeds the quantity demanded, the greater the surplus (excess supply) and the greater the pressure for the price to fall. See pages 95-97.

18. a As discussed on page 95, there is a surplus (excess supply) when the price is above equilibrium. A surplus will motivate sellers to reduce price to rid themselves of their excess supplies. As the price falls, the quantity demand rises and the quantity supplied falls; demand and supply curves do *not* shift.

19. c   As discussed on pages 95-96 whenever price is below equilibrium, a shortage is observed, and price rises.

20. b   Since this statement says demand increases, then the demand curve shifts rightward. There is no change in the supply curve. Assuming an upward sloping supply curve, that means that price will rise and quantity will rise. See pages 98-99.

21. d   Since this statement says supply decreases, then the supply curve shifts leftward. There is no change in the demand curve. Assuming a downward sloping demand curve, that means that price will rise and quantity will fall. See pages 98-99.

22. a   The demand for bikinis would rise shifting the demand curve to the right. The supply curve does not change. This creates a temporary shortage that is eliminated over time as the market moves to its new equilibrium at a higher price and a greater quantity traded. See pages 98-99.

23. c   Only a decrease in demand will result in a decrease in quantity and a decrease in price. See pages 98-99.

24. a   An increase in demand has a tendency to increase price and increase the quantity. An increase in supply has a tendency to *decrease* the price and increase the quantity. So, on balance, we are certain of an increase in the equilibrium quantity, but we are uncertain about the impact on the price in the market. See pages 98-99.

25. a   An increase in demand causes the quantity demanded to exceed the quantity supplied, creating excess demand (a shortage). This increases the price causing movement *up* along the demand and supply curves resulting in a *greater* quantity traded in the market. See pages 98-99.

26. b   The fallacy of composition is the false assumption that what is true for a part will also be true for the whole. See page 100.

ANSWERS

POTENTIAL ESSAY QUESTIONS

The following are annotated answers. They indicate the general idea behind the answer.

1.   The shortage of parking spaces implies that permit prices are below equilibrium. The price of a permit should be increased. At least with the purchase of a permit you could be reasonably certain that a space would be available.

2.   Suppose there is an increase in demand. The demand curve shifts out to the right, creating a temporary shortage (excess demand) at the original price. As a result, buyers competitively bid up the price. As the price rises, the quantity demanded falls (movement up along the demand curve toward the new point of intersection) and the quantity supplied rises (movement up along the supply curve toward the new point of intersection). Eventually, the price rises enough until the quantity demanded is once again equal to the quantity supplied. Because there is neither a shortage nor a surplus at this new point of intersection, the new market equilibrium price and quantity is obtained. The market equilibrium price and quantity will both increase as a result of an increase in demand. *You should be able to illustrate this graphically as well.*

USING SUPPLY AND DEMAND

● CHAPTER AT A GLANCE

This review is based upon the learning objectives that open the chapter.

1. Changes (shifts) in demand and supply are what cause changes in the price and the quantity traded in real-world markets. (106-111)

   Shifts in both demand and supply can be tricky. But remember, simply locate the new point of intersection. When both curves shift, the effect on either price or quantity depends on the relative size of the shifts. Moreover, the effect on either price or quantity (one of them) will be certain, while the effect on the other will be uncertain. Note:

   ↑D and ↑S→?P;↑Q   ↑D and ↓S→↑P;? Q

    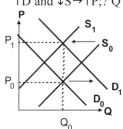

   ↓D and ↑S→↓P; ?Q   ↓D and ↓S→?P;↓ Q

    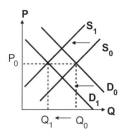

2. The determination of exchange rates—the price of currencies—can be determined by supply and demand analysis, in the same way supply and demand analysis applies to any other good. (107-109)

Exchange rates reported daily in newspapers enable us to determine the dollar price of foreign goods.

3. Price ceilings cause shortages; price floors cause surpluses. (111-115)

   A price ceiling is a legal price set by government below equilibrium. An example is rent controls. A price floor (sometimes called a price support) is a legal price set by government above equilibrium. An example is the minimum wage.

    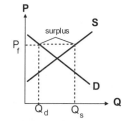

   Price Ceiling   **Price Floor**

4. Excise taxes and tariffs (excise taxes paid by foreign producers on imported goods) raise price and reduce quantity. Quantity restrictions also decrease supply (shift the supply curve up, to the left) raising the price and reducing the quantity. (115-117)

   Any excise tax imposed on suppliers shifts the supply curve up by the amount of the tax. Rarely is the tax <u>entirely</u> passed on to consumers in the form of a higher price. Quantity restrictions also decrease supply.

With tax t, price rises to P_2 and the government collects revenue shown by the shaded region. A quantity restriction of Q_2 has the same effect on price and quantity.

5. In a third-party payer system, the consumer and the one who pays the cost differ. In third-party payer systems quantity demanded, price, and total spending are greater than when the consumer pays. (117-118)

    The graph below shows the effects of a third-party payer market. In a free market, given the supply and demand curve shown, equilibrium price is P_1 and equilibrium quantity is Q_1. If the co-payment, however, is P_0, the consumer purchases quantity Q_2. The supplier will only sell that quantity at price P_2, so the third party pays the difference (P_2-P_0). Under a third-party payer system, total expenditures are larger—shown by the larger shaded square—than a free market—shown by the smaller and darker shaded square.

    Third-party payers are typically health insurance companies, Medicare or Medicaid. Consumers have little incentive to hold down costs when someone else pays. Much of the health care system in the United States today is a third-party payer system.

    See also, "Appendix A: Algebraic Representation of Supply, Demand, and Equilibrium."

● SHORT-ANSWER QUESTIONS

1. Demonstrate graphically what happens in the following situation: Income in the U.S. rose in the 1990s and more and more people began to buy luxury items such as caviar. However, about that same time, the dissolution of the Soviet Union threw suppliers of caviar from the Caspian Sea into a mire of bureaucracy, reducing their ability to export caviar. Market: Caviar sold in the United States.

2. What changes in demand or supply would increase the exchange rate value of the dollar?

3. What is a price ceiling? Demonstrate graphically the effect of a price ceiling on a market.

4. What is a price floor? Demonstrate graphically the effect of a price floor on a market.

5. Why are rent controls likely to worsen an existing shortage of housing?

6. Demonstrate graphically what happens to equilibrium price and quantity when a tariff is imposed on imports.

7. What is a third-party payer system? Name one example.

MATCHING THE TERMS
Match the terms to their definitions

___	**1.** euro	**a.**	The law that sets lowest wage a firm can legally pay an employee.
___	**2.** exchange rate	**b.**	Tax on an imported good.
___	**3.** excise tax	**c.**	Tax that is levied on a specific good.
___	**4.** minimum wage law	**d.**	The person who decides how much of the good to buy differs from the person paying for the good.
___	**5.** price ceiling		
___	**6.** price floor	**e.**	A government-imposed limit on how high a price can be charged.
___	**7.** rent control	**f.**	The price of one currency in terms of another currency.
___	**8.** tariff	**g.**	Price ceiling on rents set by government.
___	**9.** third-party payer market	**h.**	A government-imposed limit on how low a price can be charged.
		i.	The currency used by some members of the European Union.

● PROBLEMS AND APPLICATIONS

1. Suppose you are told that the price of Cadillacs has increased from last year, as has the number bought and sold. Is this an exception to the law of demand, or has there been a change in demand or supply that could account for this?

2. Suppose the exchange rate is one dollar for 125 Japanese yen. How much will a $50 pair of Levi jeans cost a Japanese consumer? How much will a 4,000,000 yen Toyota cost an American consumer?

3. The following table depicts the market supply and demand for milk in the United States.

Price in dollars per gal.	Quantity of gal. supplied in 1,000s	Quantity of gal. demanded in 1,000s
$1.50	600	800
$1.75	620	720
$2.00	640	640
$2.25	660	560
$2.50	680	480

a. Graph the market supply and demand for milk.

b. What is the equilibrium market price and quantity in the market?

c. Show the effect of a government–imposed price floor of $2.25 on the quantity supplied and quantity demanded.

d. Show the effect of a government–imposed price ceiling of $1.75 on the quantity supplied and quantity demanded.

e. What would happen to equilibrium price and quantity if the government imposes a $1 per gallon tax on the sellers and as a result, at every price supply decreases by 100,000? What price would the sellers receive?

4. Suppose the U.S. government imposes stricter entry barriers on Japanese cars imported into the United States. This could be accomplished by the U.S. government either raising tariffs or imposing a quantity restriction (such as a quota).

    a. What impact would this have on the market for Japanese cars in the United States?

    b. What impact would this likely have on the market for American-made cars in the United States?

    c. What do you think could motivate the U.S. government to pursue these stricter entry barriers on Japanese cars coming into the U.S.?

    d. Would Japanese car manufacturers prefer a tariff or a quota? Why?

5. Describe what likely happens to market price and quantity for the particular goods in each of the following cases:

    a. A technological breakthrough lowers the costs of producing tractors in India while there is an increase in incomes of all citizens in India. Market: tractors.

    b. The United States imposes a ban on the sale of oil by companies that do business with Libya and Iran. At the same time, very surprisingly, a large reserve of drillable oil is discovered in Barrington, Rhode Island. Market: Oil.

    c. In the summer of 2004, many people watched the Summer Olympics on television instead of going to the movies. At the same time, thinking that summer is the peak season for movies, Hollywood released a record number of movies. Market: Movie tickets.

    d. After a promotional visit by Michael Jordan to France, a craze for Nike Air shoes develops, while workers in Nike's manufacturing plants in China go on strike, decreasing the production of these shoes. Market: Nike shoes.

A1. The supply and demand equations for strawberries are given by $Q_s = -10 + 5P$ and $Q_d = 20 - 5P$ respectively, where P is price in dollars per quart, Q_s is millions of quarts of strawberries supplied, and Q_d is millions of quarts of strawberries demanded.

    a. What is the equilibrium market price and quantity for strawberries in the market?

b. Suppose a new preservative is introduced that prevents more strawberries from rotting on their way from the farm to the store. As a result, the supply of strawberries increases by 20 million quarts at every price. What effect does this have on market price and quantity sold?

c. Given the original supply, now suppose it has been found that the spray used on cherry trees has ill effects on those who eat the cherries. As a result, the demand for strawberries increases by 10 million quarts at every price. What effect does this have on market price for strawberries and quantity of strawberries sold?

A2. The supply and demand equations for roses are given by $Q_s = -10 + 3P$ and $Q_d = 20 - 2P$ respectively, where P is dollars per dozen roses and Q is dozens of roses in hundred thousands.

a. What is the equilibrium market price and quantity of roses sold?

b. Suppose the government decides to make it more affordable for individuals to give roses to their significant others, and sets a price ceiling for roses at $4 a dozen. What is the likely result?

c. Suppose the government decides to tax the suppliers of roses $1 per dozen roses sold. What is the equilibrium price and quantity in the market? How much do buyers pay for each dozen they buy for their significant others? How much do suppliers receive for each dozen they sell?

d. Suppose the government decides instead to impose a $1 tax on buyers for each dozen roses purchased. (Government has determined buying roses for love to be a demerit good.) What is the equilibrium price and quantity in the market? How much do the buyers pay and how much do the sellers receive?

● A BRAIN TEASER

1. Buchananland wants to restrict its number of auto imports from Zachstan. It is trying to decide whether it should impose a tariff or quantity restrictions (in this case called quotas) on Zachstani cars. With the help of a diagram, explain why auto makers in Zachstan have hired a lobbyist to persuade the government of Buchananland to set quotas instead of imposing tariffs.

● MULTIPLE CHOICE

Circle the one best answer for each of the following questions:

1. If a frost in Florida damages oranges, what will likely happen to the market for Florida oranges?
   a. Demand will increase.
   b. Demand will fall.
   c. Supply will increase.
   d. Supply will decrease.

2. Assume that the cost of shipping automobiles from the United States to Japan decreases. What will most likely happen to the selling price and quantity of cars made in the U.S. and sold in Japan?
a. The price will rise, and quantity will fall.
b. Both price and quantity will rise.
c. The price will fall, and quantity will rise.
d. The price will fall. What happens to quantity is not clear.

3. Assuming standard supply and demand curves, what will likely happen to the price and quantity of cricket bats in Trinidad as interest in cricket dwindles following the dismal performance of the national cricket team, while at the same time taxes are repealed on producing cricket bats?
a. The price will decrease, but what happens to quantity is not clear.
b. The price will decrease, and quantity will increase.
c. The price will increase, but what happens to quantity is not clear.
d. It is not clear what happens to either price or quantity.

4. A higher equilibrium price with no change in market equilibrium quantity could be caused by:
a. supply shifting in and no change in demand.
b. supply and demand both increasing.
c. a decrease in supply and an increase in demand.
d. demand and supply both shifting in.

5. A fall in the value of the euro relative to the dollar:
a. could be caused by an increase in the demand for the euro.
b. could be caused by an increase in the supply of the euro.
c. will make American-made goods cheaper for Europeans.
d. will make European-made goods more expensive for Americans.

6. An increase in the value of the dollar relative to the euro could be caused by:
a. an increase in the supply of the dollar.
b. an increase in the demand for the dollar.
c. a decrease in the demand for the dollar.
d. an increase in U.S. imports.

7. An expected decline in the value of U.S. stocks will most likely:
a. increase the supply of the euro and increase the demand for the dollar.
b. increase the supply of the dollar and increase the demand for the euro.
c. decrease the demand for the dollar and the euro.
d. increase the demand for the dollar and the euro.

8. Referring to the graph below, if there is a price ceiling imposed on this market of P_2, consumers will pay:

a. P_1 and buy quantity Q_1.
b. P_2 and buy quantity Q_2.
c. P_0 and buy quantity Q_0.
d. P_2 and buy quantity Q_0.

9. Referring to the graph below, if there is a price floor imposed on this market of P_2, consumers will pay:

a. P_1 and buy quantity Q_1.
b. P_2 and buy quantity Q_2.
c. P_0 and buy quantity Q_0.
d. P_2 and buy quantity Q_0.

10. Effective rent controls:
a. are examples of price floors.
b. cause the quantity of rental occupied housing demanded to exceed the quantity supplied.
c. create a greater amount of higher quality housing to be made available to renters.
d. create a surplus of rental occupied housing.

11. An increase in the minimum wage can be expected to:
    a. cause unemployment for some workers.
    b. cause a shortage of workers.
    c. increase employment.
    d. help businesses by reducing their costs of production.

12. A tariff:
    a. is a tax imposed on an imported good.
    b. is a quantitative restriction on the amount that one country can export to another.
    c. imposed on a good will shift the supply of that good outward to the right.
    d. will reduce the price paid by the consumer of the good.

13. Quantity restrictions on supply imposed below equilibrium quantity on a market:
    a. increase price and reduce quantity traded.
    b. increase price and increase quantity traded.
    c. decrease price and reduce quantity traded.
    d. decrease price and increase quantity traded.

14. Referring to the graph below, suppose initial supply is represented by S_0. A tax T on suppliers will raise the price that:

    a. suppliers receive net of the tax to P_1.
    b. suppliers receive net of the tax to P_2.
    c. consumers pay to P_2.
    d. consumers pay to P_3.

15. In a third-party payer system:
    a. the person who chooses the product pays the entire cost.
    b. the quantity demanded would be lower than it otherwise would be.
    c. the quantity demanded will be higher than it otherwise would be.
    d. consumers are hurt.

16. In the graph below that demonstrates a third-party payer market, suppose the consumer is required to make a co-payment of P_0. Which of the following areas represents the cost of the program to the third party?

    a. rectangle A.
    b. rectangle B.
    c. rectangle C.
    d. the sum of rectangles A, B, and C.

17. Third-party payer markets result in:
    a. a lower equilibrium price received by the supplier.
    b. a smaller quantity supplied.
    c. a smaller quantity demanded.
    d. increased total spending.

A1. The supply and demand equations for Nantucket Nectar's Kiwi-berry juice are given by $Q_s = -4 + 5P$ and $Q_d = 18 - 6P$ respectively, where price is dollars per quart and quantity is thousands of quarts. The equilibrium market price and quantity is:
    a. P = \$2, Q = 6 thousand quarts.
    b. P = \$3, Q = 5 thousand quarts.
    c. P = \$14, Q = 66 thousand quarts.
    d. P = \$22, Q = 106 thousand quarts.

A2. The supply and demand equations for sidewalk snow removal in a small town in Montana are given by $Q_s = -50 + 5P$ and $Q_d = 100 - 5P$ respectively, where price is in dollars per removal and quantity is numbers of removals per week. It snows so much that demand for sidewalk snow removals increases by 30 per week. The new equilibrium market price and quantity is:
    a. P = \$15, Q = 6 sidewalk snow removals.
    b. P = \$15, Q = 5 sidewalk snow removals.
    c. P = \$18, Q = 66 sidewalk snow removals.
    d. P = \$18, Q = 40 sidewalk snow removals.

A3. The supply and demand equations for Arizona Ice Tea in Arizona are given by $Q_s = -10 + 6P$ and $Q_d = 40 - 8P$; P is the price of each bottle in dollars; and quantity is in hundreds of thousands of bottles per month. Suppose the state government imposes a $1 per bottle tax on the suppliers. The market price the suppliers receive and the equilibrium quantity in the market are:

  a. $3 per bottle and 8 hundred thousand bottles per month.

  b. $3 per bottle and 16 hundred thousand bottles per month.

  c. $4 per bottle and 8 hundred thousand bottles per month.

  d. $4 per bottle and 16 hundred thousand bottles per month.

POTENTIAL ESSAY QUESTIONS

You may also see essay questions similar to the "Problems & Applications" and "A Brain Teaser" exercises.

1. Discuss the impact on the relative price of American exports and imports if the exchange rate value of the dollar rises.

2. Explain why a third-party payer system results in a greater quantity demanded and increases total spending.

ANSWERS

SHORT-ANSWER QUESTIONS

1. The demand curve for Russian caviar shifts out; supply shifts in; the price rises substantially. What happens to quantity depends upon the relative sizes of the shifts. (110-111)

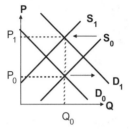

2. Either an increase in the demand or a decrease in the supply of the dollar could increase its price (exchange rate). (110-111)

3. A price ceiling is a government imposed limit on how high a price can be charged. An effective price ceiling below market equilibrium price will cause $Q_D > Q_S$ (a shortage) as shown in the graph below. (111-113)

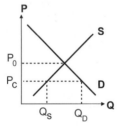

4. A price floor is a government imposed limit on how low a price can be charged. An effective price floor above market equilibrium price will cause $Q_S > Q_D$ (a surplus) as shown in the graph below. (113-115)

5. Rent controls are price ceilings and result in shortages in rental housing. As time passes and as the population rises, the demand for rental housing rises. On the supply side, other ventures become more lucrative relative to renting out housing. Owners have less incentive to repair existing buildings, let alone build new ones, reducing the supply of rental housing over time. As a result, the shortage becomes more acute over time (112-113)

6. A tariff is an excise tax paid by foreign producers on an imported good. As a tariff of t is imposed, the supply curve shifts upward to S_1 by the amount of the tariff. The equilibrium price goes up and quantity goes down. (115-116)

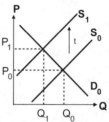

7. In a third-party payer system the person who decides how much of a good to buy differs from the person who pays for the good. One example is the health care system in the United States today. (117-118)

ANSWERS

MATCHING

1-i; 2-f; 3-c; 4-a; 5-e; 6-h; 7-g; 8-b; 9-d;

ANSWERS

PROBLEMS AND APPLICATIONS

1. This is not an exception to the law of demand (there are very few exceptions). Instead, an increase in demand could account for a higher price and a greater amount bought and sold, as is illustrated in the figure below. (110-111)

2. The Levi jeans will cost the Japanese consumer 6,250 yen (125x50). The Toyota will cost the American consumer $32,000 (4,000,000/125). (107-109)

3. a. The market supply and demand for milk is graphed below. (box on 108, 110-111)

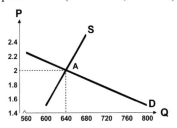

b. The equilibrium market price is $2 and equilibrium quantity in the market is 640 thousand gallons of milk because the quantity supplied equals the quantity demanded. This is point A on the graph above. (box on 108, 110-111)

c. A government–imposed price floor of $2.25 is shown in the figure below. Since it is a price above market price, quantity supplied (660) exceeds quantity demanded (560) by 100 thousand gallons. (113-115)

d. A government-imposed price ceiling of $1.75 is below market price. Quantity supplied (620 thousand gallons) will be less than quantity demanded (720 thousand gallons) by 100 thousand gallons, as shown below. (111-113)

e. Because of the tax, the quantity supplied at every price level will decline by 100 thousand gallons. The supply and demand table will change as follows:

Price in dollars per gal.	Quantity of gal. supplied 1,000s	Quantity of gal. demanded 1,000s
$1.50	500	800
$1.75	520	720
$2.00	540	640
$2.25	560	560
$2.50	580	480

The market equilibrium price would be $2.25 and the equilibrium quantity would be 560 thousand gallons. Since the sellers will have to pay $1 tax on every gallon they sell, they will receive $1.25 per gallon of milk. (115-116)

4. a. A higher tariff or a stricter quota imposed on Japanese cars would decrease the supply of Japanese cars in the United States. The upward (leftward) shift of the supply curve, such as from S_1 to S_2 shown in the figure below, creates a temporary shortage (excess demand) at the original price that puts upward pressure on the prices of Japanese cars. The result over time will be higher prices for Japanese cars, as well as a decrease in the amount bought and sold in the U.S. market, as shown below. (115-117)

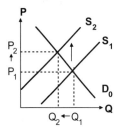

b. Because Japanese and American-made cars are substitutes for each other, some people will switch from buying the now relatively more expensive Japanese cars (law of demand in action) to buying more American-made cars. (Notice that "relative" prices are what are relevant.) This increases the demand for American-made cars, increasing their prices as well as the amount bought and sold. This is illustrated in the figure below. (115-117)

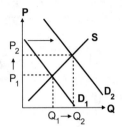

c. These trade barriers may be advocated by American car manufacturers. They could obviously benefit from the higher prices and greater sales. American automotive workers could also benefit from the greater job security that comes with more cars being produced and sold. These "special interest groups" may put political pressure on government, and the government may succumb to that pressure. (115-117)

d. The Japanese would prefer a quota over a tariff. This is because a tariff would require them to pay taxes to the U.S. government; while a quota would not. (115-117)

5. a. The supply curve will shift out from S_0 to S_1 as the new technology makes it cheaper to produce tractors. Increased incomes will shift the demand for tractors out from D_0 to D_1. Equilibrium price may go up, remain the same, or go down, depending on the relative shifts in the two curves. Equilibrium quantity, however, will definitely increase. (110-111)

b. The ban on the companies doing business with Libya and Iran will shift the supply curve in from S_0 to S_1. The discovery of oil will, however, shift it back out to possibly S_2. Depending on the relative shifts, equilibrium price and quantity will change. In the case shown in the diagram, the shift resulting from the discovery of

the new oil source dominates the shift resulting from the ban, and the equilibrium price falls and quantity goes up. (110-111)

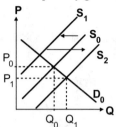

c. With more people watching the Olympics, the demand for movies shifts in from D_0 to D_1. At the same time the increased supply of movies will shift the supply curve out from S_0 to S_1. Equilibrium price will fall, while the change in equilibrium quantity will depend on the relative shifts in the curves. (110-111)

d. With more people demanding Nike Air shoes, the demand curve will shift out from D_0 to D_1. The worker strike will, however, reduce supply and shift it in from S_0 to S_1. The resulting equilibrium price will be higher, while the change in quantity depends on the relative shifts in the curves. (110-111)

A1. a. Equating Q_s to Q_d and then solving for equilibrium price gives us $3 per quart. Substituting $3 into the demand and supply equations, we find that equilibrium quantity is 5 million quarts. (123)

b. Since supply increases by 20 million quarts, the new supply equation is $Q_s = 10 + 5P$. Equating this with the demand equation, we find the new equilibrium price to be $1 per quart. Substituting into either the new supply equation or the demand equation we find that equilibrium quantity is 15 million quarts. (124-125)

c. With demand increasing, the new demand equation is $Q_d = 30 - 5P$. Setting Q_s equal to Q_d and solving for price we find equilibrium price to be $4 per quart. Substituting this into either the new demand or the supply equation we find equilibrium quantity to be 10 million quarts. (124-125)

A2. a. Equating Q_s and Q_d, then solving gives equilibrium price $6 and quantity 8 hundred thousand dozen. (123)

b. If price ceiling is set at $4, $Q_s = 2$, and $Q_d = 12$; resulting in a shortage of ten hundred thousand dozen. (125)

c. If a $1 tax is imposed on suppliers, the new supply equation will be $Q_s = -10 + 3(P-1) = -13 + 3P$. Equating this with Q_d gives equilibrium price $6.60 and quantity 6.8 hundred thousand. Buyers pay $6.60 for each dozen they buy, and the sellers receive $1 less than that, or $5.60, for each dozen they sell. (125-126)

d. As a result of the tax, the new demand equation will be $Q_d = 20 - 2(P+1) = 18 - 2P$. Equating this with Q_s gives equilibrium price $5.60 and quantity 6.8 hundred thousand. Buyers pay $6.60 (P + 1) for each dozen they buy, and the sellers receive $5.60 for each dozen they sell. (125-126)

ANSWERS

A BRAIN TEASER

1. The supply and demand equilibrium are at price P_e and quality Q_e. If quotas for Zachstani cars are set at Q_2, the price received for each car sold is P_2, which is well above P_t, the price they would normally sell for at that quantity. A tariff of $t (P_2 - P_t)$ would have to be imposed to

reduce imports to Q_2 reflected by the supply curve shifting in to S_1. In both cases, consumers pay Zachstan producers P_2 for each car. In the case of the quota, Zachstan producers keep P_2 for each car. In the case of the tariff, Zachstan producers must give up t to the government for each car sold. Because with quotas the price received (and therefore profits) are higher, they have the lobbyist lobbying for quotas. (115-117)

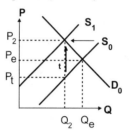

ANSWERS

MULTIPLE CHOICE

1. d A frost will reduce the quantity of oranges available for sale at every price. Supply will decrease. See pages 110-111.

2. c The supply curve will shift out, market price will fall and the quantity will rise. See pages 110-111.

3. a Demand for cricket bats will fall, shifting the demand curve in, while the tax repeal will shift the supply curve out. Price will fall, and quantity may change depending on the relative shifts of the supply and demand curves. See pages 110-111.

4. c When the demand curve shifts out, while the supply curve shifts in, the price rises and the quantity can remain the same. See pages 110-111.

5. b The analysis of currencies is the same as the analysis for any other good. A shift of supply out and to the right will result in a lower price. A fall in the value of the euro means it will take fewer dollars to purchase one euro, making European-made goods cheaper for Americans and American-made goods more expensive for Europeans. See pages 107-109.

6. b An increase in the price of anything would require an increase in demand or a decrease in supply. An increase in U.S. imports will increase the supply of dollars lowering the price of the dollar. See pages 107-109.

7. b Falling U.S. stock prices would encourage people to get out of the U.S. stock market and place their funds elsewhere, for example, in European financial markets. Therefore, people would sell (supply) dollars and buy (demand) more euros. See pages 107-109.

8. a As discussed on pages 111-113, a price ceiling above equilibrium price will not affect the market price or quantity. Equilibrium price and quantity, in this case will be determined by the intersection of the supply and demand curves—at price P_1 and quantity Q_1.

9. d At a price of P_2 the quantity demanded by consumers is Q_0. The quantity supplied by sellers would be Q_2 at price P_2. A surplus of $Q_2 - Q_0$ would put downward pressure on price. However, government does not allow a lower price. So, the equilibrium price and quantity of P_1 and Q_1 would not prevail when government intervenes with a price floor. See pages 113-115.

10. b Rent controls are price ceilings and therefore cause the quantity demanded to exceed the quantity supplied. Indeed, the quantity demanded rises while the quantity supplied falls creating a shortage. See pages 111-113.

11. a Because the minimum wage is a price floor it increases the quantity supplied and decreases the quantity demanded (*decreasing* employment) and creating a *surplus* of workers (causing some unemployment). The higher minimum wage would *increase* costs of production to businesses. See pages 113-115.

12. a The correct answer is a by definition. Also, a tariff will decrease supply, shifting the supply curve inward to the left. This causes the price consumers must pay to rise. See pages 115-116.

13. a Quantity restrictions reduce supply and create a higher price and lower quantity traded in a market. See pages 116-117.

14. c A tax shifts the supply curve up by the amount of the tax. The price consumers pay is determined by the price where the demand curve and the after-tax supply curve intersect. The after-tax price suppliers receive falls to P_0, the new equilibrium price less the tax (P_2–T). See pages 115-116.

15. c In a third-party payer system the person who chooses the product pays some but not all of the cost. As a result of a lower effective price to the consumer, the quantity demanded will be higher than otherwise. See pages 117-118.

16. a At a price of P_0, the consumer demands quantity Q_1. The supplier requires a price of P_1 for that quantity. Therefore, total expenditures are P_1 times Q_1 or areas A, B, and C. Of these, consumers pay areas B and C. The third party pays area A. See pages 117-118.

17. d In third-party payer markets the quantity demanded, price, and total spending are greater than when the consumer pays. See pages 115-116.

A1. a Equating the supply and demand equations gives equilibrium P = $2. Substituting this into either the supply or demand equation tells us that Q = 6 thousand quarts. See page 123.

A2. d The new demand becomes $Q_d = 130 - 5P$. Equating the supply and demand equations gives equilibrium P = $18. Substituting this into either the supply or demand equation tells us that Q = 40 sidewalk snow removals. See pages 124-125.

A3. a   A $1 per bottle tax on suppliers makes the supply equation $Q_s = -10 + 6(P - 1) = -16 + 6P$. Equating this with the demand equation gives equilibrium $P = \$4$ and $Q = 8$ hundred thousand. The supplier receives $3 (\$4 - \$1). See pages 125-126.

━━━━━━ ANSWERS ━━━━━━

POTENTIAL ESSAY QUESTIONS

The following are annotated answers. They indicate the general idea behind the answer.

1.   An increase in the exchange rate value of the dollar means that the dollar will buy more units of foreign currencies. Therefore, the relative price of foreign products imported into the United States will decrease and Americans will import more. Likewise, a stronger dollar will make American products relatively more expensive to foreigners. Foreigners will buy fewer American products and the United States will export less. If U.S. imports rise and exports fall, the U.S. trade deficit rises.

2.   Because part of the costs of obtaining a good or service in a third-party payer system is paid by someone other than the consumer, the effective price to the consumer is lower and the quantity demanded is greater. At this higher quantity demanded the price charged by sellers is greater. The result is greater consumption at a higher price and therefore greater total spending on the good or service. See Figure 5-7 on page 115 for a graphic illustration of this.

THINKING LIKE A MODERN ECONOMIST

CHAPTER AT A GLANCE

This review is based upon the learning objectives that open the chapter.

1. <u>Traditional building-blocks</u> are the assumptions that (1) people are completely rational and (2) are self-interested.

   <u>Behavioral building-blocks</u> are the assumptions that (1) people behave purposefully and (2) follow their enlightened self-interest. (128-129)

   Traditional → people are completely rational.
   Behavioral → people are predictably irrational.

2a. <u>Heuristic models</u> are models that are expressed informally in words. They are verbal rather than mathematical.

   <u>Heuristic models</u> are merely stepping stones to more formal models; they are not sufficiently precise to test scientifically.
   (128, 134-139)

   Heuristic = Informal = Non-mathematical = Verbal

2b. <u>Traditional heuristic models</u> are informal, verbal models that are based on the narrow assumptions of complete rationality and self-interest. (134-136)

   <u>Behavioral heuristic models</u> are informal, verbal models that are based on the broader assumptions of purposeful action and enlightened self-interest. (136-139)

3. <u>Empirical models</u> are based on statistical patterns in the data. They are created by first collecting and analyzing data and then formulating an hypothesis.

   <u>Formal models</u> begin with assumptions that are combined to formulate an hypothesis. The hypotheses are tested against the data. (141, 146)

   - *Empirical models: collect data then formulate hypotheses.*
   - *Formal models: formulate hypotheses then test against the data.*

4. Modern economists use many types of formal models. Three are: butterfly effect models, game theory models, and ACE models. (144-145)

   Butterfly effect models are models in which a small change causes a large effect.

   Game theory models are models that focus on strategic interaction among individuals.

   An agent based computational economic (ACE) model is a culture dish approach to the study of economic phenomenon in which agents are allowed to interact in a computationally constructed environment and the researcher observes the results of that interaction. This approach is fundamentally different from standard modeling; it is computer-based and has no equations to be solved.

5. Traditional economists tend to have one framework from which they derive policy precepts. Modern economists allow for multiple frameworks and multiple policy precepts. (148-149)

Traditional economics suggests that the market is likely to be the best way to deal with a problem, and that, left alone, the market will guide people toward doing the best they, and society, can, given the constraints.

Modern economics in general is less sure that the market will solve every problem; while it accepts the useful functions of the market, it also recognizes the limitations of the market.

● SHORT-ANSWER QUESTIONS

1. How do traditional building-blocks differ from behavioral building-blocks?

2. Define the inductive approach and the deductive approach. Which of the reasoning approaches does traditional economics use? What about modern economics?

3. What is a model?

4. How do traditional heuristic models differ from behavioral heuristic models? Give an example of each.

5. How do empirical models differ from formal models? Give an example of each.

6. Describe the tradeoff between simplicity and complexity that exists for models.

7. List and define three types of formal models used by modern economists.

8. How and why do modern economics and traditional economics differ in their policy prescriptions? Give a specific example.

MATCHING THE TERMS
Match the terms to their definitions

____ 1. agent-based computational economic (ACE) model	**a.** An economist who is willing to use a wider range of models than did earlier economists.
____ 2. behavioral economics	**b.** Behavior such as habits and rules of thumb that may be incompatible with the traditional economic understanding of rationality.
____ 3. butterfly effect model	**c.** A model in which one analyzes the strategic interaction of individuals when they take into account the likely response of other people to their actions.
____ 4. coefficient of determination	
____ 5. econometrics	**d.** When people value something more just because they have it.
____ 6. empirical model	**e.** Microeconomic analysis that uses a broader set of building-blocks than rationality and self-interest used in traditional economics.
____ 7. endowment effect	
____ 8. enlightened self-interest	
____ 9. game theory model	**f.** A model in which the path to equilibrium affects the equilibrium.
____ 10. heuristic model	**g.** A simplified representation of the problem or question that captures the essential issues.
____ 11. model	
____ 12. modern economist	**h.** An economist who studies the logical implications of rationality and self-interest in relatively simple algebraic or graphical models, such as the supply and demand model.
____ 13. natural experiment	
____ 14. path-dependent model	
____ 15. pre-commitment strategy	**i.** Models that statistically discover a pattern in the data.
____ 16. purposeful behavior	**j.** An equilibrium in a model in which people's beliefs become self-fulfilling.
____ 17. regression model	
____ 18. self-confirming equilibrium	**k.** A model that is expressed informally in words.
____ 19. traditional economist	**l.** A model that uses a culture dish approach to the study of economic phenomena in which agents are allowed to interact in a computationally constructed environment and the researcher observes the results of that interaction.
	m. An empirical model in which one statistically relates one set of variables to another.
	n. A measure of the proportion of the variability in the data that is accounted for by the statistical model.
	o. An event created by nature that can serve as an experiment.
	p. When people can care about other people as well as themselves.
	q. A model in which a small change causes a large effect.
	r. A strategy in which people consciously place limitations on their future actions, thereby limiting their choices.
	s. The statistical analysis of economic data.

● PROBLEMS AND APPLICATIONS

1. You are the research assistant to Princeton economics professor Orley Ashenfelter. Together you have been working on a new regression model to determine the quality of wine grown in Spirits-land. After collecting and analyzing your data, you have come up with the relationship below.

a. Use the equation to predict the quality of wine for each year. Write the values in the table.

Wine quality = 8 + 0.1(winter rainfall) + 0.002(average growing season temperature) − 0.05(harvest rainfall)

	Wine Quality	Winter rainfall	Average growing season temperature	Harvest rainfall
2006		4	75	2
2007		4	75	2
2008		10	80	6
2009		7	60	15

    b. Is this an empirical or a formal model? Why?

2. Complete the following table.

	Earlier Economics	Modern Economics	
		Behavioral Economists	**Traditional Economists**
Assumptions	1.	1.	1.
	2.	2.	2.
Approach			
Types of models			

3. State for each of the following if it is an example of an empirical model or if it is an example of a formal model. And then explain why.

    a. An equation that is derived from last semester's data that summarizes the statistical relationship between the number of students and the average final grade in a particular professor's class.

    b. A model that uses production possibility curves for Portugal and Britain with regard to wheat and wine production to show how comparative advantage and specialization allow both countries to consume outside of their individual production possibility curves.

    c. A supply and demand model for the price of livestock.

    d. An equation that is derived from last year's data that summarizes the statistical relationship between the number of livestock sold and the average price of livestock.

    e. A model that uses equation $Qs = -5 + 2P$ for quantity supplied of livestock and the equation $Qd = 10 - P$ for quantity demanded of livestock.

● A BRAIN TEASER

1. Two economists are walking down the street. One says to the other "Look! A $100 bill!" The other one says "Don't bother picking it up. If it were really a hundred dollar bill, someone would have picked it up already."

Which of these two economists is more likely to be a behavioral economist? Which one is more likely to be a traditional economist? Why?

● MULTIPLE CHOICE

Circle the one best answer for each of the following questions:

1. In modern economics supply and demand is considered:
   a. the holy grail of economics.
   b. an important stepping stone, but just a stepping stone.
   c. the glue that holds economics together.
   d. an empirical model.

2. What is the "glue" that holds economics together?
   a. Modeling.
   b. Supply and demand.
   c. Economic theories.
   d. Data analysis.

3. Traditional economists assume:
   a. complete rationality and enlightened self-interest.
   b. purposeful behavior and enlightened self-interest.
   c. complete rationality and self-interest.
   d. purposeful behavior and self-interest.

4. Behavioral economists assume:
   a. complete rationality and enlightened self-interest.
   b. complete rationality and self-interest.
   c. purposeful behavior and self-interest.
   d. purposeful behavior and enlightened self-interest.

5. Which of the choices below are examples of models?
   a. A small replica of a proposed house.
   b. A computer simulation that simulates the growth of bacteria.
   c. The online game Second Life.
   d. All of the above.

6. Behavioral economists argue:
   a. that the supply/demand model should be discarded.
   b. traditional building-blocks do not explain everything.
   c. models built on traditional building-blocks are irrelevant.
   d. All of the above.

7. What real-world behaviors do behavioral economists incorporate into their models?
   a. That people make choices based on rules of thumb.
   b. Endowment effects.
   c. Pre-commitment strategies.
   d. All of the above.

8. What type of economist is most likely to rely primarily on deductive reasoning?
   a. Behavioral economists.
   b. Modern economists.
   c. Traditional economists.
   d. Modern traditional economists.

9. Heuristic models are:
   a. informal and verbal simplified representations that capture the essential issues of a problem.
   b. models based on the behavioral building-blocks of purposeful behavior and enlightened self-interest.
   c. models that statistically discover a pattern in the data.
   d. models that are based only on formal logical relationships.

10. Why are heuristic models limited?
    a. They are not sufficiently precise, making their validity difficult to test.
    b. Their traditional building-blocks make them too abstract to be of practical use.
    c. Their behavioral building-blocks make them too dependent on context.
    d. They are too mathematical and reliant on theory.

11. Which types of economists rely on empirical work?
    a. Traditional economists.
    b. Behavioral economists.
    c. Modern traditional economists.
    d. All modern economists.

12. An empirical economist uses:
    a. deductive reasoning only.
    b. econometrics and empirical models.
    c. ACE models only.
    d. inductive methods only.

13. Econometrics is:
   a. the statistical analysis of economic data.
   b. the measure of the proportion of the variability in data accounted for by the statistical model.
   c. the computationally constructed environment in an agent based computation economic model.
   d. the parameters of stranger attractor models.

14. All of the following are formal models *except*:
   a. butterfly effect models.
   b. game theory models.
   c. supply and demand models.
   d. heuristic models.

15. With regard to policy, traditional economists generally are more likely than behavioral economists to suggest that:
   a. the market is likely to be the best way to deal with a problem.
   b. there are limitations of the market.
   c. because there are multiple frameworks within which a problem can be thought about, there is fundamental ambiguity about the appropriate policy.
   d. there is a potential role for government interventions and public policy in the economy even when there are no externalities.

16. With regard to policy, behavioral economists are more likely than traditional economists to suggest that:
   a. free market policy guarantees both liberty and prosperity.
   b. there is an important role for government intervention and public policy even when there are no externalities.
   c. the market is likely to be the best way to deal with a problem.
   d. there is no ambiguity about what policy should be.

● POTENTIAL ESSAY QUESTIONS

You may also see essay questions similar to the "Problems & Applications" and "A Brain Teaser" exercises.

1. Respond to the following statement: "Formal models, as abstract simplifications (based on theories) of problems or issues, do a poor job of describing what goes on in the real world. Economists should 'bring the model to the data' and concentrate on empirical models instead."

2. When housing bubbles burst, people are sometimes unwilling to sell their house for less than they bought it for. What assumptions or building blocks does this call into question? Which perspective (traditional or behavioral) provides a better explanation for this phenomenon? Why?

3. Behavioral economists argue that people tend to make choices based on rules of thumb. How could traditional economists reconcile their assumption that people are rational with this use of rules of thumb?

━━━━━ ANSWERS ━━━━━

SHORT-ANSWER QUESTIONS

1. The traditional building-blocks are the assumptions that people are (1) completely rational and (2) self-interested. Behavioral building-blocks are the assumptions that people (1) behave purposefully and (2) follow their enlightened self-interest.

   Traditional building-blocks are narrower and more restrictive than behavioral building-blocks. As a result, models based on traditional building-blocks are more analytically powerful; they provide simplicity and insight by high-lighting the relevant general issues. Models based on behavioral building-blocks provide less clear-cut results but capture how people actually behave. (128-129)

2. An inductive approach is an approach to understanding a problem or question in which understanding is developed empirically from statistically analyzing what is observed in the data. A deductive approach is an approach to understanding a problem or question that begins with certain self-evident principles from which implications are logically deduced. Traditional economics is typically characterized as a deductive approach and modern economics involves more use of induction. (128)

3. A model is a simplified representation of a problem or question that captures the essential issues. (127)

4. A heuristic model is a model that is expressed informally in words. Traditional heuristic models are informal, verbal models that are based on the narrow assumptions of complete rationality and self-interest. Behavioral heuristic models are informal, verbal models that are based on the broader assumptions of purposeful action and enlightened self-interest. The broader assumptions of behavioral heuristic models allow for a much wider range of models and sets of explanations, as well as a much wider range of policy interventions, compared to traditional heuristic models. Behavioral heuristic models take social dimensions of problems into account; traditional heuristic models don't.

Economists Steven Landsburg's models *"How More Sex is Safer Sex"* and *"Why Car Insurance Costs More Some Places than others"* are examples of traditional heuristic models. Economist Robert Frank's models *"Why are People More Likely to Return Cash than a Lampshade?"* and *"Why Don't More People Wear Velcro Shoes?"* are examples of behavioral heuristic models. (134-138)

5. Empirical models begin with a pattern found in the data. (They are created by first collecting and analyzing data and then formulating an hypothesis.) Formal models are those derived by first formulating the hypothesis and then testing it with data.

   Empirical models, by "letting the data speak," quantifiably and scientifically support the implications and conclusions of heuristic models. Simple relationships derived from data help explain and sometimes predict outcomes in the real world. However, because of the impossibility of controlled experiments, "letting the data speak" will not necessarily provide definitive answers. Formal models rely on theoretical models to guide them in interpreting data and drawing out policy implications from their work. But because of the almost infinite number of potential interrelationships, out-comes, and models, there is a formal theoretical model that can arrive at just about any possible conclusion. An example of an empirical model is the regression model. An example of a formal model is the butterfly effect model. (139-144)

6. Each new relationship added to a model involves an additional level of technical difficulty. The more complex the model, the harder it is to arrive at a conclusion. (143-144)

7. Modern economists use many types of formal models. Here are three: (1) Butterfly effect models – models in which a small change causes a large effect. In these models, because a small change could tip the economy into a low-growth, high-unemployment equilibrium that would be difficult to escape, there is a serious potential for economic depression. (2) Game theory models – models in which one analyzes the strategic interaction of individuals when they take into account the likely re-sponse of other people to their actions. Game

theory is the subject of most graduate micro-economic studies and courses. (3) Agent based computational economic (ACE) models – a culture dish approach to the study of economic phenomenon in which agents (encapsulated collections of data and methods representing an entity residing in that environ-ment on the computer) are allowed to interact in a computationally constructed environment and the researcher observes the results of that interaction. This approach is fundamentally different from standard modeling; it is com-puter-based and has no equations to be solved. (142-145)

8. Traditional economics and modern economics differ significantly in their policy prescriptions because they use different assumptions and methodologies. Traditional economics sug-gests that the market is likely to be the best way to deal with a problem, and that, left alone, the market will guide people toward doing the best they, and society, can, given the con-straints. Modern economics in general is less sure that the market will solve every problem; while it accepts the useful functions of the market it also recognizes the limitations of the market. The difference in policy prescriptions occurs because of the different assumptions and viewpoints underlying the two perspec-tives. Traditional economics has more narrow assumptions. Modern economics has broad assumptions. Traditional economics tends to favor policies directed at achieving more growth. Behavioral economics is more likely to allow for the distribution of income to be taken into account. (148-149)

ANSWERS

MATCHING

1-l; 2-e; 3-q; 4-n; 5-s; 6-i; 7-d; 8-p; 9-c; 10-k; 11-g; 12-a; 13-o; 14-f; 15-r; 16-b; 17-m;18-j; 19-h.

ANSWERS

PROBLEMS AND APPLICATIONS

1. **a.**   (140-141)

	Wine Quality	Winter rainfall	Average growing season temperature	Harvest rainfall
2006	8.45	4	75	2
2007	8.45	4	75	2
2008	8.86	10	80	6
2009	8.07	7	60	15

b.   This is an empirical model. It statistically discovers a pattern in the data. In addition it is a regression model, that is, an empirical tool in which one statistically relates one set of variables to another. (139-143)

2. (129-134)

	Earlier Economics	Modern Economics	
		Behavioral Economists	**Traditional Economists**
Assumptions	Rationality	Purposeful behavior	Rationality
	Self-interest	Enlightened Self-interest	Self-interest
Approach	Primarily deduction	Induction and deduction; emphas-is on experimental economics and empirical models	Induction and deduction; em-phasis on empirical models
Types of models	Simple supply demand models	All types including highly complex mathematical models and ACE models	All types in-cluding highly complex mathematical models and ACE models

3. **a.**   This is an example of an empirical model, specifically a regression model. An empirical relationship is derived using the concept of goodness-of-fit that results in an algebraic representation of a pattern in the data. Because the model is derived from data and not based on theory, it is an empirical model. (139-143)

b. This is an example of a formal model. The model makes use of the theory of comparative advantage to highlight the important implications specialization and division-of-labor have for international trade. Because the model is based on a theory and not derived from data, it is a formal model. (139-145)

c. This is an example of a formal model. The model makes use of the invisible hand theorem. Because the model is carefully based on deductive reasoning, it is a formal model. (139-145)

d. This is an example of an empirical model. A mathematical relationship is derived using the concept of goodness-of-fit that results in an algebraic representation of a pattern in the data. Because the model is derived from data, it is an empirical model. (139-145)

e. This is an example of a formal model. While the model is expressed algebraically it is still based not on data analysis, but on the invisible hand theorem. Because the model is carefully based on deductive reasoning, it is a formal model. (139-145)

ANSWERS

A BRAIN TEASER

1. The economist who acknowledged that there was a $100 bill on the street is more likely to be a behavioral economist because a behavioral economist is likely to allow for the possibility of predictable irrationality. The economist who said not to bother picking it up is more likely to be a traditional economist because a traditional economist is likely to believe that people make choices based on marginal cost and marginal benefit. If there were a real $100 bill on the ground, someone would have already picked it up. So, it won't be there. The behavioral economist will likely put less faith in people's rationality and will likely argue that one would likely regret not having checked to see if the $100 is real because he is less sure of the relevance of the deductive model to the real world and will also likely feel loss aversion for not having checked.

Behavioral economists inductively derive the principles and assumptions on which they base their models. They decide what assumptions are justified based on what behaviors they observe in the real-world. Behavioral economists' two main assumptions are that people behave purposefully and follow their enlightened self-interest.

Traditional economists deduce self-evident principles that are narrower and more restrictive on which they build their models. Traditional economists' assumptions are that people are completely rational and self-interested.

So, because the behavioral economist has broader assumptions on which he builds his models, he is more likely to acknowledge that there is unclaimed money on the street.

Because the traditional economist has narrower assumptions on which he builds his models, he is less likely to accept the irrational possibility that there is unclaimed money on the street. Because people employ maximizing behavior and as the market is efficient, there should be no money on the street. The existence of the money is incompatible with the assumptions of the traditional economist. (129-131)

ANSWERS

MULTIPLE CHOICE

1. b   As discussed on pages 127 and 128, the author states that his goal in including this chapter is to disabuse you from thinking that the supply and demand model is the holy grail of economics. He also points out that models are the glue that holds economics together. The supply and demand model is not an empirical model. He also says how supply and demand is just a stepping stone.

2. a   As discussed on page 127, modeling is the glue that holds modern economics together.

3. c   As discussed on page 129, traditional economists are economists who study the logical implications of rationality and self-interest.

4. d   As discussed on page 129, behavioral economists are economists who use a broader set of building-blocks than rationality and self-interest. They believe rationality should be broadened to purposeful behavior and self-interest to enlightened self-interest.

5. d   On pages 129 and 130 several different examples are given of what might be considered models. The proposed house, the computer simulation, and Second Life are all mentioned as possible examples.

6. b   As discussed on pages 129 and 130, behavioral economists do not advocate discarding the supply/demand model. Behavioral economists recognize that traditional building-blocks do not explain everything.

7. d   As discussed on pages 129-132, behavioral economists incorporate the idea that people will make choices based on rules of thumb into their models. Behavioral economists also incorporate endowment effects and pre-commitment strategies into their models.

8. c   As discussed on pages 128 and 129, traditional economists use primarily deductive reasoning.

9. a   As discussed on page 128, a heuristic model is an informal or verbal model.

10. a   As discussed on pages 138 and 139, heuristic means verbal and informal. Heuristic models are limited because they are not sufficiently precise, making their validity difficult to test.

11. d   As discussed on pages 139 and 140, because economists try to understand the real world at some point all rely on empirical work.

12. b   As discussed on pages 139 and 140, empirical economists can use traditional assumptions and deduction. What distinguishes them from other economists is their reliance on statistical techniques such as econometrics and models based on data (empirical models).

13. a   As discussed on page 139, econometrics is the statistical analysis of economic data.

14. d   As discussed on pages 142-145, butterfly effect models, game theory models, and supply/demand models are all formal models.

15. a   As discussed on pages 148 and 149, traditional economists are likely to believe that markets are the best way to deal with a problem. The other options describe behavioral economists.

16. b   As discussed on pages 148 and 149, behavioral economists are much more likely to support government intervention. Traditional economists are much more likely to support the market as the way to deal with a problem and see much less ambiguity.

◼ ANSWERS ◼

POTENTIAL ESSAY QUESTIONS

The following are annotated answers. They indicate the general idea behind the answer.

1.   It is true that "letting the data speak" and "bringing the model to the data" will ground theory in mathematics and science. What primarily distinguishes modern economists from other social scientists is economists' reliance on formal empirical methods. Modern economics is based on experiments that can be replicated, or on statistical analysis of real-world observations. With the amount of data and computing power available increasing exponentially, empirical analysis and statistics is likely to play an increasingly significant role in modern economics.

However, data by themselves have no meaning. Data must be interpreted and given meaning by economists. How a modern economist interprets the data depends on what model and building-blocks he or she is implicitly or explicitly using. Data must be organized by theories.

Economics is not a laboratory science. Moral and practical problems severely limit when controlled experiments can be utilized. Given this limited ability to conduct controlled experiments, letting the data speak will not necessarily provide the definitive answer. As a result, economists need theoretical models to guide them in interpreting data and drawing out policy implications from their work.

2. I'll start with a humorous quote: "Economists tend to think people are crazy because they won't sell their homes for less than they paid for them—and people think economists are crazy for thinking things exactly like that" – Professor Christopher Mayer.

The loss-averse behavior of people who don't want to sell their homes for less than they bought them for is an example of predictably irrational behavior. This behavior is irrational because the market is the means for determining how much something is worth. In this situation, it is irrational to take into account the price you paid for your house. This irrationality calls into question the traditional assumption that people are completely rational.

Behavioral economics, which says that people are not perfectly rational but instead are predictably irrational, provides an alternative explanation for this phenomenon. According to behavioral economics, people take things beside economic factors, such as social factors, into account when making a decision. They will experience severe loss-aversion if they sell their house for less than the price they paid. Thus, they will refuse to lower the asking price on their house.

3. The traditional assumptions and building-blocks of economics, while narrow, can still be used to explain what seems to be irrational behavior. Take, for example, when people make choices based on rules of thumb rather than using the economic decision rule and calculating the marginal costs and benefits.

A behavioral economist would describe this as predictably irrational behavior. People "do what they see others doing" without rationally weighing the costs and benefits of each decision. This fits nicely with the behavioral assumption of purposeful behavior.

In this case, purposeful behavior reduces the costs of making decisions.

However, this behavior can also be construed as rational. Part of rationally weighing the costs and benefits of each decision involves calculating the opportunity cost. There is an opportunity cost, not only for the decision, but for the decision to weigh the costs and benefits. The opportunity cost of weighing the costs and benefits is the time it takes to calculate and compare the marginal cost with the marginal benefit. Because time is a scarce commodity, it is highly valued. If people were to rationally compare the marginal cost with the marginal benefit of every single decision in their lives then they would use up significant amounts of valuable time. It is also unnecessary. Therefore, it can be considered rational to forgo weighing the costs and benefits and instead make choices based on rules of thumb. That means, in some cases, it is rational to be irrational.

Pretest
Chapters 1 - 6

I

Take this test in test conditions, giving yourself a limited amount of time to complete the questions. Ideally, check with your professor to see how much time he or she allows for an average multiple choice question and multiply this by 26. This is the time limit you should set for yourself for this pretest. If you do not know how much time your teacher would allow, we suggest 1 minute per question, or about 25 minutes.

1. You bought stock A for $10 and stock B for $50. The price of each is currently $20. Assuming no tax issues, which should you sell if you need money?
   a. Stock A.
   b. Stock B.
   c. There is not enough information to tell which to sell.
   d. You should sell an equal amount of both.

2. The opportunity cost of reading Chapter 1 of a 38 chapter text:
   a. is about 1/38 of the price you paid for the book because the chapter is about 1/38 of the book.
   b. zero since you have already paid for the book
   c. has nothing to do with the price you paid for the book.
   d. is 1/38 the price of the book plus 1/38 the price of the tuition.

3. If at Female College there are significantly more females than males (and there are not a significant number of gays or off-campus dating opportunities), economic forces:
   a. will likely be pushing for females to pay on dates.
   b. will likely be pushing for males to pay on dates.
   c. will likely be pushing for neither to pay on dates.
   d. are irrelevant to this issue. Everyone knows that the males always should pay.

4. The statement, "The distribution of income should be left to the market," is:
   a. a positive statement.
   b. a normative statement.
   c. an art-of-economics statement.
   d. an objective statement.

5. If the opportunity cost of good X in terms of good Y is 2Y, so you'll have to give up 2Y to get one X, the production possibility curve could look like:
   a. A only.
   b. B only.
   c. C only.
   d. A, B or C.

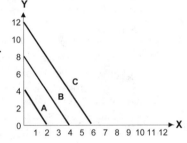

6. Given the accompanying production possibility curve, when you're moving from point C to point B the opportunity cost of butter in terms of guns is:
   a. 1/3.
   b. 1.
   c. 2.
   d. 3/2.

7. If countries A and B have production possibility curves A and B respectively, country A has a comparative advantage in the production of:
   a. no good.
   b. both goods.
   c. good X only.
   d. good Y only.

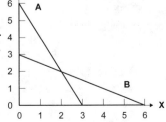

8. Outsourcing in the United States is evidence that:
   a. the United States does not have any comparative advantages.
   b. the U.S. dollar is valued too low.
   c. the law of one price doesn't hold.
   d. the law of one price is affecting global production.

9. According to the law of one price:
   a. wages will eventually be the same for every industry.
   b. wages will eventually be the same in every country.
   c. wage differences cannot continue unless they reflect differences in productivity.
   d. wage differences can continue as long as product prices can differ among countries.

10. In theory, socialism is an economic system:
    a. that tries to organize society in the same ways as most families organize, striving to see that individuals get what they need.
    b. based on central planning and government ownership of the means of production.
    c. based on private property rights.
    d. based on markets.

11. In practice, in command or socialist economies, the "what to produce" decision is most often made by:
    a. consumers.
    b. the market.
    c. government.
    d. firms.

12. The largest percentage of business receipts are by:
    a. partnerships.
    b. sole proprietorships.
    c. corporations.
    d. nonprofit companies.

13. The largest percentage of state and local expenditures is on:
    a. education.
    b. health and medical care.
    c. highways.
    d. income security.

14. There are many more substitutes for good A than for good B.
    a. The demand curve for good B will likely shift out further.
    b. The demand curve for good B will likely be flatter.
    c. You can't say anything about the likely relative flatness of the demand curves.
    d. The demand curve for good A will likely be flatter.

15. If the price of air conditioners falls, there will be:
    a. an increase in demand for air conditioners.
    b. an increase in the quantity of air conditioners demanded.
    c. an increase in the quantity of air conditioners supplied.
    d. a shift out of the supply for air conditioners.

16. The law of supply states that:
    a. quantity supplied increases as price increases, other things constant.
    b. quantity supplied decreases as price increases, other things constant.
    c. more of a good will be supplied the higher its price, other things changing proportionately.
    d. less of a good will be supplied the higher its price, other things changing proportionately.

17. If at some price the quantity supplied exceeds the quantity demanded then:
    a. a surplus (excess supply) exists and the price will fall over time as sellers competitively bid down the price.
    b. a shortage (excess demand) exists and the price will rise over time as buyers competitively bid up the price.
    c. the price is below equilibrium.
    d. equilibrium will be reestablished as the demand curve shifts to the left.

18. An increase in demand for a good will cause:
    a. excess demand (a shortage) until price changes.
    b. movement down along the demand curve as price changes.
    c. movement down along the supply curve as price changes.
    d. a higher price and a smaller quantity traded in the market.

19. A higher equilibrium price with no change in market equilibrium quantity could be caused by:
   a. supply shifting in and no change in demand.
   b. supply and demand both increasing.
   c. a decrease in supply and an increase in demand.
   d. demand and supply both shifting in.

20. Effective rent controls:
   a. are examples of price floors.
   b. cause the quantity of rental occupied housing demanded to exceed the quantity supplied.
   c. create a greater amount of higher quality housing to be made available to renters.
   d. create a surplus of rental occupied housing.

21. Referring to the graph below, suppose initial supply is represented by S_0. A tax T on suppliers will raise the price that:

   a. suppliers receive net of the tax to P_1.
   b. suppliers receive net of the tax to P_2.
   c. consumers pay to P_2.
   d. consumers pay to P_3.

22. Third-party payer markets result in:
   a. a lower equilibrium price received by the supplier.
   b. a smaller quantity supplied.
   c. a smaller quantity demanded.
   d. increased total spending.

23. Behavioral economists argue:
   a. that the supply/demand model should be discarded.
   b. traditional building-blocks do not explain everything.
   c. models built on traditional building-blocks are irrelevant.
   d. All of the above.

24. What type of economist is most likely to rely primarily on deductive reasoning?
   a. Behavioral economists.
   b. Modern economists.
   c. Traditional economists.
   d. Modern traditional economists.

25. With regard to policy, traditional economists generally are more likely than behavioral economists to suggest that:
   a. the market is likely to be the best way to deal with a problem.
   b. there are limitations of the market.
   c. because there are multiple frameworks within which a problem can be thought about, there is fundamental ambiguity about the appropriate policy.
   d. there is a potential role for government interventions and public policy in the economy even when there are no externalities.

26. With regard to policy, behavioral economists are more likely than traditional economists to suggest that:
   a. free market policy guarantees both liberty and prosperity.
   b. there is an important role for government intervention and public policy even when there are no externalities.
   c. the market is likely to be the best way to deal with a problem.
   d. there is no ambiguity about what policy should be.

━━━━━━━ ANSWERS ━━━━━━━

1.	c	(1:5)		14.	d	(4:2)
2.	c	(1:11)		15.	b	(4:4)
3.	a	(1:13)		16.	a	(4:13)
4.	b	(1:17)		17.	a	(4:18)
5.	d	(2:3)		18.	a	(4:25)
6.	d	(2:6)		19.	c	(5:4)
7.	d	(2:12)		20.	b	(5:10)
8.	d	(2:16)		21.	c	(5:14)
9.	c	(2:18)		22.	d	(5:17)
10.	a	(3:2)		23.	b	(6:6)
11.	c	(3:5)		24.	c	(6:8)
12.	c	(3:9)		25.	a	(6:15)
13.	a	(3:13)		26.	b	(6:16)

Key: The figures in parentheses refer to multiple choice question and chapter numbers. For example (1:2) is multiple choice question 2 from chapter 1.

DESCRIBING SUPPLY AND DEMAND: ELASTICITIES

CHAPTER AT A GLANCE

This review is based upon the learning objectives that open the chapter.

1. Elasticity is defined as percentage change in quantity divided by percentage change in some variable that affects demand or supply. The most commonly used elasticity concept is price elasticity of demand. (154)

   The price elasticity of <u>demand</u> measures <u>buyer</u> responsiveness to a price change. It equals the percentage change in <u>quantity demanded</u> divided by the percentage change in price.

   The price elasticity of <u>supply</u> measures <u>seller</u> responsiveness to a price change. It equals the percentage change in <u>quantity supplied</u> divided by the percentage change in price.

2. To calculate price elasticity of a price range, calculate the percentage change at the midpoint of the range. (156-157)

   $$\text{Price Elasticity} = \frac{\text{percent change in quantity}}{\text{percent change in price}}$$

   $$\text{Percentage change in quantity} = \frac{Q_2 - Q_1}{1/2\,(Q_1 + Q_2)}$$

   $$\text{Percentage change in price} = \frac{P_2 - P_1}{1/2\,(P_1 + P_2)}$$

   ✔ *Elasticity is not the same as slope!*

3. Five elasticity terms listed from most to least elastic are: perfectly elastic (E = infinity); elastic ($E > 1$); unit elastic ($E = 1$); inelastic ($E < 1$); and perfectly inelastic ($E = 0$). (158-162)

   Consider the price elasticity of demand for a good.

   - *A <u>perfectly elastic</u> demand curve is a horizontal line.*
   - *An <u>elastic</u> demand for a good means buyers are relatively responsive to a price change (the percentage change in the quantity demanded is greater than the percentage change in the price).*
   - *When the demand for an item is <u>unit elastic</u>, buyers are neither relatively responsive nor unresponsive—(the percentage change in the quantity demanded equals the percentage change in the price).*
   - *An <u>in</u>elastic demand for a good means buyers are relatively <u>un</u>responsive to a price change (the percentage change in the quantity demanded is less than the percentage change in the price).*
   - *A <u>perfectly inelastic</u> demand curve is a vertical line, indicating there is no change in the quantity demanded given a change in the price.*

4. The more substitutes, the more elastic the demand and the more elastic the supply. (162-163)

   The number of substitutes a good has is affected by several factors. Four of the most important determinants of substitutability that give rise to a <u>greater</u> elasticity of demand for a good are:

- *The time period being considered: the longer the time interval, the larger the elasticity.*
- *The degree to which the good is a luxury: luxuries have greater elasticities.*
- *The market definition: the more specifically the good is defined the greater the elasticity. (e.g. there are more substitutes for Swiss cheese than for dairy products in general.)*
- *The importance of the good in one's budget: the greater the price relative to one's budget, the greater the elasticity.*

As for the elasticity of supply: the greater the amount of time under consideration, the greater the elasticity of supply (this is because the greater the amount of time, the greater the ability of sellers to respond to the price change).

5. With elastic demands, a rise in price decreases total revenue. With inelastic demands, a rise in price increases total revenue. (166-169)

Therefore, firms have a strong incentive to separate people according to their price elasticity of demand. People with a more inelastic demand are charged a higher price. Economists call this price discrimination.

✔ *Know the relationship between the price elasticity of demand and total revenue:*

Elastic: *↑P→↓TR;   ↓P →↑TR*
Unit Elastic: ↑P or↓P→ no change in TR
Inelastic: *↑P→↑TR;   ↓P →↓TR*

So↓P when demand is elastic and ↑P when demand is inelastic to increase TR.

6. Income elasticity of demand shows the responsiveness of demand to changes in income. Cross-price elasticity shows the responsiveness of demand to changes in prices of other goods. (168-171)

Income elasticity of demand equals the percentage change in quantity demanded divided by the percentage change in income. Normal goods have income elasticities greater than zero while inferior goods have negative income elasticities. Moreover, luxuries have an income elasticity greater than 1 while necessities have an income elasticity less than 1 (but still positive).

Cross-price elasticity of demand equals the percentage change in quantity demanded divided by the percentage change in the price of another good. Substitutes have positive cross-price elasticities; complements have negative cross-price elasticities.

7. Figure 7-6 reviews the effect of shifts in demand and supply with various elasticities. (172-173)

Knowledge of elasticity enables us to determine to what extent the equilibrium quantity and the equilibrium price will change given a change in demand and supply. For example, if demand is highly inelastic and supply shifts in to the left, the price rises significantly while the quantity hardly decreases at all.

More precisely, when demand shifts:

$\%\Delta$ in price = (%Δ in demand) / $(E_D + E_S)$

and when supply shifts:

$\%\Delta$ in price = (%Δ in supply) / $(E_D + E_S)$

SHORT-ANSWER QUESTIONS

1. Define the concepts *price elasticity of demand* and *price elasticity of supply*.

2. If the price of a good changes by 30 percent and quantity demanded for that same good remains unchanged, what is the price elasticity of demand for that good?

3. If price elasticity of supply is 4 and price changes by 10 percent, by what percent will the quantity supplied change?

4. Define the terms *elastic*, *inelastic*, and *unit elastic* as applied to points on supply and demand curves.

5. What are the four main determinants of the price elasticity of demand?

6. What is the main determinant of the price elasticity of supply?

7. In each of the following cases, state what will be the effect of a rise in price on total revenue:

   a. Demand is inelastic.

   b. Demand is elastic.

   c. Demand is unit elastic.

8. Define income elasticity of demand. How do the income elasticities of demand differ among normal goods, necessities, luxuries, and inferior goods?

9. Define cross-price elasticity of demand.

11. Explain how using the concept *elasticity* makes supply and demand analysis more useful.

10. What is a complementary good? What is the general value of the cross-price elasticity of demand for a complementary good? What is a substitute good? What is the general value of the cross-price elasticity of demand for a substitute good?

MATCHING THE TERMS
Match the terms to their definitions

____ **1.** complements
____ **2.** cross-price elasticity of demand
____ **3.** elastic
____ **4.** elasticity
____ **5.** inelastic
____ **6.** income elasticity of demand
____ **7.** inferior goods
____ **8.** luxury
____ **9.** necessity
____ **10.** normal goods
____ **11.** perfectly elastic demand curves
____ **12.** perfectly inelastic demand curves
____ **13.** price elasticity of demand
____ **14.** price elasticity of supply
____ **15.** substitutes
____ **16.** unit elastic

a. A measure of the percent change in the quantity demanded divided by the percent change in the price of that good.
b. Goods whose consumption decreases when income increases.
c. Goods that can be used in place of one another.
d. Goods that are used in conjunction with other goods.
e. Goods whose consumption increases with an increase in income.
f. Horizontal demand curves. E_d = infinity.
g. % change in quantity is greater than % change in price. $E > 1$.
h. % change in quantity is less than % change in price. $E < 1$.
i. A good that has an income elasticity between 0 and 1.
j. For points on curves, the case that the percentage change in quantity is equal to the percentage change in price. $E_d = 1$.
k. Vertical demand curves. $E_d = 0$.
l. The percentage change in quantity demanded divided by percentage change in income.
m. The percentage change in quantity demanded of one good divided by the percentage change in the price of a related good.
n. Refers to responsiveness.
o. A good that has an income elasticity greater than one.
p. A measure of the percent change in the quantity supplied divided by the percent change in the price of that good.

● PROBLEMS AND APPLICATIONS

1. Assume the price elasticity of demand for a good is 0.5 (after we take the absolute value—drop the negative sign). If there is a 10% decrease in the price, what would happen to the percentage change in the quantity demanded? What if the price were to rise by 15%?

2. Calculate the price elasticity for each of the following. State whether price elasticity of demand is elastic, unit elastic, or inelastic. Will revenue rise, decline, or stay the same with the given change in price?

   a. The price of pens rises 5%; the quantity demanded falls 10%.

   b. The price of a ticket to a Boston Red Sox baseball game rises from $10 to $12 a game. The quantity of tickets sold falls from 160,000 tickets to 144,000.

   c. The price of an economics textbook declines from $50 to $47.50. Quantity demanded rises from 1,000 to 1,075.

   d. The price of water beds rises from $500 to $600. Quantity demanded falls from 100,000 to 80,000.

3. Suppose that in deciding what price to set for the video *Shrek II*, Disney decided to either charge $12.95 or $15.95. It estimated the demand to be quite elastic. What price did it most likely charge and why?

4. Calculate the price elasticity of the following products. State whether elasticity of supply is elastic, unit elastic, or inelastic.

   a. Cocoa Puffs: The price of a 14-oz. box of Cocoa Puffs rises 4 percent while quantity supplied rises 15 percent.

   b. Japanese yen: The price of Japanese yen in terms of dollars rises from 100 yen per dollar to 110 yen per dollar. Its quantity supplied rises from 5,000,000 yen to 5,300,000 yen per year.

c. Jansport backpacks: The price of Jansport backpacks falls from $30 a pack to $25 a pack. The quantity supplied falls from 150,000 to 125,000 per week.

5. Calculate the income elasticity of demand for the following goods. State whether each is a luxury, a necessity, or an inferior good.

a. As average income per student rises from $10,000 to $12,000 a year, demand for ice cream cones increases from 30,000 cones to 37,500 cones per year.

b. As income decreases from 120,000 to 100,000 Mexican pesos per year, demand for margarine increases from 50 to 60 pounds per year.

c. As income decreases from $20,000 to $18,000 per year, demand for summer cottages in Vermont decreases from 80 to 75.

6. Determine the cross-price elasticity of demand for the following examples. Are they substitutes or complements? How do you know?

a. The price of a pizza rises from $9 to $12, and the quantity demanded of Big Macs increases from 3 million to 4 million burgers per year.

b. The price of hot dogs falls from $4 a pound to $2 a pound, and the quantity demanded of mustard increases from 15 tons to 20 tons per year.

7. What will likely happen to equilibrium price and quantity in the following cases?

a. Demand is highly inelastic. The supply curve shifts out.

b. Supply is highly inelastic. The demand curve shifts out.

c. Supply is highly elastic. The demand curve shifts in.

8. Suppose demand shifts out to the right by 10 percent, the elasticity of demand is 1.2, and the elasticity of supply is 0.8. How much will price change?

● A BRAIN TEASER

1. Farmers have a relatively inelastic demand for their crops. Suppose there is a bumper crop year (an unusually large harvest). Will farmers be happy or sad about the news there has been an unusually large amount of their crops produced this year? Why?

● MULTIPLE CHOICE

Circle the one best answer for each of the following questions:

1. The definition of price elasticity of demand is:
    a. the change in quantity demanded divided by the change in price.
    b. the percentage change in quantity demanded divided by the percentage change in price.
    c. the percentage change in price divided by the percentage change in quantity demanded.
    d. the percentage change in the quantity supplied divided by the percentage change in price.

2. When the price of a good was raised from $10 to $11, the quantity demanded fell from 100 to 99. The price elasticity of demand is approximately:
    a. .1.
    b. 1.
    c. 10.
    d. 100.

3. If a firm can sell 1,200 units at a price of $14 per unit and 2,000 units at a price of $10 per unit, we can conclude:
    a. the price elasticity of demand for that good is 1.5.
    b. that the demand for this good is inelastic.
    c. that a price reduction would decrease the firm's total revenue.
    d. there must be very few substitutes for this good.

4. As the manager of a hotel, you want to increase the number of occupancies by 12%. It has been determined that the price elasticity of demand for rooms in your hotel is 2. This information implies:
    a. the demand for rooms in your hotel is inelastic.
    b. if you lower your rates by 6% then you will increase the number of occupancies by 12%.
    c. if you were able to raise your rates your total revenue would rise.
    d. there must be few substitutes for your hotel services.

5. A rise in price has just increased total revenue, other things constant. One would surmise that the demand for the firm's product is:
    a. inelastic.
    b. elastic.
    c. unit elastic.
    d. none of the above.

6. As a manager, you have determined that the demand for your good is quite elastic. Therefore:
    a. increasing the price of your good will increase revenues.
    b. decreasing the price of your good will increase revenues.
    c. increasing the price of your good will have no impact on the quantity demanded.
    d. any change in your price will not impact revenues.

7. In reference to the graph below, which of the following is true?

    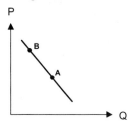

    a. Point B is more elastic than point A.
    b. Point A is more elastic than point B.
    c. Points A and B have equal elasticity.
    d. One cannot say anything about the elasticities without more information.

8.   The elasticity of the curve below is:

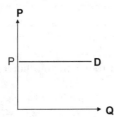

a. perfectly elastic.
b. perfectly inelastic.
c. unit elastic.
d. partially inelastic.

9.   The more a good is a necessity:
a. the more elastic its demand curve.
b. the more inelastic its demand curve.
c. the more unit elastic its demand curve.
d. the flatter the demand curve.

10. The more specifically or narrowly a good is defined the:
a. more substitutes it has and therefore the more elastic its demand curve.
b. more substitutes it has and therefore the more inelastic its demand curve.
c. fewer substitutes it has and therefore the more inelastic its demand curve.
d. more unit elastic its demand curve.

11. In the long run, the elasticity of demand is generally:
a. greater than in the short run.
b. smaller than in the short run.
c. the same as in the short run.
d. unrelated to the elasticity in the short run.

12. When price changes from 4 to 5, output supplied changes from 50 to 60. The elasticity of supply is approximately:
a. .5.
b. .8.
c. 1.25.
d. .25.

13. In the graph below, point A on the supply curve, S, is:

a. elastic.
b. inelastic.
c. unitary elastic.
d. unknown because one cannot say from the graph.

14. In the graph below, point A on the supply curve, S, is:

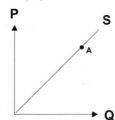

a. elastic.
b. inelastic.
c. unitary elastic.
d. unknown because one cannot say from the graph.

15. The supply curve in the graph below is:

a. perfectly inelastic.
b. perfectly elastic.
c. unit elastic.
d. showing that its elasticity changes at various points.

16. A good whose consumption decreases when income increases is generally called:
a. a normal good.
b. an inferior good.
c. a substitute good.
d. a complementary good.

17. Two goods are substitutes when they:
a. are goods that are used in conjunction with each other.
b. have negative income elasticities.
c. have positive income elasticities.
d. have positive cross-price elasticities.

18. Price discrimination is most likely to occur in markets:
    a. when all individuals have equal elasticities.
    b. when some individuals have highly inelastic demands and some have highly elastic demands.
    c. in which the elasticity of demand is 1.
    d. in which the elasticity of demand is 0.

19. A significant price rise with virtually no change in quantity would most likely be caused by a highly:
    a. elastic demand and supply shifts to the right.
    b. inelastic supply and a shift in demand to the right.
    c. inelastic demand and supply shifts out.
    d. elastic supply and demand shifts in.

20. A significant quantity rise with virtually no change in price would most likely be caused by a highly:
    a. elastic demand and supply shifts to the right.
    b. inelastic supply and demand shifts to the right.
    c. inelastic demand and supply shifts to the right.
    d. elastic supply and demand shifts to the left.

21. A significant price decline with virtually no change in quantity would most likely be caused by:
    a. a highly elastic demand and supply shifts to the right.
    b. a highly inelastic supply and demand shifts to the right.
    c. a highly inelastic demand and supply shifts out.
    d. a highly elastic supply and demand shifts in.

22. If supply increases by 4 percent, the elasticity of demand is 0.5, and the elasticity of supply is 1.5, then the price will:
    a. increase by 8 percent.
    b. increase by 2 percent.
    c. decrease by 8 percent.
    d. decrease by 2 percent.

POTENTIAL ESSAY QUESTIONS

You may also see essay questions similar to the "Problems & Applications" and "A Brain Teaser" exercises.

1. What can cause some products to exhibit elastic demand while others have inelastic demand?

2. Why are some businesses interested in trying to determine which consumers have an elastic demand and which have an inelastic demand for the product being sold?

ANSWERS

SHORT-ANSWER QUESTIONS

1. *Price elasticity of demand* is the percentage change in quantity demanded divided by the percentage change in price. *Price elasticity of supply* is the percentage change in quantity supplied divided by the percentage change in price. (154)

2. Price elasticity of demand is the percentage change in quantity demanded divided by the percentage change in price. Since the quantity demanded has not changed, the price elasticity of demand is zero. In other words, demand is perfectly inelastic. (154, 158)

3. Price elasticity of supply is the percentage change in quantity supplied divided by the percentage change in price. Thus, if the elasticity of supply is 4 and price changes by 10%, quantity supplied will change by 40%. (154)

4. For elastic points, the percentage change in quantity is greater than the percentage change in price. For inelastic points, the percentage change in quantity is less than the percentage change in price. For unit elastic points, the percentage change in quantity is equal to the percentage change in price. (155, 158)

5. The four main determinants of price elasticity of demand are (1) the time interval considered, (2) whether the good is a necessity or a luxury, (3) how specifically the good is defined, and (4) its price as a percentage of one's total expenditures. The larger the time interval, the more elastic is demand. The more a good is a luxury, the more demand is elastic. The more specifically a good is defined, the more elastic is demand. The more a good's price is a percentage of one's expenditures, the more elastic is demand. (162-163)

6. Price elasticity of supply essentially depends on the time period considered: the longer the time period, the more elastic the supply curve, because there are more options for change. Also, the easier it is to substitute production of a good, the more elastic the supply curve. (163)

7. **a.** If demand is inelastic, the percent fall in quantity demanded will be *less than* the percent rise in price. So a rise in price will increase total revenue. (166-167)
   b. If demand is elastic, the percent fall in quantity demanded will be *greater than* the percent rise in price. So a rise in price will reduce total revenue. (166-167)
   c. If demand is unit elastic, the percent fall in quantity demanded will *equal* the percent rise in price. So a rise in price will not change total revenue. (166-167)

8. Income elasticity of demand is the percentage change in demand divided by the percentage change in income. Normal goods have positive income elasticities. Luxury goods have positive income elasticities greater than one, while necessities have positive income elasticities less than one. Inferior goods have negative income elasticities. (168-170)

9. Cross-price elasticity of demand is the percentage change in quantity demanded of one good divided by the percentage change in the price of another good. (168)

10. A complementary good is a good whose consumption goes down when the price of the other good (for which it is a complement) goes up. Complements have negative cross-price elasticities. A substitute good is a good whose consumption goes up when the price of the other good (for which it is a substitute) goes up. Substitutes have positive cross-price elasticities. (170-171)

11. Knowledge of elasticity enables us to determine *to what extent* there will be a change in the equilibrium quantity and the equilibrium price, given a change in demand and supply. (172-173)

ANSWERS

MATCHING

1-d; 2-m; 3-g; 4-n; 5-h; 6-l; 7-b; 8-o; 9-i; 10-e; 11-f; 12-k; 13-a; 14-p; 15-c; 16-j.

ANSWERS

PROBLEMS AND APPLICATIONS

1. Given that the $E_d = 0.5$, and the price falls by 10%, the quantity demanded will rise by 5%. [The trick is to multiply the E_d number (0.5), by the percentage change in the price (10) to get the percentage change in the quantity demanded (5). But remember, the law of demand tells us that the quantity demanded moves in the opposite direction from the change in the price.] If the price were to rise by 15%, the quantity demanded would fall by 7.5% (0.5 × 15 = 7.5). (154-155)

2. Price elasticity of demand is the percent change in quantity demanded divided by the percent change in price. Demand is elastic if the price elasticity is greater than one (always drop the negative sign—take the absolute value); a rise in price will lower total revenue. Demand is inelastic if the price elasticity is less than one; a rise in price will increase total revenue. Demand is unit elastic if the price elasticity is equal to one; a rise in price leaves total revenue unchanged. (154-155, 166-168)

    a. Price elasticity of demand is 10%/5% = 2. Since 2 > 1, demand is elastic. Total revenue falls.

    b. Price elasticity of demand is [(144,000−160,000)/152,000]/[(12−10)/11] = 0.58. Since 0.58 < 1, demand is inelastic. Total revenue rises.

    c. Price elasticity of demand is [(1,075−1,000)/1,037.5]/[(47.5−50)/48.75] = 1.41. Since 1.41 > 1, demand is elastic. Total revenue rises.

    d. Price elasticity of demand is [(80,000−100,000)/90,000]/[(600−500)/550] = 1.2. Since 1.2 > 1, demand is elastic. Total revenue falls.

3. It would charge the lower price, $12.95, because a lower price will increase total revenue when demand is elastic. (166-168)

4. a. Price elasticity of supply is 15%/4% = 3.75. Since 3.75 > 1, supply is elastic. (154-155)

    b. Price elasticity of supply is [(5,300,000−5,000,000)/5,150,000]/ [(110−100)/105] = 0.61. Since 0.61 < 1, supply is inelastic. (154-155)

    c. Price elasticity of supply is [(125,000−150,000)/137,500]/[25−30/27.5] = 1. Since 1 = 1, supply is unit elastic. (154-155)

5. a. The income elasticity of demand is [(37,500−30,000)/33,750]/[(12,000−10,000)/11,000]=1.22. Since 1.22>1, ice cream cones are a luxury good. (168-170)

    b. The income elasticity of demand is [(60−50)/55]/[(100,000−120,000)/110,000] = −1. Since −1 < 0, margarine is an inferior good. (168-170)

    c. The income elasticity of demand is [(75−80)/77.5]/[(18,000−20,000)/19,000] = 0.61. Since 0 < 0.61 < 1, summer cottages are a necessity. (168-170)

6. a. The cross-price elasticity of demand is [(4,000,000−3,000,000)/3,500,000]/[(12−9)/10.5] = 1. Since 1 > 0, pizzas and Big Macs are substitutes. (168, 170-171)

    b. The cross-price elasticity of demand is [(20−15)/17.5]/[(2−4)/3] = −0.43. Since −0.43 < 0, hot dogs and mustard are complements. (168, 170-171)

7. a. The price will fall considerably but quantity will not rise significantly, as shown below. (172-173)

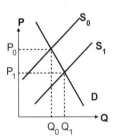

b. The price will rise considerably but quantity will not rise significantly, as shown below. (172-173)

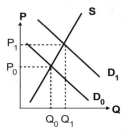

c. The quantity will fall considerably, but price will not fall significantly, as shown below. (172-173)

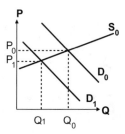

8. When demand shifts, the percent change in price = (percent change in demand)/(E_D+E_S)= 10/2=5 percent. In this case, because demand increases, the price rises by 5 percent. (172-173)

◼ ANSWERS ◼

A BRAIN TEASER

1. They will be sad. The bumper crop year will increase the supply of the crop and reduce the price significantly. A fall in the price given the inelastic demand will decrease total revenues—farmers' incomes will fall. (166-168)

◼ ANSWERS ◼

MULTIPLE CHOICE

1. b The price elasticity of demand is the percentage change in quantity demanded divided by the percentage change in price. Option d is the definition of the price elasticity of supply. See pages 154-155.

2. a Substituting in the basic formula for elasticity gives .01/.1 = .1. See pages 154-157.

3. a Using the formula for elasticity of demand (percent change in quantity divided by percent change in price = .5/.33) gives 1.5 (out of convention we always take the absolute value). Therefore, the good is elastic because its absolute value is greater than one and it likely has many substitutes. A price fall would increase the firm's total revenue. See pages 154-157.

4. b The price elasticity of demand of 2 means that every 1% change in the price will cause a 2% change in the quantity demanded. To obtain a 12% increase in the quantity demanded means the price must fall by 6%. See the formula for elasticity of demand on page 154.

5. a The revenue gain from the increase in price had to exceed the loss from the reduction in quantity, so the demand must be inelastic. See pages 166-168.

6. b When a good is price–elastic then a price decrease will result in a proportionately larger increase in the quantity demanded and revenues will rise. See pages 166-168.

7. a The elasticity changes along a straight line demand curve from highly elastic in upper portions of the demand curve to highly inelastic in the lower portions of the curve. See pages 158-159.

8. a A horizontal demand curve is perfectly elastic because the percentage change in quantity is infinite. See Figure 7-2 on page 158.

9. b Necessities tend to have few substitutes and the fewer the substitutes, the more inelastic the demand curve. See pages 160-162.

10. a The more specifically or narrowly a good is defined, the more substitutes it tends to have and the greater its elasticity of demand. See page 162.

11. a The greater the time period under consideration, the greater the possibility for substitution and, therefore, the greater the elasticity of demand. See page 162.

12. b Elasticity of supply is the percent change in quantity divided by the percent change in price: 18% / 22% = .8. See pages 154-157.

13. a You can either calculate the elasticity (percent change in quantity divided by the percent change in price) or you can use the trick in the "Added Dimension" box (any straight line supply curve that intersects the vertical axis is elastic) on page 161.

14. c Use the trick in the "Added Dimension" box (any straight line supply curve going through the origin will be unit elastic) on page 161.

15. a For a vertical supply curve, the percent change in quantity becomes zero, so the elasticity becomes zero, making supply perfectly inelastic. See pages 158-159.

16. b People buy fewer inferior goods when income rises. See pages 169-170.

17. d When the price of a good increases and this increases the demand for its substitute, then the cross-price elasticity of demand is positive. See page 170.

18. b Price discrimination requires separating consumers by their elasticities and charging higher prices to individuals who have inelastic demands. See pages 172-173.

19. b Since price rose significantly while quantity remained virtually unchanged, either demand or supply is inelastic. Since price rose, either demand shifted out or supply shifted in. Only option b fits these conditions. See pages 172-173.

20. a Since quantity rose significantly while price remained virtually unchanged either demand or supply is elastic. Since quantity rose, either demand shifted out or supply shifted out. Only option a fits these conditions. See pages 172-173.

21. c Since price declined significantly while quantity remained virtually unchanged, either demand or supply is inelastic. Since price declined, either demand shifted in or supply shifted out. Only option c fits these conditions. See pages 172-173.

22. d When supply shifts, the percent change in price = (percent change in supply)/(E_D+E_S) = 4/2=2. Because supply increased, the price decreases by 2 percent. See pages 172-173.

■■■■ ANSWERS ■■■■

POTENTIAL ESSAY QUESTIONS

The following are annotated answers. They indicate the general idea behind the answer.

1. As a general rule, the more substitutes a good has, the more elastic is its demand. The number of substitutes is, in turn, affected by the time interval under consideration, whether the good is considered a necessity or a luxury, the specificity with which the good is defined, and the relative prices of the good compared to one's income.

2. In order to maximize revenues firms will try to charge a higher price for the product to those consumers that have a more inelastic demand (because an increase in the price increases total revenue) and a lower price to those that have an elastic demand (because a decrease in the price increases total revenue).

TAXATION AND GOVERNMENT INTERVENTION

● CHAPTER AT A GLANCE

This review is based upon the learning objectives that open the chapter.

1.   Equilibrium maximizes consumer and producer surplus (179-181)

     Consumer surplus is the difference between the price buyers would have been willing to pay and the price they actually had to pay. Equal to Area A in the graph below.

     Producer surplus is the difference between the price sellers would have been willing to accept and the price they actually received as payment. Equal to Area B in the graph below.

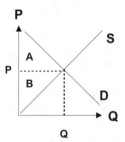

Hint: To answer numerical problems calculating producer and consumer surplus, remember the formula for the area of a triangle is 1/2 base × height.

2.   The burden of taxation to society is the loss of consumer and producer surplus caused by the tax. (181-183)

     Total cost to consumers and producers is more than tax revenue. Refer to the graph below. Suppose a per unit tax "t" is paid by suppliers. Consumers pay rectangle B in tax revenue and lose area C in consumer surplus. Producers pay area D in tax revenue and lose area E in producer surplus. The triangular area represented by areas C (lost consumer surplus) and E (lost producer surplus) represents a cost of taxation in excess of the revenue paid to government. It is lost consumer and producer surplus that is not gained by government. This loss of consumer

and producer surplus from a tax is known as "deadweight loss." Graphically, deadweight loss is shown by the "welfare loss triangle"— area C + E.

3.   The person who physically pays a tax is not necessarily the person who bears the burden of the tax. Who bears the burden of the tax (also known as tax incidence) depends upon who is best able to change his behavior in response to the tax, or who has the greater elasticity. (183-185)

     The more inelastic one's relative supply and demand, the larger the burden of the tax one will bear.

     The general rule about elasticities and tax burden is this: if demand is more inelastic than supply, demanders will pay a higher percentage of the tax. If supply is more inelastic than demand, suppliers will pay a higher share. More specifically:

     fraction of tax borne by demander = price elasticity of supply divided by the sum of the price elasticity of demand and supply $= E_S / (E_D + E_S)$.

     fraction of tax borne by supplier = price elasticity of demand divided by the sum of the price elasticity of demand and supply $= E_D / (E_D + E_S)$.

4. A price ceiling is, in essence, an implicit tax on producers and an implicit subsidy to consumers. (187-189)

Refer to the graph below. With an effective price ceiling of P_1 the quantity supplied (and the amount consumed) falls from Q_e to Q_1. The welfare loss equals area C + E. This is the same effect as a tax. However, the loss of producer surplus, area D, is now transferred to consumers. It is as if government places a tax on suppliers and then gives that tax revenue to consumers when they consume the good.

5. Rent seeking is an activity designed to transfer surplus from one group to another. If demand is inelastic, suppliers have an incentive to restrict supply to raise the price because this will raise their revenue. When the supply of a good is inelastic, consumers have an incentive to hold the price down. (188-190)

For example, the demand for food is inelastic. Farmers have an incentive to lobby government to restrict supply or to create a price floor for their commodities (sometimes called price supports) because they will be better off.

On the other hand, when the supply of a good is inelastic like that of rental-occupied housing, and demand rises, rental rates will rise significantly and consumers will scream for rent controls.

Government sometimes succumbs to political pressure for price controls (price floors and price ceilings). However, price controls create surpluses and shortages that only become more severe over time.

6. The general rule of political economy is when small groups are helped by a government action and large groups are hurt by that same action, the small group tends to lobby more effectively than the larger group. (190)

Because of the rule, policies tend to reflect the interests of small groups.

An example is the farm lobby. Farmers have been effective in getting government to hold up farm prices by restricting supply even though taxpayers are worse off.

● SHORT-ANSWER QUESTIONS

1. What are consumer surplus and producer surplus? How are they related to demand and supply curves?

2. What happens to combined consumer and producer surplus when government sets a price floor above equilibrium price?

3. What is the burden of taxation to society?

4. What is the general rule about who bears the relative burden of a tax?

5. What is the general rule about elasticities and tax burden?

6. For whom is a price ceiling an implicit tax? For whom is a price ceiling an implicit subsidy?

7. For whom is a price floor an implicit tax? For whom is a price floor an implicit subsidy?

8. What is an important similarity and an important difference between taxes and price controls (price ceilings and price floors)?

9. What is rent seeking and how is rent seeking related to elasticity?

10. What is the general rule of political economy in a democracy?

MATCHING THE TERMS
Match the terms to their definitions

___ 1.	consumer surplus	a.	A tax that is levied on a specific good.
___ 2.	deadweight loss	b.	Economist who integrates an economic analysis of politics with the analysis of the economy.
___ 3.	excise tax	c.	A geometric representation of the welfare cost in terms of misallocated resources caused by a deviation from a supply-demand equilibrium.
___ 4.	general rule of political economy	d.	The loss to society of consumer and producer surplus from a tax.
___ 5.	price ceiling	e.	A government-set price above which price may not rise.
___ 6.	price floor	f.	Activity designed to transfer surplus from one group to another.
___ 7.	producer surplus	g.	A government-set price below which price may not fall.
___ 8.	public choice economist	h.	The value the consumer gets from buying a product less its price.
___ 9.	rent-seeking activity	i.	The price the producer sells a product for less the cost of producing it.
___ 10.	welfare loss triangle	j.	Small groups that are significantly affected by a government policy will lobby more effectively than large groups that are equally affected by that same policy.

PROBLEMS AND APPLICATIONS

1. Refer to the graph below when answering the following questions.

a. Given supply curve S_0, what is the area representing consumer surplus at the market equilibrium price?

b. Given supply curve S_0, what is the area representing producer surplus at the market equilibrium price?

c. Now suppose a per unit tax, t, paid by the supplier shifts the supply curve up from S_0 to S_1. Equilibrium price rises from P_e to P_1 and equilibrium quantity falls from Q_0 to Q_1. What area represents consumer surplus after the tax?

d. After the tax, what area represents what consumers pay in tax revenue to government?

e. What area represents lost consumer surplus caused by the tax and not gained by government?

f. What area represents producer surplus after the tax?

g. After the tax, what area represents what producers pay in tax revenue to government?

h. What area represents lost producer surplus caused by the tax and not gained by government?

i. What area represents deadweight loss; that is, what is the welfare loss triangle?

2. The supply and demand for foreign cars in
    Bangladesh is shown in the graph below.
    Suppose the government imposes a tax on
    supply of 10,000 takas per car. The new
    equilibrium price and quantity are shown in the
    graph below.

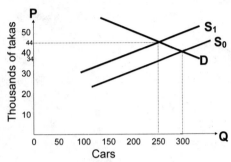

a. What would be the tax paid by consum-
    ers? Suppliers? What price do suppliers
    with and without the tax receive?

b. Demonstrate graphically the tax paid by
    each.

c. From your answer to (b), what can you
    conclude about the relative elasticities of
    the supply and demand curves?

3. What is the deadweight loss from the tax equal
    to in question #2?

4. Suppose the price elasticity of supply is 0.5
    and the price elasticity of demand is 1.5. If the
    government imposes a tax on the good, what
    percentage of the tax is borne by buyers?

5. a. If government, given its targeted revenue
        from a tax, wants to have as large an effect
        on individual actions as possible, should
        it tax goods with an inelastic or elastic
        demand? Why?

    b. If government wants to raise revenues
        from a tax and minimize welfare loss,
        should it tax goods with *inelastic* demand
        or supply, or *elastic* demand or supply?
        Why?

6. Refer to the graph below when answering the
    following questions.

    a. In market equilibrium, what area repre-
        sents consumer surplus? Producer
        surplus?

    b. Suppose government imposes a price
        ceiling of P_1. What happens to the
        quantity demanded and the quantity
        supplied?

    c. What happens to consumer and producer
        surplus as a result of the price ceiling?

d. What is the welfare loss triangle as a result of the price ceiling?

e. How is a price ceiling equivalent to a tax on producers and a subsidy to consumers?

f. Suppose that instead of government imposing a price ceiling, it imposed a tax that reduced the quantity supplied to Q_1. What is an essential similarity between the two outcomes? What is an essential difference?

7. How could the fact that farmers lobby government to restrict the supply of agricultural production or to pursue agricultural price supports (price floors) be viewed as rent-seeking activity?

8. Why will shortages that result from price ceilings, and surpluses that result from price floors, become more acute over time?

● A BRAIN TEASER

1. Who bears the larger burden of an excise tax on cigarettes: smokers or tobacco companies? If government increases the tax on cigarettes, what will happen to government's tax revenues?

● MULTIPLE CHOICE

Circle the one best answer for each of the following questions:

1. Refer to the graph below. The amount of consumer surplus at market equilibrium is:
a. $18.
b. $9.
c. $72.
d. $36.

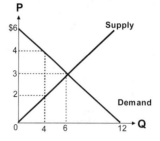

2. Refer to the graph in Question #1. The lost combined consumer and producer surplus from a price of $4 is:
a. $2.
b. $4.
c. $12.
d. $36.

3. Assume equilibrium in the graph below. What area represents consumer surplus?
a. A + B + C.
b. D + C + E.
c. E.
d. E + F.

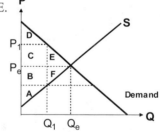

4. Refer to the graph for Question #3. Assume equilibrium. What area represents the welfare loss from a price floor of P_1?
a. B + C + E + F.
b. C + B.
c. B.
d. E + F.

5. Refer to the graph below. If a per unit tax, t, is paid by sellers:

   a. producer surplus is represented by areas A, B, and C before the tax and A after the tax.
   b. consumer surplus is represented by areas D, E and F before the tax and B after the tax.
   c. the tax, t, imposes a deadweight loss represented by the welfare loss triangle- areas C and E.
   d. consumers lose surplus given by area E while producers lose surplus given by area C.

6. Refer to the graph in Question #5. If a per unit tax, t, is paid by sellers, which of the following is true?
   a. Tax revenue paid equals the tax, t, times the equilibrium quantity, Q_1, or areas B and D.
   b. The total cost to consumers and producers is less than tax revenue to government.
   c. Producers pay area B in tax revenue and also lose area C in producer surplus.
   d. Consumers pay area D in tax revenue and lose area E in consumer surplus.

7. Deadweight loss from a tax is:
   a. the loss of consumer surplus from a tax.
   b. the loss of producer surplus from a tax.
   c. the loss of consumer *and* producer surplus from a tax.
   d. the amount of tax revenues collected by government.

8. The welfare loss triangle is a geometric representation of the:
   a. lost quantity traded that would have otherwise benefited both consumers and producers.
   b. amount of tax paid by consumers and businesses.
   c. consumer surplus after a tax.
   d. producer surplus after a tax.

9. The burden of a tax is:
   a. most heavily borne by those with the more inelastic demand or supply.
   b. most heavily borne by those with the more elastic demand or supply.
   c. usually equally split between buyers and sellers.
   d. usually passed on to consumers in the form of a higher price.

10. How much of a $100 tax will consumers pay if the price elasticity of demand is 3 and the price elasticity of supply is 2?
   a. $50.
   b. $40.
   c. $30.
   d. $20.

11. How much of a $100 tax will consumers pay if the price elasticity of supply is 2 and the price elasticity of demand is 4?
   a. $20.
   b. $33.
   c. $40.
   d. $60.

12. Social Security taxes are:
   a. levied by government more heavily on employees than employers, even though the burden of the tax is most heavily borne by employers.
   b. most heavily borne by employers if the demand for labor tends to be more inelastic than supply.
   c. most heavily borne by workers if the demand for labor tends to be more inelastic than the supply of labor.
   d. most heavily borne by workers if the supply of labor tends to be more inelastic than the demand for labor.

13. An effective price ceiling:
   a. is a government-set price above market equilibrium price.
   b. is an implicit tax on producers and an implicit subsidy to consumers.
   c. will create a surplus.
   d. causes an increase in consumer and producer surplus.

14. Refer to the graph below. A price ceiling of P$_1$ will:

   a. create a shortage of Q$_e$ – Q$_1$.
   b. transfer surplus D from producers to consumers.
   c. create a deadweight loss equal to areas A + B + C.
   d. increase combined producer and consumer surplus by triangles C and E.

15. Rent-seeking activity is designed to:
   a. produce additional revenue for government.
   b. minimize welfare loss.
   c. maximize welfare loss.
   d. transfer surplus from one group to another.

16. The general rule of political economy in a democracy states:
   a. small groups that are significantly affected by a government policy will lobby more effectively than will large groups who are equally affected by that policy.
   b. large groups that are significantly affected by a government policy will lobby more effectively than small groups who are equally affected by that policy.
   c. large groups will always win in majority rule situations.
   d. Congress will always be inefficient.

17. In which case will a price floor result in the greatest excess supply?
   a. When both demand and supply are highly inelastic.
   b. When both demand and supply are highly elastic.
   c. When demand is elastic and supply is inelastic.
   d. When demand is inelastic and supply is elastic.

● POTENTIAL ESSAY QUESTIONS

You may also see essay questions similar to the "Problems & Applications" and "A Brain Teaser" exercises.

1. Discuss the relationship between elasticity and tax burden.

2. What are the basic similarities and differences between the effects of taxes and price controls?

■■■■ ANSWERS ■■■■

SHORT-ANSWER QUESTIONS

1. Consumer surplus is the difference between the price buyers are willing to pay (shown by the demand curve) and the price they actually pay. Producer surplus is the difference between what the sellers are willing to accept as payment (shown by the supply curve) and what they actually receive as payment. (179-181)

2. A price floor above equilibrium price will result in a lower quantity purchased and therefore a lower combined producer and consumer surplus. (187-188, especially Figure 8-4)

3. The burden of taxation to society is the loss of consumer and producer surplus caused by the tax. (181-183)

4. The relative burden of a tax (also known as a tax incidence) follows the general rule: *The more inelastic one's relative supply and demand, the larger the burden of the tax one will bear.* (183-185)

5. The general rule about elasticities and tax burden is this: *if demand is more inelastic than supply, consumers pay a higher percentage of the tax. If supply is more inelastic than demand, suppliers pay a higher share.* (183-185)

6. A price ceiling (a government-set price below market equilibrium price) is an implicit tax on producers and an implicit subsidy to consumers. (186-187)

7. A price floor (a government-set price above market equilibrium price) is in essence an implicit tax on consumers and an implicit subsidy to producers. (187-188)

8. An important similarity between taxes and price controls (which include price ceilings and price floors) is that they all create a loss of consumer and producer surplus shown graphically by a welfare loss triangle. An important difference between taxes and price controls is that price controls create surpluses (in the case of a price floor) and shortages (in the case of a price ceiling), while taxes do not create surpluses or shortages. (187-188)

9. Rent seeking is an activity designed to transfer surplus (consumer or producer surplus) from one group to another. The more inelastic the demand, the greater the incentive suppliers have to drive the price up because this will increase their revenue and lower their cost, which raises their profits. The more inelastic supply, the greater the incentive consumers have to lobby government to set a price ceiling because it will result in a larger transfer of surplus to themselves. (188-190)

10. The general rule of political economy in a democracy is that small groups that are significantly affected by a government policy will lobby more effectively than large groups that are equally affected by that same policy. (190)

■■■■ ANSWERS ■■■■

MATCHING

1-h; 2-d; 3-a; 4-j; 5-e; 6-g; 7-i; 8-b; 9-f; 10-c.

■■■■ ANSWERS ■■■■

PROBLEMS AND APPLICATIONS

1. a. Area A + B + C represents consumer surplus at the market equilibrium price. (181-183 and Figure 8-2)
    b. Area D + E + F represents producer surplus at the market equilibrium price. (181-183 and Figure 8-2)
    c. Area A is consumer surplus after the tax. (181-183 and Figure 8-2)
    d. Area B is what consumers pay in tax revenues to government. This represents lost consumer surplus gained by government. (181-183 and Figure 8-2)
    e. Area C is lost consumer surplus not gained by government. (181-183 and Figure 8-2)
    f. Area F is producer surplus after the tax. (181-183 and Figure 8-2)
    g. Area D is what producers pay in tax revenues to government. This represents lost producer surplus gained by government. (181-183 and Figure 8-2)

h. Area E represents lost producer surplus not gained by government. (181-183 and Figure 8-2)

i. Area C + E is the deadweight loss from a tax. This area is the welfare loss triangle. (181-183 and Figure 8-2)

2. a. The consumers now have to pay 44,000 takas per car, which is 4,000 takas more than before. Their tax burden is (4,000 × 250) = 1,000,000 takas. Suppliers now receive 34,000 takas (44,000-10,000) on each car they sell, which is 6,000 takas less per car than before the tax. Their tax burden is (6,000 × 250) = 1,500,000 takas. (181-185, especially Figure 8-3)

b. The graph above shows the relative taxes paid by consumers and producers. The upper shaded portion is consumers' tax burden. The lower shaded portion is suppliers' tax burden. (181-185, especially Figure 8-3)

c. Since the supplier's tax burden is greater, the supply curve is more inelastic than the demand curve. (181-185, especially Figure 8-3)

3. The deadweight loss of a tax is shown by a welfare loss triangle. In this case that triangle has a base of 10,000 takas and a height of 50 cars (when the triangle is turned on its side). The area of that triangle = ½ x base x height = ½ x 10,000 x 50 = 250,000 takas. (180)

4. The tax borne by buyers equals the price elasticity of supply divided by the sum of the price elasticities of supply and demand (0.5/2)= .25 or 1/4. Producers bear the other 75 percent or 3/4 of the tax. Producers pay the largest fraction (percentage) of a tax when demand is elastic and supply is inelastic. The one with the greater inelasticity bears the biggest burden of a tax. (183-185)

5. a. Government should tax goods with *elastic* demand if it wishes to have as large an effect on individual actions as possible. This is because an elastic demand means there are many substitutes buyers can turn to in response to the higher price as a result of the tax. Buyers will cut back on their consumption rather dramatically. (185-186)

b. Government should tax goods with *inelastic* demand or supply if it wishes to raise revenues and minimize welfare loss. Revenues to government will rise because an inelastic demand or supply means there are few substitutes or alternatives for buyers and sellers to turn to. Graphically, an inelastic demand or supply will minimize welfare loss because the welfare loss triangle will be smaller the steeper (the more inelastic) the demand or supply curves. (185-186, Figure 8-3, and the "Reminder" box on page 183)

6. a. Market equilibrium is P_e and Q_e. Consumer surplus is area A + B + C. Producer surplus is area D + E + F. (179-181, especially Figure 8-2)

b. As a result of the price ceiling, the quantity supplied falls from Q_e to Q_1 and the quantity demanded rises from Q_e to Q_2. This creates a shortage of $Q_2 - Q_1$. (186-188, especially Figure 8-4)

c. Consumer surplus becomes area A + B + D. Producer surplus becomes area F. (186-188, especially Figure 8-4)

d. The welfare loss triangle is area C + E. (186-188, especially Figure 8-4)

e. A price ceiling is equivalent to a tax on producers and a subsidy to consumers because area D is transferred from producers to consumers as a result of the price ceiling. (186-188, especially Figure 8-4)

f. The welfare loss would be the same (the welfare loss triangle would still be area C + E). However, an essential difference between the two is that a price ceiling creates a shortage, while a tax would not. Another difference is who gets the surplus. In the case of the tax, government gets areas B and D as tax revenue. (186-188, especially Figure 8-4)

7. Because the demand for agricultural goods is inelastic, farmers have an incentive to get government to restrict supply or create a price floor, thereby raising their revenue (their income). This is rent seeking because farmers are attempting to shift consumer surplus to themselves. (188-189)

8. Price ceilings and price floors create greater shortages and surpluses over time because in the long run, supply and demand tend to be more elastic than in the short run. (191-193)

ANSWERS

A BRAIN TEASER

1. Smokers will bear the biggest burden of the cigarette tax because the demand for cigarettes is inelastic (for those "hooked" on smoking there are few substitutes for cigarettes). If government increases the cigarette tax, this will increase the price by a greater percentage than the quantity demanded falls (because demand is inelastic). That is, few people stop smoking. Therefore, tax revenues to government rise. (181-183)

ANSWERS

MULTIPLE CHOICE

1. b The consumer surplus triangle has a base of 6 (the equilibrium quantity) and a height of $3 (6 - 3). Since the area of a triangle is ½ (base x height), the consumer surplus is ½(3 x 6) = $9. See page 180 and Figure 8-1.

2. a The lost consumer and producer surplus when price rises to $4 is the triangle that has a height (looked at sideways) of 2 (6 – 4) and a base of 2 (4 - 2). Since the area of a triangle is ½ (base x height), the lost surplus is ½(2 x 2) = $2. See page 180 and Figure 8-1.

3. b Consumer surplus is the area under the demand curve above the equilibrium price. See page 182 and Figure 8-2.

4. d The loss to consumers is E and C (but C is gained by producers). The loss to producers is F. So the total loss is E + F. See page 182 and Figure 8-2.

5. c The incorrect options have consumer and producer surplus confused. Deadweight loss is surplus lost by consumers and producers but not gained by anyone. It is a net loss to society because of deviation from market equilibrium. See page 182 and Figure 8-2.

6. a Tax revenue is the tax per unit times the units sold, area B + D. To be correct, option b should read "is *greater* than." Options c and d would be correct if we reversed the terms consumer and producer, as well as the terms consumer surplus and producer surplus. See page 182 and Figure 8-2.

7. c Deadweight loss is the loss of consumer and producer surplus from a tax. See pages 181-183.

8. a The welfare loss triangle is the cost of taxation in *excess* of the revenue paid to government. Moreover, it represents the *loss* of consumer *and* producer surplus from a tax. See pages 181-183.

9. a Those with inelastic demand or supply are less able to change their behavior and therefore bear a greater share of the tax. See pages 183-184.

10. b The fraction of a tax borne by consumers equals the price elasticity of supply divided by the sum of the price elasticity of demand and supply (2/5= 0.4). 4/10 or 40 percent of $100 is $40. See page 185.

11. b The fraction of a tax borne by consumers equals the price elasticity of supply divided by the sum of the price elasticity of demand and supply (2/6 = 1/3). One third of $100 is $33.33. See page 185.

12. d Government divides the taxes among employees and employers equally. However, since the supply of labor is

relatively more inelastic, employees bear the greater burden of Social Security taxes. See pages 185-186.

13. b A price ceiling is a government-set price *below* equilibrium and creates a *shortage*. A price ceiling reduces consumer and producer surplus, but a portion of the lost producer surplus is transferred to consumers. A price ceiling creates welfare loss just like taxes do. See pages 187-189.

14. b A price ceiling creates a shortage equal to $Q_2 - Q_1$. Producer surplus D is transferred to consumers because of the lower price. Producer and consumer surplus *falls* by areas C and E (the welfare loss triangle). See pages 187-189, especially Figure 8-4.

15. d Rent-seeking activity is designed to transfer surplus from one group to another—whether it be from producers to consumers or the other way around. See page 189.

16. a Congress may always be inefficient, but this is not the general rule of political economy. See page 190.

17. b When both parties have the greatest possibility of change, there will be the greatest surplus. This occurs in the long run when both demand and supply are more elastic. See pages 189-190.

■ ANSWERS ■

POTENTIAL ESSAY QUESTIONS

The following are annotated answers. They indicate the general idea behind the answer.

1. The general rule about elasticities and tax burden is this: if demand is more inelastic than supply, consumers will pay a higher percentage of the tax. If supply is more inelastic than demand, suppliers will pay a higher share.

2. Price controls and taxes are similar in that they both create welfare loss. They differ in that price controls create shortages (in the case of a price ceiling) and surpluses (in the case of a price floor), while taxes do not. Another difference is who gets the surplus. For a tax, government gets some of the surplus as tax revenue.

INTERNATIONAL TRADE POLICY, COMPARATIVE ADVANTAGE, AND OUTSOURCING

9

This review is based upon the learning objectives that open the chapter.

1. The primary trading partners of the United States are Canada, Mexico, the European Union, and the Pacific Rim countries. (199-202)

   A trade balance is the difference between a country's exports and imports. When imports exceed exports, a country has a trade deficit. When exports exceed imports a country has a trade surplus. Because the United States has had large trade deficits since the 1970s, it is a net debtor nation.

   The nature of trade is continually changing. The United States is importing more and more high-tech goods and services from India and China and other East Asian countries.

   Outsourcing is a type of trade. Outsourcing is a larger phenomenon today compared to 30 years ago because countries where jobs are outsourced today—China and India—are much larger.

2. The principle of comparative advantage states that as long as the relative opportunity costs of producing goods differ among countries, there are potential gains from trade. (203-205)

   When countries specialize in the production of those goods for which each has a <u>comparative advantage</u> and then trade, all economies involved benefit.

   A country has a comparative advantage in producing good "x" if its opportunity cost of producing good "x" is lower.

3. Three determinants of the gains of trade are: (205-206)

- The more competition, the less the trader gets.
- Smaller countries get a larger proportion of the gain than larger countries.
- Countries producing goods with economies of scale get a larger gain from trade.

   Also: countries which specialize and trade along the lines of comparative advantage are able to consume more than if they did not undertake trade (they are able to escape the confines of their own production possibility curves).

4. Three reasons for differences between economists' and laypeople's views of trade are: (1) gains from trade are often stealth gains, (2) comparative advantage is determined by more than wages, and (3) nations trade more than just manufactured goods. (206-207)

   The gains from trade in the form of low consumer prices tend to be widespread and not easily recognizable, while the costs in jobs lost tend to be concentrated and readily identifiable. But, the gains outweigh the costs over time. Convincing the public of this remains a challenge, especially for policymakers.

5. Transferable comparative advantages will tend to erode over time; inherent comparative advantages will not. (209-211)

   The U.S. has comparative advantages due to its skilled workforce, institutions, and infrastructure, among other things. Some of these are inherent comparative advantages, while others are transferable comparative advantages. The law of one price and the convergence hypothesis will work to erode any transferable comparative advantages over time. The degree to which, and how quickly, the United States loses some of its comparative advantages depends on how transferable they are.

6. Three policies used to restrict trade are: (211-215)
- tariffs: taxes on internationally traded goods;
- quotas: quantity limits placed on imports; and
- regulatory trade restrictions: government-imposed procedural rules that limit imports.

Countries can also restrict trade through: voluntary restraint agreements, embargoes, and nationalistic appeals.

Arguments for restricting trade include:
- *Unequal internal distribution of the gains from trade;*
- *Haggling by companies over the gains from trade;*
- *Haggling by countries over trade restrictions;*
- *Specialized production; learning by doing; and economies of scale;*
- *Macroeconomic aspects of trade;*
- *National security;*
- *International politics;*
- *Increased revenue brought in by tariffs.*

Understand these motives for trade barriers and be able to explain why they may be fallacious.

7. Economists generally oppose trade restrictions because: (221-222)
- from a global perspective, free trade increases total output;
- international trade provides competition for domestic companies;
- restrictions based on national security are often abused or evaded; and
- trade restrictions are addictive.

Economists generally argue that the benefits of free trade outweigh the costs—especially over time.

Trade restrictions limit the supply of an imported good, increasing its price and decreasing quantity. Governments prefer tariffs over quotas because they generate tax revenues, while companies prefer quotas.

8. Free trade associations help trade by reducing barriers to trade among member nations. Free trade associations could hinder trade by building up barriers to trade with nations outside the association. (222-224)

A free trade association is a group of countries that allows free trade among its members and puts up common barriers against all other countries' goods.

The WTO and GATT are important international economic organizations designed to reduce trade barriers among all countries.

● SHORT-ANSWER QUESTIONS

1. Who are the primary trading partners of the United States?

2. How has U.S. trade with the rest of the world changed in recent years?

3. What is the principle of comparative advantage?

4. What are three determinants of the gains of trade?

5. What are three reasons laypeople's and economists' views of trade differ?

6. What are four sources of comparative advantages for the United States?

7. Why is the United States losing some of its comparative advantages?

8. In a talk to first-year members of Congress you are asked what they can do to restrict trade. You oblige.

9. You reveal to these first-year members of Congress that you believe in free trade. Hands fly up from people just waiting to tell you why they want to restrict trade. What are some of their reasons?

10. After listening to their remarks, you gather your thoughts and offer them reasons why you generally oppose trade restrictions. What do you say?

11. The first-year members of Congress ask you how the nation joining a free trade association could help and hinder international trade. What do you say?

MATCHING THE TERMS
Match the terms to their definitions

___ 1.	balance of trade	a.	A tax governments place on internationally traded goods—generally imports.
___ 2.	comparative advantage	b.	All-out restriction on import or export of a good.
___ 3.	economies of scale	c.	As long as the relative opportunity costs of producing goods differ among countries, there are potential gains from trade, even if one country has an absolute advantage in everything.
___ 4.	embargo		
___ 5.	free trade association		
___ 6.	General Agreement on Tariffs and Trade (GATT)	d.	Costs per unit output go down as output increases.
		e.	Country that will pay as low a tariff on its exports as will any other country.
___ 7.	infant industry argument	f.	Demanding a larger share of the gains of trade than you might get normally.
___ 8.	inherent comparative advantage	g.	Government-imposed procedural rule that limits imports.
___ 9.	learning by doing	h.	Group of countries that allow free trade among its members and put up common barriers against all other countries' goods.
___ 10.	most-favored nation		
___ 11.	quota	i.	Periodic international conference held in the past to reduce trade barriers.
___ 12.	regulatory trade restriction	j.	Program designed to compensate losers for reductions in trade restrictions.
___ 13.	strategic bargaining	k.	Quantity limit placed on imports.
___ 14.	strategic trade policy	l.	An organization whose functions are generally the same as were those of GATT—to promote free and fair trade among countries.
___ 15.	tariff		
___ 16.	trade adjustment assistance program	m.	With initial protection, an industry will be able to become competitive.
		n.	You become better at a task the more you perform it.
___ 17.	transferable comparative advantage	o.	The difference between the value of exports and the value of imports.
___ 18.	World Trade Organization (WTO)	p.	Threatening to implement tariffs to bring about a reduction in tariffs or some other concessions from the other country.
		q.	Comparative advantage based on factors that are relatively unchangeable.
		r.	Comparative advantage based on factors that can change relatively easily.

● PROBLEMS AND APPLICATIONS

1.　a.　State whether there is a basis for trade in the following:

Case 1: In Country A the opportunity cost of producing one widget is two wadgets. In Country B the opportunity cost of producing two widgets is four wadgets.

Case 2: In Country C the opportunity cost of producing one widget is two wadgets. In Country D the opportunity cost of producing two widgets is one wadget.

Case 3: In Country E the opportunity cost of producing one widget is two wadgets. In Country F the opportunity cost of producing one widget is four wadgets.

b. On what general principle did you base your reasoning?

c. Assume that in Case 3 there are constant marginal returns and constant returns to scale. Country E is currently producing 10 widgets and 4 wadgets. Country F is currently producing 20 widgets and 20 wadgets. Can you make an offer involving trade that will make both countries better off?

d. How would your answer differ if each country experiences economies of scale?

2. Suppose Country A and Country B are potential trading partners. Each country produces two goods: fish and wine. If Country A devotes all of its resources to producing fish, it can produce 1,000 fish, and if it devotes all of its resources to producing wine, it can produce 2,000 bottles of wine. If Country B devotes all of its resources to producing fish, it can produce 3,000 fish, and if it devotes all of its resources to producing wine it can produce 3,000 bottles of wine. For simplicity, assume the production possibility curves of these countries are straight lines.

a. Draw the production possibility curve for Country A on the axes below. In Country A, what is the opportunity cost of one bottle of wine in terms of fish?

b. Draw the production possibility curve for Country B on the axes for (a). In Country B, what is the opportunity cost of one bottle of wine in terms of fish?

c. Does Country A have a comparative advantage in producing either wine or fish? Does Country B have a comparative advantage in producing either wine or fish?

d. Suppose Country A specialized in that good for which it has a comparative advantage and Country B specialized in that good for which it has a comparative advantage. Each country would then trade the good it produced for the good the other country produced. What would be a fair exchange of goods?

3. Suppose two countries A and B have the following production possibility tables:

% Resources devoted to Machines	Country A Production Machines	Food	Country B Production Machines	Food
A	100	200	0	40	0
B	80	160	8	32	40
C	60	120	16	28	80
D	40	80	24	24	120
E	20	40	32	16	160
F	0	0	40	0	200

a. Draw the production possibility curves for Country A and Country B on the axes below.

b. Which country has the comparative advantage in the production of food?

c. Suppose each country specializes in the production of one good. Explain how Country A can end up with 50 food units and 150 machines and Country B can end up with 150 food units and 50 machines. Both points are outside the production possibility curve for each country without trade.

4. State whether the trade restriction is a quota, tariff, or regulatory trade restriction.

a. The EU (European Union) requires beef to be free of growth-inducing hormones in order to be traded in EU markets.

b. Hong Kong has maintained rice import controls on quantity since 1955 in order to keep local rice importers in business and to secure a steady wartime food supply.

c. To encourage domestic production of automobile parts, Japan limits the importation of automobile parts according to a rigid schedule of numbers.

d. The United States charges French wineries 10% of the value of each case of French wine imported into the United States.

5. Suppose the U.S. is considering trade restrictions against EU-produced hams. Given the demand and supply curves drawn below, show a tariff and a quota that would result in the same exports of ham to the United States.

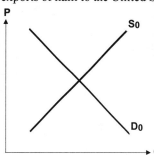

a. Would a tariff or a quota result in higher government revenue?

b. Which would the EU prefer?

c. Which would American ham producers prefer?

d. Which would American consumers prefer?

● A BRAIN TEASER

1. What are the benefits and the costs to a nation of lower trade barriers? Which are greater for the nation: the benefits or the costs of free trade?

● MULTIPLE CHOICE

Circle the one best answer for each of the following questions:

1. If a nation is a debtor nation it:
   a. is currently running a trade deficit.
   b. is currently running a trade surplus.
   c. has run trade deficits in the past.
   d. has run trade surpluses in the past.

2. If a country has a trade deficit, it is:
   a. consuming more than it is producing.
   b. lending to foreigners.
   c. buying financial assets.
   d. buying real assets.

3. Compared to the past, the United States is now:
   a. importing more high-tech goods and services from India and China and other East Asian countries.
   b. importing more goods and services that are lower down the technological ladder.
   c. outsourcing less to newly emerging industrialized countries like China and India.
   d. facing less competition from newly emerging industrialized countries like China and India.

4. Refer to the graph below. Given these production possibility curves, you would suggest that:

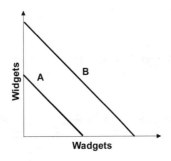

   a. Country A should specialize in widgets and Country B in wadgets.
   b. no trade should take place.
   c. Country A should specialize in wadgets and Country B in widgets.
   d. Both countries should produce an equal amount of each.

5. Refer to the graph below. The graph demonstrates Saudi Arabia's and the United States' production possibility curves for widgets and wadgets. Given these production possibility curves, you would suggest that:

   a. Saudi Arabia specialize in widgets and the United States in wadgets.
   b. No trade should take place.
   c. Saudi Arabia specialize in wadgets and the United States in widgets.
   d. Both countries should produce an equal amount of each.

6. If a nation has a comparative advantage in the production of good X then:
   a. it can produce good X at the lowest opportunity cost.
   b. it will import good X.
   c. it can produce more of good X than any other nation.
   d. the opportunity cost of producing an additional unit of good X is greater than for any other nation.

7. A widget has an opportunity cost of 4 wadgets in Saudi Arabia and 2 wadgets in the United States. Given these opportunity costs, you would suggest that:
   a. Saudi Arabia specialize in widgets and the United States in wadgets.
   b. no trade should take place.
   c. Saudi Arabia specialize in wadgets and the United States in widgets.
   d. both countries should produce an equal amount of each.

8. Country A's cost of widgets is $4.00 and cost of wadgets is $8.00. Country B's cost of widgets is 8 euros and cost of wadgets is 16 euros. Which of the following would you suggest?

a. Country A should specialize in widgets and Country B in wadgets.

b. Trade of widgets for wadgets would not benefit the countries.

c. Country A should specialize in wadgets and Country B in widgets.

d. Both countries should produce an equal amount of each.

9. In considering the distribution of the gains from trade:

a. smaller countries usually get a larger proportion of the gains from trade.

b. larger countries usually get a larger proportion of the gains from trade.

c. the gains are generally split equally between small and large countries.

d. no statement can be made about the general nature of the split.

10. Which of the following statements correctly summarizes a difference between the layperson's and the economists' views of the net benefits of trade?

a. Economists often argue that the gains from trade in the form of low consumer prices tend to be widespread and not easily recognizable while the costs in jobs lost tend to be concentrated and readily identifiable.

b. Economists often argue that most U.S. jobs are at risk of outsourcing while laypeople intuitively recognize that inherent in comparative advantage is that each country has a comparative advantage in the production of some good.

c. Economists focus on trade in manufactured goods while laypeople also focus on trade involving the services of people who manage the trade.

d. Economists most often argue that the costs of trade outweigh the benefits while laypeople often argue that the benefits of trade outweigh the costs.

11. Transferable comparative advantages are:

a. based on factors that are relatively unchangeable.

b. based on factors that can change relatively easily.

c. becoming more like inherent comparative advantages with technological innovations.

d. rarely eroded over time.

12. Trade restrictions tend to:

a. increase competition.

b. increase prices to consumers.

c. benefit consumers.

d. have economic benefits that outweigh the economic costs.

13. A tariff is a:

a. tax government places on internationally-traded goods.

b. quantity limit placed on imports.

c. total restriction on imports.

d. government-imposed procedural rule that limits imports.

14. An embargo is a:

a. tax government places on imports.

b. quantity limit placed on imports.

c. total restriction on imports.

d. government-imposed procedural rule that limits imports.

15. For governments:

a. tariffs are preferred over quotas because tariffs can help them collect revenues.

b. quotas are preferred over tariffs because quotas can help them collect revenues.

c. neither quotas nor tariffs can help collect revenues.

d. both quotas and tariffs are sources of revenues.

16. Reasons for restricting trade include all of the following *except:*

a. the existence of learning by doing and economies of scale.

b. national security reasons.

c. the increased revenue brought in from tariffs.

d. the fact that trade decreases competitive pressures at home.

17. Economists generally oppose trade restrictions
    for all of the following reasons *except:*
    a. from a global perspective, free trade in-
       creases total output.
    b. the infant industry argument.
    c. trade restrictions lead to retaliation.
    d. international politics.

18. Free trade associations tend to:
    a. reduce restrictions on trade and thereby
       always expand free trade.
    b. lower trade barriers for all countries.
    c. replace multinational negotiations, and
       thereby always hurt free trade.
    d. expand, but also reduce, free trade.

● POTENTIAL ESSAY QUESTIONS

You may also see essay questions similar to the "Problems & Applications" and "A Brain Teaser" exercises.

1. What is the difference between a tariff and a
    quota? Why do governments prefer tariffs
    while foreign producers prefer quotas? What is
    the result of tariffs and quotas on the price and
    equilibrium quantity of the imported good?

2. What are six ways in which a country may
    restrict trade? Why do most economists
    support free trade and oppose trade restric-
    tions?

ANSWERS

SHORT-ANSWER QUESTIONS

1. The primary trading partners of the United States are Canada, Mexico, the European Union, and Pacific Rim countries. (200-202)

2. The kinds of goods and services the U.S. imports have shifted from primarily basic manufacturing goods and raw commodities to high-tech manufacturing goods and services from developing countries such as India, China, and other East Asian countries. In addition, more and more production of more sophisticated goods and services is being outsourced to these countries because their economies are much larger. (200-202)

3. The principle of comparative advantage is that as long as the relative opportunity costs of production differ among countries, there are potential gains from trade, even if one country has an absolute advantage in everything. (203)

4. Three determinants of the gains of trade are (1) the more competition, the less the trader gets and the more will go to the countries who are trading; (2) smaller countries get a larger proportion of the gain than larger countries; and (3) countries producing goods with economies of scale get a larger gain from trade. (205-206)

5. Three reasons for differences between economists' and laypeople's views of trade are: (1) gains from trade are often stealth gains, (2) comparative advantage is determined by more than wages, and (3) nations trade more than just manufactured goods. (206-209)

6. The United States has comparative advantages due to: (1) skills of the U.S. labor force, (2) U.S. governmental institutions, (3) U.S. physical and technological infrastructure, (4) English is the international language of business, (5) wealth from past production, (6) U.S. natural resources, (7) cachet, (8) inertia, (9) U.S. intellectual property rights, and (10) a relatively open immigration policy. (209-210)

7. The United States is losing some of its transferable comparative advantages (as opposed to inherent comparative advantages) because economic forces push to spread technologies, which eliminates transferable comparative advantages. These economic forces include lower wages, a growing entrepreneurial spirit, institutions conducive to production in developing countries and exchange rate adjustments. (210-211)

8. Three policies countries use to restrict trade are (1) tariffs, (2) quotas, and (3) regulatory trade restrictions. There are others. (211-215)

9. Their answers might include: (1) although foreign competition might make society better off, some people may lose their jobs because of foreign competition (unequal internal distribution of the gains from trade); (2) some foreign companies are taking tough bargaining positions, and restricting trade is our only weapon against that (haggling by companies over trade restrictions); (3) some foreign countries are threatening us with trade restrictions (haggling by countries over the gains from trade); (4) trade restrictions will protect new U.S. industries until they learn to be competitive (learning by doing and economies of scale); (5) imports hurt U.S. domestic income in the short run, and the economy needs to grow in the short run (trade can reduce domestic output in the short run); (6) some restrictions are needed to protect our national security; (7) we do not want to trade with countries who violate our human rights standards or whose ideology conflicts with our democratic ideals (international politics may dominate trade considerations); and (8) tariffs bring in revenue for the U.S. government. (215-221)

10. I would say that I generally oppose trade restrictions because (1) from a global perspective, free trade increases total output, (2) international trade provides competition for domestic companies, (3) restrictions based on national security are often abused, and (4) trade restrictions are addictive. (221-222)

11. Free trade associations promote trade among members by reducing barriers to trade among the member nations. However, free trade associations could hinder trade by building up barriers to trade with nations outside the association. (222-224)

━━━ ● ━━━ ANSWERS ━━━ ● ━━━

MATCHING

1-o; 2-c; 3-d; 4-b; 5-h; 6-i; 7-m; 8-q; 9-n; 10-e; 11-k; 12-g; 13-f; 14-p; 15-a; 16-j; 17-r; 18-l.

━━━ ● ━━━ ANSWERS ━━━ ● ━━━

PROBLEMS AND APPLICATIONS

1. **a.** There is a basis for trade in Cases 2 and 3 because opportunity costs differ. (203-205)

    b. The general principle is that there are gains from trade to be made when each country has a comparative advantage in a different good. (203-205)

    c. I would have country E specialize in widgets and country F specialize in wadgets. Since country E is currently producing 10 widgets and 4 wadgets, I would have it produce 12 widgets and no wadgets, promising that I will give it 5 wadgets for the extra two widgets it produced. I would have Country F produce 28 wadgets and 18 widgets, promising that I will give it 2 widgets in return for 7 of its wadgets. After I made this trade both countries are one wadget better off. I am two wadgets better off. (These two wadgets are the return to me for organizing the trade.) (203-205)

    d. If there were economies of scale, there would be an even stronger argument for trade. (203-205)

2. **a.** The production possibility curve for Country A is the curve labeled A in the graph below. In Country A the opportunity cost of one bottle of wine is 1/2 fish. Each fish forgone frees up resources sufficient to make two bottles of wine. (203-205)

    b. The production possibility curve for Country B is the curve labeled B in the graph above. In Country B the opportu-

nity cost of one bottle of wine is one fish. Each fish forgone frees up resources sufficient to make one bottle of wine. (203-205)

    c. Country A has a comparative advantage in wine because it has to give up only 1/2 a fish for each bottle of wine while Country B has to give up 1 fish for each bottle of wine. Country B must necessarily have a comparative advantage in fish. (203-205)

    d. A fair exchange for B would be giving up one fish for one bottle of wine or better because that is its opportunity cost of producing one fish. A fair exchange for A would be giving up two bottles of wine for 1 fish or better since its opportunity cost of producing two bottles of wine is one fish. Any exchange between these two, such as 2 fish for 3 bottles of wine, would be a fair exchange. (203-205)

3. **a.** The production possibility curves for Country A and Country B are drawn below. (204)

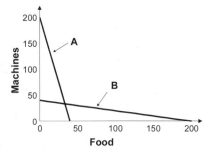

    b. Country B has the comparative advantage in the production of food since it has to give up only 1/5 machine to produce one unit of food while Country A has to give up 5 machines to produce one unit of food. (203-205)

    c. Country A would be willing to supply 5 machines for 1 unit of food. Country A would be willing to supply 5 units of foods for one machine. Let's suppose they trade 1 for 1. Country A would produce 200 machines, selling 50 to Country B for 50 units of foods. Country B would produce 200 food units, and sell 50 to Country A for 50 machines. This way they each reach their higher desired level of consumption. (203-205)

4. **a.** Regulatory trade restriction because this is a regulation that has the final effect of reducing imports without a tax or numerical limitation. (211-215)

b. Quota. It is a numerical restriction on the amount of rice entering the country. (211-215)

c. Quota because it is a numerical restriction on imports. (211-215)

d. Tariff because it is a tax on imports. (211-215)

5. A tariff would shift the supply curve up by the amount of the tariff. A quota with the same result would be at Q_1. Equilibrium quantity would fall from Q_0 to Q_1. Equilibrium price would rise from P_0 to P_1. This is shown on the graph below. (211-214 and Figure 9-5)

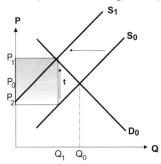

a. The government receives no revenue from the quota, but receives the shaded region as revenue from the tariff as shown on the graph above. (211-214 and Figure 9-5)

b. The EU would prefer the quota since it will receive a higher price, P_1, for the same quantity of goods, Q_1 as it would with a tariff. With a tariff it would receive P_2, for Q_1. (211-214 and Figure 9-5)

c. American ham producers prefer the quota because any increase in domestic demand would be met by domestic supply. (211-214)

d. American consumers do not prefer either since the resulting price and quantity is the same with both. If, however, the tariff revenue were to lead to lower taxes or higher government services, they might prefer the tariff over the quota. They also might prefer the tariff to the quota because any increase in domestic demand will be partially met with imports, keeping domestic producers more efficient than under a quota system. (211-214)

ANSWERS

A BRAIN TEASER

1. The benefits of lower trade barriers are a wider variety of higher quality, lower-priced products made available to consumers. This translates into an increase in the average absolute standard of living for the nation. The costs of lower trade barriers to a nation are the loss of jobs in those industries that find it difficult to compete in the global economy. The economic benefits of free trade outweigh the costs, at least over time. This is why economists generally favor free trade. (221-222)

ANSWERS

MULTIPLE CHOICE

1. c A debtor nation may currently be running a surplus or a deficit. Debt is accumulated deficits. A debtor nation could be running a surplus if it ran deficits in the past. See pages 202-203.

2. a If a country has a trade deficit, it is importing (consuming) more than it is exporting (producing). See pages 202-203.

3. a The U.S. is importing more and more high-tech goods and services that are higher up the technological ladder from India and China and other East Asian countries. The U.S. is outsourcing more to these newly emerging industrialized countries and is therefore facing more competition from these nations. See pages 200-202.

4. b Since the curves have the same slope, no country has a comparative advantage in either good and there is no basis for trade. See pages 203-205 and Figure 9-3.

5. a The opportunity cost for Saudi Arabia of wadgets in terms of widgets is higher than the opportunity cost for the United States. So Saudi Arabia should specialize in widgets and the United States in wadgets. See pages 203-205 and Figure 9-3.

6. a A comparative advantage in the production of X means the nation can produce that good with a lower opportunity cost. Because the nation is relatively more efficient at producing X, it will specialize in its production and export that good. Answer c may be true, but it is also possible to have a comparative advantage in X without being able to produce more of X than any other nation. See pages 203-205.

7. c The opportunity cost for the United States of wadgets in terms of widgets is higher than the opportunity cost for Saudi Arabia. So the United States should specialize in widgets and Saudi Arabia in wadgets. See pages 203-205.

8. b The opportunity cost of widgets and wadgets is equal in both countries so neither country has a comparative advantage in either good and there is no basis for trade. See pages 203-205.

9. a Smaller countries usually find that their production possibilities are changed more, and hence they benefit more. See pages 205-206.

10. a It is because the costs of trade are more visible than the benefits that many laypeople oppose free trade. Switching "economists" and "laypeople" would make options b through d correct. See pages 206-209.

11. b Transferable comparative advantages are based on factors that can change relatively easily and will tend to erode over time. Technological innovations are turning inherent comparative advantages into transferable comparative advantages. See page 210.

12. b Trade restrictions reduce competition and therefore increase prices to consumers. Thus, consumers are hurt. The benefits of trade restrictions go to the domestic producers that do not have to compete as aggressively. The economic costs of trade restrictions (in the form of higher prices consumers must pay) far outweigh their benefits (which go to the protected domestic industries in the form of higher profits and more secure jobs). See pages 211-215.

13. a A tariff is a tax placed on imported goods. See page 212.

14. c An embargo is an all-out restriction on the trade of goods with another country. See page 214.

15. a Governments prefer tariffs because they generate revenues, quotas do not. See pages 212-214.

16. d Trade increases competitive pressures at home and increases competitiveness. See pages 215-221.

17. b The infant industry argument is an argument in favor of trade restrictions. Economists' response to the infant industry argument is that history shows that few infant industries have ever grown up. See pages 221-222.

18. d While free trade associations may work toward lowering trade barriers among member nations, they may result in higher trade barriers for nonmember countries. See pages 222-224.

■━━━━ ANSWERS ━━━━■

POTENTIAL ESSAY QUESTIONS

The following are annotated answers. They indicate the general idea behind the answer.

1. A tariff is a tax on an imported item. A quota is a quantity limitation. Tariffs are preferred by governments because they raise revenues and are disliked by foreign producers because they require tax payments to the imposing government. However, notice that both tariffs and quotas raise prices and decrease the quantity of imported goods bought and sold.

2. Countries use a variety of policies to restrict trade. These include:
● Tariffs.
● Quotas.
● Voluntary restraint agreements.
● Embargoes.
● Regulatory trade restrictions.
● Nationalistic appeals.

Economists generally oppose trade restrictions because: (1) from a global perspective, free trade increases total output—it raises standards of living; (2) international trade provides competition for domestic companies; (3) restrictions based on national security are often abused or evaded; and (4) trade restrictions often become addictive for domestic firms that benefit. Free trade forces domestic firms to be efficient—to provide higher quality goods at cheaper prices. Economists argue that trade restrictions may create some short-run benefits, but the costs (or harm done, which includes higher prices domestic consumers must pay) outweigh the benefits over time.

THE LOGIC OF INDIVIDUAL CHOICE

CHAPTER AT A GLANCE

This review is based upon the learning objectives that open the chapter.

1. The principle of diminishing marginal utility states that after some point, the marginal utility received from each additional unit of a good decreases with each unit consumed, other things equal. (235)

    Marginal means "extra."
    Utility means "satisfaction."

2. The principle of rational choice tells us to spend our money on those goods that give us the most marginal utility per dollar. (233-235)

    If $MU_x/P_x > MU_y/P_y$, choose to consume an additional unit of good x;

    If $MU_x/P_x < MU_y/P_y$, choose to consume an additional unit of good y;

    If $MU_x/P_x = MU_y/P_y$, you are maximizing utility; you cannot increase your utility by adjusting your choices.

    $MU_x/P_x = MU_y/P_y$ *means the extra satisfaction per last dollar spent on x equals that for y.*

3. When the ratios of the marginal utility to the price of goods are equal, you're maximizing utility; that is the utility maximizing rule. (235-237)

    The equality: $MU_x/P_x = MU_y/P_y$ implies a combination of quantities of goods x and y consumed that will maximize your satisfaction given your budget, preferences, and the prices of x and y. No other combination of goods x and y will satisfy you as much.

4a. According to the principle of rational choice, if there is diminishing marginal utility and the

price of a good goes up, we consume less of that good. Hence, the principle of rational choice leads to the law of demand. (238-240)

If $MU_x/P_x = MU_y/P_y$ and then P_x increases, we get $MU_x/P_x < MU_y/P_y$ and we buy more of y and buy less of x.

The law of demand tells us that less will be purchased at higher prices. There are two effects that account for this – the income effect and the substitution effect.

4b. According to the principle of rational choice, if there is diminishing marginal utility and the price of supplying a good goes up, you supply more of that good. (240-241)

Consider labor. As the wage rate goes up, you will be willing to work more hours. Note that the law of supply can be derived from the principle of rational choice.

5. Three assumptions of the theory of choice are: decision making is costless, tastes are given, and individuals' maximize utility. (241-245)

    We must understand that these three assumptions don't always hold. The ultimatum game suggests that people care about fairness as well as maximizing their total utility. The status quo bias suggests that actions are based on perceived norms.

6. Behavioral economists look at choices in ways other than utility maximization. (242)

    Behavorial economists build upon traditional economics by conducting experiments to reveal how people make decisions.

    See also, Appendix A: "Indifference Curve Analysis."

● SHORT-ANSWER QUESTIONS

1. What is marginal utility?

2. Suppose you and your friend are studying hard for an economics exam. You have a craving for double cheese pizza. You order a large. Your mouth is watering as you sink your teeth into the first slice. Oh, the pleasure! You eagerly reach for the second slice. The additional pleasure that you get from this slice is less than that from the first. The third and fourth slice each give you even less pleasure. What principle does this describe? State the principle in general terms.

3. Suppose you had $8 to spend. You like going to see Ben Affeck movies a lot, but you like to see John Turturro movies even more. If these were your only choices to spend the $8 on, which movie would you go to see? Show how your choice follows the principle of rational choice.

4. What are the formulas that embody the principle of rational choice?

5. Explain why you're maximizing utility when the ratios of the marginal utility to the price of goods are equal.

6. Suppose you are maximizing utility by consuming two Big Macs at $2 apiece and three ice cream cones at $1 apiece. What happens to the number of Big Macs and ice cream cones consumed if the price of an ice cream cone rises to $2? How does this change in consumption account for the law of demand?

7. Why can economists believe there are many explanations of individual choice, but nonetheless focus on self-interest?

8. Describe the ultimatum game. What have economists learned about people's tastes from the ultimatum game? What are the implications for the theory of rational choice?

MATCHING THE TERMS

Match the terms to their definitions

____ 1. conspicuous consumption

____ 2. income effect

____ 3. marginal utility

____ 4. principle of diminishing marginal utility

____ 5. principle of rational choice

____ 6. status quo bias

____ 7. substitution effect

____ 8. total utility

____ 9. ultimatum game

____ 10. utility

____ 11. utility maximizing rule

a. As you consume more of a good, at some point, consuming another unit of the good will yield less additional pleasure compared to the preceding unit.

b. A rule stating that one should consume that combination of goods where the ratios of their marginal utilities to their prices are equal.

c. A measure of the pleasure or satisfaction one gets from consuming a good or service.

d. Spend your money on those goods that give you the most marginal utility per dollar.

e. The satisfaction one gets from consuming one additional unit of a product above and beyond what has already been consumed up to that point.

f. The total satisfaction one gets from a product.

g. Consumption of goods not for one's direct pleasure, but simply to show off.

h. Individuals' actions are influenced by the current situation even when that situation is not important to the decision.

i. An exercise that demonstrates people care about fairness as well as personal total utility.

j. The reduction in quantity demanded because the price increase has made us poorer.

k. The reduction in quantity demanded because the relative price has risen.

● PROBLEMS AND APPLICATIONS

1. a. Fill in the blanks for the following table that shows how marginal utility and total utility change as more and more chocolate chip cookies are consumed. (Marginal utility refers to the marginal utility of increasing to that row; e.g., the marginal utility of going from 0 to 1 is 20.)

Number of choc. chip cookies	Total utility	Marginal utility
1	___	20
2	37	___
3	51	___
4	___	11
5	___	8
6	___	5
7	77	___
8	___	–1

b. On the axes below, graph the total utility curve of the table above.

c. Graph the marginal utility curve on the axes for b.

d. Is the principle of diminishing marginal utility operative in this case? Explain your answer.

e. At what point does the principle of diminishing marginal utility take effect? At what point does marginal utility become zero?

2. Using the principle of rational choice, choose the best option in each case:

a. A $2 slice of pizza giving you 80 units of utility and a $2 hero sandwich giving you 60 units of utility.

b. A $40,000 BMW giving you 200,000 units of utility and a $20,000 Toyota giving you 120,000 units of utility.

c. Taking an economics course that meets 3 times a week for ten weeks giving 900 units of utility or taking a history course that meets 2 times a week for ten weeks giving 800 units of utility. Both class periods last 50 minutes. There is no homework or studying.

d. Taking Tory out for a date at the Four Seasons restaurant in New York City at a cost of $120 which gives you 600 units of utility and taking Sam out at the corner pizza place at a cost of $15 which gives you 60 units of utility. (Tory is short for Victoria or Torrence and Sam is short for Samantha or Samuel — you choose which.)

3. Suppose you are taking courses from two different colleges, both on a part-time basis. One college offers only science courses. The other offers only humanities courses. Each class meets for the same amount of time and

you have an unlimited number of hours you can devote to course work, but only $10,500 to devote to tuition. Science courses cost $1,500 a course and humanities courses cost $3,000 a course. You are taking the courses for enjoyment and you have estimated the utility from the consumption of these courses as presented in the following table:

Number of courses	Science Total utility	Humanities Total utility
0	0	0
1	4,500	7,500
2	7,500	12,000
3	9,750	15,750
4	11,250	18,750
5	11,750	21,000
6	12,000	22,500

a. How many science courses and how many humanities courses should you take (assuming you follow the principle of rational choice)?

b. Suppose the price of humanities courses falls to $1,000 a course, how would your answer to (a) change?

A1. Suppose you have a budget constraint of $10 to spend on pens and notebooks. Pens are 50 cents apiece and notebooks are $1 apiece. Draw the budget constraint, putting pens on the vertical axis and notebooks on the horizontal axis.

a. What is the slope of the line?

b. What happens to the budget constraint if your income available to spend falls to $8? What is the slope of the new curve? Show this graphically on the graph for (a).

c. Given the new $8 budget constraint, now suppose the price of notebooks rises to $2 apiece. What happens to the budget constraint? Show this graphically using the same axes as in the graph for (a) and (b).

A2. Suppose the following table depicts your indifference between combinations of pens and notebooks:

	Notebooks	**Pens**
A	12	6
B	8	7
C	6	8
D	5	10
E	4	14

a. Graph the indifference curve on the axes below, with pens on the vertical axis and notebooks on the horizontal axis.

b. What is the marginal rate of substitution between combinations C and D?

c. Combine the indifference curve from question A2 with the $10 budget constraint from question A1 on the graph above. What is the combination of goods you will choose using the principle of rational choice?

A BRAIN TEASER

1. The wedding industry is a $32 billion business. Weddings tend to be a onetime expense, with lavish expenditures on first marriages per wedding and smaller expenditures on later marriages. Would you expect the profit margins on wedding supplies to be higher or lower than for grocery stores? Why?

MULTIPLE CHOICE

Circle the one best answer for each of the following questions:

1. The principle of diminishing marginal utility says that after some point the marginal utility received from each additional unit of a good:
a. remains constant with each good consumed.
b. increases with each unit consumed.
c. decreases with each unit consumed.
d. approaches infinity with each good consumed.

2. The utility gained from eating one slice of pizza is 30 and the utility gained from eating a second slice of pizza is 20. From this we know:
a. the marginal utility of the second slice of pizza is 50.
b. the total utility of the second slice of pizza is 50.
c. the marginal utility of the second slice of pizza is 20.
d. there is not enough information to compute the marginal utility.

3. With regard to utility, it is true that
a. the total satisfaction one gets from one's consumption of a product is called marginal utility.
b. if you buy one Big Mac that gives you marginal utility of 400 and a second one that gives you marginal utility of 250, total utility of eating two Big Macs is 650.
c. according to the law of diminishing marginal utility, the more we consume of something, the smaller the total satisfaction received from that good.
d. when choosing between two goods, a rational consumer will choose that product that gives the greatest total utility per dollar.

4. The principle of rational choice specifically states that you choose how to spend additional income based on what gives you:
    a. the most total utility for that dollar.
    b. the most marginal utility for that dollar.
    c. the most average utility for that dollar.
    d. the least total utility for that dollar.

5. The price of good A is $1; the price of good B is $2. The marginal utility you get from good A is 40; the marginal utility you get from good B is 60. Assuming you can make marginal changes, you should:
    a. consume more of good A and less of good B.
    b. consume more of good B and less of good A.
    c. keep consuming equal amounts of both goods.
    d. realize that you don't have enough information to answer the question.

6. The price of good A is $2; the price of good B is $2. The marginal utility you get from good A is 40; the marginal utility you get from good B is 60. Assuming you can make marginal changes, you should:
    a. consume more of good A and less of good B.
    b. consume more of good B and less of good A.
    c. keep consuming equal amounts of both goods.
    d. realize that you don't have enough information to answer the question.

7. The price of good A is $1; the price of good B is $2. The marginal utility you get from good A is 40; the marginal utility you get from good B is 80. Assuming you can make marginal changes, you should:
    a. consume more of good A and less of good B.
    b. consume more of good B and less of good A.
    c. keep consuming the amount of both goods that you are currently consuming.
    d. realize that you don't have enough information to answer the question.

8. Dennis is deciding where to spend his spring break. If he goes to Vail, Colorado, the trip will give him 10,000 units of utility (satisfaction) and will cost him $500. If, instead, he travels to Padre Island, Texas, the trip will give him 6,000 units of pleasure and will cost him $400. Dennis should go to:
    a. Vail because his total pleasure will be greater.
    b. Padre Island because it is cheaper.
    c. Vail because his pleasure per dollar spent will be greater.
    d. Padre Island because his pleasure per dollar spent will be greater.

9. Economists assume that consumers will choose to purchase and consume:
    a. those goods that cost the least.
    b. those goods with the highest total utility.
    c. that combination of goods at which marginal utilities per dollar spent are equal.
    d. that combination of goods for which total utilities per dollar spent are equal.

10. The rational consumer will buy more of good X when:
    a. $MU_X/P_X < MU_Y/P_Y$.
    b. $MU_X/P_X > MU_Y/P_Y$.
    c. $MU_X/P_X = MU_Y/P_Y$.
    d. the price of good X increases.

11. If $MU_X/P_X = MU_Y/P_Y$ and the price of Y decreases, then the rational consumer will:
    a. continue consuming the same combination of X and Y.
    b. buy more of Y.
    c. buy more of X.
    d. buy less of X and Y.

12. For inferior goods, when price falls,
    a. the substitution effect leads to consuming less of the good.
    b. the income effect leads to consuming more of the good.
    c. the income effect leads to consuming less of the good.
    d. the income and substitutions effects both lead to consuming more of the good.

13. If your marginal utility of additional income is 60 units of utility, your opportunity cost of working is $5.00 per hour, and you are currently working 10 hours per week at $6.00 per hour, what is the minimum wage that you will require to work another hour?
    a. 60 units of utility.
    b. $5.00.
    c. $6.00.
    d. Insufficient information has been given to answer this question.

14. The theory of bounded rationality suggests that:
   a. all goods will be normal goods.
   b. all goods will be substitutes.
   c. many of our decisions are based on rules of thumb.
   d. individual tastes will be bounded and hence there will be diminishing marginal utility.

15. A focal point equilibrium is an equilibrium in which a set of goods is consumed:
   a. because the goods are subjectively preferred to all other goods.
   b. because the goods are objectively preferred to all other goods.
   c. not because the goods are necessarily preferred to all other goods, but simply because through luck, or advertising, they have become the goods to which people gravitate.
   d. through luck, or advertising, they have become focal points to which people gravitate despite the fact that other goods are definitely preferred.

16. Economists' theory of choice assumes:
   a. decision-making has costs.
   b. peoples' preferences are given, and are not shaped by society.
   c. people do not always make decisions that are rational.
   d. people maximize many things, one of which is utility.

17. Behavioral economists find that people:
   a. always give the same answer regardless of how questions are posed.
   b. care only about maximizing their own utility, not fairness.
   c. tend to make choices consistent with the perceived norm.
   d. can handle decisions with 2 choices just as easily as decisions with 5 choices.

A1. Refer to the graph below. The budget constraint reflects a relative price of chocolate (in terms of soda) of:
   a. one-fourth.
   b. one-half.
   c. one.
   d. two.

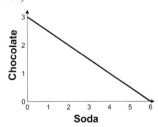

A2. Refer to the graph below on the left. If the price of chocolate falls, the budget constraint will:
   a. rotate out and become flatter.
   b. rotate in but keep the same slope.
   c. rotate in and become steeper.
   d. rotate out and become steeper.

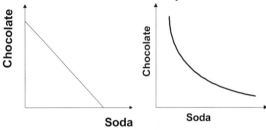

A3. Refer to the graph above on the right. The absolute value of the slope of the indifference curve represents:
   a. the marginal utility of chocolate divided by the marginal utility of soda.
   b. the marginal utility of soda divided by the marginal utility of chocolate.
   c. the marginal utility of soda times the marginal utility of chocolate.
   d. the marginal utility of chocolate divided by the price of chocolate.

A4. Refer to the graph below. The equilibrium in the indifference curve model is at point:
   a. A.
   b. B.
   c. C.
   d. D.

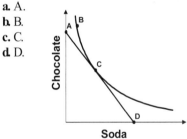

● POTENTIAL ESSAY QUESTIONS

You may also see essay questions similar to the "Problems & Applications" and "A Brain Teaser" exercises.

1. Discuss the principle of diminishing marginal utility. How is this related to the principle of rational choice and the law of demand?

2. Distinguish between the income and substitution effects.

ANSWERS

SHORT-ANSWER QUESTIONS

1. Marginal utility refers to the satisfaction one gets from the consumption of an incremental or additional product above and beyond what has already been consumed up to that point. (231-232)

2. The fact that you enjoy each subsequent slice less and less follows the principle of diminishing marginal utility. It states that after some point, the marginal utility received from each additional unit of a good decreases with each unit consumed. (235)

3. You would choose to see the John Turturro movie because it would give more pleasure for the same amount of money. This decision follows the principle of rational choice which tells us to spend our money on those goods that give us the most marginal utility per dollar. (233-235)

4. The formulas that embody the principle of rational choice are:
   If $MU_x/P_x > MU_y/P_y$, choose to consume an additional unit of good x;
   If $MU_x/P_x < MU_y/P_y$, choose to consume an additional unit of good y;
   If $MU_x/P_x = MU_y/P_y$, you're maximizing utility. (233-235)

5. If the ratios of the marginal utility to the price of goods are equal, you cannot adjust your spending in any way to increase total utility. Changing your spending will result in additional total utility for that good you increased. But that additional utility is less than the decrease in utility for that good that you have given up. Thus, the marginal utilities per dollar are no longer equal and overall total utility has fallen. Total utility is maximized where the ratios of the marginal utility to the price of goods are equal. (235-237)

6. If you were initially maximizing utility, it must be that $MU_{Big\ Macs}/\$2 = MU_{i.c.}/\$1$. If the price of ice cream cones rises, then you are no longer maximizing utility because $MU_{Big\ Macs}/\$2 > MU_{i.c.}/\$2$. To once again maximize utility, you would raise the marginal utility of ice cream cones and lower the marginal utility of Big Macs by choosing to consume more Big Macs and fewer ice cream cones because the marginal utility per dollar spent on Big Macs is greater than that for ice cream cones. You would adjust your consumption to the point where the marginal utilities per dollar were once again equal. The price of ice cream cones *relative to Big Macs* rose and the quantity demanded fell; and the price of Big Macs *relative to ice creams* fell and the quantity demanded rose. This is the law of demand in action. (238-240)

7. Economists believe there are many explanations of individual choice, but nonetheless they focus on self-interest because their simple self-interest theory cuts through many complications and in doing so often captures a part of reality other approaches miss. (245-246)

8. The ultimatum game is a game in which one person is given a sum of money that they can then share with another person. The person with the money can offer the other person any amount of that sum. If the offer is accepted, both people keep the money as negotiated. If the offer is rejected, all money must be returned. While economic theory suggests any offer would be accepted, offers that aren't close to half the sum are generally rejected. This suggests that people care about fairness as well as maximizing their total utility. The implications are that the assumptions of the theory of rational choice do not always hold true in reality. (245)

ANSWERS

MATCHING

1-g; 2-j; 3-e; 4-a; 5-d; 6-h; 7-k; 8-f; 9-i; 10-c; 11-b.

ANSWERS

PROBLEMS AND APPLICATIONS

1. **a.** This question tests the concepts of marginal utility, total utility, and the principle of diminishing marginal utility. Marginal utility is the satisfaction one gets from the consumption of an *incremental* product. Total utility is the total satisfaction from all units consumed up to that point of

consumption; it is the sum of all marginal utilities from consumption. (231-232)

Number of choc. chip cookies	Total utility	Marginal utility
1	20	20
2	37	17
3	51	14
4	62	11
5	70	8
6	75	5
7	77	2
8	76	−1

b.   The total utility curve is shown below. It is bowed downward because the marginal utility diminishes as more cookies are consumed.(232-233, especially Figure 10-1)

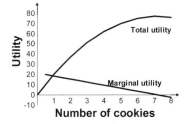

c.   The marginal utility curve is shown above. Its slope is always negative because the marginal utility of each additional cookie is always declining. (232-233, especially Figure 10-1)

d.   The principle of diminishing marginal utility is operative in this case. It states that as more of a good is consumed, beyond some point the additional units of consumption will yield fewer units of utility than the previous units. This is shown in the table by the third column. Its values are always declining. (231-233)

e.   The principle of diminishing marginal utility operates from the second cookie on. The second cookie gave less pleasure than the first cookie. This is true throughout, from 2 through 8. Marginal utility becomes zero between 7 and 8 cookies. The marginal utility of the 7th cookie is 2, but the marginal utility of the 8th is −1. (232)

2.   The principle of rational choice, discussed on page 192, states: Spend your money on those goods that give you the most marginal utility (MU) per dollar. (233-234)

a.   Choose the $2 slice of pizza. Marginal utility per dollar of the slice of pizza is 80 units of utility/$2 = 40 units of utility per dollar. Marginal utility per dollar of a hero sandwich is 60/ $2 = 30 units of utility per dollar. 40>30.

b.   Choose the $20,000 Toyota. Marginal utility per dollar for the Toyota is 120,000 units of utility/$20,000 = 6 units of utility per dollar. Marginal utility per dollar for the BMW is 200,000/$40,000 = 5 units of utility per dollar. 6>5.

c.   Choose the history course. Here the two alternatives have a cost in time, not money. The analysis is the same. Just calculate the marginal utility per minute and choose the one with the higher marginal utility per minute. Marginal utility per minute for the economics course is 900 units of utility/1500 minutes = 0.6 units of utility per minute. Marginal utility per minute for the history course is 800 units of utility/ 1000 minutes = 0.8 units of utility per minute. 0.8 > 0.6.

d.   Take Tory out on a date to the Four Seasons. Marginal utility per dollar for taking Tory out is 600 units of utility/ $120 = 5 units of utility per dollar. Marginal utility per dollar for taking Sam out is 60 units of utility/ $15 = 4 units of utility per dollar. 5 > 4.

3.   This tests your understanding of the principle of rational choice, which states that a rational individual will adjust consumption of all goods until the marginal utilities per dollar are equal. (233-238)

a.   You should take 3 science courses and 2 humanities courses, given your budget constraint of $10,500. To determine this, first you must calculate the marginal utilities, and then the marginal utilities per dollar when you are spending all your money. We show the calculations to arrive at the answer in the table on the next page. Following the principle of rational choice, select that combination where the marginal utilities per dollar are equal. Looking only at those combinations where you are spending all your money, this is at the combination of 3 science courses and 2 humanities courses. We reached this conclusion by figuring out different combinations of courses beginning with 6 science courses, calculating how many humanities courses could be purchased with the remaining funds, and comparing marginal utilities per dollar. If the marginal utility per dollar of science courses is lower than that for humanities course, choose one less science course and repeat the calculation. Keep doing this until the marginal utilities per dollar are the same for both.

SCIENCE COURSES

Number of Courses	Total utility	Marginal utility	MU per $
0	0	0	0
1	4,500	4,500	3
2	7,500	3,000	2
3	9,750	2,250	1.5
4	11,250	1,500	1
5	11,750	500	0.33
6	12,000	250	0.17

HUMANITIES COURSES

Number of Courses	Total utility	Marginal utility	MU per $
0	0	0	0
1	7,500	7,500	2.5
2	12,000	4,500	1.5
3	15,750	3,750	1.25
4	18,750	3,000	1
5	21,000	2,250	0.75
6	22,500	1,500	0.5

b. Now you should take 3 science courses and 6 humanities courses, given your budget constraint of $10,500. First you must calculate the marginal utilities and then the marginal utilities per dollar. This is shown in the accompanying table. Next, following the principle of rational choice, select that combination where the marginal utilities per dollar are equal and you cannot buy any more courses. This is at the combination of 3 science courses and 6 humanities courses.

SCIENCE COURSES

Number of Courses	Total utility	Marginal utility	MU per $
0	0	0	0
1	4,500	4,500	3
2	7,500	3,000	2
3	9,750	2,250	1.5
4	11,250	1,500	1
5	11,750	500	0.33
6	12,000	250	0.17

HUMANITIES COURSES

Number of Courses	Total utility	Marginal utility	MU per $
0	0	0	0
1	7,500	7,500	7.5
2	12,000	4,500	4.5
3	15,750	3,750	3.75
4	18,750	3,000	3
5	21,000	2,250	2.25
6	22,500	1,500	1.5

A1. The budget constraint is drawn below. It was constructed by first finding out the y-intercept —how many pens could be bought with the entire $10: 20 pens—and then finding out the x-intercept—how many notebooks could be bought with the entire $10: 10 notebooks. Connect these points to get the budget constraint. (250-251)

a. The slope of the budget constraint is $-P_{notebooks}/P_{pens} = -\$1/0.50 = -2$.

b. The budget constraint shifts in, intersecting the pen axis at 16 and the notebook axis at 8. To find this, use the process described above to find the initial budget constraint. Since relative prices did not change, the slope is still -2. This is shown below.

c. Since relative prices changed, the budget constraint rotates. To find the new budget constraint, find first how many notebooks can be bought at their new price: 4. The y-intercept remains at 16 since the price of pens did not change. The budget constraint rotates in along the notebook axis and intersects it at 4 notebooks. Since notebooks became more expensive, the slope became steeper. The slope of the line is $-P_{notebooks} / P_{pens} = -\$2/0.50 = -4$. This is shown below.

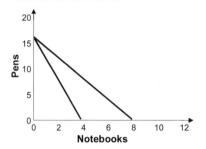

A2. a. To graph the indifference curve, plot each set of points which give the same utility. This is done below. (251-253)

b. The marginal rate of substitution between the combinations C and D is equal to the slope between C and D, $MU_{notebooks} / MU_{pens} = -2$. (252)

c. To find where you maximize utility given the budget constraint, find that point where the slope of the budget constraint equals the marginal rate of substitution between pens and notebooks. This is at points between C and D shown in the graph below. At points between C and D, the slope of the budget constraint is equal to the marginal rate of substitution: $MU_{ntbks} / MU_{pens} = -2 = -P_{ntbks} / P_{pens}$. The budget constraint is tangent to the indifference curve at points between C and D. This implies that any other indifference curve that intersects the budget constraint line gives you less total utility than does the current indifference curve. A rational choice maximizes your own utility. Hence, you should choose combinations represented by points between C and D. (253)

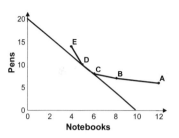

A BRAIN TEASER

1. Higher, because the marginal utility on marriages is very high–especially for the first marriage. That is, people are willing to pay dearly for a memorable event. Moreover, there is a very inelastic demand (there are few "acceptable" substitutes) for the services and supplies provided for weddings. This, too, has a tendency to result in high prices. Moreover, there's more to life than a literal application of the rational choice model. We do crazy things just for the sake of doing crazy things. We follow rules of thumb–such as, we don't want to be seen as a "cheap skate" on our child's (or our future spouse's) wedding day. Moreover, we are more apt to be conspicuous consumers when it comes to weddings. All of these elements are not nearly as strong for grocery store shopping (241-242)

MULTIPLE CHOICE

1. c   The principle of diminishing marginal utility says that after some point, the additional satisfaction one gets from consuming additional units declines. See page 233.

2. c   When we say that the utility of the second slice of pizza is 20, we mean we are getting an additional 20 units of utility, so the marginal utility of the second slice is 20. See page 231-232.

3. b   Options a, c, and d would be true statements if "total" was changed to "mar-

ginal." See pages 231-232, especially the table in Figure 10-1.

4. b   You are better off by choosing to spend an additional sum of money on the good that provides you the greatest marginal utility per dollar. See pages 233-237.

5. a   Applying the rational choice rule, you divide the MU by the price. Increase consumption of the good that gives the greater marginal utility per dollar. Since 40/1 is greater than 60/2 then increase consumption of A and decrease consumption of B. See pages 233-237.

6. b   Increase the consumption of that good that provides the greatest MU/P. Since 40/2 is less than 60/2 you consume more of good B. See pages 233-237.

7. c   Increase the consumption of that good that provides the greatest MU/P. Since 40/1 equals 80/2 you continue to consume the same amounts of both goods you are currently consuming. See pages 233-237.

8. c   The trip to Vail will give Dennis the greatest marginal utility per dollar spent. See pages 233-237.

9. c   This is the rational choice. See page 235.

10. b   When $MU_X/P_X > MU_Y/P_Y$ the marginal utility for the money spent on good X exceeds that for good Y. You are getting more satisfaction for the last dollar spent on good X. Therefore, buy more of good X. See page 234.

11. b   A decrease in the price of Y will cause $MU_X/P_X < MU_Y/P_Y$. Therefore, one should buy more of good Y (and less of good X). See page 238.

12. c   For an inferior good, when income rises, less of the good is consumed. If the price of a good falls, the price decline has made the person richer (the purchasing power of their income has risen). Considering this effect alone, the price decline will result in consuming less of the good. The substi-

tution effect will work in the opposite direction, offsetting the income effect. The net effect is unknown. Quantity demanded may rise, fall, or remain the same. See pages 239-240.

13. b   Only the opportunity cost is needed to determine what would be required to get you to work another hour. See pages 240-241.

14. c   The theory of bounded rationality suggests that many of our decisions are based on rules of thumb rather than on the principle of rational choice. See page 241.

15. c   A focal point equilibrium may be the preferred equilibrium but it does not necessarily have to be the preferred equilibrium if individuals had better information. See page 242.

16. b   Economists' theory of choice assumes that decision-making is costless, people's preferences are given (and are not shaped by society), and individuals are rational and attempt to maximize utility. See pages 242-243.

17. c   Behavioral economists have found that people tend to make decisions consistent with the perceived norm. This is the status quo bias. They also find that decisions are not costless. The greater the number of choices, the more costly the decision. Also people care about fairness as well as maximizing utility. See page 242.

A1. d   Divide the intercept on the soda axis by the intercept on the chocolate axis to find the price of chocolate in terms of soda. One can buy either 6 sodas or 3 chocolates, or, 2 sodas or 1 chocolate. See page 251.

A2. d   A fall in the price of chocolate means that the same amount of soda will give more pieces of chocolate, so the budget constraint rotates up from the intersection of the soda axis, becoming steeper. See page 251.

A3. b   A movement down the curve represents the soda needed to compensate the individual—i. e., keep her utility constant—for giving up some chocolate. See pages 251-252.

A4. c   The equilibrium is where the indifference curve is tangent to the budget constraint. See page 253.

━━━━━━ ANSWERS ━━━━━━

POTENTIAL ESSAY QUESTIONS

The following are annotated answers. They indicate the general idea behind the answer.

1. As we consume more of any good or service the marginal utility declines. We consume combinations of goods and services for which their marginal utilities in relation to their prices are equal. If the price for good X falls, the marginal utility of good X in relation to its price will be greater than for other goods and services. We are simply getting more satisfaction for the money spent on the last unit of good X consumed. Therefore, we buy more of good X. So as the price of good X falls we find it rational to buy more of good X. This is the law of demand.

2. When the price of a good rises, the quantity demanded generally will fall. There are two forces that lead to this. First, because the price of the good relative to other goods has increased, consumers will substitute other goods whose prices have not risen for the good whose price has risen. This is called the substitution effect. The rise in the price of the good has also reduced the purchasing power of the income of consumers. Consumers just cannot buy as much as before because the price increase has made them poorer. The decline in quantity demanded because the price increase has made consumers poorer is called the income effect.

GAME THEORY, STRATEGIC DECISION MAKING, AND BEHAVIORAL ECONOMICS

● CHAPTER AT A GLANCE

This review is based upon the learning objectives that open the chapter.

1. Game theory can be structured to reflect the assumptions of a variety of models, making it more flexible than economists' traditional models of market behavior. (256)

    Game theory looks at strategic interaction among individuals and firms.

2. A prisoner's dilemma game is a game where the decision of one player affects the outcome for both players. The two players must make simultaneous decisions. (257-259)

    The prisoner's dilemma can be illustrated with pay-off matrix. See page 258 in the textbook for an example. Players are assumed to make the best choice for themselves given the expected decision of the other player.

3. A Nash equilibrium is the set of strategies for each player in a game where no one can improve his or her payoff by changing strategy unilaterally. (259)

    A Nash equilibrium assumes players do not collude.

4. A dominant strategy is preferred regardless of one's opponent's move. A mixed strategy is choosing randomly. (259-262)

    The best strategy for rock, paper, scissors is a mixed strategy. It keeps your opponent guessing. The classic prisoner's dilemma game has a dominant strategy of each prisoner confessing.

5. Loss aversion and framing effects are examples of findings in behavioral economics that challenge the assumptions of the standard model. (269-270)

    Once people acquire something, they tend to want to keep it. This is loss aversion.

    The way a question is framed affects the decision, even if the outcomes are the same. This is framing effects.

6. It only takes a few individuals to act as the model assumes (that is, are rational) for the predictions of the traditional model to hold. (270-271)

    Those individuals who are rational will be able to take advantage of the irrationality of others.

● SHORT-ANSWER QUESTIONS

1. There are two roommates. Both want to have a television for the apartment that costs $300, although neither has revealed that information to the other. Each values TV watching at $325. If only one roommate expresses the desire to have a TV, he will pay the entire cost. If both express a desire to have a TV, they will split the cost. If neither expresses a desire to have a TV, they don't get one. Draw a payoff matrix showing the gain of each roommate that reflects the situation and explain the strategic decision for each individual. How would their answer differ if they could cooperate?

2. Does the prisoner's dilemma game have a Nash equilibrium? Why or why not?

3. How would you expect the results of a single play ultimatum game to differ from a repeated play ultimatum game?

4. If a game arrives at a Nash equilibrium, is that Nash equilibrium to be preferred to a cooperative equilibrium?

5. In the 2/3rds game what is the Nash equilibrium? Would you expect it to be reached?

6. Is it true that in a Vickrey auction since the winner only pays the second-highest bid, winners can be expected to do better than in normal "highest bidder" auctions? Why?

7. In showing houses real estate agents sometimes show either expensive or run-down houses first, and then bring the client to the house they believe is best for them. Why?

8. Professor of Law Cass Sunstein asked two different groups of law students the following questions:

    Group 1: Under existing regulation of arsenic in drinking water, you face an annual cancer risk of 1 in 500,000. The government is proposing to tighten the regulation, in a way that would decrease the risk to 1 in 600,000. How much would you be willing to pay each year, in increased water bills, to favor the government's proposal? Choose one (a-f).

    a. $25; b. $50; c. $100; d. $200; e. $400; f. over $400.

    Group 2: Under existing regulation of arsenic in drinking water, you face an annual cancer risk of 1 in 600,000. The national government is proposing to loosen the regulation, in a way that would increase the risk to 1 in 500,000. How much would you have to be paid each year, in reduced water bills, to favor the government's proposal? Choose one (a-f).

    a. $25; b. $50; c. $100; d. $200; e. $400; f. over $400.

    While the value of each proposal was identical in terms of the probabilistic loss of life, the first group's median answer was $25 while the second group's median answer was $100. How would you explain the difference?

9. When an economist says that he doesn't care whether most people are rational or not, but only cares that "no money is left on the table," what does he or she mean?

MATCHING THE TERMS
Match the terms to their definitions

___ 1. backward induction

___ 2. cheap talk

___ 3. cooperative game

___ 4. dominant strategy

___ 5. framing effect

___ 6. game theory

___ 7. mixed strategy

___ 8. Nash equilibrium

___ 9. noncooperative game

___ 10. payoff matrix

___ 11. prisoner's dilemma

___ 12. screening question

___ 13. sequential game

___ 14. simultaneous move game

___ 15. Vickrey auction

a. The tendency of people to base their choices on how the choice is presented.

b. A sealed-bid auction where the highest bidder wins but pays the price bid by the next-highest bidder.

c. A strategy of choosing randomly among moves.

d. You begin with a desired outcome and then determine the decisions that could have led you to that outcome.

e. A game in which each player is out for him or herself and agreements are either not possible or not enforceable.

f. A game in which players can form coalitions and enforce the will of the coalition on its members.

g. A question structured in a way to extract strategic information about the person answering.

h. A game where players make their decisions at the same time as other players without knowing what choice the other players have made.

i. A game where players make decisions one after another; so one player responds to the known decisions of other players.

j. A set of strategies for each player in the game in which no player can improve his or her payoff by changing their strategy unilaterally.

k. A strategy that is desired by a player regardless of the opponent's move.

l. Communication that occurs before the game is played that carries no cost and is backed up only by trust, and not any enforceable agreement.

m. A table that shows the outcome of every choice by every player, given the possible choices of all other players.

m. A well-known two-person game that demonstrates the difficulty of cooperative behavior in certain circumstances.

o. Formal economic reasoning applied to situations in which decisions are interdependent.

PROBLEMS AND APPLICATIONS

1. A famous game developed by O. Hayword is called the Battle of Bismarck Sea. In the game, a Japanese admiral has to transport troops to New Guinea. He can take the rainy northern route or the sunny southern route. The United States knows the convoy will sail, and wants to attack it, but does not know which route the Japanese will take. The Americans have only enough reconnaissance planes to check out one route. If they explore the southern route and find the Japanese took that route, they will likely get three days of bombing in, but only one day of bombing in if the Japanese take the northern route. If the United States explores the northern route and find the Japanese, they will only get two days of bombing in because one of the days will have weather too bad to bomb. If instead the Japanese took the Southern route, they get in 2 days of bombing.

   a. Construct a payoff matrix with days of bombing as the positive payoff for the United States and the negative payoff for the Japanese.

b. What is the United States's dominant strategy?

c. What is the Japanese dominant strategy?

d. If the Japanese have a dominant strategy what does it make sense for the United States to do?

2. To show their bravery some boys have played a game of chicken in which they drive cars headed directly towards each other, to see who is the first one to swerve off, which means you are a chicken and you lose face. Assume that if you are chicken you get a payoff of one and the other gets 3; if you both swerve at the last minute, you each get a payoff of 2, and if you both go straight, you die which is denoted by a payoff of zero.

a. Draw the relevant payoff matrix.

b. What is the Nash equilibrium in the game?

c. If you have a reputation for being crazy, can that affect the outcome of the game?

d. How would your play differ if the other driver made it clear that they would decide whether to swerve or not by flipping a coin, and would not make a rational choice?

3. Consider the following pay-off matrixes:

a.

	H	T
H	+1, −1	0, 0
T	0, 0	−1, +1

b.

	H	T
H	+1, −1	+1, −1
T	−1, +1	−1, +1

c.

	H	T
H	+2, −1	+1, −1
T	−1, +1	−1, +2

d.

	H	T
H	3, 3	0, 2
T	2, 0	1, 1

a. For each of the payoff matrices listed, is there a dominant strategy for Player A (whose options are the rows and whose payoffs are specified by the first value in each square). If so, what is it?

b. If you were playing the game specified by payoff matrix *a* 100 times, what percentage of the time should you call heads (H)?

A BRAIN TEASER

1. You have been captured by the "evil one" who has put you in a soundproof box which has one button in it. It is 11:45 AM. You find the following information written on the wall of the box. As part of my PhD dissertation, I have captured you and 200 of your fellow students and put you each into a separate box. If any of you pushes the button, cynide gas

will be released into your box, which will kill you instantly, but the others will live. However, if no one pushes the button before 12:00, the cynide gas will be released in all the boxes, and you will all die. Do you push the button or not? Explain your reasonings.

● MULTIPLE CHOICE

Circle the one best answer for each of the following questions:

1. Game theory is best described as:
   a. formal economic reasoning applied to situations in which decisions are independent.
   b. formal economic reasoning applied to situations in which decisions are interdependent.
   c. the analysis of dilemmas facing prisoners.
   d. a recreational activity of economists.

2. Game theory is a tool:
   a. used only by economists to study strategic interaction where agents' decisions are independent.
   b. used by economists and other social scientists to study strategic interaction where agents' decisions are independent.
   c. used only by economists to study strategic interaction where agents' decisions are interdependent.
   d. used by economists and other social scientists to study strategic interaction where agents' decisions are interdependent.

3. The economic way of thinking is best described as:
   a. create a simple model, empirically test it, and use it to guide your analysis.
   b. translate a problem to a graph and solve for an equilibrium.
   c. analyze all aspects of a problem and use that analysis to guide your thinking about the problem.
   d. create a simple model and use it to guide your analysis.

4. A payoff matrix shows:
   a. the payoffs that one player must make to the other player.
   b. the payoff for each choice of each player.
   c. the best choices for each player.
   d. the best and worst choices for each player.

5. The following payoff matrix represents a:

	A	A
B	A: 1, B: 100	A: 0, B: 1
B	A: 2, B: 0	A: 5, B: 2

   a. zero sum game.
   b. non-zero sum game.
   c. repeated game.
   d. sequential game.

6. The Nash equilibrium solution for the following payoff matrix is:

	A	A
B	A: 1, B: 100	A: 0, B: 1
B	A: 2, B: 0	A: 5, B: 2

   a. 1, 100.
   b. 2, 0.
   c. 0, 1.
   d. There is more than one equilibrium solution.

7. If individuals can cooperate and share the gains, which payoff is the most likely?

	A	A
B	A: 1, B: 100	A: 0, B: 1
B	A: 2, B: 0	A: 5, B: 2

   a. 1, 100.
   b. 2, 0.
   c. 0, 1.
   d. 5, 2.

8. The prisoner's dilemma is a well-known game in which:
   a. cooperation is costless.
   b. independent action is not necessarily the best joint action, but is the best independent action.
   c. firms always cheat.
   d. firms never cheat.

9. Generally, a repeated game will have:
   a. the same solution as a single play game.
   b. the same solution as a simultaneous play game.
   c. a different solution than a single play game.
   d. a different solution than a simultaneous play game.

10. If play in a game consistently deviates from the predicted play, the most likely reason is:
    a. players must not be rational.
    b. player's decisions are not described by the assumptions of the game.
    c. the game is incorrectly structured.
    d. economic reasoning is wrong.

11. In the game rock/paper/scissors, you should:
    a. generally choose rock because it breaks scissors.
    b. generally choose paper because it covers rock.
    c. generally choose scissors because it cuts paper.
    d. look for a pattern in your opponents play and choose accordingly.

12. Assuming the standard assumptions, in a single play ultimatum game, the first player's best strategy is to:
    a. split the money evenly with a bit more going to yourself.
    b. give most money to the opponent.
    c. give most money to yourself.
    d. take all the money for yourself.

13. Assuming the traditional assumptions, in an infinitely long repeated play ultimatum game, the first player's best strategy is most likely to:
    a. split the money evenly with a bit more going to yourself.
    b. give most money to the opponent.
    c. give most money to yourself.
    d. take all the money for yourself.

14. In the 2/3rds game, in which you are to choose a number which is 2/3rds of the average chosen by the group, the Nash equilibrium is:
    a. zero.
    b. 11.
    c. 22.
    d. 33.

15. In a Vickrey auction:
    a. since the bidder pays only the next highest bid, he gets a better price than in a standard auction.

    b. even though the bidder pays only the next highest bid, he does not get a better price than in a standard auction.
    c. since the bidder pays the highest price, he pays a higher price than in a standard auction.
    d. even though the bidder pays the highest price, he does not get a better price than in a standard auction.

16. In the "trust game" a player is given money, which he can either keep, or give to someone else. If he gives the money to someone else, that money is tripled, and the second person can return some portion to the first player. The Nash equilibrium in this game is:
    a. for the first player to keep the entire sum.
    b. for the first player to keep half the money and give the other half to the second player.
    c. for the first player to give the entire sum to the other player.
    d. There is no Nash equilibrium for this game.

17. The fact that restaurants offer early-bird specials instead of peak-time surcharges is an example of:
    a. loss aversion.
    b. framing effects.
    c. non-zero sum game.
    d. irrational behavior.

18. Charlotte owns two stocks—stock A and stock B. She bought stock A for $60 and stock B for $10. Both are now valued at $50. The fact that Charlotte prefers to sell stock B because she will realize a gain instead of stock A because she will realize a loss is an example of:
    a. loss aversion.
    b. framing effects.
    c. non-zero sum game.
    d. band-wagon effects.

19. If most people don't conform to the assumptions of the standard model:
    a. the outcome of the model could not be true.
    b. the outcome of the model could still be true.
    c. society will have to better educate its people.
    d. the assumptions have to be revised.

POTENTIAL ESSAY QUESTIONS

You may also see essay questions similar to the "Problems & Applications" and "A Brain Teaser" exercises.

1. You are thinking of buying some shares of stock, and you know that people will be retiring soon and selling off their stock to finance their retirement. Thus, the stock market can be expected to fall, and you would be best off if you sold your stock now. If the assumptions of this question are correct, is the reasoning correct?

2. Martin Shubik, a famous game theorist, has designed the following game called the dollar auction. In it, a dollar bill is auctioned according to two rules.
    a. The dollar bill goes to the highest bidder.
    b. The second highest bidder also has to pay the amount of the last bid but he gets nothing in return.
    What would be your strategy in this game? Is it possible for the bidding to exceed $1.00?

3. Can a policy of a pre-emptive war be justified on game theoretic grounds?

ANSWERS

SHORT-ANSWER QUESTIONS

1.

	A wants TV	A doesn't want TV
B wants TV	175,175	325,25
B doesn't want TV	25,325	0,0

If player A states he wants the TV, then player B's best strategy is to state that he doesn't want it. If player A states that he doesn't want the TV then player B's best strategy is to state that he wants it. The reverse is true for Player B. There are no dominant strategies, but two Nash equilibria. If the players could cooperate, there would likely be a push for both saying they wanted the TV, and they would split the costs. (257-259)

2. The prisoner's dilemma game has a Nash equilibrium because there is an outcome (both confess) if each player follows his best strategy and assumes that the other player follows his or her best strategy, and no player can do better by changing strategy unilaterally. (257-259)

3. I would expect more money to be shared in a repeated-play ultimatum game since it would allow for signals of willingness to share to be sent by the first player, and for the second player to punish the first player if he does not share. (263)

4. No, cooperative equilibria can lead to better outcomes for both players. The Nash equilibrium is best only for those games in which no cooperation is allowed or possible. (259-263)

5. The Nash equilibrium in the 2/3rds game is zero. It would probably not be reached regardless of how many times the game is played, because all individuals would not be expected to be following the "best" strategy. (263-264)

6. No, it is not true. The reason is that the bidder's strategy changes, so that each bidder now has an incentive to bid his true reservation price rather than simply the price that beats the next highest bidder. This happens only if the auction is a sealed-bid auction. (268)

7. This is probably explained by their trying to take advantage of framing effects. By showing expensive or run down houses first, the agent changes the frame of reference for the client and makes them more likely to see the final house as a good buy. (269-270)

8. I would explain the results in terms of loss aversion. Since people already had safer drinking water, they were less likely to give it up (require a higher payment) to lose that safety than they were willing to pay to gain that increased safety. What people are more likely to keep is what they have (safe water or money). (269-270)

9. For the predictions of economic theory to hold true, only a portion of the population has to exhibit "rational" behavior. The "rational" ones will devise schemes to take advantage of other people's irrationality and transfer money that the irrational ones leave on the table to themselves. This makes the system operate as if all people were rational. (269-271)

ANSWERS

MATCHING

1-d; 2-l; 3-f; 4-k; 5-a; 6-o; 7-c; 8-j; 9-e; 10-m; 11-n; 12-g; 13-i; 14-h; 15-b.

ANSWERS

PROBLEMS AND APPLICATIONS

1. a. (262-263)

	Japan Northern route	Japan Southern route
US Northern route	2, −2	2, −2
US Southern route	1, −1	3, −3

b. The United States does not have a dominant strategy. They do better by choosing north if the Japanese choose north, but better by choosing south if the Japanese choose south. (257-259)

c. The Japanese have a dominant strategy since they come out better off if they go north. If they go south and the United States chooses south, they are bombed for three days. (262)

d. Since the Japanese have a dominant strategy, it makes sense for the United States to do the reconnaissance on the Northern Route. (257-259)

2. a. The game of "chicken" can be described by the following payoff matrix. (262-263)

	Swerve	Go straight
Swerve	2, 2	1, 3
Go straight	3, 1	0, 0

b. There are two Nash equilibria in this game—the upper right and lower left payoffs. If the other person is swerving, which is the best option, then it is in your interest to go straight. But the same reasoning holds for the other player, which is why it is called a game of chicken. (257-259)

c. Yes, if you are known as crazy, you are expected to go straight, and this changes the other player's dominant strategy to become one of swerving. (262)

d. This again changes the strategy for the other player, since there is now a 50% chance that you are going to swerve. It will make him more likely to swerve. (257-259)

3. a. In a, b, and c, the dominant strategy is heads. A has no dominant strategy for d. (260-262)

b. Because there is a benefit to predicting the other person's choice, you should have a mixed strategy. You should play heads or tails randomly with equal probability. (260-262)

━━━━ ANSWERS ━━━━

BRAIN TEASER

1. There is no answer to this question which is an example of what is called the volunteer's dilemma. The best outcome is for one person to push the button, but there is no way of

determining whether your doing so would save the others or not, because you don't know if anyone else has pushed the button already. (257-259)

━━━━ ANSWERS ━━━━

MULTIPLE CHOICE

1. b The best description is b. "c" and "d" are too narrow, and "a" is incorrect since the strategic element of game theory emphasizes agent interdependence. See page 256.

2. d Since game theory is used by all social scientists, the answer must be b or d, and since game theory studies interdependent decisions, the answer must be d. See pages 260-261.

3. a As the Solow quote emphasizes in the text, the economic approach involves modeling and empirically testing of that model. See pages 260-261.

4. b The payoff matrix is a table showing the outcome of every choice of every player, so b is the best answer. See page 258.

5. b It is a non-zero sum game because the gains of one individual do not offset the losses to the other. See pages 262-264.

6. d There are two Nash equilibria. Assuming the individuals can expect the other player to choose the outcome that maximizes his payoff, the best that the players can do is to follow this strategy. See pages 259-260 and Figure 11-1 on page 258.

7. a I would expect that a is the most likely since it has the higher combined payoff, and I would expect that some sharing arrangement would be made. See page 269 and Figure 11-1.

8. b In the prisoner's dilemma game, cooperation is beneficial for both prisoners, but difficult to achieve. Firms do not always get together. There may or may not be cheating, but firms expect others to cheat. See Figure 11-1 on page 258.

9. c   Simultaneous play games could be repeated or single play games so b and d are not possibilities. Since repeated games offer more possibilities for implicit cooperation than single-play games do, a repeated game generally will have a different solution than a single play game. See pages 260 and 263.

10. b   Games require strict assumptions, which are often not met in real life, which is the most likely reason why games deviate from predicted play. See pages 260-262.

11. d   In games, you should use backward induction to determine your play. Backward induction requires you to look for a pattern and take advantage of it. See pages 260-262.

12. c   Since the game is played only once, the other person should accept any offer that gives him more than zero, so c is the best answer. See pages 263.

13. a   Since the game is being played again and again, the other person will likely punish you if you give most of the money to yourself and thus a is most likely the best strategy. See pages 260 and 263.

14. a   The Nash equilibrium is zero since choosing 2/3rds of an average always drives the choice down, and through backward induction approaches zero. See pages 263-264.

15. b   In a Vickrey auction, the bidder pays the second-highest price, so the answer must be a or b. It is "b" because the bidder's strategy changes, since they now have an incentive to bid the full value of the good, rather than to make a bid that just beats the next highest bidder. See page 268.

16. a   Since the second player will be assumed to keep all the money he is given and not return any to the first player, the Nash equilibrium is for the first player to keep all the money. See pages 268-270.

17. b   The effect of charging peak-time eaters more is the same as charging non-peak time eaters less. Restaurants advertise that they discount off-peak dinners as a way to frame the practice as a discount rather than a surcharge to peak eaters. See pages 269-270.

18. a   This is an example of loss aversion. Although past price of a stock ought not to determine which is sold, people often sell the one whose price has risen to avoid realizing a loss. See pages 269-270.

19. b   Even if most people don't conform to the standard model, if at least some do, they will take advantage of those who do not, which may result in the identical aggregate outcome. See pages 269-271.

━━━━━ ANSWERS ━━━━━

POTENTIAL ESSAY QUESTIONS

The following are annotated answers. They indicate the general idea behind the answer.

1. Other things equal, a greater number of retirees would mean that more people will be selling stocks and that stock prices will fall. But other things don't remain equal. Other stock market investors likely have already realized this same probability and have already sold off their stocks. Thus, if people are rational, one would expect that the current price of stocks already reflects the effect of the greater number of retirees on future stock prices. When one thinks strategically, one realizes that other people who have just as much information as you do, are likely to have acted on it, and eliminated the possibility of gain from simple insights.

2. My strategy would be to not enter into the game since it is most likely that the dollar will go for more than $1.00, since the second highest bidder's best strategy is to bid one cent higher. Here's why. Say the highest bid is $0.99 and the next highest is $0.98. If the bidding ends there, the 2nd highest bidder pays $0.98 and gets nothing. If, instead, she bids $1.00, she becomes the highest bidder and cuts her $0.98 losses to zero. But wait. Now the person who bid $.99 is the second-highest

bidder and is therefore out $.99. So, he, then has an incentive to bid $1.01 to win the $1 so that he loses only 0.01 instead of $.99. This bidding can go on forever. Since in this game, the best strategy once people have entered the bidding process is for the bidding to go on forever, the best strategy is not to enter the game, (or to make an agreement with the other bidders to collude and split the profits or losses).

3. One could argue that a policy of a pre-emptive war can be justified on game-theoretic grounds if one assumes that there is a first-mover advantage (striking pre-emptively gives one an advantage in a likely war) or if the cost of not striking pre-emptively is greater than a pre-emptive strike. Of course, that also holds for the other side, and cooperating and diplomacy are almost always the best joint strategy.

PRODUCTION AND COST ANALYSIS I

● **CHAPTER AT A GLANCE**

This review is based upon the learning objectives that open the chapter.

1. Accounting profit is explicit revenue less explicit cost. Economists include implicit revenue and cost in their determination of profit. (277-279)

   Economic profit = (explicit and implicit revenue) – (explicit and implicit cost).

   Implicit revenue includes the increases in the value of assets owned by the firm.

   Implicit costs include the opportunity cost of time and capital provided by the owners of the firm. Accountants do not include these implicit revenues and costs in their calculations of profit.

2. A long-run decision is a decision in which the firm can choose among all possible production techniques. A short-run decision is a decision in which the firm is constrained in regard to what production decisions it can make. (279-280)

   Long run → all inputs are variable → all costs are variable.

   Short run → at least one input is fixed → some costs are fixed and some are variable (vary with the production level).

3. The law of diminishing marginal productivity states that as more and more of a variable input is added to an existing fixed input, at some point the additional output one gets from the additional input will fall. (281-283)

   Sometimes called "flowerpot law." Its existence eventually causes costs of production to rise.

   Study all tables and figures in this chapter! Marginal product is the extra output from an additional unit of an input.

Marginal productivity declines because of the law of diminishing marginal productivity. It is because of diminishing marginal productivity that costs of production eventually rise.

4. The most important categories of costs are shown in Table 12-1. Notice total costs, marginal costs, average fixed costs, average variable costs, and average total costs can be calculated given fixed costs and variable costs at each level of output. (283-285)

✔ *Know how to calculate all 7 short-run cost figures! (FC, VC, TC, MC, AFC, AVC, and ATC). Notice the two ways to calculate each:*

TC	$=$	$FC + VC \ (= ATC \times Q)$
VC	$=$	$TC - FC \ (= AVC \times Q)$
FC	$=$	$TC - VC \ (= AFC \times Q)$
MC	$=$	$\Delta TC/\Delta Q \ (= \Delta TVC/\Delta Q)$
ATC	$=$	$TC/Q \ (= AFC + AVC)$
AVC	$=$	$VC/Q \ (= ATC - AFC)$
AFC	$=$	$FC/Q \ (= ATC - AVC)$

5. The marginal cost curve goes through the minimum point of the average total cost curve and average variable cost curve; each of these curves is U-shaped. The average fixed cost curve slopes down continuously. (285-289)

   See Figure 12-2b. Remember that all cost curves (except FC and AFC) are shaped the way they are because of increasing and diminishing marginal productivity!

6. When marginal and average productivity are rising, marginal and average cost curves are falling. When marginal and average productivity are falling, marginal and average cost curves are rising. (287-289)

   Figure 12-3 in the textbook on page 287 shows how marginal productivity and marginal costs are mirror images of one another. The same is true for average productivity and average cost.

✔ *Study the "Reminder" box "Review of Costs."*

● SHORT-ANSWER QUESTIONS

1. What is the difference between accounting profit and economic profit?

2. Suppose you are the president of a corporation who is designing a 2-year plan of operations and a 10-year plan of operations. How would those plans differ?

3. Suppose you are a novice gardener. You plant one seed in a flower pot and watch it grow into a stalk of wheat with plump wheat berries. The next year, you plant two seeds in that pot and harvest double the amount of wheat berries. You deduce that at this rate, you can provide the world's supply of wheat berries in your little pot. Why is this obviously not true? What principle is your answer based on?

4. What is the algebraic relationship between total cost, total variable cost, and total fixed cost? What is the algebraic relationship between average total cost, average variable cost, and average fixed cost? What is marginal cost equal to?

5. What does the marginal cost curve measure?

6. What does the average variable cost curve measure?

7. What does the average fixed cost curve measure?

8. What does the average total cost curve measure?

9. How does the law of diminishing marginal productivity affect the shape of short-run cost curves?

10. Where does the marginal cost curve intersect the average total cost and average variable cost curves? Explain why the relationship between marginal cost and average cost is how you have described it.

11. Draw typical *AFC*, *AVC*, *ATC*, and *MC* curves on the same graph, making sure to maintain the relationships among them.

MATCHING THE TERMS
Match the terms to their definitions

___ 1. average fixed cost

___ 2. average product

___ 3. average total cost

___ 4. average variable cost

___ 5. economic profit

___ 6. fixed costs

___ 7. law of diminishing marginal productivity

___ 8. long-run decision

___ 9. marginal cost

___ 10. marginal product

___ 11. production function

___ 12. profit

___ 13. short-run decision

___ 14. total cost

___ 15. variable costs

a. A decision in which the firm can choose among all possible production techniques.

b. Additional output forthcoming from an additional input, other inputs constant.

c. As more and more of a variable input is added to an existing fixed input, after some point the additional output one gets from the additional input will fall.

d. Total revenue minus total cost.

e. Costs that are spent and cannot be changed in the period of time under consideration.

f. Equation that describes the relationships between inputs and outputs, telling the maximum amount of output that can be derived from a given number of inputs.

g. Firm is constrained in regard to what production decisions it can make.

h. Fixed cost divided by quantity produced.

i. Sum of fixed and variable costs.

j. Variable cost divided by quantity produced.

k. The costs of variable inputs.

l. The cost of changing the level of output by one unit.

m. Total output divided by the quantity of the input.

n. Total cost divided by the quantity produced.

o. Explicit and implicit revenue minus explicit and implicit cost.

● PROBLEMS AND APPLICATIONS

1. Suppose you and a friend are thinking about opening a fast food vending service at a nearby resort during your summer break. This will entail serving pizzas out of a vendor's truck. This venture is an alternative to working at a factory job where you could each earn $7,000 over the summer break. A fully equipped truck could be leased for $10,000. Insurance and other miscellaneous operating expenses total $1,000. Given your projected sales revenues of $33,000 you anticipate your variable costs to total $8,000. Together, you and your friend have just enough money in the bank to cover all of the summer's fixed and variable costs of the business. If you pull that

money out of the bank, you will have to collectively forgo $500 in interest income for the summer.

a. What would be the accounting profit for your business?

b. What would be the economic profit for your business?

2. Find *TC, AFC, AVC, ATC,* and *MC* for the following table. Also, graph the TC curve on one graph and graph AFC, AVC, ATC, and MC on another graph.

Units	FC	VC	TC	MC	AFC	AVC	ATC
0	50	0					
1	50	90					
2	50	120					
3	50	165					
4	50	220					
5	50	290					

3. You are presented with the following table on average productivity. Labor is your only variable cost. The price of labor is $20 per hour, and the fixed cost is $50.

Labor	TP	MP	AP	TC	MC	AVC
1	2					
2	6					
3	15					
4	20					
5	23					
6	24					

a. Fill in the table above for marginal product (MP), average product (AP), total cost (TC), marginal cost (MC), and average variable costs (AVC).

b. Graph the average variable cost curve.

c. Show that the graph you drew in 3(b) is the approximate mirror image of the average productivity curve.

d. Graph the marginal cost and the marginal productivity curves. Show that they are approximate mirror images of each other.

e.   What is the relationship between marginal
cost (*MC*) and average cost (*AVC* and
ATC)? What is the relationship between
marginal product (*MP*) and average
product (*AP*)?

4.   A firm has fixed cost of $50. Variable costs
are as follows:

Units	VC
1	75
2	110
3	150
4	200
5	260
6	335

a.   Graph *AFC*, *ATC*, *AVC,* and *MC* curves
on the axes below from the information
provided in the table above (all on the
same graph).

b.   Explain the relationships between the *MC*
curve and *ATC* and *AVC* curves and
between the *ATC* and *AVC* curves.

c.   Suppose fixed costs fall to $20. Graph new
AFC, ATC, AVC, and *MC* curves.

d.   Which curves shifted? Why?

5.   A box of Wheaties cereal with a wholesale
price of $1.60 has the following costs:

Labor:	$ 0.15
Materials:	0.30
Sales cost:	0.30
Advertising:	0.15
Research and Development:	0.15
Rent on factory building and equipment:	0.15
Owner's profit:	0.40

a.   Which are likely variable costs?

b.   Which are likely fixed costs?

c.   If output were to rise, what would likely
happen to *ATC*?

● A BRAIN TEASER

1. Refer to the cost curves for a firm shown below when answering the following questions. Assume the firm is currently producing 100 units of output.

a. What is the number representing the marginal cost of producing the 100th unit of output? What geometric line segment represents that number?

b. What is ATC when output is 100? What geometric line segment represents that number?

c. What is AVC when output is 100? What geometric line segment represents that number?

d. What is AFC when output is 100? What geometric line segment represents that number?

e. What is TC when output is 100? What geometric *area* represents that number?

f. What is VC when output is 100? What geometric *area* represents that number?

g. What is FC when output is 100? What geometric *area* represents that number?

h. Why does the vertical distance between the AVC and ATC curves decrease as output expands?

● MULTIPLE CHOICE

Circle the one best answer for each of the following questions:

1. Economic profit:
   a. equals explicit and implicit revenues minus explicit and implicit costs.
   b. is the same as accounting profit.
   c. will always be larger than an accounting profit.
   d. does not include the opportunity cost of the entrepreneur in the total revenue calculation.

2. The difference between the short run and the long run in the cost model is that:
   a. the short run pertains to a period of time less than one year; long run is longer than one year.
   b. in the short run at least one input (factor of production) is fixed; in the long run all inputs are variable.
   c. in the short run some costs are fixed; in the long run all costs are fixed.
   d. in the short run all costs are variable; in the long run all costs are fixed.

3. In a short-run decision:
   a. a firm has more options than in the long run.
   b. a firm has fewer options than in the long run.
   c. a firm has the same number of options as in the long run.
   d. there is no relation between the number of options a firm has and whether it is a short-run decision or a long-run decision.

4. If a firm can produce 560 units of output with 5 workers and 600 units of output with 6 workers then the:
   a. marginal product of the 6th worker is 100 units.
   b. marginal product of the 6th worker is 40 units.
   c. average product of 6 workers is 70 units.
   d. average product of 5 workers is 100 units.

5. Refer to the graph below. The range marked "A" shows:

a. increasing marginal productivity.
b. diminishing marginal productivity.
c. diminishing absolute productivity.
d. diminishing absolute marginal productivity.

6. The law of diminishing marginal productivity:
a. states that as more and more of a variable input is added to an existing fixed input, after some point the additional output one gets from the additional input will fall.
b. states that as more and more of a variable input is added to an existing fixed input, after some point the additional output one gets from the additional input will rise.
c. explains why marginal costs of production fall as additional units of output are produced.
d. explains why average productivity always rises.

7. When the law of diminishing marginal productivity is operating:
a. increasing returns to scale are realized.
b. marginal productivity is falling and average productivity is rising.
c. marginal productivity is falling and marginal costs are rising.
d. marginal productivity is rising and marginal costs are rising.

8. Five workers are producing a total of 28 units of output. A worker's marginal product:
a. is 5.
b. is 28.
c. is 28 divided by 5.
d. cannot be determined from the information provided.

9. The firm is producing an output of 24 and has total costs of 260. Its marginal cost:
a. equals 10.83.
b. equals 8.75.
c. equals 260.
d. cannot be determined from the information provided.

10. Fixed costs:
a. are costs that do not change with the output level.
b. equal total costs plus variable costs.
c. equal average fixed costs divided by the output level.
d. rise at first then decline as output rises.

11. Concerning costs of production, it is true that:
a. if a firm shuts down for a month its total costs for the month will equal its fixed costs for the month.
b. average variable costs equal total variable costs multiplied by the output level.
c. marginal costs equal the change in total costs divided by the change in variable costs.
d. marginal cost equals average total cost multiplied by the output level.

12. A firm is producing 100 units of output at a total cost of $800. The firm's average variable cost is $5 per unit. The firm's:
a. marginal cost is $8.
b. total variable cost is $300.
c. average fixed cost is $3.
d. average total cost is $500.

13. The only variable input used in the production of pickles in a small factory is labor. Currently 5 workers are employed; each works 40 hours per week and is paid $15 per hour. If fixed costs are $4,000 per week and total output is 4,000 jars of pickles per week, then:
a. average fixed cost is $16,000.
b. total costs are $7,000.
c. total variable costs are $4,000.
d. average total costs are $0.75.

14. A firm's total fixed costs are $100; total variable costs are $200; and average fixed costs are $20. The firm's total output:
   a. is 1.
   b. is 5.
   c. is 10.
   d. cannot be determined from the information provided.

15. Refer to the graph below. The curves in the graph are:

   a. correctly drawn.
   b. incorrectly drawn because the average total cost curve is above the average variable cost curve.
   c. incorrectly drawn because the marginal cost curve is positioned wrong.
   d. incorrectly drawn because marginal cost and average variable costs are confused.

16. Refer to the graph below. The curve represented is most likely:

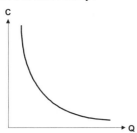

   a. an average total cost curve.
   b. an average variable cost curve.
   c. an average fixed cost curve.
   d. a total cost curve.

17. Concerning costs and cost curves for a firm, it is true that:
   a. if a firm increases its output from 100 to 101 and total costs increase from $55 to $60 then marginal cost of producing the 101st unit of output is $115.
   b. if marginal cost exceeds average total cost then average total cost is falling.
   c. the vertical distance between the average total and average variable cost curves at any given output level equals average fixed cost at that output level.
   d. the marginal cost curve intersects the average variable and average total cost curves when they are sloping downward.

18. If marginal cost exceeds average total cost then:
   a. average total cost is falling.
   b. average total cost is at its low point.
   c. average total cost is rising.
   d. marginal cost is at its low point.

19. Marginal cost reaches its minimum at a production level in which:
   a. average total cost is at its minimum.
   b. average variable cost is at its minimum.
   c. average productivity is at its maximum.
   d. marginal productivity is at its maximum.

● POTENTIAL ESSAY QUESTIONS

You may also see essay questions similar to the "Problems & Applications" and "A Brain Teaser" exercises.

1. Describe the relationship between the law of diminishing marginal productivity and costs of production in the short run.

2. Distinguish the various kinds of cost curves and describe the relationship between them.

■■■■■■ ANSWERS ■■■■■■

SHORT-ANSWER QUESTIONS

1. Accounting profit = explicit revenue – explicit cost. Economic profit = (explicit *and* implicit revenue) – (explicit *and* implicit cost). Implicit revenue includes the increases in the value of assets owned by the firm. Implicit costs include the opportunity cost of time and capital provided by the owners of the firm. Accountants do not include these implicit revenues and costs in their calculations of profit. (277-279)

2. In a long-run planning decision, a firm chooses among all possible production techniques. In a short-run planning decision, the firm has fewer options. (279-280)

3. This is obviously not true because eventually each additional seed you add will produce fewer and fewer berries. At some point, the plants will choke one another out. This follows from the law of diminishing marginal productivity: as more and more of a variable input is added to an existing fixed input, after some point the additional output one gets from the additional input will fall. (281-283)

4. $TC = VC + FC$. $ATC = AVC + AFC$. $MC = \Delta TC/\Delta Q \, (= \Delta TVC/\Delta Q)$. (282-285)

5. A marginal cost curve measures the change in cost associated with a change in output. It is the extra cost of producing an additional unit of output. (284-286)

6. An average variable cost curve measures variable cost averaged over total output. (284-286)

7. An average fixed cost curve measures fixed costs averaged over total output. (284-286)

8. An average total cost curve measures total cost (variable plus fixed cost) averaged over total output. (284-286)

9. The law of diminishing marginal productivity means that eventually marginal productivity falls. When that happens, short-run costs (except fixed costs) begin to rise. When marginal and average productivity are rising, marginal and average cost curves are falling. When marginal and average productivity are falling, marginal and average cost curves are rising. (284-286)

10. The marginal cost curve intersects the average total and average variable cost curves at their minimum points. The marginal cost curve intersects these average cost curves at their minimum points because when marginal cost exceeds average cost, average cost must be rising; when marginal cost is less than average cost, average cost must be falling. (288-289)

11. Typical *AFC, AVC, ATC,* and *MC* curves are graphed below. Since fixed costs are the same for all levels of output, the *AFC* curve is always falling as the same fixed costs are spread over larger and larger levels of output. The *MC* curve first declines because of increasing marginal productivity but then rises because decreasing marginal productivity eventually sets in. The *MC* curve intersects the *AVC* and *ATC* curves at their minimum points. This is true because if marginal cost is below average cost, average cost must be falling and if marginal cost is above average cost, average cost must be rising. (288-289, especially Figure 12-2(b) and Figure 12-4)

■■■■■■ ANSWERS ■■■■■■

MATCHING

1-h; 2-m; 3-n; 4-j; 5-o; 6-e; 7-c; 8-a; 9-l; 10-b; 11-f; 12-d; 13-g; 14-i; 15-k.

■■■■■■ ANSWERS ■■■■■■

PROBLEMS AND APPLICATIONS

1. **a.** Accounting profit = explicit revenue – explicit cost = $33,000 – ($10,000 + $1,000 + $8,000) = $14,000 accounting profit. (277-279)

b. Economic profit = (explicit and implicit revenue) − (explicit and implicit cost) = ($33,000) − ($7,000 + $7,000 + $10,000 + $1,000 + $8,000 + $500) = − $500; $500 economic loss. (277-279)

2. By definition, $TC = FC + VC$, $AFC = FC/Q$, $AVC = VC/Q$, $ATC = AFC + AVC$, and $MC =$ the change in TC per unit of output. Using this information, we completed the following table. (Marginal cost refers to the marginal cost of increasing output to that row, e.g., the marginal cost of going from 0 to 1 is 90.) (284-286)

Units	TC	MC	AFC	AVC	ATC
0	50	—	—	—	—
1	140	90	50.00	90	140.00
2	170	30	25.00	60	85.00
3	215	45	16.67	55	71.67
4	270	55	12.50	55	67.50
5	340	70	10.00	58	68.00

The total cost curve is shown below. The *ATC, AVC, MC,* and *AFC* curves are also shown below. (284-286; Figure 12-2)

3. **a.** $AP = TP/Q$, $MP =$ change in TP, TC is (Labor $\times$ 20) + FC, $MC =$ change in TC divided by the change in TP (or Q). AVC is VC/Q. Using these definitions, we completed the following table. (Marginal cost refers to the marginal cost of increasing to that row, e.g., the marginal cost of increasing total product from 2 to 6 is 5.00.) (281-283; Figure 12-1 and Table 12-1)

Labor	TP	MP	AP	TC	MC	AVC
1	2	—	2.0	70	—	10.00
2	6	4	3.0	90	5.00	6.67
3	15	9	5.0	110	2.22	4.00
4	20	5	5.0	130	4.00	4.00
5	23	3	4.6	150	6.67	4.35
6	24	1	4.0	170	20.00	5.00

b. The average variable cost curve is shown below. (285-286; Figure 12-2)

c. The *AP* and *AVC* curves are shown below. They are the mirror images of one another in that the maximum point on the *AP* curve occurs at the same quantity as the minimum point on the *AVC* curve. Also, when the *AP* curve is falling, *AVC* is rising, and vice versa. This is because as productivity falls, costs per unit rise, and as productivity increases, costs per unit decrease. (287-288; Figure 12-3)

d. The marginal cost and marginal productivity curves are shown below. The maximum point on the *MP* curve occurs at the same quantity as the minimum point on the *MC* curve. When the *MP* curve is falling *MC* is rising, and vice versa. This is because as productivity falls, costs per unit rise and as productivity increases, costs per unit decrease. (287-289, Figure 12-3)

e. When the *MC* curve is below the *AVC* (or *ATC*) curve, the *AVC* (or *ATC*) curve is falling. The *MC* curve intersects with the *AVC* (or *ATC*) curve at its minimum point. When the *MC* curve is above the *AVC* (or *ATC*) curve, the *AVC* (*ATC*) curve is rising. The same goes for marginal product and average product. When marginal product is below average product, average product is falling and when marginal product is above average product, average product is rising. (289-289)

4. a. To graph the *ATC, AFC, AVC,* and *MC* curves, first determine the values of these curves for units 1 through 6. *TC = FC + VC, AFC = FC/Q, AVC = VC/Q, ATC = AFC + AVC,* and *MC* = the change in *TC*. These values are shown in the table below. The curves are also shown below. (Marginal cost refers to the marginal cost of increasing to that row, e.g., the marginal cost of going from 0 to 1 is 75.) (284-286)

Units	VC	ATC	AVC	AFC	MC
1	75	125	75	50	75
2	110	80	55	25	35
3	150	66.67	50	16.67	40
4	200	62.5	50	12.5	50
5	260	62	52	10	60
6	335	64.17	55.83	8.33	75

b. The *MC* curve goes through the minimum points of both the *ATC* and *AVC* curves, which are rising when they are below the *MC* curve, and falling when they are above the *MC* curve. *ATC* and *AVC* curves are both U-shaped. Because of fixed costs, the *AVC* curve is always below the *ATC* curve, but the two curves converge as output increases (because AFC equals ATC – AVC, and AFC decreases as output increases). (288-289)

c. The curves are shown below. (288-289)

Units	VC	ATC	AVC	AFC	MC
1	75	95	75	20	75
2	110	65	55	10	35
3	150	56.67	50	6.67	40
4	200	55	50	5	50
5	260	56	52	4	60
6	335	59.17	55.83	3.33	75

d. Only the *AFC* and *ATC* curves shifted because they are the only curves that depend on fixed costs. All the others are based only on variable costs. Because the fixed cost falls to $20, the average fixed cost must fall as well. (288-289)

5. a. Labor and material costs are variable costs since they will rise and fall as production of Wheaties rises and falls. (282-283)

b. Sales, advertising, R&D, and rent on factory building and equipment are fixed costs since they are most likely independent of the level of Wheaties produced. (282-283)

c. Because fixed cost is high in this production process, almost equal to half of the revenue, an increase in output is likely to reduce *AFC*. If *AVC* does not rise more then *ATC* would likely fall as well. (282-283)

■■■■■ ANSWERS ■■■■■

A BRAIN TEASER

1. a. MC for the 100th unit of output is equal to $13 (the extra cost of producing that 100th unit is $13), or line segment 0M. (The line segment 0M simply represents the distance or amount of $13). (285-289)

b. ATC = $9, or line segment 0T, when output is 100. (285-289)

c. AVC = $5, or line segment 0V, when output is 100. (285-289)

d. AFC = $4. Note that AFC = ATC − AVC. The line segment representing AFC is line segment AB, which is also equal to line segment VT. Recall that, at a given output level, the vertical distance between the ATC and AVC curves equals AFC at that particular output level. (285-289)

e. TC = $900. (Note that TC = ATC × Q = $9 × 100 = $900). The geometric area representing TC is area 0TBQ. (Note that the area 0TBQ is equal to a width multiplied by a length. Think of the width as line segment 0T, representing ATC. Think of the length as line segment 0Q, representing the output level, Q. 0T multiplied by 0Q equals area 0TBQ.) (285-289)

f. VC = $500 (VC = AVC × Q = $5 × 100 = $500), or area 0VAQ (0VAQ = line segment 0V multiplied by line segment 0Q). (285-289)

g. FC = $400 (FC = AFC × Q = $4 × 100 = $400; or, FC = TC − VC = $900 − $500 = $400). The area representing FC is area VTBA. (FC = TC − VC = 0TBQ − 0VAQ = VTBA). (285-289)

Note that one can obtain all seven (7) short-run cost numbers when only provided with the MC, AVC, and ATC curves! Remember how to do this. It will come in handy later.

h. Because the vertical distance between the ATC and AVC curves equals AFC, and AFC decreases as output increases, then the vertical distance between the ATC and AVC curves decreases as output increases. (285-289)

ANSWERS

MULTIPLE CHOICE

1. a   Economic profit is explicit and implicit revenue minus explicit and implicit costs. Economists include opportunity costs in total cost. Since implicit revenue might be positive and greater than implicit cost, economic profit could be higher than accounting profit but that is not always the case. Indeed, economic profit is typically smaller than an accounting profit because implicit costs usually exceed implicit revenue. See pages 277-279.

2. b   There is no set calendar time associated with the short run or the long run. In the short run some costs are fixed; in the long run all costs are variable costs—because nothing is fixed in the long run. See pages 279-280.

3. b   The longer the time period, the more numerous the options. See pages 279-280.

4. b   Marginal product is the change in total product. That is, 600 − 560 = 40. Average product is total product divided by the number of workers. Average product of 5 workers is 112 and the average product of 6 workers is 100. See pages 279-281, especially Figure 12-1.

5. b   A bowed downward production function has marginal product decreasing as output increases. See Figure 12-1 on page 281.

6. a   Because of diminishing marginal productivity, marginal costs of production rise as additional units are produced. In addition, diminishing marginal productivity causes average productivity to fall. See pages 281-283.

7. c   When marginal productivity is falling, more inputs are necessary to increase production by the same amount. Thus, marginal costs are rising. See pages 281-283, and 287-288.

8. d   To determine marginal product you need to know the change in total product as you add a worker. See pages 281-283.

9. d   To determine marginal costs one must know the change in costs associated with a change in quantity. See pages 284-285.

10. a   Fixed costs remain constant no matter what output is. Also, fixed costs equal total costs minus variable costs. Moreover, fixed costs equal average fixed costs multiplied by the output level. See pages 283-284.

11. a Total costs equal fixed costs when a firm shuts down. This is because there are no variable costs when a firm shuts down. Average variable costs equal total variable costs *divided* by the output level. Marginal costs equal the change in total costs divided by the change in *the output level*. *Total cost* equals average total cost multiplied by the output level. See pages 284-285.

12. c Average total cost equals total cost divided by output ($800/100 = $8). Average fixed cost equals average total cost minus average variable cost ($8–$5 = $3). See pages 284-285.

13. b 5 workers times 40 hours times $15 is $3,000. These are variable costs. Add this to fixed cost to get total cost. Average total cost is $7,000 divided by 4,000, or $1.75. Average fixed cost is $4,000 divided by 4,000, or $1. See pages 284-285.

14. b Average fixed costs equal total fixed costs divided by output. If the firm's total fixed costs are $100 and average fixed costs are $20, the quantity must be 100/20 = 5. See pages 284-285.

15. a The *ATC* curve is above the *AVC* curve and the *MC* curve goes through the minimum points of the *AVC* and the *ATC* curves. The *AFC* curve is always falling. See Figure 12-2 on page 285.

16. c Only the average fixed cost curve falls continuously. See Figure 12-2 on page 285.

17. c $AFC = ATC - AVC$. See pages 284 and 285.

18. c If marginal cost exceeds average total cost, average total cost is rising. Marginal cost reaches a minimum well below average total cost. See pages 288-289 and Figure 12-4.

19. d When marginal productivity is at its maximum then the extra cost of producing

additional units (marginal cost) reaches its minimum. See page 287-288 and Figure 12-3.

━━━ ANSWERS ━━━

POTENTIAL ESSAY QUESTIONS

The following are annotated answers. They indicate the general idea behind the answer.

1. When marginal productivity is increasing, costs of production (except fixed cost, which do not vary with the output level) are falling. When marginal productivity is decreasing, costs of production (except fixed cost, which do not vary with the output level) are rising.

2. When productivity is falling, marginal cost and therefore average variable (and average total) costs must be rising.

✔ *Know how to calculate all 7 short-run costs!*

PRODUCTION AND COST ANALYSIS II

13

CHAPTER AT A GLANCE

This review is based upon the learning objectives that open the chapter.

1. Technical efficiency is efficiency that does not consider costs of inputs. But the least-cost technically efficient process is the economically efficient process. (296)

    Firms try to be economically efficient because they want to minimize costs to maximize profits.

2. In the long run all inputs are variable, so only economies and diseconomies of scale can influence the shape of the long-run cost curve. (296-301)

    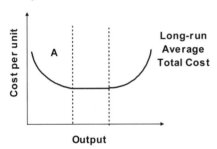

    Note that in the long run, as quantity of production increases, the firm is using ever-larger scales of operation (larger plant or factory sizes).

    If you double all inputs and per-unit costs fall (rise), the firm is experiencing economies (diseconomies) of scale.

    If per-unit (or average) costs do not change, the firm is experiencing constant returns to scale.

    Don't get short-run costs confused with long-run costs. The U-shape of short-run average variable and average total cost curves reflects increasing and diminishing marginal productivity. The U-shape of the long-run average total cost curve reflects economies and diseconomies of scale.

3. The envelope relationship is the relationship showing that, at the planned output level, short-run average total cost equals long-run average total cost, but at all other levels of output, short-run average total cost is higher than long-run average total cost. (301-302)

    See Figure 13-2 in the textbook (page 301)

    $SRATC_2$ is the appropriate plant size to produce Q_1 because costs per unit are lower.

4. The expected price per unit must exceed the opportunity cost of supplying the good for a good to be supplied. (303)

    Potential economic profit motivates entrepreneurs to supply those goods demanded by consumers. The greater the demand, the greater the price, the greater the profit potential, and the greater the quantity supplied.

5. Some of the problems of using cost analysis in the real world include: (303-308)
    *   Economies of scope;
    *   Learning by doing and technological change;
    *   Many dimensions; and
    *   Unmeasured costs such as opportunity costs.

    See also, Appendix A: "Isocost/Isoquant Analysis."

SHORT-ANSWER QUESTIONS

1. You are consulting for a firm. Through analysis the firm has determined that the best it can do is produce 100 tons of wheat per day with 10 workers and 1 acre of land or 100 tons of wheat per day with 10 acres of land and 1 worker. You are asked to choose the most efficient method of production. What do you advise?

2. After having read your report, the executives come running after you. They tell you that they have forgotten to tell you that an acre of land costs $40 an acre per day and workers can be hired for $100 a day. They wonder whether your answer to Question 1 changes.

3. The cost of developing a typical introductory economics textbook is well over $1 million. Once the textbook is developed and ready to print, the actual print costs for large runs are about $6 per book. What do these facts suggest about the shape of the long-run average total cost curve of producing textbooks?

4. What is the envelope relationship between short-run cost curves and long-run cost curves?

5. Why does an entrepreneur start a business? How are the decisions by the entrepreneur central to all supply decisions?

6. Suppose you are giving a talk on costs to decision-makers of firms. Without caveat, you have presented the cost curves as taught to you in this text. What are some likely problems your audience might have with your presentation?

MATCHING THE TERMS
Match the terms to their definitions

___ 1. constant returns to scale

___ 2. diseconomies of scale

___ 3. economically efficient

___ 4. economies of scale

___ 5. economies of scope

___ 6. entrepreneur

___ 7. indivisible setup cost

___ 8. learning by doing

___ 9. minimum efficient level of production

___ 10. monitoring costs

___ 11. team spirit

___ 12. technical efficiency

___ 13. technological change

a. A decrease in per-unit costs as a result of an increase in output.

b. An increase in per-unit costs as a result of an increase in output.

c. An increase in the range of production techniques that provides new ways of producing goods and the production of new goods.

d. Becoming more proficient at doing something by actually doing it.

e. Where long-run average total costs do not change with an increase in output.

f. Individual who sees an opportunity to sell an item at a price higher than the average cost of producing it.

g. The costs of producing products are interdependent so that producing one good lowers the cost of producing another.

h. The level of production run that spreads out setup costs sufficiently for a firm to undertake production profitably.

i. The cost of an indivisible input for which a certain minimum amount of production must be undertaken before the input becomes economically feasible to use.

j. Using the method of production that produces a given level of output at the lowest possible cost.

k. A situation in which as few inputs as possible are used to produce a given output.

l. Costs incurred by the organizer of production in seeing to it that the employees do what they're supposed to do.

m. The feelings of friendship and being part of something that bring out people's best efforts.

PROBLEMS AND APPLICATIONS

1. In some developing countries relatively primitive labor-intensive production processes are often used. Farming is an example. Why might a firm be economically efficient by not using the latest technology in the production process?

2. The following table represents long-run total costs:

Q	TC	LRATC
1	60	
2	66	
3	69	
4	72	
5	75	
6	90	
7	126	
8	184	
9	297	
10	600	

a. Calculate the long-run average total cost in the column provided.

b. Graph the *LRATC* curve on the graph below.

c. Label the area of economies of scale and the area of diseconomies of scale on the graph.

3. How can the extent to which economies and diseconomies of scale are present in an industry help account for the size and the number of firms in that industry? That is, if economies of scale were quite extensive in a particular industry, would you expect a large number of relatively small firms, or a small number of relatively large firms to be operating within that industry? What if diseconomies of scale set in at a relatively small output level?

4. What could help account for computer hardware manufacturers getting increasingly more involved with the development and production of computer software? Or, the airline passenger service businesses getting involved in air parcel and small package delivery service, and soft drink manufacturers buying up fast food restaurants (e.g. Pepsi-Cola company buying up Kentucky Fried Chicken and Pizza Hut—to name just a few)?

A1. Suppose the following table depicts the combinations of factors of production that result in the production of 100 units of bhindi.

	Labor	Machinery
A	25	4
B	20	5
C	10	10
D	5	20
E	4	25

a. Graph the isoquant curve for this table on the graph below, with machinery on the vertical axis and labor on the horizontal axis.

b. What is the marginal rate of substitution between combinations C and D?

A2. Suppose you had $120 available to produce the same product (bhindi) as in the previous question. Labor costs are $4 per person and machinery costs are $8 per unit. Draw the isocost line with machinery on the vertical axis and labor on the horizontal axis.

a. What is the slope of the line?

b. What happens to the isocost line if you frivolously spend $40 of your $120 on entertaining your good-for-nothing boyfriend Kyle? What is the slope of your new isocost line? Show this graphically.

c. Suppose the labor union raises labor costs to $10 per person. What happens to the isocost line? Show this graphically.

d. Combine the isoquant curve from *A1* with the original isocost line from *A2* on the graph below. What combination of labor and machinery will you choose for the economically efficient point of production?

● A BRAIN TEASER

1. Explain why when long-run average total costs are decreasing, and economies of scale are experienced, it may be better for a firm to operate a larger plant with some excess capacity (not operating at that scale of operation's minimum average total costs), as opposed to using a smaller plant that is operating at peak efficiency (at that plant's

minimum average total costs). *(Hint: You may want to graph a long-run average cost curve as an envelope of short-run average cost curves and use that graph as a visual aid in helping you answer this question.)*

● MULTIPLE CHOICE

Circle the one best answer for each of the following questions:

1. Which of the following concerning technical and economic efficiency is true?
   a. Many different production processes can be economically efficient, but only the method that involves the lowest possible cost is technically efficient.
   b. To achieve technical efficiency, managers must use the most up-to-date technology.
   c. The economically efficient method of production is the same in all countries.
   d. To achieve economic efficiency, managers need to use the least costly input combination.

2. The long run average total cost of production:
   a. rises as output increases when we experience economies of scale.
   b. is explained by decreasing marginal productivity.
   c. passes through the minimum point of each short-run average total cost curve.
   d. is considered to be an envelope curve because each short-run average total cost curve touches it at only one level of output.

3. Indivisible setup costs refer to:
   a. the cost of an indivisible input for which a certain minimum amount of production must be undertaken before production becomes economically feasible.
   b. the cost of an indivisible input for which a certain maximum amount of production must be undertaken before production becomes economically feasible.
   c. the cost of an indivisible input whose cost is invisible.
   d. the cost of an indivisible input whose cost of production is lower because an interdependent good is also being produced.

4. Economies of scale:
   a. account for the upward-sloping portion of the long-run average total cost curve.
   b. exist because of the difficulties in coordinating and managing a large business enterprise.
   c. imply an increase in per-unit costs of production associated with an increase in output.
   d. arise because large indivisible setup costs are spread out among a larger level of output and because of the efficiencies of greater labor and management specialization.

5. Refer to the graph below. The section of the long-run average total cost curve marked as "A" represents:

   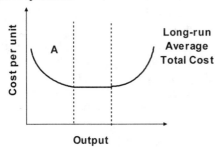

   a. economies of scale.
   b. diseconomies of scale.
   c. diminishing marginal productivity.
   d. increasing marginal productivity.

6. Explanations for diseconomies of scale include all of the following *except:*
   a. as firm size increases, monitoring costs generally increase.
   b. as firm size increases, team spirit or morale generally decreases.
   c. as firm size increases, monitoring costs generally decrease, thereby increasing other costs.
   d. All of the above are explanations.

7. Which of the following is associated with diseconomies of scale?
   a. Producing 1,000 lawn mowers costs $100,000 while producing 2,000 lawn mowers costs $220,000.
   b. 50 workers and 5 machines produce 1,000 units of output while 100 workers and 10 machines produce 2,500 units of output.

c. 50 workers and 5 machines produce 1,000 units of output while 60 workers and 5 machines produce 1,200 units of output.
d. Producing 1,000 lawn mowers costs $100,000 while producing 2,000 lawn mowers costs $150,000.

8. Refer to the graph below. Which of the following statements about the graph is true?

   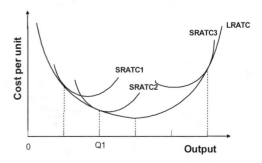

   a. The scale of operation associated with $SRATC_3$ is realizing some economies of scale.
   b. $SRATC_2$ is a smaller scale of operation than $SRATC_1$.
   c. The lowest-cost scale of operation to produce Q_1 is $SRATC_1$.
   d. The lowest-cost scale of operation to produce Q_1 is $SRATC_2$.

9. Constant returns to scale:
   a. refer to the upward sloping portion of the long-run ATC curve.
   b. refer to the downward sloping portion of the long-run ATC curve.
   c. means long-run average total costs do not change with an increase in output.
   d. are a result of rising monitoring costs and a loss of team spirit.

10. The envelope relationship refers to the fact that the:
    a. short-run average cost curve forms an envelope around long-run average cost curves.
    b. long-run average cost curve forms an envelope around short-run average cost curves.
    c. average cost curve forms an envelope around the marginal cost curve.
    d. marginal cost curve forms an envelope around the average cost curve.

11. Economies of scope occur when:
    a. firms increase production of a good, and that good's cost falls.
    b. firms increase their long-run vision and costs fall.
    c. the costs of production of one product fall when the firm increases the production of another product.
    d. technological change lowers cost of production.

12. Learning by doing and increases in technology cause the long-run:
    a. average cost curve to be downward sloping.
    b. average cost curve to be upward sloping.
    c. average cost curve to shift down.
    d. marginal cost curve to be downward sloping.

13. Total revenue is $1,000; explicit measurable costs are $500. Accounting profit:
    a. is $1,000.
    b. is $500.
    c. is $200.
    d. cannot be determined from the figures given.

14. A business owner makes 400 items by hand in 500 hours. She could have earned $20 an hour working for someone else. If the items sell for $50 each and the explicit costs total $12,000, then:
    a. total revenue equals $10,000.
    b. implicit costs equal $20,000.
    c. the accounting profits equal $10,000.
    d. the economic loss equals $2,000.

A1. Refer to the graph below. The isocost line represents a price of machinery (in terms of labor) of:
    a. one-eighth unit of labor.
    b. one-fourth unit of labor.
    c. one-half unit of labor.
    d. two units of labor.

A2. Refer to the graph for Question A1. If the price of machinery increases, the isocost line will rotate :
    a. in and become flatter.
    b. in and become steeper.
    c. out and become flatter.
    d. out and become steeper.

A3. The economically efficient point in the isoquant model in the graph below is at point:
    a. A.
    b. B.
    c. C.
    d. D.

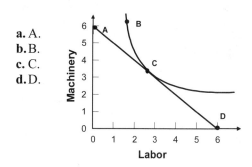

● POTENTIAL ESSAY QUESTIONS

You may also see essay questions similar to the "Problems & Applications" and "A Brain Teaser" exercises.

1. What are economies and diseconomies of scale? Why do they exist?

2. Discuss some of the problems of using cost analysis in the real world.

ANSWERS

SHORT-ANSWER QUESTIONS

1. You tell them that both methods are of equal
    technical efficiency, but you cannot determine
    which is more economically efficient. To make
    this decision you would need to know the
    relative prices of each input. (296)

2. You smile and say that is exactly the informa-
    tion you need to tell them the most economi-
    cally efficient method of production. At these
    prices, the first method of production costs
    $1,040 per 100 tons and the second method
    costs $500 per 100 tons. The second method is
    the economically efficient method. Technical
    efficiency means as few inputs as possible are
    used to produce a given output. It does not
    consider the costs of inputs. Economic
    efficiency means using that combination of
    inputs with the lowest possible cost for a given
    output. (296)

3. Because of the large indivisible setup costs,
    large economies of scale are possible in
    printing books. These economies of scale
    suggest that the long-run average total cost
    curve is steeply downward sloping. As
    production expands, economies of scale
    dominate and cost per unit declines. After
    some point, as output increases, however,
    diseconomies could set in and cost per unit
    could rise. This would lead to a U-shaped
    average total cost curve in the long run. (296-
    301)

4. The envelope relationship is the relationship
    between short-run and long-run average total
    costs. At the planned output level, short-run
    average total cost equals long-run average total
    cost, but at all other levels of output, short-run
    average total cost is higher than long-run
    average total cost. (301-302)

5. An entrepreneur will supply a good if the
    expected price of the good exceeds the cost of
    producing it. This difference is the
    entrepreneur's expected profit. It is the profit
    incentive that underlies production in an
    economy. (303)

6. Since your audience is working with the real
    world, they will see that actual production
    processes diverge from textbook analysis.

Some of the problems the audience might list
are (1) economies of scope; (2) learning by
doing and technological change; (3) the supply
decision is multidimensional; and (4) the
relevant costs are not always the ones you find
in a firm's accounts. (303-308)

ANSWERS

MATCHING

1-e; 2-b; 3-j; 4-a; 5-g; 6-f; 7-i; 8-d; 9-h; 10-l; 11-
m; 12-k; 13-c.

ANSWERS

PROBLEMS AND APPLICATIONS

1. Using the latest technology in combination
    with the required inputs may be a more costly
    production process than using more primitive
    techniques—especially when labor is cheap.
    What a firm wants to do is to use whatever
    combination of inputs that minimizes costs of
    production so that it can remain price competi-
    tive in the market. (296)

2. Before graphing *LRATC*, first calculate the
    figures. $LRATC = TC/Q$. (296-299)

    a.

Q	TC	LRATC
1	60	60
2	66	33
3	69	23
4	72	18
5	75	15
6	90	15
7	126	18
8	184	23
9	297	33
10	600	60

    b. The graph shown below plots the values
        from the table above to show the *LRATC*
        curve. (See Figure 13-1 on page 298)

c. As shown in the figure, economies of scale is to the left of $Q = 5$, where *LRATC* is falling. Diseconomies of scale is to the right of $Q = 6$, where *LRATC* is rising. (See Figure 13-1 and page 298)

3. If economies of scale are quite extensive in an industry (i.e., larger and larger scales of operation result in lower and lower long-run average total costs of production) one would expect a relatively small number of very large firms. This is because all firms will be trying to reduce their costs by expanding, to lower their prices, and to gain a greater share of the market. You have to "get big or get out"—or be driven out of business by your competitor's lower prices. On the other hand, if diseconomies of scale set in at a relatively small output level, then you would expect a relatively large number of relatively small firms. (296-301)

4. Economies of scope can explain this. It is cheaper for these firms to produce, market, or distribute these goods or services when they are already involved in producing the other. Indeed, this concept seems to explain best why firms produce multiple rather than single products. (304-305)

A1. a. To graph the isoquant curve, plot each of the combinations of labor and machinery which generate the same (100) units of production of bhindi, as is done in the graph below. (312)

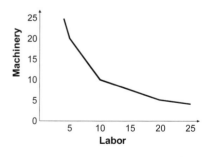

b. The marginal rate of substitution between combinations C and D is equal to the absolute value of the slope between C and D, $MP_{labor}/MP_{machinery} = 2$. (313)

A2. a. The x-axis (labor axis) intercept is 30 ($120/$4), and the y-axis (machinery axis) intercept is 15 ($120/$8). The slope of the line is $-P_{labor}/P_{machinery} = -4/8 = -1/2$. It is shown in the graph below. (313-314).

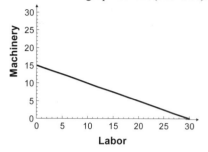

b. The isocost line shifts in to the left as money available for production is reduced to $80. Now maximum 20 units of labor or 10 units of machinery can be purchased. Since the relative price of labor and machinery doesn't change, the slope of the isocost line remains $-1/2$. This is shown in the graph below. (313-314)

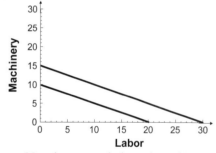

c. Now because relative prices change, the isocost line rotates. To find the new isocost line, find first how many units of labor can be purchased for $120 at the new price $10. The isocost line rotates along the labor axis and intersects it at 12 units of labor. The y intercept remains the same at 15 since the price of machinery did not change. Since labor becomes more expensive, the slope becomes steeper. The slope of the line now is $-P_{labor}/P_{machinery} = -10/8 = -1.25$. This is shown in the graph below. 313-314)

d To find the most economically efficient combination of inputs, find that point where the slope of the isocost line equals the slope of the isoquant curve (which is the marginal rate of substitution between labor and machinery). This is at points between B and C where $-MP_{labor}/MP_{machinery} = -1/2 = -P_{labor}/P_{machinery}$. The isocost line is tangent to the isoquant curve at points between B and C. This implies that any other isoquant curve that intersects the isocost line is less economically efficient. This is shown in the graph below. (314-315)

ANSWERS

A BRAIN TEASER

1. This is best explained by viewing a long-run average total cost (LRATC) curve. See the graph below. Note that the downward sloping portion of the LRATC curve indicates decreasing LRATC and therefore economies of scale. Also, one needs to keep in mind that a LRATC curve is really an envelope of short-run average total cost (SRATC) curves, and that each SRATC curve is associated with a larger scale of operation (or plant size) as the quantity increases. Also note that a firm's objective is to find that scale of operation (or plant size) that minimizes LRATC given the targeted output level it wishes to produce. This is shown as that scale of operation where its SRATC curve is just tangent to the LRATC curve at the targeted output level.

    Now suppose that a firm has determined that the profit maximizing quantity it should produce, given the market demand for its product, is Q_1—this is the targeted output level. To produce Q_1, the firm should use the plant size associated with $SRATC_2$—this curve is just tangent to the LRATC curve. No other plant size can produce Q_1 cheaper, even though this scale of operation is not operating at its minimum average total costs (we are not at the low point on $SRATC_2$). Notice that $SRATC_1$ is a smaller plant size. It could produce Q_1 at its minimum average total costs (at the low point on $SRATC_1$). But the per-unit costs associated with this smaller plant size are higher (note that $SRATC_1$ lies above $SRATC_2$).

    The idea, in the long run, is to minimize long-run average total costs (even if that means operating with a scale of operation that has some excess productive capacity—not operating at its SRATC curve's low point). (See Figure 13-2 on page 301)

ANSWERS

MULTIPLE CHOICE

1. **d** Economic efficiency means producing with least cost while technical efficiency means producing with the least number of inputs. Many combinations are technically efficient. Which is economically efficient depends upon the costs of each input. Because inputs to production have different costs in various countries, an economically efficient method of production in one country might not be the same method in another country. See page 296.

2. **d** Economies of scale cause the LRATC curve to decrease (slope downward). Long run costs are *not* related to marginal productivity. The curve is not tangent to the low points of all SRATC curves. See pages 296-301.

3. a This is the definition of indivisible setup costs found on page 297. Note that huge setup costs require high levels of production to get per-unit production costs down to a level where production is profitable.

4. d Economies of scale cause the LRATC curve to slope downward. Per unit production costs fall. Difficulties in coordinating and managing a large business cause *dis*economies of scale. See pages 296-299.

5. a Economies of scale cause the LRATC curve to slope downward. The law of diminishing marginal productivity relates to short-run curves only. See Figure 13-1 on page 298.

6. c Monitoring costs generally rise as a firm enlarges. Moreover, there is no reason to assume that decreasing monitoring costs will cause other costs to increase. See page 299.

7. a Economies and diseconomies of scale relate to instances where all inputs are varied. That eliminates the option where only the number of workers is increased as a possibility. Diseconomies of scale exist when *average* costs rise. Average costs rise in (a) from $100 to $110. See pages 296-299.

8. d The lowest-cost scale of operation is on the SRATC curve that is tangent to the LRATC curve at that level of output. The scale of operation represented by $SRATC_3$ suffers from diseconomies of scale. See pages 301-303, especially Figure 13-2.

9. c Constant returns to scale refer to the flat portion of the LRATC curve where long-run average total costs remain constant when output increases. See page 299.

10. b As discussed on pages 301-303 (including Figure 13-2), the long-run average cost curve forms an envelope around short-run average cost curves.

11. c As discussed on page 304, c is the definition of economies of scope. Economies of scope play an important role in firms' decisions about what combinations of goods to produce.

12. c Learning by doing reduces average costs at every level of output. This is shown by a downward shift in the average cost curve. See page 305.

13. b Accounting profit is total revenue minus explicit measurable costs. See pages 307-308.

14. d Total revenue equals $20,000 ($50 × 400). Implicit costs ($20 × 500 = $10,000) plus explicit costs ($12,000) equal $22,000. Economic loss is $2,000. Accounting profit equals $8,000. See pages 307-308.

A1. c To get one unit of machinery one must give up one-half unit of labor. See pages 312-313.

A2. a A rise in the price of machinery means that the same amount of funds will purchase less machinery, so the isocost line rotates down from the intersection of the labor axis, hence becoming flatter. See pages 313-314.

A3. c The economically efficient point is where the isoquant curve is tangent to the isocost line. See pages 314-315.

■■■■■ ANSWERS ■■■■■

POTENTIAL ESSAY QUESTIONS

The following are annotated answers. They indicate the general idea behind the answer.

1. Economies of scale have lower average total costs of production as larger scales of operation are used. They result from greater specialization of labor and management.
   Diseconomies of scale arise when larger scales of operation are used and higher average total costs of production are experienced.
   Diseconomies of scale arise because management loses control over operations. That is, monitoring costs rise and there is often a loss of team spirit.

2. Some of the problems of using cost analysis in the real world include: (1) economies of scope; (2) learning by doing and technological change; (3) many dimensions; and (4) unmeasured costs such as opportunity cost.

Pretest
Chapters 7 - 13

Take this test in test conditions, giving yourself a limited amount of time to complete the questions. Ideally, check with your professor to see how much time he or she allows for an average multiple choice question and multiply this by 30. This is the time limit you should set for yourself for this pretest. If you do not know how much time your teacher would allow, we suggest 1 minute per question, or 30 minutes.

1. When the price of a good was raised from $10 to $11, the quantity demanded fell from 100 to 99. The price elasticity of demand is approximately:
   a. .1.
   b. 1.
   c. 10.
   d. 100.

2. As a manager, you have determined that the demand for your good is quite elastic. Therefore:
   a. increasing the price of your good will increase revenues.
   b. decreasing the price of your good will increase revenues.
   c. increasing the price of your good will have no impact on the quantity demanded.
   d. any change in your price will not impact revenues.

3. In the graph below, point A on the supply curve, S, is:

   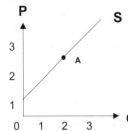

   a. elastic.
   b. inelastic.
   c. unitary elastic.
   d. unknown because one cannot say from the graph.

4. A significant price rise with virtually no change in quantity would most likely be caused by a highly:
   a. elastic demand and supply shifts to the right.
   b. inelastic supply and a shift in demand to the right.
   c. inelastic demand and supply shifts out.
   d. elastic supply and demand shifts in.

5. If supply increases by 4 percent, the elasticity of demand is 0.5, and the elasticity of supply is 1.5, then the price will:
   a. increase by 8 percent.
   b. increase by 2 percent.
   c. decrease by 8 percent.
   d. decrease by 2 percent.

6. Assume equilibrium in the graph below. What area represents consumer surplus?
   a. A+B+C.
   b. D+C+E.
   c. E.
   d. E+F.

   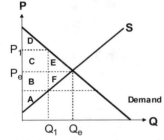

7. Refer to the graph below. If a per unit tax, t, is paid by sellers:

   a. producer surplus is represented by areas A, B, and C before the tax and A after the tax.
   b. consumer surplus is represented by areas D, E, and F before the tax and B after the tax.
   c. the tax, t, imposes a deadweight loss represented by the welfare loss triangle-areas C and E.
   d. consumers lose surplus given by area E while producers lose surplus given by area C.

8. The burden of a tax is:
   a. most heavily borne by those with the more inelastic demand or supply.
   b. most heavily borne by those with the more elastic demand or supply.
   c. usually equally split between buyers and sellers.
   d. usually passed on to consumers in the form of a higher price.

9. How much of a $100 tax will consumers pay if the price elasticity of demand is 3 and the price elasticity of supply is 2?
   a. $50.
   b. $40
   c. $30.
   d. $20.

10. In which case will a price floor result in the greatest excess supply?
    a. When both demand and supply are highly inelastic.
    b. When both demand and supply are highly elastic.
    c. When demand is elastic and supply is inelastic.
    d. When demand is inelastic and supply is elastic.

11. Refer to the graph below. The graph demonstrates Saudi Arabia's and the United States' production possibility curves for widgets and wadgets. Given these production possibility curves, you would suggest that:

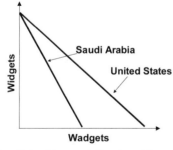

    a. Saudi Arabia specialize in widgets and the United States in wadgets.
    b. No trade should take place.
    c. Saudi Arabia specialize in wadgets and the United States in widgets.
    d. Both countries should produce an equal amount of each.

12. Country A's cost of widgets is $4.00 and cost of wadgets is $8.00. Country B's cost of widgets is 8 euros and cost of wadgets is 16 euros. Which of the following would you suggest?
    a. Country A should specialize in widgets and Country B in wadgets.
    b. Trade of widgets for wadgets would not benefit the countries.
    c. Country A should specialize in wadgets and Country B in widgets.
    d. Both countries should produce an equal amount of each.

13. Transferable comparative advantages are:
    a. based on factors that are relatively unchangeable.
    b. based on factors that can change relatively easily.
    c. becoming more like inherent comparative advantages with technological innovations.
    d. rarely eroded over time.

14. Economists generally oppose trade restrictions for all of the following reasons *except:*
    a. from a global perspective, free trade increases total output.
    b. the infant industry argument.
    c. trade restrictions lead to retaliation.
    d. international politics.

15. The utility gained from eating one slice of pizza is 30 and the utility gained from eating a second slice of pizza is 20. From this we know:
    a. the marginal utility of the second slice of pizza is 50.
    b. the total utility of the second slice of pizza is 50.
    c. the marginal utility of the second slice of pizza is 20.
    d. there is not enough information to compute the marginal utility.

16. The price of good A is $1; the price of good B is $2. The marginal utility you get from good A is 40; the marginal utility you get from good B is 60. Assuming you can make marginal changes, you should:
    a. consume more of good A and less of good B.
    b. consume more of good B and less of good A.
    c. keep consuming equal amounts of both goods.
    d. realize that you don't have enough information to answer the question.

17. The rational consumer will buy more of good X when:
   a. $MU_X/P_X < MU_Y/P_Y$.
   b. $MU_X/P_X > MU_Y/P_Y$.
   c. $MU_X/P_X = MU_Y/P_Y$.
   d. the price of good X increases.

18. Game theory is a tool:
   a. used only by economists to study strategic interaction where agents' decisions are independent.
   b. used by economists and other social scientists to study strategic interaction where agents' decisions are independent.
   c. used only by economists to study strategic interaction where agents' decisions are interdependent.
   d. used by economists and other social scientists to study strategic interaction where agents' decisions are interdependent.

19. The Nash equilibrium solution for the following payoff matrix is:

	A	A
B	A: 1, B: 100	A: 0, B: 1
B	A: 2, B: 0	A: 5, B: 2

   a. 1, 100.
   b. 2, 0.
   c. 0, 1.
   d. There is more than one equilibrium solution.

20. If individuals can cooperate and share the gains, which payoff is the most likely?

	A	A
B	A: 1, B: 100	A: 0, B: 1
B	A: 2, B: 0	A: 5, B: 2

   a. 1, 100.
   b. 2, 0.
   c. 0, 1.
   d. 5, 2.

21. In the "trust game" a player is given money, which he can either keep, or give to someone else. If he gives the money to someone else, that money is tripled, and the second person can return some portion to the first player. The Nash equilibrium in this game is:
   a. for the first player to keep the entire sum.
   b. for the first player to keep half the money and give the other half to the second player.
   c. for the first player to give the entire sum to the other player.
   d. There is no Nash equilibrium for this game.

22. If most people don't conform to the assumptions of the standard model:
   a. the outcome of the model could not be true.
   b. the outcome of the model could still be true.
   c. society will have to better educate its people.
   d. the assumptions have to be revised.

23. Refer to the graph below. The range marked "A" shows:

   a. increasing marginal productivity.
   b. diminishing marginal productivity.
   c. diminishing absolute productivity.
   d. diminishing absolute marginal productivity.

24. Five workers are producing a total of 28 units of output. A worker's marginal product:
   a. is 5.
   b. is 28.
   c. is 28 divided by 5.
   d. cannot be determined from the information provided.

25. A firm is producing 100 units of output at a total cost of $800. The firm's average variable cost is $5 per unit. The firm's:
   a. marginal cost is $8.
   b. total variable cost is $300.
   c. average fixed cost is $3.
   d. average total cost is $500.

26. Refer to the graph below. The curves in the graph are:

   a. correctly drawn.
   b. incorrectly drawn because the average total cost curve is above the average variable cost curve.
   c. incorrectly drawn because the marginal cost curve is positioned wrong.
   d. incorrectly drawn because marginal cost and average variable costs are confused.

27. Which of the following concerning technical and economic efficiency is true?

   a. Many different production processes can be economically efficient, but only the method that involves the lowest possible cost is technically efficient.

   b. To achieve technical efficiency, managers must use the most up-to-date technology.

   c. The economically efficient method of production is the same in all countries.

   d. To achieve economic efficiency, managers need to use the least costly input combination.

28. Economies of scale:

   a. account for the upward-sloping portion of the long-run average total cost curve.

   b. exist because of the difficulties in coordinating and managing a large business enterprise.

   c. imply an increase in per-unit costs of production associated with an increase in output.

   d. arise because large indivisible setup costs are spread out among a larger level of output and because of the efficiencies of greater labor and management specialization.

29. Constant returns to scale:

   a. refer to the upward sloping portion of the long-run ATC curve.

   b. refer to the downward sloping portion of the long-run ATC curve.

   c. means long-run average total costs do not change with an increase in output.

   d. are a result of rising monitoring costs and a loss of team spirit.

30. The envelope relationship refers to the fact that the:

   a. short-run average cost curve forms an envelope around long-run average cost curves.

   b. long-run average cost curve forms an envelope around short-run average cost curves.

   c. average cost curve forms an envelope around the marginal cost curve.

   d. marginal cost curve forms an envelope around the average cost curve.

━━━━━━━━━   ANSWERS   ━━━━━━━━━

1.	a	(7:2)		**16.**	a	(10:5)
2.	b	(7:6)		**17.**	b	(10:10)
3.	a	(7:13)		**18.**	d	(11:2)
4.	b	(7:19)		**19.**	d	(11:6)
5.	d	(7:22)		**20.**	a	(11:7)
6.	b	(8:3)		**21.**	a	(11:16)
7.	c	(8:5)		**22.**	b	(11:19)
8.	a	(8:9)		**23.**	b	(12:5)
9.	b	(8:10)		**24.**	d	(12:8)
10.	b	(8:17)		**25.**	c	(12:12)
11.	a	(9:5)		**26.**	a	(12:15)
12.	b	(9:8)		**27.**	d	(13:1)
13.	b	(9:11)		**28.**	d	(13:4)
14.	b	(9:17)		**29.**	c	(13:9)
15.	c	(10:2)		**30.**	b	(13:10)

Key: The figures in parentheses refer to multiple choice question and chapter numbers. For example (1:2) is multiple choice question 2 from chapter 1.

PERFECT COMPETITION

CHAPTER AT A GLANCE

This review is based upon the learning objectives that open the chapter.

1. Six conditions for a market to be perfectly competitive are: (317-318)

    - Both buyers and sellers are price takers.
    - Large number of firms.
    - No barriers to entry.
    - Identical product.
    - Complete information.
    - Profit-maximizing entrepreneurial firms.

    Compare these with the non-competitive markets (next 2 chapters).

2. If marginal revenue does not equal marginal cost, a firm can increase profit by changing output. Therefore, profit is maximized when MC = MR = P. (321-323)

    P = MR for a perfectly competitive firm.

    In general, for any firm, if
    MR > MC, increase Q.
    MR = MC, profit is maximized.
    MR < MC, decrease Q.

3. Because the marginal cost curve tells us how much of a produced good a firm will supply at a given price, the marginal cost curve is the firm's supply curve. (323)

    A firm's short-run supply curve is its MC curve above minimum AVC. This is because at any P greater than minimum AVC, a competitive firm will produce where P = MR = MC.

4. The profit-maximizing output can be determined in a table (as in Table 14-1 on page 325) or in a graph (as in Figure 14-5 on page 326). (325-328)

    Just find that output level at which MR = MC. This is shown graphically where the two curves intersect. (Remember: the demand curve facing the firm is also its MR curve and it is horizontal at the market price).

5. The market supply curve is the horizontal sum of all the firms' marginal cost curves, taking account of any changes in input prices that might occur. (328-329)

    At each price, draw a vertical line from the marginal cost curve to the quantity axis to determine the quantity supplied by each firm in the market. Then add the quantity supplied by each firm at each price to obtain the market supply curve.

6. Since profits create incentives for new firms to enter, output will increase, and the price will fall until zero profits are being made. (329-331)

Over time if economic profits are earned, the number of sellers increases, increasing market supply and decreasing market price. The lower market price decreases firms' profits until the economic profits are competed away. Note that a zero economic profit (a normal profit) is earned by competitive firms in the long run.

7. The long-run market supply curve may be upward sloping, horizontal, or downward sloping, depending on what happens to input prices as an industry expands. (332-333)

    If the demand for an industry's product increases, the industry will expand (more of the good is produced) and:

    - *An increasing-cost industry has an upward-sloping long-run market supply curve reflecting higher input prices as the industry expands.*

    - *A constant-cost industry has a horizontal long-run market supply curve reflecting no change in input prices as the industry expands.*

    - *A decreasing-cost industry has a down-ward-sloping long-run market supply curve reflecting lower input prices as the industry expands.*

● SHORT-ANSWER QUESTIONS

1. How is competition as a process different from competition as a state?

2. What are six necessary conditions for perfect competition?

3. You are advising a vendor of ice cream at a beach. There are plenty of vendors on the beach and plenty more waiting to begin selling. Your client can't seem to change the market price for ice cream, but she still wants to make sure she maximizes profits. What do you advise she do? She knows all her costs of doing business.

4. You are given a competitive firm's marginal cost curve and asked to determine the supply curve for that firm. What do you say?

5. Given the following table, what is the profit-maximizing output and profit of a perfect competitor?

P=MR	Q	FC	VC
35	0	10	0
35	1	10	20
35	2	10	38
35	3	10	50
35	4	10	77
35	5	10	112
35	6	10	156

6. On the graph below, show the output and short-run profit of a perfect competitor.

7. When should a firm shut down?

8. How are firms' marginal cost curves and the market supply curve related?

9. Given the graph below, showing a representative firm in a competitive market, what will happen in the long run? Explain, using the graph and words.

10. Suppose the owners of a small drug store decided to close their store after Wal-Mart opened a store nearby. Assuming the market was competitive before and after Wal-Mart opened its store, show graphically and explain with words the likely conditions for the small drug store before and after Wal-Mart opened.

11. What does the long-run market supply curve look like in an increasing-cost industry? Why? What about the constant-cost and decreasing-cost industries?

MATCHING THE TERMS
Match the terms to their definitions

___	1.	barriers to entry	**a.** Firm or individual who takes the market price as given.
___	2.	marginal cost	**b.** Anything that prevents other firms from entering a market.
___	3.	marginal revenue	**c.** The change in total cost associated with a change in quantity.
___	4.	market supply curve	**d.** The change in total revenue associated with a change in
___	5.	normal profit	quantity.
___	6.	perfectly competitive market	**e.** Market in which economic forces operate unimpeded.
			f. Point at which the firm will gain more by temporarily shutting
___	7.	price taker	down than it will by staying in business.
___	8.	profit-maximizing condition	**g.** The horizontal sum of all the firms' marginal cost curves, taking account of any changes in input prices that might occur.
___	9.	shutdown point	**h.** The amount of money the owners of a business would have received in their next-best alternative.
			i. Produce where MC = MR.

● PROBLEMS AND APPLICATIONS

1. The following table shows the total cost for a product that sells for $20 a unit.

Q	TC
0	30
1	55
2	75
3	85
4	100
5	120
6	145
7	185
8	240
9	310
10	395

   a. What is the output level for a profit-maximizing firm? Use the space to the right of the table to work out your answer.

   b. How does your answer change if price rises to $25?

   c. Calculate profit in part *a* and *b* above.

   d. Should the firm stay in business at *P* = $20? At $25?

   e. Suppose *P* = $15, what output level maximizes profit? What is the profit? Should the firm stay in business?

2. The following cost curves are for a representative firm in a competitive market.

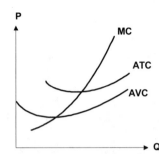

   a. Label the minimum point of the *ATC* and *AVC* curves as A and B respectively. Explain your answer.

   b. Draw a demand curve for this firm on that same graph, assuming the market is in equilibrium. Explain why you have drawn it this way.

   c. Illustrate the long-run equilibrium price and quantity for the firm on that same graph. Is the firm earning economic profit? Explain your answer.

3. Consider the market demand and supply curves below on the left and a representative firm's cost curves below on the right.

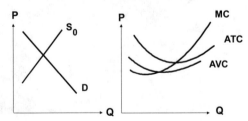

   a. Is this representative firm earning economic profit, loss, or zero profit? Shade the area for profit or loss, or label the point of zero profit.

b. In the long run, what will happen?

c. Beginning with the long-run equilibrium in *b*, show the effect of a decrease in demand on profit. What will happen in the long run to supply, price, and profit?

4. What is wrong with each of the following graphs?

a.

b.

c.

d.

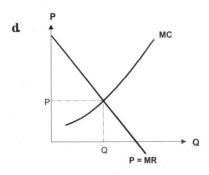

A BRAIN TEASER

1. Suppose a competitive firm experiences a sudden increase in its fixed costs. For example, suppose property taxes increase dramatically. What impact, if any, will this have on the firm's profit-maximizing quantity to produce? What will happen to the firm's profit?

MULTIPLE CHOICE

Circle the one best answer for each of the following questions:

1. Which of the following is a requirement of a perfectly competitive market?
   a. Buyers and sellers are price takers.
   b. There are barriers to entry.
   c. There are indivisible setup costs.
   d. Selling firms maximize sales.

2. In a perfectly competitive market:
   a. firms sell a differentiated product where one firm's output can be distinguished from another firm's output.
   b. there are so many firms selling output in the market that no one individual firm has the ability to control the market price.
   c. economic profits can be earned in the long run.
   d. there are very strong barriers to entry that can prevent potential competitors from entering the market.

3. Refer to the graph below. The perceived demand curve faced by an individual firm in a competitive market is best represented by which of the following?
   a. A.
   b. B.
   c. C.
   d. D.

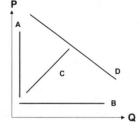

4. Refer to the graph below. The market demand curve in a competitive market is best represented by which of the following?
   a. A.
   b. B.
   c. C.
   d. D.

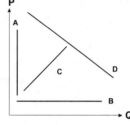

5. Refer to the graph below. A competitive firm is producing at output A.

   a. It could increase profits by increasing output.
   b. It could increase profits by decreasing output.
   c. It cannot increase profits.
   d. One can say nothing about profits from the diagram.

6. Refer to the graph below. A competitive firm is producing at output A.

   a. It could increase profits by increasing output.
   b. It could increase profits by decreasing output.
   c. It cannot increase profits.
   d. One can say nothing about profits from the diagram.

7. In order to maximize profits (or minimize losses) a firm should produce at that output level at which:
   a. total revenue is maximized.
   b. average total costs are minimized.
   c. marginal revenue equals marginal cost.
   d. marginal revenue exceeds marginal cost by the greatest amount.

8. Price in a competitive market is $6. The firm's marginal cost is $4 and the marginal cost curve has the normal shape. What would you advise the firm to do?
   a. Raise its price.
   b. Increase its output.
   c. Decrease its output.
   d. Lower its price.

9. In a competitive market, which of the following is the firm's supply curve?
   a. The average variable cost curve.
   b. The marginal cost curve.
   c. The average total cost curve.
   d. The average revenue curve.

10. If a firm is producing at an output level at which:
    a. marginal revenue exceeds marginal cost, then the firm should reduce its output level to maximize profits.
    b. marginal revenue is less than marginal cost, then the firm should expand its output level to maximize profits.
    c. price exceeds average total costs, then the firm is earning an economic profit.
    d. price is less than minimum average total cost but greater than average variable cost, then the firm should shut down.

11. Refer to the graph below. The firm's profit in this case will be measured by:

a. the rectangle ABEF.
b. the rectangle ACDF.
c. the rectangle ABHG.
d. the rectangle BCDE.

12. Refer to the graph below. How low must the price fall before the firm will decide to shut down?

a. Approximately $40.
b. Approximately $35.
c. Approximately $18.
d. Approximately $12.

13. Refer to the graph below. This firm:

a. is earning an economic profit equal to $2,000.
b. should produce 100 units of output and charge a price of $40.
c. is incurring total costs equal to $80.
d. should shut down because price is less than minimum average variable cost.

14. In the graph below for a perfectly competitive firm:

a. at P_2 the firm is incurring an economic loss but should remain in operation to minimize losses.
b. at P_3 a zero economic profit is being earned.
c. at P_4 an economic profit is earned.
d. all of the above.

15. Normal profits are:
a. approximately 6 percent of costs.
b. approximately 8 percent of costs.
c. returns to the owners of business for the opportunity cost of their implicit inputs.
d. generally larger than accounting profits.

16. In the long-run competitive equilibrium the average firm:
a. will be going out of business.
b. will be expanding.
c. will be making only a normal profit.
d. won't even be making a normal profit.

17. In a competitive market for good X, the price of a complementary good falls. If it is a constant-cost industry, we know that in the long run, equilibrium quantity will:
a. increase and equilibrium price will remain the same.
b. increase and equilibrium price will increase.
c. decrease and equilibrium price will increase.
d. decrease and equilibrium price will remain the same.

18. In an increasing-cost industry, the long-run market supply curve will be:
a. upward sloping.
b. horizontal.
c. vertical.
d. downward-sloping.

● POTENTIAL ESSAY QUESTIONS

You may also see essay questions similar to the "Problems & Applications" and "A Brain Teaser" exercises.

1. Describe how to find a competitive firm's price, level of output, and profit given the firm's marginal cost curve and average total cost curve.

2. According to the textbook author, there are four major things to remember when considering a perfectly competitive industry. What are these four things?

■■■■ ANSWERS ■■■■

SHORT-ANSWER QUESTIONS

1. Competition as a process is a rivalry among firms, with one firm trying to take away market share from another firm. Competition as a state is the end result of the competitive process under certain conditions. (317)

2. The six conditions necessary for perfect competition are that (1) buyers and sellers are both price takers, (2) the number of firms is large, (3) there are no barriers to entry, (4) firms' products are identical, (5) there is complete information, and (6) selling firms are profit maximizing entrepreneurial firms. (317-318)

3. It is clear that she is in a competitive market. She has no control over prices—she is a price-taker. I would advise that she calculate her marginal cost at various levels of output and sell the number of ice creams where marginal cost equals price. This will maximize her profit. To see why, for a perfect competitor, producing where $MC = P$ maximizes total profit, you must first understand that $MR = P$ for a perfect competitor. By definition a competitive firm takes price as given, so the incremental revenue, marginal revenue, of selling an additional unit is that unit's price. If we prove that a perfect competitor maximizes profit when $MC = MR$, we simultaneously prove that profit is maximized at output where $MC = P$. If marginal revenue does not equal marginal cost, a firm can increase profit by changing output. If a firm produces where $MC < MR$, it is earning a profit per unit and the firm can increase total profits by producing more until MC is no longer less than MR. If $MC > MR$, the firm is incurring a loss for that last unit; it can increase profits by reducing output until MC is no longer greater than MR. Given these conditions, the firm maximizes profit where $MC = MR$ or $MC = P$. (320-322)

4. The marginal cost curve (above the AVC curve) is the supply curve for a perfectly competitive firm because the marginal cost curve tells us how much of a produced good a firm will supply at a given price. (323, especially Figure 14-3)

5. To find where the profit-maximizing competitive firm produces, we need to know MR and MC. We know MR. We need to calculate MC, the change in VC. We do this in column 5 in the table below. To calculate profit we need to know ATC. It is the sum of FC and VC divided by Q and is shown in column 7. (Marginal cost refers to the marginal cost of increasing to that row, e.g., the marginal cost of going from 0 to 1 is 20.)

P=MR	Q	FC	VC	MC	TC	ATC	TR	Profit
35	0	10	—	—	10	—	0	−10
35	1	10	20	20	30	30	35	5
35	2	10	38	18	48	24	70	22
35	3	10	50	12	60	20	105	45
35	4	10	77	27	87	21.75	140	53
35	5	10	112	35	122	24.4	175	53
35	6	10	156	44	166	27.67	210	44

Looking at the table, we see that $MC = MR$ at $Q = 5$. Profit is $(P - ATC) \times Q = 10.6 \times 5 = 53$. Alternatively, Profit = TR −TC = $(P \times Q)$ − TC = $(35 \times 5) - 122 = 175 - 122 = 53$. Notice that when producing where MR = MC profit is as high or higher than at any other level of output. Increase output until MR = MC. This way you know you will be maximizing profits (minimizing losses). (323-325, especially Table 14-1)

6. The output of a perfect competitor is shown by the intersection of the marginal cost curve and the marginal revenue curve. On the graph below it is at Q^*. Profit for a perfect competitor is the profit per unit, the difference between the price for which each unit is sold and the average cost of each unit, times the number of units sold. Graphically, profit per unit is the vertical distance from the MR curve to the ATC curve. Multiply this by Q^* to get profit. It is the shaded region in the graph. (326-329)

7. A firm should shut down if $P \leq$ minimum AVC. (Alternatively, a firm should shut down if losses are greater than total fixed costs; or, total revenue is less than total variable costs.) (328)

8. The market supply curve is the horizontal sum of all firms' marginal cost curves, taking account of any changes in input prices that might occur. (328-329)

9. The graph below shows a representative firm in a competitive market making an economic profit when price is P^*. Since profits create incentives for new firms to enter, output will increase and the price will fall to P_1 until zero profits are being made. (329-331)

10. Before Wal-Mart opened a store, the small drug store produced Q^* at a given competitive price of P^* and earned normal profits. Since Wal-Mart is a discount drug store, opening its store in the market most likely pushed prices down to P_1. Given the new price level, the small drug store now reduced output to Q_1 and incurred a loss. Eventually, all costs are variable and the ATC curve becomes the AVC curve and prices now are below the shutdown point. This is shown in the graph below. (329-331)

11. In an increasing-cost industry the long-run market supply curve is upward sloping because of higher input prices as the industry

expands. The constant-cost industry's long-run market supply curve is horizontal because of constant input prices as the industry expands. The decreasing-cost industry's long-run market supply curve is downward sloping because of lower input prices as the industry expands. (332-333)

━━━ ANSWERS ━━━

MATCHING

1-b; 2-c; 3-d; 4-g; 5-h; 6-e; 7-a; 8-i; 9-f.

━━━ ANSWERS ━━━

PROBLEMS AND APPLICATIONS

1. To find the profit-maximizing level of output, first we determine marginal costs for the firm. We also show the values for a number of other costs. We use the formulas for these costs: MC = change in total cost, FC = $30 (costs when $Q = 0$); VC = $TC - FC$, $AVC = VC/Q$. (Marginal cost refers to the marginal cost of increasing to that row, e.g., the marginal cost of going from 0 to 1 is 25.) (321-323, especially Figure 14-2)

Q	TC	MC	VC	FC	AVC
0	30	0	0	30	0
1	55	25	25	30	25
2	75	20	45	30	22.5
3	85	10	55	30	18.3
4	100	15	70	30	17.5
5	120	20	90	30	18
6	145	25	115	30	19.2
7	185	40	155	30	22.1
8	240	55	210	30	26.25
9	310	70	280	30	31.1
10	395	85	365	30	36.5

a. A profit-maximizing firm will produce at the output level where $MC = MR$. Since MR = market price for the competitive firm, MR =$20. MC = 20 at 2 units and 5 units. It will not choose to produce 2 units because marginal costs are declining and the firm would make additional profit by increasing output above 2. So, the profit maximizing output level is at 5 units. (320-322 and 323-325)

b. If price rises to $25, so does *MR*. *MC* = *25* at 6 units. (321-322)

c. In (a), profit = total revenue − total costs at 5 units: $(5 \times \$20) - \$120 = -\$20$, an economic loss. In (b), profit = total revenue − total costs at 6 units: $(6 \times \$25) - \$145 = \$5$. (323-325)

d. The firm will stay in business at $P = \$20$ or 25, since $P > AVC$ at both these prices. (328)

e. At $P = \$15$, the profit-maximizing level of output is 4 units. The profit in this case is −$40 (loss of $40). Since $P < AVC$ in this case, the firm should temporarily shut down its business. (328)

2. a. As shown in the graph below, points A and B are the minimum of the *ATC* and *AVC* curves. It is where they intersect the *MC* curve. From an earlier chapter, we know that the *MC* curve goes through the *ATC* and *AVC* curves at their minimum points. (Figure 14-5 on page 326)

b. A demand curve for the representative firm is drawn in the graph above. It is a horizontal line because an individual firm in a competitive market is a price taker; the demand for its product is perfectly elastic. (320)

c. As illustrated above, the long-run equilibrium position occurs when the demand curve is tangent to the *ATC* curve because it is only at this point that economic profit for the firm is equal to zero. There is no incentive for new firms to enter the market, nor would existing firms exit the market. The long-run equilibrium is reached. (Figure 14-6 on page 329)

3. a. As shown by the shaded region on the following graph, the representative firm is earning an economic profit. (326-329)

b. Refer to the graphs below. More firms will enter the market to share the profit. But as market supply increases from S_0 to S_1, the market price falls which in turn reduces the profit margin for all the firms. This process continues until price falls to P_1 where there is no more economic profit. This assumes a constant-cost industry. (332-333)

c. As shown on the graphs below, a decrease in market demand from D_0 to D_1, results in a fall of market price from P_0 to P_1 which in turn causes each firm in the market to make a loss. The losses will cause some firms to exit the market. Hence, market supply shrinks from S_0 to S_1, until prices rise from P_1 to P_0. In the long run, price returns to the original level. Each firm still has zero economic profit. This assumes a constant-cost industry. (332-333)

4. a. The curve labeled *AVC* is really an *AFC* curve. The correct *AVC* curve would intersect the *MC* at the minimum point of the *AVC* curve and rise thereafter. (Figure 14-5 on page 326)

b. Loss is mis-labeled in the graph. Loss and profit are measured by the vertical difference between price and average total costs, not average variable costs. Here, economic profit is zero (there is no loss). (Figure 14-5 on page 326)

c. Output should be where *MC = MR = P,* not where *ATC = MC.* A competitive firm will maximize profits where *MC = MR = P.* (Figure 14-5 on page 326)

d. A competitive firm faces a horizontal demand curve since it cannot affect prices. Here it is downward-sloping. (Figure 14-5 on page 326)

■■■■■■■   ANSWERS   ■■■■■■■

A BRAIN TEASER

1. An increase in fixed costs (FC) will increase average total cost (ATC). Average variable cost (AVC) and marginal cost (MC) will remain unchanged. The ATC curve will shift up. Because MC has not changed (the MC curve has not shifted), and assuming the price in the competitive market (MR for the firm) has not changed, the profit- maximizing output level will not change for the firm. However, its profits will decrease because of higher costs. (325-327)

■■■■■■■   ANSWERS   ■■■■■■■

MULTIPLE CHOICE

1. a   In a competitive market, firms are profit-maximizing, not sales-maximizing firms. Buyers and sellers are pricetakers because each one cannot affect the market. See pages 317-318.

2. b   Competitive firms sell a homogenous product, there are no barriers to entry, and they cannot earn economic profits in the long run. See pages 317-318 and 329-331.

3. b   Although the market demand curve is downward sloping, individual firms are so small in relation to the market that they perceive their demand curves as horizontal. See page 320 and Figure 14-1.

4. d   The market demand curve is downward sloping. See page 320 and Figure 14-1.

5. a   For the perfectly competitive firm P = MR. If P > MC, increase output to increase profits. See pages 321-322, especially Figure 14-2.

6. b   For the perfectly competitive firm P = MR. If P < MC, decrease output to increase profits. See pages 321-322, especially Figure 14-2.

7. c   Any firm maximizes profit by producing where marginal revenue equals marginal cost. Also note, for the perfectly competitive firm, price equals marginal revenue. See pages 321-322.

8. b   Since P > MC, increase output until MC = P = MR, the profit-maximizing level of output. See pages 325-326.

9. b   Since a perfect competitor chooses to produce where P = MC, the marginal cost curve is the firm's supply curve (above minimum average variable cost). See page 323.

10. c   Profit per unit = (P – ATC). Total profit equals profit per unit times quantity. To maximize profits (or minimize losses), firms will produce where marginal revenue equals marginal cost. Firms will shut down if price is less than average variable costs. See pages 323-328.

11. b   Output is determined where marginal cost equals price (and price equals marginal revenue for the competitive firm). To determine profit one finds the rectangle formed by ATC at the output level and price determined by where marginal cost equals price. See Figure 14-5, page 326.

12. c   The shutdown point is where the marginal cost equals minimum average variable cost. See page 328.

13. a   Quantity is where P = MR = MC. Profit is (P – ATC) times quantity produced. Total cost is ATC times quantity. See pages 326-328.

14. d If P > ATC an economic profit is earned. If P = ATC a zero economic profit (a normal profit) is earned. If P < ATC but above minimum AVC, the firm is incurring an economic loss but should remain in operation to minimize losses. See pages 326-328.

15. c See definition of normal profit in the textbook on page 330.

16. c The zero profit condition for long-run competitive equilibrium discussed in the text includes a normal profit. See pages 329-331.

17. a If the price of a complement falls, the demand for X will increase, increasing quantity and increasing price in the short run. Economic profits will induce new firms to enter the market over time and the supply curve will shift to the right. Since it is a constant-cost industry, the long-run supply curve is horizontal—price remains the same while output rises. See pages 331-333.

18. a If an industry expands and this increases input prices then the long-run market supply curve will be upward sloping. See pages 332-333.

ANSWERS

POTENTIAL ESSAY QUESTIONS

The following are annotated answers. They indicate the general idea behind the answer.

1. To find a competitive firm's price, level of output, and profit given the firm's marginal cost curve and average total cost curve, do the following: (See the "A Reminder" box on page 330)
   1. Determine the market price where market supply and demand curves intersect. This is the price the competitive firm accepts for its products. Draw a horizontal marginal revenue (MR) curve at this market price.
   2. Determine the profit-maximizing level of output by finding the level of output where the MR and MC curves intersect.
   3. Determine profit by subtracting average total costs at the profit-maximizing level of output from the price and multiplying by the firm's output.

   If you are determining profit graphically, find the point at which MR = MC. Extend a line down to the ATC curve. Extend a line from that point to the vertical axis. To complete the box indicating profit, go up the vertical axis to the market price.

2. Four things to remember when considering a perfectly competitive industry: (See "A Reminder" box on page 333)
   1. The profit-maximizing condition for perfectly competitive firms is MC = MR = P.
   2. To determine profit or loss at the profit-maximizing level of output, subtract average total cost at that level of output from price and multiply the result by the output level.
   3. Firms will shut down production if price is equal to or falls below the minimum of their average variable costs.
   4. A competitive firm is in long-run equilibrium only when it is earning zero economic profit, or where price equals the minimum of long-run average total costs.

MONOPOLY

15

CHAPTER AT A GLANCE

This review is based upon the learning objectives that open the chapter.

1. A competitive firm produces where marginal revenue equals price. A monopolist does not. The monopolist takes into account the fact that its decision can affect price. (340-341)

   The monopolist faces the market demand curve. It must reduce P to sell more. Hence, MR < P.

2. The general rule that any firm must follow to maximize profit is: Produce at an output level at which MC = MR. (343-344)

   If MR > MC then increase Q.

   If MR = MC then the firm is maximizing profit (minimizing loss).

   If MR < MC then decrease Q.

3. To find a monopolist's level of output, price, and profit, follow these four steps: (341-344 and especially Figures 15-1, 15-2, and 15-3, and "A Reminder" on page 346)

   a. Draw the marginal revenue curve.

   b. Determine the output the monopolist will produce: The profit-maximizing level of output is where MR and MC curves intersect. *(See the graph in the next column.)*

   c. Determine the price the monopolist will charge: Extend a line from where MR = MC up to the demand curve. Where this line intersects the demand curve is the monopolist's price. *(See the graph at the top of the next column.)*

   d. Determine the profit the monopolist will earn: Subtract the *ATC* from price at the profit-maximizing level of output to get profit per unit. Multiply profit per unit by quantity of output to get total profit. *(See the graph below.)*

4. The welfare loss from monopoly is the triangle in the graph below. It is not the loss that most people consider. They are often interested in normative losses that the graph does not capture. (347-348)

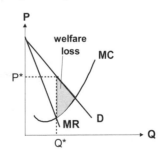

Because monopolists reduce output and charge a price that is higher than marginal cost, monopolies create a welfare loss to society.

5. When a monopolist price discriminates, it charges individuals high up on the demand curve higher prices and those low on the demand curve lower prices. (348-349)

    If a monopolist can (1) identify groups of customers who have different elasticities of demand, (2) separate them in some way, and (3) limit their ability to re-sell its product between groups, it can price discriminate.

    A price discriminating monopolist earns more profit than a normal monopolist because it can charge a higher price to those with less elastic demands and a lower price to those with more elastic demands. Price discrimination increases profits.

6. If there were no barriers to entry, profit-maximizing firms would always compete away monopoly profits. (349-353)

✔   *Know the different types of barriers to entry. The stronger the barriers to entry, the stronger the monopoly power (the greater the ability to charge a higher price) and the greater the ability to earn economic profits over time.*

7. Normative arguments against monopoly include:
    - monopolies are inconsistent with freedom,
    - the distributional effects of monopoly are unfair, and
    - monopolies encourage people to waste time and money trying to get monopolies. (353)

Possible economic profits from monopoly lead potential monopolists to spend money to get government to give them a monopoly.

See also, Appendix A: "The Algebra of Competitive and Monopolistic Firms."

SHORT-ANSWER QUESTIONS

1. What is the key difference between the decisions by monopolists and the collective decisions of competing firms with regard to setting price and production levels?

2. The president of Corning Fiberglass comes to you for advice. The firm has patented its pink fiberglass. It seems to be able to set its own price. In fact, you can say it has a monopoly on its shade of pink fiberglass. It wants you to tell it how to maximize profits. What information would you ask the president for, and what would you do with that information?

3. Calculate a monopolist's price, output, and profit using the following table:

Q	Price	Total cost
0	$36	$47
1	33	48
2	30	50
3	27	58
4	24	73
5	21	89
6	18	113
7	15	153
8	12	209
9	9	289

4. Show a monopolist's price, output, and profit using the graph below.

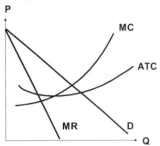

5. Show graphically the welfare loss from monopoly on the axes below.

6. Why will a price discriminating monopolist earn more profit than a normal monopolist?

7. Why, without barriers to entry, would there be no monopoly?

8. After seeing your answer to question 5, a group of consumers are outraged. "Why," they say, "that doesn't come close to the harm monopolists inflict on us." Why might the welfare loss from monopoly you demonstrated underestimate their view of the loss from monopoly?

MATCHING THE TERMS
Match the terms to their definitions

___ 1. monopoly

___ 2. natural monopoly

___ 3. patent

___ 4. price discriminate

___ 5. MR = MC

a. A legal protection of a technical innovation that gives the person holding the patent sole right to use that innovation.

b. The condition under which a monopolist (or any firm) is maximizing profit.

c. Monopolies that exist because economies of scale create a barrier to entry.

d. To charge a different price to different individuals or groups of individuals.

e. A market structure in which one firm makes up the entire market.

PROBLEMS AND APPLICATIONS

1. What are some real-world examples of monopolies?

2. Consider the following graph for a monopoly.

   a. Indicate on the graph the monopolist's output and price. Shade the area representing any economic profit (or loss).

   b. If this monopolist earns economic profits, then what is expected to happen over time? What if economic losses were incurred?

3. Consider the following graph for a monopoly.

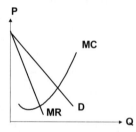

   a. Illustrate the output level and price charged by the monopoly on the graph.

   b. What would the price and output level be if this were a competitive market?

   c. Illustrate the area representing welfare loss on the graph. Explain what is meant by "welfare loss" associated with a monopoly.

4. The following table represents the market for Corning Fiberglass. Corning is the sole producer of fiberglass.

Q	Price	TC
0	—	60
1	46	65
2	42	81
3	38	111
4	34	145
5	30	189
6	24	249

a. Determine the profit-maximizing price and output.

b. What is the monopolist's profit?

c. Suppose the market is competitive, what is output and price? Would this company stay in business?

A1. Suppose the marginal costs, and therefore the market supply, for Mimi Chocolates is given by $P = Q_s/2 + 3$. The market demand is given by $Q_d = 10 - 2P$.

a. What is the equilibrium price and quantity if the market for chocolates is perfectly competitive?

b. If Mimi Chocolates has a monopoly in the market, what will be the price and the quantity produced in the market?

● A BRAIN TEASER

1. Suppose you are in the business of staging concerts. You have just contracted to stage a concert featuring a red-hot rock group. The total cost of staging the concert is $10,000. This total cost is independent of how many people attend the concert. Your market research indicates that attendance at the concert will vary depending on the price of an admission ticket, as shown below. What ticket price should you charge to maximize profit? Briefly explain.

Ticket Price	Attendance
$20	771
$18	979
$16	1,133
$14	1,327
$12	1,559
$10	1,625
$ 8	1,803

● MULTIPLE CHOICE

Circle the one best answer for each of the following questions:

1. Monopoly is the market structure in which:
   a. one firm makes up the entire market.
   b. two firms make up the entire market.
   c. the market is made up of a few big firms.
   d. firms make a supernormal profit.

2. Which of the following is *false*?
   a. A monopoly is a price-maker, whereas a competitive firm is a price-taker.
   b. The monopolist produces where MR = MC while the perfect competitor does not.
   c. The monopoly's marginal revenue curve lies below the demand curve whereas the

competitive firm's marginal revenue curve is horizontal at the market price.

d. A monopolist is protected by barriers to entry whereas a competitive firm is not.

3. A profit-maximizing monopolist will:
a. produce an output level at which MR > MC.
b. produce an output level at which P > MC.
c. always earn an economic profit in the short run.
d. increase production when MR < MC.

4. Refer to the graph below. Which curve is the marginal revenue curve for the market demand curve D faced by a monopolist?
a. Curve A.
b. Curve B.
c. Curve C.
d. Curve D.

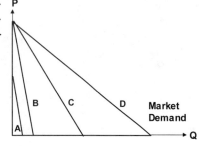

5. Refer to the graph below. A monopolist would most likely produce quantity shown by:
a. A.
b. B.
c. C.
d. D.

6. Refer to the graph below. Which rectangle represents the monopolist's profit?
a. A.
b. A + B + C.
c. C + D.
d. None of the above.

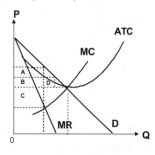

7. Refer to the graph below. The monopolist represented is:

a. making a profit.
b. making a loss.
c. making zero profit.
d. unable to determine what kind of profit it is making.

8. Refer to the graph below. Which of the following statements about the market represented is true?

a. A monopolist would charge price P_2 and produce output Q_2.
b. A monopolist would charge price P_1 and produce output Q_1.
c. A competitive market would charge price P_2 and produce output Q_2.
d. A monopolist would earn a profit per unit equal to P_3 minus P_1.

9. Refer to the graph for Question #8. Which of the following statements about the effect of the monopolist represented is true?
a. Triangle *bac* represents the lost producer surplus to society due to the monopoly.
b. Triangle *dbc* represents the lost consumer surplus to society due to the monopoly.
c. Triangle *dac* represents the welfare loss to society due to the monopoly.
d. Lost production due to the monopoly is equal to Q_1.

10. Refer to the graph below. This monopolist is:

   a. earning a profit of $600.
   b. earning a profit of $800.
   c. breaking even.
   d. incurring a loss of $300.

11. A price-discriminating monopolist:
   a. charges different prices to customers with different elasticities of demand.
   b. will earn a lower profit than a non-price-discriminating monopolist.
   c. will have a marginal revenue curve that lies above its demand curve.
   d. is trying to allow some people to purchase the good who could not normally afford to do so.

12. Price discrimination requires:
   a. identifying groups of customers with different elasticities.
   b. separating customers in some way.
   c. limiting customers' ability to re-sell the product between different groups.
   d. all of the other options listed to be successful.

13. A natural monopoly is a monopoly:
   a. that exists because of economies of scale.
   b. that is created by natural law.
   c. where natural legal barriers prevent entry.
   d. in which patents exist.

14. Refer to the graph below. Which area represents the welfare loss due to a monopolist?
   a. A.
   b. A + B.
   c. B + C.
   d. A + B + C.

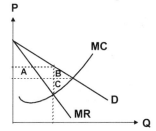

15. For a monopolist to earn an economic profit in the long run, which of the following must happen?
   a. There are barriers to entry.
   b. Average total costs must fall.
   c. Welfare loss due to monopoly must increase.
   d. Fixed costs must be eliminated.

16. Which of the following statements is *least* likely to explain public ire against monopolies?
   a. Monopolies are inconsistent with freedom.
   b. The distributional effects of monopolies are unfair.
   c. Monopolies encourage people to waste time and money trying to get monopolies.
   d. Monopolies sometimes exist because of an ability to produce superior products.

A1. Suppose the marginal costs, and therefore the market supply, for ketchup in Mexico is given by $P = Q_s/2 + 1$. The market demand is given by, $Q_d = 20 - 4P$. If there is a monopoly in the ketchup market the price and the quantity produced are:
   a. $P = 11/3$, $Q = 16/3$.
   b. $P = 11/3$, $Q = 4$.
   c. $P = 3$, $Q = 4$.
   d. $P = 4$, $Q = 4$.

● POTENTIAL ESSAY QUESTIONS

You may also see essay questions similar to the "Problems & Applications" and "A Brain Teaser" exercises.

1. What is the objective of price discrimination? What conditions must be present for a firm to be able to price discriminate?

2. What are three normative arguments against monopoly?

ANSWERS

SHORT-ANSWER QUESTIONS

1. For a competitive firm, marginal revenue equals price regardless of output. But for a monopolist, price depends on output. A monopolist must take into account the fact that its output decisions can affect price. Its marginal revenue does not equal the price it charges. Instead, $MR < P$ for the monopolist. (340-343)

2. You tell the president that the firm needs to know its marginal costs and its marginal revenues. To maximize profits, it should produce where $MR = MC$. A monopolist produces where $MC = MR$ to maximize total profit for the same reasons a perfectly competitive firm does. If $MC < MR$, it can increase total profits by producing more. If $MC > MR$, it can increase total profits by decreasing output. It is only where $MC = MR$ that it cannot increase profits by changing output. (343-344)

3. To calculate a monopolist's output, first calculate total revenue ($P \times Q$) for each output level. Then calculate marginal revenue (the change in total revenue). Find where $MR = MC$. This is at 4 units and a price of $24. Profit is calculated as total revenue minus total cost: $23. Notice that profit is maximized at an output where $MR = MC$. Profits are as high or higher here than at any other output level. (Marginal cost refers to the marginal cost of increasing to that row, e.g., the marginal cost of going from 0 to 1 is 1. The same goes for marginal revenue.) (343-344)

Q	Price	Total revenue	Marginal revenue	Total cost	Marginal cost
0	$36	0	—	$47	—
1	33	33	33	48	1
2	30	60	27	50	2
3	27	81	21	58	8
4	24	96	15	73	15
5	21	105	9	89	16
6	18	108	3	113	24
7	15	105	−3	153	40
8	12	96	−9	209	56
9	9	81	−15	289	80

4. A monopolist's output is set where $MC = MR$ (where the MC and MR curves intersect). Extend a line vertically; it sets price where that line intersects the demand curve, here at P^*. Profit is determined by dropping a vertical line from the price the monopolist charges to the ATC curve and multiplying by Q^*. This is the shaded region in the graph below. (344-347; especially the "A Reminder" box on page 346)

5. Welfare loss from monopoly is shown as the shaded region on the graph below. (347)

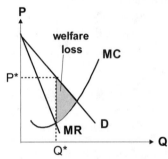

6. If a monopolist can (1) identify groups of customers who have different elasticities of demand, (2) separate them in some way, and (3) limit their ability to re-sell its product between groups, it can price discriminate. A price discriminating monopolist earns more profit than a normal monopolist because it can increase output without reducing the price it charged for previous units. It can charge a higher price to those with less elastic demands and a lower price to those with more elastic demands. Price discrimination increases profits. (348-349)

7. Without barriers to entry there would be no monopoly because profit-maximizing firms would always enter to compete away monopoly profits. (349-353)

8. You first think that they are wrong. They simply do not understand the model. Upon further reflection, you realize that your model does not include normative arguments against monopoly. These include: (1) monopolies are inconsistent with freedom, (2) the distributional effects of monopoly are unfair, and (3) monopolies encourage people to waste time and money trying to get monopolies. (353)

ANSWERS

MATCHING

1-e; 2-c; 3-a; 4-d; 5-b.

ANSWERS

PROBLEMS AND APPLICATIONS

1. Your local cable television, water, gas, and electric companies are a few examples. In some small towns the only grocery store in town will behave as a monopoly. Note that it may be helpful to think in terms of regional markets, and in terms of the number of suitable substitutes available for the good or service. The smaller the number of suitable substitutes the greater the monopoly power. (340-342)

2. **a.** The monopolist will produce Q* and charge price P*. Because $P > ATC$ the monopoly is earning an economic profit shown as the shaded area in the graph below. (344-345)

    b. Economic profits always attract other businesses. However, because the barriers to entry in a monopoly are so strong, potential competitors will find it very difficult to enter this market. Therefore,

economic profits are likely to persist for some time. If losses are incurred by a monopolist, like any other firm, the monopolist will shut down if $P < AVC$ in the short run. No firm can sustain losses in the long run. (349)

3. **a.** See the graph below. The monopoly would produce Q_m and charge price P_m. (344-345)

    b. See the graph below. The competitive outcome would be Q_c and P_c. (As you would expect, the monopolist charges a higher price and produces less than if the market were competitive.) (345-346 and especially Figure 15-1)

    c. The shaded area in the graph below illustrates welfare loss. Welfare loss is the amount by which the marginal benefits to society (measured by the prices people are willing to pay along the demand curve) exceed the marginal costs to society (measured by points along the marginal cost curve) for those units that would be produced in a competitive market but are not produced in a non-competitive market. (347-348)

4. To answer the following questions, first calculate *MC, MR,* and *AVC. MC* is the change in *TC, AVC* is *VC/Q,* and *MR* is the change in *TR,* where *TR* is $P \times Q$. This is shown below. (Marginal cost refers to the marginal cost of increasing to that row, e.g., the marginal cost of going from 0 to 1 is 5. The same goes for marginal revenue.) (343-344 and Table 15-1 on page 341)

Q	Price	TC	MC	TR	MR	AVC
0	—	60	—	0	—	0
1	46	65	5	46	46	5
2	42	81	16	84	38	10.5
3	38	111	30	114	30	17.00
4	34	145	34	136	22	21.25
5	30	189	44	150	14	25.8
6	24	249	60	144	−6	31.5

a.   Monopolists maximize profits where $MR = MC$. $MR = MC$ at 3 units. Corning will charge a price of $38. (343-344)

b.   Profit = total revenue minus total costs = $3. (343-344)

c.   If the market were competitive, then the firm would produce where $MC = P$. So Q is 4 units and $P = \$34$. Profit = total revenue − total costs = −$9. The firm will still stay in business in the short run since $P > AVC$. (344)

A1. a.   Rewriting the marginal cost equation with quantity supplied on the left gives: $Q_s = 2P - 6$. Setting this equal to quantity demanded gives equilibrium price at 4 and quantity at 2. (359-360)

b.   Specifying the demand curve in terms of quantity demanded gives: $P = 5 - Q/2$. Multiplying this by Q gives total revenue $TR = 5Q - Q^2/2$. The marginal revenue is the first derivative of this. Thus, $MR = 5 - Q$. By setting $MR = MC$ and solving for Q we get the quantity that would be produced if the chocolate market were a monopoly. (359-360)

$$5 - Q = Q/2 + 3$$
$$3/2Q = 2$$
$$Q = 4/3, \text{ or } 1.33.$$

The monopolist charges the price that consumers are willing to pay for that quantity. Substituting $Q = 4/3$ into the demand equation gives $P = 13/3$, or 4.33. You can see that if there is a monopoly in the market, the price charged is higher than the competitive market price; also, the quantity produced is lower. (347)

ANSWERS

A BRAIN TEASER

1.   The profit-maximizing price is $12. It generates maximum revenues of $18,708. Since all costs of staging the concert are fixed (sunk) costs, a price which maximizes revenues also maximizes profit. Profit will equal $8,708 (TR − TC = $18,708 − $10,000). (343-344)

ANSWERS

MULTIPLE CHOICE

1.   a   Monopoly means one firm; that firm may or may not make a supernormal profit. See page 339.

2.   b   Both monopolies and competitive firms produce where MR = MC. Recall that P = MR for a competitive firm. So , the profit-maximizing rule for a competitive firm is sometimes written: produce where P = MC. See page 344.

3.   b   A monopolist produces where MR = MC. Since MR is below the demand curve, this means the monopolist produces where P > MC. If MR > MC, it will *increase* production. If MR < MC, it will *decrease* production. See pages 343-344.

4.   c   The marginal revenue curve equals the demand curve at the vertical axis and bisects the distance between the origin and the point where the demand curve intersects the horizontal axis. See page 343, "Added Dimension."

5.   a   Output is determined where marginal revenue equals marginal cost. This is shown where the MR and MC curves intersect. See pages 341-344, especially Figure 15-1.

6.   a   Output is determined where marginal revenue equals marginal cost. Profit is determined by the rectangle created by the relevant price and average cost at that output. See pages 345-346, and "A Reminder" on page 346.

7.   c   A monopolist produces where MC = MR and charges a price determined by the demand curve. Since P = ATC, the monopolist is earning no profit. See Figure 15-4a on page 347.

8.   c   A monopolist produces where MC = MR and charges a price determined by the demand curve. This results in a price of P_3 and output Q_1. The profit per unit is P_3 minus P_2. A perfectly competitive market produces where MC intersects the market demand curve. See Figure 15-1 on page 342.

9. c A monopolist produces where MC = MR and charges a price determined by the demand curve. A perfectly competitive market produces where MC intersects the market demand curve. Welfare loss is lost consumer and producer surplus due to the decline in output. This is the triangle above the MC curve, below the demand curve and between Q_1 and Q_2. See pages 347-348, especially Figure 15-5.

10. d The monopolist produces where MC = MR, or 100, and charges a price determined by the demand curve, or $11. Because ATC = $14, the monopolist is losing $3 per unit. $3 x 100 = $300 loss. See pages 343-344 and Figure 15-3 on page 346.

11. a By segmenting the market into groups of customers with different elasticities of demand a price-discriminating monopolist can increase profits by charging higher (lower) prices to consumers with a more inelastic (elastic) demand. See pages 348-349.

12. d By segmenting the market into groups of customers with different elasticities of demand a price-discriminating monopolist can increase profits by charging higher (lower) prices to consumers with a more inelastic (elastic) demand. This requires all the options listed. See pages 348-349.

13. a If large fixed (setup) costs create barriers to entry for an industry and average total costs decline as output rises, it is more efficient for there to be only one producer. This industry is known as a natural monopoly. See pages 349-354.

14. c A monopolist produces where MC = MR and charges a price determined by the demand curve. A perfectly competitive market produces where MC intersects the market demand curve. Welfare loss is lost consumer and producer surplus due to the decline in output. This is the triangle above the MC curve, below the demand curve and between the two levels of output. See pages 348-349, especially Figure 15-5.

15. a If there were no barriers to entry, competitors would enter the market and drive down price until only normal profits were earned. See page 349.

16. d As discussed on page 353, monopolies based on ability usually don't provoke the public's ire. Often in the public's mind such monopolies are "just monopolies."

A1. d Specifying the demand curve in terms of quantity produced gives: $P = 5 - Q/4$. Multiplying this by Q gives total revenue $TR = 5Q - Q^2/4$. The marginal revenue is the first derivative of this. Thus, $MR = 5 - Q/2$. By setting MR = MC and solving for Q we get the quantity produced: $5 - Q/2 = Q/2 + 1$; $Q = 4$. The monopolist charges the price that consumers are willing to pay for that quantity. Substituting $Q = 4$ into the demand equation gives $P = 4$. Thus, *d* is the correct answer. See pages 359-360.

■■■ ANSWERS ■■■

POTENTIAL ESSAY QUESTIONS

The following are annotated answers. They indicate the general idea behind the answer.

1. The objective of price discrimination is to increase profits. In order to price discriminate, a firm must be able to segment its markets or customers. It must also be able to determine which markets or customers have the more inelastic demand for the good or service, and then charge those people the higher price. Finally, the product cannot be easily resold.

2. Normative arguments against monopoly include (1) monopolies are inconsistent with freedom, (2) the distributional effects of monopoly are unfair, and (3) monopolies encourage people to waste time and money trying to get monopolies.

MONOPOLISTIC COMPETITION AND OLIGOPOLY

CHAPTER AT A GLANCE

This review is based upon the learning objectives that open the chapter.

1. Four distinguishing characteristics of monopolistic competition are: (361-363)

   1. Many sellers.
   2. Differentiated products.
   3. Multiple dimensions of competition.
   4. Easy entry of new firms in the long run.

   ✔ *Know these as well as the distinguishing characteristics of all 4 market models.*

2. The equilibrium of a monopolistic competitor is: (363-364)

   Notice the tangency between the D and ATC curves at output where MR = MC. Also note only a zero economic profit in the long run (P=ATC). But because P>MC this implies underproduction from society's perspective and hence some welfare loss.

3. The central element of oligopoly is that there are a small number of firms in an industry so that, in any decision it makes, each firm must take into account the expected reaction of other firms. (367)

   Oligopolistic firms are mutually interdependent and can be collusive or non-collusive. If they collude and form a cartel, they can increase their collective profits. Although there is a tendency for collusion (getting together to avoid competing), holding firms to an agreement is difficult because each firm has a tendency to cheat.

4. In the contestable market model of oligopoly, pricing and entry decisions are based only on barriers to entry and exit, not on market structure. Thus, even if the industry contains only one firm, it could still be a competitive market if entry is open. (367-371)

   Two extreme models of oligopoly behavior:

   - Cartel model: Firms set a monopoly price.
   - Contestable market model: An oligopoly with no barriers sets a competitive price.

   Most real-world oligopolies are between these extremes.

5. To measure industry structure, economists use one of two methods: the concentration ratio or a Herfindahl index. (374)

   A concentration ratio is the value of sales by the top firms of an industry stated as a percentage of total industry sales. For example, a four-firm concentration ratio of 60% means the four largest firms account for 60% of total industry sales.

   A Herfindahl Index is a method used by economists (and the Department of Justice) to classify how competitive an industry is. A Herfindahl Index has 2 advantages over a concentration ratio: (1) it takes into account all firms in an industry, and (2) it gives extra weight to firms with especially large shares of the market.

● SHORT-ANSWER QUESTIONS

1. The soap industry is characterized by monopolistic competition. There are many types of soap: Ivory, Irish Spring, Lever, and so on. When one firm lowers its price it won't calculate the reaction of the other firms. In the automobile market, which is oligopolistic, GM does worry about how Chrysler prices its cars. Based on level of competition, what distinguishes these two (monopolistically competitive vs. oligopolistic) markets?

2. Show graphically the equilibrium of a monopolistic competitor.

3. State the central element of oligopoly and the two basic types of oligopolies.

4. Major oil producers in the world have formed a tight cartel, OPEC. At times, the cartel has fallen apart. What are the reasons the major oil producers have a powerful desire to keep OPEC strong?

5. How does the contestable market theory lead to determining competitiveness by performance rather than structure?

6. What is the 4-firm concentration ratio for an industry in which 10 firms all have 10% of the market?

7. What is a Herfindahl index for an industry in which 10 firms all have 10% of the market?

MATCHING THE TERMS
Match the terms to their definitions

___ **1.** cartel

___ **2.** cartel model of oligopoly

___ **3.** concentration ratio

___ **4.** contestable market model

___ **5.** Herfindahl Index

___ **6.** implicit collusion

___ **7.** market structure

___ **8.** monopolistic competition

___ **9.** North American Industry Classification System (NAICS)

___ **10.** oligopoly

___ **11.** strategic decision making

a. A market structure in which many firms sell differentiated products.

b. A market structure with a few interdependent firms.

c. A combination of firms that acts like a single firm.

d. A model that bases pricing and output decisions on entry and exit conditions, not on market structure.

e. The physical characteristics of the market within which firms interact.

f. An index of market concentration calculated by adding the squared values of the individual market shares of all firms in the industry.

g. An industry classification that categorizes firms by type of economic activity and groups firms with like production processes.

h. Multiple firms making the same pricing decisions even though they have not consulted with one another.

i. A model that assumes that oligopolies act as if they were monopolists that have assigned output quotas to individual member firms of the oligopoly so that total output is consistent with joint profit maximization.

j. Taking explicit account of a rival's expected response to a decision you are making.

k. The value of sales by the top firms of an industry stated as a percentage of total industry sales.

PROBLEMS AND APPLICATIONS

1. Given the following demand and marginal revenue curves, add a marginal cost curve.

a. Label profit-maximizing price and output for a monopolist. Label profit-maximizing price and output for a monopolistically competitive firm.

b. Add an average total cost curve that is consistent with long-run equilibrium in a market characterized by monopolistic competition. What is the economic profit? Explain your answer.

2. For each of the following graphs state whether it characterizes perfect competition, monopoly, or monopolistic competition in the long run. Explain your answer.

(a)

(b)

(c)

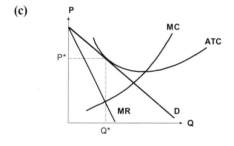

3. For each of the following calculate the four-firm concentration ratio and the Herfindahl index.

    a. 20 firms in the market each having equal shares.

    b. 10 firms are in the market. One firm has 91% of market share. The remaining 9 firms share the remaining market equally.

    c. The industry's top firm has 31% of the market and the next three have 2% apiece. There are 63 remaining firms, each with a 1% share.

    d. 4 firms equally share the market.

    e. Rank each of these markets by how competitive they are: from the most to least competitive, first using the concentration ratio and then the Herfindahl index. Do they differ? Why or why not?

4. Fill in the following table, which captures the central differences among various market structures.

	Monopoly	Oligopoly	Monopolistic Competition	Perfect Competition
Number of Firms				
Pricing Decisions				
Output Decisions				
Profit				

A1. Suppose there are two ice-cream stands on opposite sides of the road: Ben's stand and Jerry's stand. Each has identical costs of 25 cents a cone. Each has the option of charging $1 a cone or $1.50 a cone. If Ben and Jerry collude, both charging $1.50 a cone, each will sell 50 cones each day. Ben thinks that he would sell more cones if he sells his at $1 a cone. If he does this, he will sell 80 cones and Jerry will sell 20. Jerry is considering the same strategy. If they both charge $1, each will sell 50 cones per day.

    a. Construct a payoff matrix for Ben and Jerry.

    b. If the stand is to be in business only one day, what would you advise Ben?

    c. If the stands are to be in business all summer long, what would you advise Ben?

⬤ A BRAIN TEASER

1. Advertising firms often argue, "Advertising doesn't cost, it pays!" How would you respond?

⬤ MULTIPLE CHOICE

Circle the one best answer for each of the following questions:

1. In a market there are many firms selling differentiated products. This market is:
    a. a competitive market.
    b. a monopolistically competitive market.
    c. an oligopolistic market.
    d. a monopoly.

2. Several firms are operating in a market where they take the other firms' response to their actions into account. This market is:
    a. a competitive market.
    b. a monopolistically competitive market.
    c. an oligopolistic market.
    d. a monopoly.

3. Strategic decision making is most important in:
    a. competitive markets.
    b. monopolistically competitive markets.
    c. oligopolistic markets.
    d. monopolistic markets.

4. At the equilibrium output for a monopolistic competitor:
    a. price equals marginal cost equals marginal revenue.
    b. price equals average total cost equals marginal revenue.
    c. marginal cost equals marginal revenue equals average total costs.
    d. price equals average total cost and marginal cost equals marginal revenue.

5. Refer to the graph below. Which of the following is the output chosen by the monopolistically competitive firm?

    a. Q_1.
    b. Q_2.
    c. Q_3.
    d. Output cannot be determined.

6. In long-run equilibrium, a monopolistically competitive firm:
    a. makes a loss.
    b. makes only a normal profit.
    c. makes a monopolistic profit.
    d. may make a loss or a profit.

7. Goals of advertising include shifting the firm's demand curve to the:
    a. left and making it more elastic.
    b. left and making it more inelastic.
    c. right and making it more elastic.
    d. right and making it more inelastic.

8. In the cartel model of oligopoly, the firms would decide how much to produce where:
    a. marginal cost equals marginal revenue.
    b. marginal cost equals price.
    c. marginal cost equals average total cost.
    d. the kink in the demand curve is.

9. According to the kinked demand curve theory of sticky prices, in an oligopolistic market:
    a. a price decrease by one firm will not be followed by the other firms.
    b. a price increase by one firm will be followed by the other firms.
    c. the kinked demand curve is inelastic in the upper portion and elastic in the lower portion of the curve.
    d. the kinked demand curve is elastic in the upper portion and inelastic in the lower portion of the curve.

10. In a contestable market model of oligopoly, prices are determined by:
    a. costs and barriers to exit.
    b. costs and barriers to entry.
    c. costs, barriers to entry, and barriers to exit.
    d. costs alone.

11. There is only one firm in the market. The economist analyzing that market has said she would expect the price to equal the firm's average total costs.
    a. She must be analyzing this market using a contestable market model.
    b. She must be analyzing this market using a game theory model.
    c. She must be analyzing this market using a cartel model.
    d. She must not be an economist, because that answer is clearly wrong.

12. In the NAICS classification system, the broadest classification would be:
    a. a two-digit industry.
    b. a three-digit industry.
    c. a four-digit industry.
    d. a five-digit industry.

13. The top four firms in the industry have 10 percent, 8 percent, 8 percent, and 6 percent of the market. The four-firm concentration ratio of this market is:
    a. 8.
    b. 32.
    c. 66.
    d. 264.

14. The top four firms in the industry have 10 percent, 8 percent, 8 percent, and 6 percent of the market. The Herfindahl index of this market is closest to which of the following?
    a. 8.
    b. 32.
    c. 66.
    d. 264.

15. A market has the following characteristics: There is strategic decision-making, output is somewhat restricted, there are few firms, and some long-run economic profits are possible. This market is:
    a. a monopoly.
    b. an oligopoly.
    c. monopolistically competitive.
    d. perfectly competitive.

A1. Strategic decision making is most important in:
    a. competitive markets.
    b. monopolistically competitive markets.
    c. oligopolistic markets.
    d. monopolistic markets.

A2. If a firm promises to always sell its goods at a lower price than its competitors with a double the difference back guarantee, the customer:
    a. will be better off because he will get a lower price from that firm.
    b. will be better off because the other firm will be forced to lower its price as well.
    c. may be worse off because the guarantee will push other firms out of business.
    d. may be worse off because it will discourage price competition by other firms.

● POTENTIAL ESSAY QUESTIONS

You may also see essay questions similar to the "Problems & Applications" and "A Brain Teaser" exercises.

1. What is the "monopolistic" element and the "competitive" element of monopolistic competition?

2. What is the difference between the contestable market model and the cartel model of oligopoly? How are they related?

ANSWERS

SHORT-ANSWER QUESTIONS

1. The distinguishing characteristics are: (1) In the soap industry there are many sellers in a highly competitive market. In the automobile industry there are about 5 big producers. (2) In the soap industry, the different labels are distinct, but firms still act independently. In the automobile industry, the products are distinct and the firms do not act independently. (3) In the soap industry, there is easy entry of new firms in the long run so there are no long-run profits. In the auto industry entry is not easy. In both industries firms compete on more than price; they also compete on image. (361-363, 366)

2. The equilibrium of a monopolistic competitor is shown in the graph below. A monopolistic competitor earns no economic profit, so the price equals *ATC*. (363-364)

3. The central element of oligopoly is that there are a small number of firms in an industry so that, in any decision it makes, each firm must take into account the expected reaction of other firms. Oligopolistic firms are mutually interdependent and can be collusive or non-collusive. (367)

4. Since there are only a few large oil-producing nations, together they are an oligopoly. Oil-producing nations have a powerful desire to keep OPEC strong because as a cartel it can increase the profits going to the combination of oil-producing nations by reducing output. (367-369)

5. In the contestable market theory, pricing decisions are based on the threat of new entrants into the market, not market share. Thus, even if the industry has only one firm, it could still price competitively. (370-371)

6. A concentration ratio is the value of sales by the top firms of an industry stated as a percentage of total industry sales. A 4-firm concentration ratio is calculated by adding together the market shares of the four firms with the largest market shares. In the case given, the 4-firm concentration ratio is 40. (373-374)

7. A Herfindahl index is a method used by economists to classify how competitive an industry is. It is calculated by summing the squares of the market shares of all the firms in the industry. In this case the Herfindahl index is $10 \times 10^2 = 1000$. (374)

ANSWERS

MATCHING

1-c; 2-i; 3-k; 4-d; 5-f; 6-h; 7-e; 8-a; 9-g; 10-b; 11-j.

ANSWERS

PROBLEMS AND APPLICATIONS

1. **a.** The graph below shows a typical marginal cost curve for a firm. The profit-maximizing level of output for a monopolist is where $MC = MR$. It will set price by extending the quantity line to the demand curve and extending a horizontal line to the price axis. This is the price a monopolistically competitive firm would charge. All this is labeled as Q^* and P^* respectively. The profit maximizing price and output procedure for a monopolistically competitive firm is the same as for a monopolist. (363-364)

b. The average total cost curve consistent with long-run equilibrium in a market characterized by monopolistic competition is drawn on the graph above. It is tangent to the demand curve at the profit-maximizing price and quantity combination. Economic profit is zero. It is drawn this way because competition implies zero economic profit in the long run. (363-364)

2. a. This graph depicts perfect competition because the demand curve facing the firm is horizontal and zero economic profit is earned. (364-365; especially Figure 16-2)

b. This graph depicts a monopolist because it faces a downward-sloping demand curve and it is earning economic profit. (364-365)

c. This graph depicts a monopolistic competitor because it faces a downward-sloping demand curve and its economic profit is zero. (It could also depict a monopolist if it so happens that the *ATC* curve is drawn as given.) (364-365)

3. A four-firm concentration ratio is the percent of total industry sales accounted for by the top four firms. It is calculated by adding together the top four firms' market shares. The Herfindahl index is calculated by adding the squared value of the market shares of *all* the firms in the industry. (373-374)

a. Four-firm concentration ratio $= 5+5+5+5 = 20$. Herfindahl index is $20 \times 5^2 = 500$.

b. Four-firm concentration ratio $= 91+1+1+1 = 94$. Herfindahl index is $91^2+1^2+1^2+1^2+1^2+1^2+1^2+1^2+1^2+1^2 = 8,290$.

c. Four-firm concentration ratio $= 31+2+2+2 = 37$. Herfindahl index is $31^2+2^2+2^2+2^2+63 \times 1^2 = 1,036$.

d. Four-firm concentration ratio $= 25+25+25+25 = 100$. Herfindahl index is $25^2+25^2+25^2+25^2 = 2,500$.

e. A higher concentration ratio and Herfindahl index indicates that the market is less competitive. The ranking using the four-firm concentration ratio is a (20), c (37), b (94), d (100). Using the Herfindahl index, the ranking is a (500), c (1036), d (2500), b (8290). They differ because the Herfindahl index takes into account *all* the firms in the market and gives extra weight to a single firm with an especially large share of the market (this accounts for the difference in the ranking of b).

4. See the following table. (372)

	Monopoly	Oligopoly	Monopolistic Competition	Perfect Competition
Number of Firms	One	Few	Many	Almost Infinite
Pricing Decisions	MC=MR	Strategic pricing between monopoly and perfect competition	MC=MR	MC=MR=P
Output Decisions	Most output restricted	Output somewhat restricted	Output restricted relatively little by product differentiation	No output restriction
Profit	Possibility of long-run economic profit	Some long-run economic profit	No long-run-economic profit possible	No long-run economic profit possible

A1. a. The payoff matrix is shown below. Ben's strategies are listed vertically. Jerry's strategies are listed horizontally. The first number in each cell is Ben's profits calculated as quantity times profit per unit. The second number is Jerry's profit calculated in the same way. (381-382 and Figure 16.3)

		Jerry's Price	
		$1.50	$1.00
Ben's Price	$1.50	$62.50/$62.50	$25/$60
	$1.00	$60/$25	$37.50/$37.50

b. If the stand is to be in business only one day I would tell Ben that his profit-maximizing strategy is to charge $1. Expected profit of charging $1.50 is $43.75 ((62.5+25)/2), assuming it is equally likely that Jerry will charge $1.50 or $1.00. Expected profit of charging $1.00 is $48.75 ((60+37.5)/2), assuming it is equally likely that Jerry will charge $1.50 or $1.00. He should charge $1.00. (381-382)

c. If they were going to sell ice cream all summer long I would recommend that Ben and Jerry develop some level of trust between themselves and collude to charge $1.50 each. This way, they maximize joint profits. (381-382)

ANSWERS

A BRAIN TEASER

1. Advertising does cost money, but if advertising increases total production and if there are economies of scale, advertising could even lower long-run average total cost. In addition, advertising is designed to increase demand and to make it more inelastic. If a firm has some market control, the firm can translate this into a higher profit per unit. Advertising pays off only when additional revenues outweigh any additional costs due to advertising. (366-367)

ANSWERS

MULTIPLE CHOICE

1. b   A monopolistically competitive market has many firms selling differentiated products. See page 361.

2. c   An oligopoly is a market in which a few firms engage in strategic decision making. See page 367.

3. c   It is within oligopolies that firms explicitly take other firms' expected reactions into account, so it is oligopoly where strategic decision making is most important. See page 361.

4. d   The equilibrium output is determined where marginal costs equal marginal revenue. At that output average total costs equal price, but that price does not equal either marginal cost or marginal revenue. See pages 363-364 and Figure 16-1.

5. a   The equilibrium output is determined where marginal cost equals marginal revenue. See pages 363-364 and Figure 16-1.

6. b   In long-run equilibrium, a monopolistically competitive firm must make zero profit (a normal profit), so that no entry is induced. See pages 363-364.

7. d   By shifting the firm's demand curve to the right and making it more inelastic, advertising allows the firm to charge a higher price and to earn a higher profit per unit. See page 366.

8. a   The cartel model has the oligopoly acting like a monopolist. See pages 367-369.

9. d   Because a price increase is not followed by other firms and sales plummet, the demand curve is elastic in the upper portion. However, a price decrease is followed by others and revenues fall. Thus, demand is inelastic in the lower portion of the curve. See pages 369-370.

10. c   Costs determine reference price, and barriers to both entry and exit determine the degree to which price deviates from cost. See page 371.

11. a   In a contestable market model, exit and entry conditions determine the firm's price and output decisions. Thus, if there are no barriers to entry and exit, even if there is only one firm in the industry, the firm will produce where price equals the firm's average total costs. See page 370.

12. a   In the North American Industry Classification System (NAICS), the more numbers, the greater the particular subdivisions, so the answer is a two-digit sector. See page 373.

13. b   The concentration ratio is calculated by summing the market shares of the top four firms. See page 371 .

14. d   The Herfindahl index sums the squares of the market shares of all firms in the industry. Squaring these market shares and adding them gives 264, so the Herfindahl index exceeds 264 if there are more than four firms. See page 374.

15. b   An oligopoly is a market in which a few firms operate, each taking into consideration other firms' behavior when making decisions. Because output is somewhat restricted, some long-run profit is possible. See page 367.

A1. c   It is within oligopolies that firms explicitly take other firms' expected reactions into account, so it is oligopoly where strategic decision making is most important. See pages 381-382.

A2. d   The best answer here is "d" since strategically, such guarantees reduce the gains from competing on price. See pages 381-382.

ANSWERS

POTENTIAL ESSAY QUESTIONS

The following are annotated answers. They indicate the general idea behind the answer.

1.   The "monopolistic" element is the ability to charge a higher-than-competitive price that is directly related to the success the firm has in differentiating its product from its competitors. The "competitive" element is that there are many sellers who are able to earn only a zero economic profit in the long run because of the weak barriers to entry into the market (the only real barrier to entry is the an ability to differentiate the product from competitors).

2.   The cartel model argues that oligopolists will come together to behave as a monopoly in terms of their pricing and output decisions because it is in their self-interest to do so— they'll make more money. (However, there is always a tendency for a firm to want to "cheat" and the mere rumor of cheating can cause a breakdown of the collusion.) The contestable market model argues that an industry that looks like an oligopoly (because there are a few dominant firms in the industry) could set highly competitive prices and produce a competitive output level. What is important in pricing and output decisions, according to the contestable market model, is not the number of firms in the industry, but the strength of the barriers to entry that exist in the market. If there are few, if any, barriers to entry, then a competitive price and output level will be observed. These two models are related in that the stronger the barriers to entry, usually the fewer the number of firms, and therefore the greater the probability for collusion.

REAL-WORLD COMPETITION AND TECHNOLOGY

● CHAPTER AT A GLANCE

This review is based upon the learning objectives that open the chapter.

1. The monitoring problem is that employees' incentives differ from the owner's incentives. By changing employees' incentives, the efficiency of the firm can sometimes be improved. (385-386)

   Self-interest-seeking managers are interested in maximizing firm profit only if the structure of the firm requires them to do so.

   An incentive-compatible contract is needed to match the goals of managers with owners.

2. Corporate takeovers, or simply the threat of a takeover, can improve firms' efficiency. (388-389)

   Because corporate takeovers often mean a change in management, takeovers pressure managers to maintain a certain level of efficiency (to avoid X-inefficiency) so the firm does not become the target of a takeover.

3. When competitive pressures get strong, individuals often fight back through social and political pressures. Competition is a process— a fight between the forces of monopolization and the forces of competition. (390)

   Everyone applauds competition, except for themselves.

   Competitive markets will exist if producers or consumers don't collude.

4. Actions firms take to break down monopoly include (1) lobbying government to change the law underpinning that monopoly if the monopoly is a legal monopoly and (2) making slight modifications to a monopolist's patent within the limits of the law. (391-394)

   Firms protect their monopolies by (1) advertising and lobbying government, (2) producing products as nearly unique as possible, and (3) charging low prices.

   Firms will spend money and time to obtain monopoly power until the marginal cost equals the marginal benefit.

5. Oligopoly tends to be most conducive to technological change. (397-398)

   Since the typical oligopolist realizes on-going economic profit, it has the funds to carry out research and development. Moreover, the belief that its competitors are innovating also forces it to do so.

   Oligopolists are constantly searching for new ways to get an edge on competitors, so most technological advance takes place in oligopolistic industries.

● SHORT-ANSWER QUESTIONS

1. Is the high pay that top-level management receives an example of the monitoring problem?

2. What are the implications of the monitoring problem for economics?

3. How can corporate takeovers improve firms' efficiency?

4. What is meant by the phrase "Competition is a process, not a state"?

5. List two actions firms take to break down monopoly.

6. List three ways in which firms protect their monopoly.

7. Explain how technology has changed competition.

8. Which market structure is most conducive to technological advance? Why?

MATCHING THE TERMS
Match the terms to their definitions

_____ 1. corporate takeover

_____ 2. dynamic efficiency

_____ 3. incentive-compatible contract

_____ 4. lazy monopolist

_____ 5. monitoring problem

_____ 6. network externality

_____ 7. reverse engineering

_____ 8. technological development

_____ 9. technological lock-in

_____ 10. X-inefficiency

a. Problem that employees' incentives differ from the owner's incentives.

b. An agreement in which the incentives and goals of both parties match as closely as possible.

c. Firm that does not push for efficiency, but merely enjoys the position it is already in.

d. Operating less efficiently than possible, which raises costs.

e. A firm or a group of individuals issues an offer to buy up the stock of a company to gain control and to install its own managers.

f. The ability to promote cost-reducing or product-enhancing technological change.

g. Firm buying up other firms' products, disassembling them, figuring out what's special about them, and then copying them within the limits of the law.

h. When greater use of a product increases the benefit of that product to everyone.

i. When prior use of a technology makes the adoption of subsequent technologies difficult.

j. The discovery of new or improved products or methods of production.

PROBLEMS AND APPLICATIONS

1. College Retirement Equities Fund (CREF) is a pension fund for college teachers, which has billions of dollars invested in the stock market. A few years ago fund participants voted on a proposal that would have placed strict limits on the amount of compensation paid to CREF executives. Why do you think 75 percent of the participants voted against the proposal?

2. Demonstrate, using the graph below, the net gain to producers and the net loss to consumers if suppliers are able to restrict their output to Q_R. What is the net deadweight loss to society?

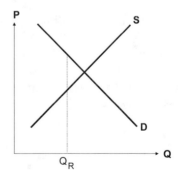

3. How can branding increase the monopoly position of a firm?

● A BRAIN TEASER

1. Consider the graph below, which represents a natural monopoly.

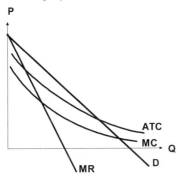

a. What price would the firm charge if it were unregulated?

b. What price would you advise to the government that the firm should be allowed to charge? Explain your answer.

c. What potential problem might your advice create over time?

● MULTIPLE CHOICE

Circle the one best answer for each of the following questions:

1. The *best* definition of an incentive-compatible contract is:
   a. a contract with sympathetic incentives.
   b. a contract with compatible incentives.
   c. a contract in which the incentive structure makes the managers' goals correspond with the firm's goals as much as possible.
   d. a contract that pays bonuses.

2. A firm is making no profit. If there is X-inefficiency, what can we conclude?
   a. The firm is operating at least cost.
   b. The firm is operating using the fewest inputs possible.
   c. The firm is operating less efficiently than economically possible.
   d. We can say nothing about the efficiency of the firm.

3. The goals of managers are generally:
   a. identical to the goals of owners.
   b. identical to the goals of workers.
   c. totally inconsistent with the goals of owners.
   d. somewhat inconsistent with the goals of owners.

4. When there is little competitive pressure, large organizations have a tendency to make decisions that:
   a. benefit the consumer.
   b. benefit the managers.
   c. benefit the government.
   d. do not benefit anyone.

5. Economists would expect that generally:
   a. for-profit firms operate more efficiently than nonprofit firms.
   b. nonprofit firms operate more efficiently than for-profit firms.
   c. for-profit firms operate equally efficiently as nonprofit firms.
   d. nonprofit firms cannot exist because they operate so inefficiently.

6. Refer to the graph below. If suppliers restrict output to OL, what area represents the welfare loss to society?
    a. A + B.
    b. B + C.
    c. C + D.
    d. A + D.

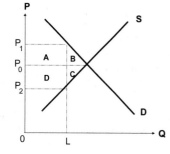

7. A patent is:
    a. a type of reverse engineering.
    b. a type of natural monopoly.
    c. a type of corporate takeover.
    d. a type of legal monopoly.

8. If average total costs are decreasing throughout the relevant range of production, the industry will be:
    a. a natural monopoly.
    b. a prime target for rent-seeking.
    c. a lazy monopolist.
    d. an example of monitoring problems.

9. When regulated monopolies are allowed to pass on all cost increases to earn a normal profit, they:
    a. have a strong incentive to operate efficiently.
    b. have little incentive to operate efficiently.
    c. become a focal point of reverse engineering.
    d. will apply for a patent.

10. Ways in which firms try to protect their monopoly include all the following *except*:
    a. advertising and lobbying.
    b. charging low prices.
    c. making their product unique.
    d. reverse engineering.

11. Many economists consider competition today to be more intense than competition ten or twenty years ago because of:
    a. technological development.
    b. greater governmental regulation and more reverse engineering.
    c. more corporate takeovers and higher trade barriers.
    d. greater political tensions among governments and lower taxes.

12. Technological advance:
    a. decreases competition.
    b. decreases specialization.
    c. increases productivity.
    d. increases costs of production.

13. The market structure most conducive to technological advance is:
    a. perfect competition.
    b. monopolistic competition.
    c. oligopoly.
    d. monopoly.

14. Technological advances are most likely for markets that:
    a. earn economic profits.
    b. have one firm supplying all the output.
    c. are protected by government regulation.
    d. produce where MR = MC.

15. Network externalities:
    a. occur when greater use of a product increases the benefit of that product to everyone.
    b. inhibit the development of industry standards.
    c. make it more likely that the most efficient standards will be adopted.
    d. reduce the likelihood that an industry becomes a "winner takes all" industry.

● POTENTIAL ESSAY QUESTIONS

You may also see essay questions similar to the "Problems & Applications" and "A Brain Teaser" exercises.

1. Describe two actions firms take to break down monopoly and three they take to protect their monopoly.

2. Explain how technology has changed competition.

■ ANSWERS ■

SHORT-ANSWER QUESTIONS

1. The monitoring problem is the problem of seeing that self-seeking individuals working for an organization follow the goals of the organization rather than their own goals. The high pay that top-level management receives might be pay for performance, or it might be an example of the monitoring problem. To determine which it is, one would need to consider the specific case and determine whether there are incentive-compatible contracts (such as low base pay and high optional bonuses based on performance) that make the managers' goals consistent with the goals of the firms' owners. (385-386)

2. Economics assumes that firms and the economy operate efficiently because firms maximize profits. The monitoring problem undermines that assumption since managers, to some degree, will follow their own goals rather than the profit-maximizing goal. Firms may become lazy monopolists and exhibit X-inefficiency. So the monitoring problem has significant implications. The degree to which firms become lazy monopolists will be limited, however, by competitive pressures. (385-386)

3. Answer *2* above pointed out that when there is a monitoring problem a firm can exhibit X-inefficiency—it can have higher costs than necessary. When that happens, the firm's stock price will fall and it may be worthwhile for another firm to come in and take the inefficient firm over, eliminate the inefficiency, and develop better incentive-compatible contracts. Often, these takeovers are financed by large amounts of debt, which means that the resulting firm must make high interest payments. So even if the new firm does not establish incentive-compatible contracts, the high debt can force the firm to operate more efficiently. (388-389)

4. The basic idea of economics is that self-seeking individuals try to do the best they can for themselves—to make life as easy as possible for themselves. One of the important ways in which they can do that is to create a

monopoly for themselves. When they do that they create the possibility of profits for other individuals who come in and steal their market—thereby breaking down their monopoly. This process of monopolization and competition breaking down the resulting monopoly is pervasive in our economy and is what is meant by the phrase: "competition is a process, not a state." (391-392)

5. To acquire monopoly profits for themselves, firms will break down monopoly through political and economic means. If the monopoly is a legal monopoly, high profit will lead potential competitors to lobby to change the law underpinning that monopoly. If the law can't be changed—say, the monopolist has a patent—potential competitors will generally get around the obstacle by developing a slightly different product or by working on a new technology that avoids the monopoly but satisfies the relevant need. (391-392)

6. Three ways in which firms protect their monopoly are (1) advertising and lobbying; (2) producing products as nearly unique as possible; and (3) charging low prices that discourage entry. All these methods cost the firms money in the short run, but increase their monopoly rents (profits) in the long run. (394)

7. Technological advance is a result of specialization that allows producers to learn more about the particular aspects of production in which they specialize. As they learn more, they not only become more productive but are more likely to generate technological advances because they gain a deeper understanding of their speciality. Technology has changed competition because competitive success hinges on an ability to specialize. (396)

8. Oligopoly tends to be most conducive to technological change. Since the typical oligopolist realizes on-going economic profit, it has the funds to carry out research and development. Moreover, the belief that its competitors are innovating also forces it to do so. Oligopolists are constantly searching for new ways to get an edge on competitors, so most technological advance takes place in oligopolistic industries. (397-398)

━━━ ● ANSWERS ● ━━━

MATCHING

1-e; 2-f; 3-b; 4-c; 5-a; 6-h; 7-g; 8-j; 9-i; 10-d.

━━━ ● ANSWERS ● ━━━

PROBLEMS AND APPLICATIONS

1. The fund participants are aware of incentive-compatible contracts. Structuring CREF executive pay based on the fund's performance in the stock market increases the chances that the interests of the owners and the managers of the fund are compatible. (385-386)

2. As shown on the graph below, if suppliers restrict supply to Q_R, they will be able to charge a price of P_R, which is higher than competitive price, P_C. This gives suppliers supplying Q_R additional income, labeled A. Some suppliers are excluded from the market (Q_c-Q_R). They lose area C in producer surplus. Consumers who cannot now purchase as many goods lose consumer surplus represented by area B. Those who can afford the higher-priced good pay the higher price. Higher expenditures are represented by area A (the additional income to firms). Since A is transferred from consumers to producers, this is not a loss to society as a whole. However, areas B and C are lost by consumers and producers, respectively, but not transferred to anyone. Those areas, B and C, are the deadweight loss to society. (Figure 17-2 on page 391)

3. Branding is an important way in which firms try to differentiate their goods and services from real or potential competitors. If a firm is successful in distinguishing its product from other producers and in associating that

positive image with its brand name, then other firms will find it difficult to compete. Remember that differentiation (through branding and other means) acts as a barrier to entry, and the stronger the barriers, the greater the monopoly power. (See pages 394-395; "Real World Application")

━━━ ● ANSWERS ● ━━━

BRAIN TEASER

1. **a.** The natural monopolist would produce quantity where $MC = MR$ and charge the price that corresponds to that quantity from the demand curve. This combination is shown on the graph below as (Q_M, P_M). (392-394)

   b. I would advise the government that the natural monopolist should be regulated to charge a price where average total cost curve intersects the demand curve. This way, the monopolist earns normal profit. You cannot require that $MC = P$ because at that price $MC < ATC$, losses would be incurred, and the monopolist would not be able to survive under these circumstances. (393)

   c. The problem with this advice is that there is little incentive for the firm to keep its costs down. Why should it keep costs down if it knows it can raise its price sufficiently to cover its costs? (393)

━━━ ● ANSWERS ● ━━━

MULTIPLE CHOICE

1. c   While incentive-compatible contracts could pay bonuses, they do not necessar-

ily have to, which rules out this option. The contract with compatible incentives doesn't say what it is compatible with. See the definition of incentive-compatible contract on pages 385-386.

2. c   Whenever there is X-inefficiency, the firm is not operating at least cost. That is, it is not economically efficient. See page 388.

3. d   Managers' goals are somewhat inconsistent with the goals of the owners. However, managers do not want to get fired and competitive pressures mean managers must make sufficient profits so they don't get fired. To that degree, their goals are consistent with the goals of the owners. See pages 385-388.

4. b   When there are no competitive pressures, organizations tend to make decisions that benefit employees or the decision-makers within these organizations rather than consumers. See pages 385-388.

5. a   While for-profit firms can exhibit inefficiency, the market limits that inefficiency. See pages 385-388.

6. b   The welfare loss is the triangle made up of areas *B* and *C*. This area represents the producer and consumer surplus lost but not gained by the other. The other areas represent transfers. See page 391 and Figure 17-2.

7. d   A patent is the legal right to be the sole supplier of a product. It is a type of legal monopoly. See page 397.

8. a   A "natural monopoly" is the best answer. The other answers fit, but nowhere near as closely. The statement you are asked to complete is essentially the definition of a natural monopoly. See pages 392-393.

9. b   When you can pass on cost increases, why try to hold costs down? See page 390.

10. d   Reverse engineering is a method firms use to try to break down other firms' monopolies. See pages 391-392.

11. a   Technological development increases competition by providing more specialized products. See page 396.

12. c   Technological advance requires specialization. Specialization increases productivity and lowers costs of production. This results in more intense competition. See page 396.

13. c   Oligopoly provides the best market structure for technological advance because firms have an incentive to innovate (they face competition) and they also have the profits to devote to research and development. See pages 397-398.

14. a   Technological advance requires large amounts of investment. Only firms that earn economic profit can afford to invest in research and development. See pages 396-399.

15. a   Network externalities promote industry standards, although those standards may not be the most efficient. They also increase the likelihood that an industry becomes a "winner takes all" industry. See page 398.

━━━━━ ANSWERS ━━━━━

POTENTIAL ESSAY QUESTIONS

The following are annotated answers. They indicate the general idea behind the answer.

1.   Actions firms take to break down monopoly include (1) lobbying government to change the law underpinning that monopoly if the monopoly is a legal monopoly and (2) making slight modifications to a monopolist's patent within the limits of the law. Firms protect their monopolies by (1) advertising and lobbying government, (2) producing products as nearly unique as possible, and (3) charging low prices.

2.   Technological advance requires specialization. Specialization increases productivity and lowers costs of production. This results in intense competition.

ANTITRUST POLICY AND REGULATION

18

CHAPTER AT A GLANCE

This review is based upon the learning objectives that open the chapter.

1. Judgment by performance is the view that competitiveness of a market should be judged by the behavior of firms in that market; judgment by structure is the view that competitiveness of a market should be judged by the structure of the market. (405-406)

   Both criteria have their problems. There are no definitive criteria for judging whether a firm has violated antitrust statutes. However, since 1945, most court decisions have relied on judgment by structure for the reason of practicality.

2. Public outrage at the formation and activities of trusts such as Standard Oil led to the passage of the Sherman Act, the Clayton Act, and the Federal Trade Commission Act. (406-408)

✔ *Know what these Acts outlaw.*

3a. The IBM case was dropped by the United States, but the prosecution of the case likely led to some of IBM's problems in the 1990s. It won but it also lost. (410-412)

   Changes in technology can alter market structure (the degree of competition) rather rapidly.

3b. The AT&T case was settled by AT&T agreeing to be split up into regional companies handling local service, and AT&T itself competing in the long-distance market. (412-413)

   Up until 1982, AT&T was a regulated monopoly. Telephone services were believed to be a natural monopoly. The communications market continues to change. AT&T was bought by Bell South, a former baby Bell. The new company is still AT&T.

3c. Whether one sees Microsoft as a monopolist depends on whether one views it in a static or dynamic framework. (414-416)

   In 2000, the U.S. court ruled that Microsoft was guilty of being a monopoly and involved in anticompetitive practices. The government recommended breaking the company into two separate companies. Microsoft had the decision reversed on appeal. The case was settled through mediation. Eventually, Microsoft agreed not to undertake non-competitive practices in the future. More recently the European Commission has found Microsoft guilty of conspiring to monopolize the European market. Microsoft and the EU are still negotiating.

   Note: Since the 1980s the United States has been more lenient in antitrust cases because of a change in ideology, the globalization of the U.S. economy, and the increasing complexity of technology.

4. Horizontal mergers are companies in the same industry merging together. Vertical mergers are combinations of two companies, one of which supplies inputs to the other's production. Conglomerate mergers are combinations of unrelated businesses. (417-418)

✔ *Know the differences. Also become familiar with the various terms associated with takeovers.*

   Most antitrust policy has concerned horizontal mergers.

5. Five reasons why unrelated firms merge include: (419)
   - To achieve economies of scope;
   - To get a good buy;
   - To diversify;
   - To ward off a takeover bid; and
   - To strengthen their political-economic influence.

   When unrelated firms merge, this constitutes a conglomerate merger.

6. Other countries have historically had more lenient antitrust laws compared to U.S. antitrust laws. Perhaps the biggest change on the international front is the emergence of a strong European antitrust policy. (420-422)

   Before the European Union (EU) was formed most now member-nations had relatively weak antitrust laws because large domestic firms needed to achieve economies of scale to be profitable; nations saw the international market as the relevant market; these countries were less populist than the United States; and saw government and business as partners, not antagonists. But, since the establishment of the EU, the European Commission, the EU's antitrust agency, has become less lenient toward non-European firms.

   Antitrust issues are by nature global, but a country's antitrust laws are not.

7. The government can also affect the competitive process by (1) regulation, (2) government ownership, and (3) industrial policy. (422-425)

   Two types of regulation are price regulation and social regulation. Price regulation is regulation directed at industries that have natural monopoly elements. Social regulation is concerned with the condition under which goods and services are produced, the safety of those goods, and the side effects of production on society.

   Government-owned firms tend not to have an incentive to hold costs down.

   An industrial policy is a formal policy that government takes toward business.

● SHORT-ANSWER QUESTIONS

1. How does judging competition by structure differ from judging competition by performance?

2. What are the two provisions of the Sherman Antitrust Act? What year was it passed by Congress?

3. What was the resolution of the IBM antitrust case?

4. What was the resolution of the AT&T antitrust case?

5. What was the resolution of the Microsoft antitrust case?

6. What are horizontal, vertical, and conglomerate mergers?

7. What are five reasons why unrelated firms would want to merge?

8. How has U.S. antitrust enforcement changed over the last ten to twenty years? What contributed to the change?

9. What is perhaps one of the biggest changes on the international antitrust front in recent years?

10. List three alternatives to antitrust policy that government can use to affect the competitive process.

MATCHING THE TERMS
Match the terms to their definitions

___ **1.** acquisition	**a.** A company buys another company; the buyer has the right of direct control of the resulting venture, but does not necessarily exercise that direct control.
___ **2.** antitrust policy	
___ **3.** Clayton Antitrust Act	**b.** A merger of companies in the same industry.
___ **4.** conglomerate merger	**c.** A merger in which one company buys another that does not want to be bought.
___ **5.** deacquisition	**d.** A government's formal policy toward business.
___ **6.** European Commission	**e.** The act of combining two firms.
___ **7.** Federal Trade Commission Act	**f.** A law that made it illegal for firms to use "unfair methods of competition" and to engage in "unfair or deceptive acts or practices."
___ **8.** sovereign wealth fund	**g.** Combination of unrelated businesses.
___ **9.** horizontal merger	**h.** Combination of two companies, one of which supplies inputs to the other's production.
___ **10.** hostile takeover	**i.** An industry in which significant economies of scale make the existence of more than one firm inefficient.
___ **11.** industrial policy	
___ **12.** judgment by performance	**j.** Judging the competitiveness of markets by the number of firms in the market and their market shares.
___ **13.** judgment by structure	**k.** Judging the competitiveness of markets by the behavior of firms in that market.
___ **14.** merger	**l.** Law passed by the U.S. Congress in 1890 to attempt to regulate the competitive process.
___ **15.** natural monopoly	**m.** One company's sale of parts of another company it has bought.
___ **16.** Sherman Antitrust Act	**n.** Purchase of a firm by another firm that then takes direct control over its operations.
___ **17.** takeover	
___ **18.** vertical merger	**o.** Government's policy toward the competitive process.
	p. A law that made four specific monopolistic practices illegal.
	q. The European Union's antitrust agency.
	r. Investment funds held by governments.

● PROBLEMS AND APPLICATIONS

1. For each of the following situations determine what type of merger activity is being undertaken.

   a. Pepsi-Cola Corporation buys Pizza Hut and Kentucky Fried Chicken.

   b. A bakery corporation buys up a grocery store chain.

   c. A steel manufacturer buys up all other steel producing factories.

2. American auto manufacturers sell their models at a lower price on the west coast in an effort to remain competitive with Japanese imports. This has upset many car dealers on the east coast who view this as price discrimination and therefore a violation of antitrust. Which antitrust law are these dealers referring to? What possible defense might the auto manufacturers claim?

3. Suppose a grocery store is interested in buying a particular brand name of canned tomato soup from a food processing vendor. However, before the vendor agrees to deliver any cans of tomato soup the grocer is required to sign a contract guaranteeing that the grocery store will buy all of its canned goods from the vendor. The grocery store objects because it argues that such a requirement is against the law. Which antitrust law would the grocer argue is being broken? What possible defense might the vendor claim?

4. You're an economist in the Antitrust Division of the Justice Department. In the personal computer market, suppose Compaq has petitioned to merge with AT&T. Compaq currently has 14% of the PC market and AT&T has 3%. The other three large firms in the market, Packard Bell, IBM, and Apple, have 11%, 9%, and 8% of the PC market respectively. In the Windows-based PC market, Compaq has 18% of the market and AT&T has 5%. The other three large firms in the Windows-based PC market, Packard Bell, IBM, and Hewlett Packard, have 14%, 12%, and 9% of the PC market respectively.

    a. Calculate the approximate Herfindahl and 4-firm concentration ratios for these firms in each industry before the merger and after the merger.

    b. If you were Compaq's economist, which industry definition would you suggest using when making your petition to the Justice Department?

c. Give an argument why the merger might decrease competition.

d. Give an argument why the merger might increase competition.

● A BRAIN TEASER

1. Suppose you are advising a regulatory agency of the Federal government to regulate the prices of a monopolist depicted by the graph below.

    a. Would you recommend setting prices at point A where $MC = MR$? Why or why not?

    b. What would be the minimum price you would recommend? Why?

c. Does the monopolist still enjoy economic profit at the minimum price you determined in *b*? If so, what area on the graph represents that profit?

d. What potential problem might be associated with your recommendation?

⬤ MULTIPLE CHOICE

Circle the one best answer for each of the following questions:

1. When judging the competitiveness of markets by the behavior of firms in that market, one is using the:
   a. "judgment by performance" criteria.
   b. "judgment by structure" criteria.
   c. "judgment by merger" criteria.
   d. "judgment by antitrust" criteria.

2. When judging the competitiveness of markets by the size and number of firms in that market, one is using the:
   a. "judgment by performance" criteria.
   b. "judgment by structure" criteria.
   c. "judgment by merger" criteria.
   d. "judgment by antitrust" criteria.

3. An important law in the U.S. regulation of markets is the:
   a. Standard Oil Antitrust Act of 1890.
   b. Sherman Antitrust Act of 1890.
   c. Alcoa Antitrust Act of 1890.
   d. Lincoln Antitrust Act of 1890.

4. In the Standard Oil and American Tobacco Company antitrust cases in 1911, the Court ruled that:

   a. the two companies had a monopolistic structure and therefore should be broken up.
   b. the two companies were guilty of unfair business practices and therefore should be broken up.
   c. the Sherman Antitrust Act did not apply.
   d. the two companies had to be disbanded.

5. The Clayton Antitrust Act made all of the following monopolistic practices illegal *except*:
   a. price discrimination.
   b. tie-in contracts.
   c. interlocking directorships.
   d. creation of a natural monopoly.

6. In the ALCOA antitrust case in 1945, the Court ruled that the:
   a. company had a monopolistic structure and therefore should be broken up.
   b. company was guilty of unfair business practices and therefore should be broken up.
   c. Sherman Antitrust Act did not apply.
   d. two companies had to be disbanded.

7. The resolution of the IBM antitrust case was that:
   a. IBM was broken up.
   b. IBM was combined with AT&T.
   c. the government dropped the IBM case.
   d. IBM was allowed to stay in the large-computer market but was kept out of the personal-computer market.

8. The resolution of the AT&T antitrust case of the 1980s was:
   a. AT&T agreed to split up into three operating divisions.
   b. AT&T agreed to split up and allow the Baby Bells to be independent.
   c. AT&T was combined with MCI and Sprint.
   d. MCI and Sprint were broken off from AT&T and developed as competitors to AT&T.

9. In the Microsoft antitrust case:
   a. the government ruled that Microsoft was a monopoly and was involved in anti-competitive practices.
   b. the government divided Microsoft into two companies.
   c. Microsoft agreed to government regulation of its prices.
   d. Microsoft was forced to get out of the Internet business.

10. When two merging companies are in the same industry, their merger is called a:
    a. horizontal merger.
    b. vertical merger.
    c. conglomerate merger.
    d. takeover merger.

11. When one of two merging companies supplies one or more of the inputs to the other merging company, the merger is called a:
    a. horizontal merger.
    b. vertical merger.
    c. conglomerate merger.
    d. takeover merger.

12. When two companies that are in unrelated industries merge, the merger is called a:
    a. horizontal merger.
    b. vertical merger.
    c. conglomerate merger.
    d. takeover merger.

13. Reasons firms would want to enter into a conglomerate merger include all the following *except:*
    a. to achieve economies of scope.
    b. to diversify.
    c. to strengthen their political and economic influence.
    d. to become a natural monopoly.

14. Antitrust laws in Europe:
    a. have become less lenient toward non-European firms.
    b. tend to be stronger than in the United States.
    c. tend to be approximately the same strength as antitrust laws in the United States.
    d. do not exist; there are no antitrust laws in Europe.

15. Globalization has impacted competition and antitrust in that:
    a. U.S. antitrust policymakers increasingly see the international market (as opposed to the purely domestic market) as the relevant market when determining the degree of competition in a market.
    b. U.S. antitrust policymakers are more strictly enforcing antitrust laws to ensure firms do not take advantage of consumers.
    c. U.S. antitrust policymakers are less willing to allow large domestic firms to achieve economies of scale.
    d. we can expect fewer international jurisdictional battles in antitrust.

16. Industrial policy is:
    a. a policy of government entering into competition with business.
    b. a policy of government industries entering into competition with business.
    c. a formal policy that government takes towards business.
    d. a laissez-faire policy of government towards business.

● POTENTIAL ESSAY QUESTIONS

You may also see essay questions similar to the "Problems & Applications" and "A Brain Teaser" exercises.

1. Why has there been a more lenient approach in the United States to the enforcement of antitrust laws in recent years?

2. What is the difference between horizontal, vertical, and conglomerate mergers? Which merging activity has most U.S. antitrust policy been concerned with? What is the principal guideline used by the Department of Justice since 1982 with respect to mergers?

━━━━━ ANSWERS ━━━━━

SHORT-ANSWER QUESTIONS

1. Judging competition by structure is the view that competitiveness of a market should be judged by the number of firms in the market and their market shares. Judging competition by performance is the view that competitiveness of a market should be judged by the behavior of firms in that market. (405)

2. The two provisions of the Sherman Antitrust Act passed in 1890 are (1) every contract, combination, or conspiracy in restraint of trade is illegal and (2) every person who shall monopolize or attempt to monopolize shall be deemed guilty of a misdemeanor. (406-407)

3. The IBM case was dropped by the United States, but the prosecution likely led to IBM's problems in the 1990s. (412-413)

4. The AT&T case was settled by AT&T agreeing to be split up into regional companies handling local service and AT&T itself competing in the long-distance market. (412-413)

5. Whether one sees Microsoft as a monopolist depends on whether one views it in a static or dynamic framework. But the court did find Microsoft guilty. However, Microsoft may have still won by ending up only having to promise to not behave monopolistically in the future. (414-416)

6. A horizontal merger is a merger between two companies in the same industry. A vertical merger is a firm merging with the supplier of one (or more) of its inputs. A conglomerate merger is a merger between unrelated businesses. (417-419)

7. Five reasons why unrelated firms would want to merge are (1) to achieve economies of scope, (2) to get a good buy, (3) to diversify, (4) to ward off a takeover bid, and (5) to strengthen political-economic influence. (419)

8. Because of greater international competition, more and more, U.S. antitrust policymakers see the international market as the relevant market. The policy focus is shifting from "Is U.S. industry internally competitive so that it does not take advantage of the consumer?" to "Is U.S. industry internationally competitive so that it can compete effectively in the world economy?" (420)

9. Perhaps the biggest change on the international antitrust front is the emergence of a strong European antitrust policy. Before the European Union (EU) was established, most of the now member-countries had relatively weak antitrust laws. But now the European Commission, the EU's antitrust agency has become much less lenient toward non-European firms. Antitrust issues are by nature global, but a country's antitrust laws are not. (420-422)

10. The government can also affect the competitive process by (1) regulation, (2) government ownership, and (3) industrial policy. (422-425)

━━━━━ ANSWERS ━━━━━

MATCHING

1-a; 2-o; 3-p; 4-g; 5-m; 6-q; 7-f; 8-r; 9-b; 10-c; 11-d; 12-k; 13-j; 14-e; 15-i; 16-l; 17-n; 18-h.

━━━━━ ANSWERS ━━━━━

PROBLEMS AND APPLICATIONS

1. a. Conglomerate merger (designed to achieve economies of scope). (419)
    b. Vertical merger. (419)
    c. Horizontal merger. (417-419)

2. The Clayton Antitrust Act prohibits price discrimination if it has the effect of lessening competition. The auto manufacturers could claim that the lower prices on the west coast do not result in less competition but are instead a consequence of the intense competition that exists on the west coast. (408)

3. The Clayton Antitrust Act prohibits tie-in contracts in which the buyer must agree to deal exclusively with one seller and not to purchase goods from competing sellers. The vendor may claim that this is not reducing competition. (408)

4. **a.** The Herfindahl index is calculated by adding the squared value of the market shares of all the firms in the industry. The 4-firm concentration ratio is calculated by adding the market shares of the four firms with the largest market shares.
PC Market: Before the merger, the Herfindahl index is greater than $14^2 + 11^2 + 9^2 + 8^2 + 3^2 = 196 + 121 + 81 + 64 + 9 = 471$. The exact Herfindahl index cannot be calculated since we do not know the market shares of all the firms in the market. The 4-firm concentration ratio before the merger is $14 + 11 + 9 + 8 = 42$. The Herfindahl index after the merger is at least $17^2 + 11^2 + 9^2 + 8^2 = 289 + 121 + 81 + 64 = 555$. The 4-firm concentration ratio after the merger is $17 + 11 + 9 + 8 = 45$.
Windows-based PC market: Before the merger, the Herfindahl index is at least $18^2 + 14^2 + 12^2 + 9^2 + 5^2 = 324 + 196 + 144 + 81 + 25 = 770$. The 4-firm concentration ratio before the merger is $18 + 14 + 12 + 9 = 53$. The Herfindahl index after the merger is at least $23^2 + 14^2 + 12^2 + 9^2 = 529 + 196 + 144 + 81 = 950$. The 4-firm concentration ratio after the merger is $23 + 14 + 12 + 9 = 58$. (Chapter 16)

b. I would use the broader PC-based computer industry definition because the Herfindahl indexes and concentration ratios are lower in this market, indicating more competition. (Chapter 16)

c. The merger might be expected to decrease competition because within the PC market the Herfindahl index rises from 471 to 555 and the 4-firm concentration ratio rises from 42 to 45. This suggests the merger would result in a less competitive market. The larger merged company may have more ability to set prices above marginal costs, resulting in a loss to society. (Welfare loss with a monopoly is shown graphically in the chapter on monopoly.) (Chapters 16-17)

d. This merger might be expected to increase competition if Compaq and AT&T cannot compete separately against the other three firms in the market. A combined Compaq and AT&T might also be more competitive in a global market. Most likely, however, this merger will lower the level of domestic competition—especially if the merger would enable economies of scale and scope to be experienced. (405-406)

ANSWERS

A BRAIN TEASER

1. **a.** I would not recommend setting prices at point A where $MC = MR$ because at that point price is less than average total costs. The monopolist would be losing money and would eventually go out of business. This is shown in the graph below. (405-406 and Chapter 15 on monopoly)

b. The minimum price I would recommend would be where the marginal cost curve intersects the demand curve at point B in the graph above. This eliminates all welfare loss to society associated with a monopoly and is the competitive price and quantity. (405-406 and Chapter 15 on monopoly)

c. The monopolist still enjoys economic profit that is represented by the shaded area in the graph above. (405-406 and Chapter 15 on monopoly)

d. There may be little incentive for the monopolist to hold down its costs. (405-406 and Chapter 15 on monopoly)

ANSWERS

MULTIPLE CHOICE

1. a   "Judgment by performance" is judging the competitiveness of markets by the performance (behavior) of firms in that market. See pages 405-406.

2. b   The "judgment by structure" is judging the competitiveness of markets by their structure (the relative size and number of competitors in that market). See pages 405-406.

3. b   The Sherman Antitrust Act passed in 1890 was an early law passed to regulate the competitive process. See pages 405-406.

4. b The early cases were decided upon by the performance, or abuse, standard, not on whether the companies were monopolies. The Act applies to unfair business practices as well as to monopolistic structure. "Disbanded" would mean the companies ceased totally to exist, whereas these two companies were changed by reorganization. See pages 407-408.

5. d The Clayton Antitrust Act is a law that made four specific monopolistic practices illegal. They are price discrimination, tie-in contracts, interlocking directorships, and buying a competitor's stock to reduce competition. See page 408.

6. a In the ALCOA case, the Court applied the monopolistic structure (or judgment by structure) standard. See pages 408-409.

7. c The antitrust suit was dropped since new competitors had changed the market structure. See pages 410-412.

8. b AT&T split up into the Baby Bells. These Baby Bells then consolidated in the 1990s. See page 413.

9. a The court ruled that Microsoft was a monopoly and that it had engaged in anti-competitive practices. Essentially, Microsoft just promised not to behave monopolistically in the future. See pages 414-415.

10. a A horizontal merger is when two firms that produce the same product merge. See pages 417-419.

11. b A vertical merger is when two firms involved in different parts of the same production process merge. See pages 418-419.

12. c A conglomerate merger is when two firms producing unrelated products merge. See page 419.

13. d Unrelated firms would want to merge to achieve economies of scope, to get a good buy, to diversify, to ward off a takeover bid, or to strengthen their political-economic influence. See page 419.

14. a Most countries have weaker antitrust laws compared to the United States. Nonetheless, the European Commission, the EU's antitrust agency, has become less lenient with non-European firms. See pages 420-421.

15. a The U.S. policy focus of government is shifting from "Is U.S. industry internally competitive so that it does not take advantage of the consumer?" to "Is U.S. industry internationally competitive so that it can compete effectively in the world economy?" See page 420.

16. c Industrial policy is a formal policy government takes toward business. An example is the U.S. military-industrial complex. See pages 424-425.

ANSWERS

POTENTIAL ESSAY QUESTIONS

The following are annotated answers. They indicate the general idea behind the answer.

1. In recent years antitrust law has worked mainly through its deterrent effect. First, because of a change in American ideology "big business" is no longer viewed as necessarily being bad. Second, the market structure in the U.S. has become less relevant as the United States has become more integrated into the global economy where there is generally more competition. Third, as technologies have become more complicated, the issues in antitrust enforcement also have become more complicated for the courts to handle. More-over, the IBM, AT&T, and Microsoft cases have significantly influenced perceptions of antitrust, creating a more lenient modern approach.

2. Two companies in the same industry merging is a horizontal merger. A firm merging with the supplier of one of its inputs is a vertical merger. Two firms in unrelated industries merging is a conglomerate merger. Horizontal mergers have attracted most U.S. antitrust policy attention. The principal guideline used by the Justice Department since 1982 is to carefully consider the approval or disapproval of a merger if, after the merger, the Herfindahl index would be above 1000.

Pretest
Chapters 14 - 18

Take this test in test conditions, giving yourself a limited amount of time to complete the questions. Ideally, check with your professor to see how much time he or she allows for an average multiple choice question and multiply this by 25. This is the time limit you should set for yourself for this pretest. If you do not know how much time your teacher would allow, we suggest 1 minute per question, or 25 minutes.

1. In a perfectly competitive market:
   a. firms sell a differentiated product where one firm's output can be distinguished from another firm's output.
   b. there are so many firms selling output in the market that no one individual firm has the ability to control the market price.
   c. economic profits can be earned in the long run.
   d. there are very strong barriers to entry that can prevent potential competitors from entering the market.

2. Refer to the graph below. A competitive firm is producing at output A.

   a. It could increase profits by increasing output.
   b. It could increase profits by decreasing output.
   c. It cannot increase profits.
   d. One can say nothing about profits from the diagram.

3. In order to maximize profits (or minimize losses) a firm should produce at that output level at which:
   a. total revenue is maximized.
   b. average total cost are minimized.
   c. marginal revenue equals marginal cost.
   d. marginal revenue exceeds marginal cost by the greatest amount.

4. Refer to the graph below. The firm's profit in this case will be measured by:

   a. the rectangle ABEF.
   b. the rectangle ACDF.
   c. the rectangle ABHG.
   d. the rectangle BCDE.

5. Normal profits are:
   a. approximately 6 percent of costs.
   b. approximately 8 percent of costs.
   c. returns to the owners of business for the opportunity cost of their implicit inputs.
   d. generally larger than accounting profits.

6. Monopoly is the market structure in which:
   a. one firm makes up the entire market.
   b. two firms make up the entire market.
   c. the market is made up of a few big firms.
   d. firms make a supernormal profit.

7. A profit-maximizing monopolist will:
   a. produce an output level at which MR > MC.
   b. produce an output level at which P > MC.
   c. always earn an economic profit in the short run.
   d. increase production when MR < MC.

8. Refer to the graph below. The monopolist represented is:

  a. making a profit.
  b. making a loss.
  c. making zero profit.
  d. unable to determine what kind of profit the monopolist is making.

9. Price discrimination requires:
  a. identifying groups of customers with different elasticities.
  b. separating customers in some way.
  c. limiting customers' ability to re-sell the product between different groups.
  d. all of the other options listed to be successful.

10. Refer to the graph below. Which area represents the welfare loss due to a monopolist?
  a. A.
  b. A + B.
  c. B + C.
  d. A + B + C.

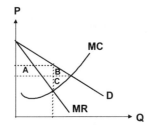

11. In a market there are many firms selling differentiated products. This market is:
  a. a competitive market.
  b. a monopolistically competitive market.
  c. an oligopoly.
  d. a monopoly.

12. Refer to the graph below. Which of the following is the output chosen by the monopolistically competitive firm?
  a. Q_1.
  b. Q_2.
  c. Q_3.
  d. Output cannot be determined.

13. In a contestable market model of oligopoly, prices are determined by:
  a. costs and barriers to exit.
  b. costs and barriers to entry.
  c. costs, barriers to entry, and barriers to exit.
  d. costs alone.

14. The top four firms in the industry have 10 percent, 8 percent, 8 percent, and 6 percent of the market. The four-firm concentration ratio of this market is:
  a. 8.
  b. 32.
  c. 66.
  d. 264.

15. A market has the following characteristics: There is strategic decision-making, output is somewhat restricted, there are few firms, and some long-run economic profits are possible. This market is:
  a. a monopoly.
  b. an oligopoly.
  c. monopolistically competitive.
  d. perfectly competitive.

16. A firm is making no profit. If there is X-inefficiency, what can we conclude?
  a. The firm is operating at least cost.
  b. The firm is operating using the fewest inputs possible.
  c. The firm is operating less efficiently than economically possible.
  d. We can say nothing about the efficiency of the firm.

17. Economists would expect that generally:
  a. for-profit firms operate more efficiently than nonprofit firms.
  b. nonprofit firms operate more efficiently than for-profit firms.
  c. for-profit firms operate equally efficiently as nonprofit firms.
  d. nonprofit firms cannot exist because they operate so inefficiently.

18. Refer to the graph below. If suppliers restrict output to OL, what area represents the welfare loss to society?

  a. A + B.
  b. B + C.
  c. C + D.
  d. A + D.

19. When regulated monopolies are allowed to pass on all cost increases to earn a normal profit, they:
a. have a strong incentive to operate efficiently.
b. have little incentive to operate efficiently.
c. become a focal point of reverse engineering.
d. will apply for a patent.

20. Technological advances are most likely for markets that:
a. earn economic profits.
b. have one firm supplying all the output.
c. are protected by government regulation.
d. produce where MR = MC.

21. When judging the competitiveness of markets by the behavior of firms in that market, one is using the:
a. "judgment by performance" criteria.
b. "judgment by structure" criteria.
c. "judgment by merger" criteria.
d. "judgment by antitrust" criteria.

22. The resolution of the IBM antitrust case was that:
a. IBM was broken up.
b. IBM was combined with AT&T.
c. the government dropped the IBM case.
d. IBM was allowed to stay in the large-computer market but was kept out of the personal-computer market.

23. In the Microsoft antitrust case:
a. the government ruled that Microsoft was a monopoly and was involved in anti-competitive practices.
b. the government divided Microsoft into two companies.
c. Microsoft agreed to government regulation of its prices.
d. Microsoft was forced to get out of the Internet business.

24. When one of two merging companies supplies one or more of the inputs to the other merging company, the merger is called a:
a. horizontal merger.
b. vertical merger.
c. conglomerate merger.
d. takeover merger.

25. Industrial policy is:
a. a policy of government entering into competition with business.
b. a policy of government industries entering into competition with business.
c. a formal policy that government takes towards business.
d. a laissez-faire policy of government towards business.

━━━━ **ANSWERS** ━━━━

1.	b	(14:2)	**14.**	b	(16:13)
2.	a	(14:5)	**15.**	b	(16:15)
3.	c	(14:7)	**16.**	c	(17:2)
4.	b	(14:11)	**17.**	a	(17:5)
5.	c	(14:15)	**18.**	b	(17:6)
6.	a	(15:1)	**19.**	b	(17:9)
7.	b	(15:3)	**20.**	a	(17:14)
8.	c	(15:7)	**21.**	a	(18:1)
9.	d	(15:12)	**22.**	c	(18:7)
10.	c	(15:14)	**23.**	a	(18:9)
11.	b	(16:1)	**24.**	b	(18:11)
12.	a	(16:5)	**25.**	c	(18:16)
13.	c	(16:10)			

Key: The figures in parentheses refer to multiple choice question and chapter numbers. For example (1:2) is multiple choice question 2 from chapter 1.

WORK AND THE LABOR MARKET

19

CHAPTER AT A GLANCE

This review is based upon the learning objectives that open the chapter.

1. An increase in the marginal tax rate is likely to reduce the quantity of labor supplied because it reduces the net wage of individuals and hence, through individuals' incentive effect, causes them to work less. (431-432)

   Higher marginal tax rates reduce the incentive to work.

2. Elasticity of market labor supply depends on: (434-435)
   • Individuals' opportunity cost of working.
   • The type of market being discussed.
   • The elasticity of individuals' supply curves.
   • Individuals entering and leaving the labor market.

   An elastic supply of labor means workers are quite responsive to a change in the wage rate. For example, an increase in the wage will result in a relatively large increase in the quantity of labor supplied (the number of people looking for work).

3. Derived demand is the demand for factors of production by firms, which depends on consumers' demands. (435-436)

   For example, if the demand for automobiles increases, the demand for automotive workers increases. It simply takes more workers to produce more cars.

4. Four factors that influence the elasticity of demand for labor are: (436)
   • The elasticity of demand for the firm's good.
   • The relative importance of the factor in the production process.
   • The possibility of, and cost of, substitution in production.
   • The degree to which marginal productivity falls with an increase in the labor.

An elastic demand for labor means employers are quite responsive to a change in the wage rate. For example, an increase in the wage rate will result in a rather dramatic reduction in the number of workers employers wish to employ.

5. A monopsony is a market in which there is only one buyer. A bilateral monopoly is a market in which a single seller faces a single buyer. (440-441)

   A monopsony will hire fewer workers (Q_m) and pay a lower wage (W_m) compared to the competitive outcome.

6. To understand real-world labor markets one must broaden the analysis. (441-443)

   What we see in the real world is a consequence of the interaction of market, social, and political forces.

7. Three types of discrimination are: (443-445)

   • Discrimination based on individual characteristics that will affect job performance.
   • Discrimination based on correctly perceived statistical characteristics of the group.
   • Discrimination based on individual characteristics that don't affect job performance or are incorrectly perceived.

   One can think of discrimination as treating individuals whom one views as equals unequally.

   See also, Appendix A: "Derived Demand."

● SHORT-ANSWER QUESTIONS

1. Use the theory of rational choice and the concept of opportunity cost to explain why firms generally offer time-and-a-half for workers to work on Thanksgiving Day.

2. Suppose Congress passes an increase in the marginal income tax rate. What is the likely effect on work effort?

3. List four factors that influence the elasticity of labor supply.

4. Explain how the demand for labor is a derived demand.

5. List four factors that influence the elasticity of labor demand.

6. Define the terms *monopsonist* and *bilateral monopoly*.

7. On average, women earn about 85 cents for every $1 earned by men. Discuss this phenomenon in terms of political forces, social forces, and market forces.

8. What are three types of discrimination?

MATCHING THE TERMS
Match the terms to their definitions

____ **1.** bilateral monopoly

____ **2.** closed shop

____ **3.** comparable worth laws

____ **4.** derived demand

____ **5.** downsizing

____ **6.** efficiency wages

____ **7.** entrepreneurship

____ **8.** incentive effect

____ **9.** labor market

____ **10.** marginal factor cost

____ **11.** monopsony

____ **12.** union shop

a. A market in which only a single firm hires labor.

b. A firm in which all workers must join the union.

c. A market with only a single seller and a single buyer.

d. A firm in which the union controls hiring.

e. Wage that is above the going market wage; paid to keep workers happy and productive.

f. Factor market in which individuals supply labor services for wages to other individuals and to firms that demand labor services.

g. Labor services that involve high degrees of organizational skills, concern, oversight, responsibility, and creativity.

h. How much a person will change his or her hours worked in response to a change in the wage rate.

i. Laws mandating comparable pay for comparable work.

j. The additional cost to a firm of hiring another worker.

k. A reduction in the workforce of major corporations, especially at the level of middle management.

l. The demand for factors of production by firms, which depends on consumers' demands.

● PROBLEMS AND APPLICATIONS

1. Use the graph below to answer the following questions.

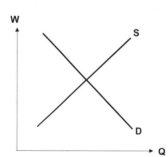

a. Label the equilibrium wage and number of workers.

b. If wages were set by the government above the equilibrium wage, what happens to the quantity supplied and the quantity demanded for labor? How do they differ?

c. Show how a technological innovation that leads to a higher demand for labor affects equilibrium wage and quantity of labor.

2. Consider again demand and supply in a labor market. For each of the following situations determine whether there would be an increase or a decrease in demand or supply of labor. Furthermore, determine the impact on the equilibrium wage rate (W) and the equilibrium quantity (Q) of labor. (You may want to use a graph of demand and supply curves for labor to help you.)

a. The demand for the product workers are producing increases.

b. It is Christmas Day, and workers value their leisure time more highly.

c. The other factory in town is now offering a higher wage rate.

d. The fringe (nonmonetary) benefits of this job have increased substantially. For example, workers are offered more lucrative health and dental coverage, better retirement programs, paid vacations, and company cars.

e. The price of a machine, which is a substitute for this labor, is now less expensive and its productivity has increased substantially due to an increase in technology. Note: the new technology does not affect worker productivity.

f. The firms in this industry have successfully convinced government to impose stricter tariffs and import quotas on a foreign good that is a substitute for the good produced by these workers.

g. The government has just adopted an "open-door" immigration policy.

h. Workers are now more productive.

3. Answer the following questions using the graph below.

a. Label the equilibrium wage and number of workers on the graph if the market is competitive.

b. Label the equilibrium wage and number of workers on the graph under a monopsonist. Compare this with the competitive outcome.

c. If there is a worker's union, what would be the equilibrium wage and level of employment?

A1. Complete the table below for a perfectly competitive firm that produces halogen light bulbs. Each light bulb sells for $1. (Marginal values refers to the marginal change of increasing to that row, i.e., the marginal physical product of going from 23 to 24 workers is 9. The same goes for marginal revenue product.)

	No. of Workers	Total Product per hour	Marginal Physical Product per hour	Average Product per hour	Marginal Revenue Product per hour
	20	200		—	
A	21	—	—	—	15
B	22	228	—	—	—
C	23	—	—	10.39	—
D	24	—	9	—	—
E	25	—	—	10.20	—
F	26	260	—	—	—

a. Draw the corresponding labor demand curve, from the values in the table.

b. Suppose the price of halogen light bulbs falls to $.50 per bulb. How does this change labor demand?

c. If halogen light bulbs sold for $1 per bulb as in (a), how many workers would the firm hire if wages were $7 per hour? How many workers would the firm hire if wages were $11 per hour?

● A BRAIN TEASER

1. Your boss has given you three possible combinations of raw materials in addition to labor and capital (machines) to produce the desired production target at the company's new production facility. Your job is to determine the least cost combination of inputs to employ. Suppose the price per unit of raw material usage per hour is $5, the wage rate per hour is $10, and the cost per hour for machines is $20. The marginal physical product (or productivity) of raw material, labor, and capital usage associated with the three combinations of input usage is summarized in the table below. Which combination of input usage will minimize the firm's costs of production to produce the desired production target at the new facility?

	MPP of Raw Material	MPP of Labor	MPP of Capital
Comb. A:	5	10	50
Comb. B:	10	20	40
Comb. C:	20	15	30

● MULTIPLE CHOICE

Circle the one best answer for each of the following questions:

1. Generally, economists believe the higher the wage:
   a. the higher the quantity of labor supplied.
   b. the greater the supply of labor.
   c. the lesser the supply of labor.
   d. the lower the quantity of labor supplied.

2. As the wage rate increases the opportunity cost of leisure:
   a. increases.
   b. decreases.
   c. remains the same.
   d. cannot be determined given the information provided.

3. An increase in the marginal tax rate will:
   a. increase the quantity of labor supplied.
   b. increase the supply of labor.
   c. decrease the supply of labor.
   d. decrease the quantity of labor supplied.

4. The irony of any need-based program is that it:
   a. increases the number of needy.
   b. decreases the number of needy.
   c. creates other needs.
   d. destroys needs.

5. Which of the following is *not* a factor influencing the elasticity of market labor supply?
   a. Individuals' opportunity cost of working.
   b. The elasticity of individuals' supply curves.
   c. The elasticity of market labor demand.
   d. Individuals entering and leaving the labor market.

6. Which of the following is *not* a reason why the labor supply for heads of households (primary workers) is more inelastic than that for secondary workers?
   a. Institutional factors, such as hours of work, are only slightly flexible.
   b. There are many more new secondary workers who can enter the market than there are primary workers.
   c. Heads of households have responsibility for seeing that there's food and shelter for the household family members.
   d. There are more secondary workers than primary workers.

7. The term "derived demand" refers to:
   a. demand by consumers for advertised products.
   b. the demand for luxury goods that is derived from cultural phenomena such as fashion.
   c. the demand for factors of production by firms.
   d. the demand for derivatives.

8. The more elastic the demand for a firm's good:
   a. the more elastic the firm's derived demand for factors.
   b. the less elastic the firm's derived demand for factors.
   c. The elasticity of demand for a firm's good has nothing to do with the firm's derived demand.
   d. The elasticity of demand could cause the elasticity of the derived demand to be either higher or lower.

9. As a factor becomes more important in the production process, the:
   a. firm's derived demand for the factor becomes less elastic.
   b. firm's derived demand for the factor becomes more elastic.
   c. firm's derived demand will not be affected.
   d. elasticity of the derived demand could become either higher or lower.

10. Economists distinguish entrepreneurship from labor because:
    a. entrepreneurship is more like capital.
    b. entrepreneurship has nothing to do with labor.
    c. entrepreneurship is such an important part of labor that it needs a specific discussion.
    d. entrepreneurs receive only profit.

11. A firm has just changed from being a competitive firm to being a monopolist. Its derived demand for labor:
    a. will increase.
    b. will decrease.
    c. might increase or might decrease.
    d. is unaffected because whether the firm is a competitive firm or a monopolist has no effect on the firm's derived demand for labor.

12. A monopsony in a labor market has:
    a. only a single seller and a single buyer of labor.
    b. only a single seller of labor.
    c. only a single buyer of labor.
    d. one seller and two buyers.

13. Compared to a competitive labor market, a monopsonist hires:
    a. fewer workers and pays them a higher wage.
    b. fewer workers and pays them a lower wage.
    c. more workers and pays them a higher wage.
    d. more workers and pays them a lower wage.

14. Which of the following cases of discrimination is likely to be most easily eliminated with market forces?
    a. A warehousing firm turns down an applicant because she is physically unable to lift boxes of the weight required by the job.
    b. An Internet firm begins a younger worker at a lower pay because younger workers are more likely to leave the job shortly after being trained.
    c. A manufacturing firm decides against hiring an individual who is black (even though the candidate is the most qualified) because the person doing the hiring is white.
    d. A retail store decides against hiring an individual who is black (even though the candidate is the most qualified) because they believe their customers will be less likely to buy from blacks.

15. Discrimination that is likely the most difficult to eliminate is discrimination that has:
    a. a social motivation.
    b. a cultural motivation.
    c. a political motivation.
    d. an economic motivation.

A1. The graph below shows the marginal revenue product of workers. If the wage is $10, approximately how many workers should it hire?
    a. 4.
    b. 8.
    c. 12.
    d. 16.

A2. The marginal product of input A is 20. The marginal product of input B is 40. The price of input A is 2. The price of input B is 3. Which of the following would be the best recommendation you could give based on this information? The firm should
    a. hire more A and less B.
    b. hire more B and less A.
    c. hire more of both A and B.
    d. not change its hiring of A and B.

● POTENTIAL ESSAY QUESTIONS

You may also see essay questions similar to the "Problems & Applications" and "A Brain Teaser" exercises.

1. What is a monopsony and how does a monopsony determine the quantity of workers employed and the wage it pays? How does this compare with the competitive labor market outcome? What is a bilateral monopoly? Could a bilateral monopoly result in a competitive labor market outcome?

2. How do market, social, and political forces interact in determining the equilibrium wage and quantity of workers employed in any real-world labor market?

ANSWERS

SHORT-ANSWER QUESTIONS

1. Work involves opportunity cost. By working one more hour, you have one less hour to devote to nonmarket activities. The theory of rational choice in the case of work means that you will supply work as long as the opportunity cost of working is less than the wage received. Since the opportunity cost of working on a holiday is greater than on other days, firms must offer workers higher wages to work on Thanksgiving Day. This demonstrates that the supply curve for labor is upward sloping: the higher the wage, the higher the quantity of labor supplied. (430-432)

2. An increase in the marginal tax rate is likely to reduce the quantity of labor supplied because it reduces the net wage of individuals and lowers the opportunity cost of not working. (431-432)

3. Factors that affect the elasticity of labor supply include (1) the individuals' opportunity costs of working, (2) the type of labor market, (3) the elasticity of the individuals' labor supplied, and (4) the individuals entering and leaving the market. (431-435)

4. Derived demand is the demand for factors of production by firms, which depends on consumers' demands. For example, if the demand for medical care increases, the demand for nurses increases. It simply takes more nurses to deliver more medical care. (435-436)

5. Factors that influence the elasticity of labor demand are (1) the elasticity of demand for the firm's good, (2) the relative importance of labor to production, (3) the possibility of, and costs of, substitution in production, and (4) the degree to which marginal productivity falls with an increase in labor. (436)

6. A *monopsonist* is the only buyer in a market. A *bilateral monopoly* is a market in which a single seller faces a single buyer. (440-441)

7. Real-world labor markets are complicated and must be explained through the interaction of political, social, and market forces. For example, the fact that women earn about 85 percent of men's earnings must be explained by these forces. Here are some of the many ways in which these forces can explain this phenomenon: It is argued that employers discriminate against women, paying them less for the same job, because they have a distaste for hiring women. This is an example of social forces at play and would result in lower wages. Women's lower pay may also result from social forces that discourage mothers from working outside the home so that women will supply labor intermittently, lowering their wage. This is an example of social forces and market forces. Comparable worth laws, anti-discrimination laws, and affirmative action laws have been passed in an effort to counteract this pay inequality. These are examples of social, political and legal forces at play in real-world labor markets. (441-443)

8. Three types of discrimination are (1) discrimination based on individual characteristics that affect job performance, (2) discrimination based on correctly perceived statistical characteristics of the group; and (3) discrimination on individual characteristics that do not affect job performance or that are incorrectly perceived. (443-445)

ANSWERS

MATCHING

1-c; 2-d; 3-i; 4-l; 5-k; 6-e; 7-g; 8-h; 9-f; 10-j; 11-a; 12-b.

ANSWERS

PROBLEMS AND APPLICATIONS

1. a. Equilibrium wage and number of workers with demand, D_0, and supply, S, are shown on the graph below as W_E and Q_E. At this point, the quantity of labor demanded equals the quantity of labor supplied. At a wage above W_E, there will be pressure for wages to fall because the quantity of labor supplied exceeds the quantity of labor demanded. At a wage below W_E, there will be pressure for wages to rise because the

quantity of labor demanded exceeds the quantity of labor supplied. (Figure 19-2 on page 437)

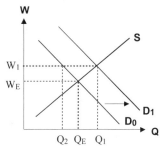

b. If wages were set by the government at W_1, the quantity of labor supplied would rise to Q_1 and the quantity of labor demanded would fall to Q_2. Quantity supplied would exceed quantity demanded. This is shown in the graph above. (Figure 19-3 on page 439)

c. A technological innovation that leads to a higher demand for labor will lead to a higher equilibrium wage and higher quantity of labor employed as the demand curve shifts to the right from D_0 to D_1. Equilibrium wage will rise to W_1 and equilibrium quantity of labor will rise to Q_1. (437-438 and Figure 19-3 on page 439)

2. a. The demand for labor would increase, increasing W and Q. (Applying concepts introduced in the appendix to this chapter, notice that the increase in the demand for the product increases the price of the product. The higher price for the product increases workers' marginal revenue product—MRP = MPP × P—which is the competitive firms' demand for labor.) (435-436, 454-456)

    b. The supply of labor would decrease on Christmas Day, which would increase W and decrease Q. (431-436 and Figure 19-3 on page 439)

    c. Supply would decrease, increasing W and decreasing Q. (431-436)

    d. Supply would increase, decreasing W and increasing Q. (431-436)

    e. Demand would decrease, decreasing W and Q. (437-439)

    f. Demand would increase, increasing W and Q. (437-439)

    g. Supply would increase, decreasing W and increasing Q. (431-436)

h. Demand would increase (according to the appendix: workers' MRP would be greater), increasing W and Q. (437-439)

3. a. If the market is competitive, the wage and employment level will be where the demand and supply curves for labor intersect. This is at W_c and Q_c respectively on the graph below. (Figure 19-4 on page 440)

    b. The monopsonist will hire workers where the marginal factor cost of labor intersects the demand for labor. A monopsonist would hire Q_m workers, less than the competitive level, and pay a wage W_m, lower than the competitive wage. (Figure 19-4 on page 440)

    c. Unions would push for higher wages than a firm in a competitive market or a monopsonist would be willing to pay. The wage would be somewhere between W_u and W_m and would depend on negotiating skills and other noneconomic forces. The number of workers hired would then be somewhere between Q_u and Q_m depending on the negotiated wage. (Figure 19-4 on page 440)

A1. Below is the completed table for a perfectly competitive firm which produces halogen light bulbs.

	No. of Workers	Total Product per hour	Marginal Physical Product per hour	Average Product per hour	Marginal Revenue Product per hour
	20	200		10	
A	21	215	15	10.24	15
B	22	228	13	10.36	13
C	23	239	11	10.39	11
D	24	248	9	10.33	9
E	25	255	7	10.2	7
F	26	260	5	10	5

We use the following relationships to fill in the table: Marginal physical product equals the change in the total product. Average product is the total product divided by the number of workers. Marginal revenue product equals marginal physical product times the price of the product. (454-456, especially Figure A19-1)

a. The corresponding labor demand curve is shown on the graph below. The demand curve shows the marginal revenue product at each quantity of labor. Labor demand is a derived demand. A firm is willing to pay a wage up to the marginal revenue product of the additional worker to hire that additional worker. That is, keep hiring workers for as long as MRP > W and stop hiring when MRP = W. (454-456, especially Figure A19-1)

b. If the price of halogen light bulbs fell to $.50 per bulb, the marginal revenue product would be halved and the demand curve for labor would shift in as shown on the accompanying graph and table. (455-456)

No. of Workers	Total Product per hour	Marginal Physical Product per hour	Average Product per hour	($0.50) Marginal Revenue Product per hour
	20	200		10	
A	21	215	15	10.24	7.5
B	22	228	13	10.36	6.5
C	23	239	11	10.39	5.5
D	24	248	9	10.33	4.5
E	25	255	7	10.2	3.5
F	26	260	5	10	2.5

c. A firm in a competitive industry will hire up to the point where the wage equals *MRP* (*MPP* times *P*). So at $1 per bulb and wages of $7 per hour, the firm would hire up to 25 workers; At $1 per bulb and a minimum wage of $11 per hour the firm would hire up to 23 workers. (456-457)

══════════ ANSWERS ══════════

A BRAIN TEASER

1. See the table on the next page. The cost minimizing condition exists at the combination of inputs (factors) employed for which the MPP/P for each input is equal. Therefore, Combination B should be adopted. For Combination A, the productivity for the money spent (MPP/P) is greater for capital than for the other inputs. Therefore, more capital and less labor and raw materials should be employed. By doing so, the firm will be able to produce the same amount at a lower cost. For Combination C, more raw materials should be employed in the production process while less labor and capital should be employed (because MPP/P for raw materials is higher).

Remember: if the cost minimization condition is not met, the firm could hire more of the input with the higher marginal product-to-price ratio and less of the other inputs, and produce the same amount of output at a lower cost. (456-457)

	MPP of Raw Material	MPP of Labor	MPP of Capital
Comb. A:	5	10	50
	(MPP/P=5/5=1)	(MPP/P=10/10=1)	(MPP/P=50/20=2.5)
Comb. B:	10	20	40
	(MPP/P=10/5=2)	(MPP/P=20/10=2)	(MPP/P=40/20=2)
Comb. C:	20	15	30
	(MPP/P=20/5=4)	(MPP/P=15/10=1.5)	(MPP/P=30/20=1.5)

ANSWERS

MULTIPLE CHOICE

1. a   The supply curve of labor is generally considered to be upward sloping. When there is a movement along the supply curve caused by an increase in the wage, the movement is called an increase in the quantity supplied, not an increase in supply. See pages 430-432.

2. a   The opportunity cost of not working increases as the wage rate rises and that is why the labor supply curve slopes upward. See pages 431-433.

3. d   An increase in the marginal tax rate will reduce the quantity of labor supplied because it reduces the net wage of individuals and hence, through individuals' incentive effect, causes them to work less. See pages 431-432.

4. a   A need-based program reduces people's incentives to prevent themselves from becoming needy, and thus a need-based program increases the number of needy. See pages 431-432.

5. c   The elasticity of demand has no impact on the elasticity of supply. See pages 434-435.

6. d   The number of primary workers compared to the number of secondary workers has nothing to do with elasticity. See pages 434-435.

7. c   Derived demand refers to the fact that the demand for factors of production is derived from the demand for a firm's goods. Because consumers demand a firm's goods, the firm demands factors of production to produce those goods. See pages 435-436.

8. a   When a rise in price will cause significant loss of revenue (which it does when demand for the good is elastic), the firm takes that into account in its decision of what to pay workers and how many workers to hire. See page 436.

9. a   As the importance of a factor to the production process rises, the less elastic is demand. This is because a more important factor has fewer substitutes. See page 436.

10. c   Entrepreneurship is a type of creative labor that is very important and needs a separate discussion. Entrepreneurs can receive more than merely profit. See page 436.

11. b   The monopolist uses marginal revenue, which is lower than the price that the competitive firm uses. Therefore, the monopolist's derived demand for labor is lower. See page 436.

12. c   While a monopoly is a market with a single seller, a monopsony is a market with a single buyer. See page 440.

13. b   A profit-maximizing monopsonist will pay a lower wage and hire fewer workers than if that labor market were competitive. See pages 440-441.

14. c   Differential treatment based upon individual characteristics that do not affect job performance is costly to firms. Market forces will work toward eliminating this type of discrimination. The warehousing firm is turning down an applicant who cannot fulfill the duties of the job. The Internet firm is basing its decision on characteristics of the group to which the

individual belongs. Although the particular individual may not quit the job, such statistical discrimination, using such rules of thumb does have a basis in keeping costs of a firm down. The final option is also costly to the firm. The easiest discrimination to eliminate is when economic incentives are working to eliminate it. See pages 443-445.

15. d   Discrimination that is economically motivated out of individuals pursuing their self-interest is most difficult to eliminate. People are least motivated to adopt change they believe may personally hurt them. See pages 443-446.

A1. b   The firm should hire workers until the wage equals the marginal revenue product. See pages 454-456.

A2. b   The marginal revenue per dollar is higher for input B so the firm should hire more of B and less of A. The other answers do not meet the cost minimization condition. See pages 456-457.

ANSWERS

POTENTIAL ESSAY QUESTIONS

The following are annotated answers. They indicate the general idea behind the answer.

1.   A monopsony is a market in which a single firm is the only buyer. The monopsonist's demand for labor is the market demand for labor. The monopsony also faces the market supply curve. The profit maximizing monopsony will hire fewer workers and pay a lower wage than the competitive outcome.

     A bilateral monopoly is a monopsony employing unionized workers. It's a bilateral monopoly because there is monopoly power on both sides of the labor market. It's possible that the monopoly power of the two sides will cancel out, giving rise to a competitive wage and quantity of labor employed.

2.   The economic forces of demand and supply, social forces, and legal or government forces all interact in the labor market. Social forces of "fairness," seniority, and discrimination as well as the political forces of child labor laws, comparable worth laws, equal opportunity laws, and laws governing unions, all affect the labor market along with the market forces of supply and demand.

WHO GETS WHAT?
THE DISTRIBUTION OF INCOME

● CHAPTER AT A GLANCE

This review is based upon the learning objectives that open the chapter.

1. A Lorenz curve is a geometric representation of the share distribution of income among families in a given country at a given time. (461-462)

    It shows the relative equality of the distribution of income. The farther below the diagonal line, the more _unequal_ the distribution of income.

2. Poverty is defined by the U.S. government as earning income equal to or less than three times an average family's minimum food expenditures as calculated by the U.S. Department of Agriculture. The official poverty measure is an absolute measure because it is based on the minimum food budget for a family. It is a relative measure because it is adjusted for average inflation. (464)

    The poverty income threshold level is approximately $21,000 for a family of four. Poverty figures, like all statistics, should be used with care. Think about some causes of poverty and the problems it poses for society.

3. The United States has less income inequality than most developing countries but more income inequality than many developed countries. (467-468)

    There is more income inequality among countries than income inequality within a country. Worldwide, income inequality is enormous. Therefore, the Lorenz curve of world income would show much more inequality than the Lorenz curve for a particular country.

4. In the United States wealth is significantly more unequally distributed than is income. (469-470)

    The bottom fifth have no net wealth while the top fifth have 80 percent of the wealth.

5. Two alternative ways to describe income distribution are the share distribution of income inequality and the income distribution according to socioeconomic characteristics. (461,470-473)

    Most Americans are in the middle class. However, income differs substantially by class and by other socioeconomic characteristics such as age, race, and gender.

6. Three problems in determining whether an equal income distribution is fair are: (1) people don't start from equivalent positions; (2) people's needs differ; and (3) people's efforts differ. (473-475)

    When most people talk about believing in equality of income, they usually mean an equality of opportunity to earn income.

    Fairness is a philosophical question. People must judge a program's fairness for themselves.

7. Three side effects of redistribution of income include:
    a. the labor/leisure incentive effect;
    b. the avoidance and evasion incentive effects;
    c. the incentive effect to look more needy than you are. (475-476)

    Income is difficult to redistribute because of incentive effects of taxes, avoidance and evasion effects of taxes, and incentive effects of redistribution programs.

8. Expenditure programs have been more successful than taxes in redistributing income. (476-480)

    On the whole, the U.S. tax system is roughly proportional, so it is not very effective as a means of redistributing income. Government spending programs are more effective than tax policy in reducing income inequality in the United States.

● SHORT-ANSWER QUESTIONS

1. What does a Lorenz curve show?

2. What is the U.S. official definition of *poverty*?

3. How is the poverty definition both an absolute and a relative measure?

4. How does income inequality in the United States compare with other countries?

5. How does the Lorenz curve for household wealth compare with the Lorenz curve for family income in the United States?

6. What are two alternative ways to describe income distribution?

7. You and your friends are having a lunchtime discussion about fairness. A friend offers a statement that since income distribution has become more unequal in the past few decades, income distribution in the United States has become less and less fair. Assume you are a contrarian. How do you respond?

8. "Nevertheless," your friend says, "I believe the current distribution is not fair. The government should do something to make the income distribution more equal." You agree to some extent, but warn that there are side effects of redistributing income. State your argument.

9. Which has been more successful in the United States in redistributing income: expenditure or taxation programs? Why?

10. What are five expenditure programs that redistribute income?

MATCHING THE TERMS
Match the terms to their definitions

___ 1. income

___ 2. Lorenz curve

___ 3. Medicare

___ 4. poverty threshold

___ 5. progressive tax

___ 6. proportional tax

___ 7. public assistance

___ 8. regressive tax

___ 9. share distribution of income

___ 10. Social Security system

___ 11. socioeconomic distribution of income

___ 12. Supplemental Security Income

___ 13. unemployment compensation

___ 14. wealth

a. A geometric representation of the share distribution of income among families in a given country at a given time.

b. The income below which a family is considered to live in poverty.

c. The relative division of total income among income groups.

d. Payments received plus or minus changes in value in a person's assets in a specific time period.

e. The value of the things individuals own less the value of what they owe.

f. The relative division or allocation of total income among relevant socioeconomic groups.

g. An average tax rate that increases with income.

h. A social insurance program that provides financial benefits to the elderly and disabled and to their dependents and/or survivors.

i. Means-tested social programs targeted to the poor and providing financial, nutritional, medical, and housing assistance.

j. An average tax rate that is constant regardless of income.

k. A multibillion-dollar medical insurance system.

l. Short-term financial assistance, regardless of need, to eligible individuals who are temporarily out of work.

m. An average tax rate that decreases with income.

n. A federal program that pays benefits, based on need, to the elderly, blind, and disabled.

● PROBLEMS AND APPLICATIONS

1. Use the Lorenz curve below to answer the following questions.

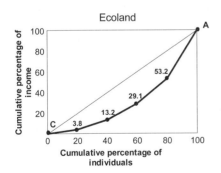

a. What percentage of total income do the top 20 percent of individuals in Ecoland receive?

b. What percentage of total income do the top 40 percent of individuals in Ecoland receive?

c.   Which value, the one in (a) or the one (b), is greater? Why?

d   What does the straight line in the diagram represent? Describe points A and C. Why is the Lorenz curve always anchored at those points?

2.   Use the following table to answer the questions.

Income quintile	% of Total Family Income		
	Eco-land	Fantasy-land	Text-land
Lowest 20%	5%	7%	2%
Second quintile	8	10	6
Third quintile	10	25	9
Fourth quintile	20	25	19
Highest 20%	57	33	64

a.   Draw a Lorenz curve for each country.

b.   Rank the countries from most equal income distribution to least equal income distribution.

3.   For each of the following state whether the tax is most likely proportional, regressive, or progressive with income.

a.   5 cent per gallon tax on gasoline.

b.   School taxes based on assessed value of a home.

c.   Sales tax of 6 percent.

d.   Medical insurance taxes of 1.45% on all income.

● A BRAIN TEASER

1.   You are completing your tax return. You are filing as a single taxpayer. Your income is $87,300. Deductions are $20,000. The rate is 10% for taxable income up to $7,550, 15% for taxable income up to $30,650, 28% of income between $30,650 and $74,200, and 33% of income above.

a.   Calculate your tax liability.

b.   Calculate your average tax rate.

c. Calculate your marginal tax rate.

d. Is the tax schedule proportional, regressive, or progressive? Explain your answer.

● MULTIPLE CHOICE

Circle the one best answer for each of the following questions:

1. The Lorenz curve is:
a. a type of supply curve.
b. a type of demand curve.
c. a geometric representation of the share distribution of income.
d. a geometric representation of the socioeconomic distribution of income.

2. Refer to the graph below. Which of the four Lorenz curves demonstrates the most income inequality?
a. A.
b. B.
c. C.
d. D.

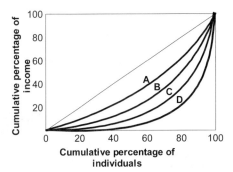

3. A family is in poverty if its income is:
a. above the poverty income threshold level.
b. less than $14,280.
c. less than three times the average food budget for that family size.
d. less than one-fifth the national average household income level for that family size.

4. The official definition of poverty is:
a. an absolute measure of poverty since it is based upon a minimum food budget determined in the 1960s.
b. a relative measure of poverty since the poverty line is defined as the income level that exceeds the income of 15 percent of all households in the United States.
c. both a relative and absolute measure of poverty since the minimum food budget is adjusted each year for average inflation in the economy.
d. neither an absolute nor relative measure of poverty since the poverty threshold changes each year.

5. If the government increases the amount of food stamps and housing assistance it gives out, the level of poverty in the United States, as officially defined:
a. will be reduced.
b. will be increased.
c. will remain unchanged.
d. cannot be determined from the information.

6. A Lorenz curve for the entire world would show:
a. more income inequality than in the United States.
b. less income inequality than in the United States.
c. approximately the same level of income inequality as in the United States.
d. no income inequality.

7. In a Lorenz curve for the United States, household wealth would:
a. show the same amount of inequality as does family income.
b. show more inequality than does family income.
c. show less inequality than does family income.
d. would show no wealth inequality at all.

8. Refer to the graph below. The Gini coefficient is shown by which area?
   a. A/B.
   b. A/(A + B).
   c. B/A.
   d. B/(A + B).

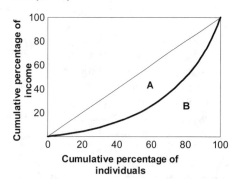

9. The U.S. class system is *best* represented by which shape?
   a. A diamond.
   b. A right-side-up pyramid with upper class on the top.
   c. A pentagon.
   d. A square.

10. Imposing a tax of 40 percent on high income workers in order to give the revenue to low income workers may not be especially effective in redistributing income if the tax:
    a. has large incentive effects.
    b. has no incentive effects.
    c. is seen as a sin tax.
    d. is not seen as a sin tax.

11. The largest government program to redistribute income is the:
    a. Social Security system.
    b. Medicaid program.
    c. Supplemental Nutritional Assistance Program (SNAP)
    d. Supplemental Security Income (SSI) program.

12. On the whole, the U.S. tax system is:
    a. unfair.
    b. roughly progressive.
    c. roughly proportional.
    d. roughly regressive.

13. In the United States, government spending programs:
    a. are less effective than tax policies in redistributing income.
    b. are more effective than tax policies in redistributing income.
    c. and tax policies are equally effective in redistributing income.
    d. and tax policies have had no measurable impact in redistributing income.

14. The U.S. federal program that pays benefits, based on need, to the elderly, blind, and disabled is called:
    a. Medicare.
    b. Medicaid.
    c. Temporary Assistance to Needy Families (TANF).
    d. Supplemental Security Income (SSI).

POTENTIAL ESSAY QUESTIONS

You may also see essay questions similar to the "Problems & Applications" and "A Brain Teaser" exercises.

1. Explain three problems in determining whether an equal income distribution is fair. When people talk about believing in the equality of income, what do they usually mean?

2. What are two direct methods through which government redistributes income? Which has generally been more successful and why?

ANSWERS

SHORT-ANSWER QUESTIONS

1. A Lorenz curve is a geometric representation of the share distribution of income among families in a given country at a given time. (461-462)

2. The official definition of *poverty* is an income equal to or less than three times an average family's minimum food expenditures as calculated by the U.S. Department of Agriculture. (464)

3. The official poverty measure is earning an absolute measure because it is based on the minimum food budget for a family. It is a relative measure because it is adjusted for average inflation. (464)

4. The United States has less income inequality than most developing countries but more income inequality than many developed countries. (467-468)

5. The Lorenz curve for household wealth is more bowed than the Lorenz curve for family income. This means that household wealth is less equally distributed than family income. (469-470 and Figure 20-5)

6. Two alternative ways to describe income distribution are the share distribution of income inequality and income distribution according to socioeconomic characteristics. (461)

7. Determining whether an equal income distribution is fair is problematic. You tell your friend that, first of all, people do not start from equivalent positions and income depends upon those initial positions. Second, people's needs differ; some people are happy with less income, while others seem to need a higher income. Lastly, people's efforts differ; some people are willing to work harder than others. Shouldn't that effort be rewarded with higher income? Equality is not synonymous with fairness. (473-475)

8. Although some might agree that a more equal distribution is desirable, there are side effects of redistributing income. They are: (1) A tax to redistribute income may result in a switch from labor to leisure and, consequently, less production and less total income. (2) An increase in taxes to redistribute income might lead to attempts to avoid or evade taxes, leading to a decrease in measured income. (3) Government programs to redistribute money may cause people to make themselves look poorer than they really are. (475-476)

9. In the United States, expenditure programs have been more successful than tax programs for redistributing income. This is because, on the whole, the U.S. tax system is roughly proportional, so it is not very effective as a means of redistributing income. (479-480)

10. Five expenditure programs to redistribute income are (1) Social Security, (2) public assistance, (3) Supplemental Security Income, (4) unemployment compensation, and (5) housing programs. (476-478)

ANSWERS

MATCHING

1-d; 2-a; 3-k; 4-b; 5-g; 6-j; 7-i; 8-m; 9-c; 10-h; 11-f; 12-n; 13-l; 14-e.

ANSWERS

PROBLEMS AND APPLICATIONS

1. **a.** 46.8%. The top 20 percent of individuals earn 46.8 percent of the income. Calculate this by starting at 80% on the horizontal axis. Draw a vertical line to the Lorenz curve. Look at the value on the vertical axis where this line intersects the Lorenz curve. This is the percent of income that the bottom 80% of individuals earn. To get the amount that the top 20% earn, subtract this number, 53.2, from 100. (461-462)

   b. 70.9%. Going through the same exercise as in 1(a) but starting at 60%, we find that the bottom 60% earn 29.1% of total income. Subtracting this from 100, we get 70.9%, the percent of total income earned by the top 40%. (461-462)

c. (b) is greater than (a). This has to be true, because the vertical axis is the *cumulative* percentage of income. If the top 20% earn a certain percentage of the total, the top 40% includes that top 20% plus more. (461-462)

d. The straight line represents the Lorenz curve if income were equally distributed. Point A says that 100% of individuals earn 100% of the income. This is true by definition. Point C says that 0% of individuals earn 0% of the income. The Lorenz curve is anchored at those points by definition. (461-462)

2. a. First we want to calculate the cumulative percentage of income for each country. We do this below by cumulatively adding together consecutive percentages.

Income quintile	Cumulative % of Income		
	Eco-land	Fantasy-land	Text-land
Lowest 20%	5%	7%	2%
Second quintile	13	17	8
Third quintile	23	42	17
Fourth quintile	43	67	36
Highest 20%	100	100	100

The Lorenz curve is the graph of these values connected. This is shown in the graph below. (461-462)

b. Fantasyland; Ecoland; Textland. The country most bowed out to the right of the diagonal line has the least equal income distribution. This is Textland. The country bowed out the least has the most equal income distribution. This is Fantasyland. Ecoland is in the middle. (461-462)

3. a. 5 cent per gallon tax on gasoline is a sales tax and sales taxes tend to be slightly regressive since poor people often spend a higher percentage of their incomes on gasoline than do rich people. (476)

b. School taxes based on assessed value of a home are considered to be roughly proportional since the value of a person's home is related to income. (476)

c. A sales tax is regressive since poor people often consume a higher percentage of their incomes than do rich people. (476)

d. Medical insurance taxes are proportional since the rate is 1.45% on all income, no matter how high or low. (476)

━━━━ **ANSWERS** ━━━━

A BRAIN TEASER

1. a. $14,482.50. First deduct $20,000 from $87,300 to get taxable income of $67,300. You pay 10% on the first $7,550, 15% on income from $7,551 to $30,650, and 28% on the remaining $36,650. Your taxes are $.10 \times \$7,550 + .15 \times 23,100 + .28 \times \$36,650 = \$755 + \$3465 + \$10,262 = \$14,482$. Since there is no income above $74,200, no income is taxed at the 33% tax rate. (476)

b. 16.5%. Your average tax rate is total taxes divided by total income: $14,482/$87,300. (476)

c. 28%. Your marginal tax rate is the rate at which your last dollar earned is taxed. This is 28%. (476)

d. The tax schedule is progressive. A progressive tax is one in which the average tax rate increases with income. As can be seen by the tax schedule, the marginal tax rate is increasing. Since the marginal tax rate is increasing, and it is above the average tax rate (because of deductions), the average tax rate is increasing too. (476)

━━━━ **ANSWERS** ━━━━

MULTIPLE CHOICE

1. c A Lorenz curve describes how income is distributed in a country. It has proportion of the population on the horizontal axis and proportion of income on the vertical axis. See pages 461-462.

2. d   A Lorenz curve describes how income is distributed in a country. It has proportion of the population on the horizontal axis and proportion of income on the vertical axis. The further the Lorenz curve is from the diagonal, the more unequally income is distributed. See pages 461-462.

3. c   A family is in poverty if its income is equal to or less than three times an average family's minimum food expenditures as calculated by the U.S. Department of Agriculture. See page 464.

4. c   The poverty threshold equals three times the minimum food budget. Thus, it is in part an absolute measure. But since it is adjusted for average inflation and not just inflation on food and since food prices have risen more slowly than average inflation, it is a relative measure. See page 464.

5. c   These aspects of income are not taken into account in determining U.S. poverty figures. See page 465.

6. a   Since world income is more unequally divided among countries, the world Lorenz curve would have to show more income inequality. See pages 467-468.

7. b   In the United States wealth is considerably less equally distributed than income. See pages 469-470.

8. b   The Gini coefficient describes the degree of income inequality. It is the area between the diagonal and the Lorenz curve divided by the total area below the diagonal. See "Added Dimension" box on page 466.

9. c   The U.S. class system is best seen as a pentagon. There is a relatively small upper class, a large middle class, and a smaller but still relatively large lower class. See pages 471-472, especially Figure 20-6.

10. a   Incentive effects can undermine attempts to redistribute income. See page 475.

11. a   As stated in the text, the Social Security system is by far the largest expenditure program to supplement income. See page 477.

12. c   The overall U.S. tax system is roughly proportional. This can be deduced from the observation that the U.S. tax system does little to redistribute income. Whether it is fair or not is a matter of opinion. See pages 479-480 and Figure 20-7.

13. b   In the United States, government spending programs are more effective than tax policies in redistributing income. See pages 479-480 .

14. d   Medicare is a multibillion-dollar medical assistance insurance system for the elderly. Medicaid is medical assistance to the poor. TANF provides assistance to needy families with children under age 19. See pages 476-478.

━━━ ANSWERS ━━━

POTENTIAL ESSAY QUESTIONS

The following are annotated answers. They indicate the general idea behind the answer.

1.   Three problems in determining whether an equal income distribution is fair are (1) people don't start from equal positions, (2) people's needs differ, and (3) people's efforts differ.

When people talk about believing in equality of income, they usually mean they believe in equality of opportunity for comparably endowed individuals to earn income. If equal opportunity of equals leads to inequality of income, that inequality in income is fair. Unfortunately, there's enormous latitude for debate on what constitutes equal opportunity of equals.

2.   The two methods are: taxation (policies that tax the rich more than the poor) and expenditures (programs that help the poor more than the rich). Most government redistribution of income works through expenditure programs (public assistance; social programs), not through taxes. This is because on the whole, the U.S. tax system is roughly proportional, so it is not very effective as a means of redistributing income.

MARKET FAILURE VERSUS GOVERNMENT FAILURE

CHAPTER AT A GLANCE

This review is based upon the learning objectives that open the chapter.

1. An externality is an effect of a decision on a third party not taken into account by the decision maker. (486-488)

   Externalities can either be negative (have undesirable social side effects in which case society would want less of the good) or positive (have desirable social side effects in which case society would want more of the good). Externalities are only one source of market failure.

   3 sources of market failure:
   - *Externalities*
   - *Public goods*
   - *Imperfect information*

   Any time a market failure exists there is a reason for possible government intervention to improve the outcome. However, government failure (government intervention in the market to improve the market failure actually making matters worse) is always a possibility. Economic policy is often a choice between market failure and government failure.

2. Ways to deal with externalities include: (1) direct regulation, (2) incentive policies (tax incentive policies and market incentive policies), and (3) voluntary solutions. (488-492)

   Economists tend to like incentive policies to deal with externalities.

   The optimal policy is one in which the marginal cost of undertaking the policy equals the marginal benefit of that policy.

3. A public good is a good that is nonexclusive (no one can be excluded from its benefits) and nonrival (consumption by one does not preclude consumption by others). (492-495)

   The public/private good differentiation is seldom clear-cut since many goods are somewhat public and somewhat private in nature, with the degree of publicness in large part determined by available technology.

It is difficult for government to decide the efficient quantity of a public good. If the public good is to be financed by a tax on citizens who benefit from it, individuals have an incentive to conceal their willingness to pay for it.

Similarly, if citizens think they will not be the ones taxed to fund the public good, but will benefit from it, they have an incentive to exaggerate their willingness to pay. We get the free rider problem with public goods.

4. Adverse selection problems can occur when buyers and sellers have different amounts of information about the good for sale. (495-499)

   When there is a lack of information or buyers and sellers don't have equal information, markets in some goods may not work well (hence, market failure). Adverse selection problems can be partially resolved by signaling.

   2 general policies to deal with informational problems are:

   - *Regulatory approach*
   - *Market approach*

5. Should government intervene in the market? It depends. (499-500)

   One needs to weigh the benefits against the costs of government intervention on a case-by-case basis and remain as objective as possible in the measurement of those benefits and costs.

   Government failure may occur because sometimes:

   - *Governments don't have an incentive to correct the problem*
   - *Governments don't have enough information to deal with the problem*
   - *Intervention is more complicated than it initially seems*
   - *The bureaucratic nature of government precludes fine-tuning*
   - *Government intervention often leads to more government intervention*

● SHORT-ANSWER QUESTIONS

1. What are three sources of market failures?

2. Suppose a steel plant begins production near your home. The resulting smoke pollutes the air you breathe. You bring a complaint to the local town board saying, "I didn't ask for that factory to be built, but I'm having to endure polluted air." The basis of your complaint is an example of what concept in economics?

3. Briefly describe the three methods of dealing with externalities.

4. Which of the methods you stated in Question #3 do most economists prefer to use when dealing with externalities?

5. What is an optimal policy?

6. Define "public good." Why is it difficult for government to decide the efficient quantity of a public good to provide?

7. What are two ways society can deal with informational problems that lead to market failures?

8. When should the government intervene in the economy?

MATCHING THE TERMS

Match the terms to their definitions

___ 1.	adverse selection problem	**a.**	A situation in which the invisible hand pushes in such a way that individual decisions do not lead to socially optimal outcomes.
___ 2.	direct regulation		
___ 3.	efficient	**b.**	Equals the marginal private costs of production plus the cost of the negative externalities associated with that production.
___ 4.	effluent fees		
___ 5.	externality	**c.**	The effect of a decision on a third party that is not taken into account by the decision maker.
___ 6.	free rider problem		
___ 7.	government failure	**d.**	The amount of a good people are allowed to use is directly limited by the government.
___ 8.	inefficient		
___ 9.	marginal social benefit	**e.**	When the effect of a decision not taken into account by the decision maker is detrimental to others.
___ 10.	marginal social cost	**f.**	Charges imposed by government on the level of pollution created.
___ 11.	market failure	**g.**	When the effect of a decision not taken into account by the decision maker is beneficial to others.
___ 12.	market incentive plan		
___ 13.	negative externality	**h.**	A plan requiring market participants to certify that they have reduced total consumption—not necessarily their own individual consumption—by a specified amount.
___ 14.	optimal policy		
___ 15.	positive externality	**i.**	A good that is nonexclusive (no one can be excluded from its benefits) and nonrival (consumption by one does not preclude consumption by others).
___ 16.	public good		
___ 17.	signaling	**j.**	Achieving a goal at the lowest cost in total resources without consideration as to who pays that cost.
___ 18.	tax incentive program		
		k.	A problem that occurs when buyers and sellers have different amounts of information about the good for sale.
		l.	When government intervention in the market to improve a market failure makes the situation worse.
		m.	Individuals' unwillingness to share in the cost of a public good.
		n.	Equals the marginal private benefit of consuming a good plus the benefit of the positive externalities resulting from consuming that good.
		o.	Achieving a goal in a more costly manner than necessary.
		p.	A policy in which the marginal cost of undertaking the policy equals the marginal benefit.
		q.	A program using a tax to create incentives for individuals to structure their activities in a way that is consistent with the desired ends.
		r.	An action taken by an informed party that reveals information to an uninformed party that offsets the false signal that caused the adverse selection problem in the first place.

● PROBLEMS AND APPLICATIONS

1. Secondhand cigarette smoke is believed to have a negative effect on the health of non-smokers. These people have not chosen to smoke, but nevertheless are negatively affected by the choice of others to smoke. Draw the market for cigarettes showing the marginal cost and marginal social cost of smoking cigarettes if this belief is correct.

a.   Demonstrate graphically the market price and quantity of cigarettes.

b.   Demonstrate graphically the efficient level of cigarettes. Explain your answer.

c.   Demonstrate graphically the tax the government would have to impose on cigarettes to arrive at the efficient level and price of cigarettes.

d.   Demonstrate graphically the tax revenue that government would collect from such a tax.

2.   A small city located by a lake has been dumping its raw sewage into the lake. This has created a public outcry by those citizens who like to fish, swim, and water-ski in the lake. The city council has surveyed the community and has estimated the social benefits associated with different levels of pollution control. These benefits, as well as the costs associated with pollution control efforts for the community, are shown in the accompanying table. What is the optimal level of pollution control? Will there still be some pollution of the lake?

Pollution Control	Total Social Benefits	Total Social Costs
1	$200,000	$40,000
2	$275,000	$75,000
3	$330,000	$110,000
4	$375,000	$145,000
5	$410,000	$180,000
6	$435,000	$215,000

3.   Assume a community has decided that there are some substantial social benefits associated with after-school organized recreational activities (such as basketball or soccer) provided to kids before many of their parents arrive home from work. The graph below shows the private demand (marginal private benefit) and society's demand (marginal social benefit) and the supply (marginal private plus social cost) of these recreational activities.

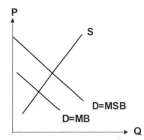

a.   Demonstrate graphically the efficient output level in the graph above. Why would this be an efficient output level?

b.   Assume the government is interested in a policy to increase the number of children spending time at these facilities. What policy would you recommend?

4.   a.   If you are willing to pay $7,000 for a used car that is a "cherry" and $2,000 for a used car that is a "lemon," how much will you be willing to offer to purchase a car if there is a 50 percent chance of purchasing a lemon?

b. If many owners of cherry cars want $4,500 for their cherries, and you are still willing to offer the same dollar amount for a used car as in part *a*, how will your estimate of the chance of getting a cherry change?

5. Suppose there are just two individuals, Bob and Susie, in a community. Bob and Susie are both interested in using a public park (a public good). Below are Bob and Susie's individual demand tables for the use of the public park per month.

Bob		Susie	
Price per month	Qty Demanded in hours per month	Price per month	Qty Demanded in hours per month
$13	4	$10	4
9	6	6	6
7	8	4	8

a. Construct a market demand table for the public park in this community.

b. Construct individual demand curves for Bob and Susie as well as the market demand curve and place them on the same graph in the space below.

● A BRAIN TEASER

1. Environmentalists are concerned about the deforestation of the United States. Some of these environmentalists have advocated government regulating the number of trees that can be cut down. As an economic adviser to the Department of the Interior you are asked to evaluate this policy and provide any recommendations. What do you say?

● MULTIPLE CHOICE

Circle the one best answer for each of the following questions:

1. All of the following are market failures *except:*
   a. positive externalities.
   b. imperfect information.
   c. negative externalities.
   d. the invisible hand.

2. An externality is:
   a. the effect of a decision on a third party not taken into account by a decision maker.
   b. another name for exports.
   c. an event that is external to the economy.
   d. the external effect of a government policy.

3. Refer to the graph below. The S curve represents the marginal private cost of production, and the D curve represents the marginal private benefit to consumers of the good. If there is a negative externality of production, and one wants to adjust the curves so that the equilibrium demonstrates the appropriate marginal social costs, either the:

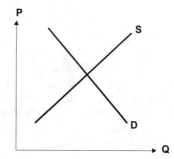

a. S curve should be shifted in to the left or the D curve should be shifted out to the right.

b. S curve should be shifted out to the right or the D curve should be shifted in to the left.

c. S curve should be shifted out to the right or the D curve should be shifted out to the right.

d. S curve should be shifted in to the left or the D curve should be shifted in to the left.

4. Refer to the graph for Question #3. The S curve represents the marginal private cost of production, and the D curve represents the marginal private benefit to consumers of the good. If there is a positive externality of consumption, and one wants to adjust the curves so that the equilibrium demonstrates the appropriate marginal social benefits, either the:

a. S curve should be shifted in to the left or the D curve should be shifted out to the right.

b. S curve should be shifted out to the right or the D curve should be shifted in to the left.

c. S curve should be shifted out to the right or the D curve should be shifted out to the right.

d. S curve should be shifted in to the left or the D curve should be shifted in to the left.

5. Which of the following is *not* one of the ways to deal with negative externalities?
a. Regulation.
b. Subsidizing producers.
c. Creating a market in the externality.
d. Voluntary solutions.

6. Refer to the graph below. If the government were attempting to set an effluent fee, the amount of that effluent fee should be:
a. P_1.
b. P_2.
c. $P_1 - P_2$.
d. $P_1 - P_3$.

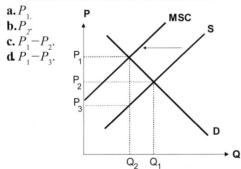

7. Mr. A is using 10 gallons of gas a day and Mr. B is using 20 gallons of gas a day. The marginal cost of reducing gas consumption

by 3 gallons a day is $8 for Mr. A and $4 for Mr. B. The government places a tax on the use of gasoline. Economists would expect:
a. Mr. A to reduce his consumption by the same amount as Mr. B.
b. Mr. A to reduce his consumption by more than Mr. B.
c. Mr. B to reduce his consumption by more than Mr. A.
d. both to reduce their consumption to zero.

8. Refer to the graph below, which shows the marginal private and social cost of fishing and the demand for fishing. The socially efficient price for consumers of fishing would be:
a. 0.
b. P_1.
c. P_2.
d. P_3.

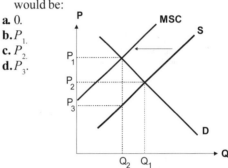

9. In addressing pollution problems, economists would most likely prefer:
a. direct regulation.
b. subsidies provided to suppliers.
c. a market incentive plan.
d. banning the production of those products that pollute.

10. Voluntary policies to resolve externalities:
a. have historically been effective in addressing externalities.
b. are generally favored by economists as the optimal policy to address externalities.
c. are generally opposed by economists because of the free rider problem.
d. are generally opposed by economists because of government failure.

11. A public good is:
a. any good traded in markets.
b. a good that is nonexclusive and nonrival.
c. a good provided only to those who pay for it.
d. rarely provided by government.

12. The optimal level of pollution control, or any other government policy, exists when the marginal benefit:
   a. exceeds the marginal cost.
   b. equals the marginal cost.
   c. is less than the marginal cost.
   d. is maximized.

13. The market demand curve for a public good is:
   a. the vertical sum of the individual demand curves at every quantity.
   b. the horizontal sum of the individual demand curves at every price.
   c. vertical at the quantity desired.
   d. always horizontal.

14. If health insurers cannot distinguish between people who have a high-risk and low-risk of medical needs, but those buying the health insurance can, the price at which insurers are willing to provide insurance to cover health care costs will be:
   a. low enough so that at least one-half of all those covered are low-insurance risks.
   b. set with the expectations that high-risk people will not purchase coverage.
   c. at a level that insurers will be unwilling to provide health coverage.
   d. at a level that many of those in good health may be unwilling to buy insurance.

15. Government failure:
   a. always outweighs market failure.
   b. sometimes outweighs market failure.
   c. never outweighs market failure.
   d. is the same as market failure.

● POTENTIAL ESSAY QUESTIONS

You may also see essay questions similar to the "Problems & Applications" and "A Brain Teaser" exercises.

1. Evaluate the benefits and costs of the regulatory versus the market approach to resolving informational problems that lead to market failure.

2. Discuss five reasons why government's solution to a market failure could worsen the market failure.

ANSWERS

SHORT-ANSWER QUESTIONS

1. Three sources of market failures are: externalities, public goods, and imperfect information. (485-486)

2. The pollution that you endure is an example of a negative externality. An externality is an effect of a decision not taken into account by the decision maker. In this case, the air pollution is the effect of steel production not taken into account by the firm. (487-488)

3. Ways to deal with externalities include (1) direct regulation, (2) incentive policies (tax incentive policies and market incentive policies), and (3) voluntary solutions. In a program of direct regulation, the government directly limits the amount of a good people are allowed to use. A tax incentive program is a program using a tax to create incentives for individuals to structure their activities in a way that is consistent with the desired ends. A market incentive program is a plan requiring market participants to certify that they have reduced total consumption—not necessarily their own individual consumption—by a specified amount. Voluntary solutions leave individuals free to choose whether to follow what is socially optimal or what is privately optimal. (488-492)

4. Economists tend to like incentive policies to deal with externalities. Direct regulation tends to be more costly to society in achieving the desired end. Voluntary policies will tend to fail because a small number of free riders often undermine the social consciousness of many in society. (489-491)

5. An optimal policy is one in which the marginal cost of undertaking the policy equals the marginal benefit of that policy. (492)

6. A public good is a good that is nonexclusive (no one can be excluded from its benefits) and nonrival (consumption by one does not preclude consumption by others). It is difficult for government to decide the efficient quantity of a public good because of the free rider problem. If the public good is to be financed by a tax on citizens who benefit from it, individuals have an incentive to conceal their willingness to pay for it. Similarly, if citizens think they will not be the ones taxed to fund the public good, but will benefit from it, they have an incentive to exaggerate their willingness to pay. (492-494)

7. Two general policies to deal with informational problems include the regulatory approach and the market approach. The regulatory approach would have government regulate the market and see that individuals provide the right information, or the government could license individuals in the market, requiring those with licenses to reveal full information about the good being sold. The market approach suggests that allowing markets for information to develop may be the best approach. (496-497)

8. The government should intervene in the economy only if the benefits outweigh the costs. One needs to weigh the benefits against the costs on a case-by-case basis and to remain as objective as possible. Government failure (government intervention only making matters worse) is always a real possibility. (499-500)

ANSWERS

MATCHING

1-k; 2-d; 3-j; 4-f; 5-c; 6-m; 7-l; 8-o; 9-n; 10-b; 11-a; 12-h; 13-e; 14-p; 15-g; 16-i; 17-r; 18-q.

ANSWERS

PROBLEMS AND APPLICATIONS

1. a. When there is a negative externality, as with the case of secondhand cigarette smoke, the supply curve which represents the marginal private cost, *S*, is lower than the marginal social cost, *MSC*. The supply curve represents the private costs of smokers who chose to smoke. The cost for society is higher, and the marginal social cost is higher, because cigarette smoke hurts those who do not smoke. The demand curve represents marginal social benefits. These curves are drawn on the next page.

Because the market does not take into account the third-party effects, equilibrium quantity is Q_e and equilibrium price is P_e. (488-489 and Figure 21-1)

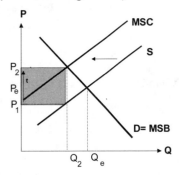

b. The efficient level of cigarettes is where marginal social costs equal marginal social benefits. This is at Q_2 and P_2. (490 and Figure 21-1)

c. The tax the government would have to impose on cigarettes to arrive at the efficient level of cigarettes is t equal to $P_2 - P_1$; it's the tax sufficient to shift the supply curve back to the marginal social cost curve. (490 and Figure 21-3)

d. This is t times the quantity of cigarettes in the market after the tax. This is shown by the shaded boxed region in the graph above. (490 and Figure 21-3)

2. See the table below. The optimal level of pollution control is 5 units, because this is the quantity of pollution control at which the marginal social benefit of the control just equals its marginal social cost. There will still be some pollution of the lake as evidenced by the increased marginal benefits associated with the 6th unit of pollution control—but that amount of pollution control is not worth it to the community given its marginal cost. (492)

Pollution Control	Total Benefits	Total Costs	Marginal Benefit	Marginal Cost
1	$200,000	$40,000	$200,000	$40,000
2	275,000	75,000	75,000	35,000
3	330,000	110,000	55,000	35,000
4	375,000	145,000	45,000	35,000
5	410,000	180,000	**35,000**	**35,000**
6	435,000	215,000	25,000	35,000

3. a. The efficient level of output (services provided in the community) is where the marginal social benefit equals the marginal social cost. This occurs at that output level, Q*, where the MSB curve intersects the supply curve as shown below. (It is reasonable to assume there is no difference between the private and social costs. So marginal social costs are given by the supply curve.) (488-489 and Figure 21-2)

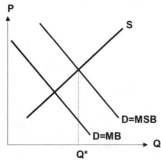

b. The private demand and/or the supply needs to be increased. This could be accomplished by subsidizing parents (increasing demand) and/or subsidizing the facilities (increasing supply). Either one of these options would increase the output level toward the efficient level where MSB = MSC. It may be much easier to administer the subsidization of the facilities. (488-489 and Figure 21-2)

4. a. Knowing that you have a 50 percent chance of buying a lemon, you will offer $4,500 (the average of $2,000 and $7,000). Given that offer price, individuals with cherries will be very hesitant to sell and will begin to exit the market, while individuals with lemons will be anxious to sell. (495)

b. If many owners of cherries want $4,500 and you are still willing to pay $4,500 for a used car then there will be more owners of cherries left in the market, increasing the chances you will be able to purchase a cherry used car. (495)

5. a. The market demand table for the public park is shown on the next page. Notice that to derive the market demand table for a public good one needs to add the marginal benefit each individual receives from the public good (the price they are

willing to pay) at each quantity. (This is just the opposite from deriving a demand table for a private good where one would have to add the quantity demanded at each price.) (495)

Price per month	Quantity Demanded in hours per month
$23	4
$15	6
$11	8

b. The lowest curve is Susie's demand curve. The middle curve is Bob's demand curve. The highest curve is the market demand curve. Notice that we vertically sum the individual demand curves to construct the market demand curve for a public good. (495 and Figure 21-4)

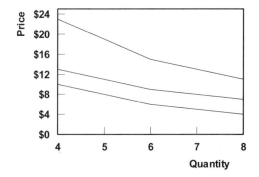

ANSWERS

A BRAIN TEASER

1. First, one must look carefully at the evidence to see if the marginal social benefit equals the marginal social cost at the current quantity of trees harvested in the timber industry. If so, then there is not a problem. After all, trees are a renewable resource. If they become scarcer, their price will rise and people will voluntarily conserve. Moreover, a higher price will increase the quantity supplied—more trees will be planted. However, if at the current market equilibrium quantity the marginal social cost exceeds the marginal social benefit, too many trees are being cut down. That is, an external cost exists. That external cost is often cited as the reduced ability of trees to clean the air—to absorb carbon dioxide. Even if we assume the external cost is sufficiently large to warrant government action, direct regulation by government often is not the most efficient approach.

Instead, a more efficient proposal may be to continue to impose a higher and higher tax on the production of lumber until supply is restricted to that quantity at which the marginal social benefit just equals the marginal social cost. At the resulting higher market price for lumber, people will voluntarily conserve trees.

Another possibility might be to subsidize people or communities to plant more trees to absorb carbon dioxide (and continue to require the timber industry to plant a new tree to replace each one cut down). This course of action may preclude the necessity to tax the timber industry. (488-492)

ANSWERS

MULTIPLE CHOICE

1. **d** An outcome where individual buyers and sellers do not have any control over price (the invisible hand) is a desirable competitive market outcome. See pages 485-486.

2. **a** An externality occurs when there is an effect of a trade on a third party. See page 486.

3. **d** A negative externality of production makes the marginal social cost higher than the marginal private cost. See pages 488-489 and Figure 21-1.

4. **a** A positive externality of consumption makes the marginal social benefit higher than the marginal private benefit. See pages 488-489 and Figure 21-2.

5. **b** Subsidizing producers would increase the production of the product. Instead, we would want to restrict the production of a product that has a negative externality. See pages 488-491.

6. d The effluent fee should be set to equate marginal social cost with marginal social benefit (which, in absence of any information to the contrary, the marginal social benefit can be assumed to be represented by the demand curve). To achieve this equality, the effluent fee needs to be sufficient to shift the supply curve up to the marginal social cost curve. See page 490 and Figure 21-3.

7. c The amount of reduction will be based on the marginal costs of reduction. Since the marginal costs of reduction are higher for Mr. A, economists would expect Mr. B to reduce his consumption by more than Mr. A. See page 490.

8. b The socially efficient price is where the marginal social cost equals the marginal social benefit (which, in absence of any information to the contrary, can be assumed to be represented by the demand curve). See pages 488-489 and Figure 21-1.

9. c Economists prefer market incentive plans because they are more efficient. See pages 488-492.

10. c Economists believe a small number of free riders will undermine the social consciousness of many in society and that eventually a voluntary policy will fail. Generally, the results of voluntary programs have not been positive. Government failure can exist only if government intervenes. The optimal government intervention exists when the marginal benefits equal the marginal costs. See pages 491.

11. b A public good is a good that is nonexclusive and whose consumption by one does not preclude its consumption by others. See page 492.

12. b Whenever the marginal benefit exceeds the marginal cost then do more of that activity. Do less whenever the marginal benefit is less than the marginal cost. See page 492.

13. a To arrive at the market demand curve for a public good we vertically add the price that each individual is willing to pay for each unit since each receives a benefit when the good is supplied. See page 493 and Figure 21-4.

14. d With certainty, insurers would not offer to provide health insurance at a price low enough so that low-risk people would purchase insurance. The only people left looking for health insurance are high-risk people. The price will rise even further until very few will buy health insurance. This is known as adverse selection. See pages 495-496.

15. b Government failure occurs when government intervention does not improve the market failure. As with almost all economic issues, there is always an "on the other hand" so the "sometimes" is the right answer. See pages 499-500.

ANSWERS

POTENTIAL ESSAY QUESTIONS

The following are annotated answers. They indicate the general idea behind the answer.

1. The regulatory approach would have government regulate the market and see that individuals provide the right information, or the government could license individuals in the market, requiring those with licenses to reveal full information about the good being sold. Although regulatory solutions have their benefits they may also create government failure. The market approach suggests that allowing markets for information to develop may be the best approach because it may at least avoid some government failure.

2. Government intervention may worsen the problems created by market failure. Government failure may occur because (1) governments don't have an incentive to correct the problem, (2) governments don't have enough information to deal with the problem, (3) intervention is more complicated than it initially seems, (4) the bureaucratic nature of government precludes fine-tuning, and (5) government intervention often leads to more government intervention.

BEHAVIORAL ECONOMICS AND MODERN ECONOMIC POLICY

22

● CHAPTER AT A GLANCE

This review is based upon the learning objectives that open the chapter.

1. Mechanism design involves identifying a goal and designing a coordination mechanism such as a market, social system or contract to achieve that goal. (508-509)

    Mechanism design economists take into account people's predictable irrationalities.

2a. Choice architecture is the context in which decisions are presented. (511-512)

    How choices are presented affects the choices people make.

2b. A nudge is the deliberate design of the choice architecture to alter people's behavior in predictably positive ways. (512)

    Nudges take into account people's predictable irrationalities.

3. A nudge policy is when government structures choices facing people so that they are free to choose what they want, but are also more likely to choose what government believes is best for them. (512-513)

    Supporters argue that nudge policies meet the criterion of libertarian paternalism: they do not restrict an individual's free choice (libertarian), but they make people more likely to make a choice that is better for themselves in the long run (paternalistic).

4. Supporters argue that nudges can be useful when (1) benefits and costs are separated by time, (2) choices are complicated and have many dimensions, and (3) choices are infrequent. (513-514)

*   *Choices where Benefits and Costs Are Separated by Time* Supporters argue that people tend to make less-than-optimal choices when the benefits and costs of their choices are separated by time. Most people weight the immediate costs and benefits more, and future costs and benefits less. Examples include weight loss, saving money, and studying.

*   *Complicated Choices with Many Dimensions* Supporters argue that people are not good at making complicated choices with many different variables involved. A nudge could help them make a better choice. Choosing what type of loan to take out in order to pay for college is an example of such a complicated choice.

*   *Infrequent Choices* Supporters argue that infrequent decisions provide little opportunity to practice making choices, evaluate feedback, or explore one's preferences, so it is particularly difficult to make the best choice. Examples of such infrequent decisions include what college to attend and what type of mortgage to take out.

5. Two types of nudge policies are (1) advantageous default option and (2) information and encouragement nudges. (514-515)

*   *Advantageous default option nudges* People tend to select the default option. By taking advantage of that tendency economic policy makers can direct people to do what they think is better for them, while still leaving people free to choose. An example is making employees opt-out of a health insurance plan.

*   *Information and encouragement nudges* Government encourages people to make certain choices that the government has decided is good for them. An example is for the government to inform people about how their energy use compares to the average.

6.   A push policy is a regulatory or tax policy to get firms or individuals to use "appropriate" nudges. (516-517).

If government can institute the behavioral economic policy directly, or if a private firm chooses to implement a policy on its own, it's a nudge. Push policies restrict free choice by the firm for the greater good and therefore can no longer claim to satisfy the libertarian paternalism criterion.

7.   Traditional economists highlight four concerns about nudge and push policies (518-520):

(1) Very few policies meet the criterion of libertarian paternalism.

Few opportunities for true nudge policies exist. In reality, most government interventions are push policies that rely on regulation to tell firms what they can and can't do.

(2) Designing helpful policies is complicated.

Designing nudge policies becomes complicated, requiring more information than government has.

(3) It isn't clear that government knows better.

Even if economists could agree that people do not always act in their own self-interest, it isn't clear that government can determine what is in people's best interest either.

(4) Government policy may make the situation worse.

Nudge policy substantially increases the potential for government failure.

● SHORT-ANSWER QUESTIONS

1. What process do modern economists follow to align people's incentives with desired ends?

2. In an effort to limit the amount of trash companies produce, Congress passes a regulation allowing each company to produce a maximum of 1,000 tons of trash per year. Is this likely an example of a mechanism designed by an economist? Why or why not? Can you suggest a potentially more efficient policy?

3. What is nudge policy? Give an example.

4. Why would a behavioral economist argue that nudges are sometimes necessary?

5. Going through her contract, an employee sees that 5% of her yearly salary is withheld to pay for health insurance. She can check a box to not have the 5% withheld and go without health insurance, but she decides to leave the box unchecked. Might this be an example of nudge policy in action? Why or why not?

6. In the example above, why can the decision to encourage employees to opt-in to a health plan be described as libertarian? In what way is it paternalistic?

7. What are three types of choices where nudges can be useful? Give an example of each.

8. What are two types of nudge policies? Give an example of each.

9. What is it called when the government uses a regulatory or tax policy to get firms to use "appropriate" nudges?

10. Seeing the "smoking kills" warning on a box of cigarettes, a shopper decides to buy a pack of gum instead. Is this an example of nudge policy in action? Why or why not?

11. Why do traditional economists reject the argument that nudge policies should be implemented whenever possible? Provide four concerns they might offer.

MATCHING THE TERMS
Match the terms to their definitions

___ 1. behavioral economic policy	**a.** Any economic policy based upon models using behavioral economic building blocks that take into account people's predictable irrational behavior.
___ 2. choice architecture	
___ 3. coordination mechanism	**b.** Economics devoted not only to studying markets, but also to designing markets and other coordinating mechanisms.
___ 4. economic engineering	
___ 5. incentive compatibility problem	**c.** Methods of coordinating people's wants with other people's desires.
___ 6. libertarian paternalistic policy	**d.** Prices that aren't paid directly, but instead are paid in terms of opportunity cost borne by the demander, and thus determine his or her action indirectly.
___ 7. mechanism design	**e.** A problem in which the incentive facing the decision maker does not match the incentive needed for the mechanism to achieve its desired end.
___ 8. nudge	
___ 9. nudge policy	**f.** Identifying a goal and then designing a mechanism such as a market, social system or contract to achieve that end.
___ 10. push policy	**g.** The context in which decisions are presented.
___ 11. shadow price	**h.** A deliberate design of the choice architecture that alters people's behavior in predictably positive ways.
	i. A policy that leaves people free to choose what they want, but encourages them to make a choice that the government believes is in their interest.
	j. A policy that leaves people free to choose, but nonetheless guides them toward a choice that a well-intentioned observer would see as good for them.
	k. A regulatory or tax policy to get firms or individuals to use "appropriate" nudges.

PROBLEMS AND APPLICATIONS

1. Indicate whether each of the following policies is libertarian, paternalistic, both, or neither.

   a. In order to encourage its students to eat a healthier lunch, a public high school eliminates french fries, pizza, and hamburgers from its menu and offers salads and sandwiches instead.

   b. A large grocery store positions its most profitable products in the front of the store and at eye level along the rows.

   c. If you choose to save 10% of your salary and access it only after you retire, your employer will supplement your savings by putting an additional 10% into your saving account. In order to opt-out of this savings plan, you must check a box in your contract saying that you do not want to have any money withheld.

2. For each of the following cases, say whether or not a nudge might be helpful. Explain why or why not.

    a. Many overweight Americans want to lose weight, but they continue to eat un-healthfully and watch TV instead of exercising.

    b. A student who needs a loan for college looks on a website and sees that there are 8 different options. She has no idea which is the best for her, so she just chooses randomly.

    c. A group of friends is trying to decide whether to go see a movie or go play a round of miniature golf.

    d. A couple is trying to choose what type of mortgage to take out on their new house.

3. Classify the following nudges as either a "potentially advantageous default nudge," an "information and encouragement nudge," "a nudge, but not one of the two specific types," or "not a nudge" and give a brief explanation.

    a. A chocolate-chip cookie cereal advertises its product on TV during programming mostly watched by children.

    b. When purchasing an expensive new laptop, the contract is written so that you must explicitly choose to opt-out of highly subsidized insurance for your computer.

    c. A college administration promotes a study in the campus newspaper showing that the average student has only one alcoholic drink per week.

    d. The government passes a new regulation requiring firms to put a label on their products if any animals were used to test the product.

4. Classify the following cases as a nudge, a push, or neither.

    a. The government passes a new regulation requiring cell phone companies to present your bill in a specific, simplified format so that you can see the source of all your costs.

    b. A variety of potato chips has the words "New, baked, not fried! Half as many calories" in big letters on its packaging.

    c. Seeing six different brands of ketchup on the supermarket shelf that all look identical, a customer just chooses one randomly.

    d. The government taxes pesticides in order to encourage organic food-production.

5. For each of the following statements, indicate whether it was likely made by a behavioral economist or a traditional economist.

   a. "Having more stuff doesn't necessarily make people happier. Relative, not absolute, income is what matters."

   b. "Designing successful nudge policies is too complicated to make it worth it."

   c. "People are rational and know their own wants and desires better than the government."

   d. "People are predictably irrational and we need to take such irrationalities into consideration when designing policy."

   e. "Price incentives are the only thing that matters to consumers."

A BRAIN TEASER

1. How might higher overall consumption lower total happiness in a society?

MULTIPLE CHOICE

Circle the one best answer for each of the following questions:

1. Which of the following is a key difference between traditional and behavioral economics?
   a. Traditional economics focuses on economic engineering, while behavioral economics is the study of free markets.
   b. Traditional economics bases its analysis on the assumption that individuals are rational and self-interested, while behavioral economics takes into account people's predictably irrational behavior.
   c. Traditional economics emphasizes the positive role that government can have in influencing people's choices, while behavioral economics emphasizes the fact that government does not know what is good for people and is often plagued by inefficiency and failures.
   d. Traditional economics considers the paternalistic component of nudges and pushes to be important, while behavioral economics puts more value on the libertarian basis of free markets.

2. Shadow prices are:
   a. extra fees that businesses such as cell phone companies hide from their customers.
   b. the cost to taxpayers of push policies put in place by the government.
   c. opportunity costs faced by the demander that indirectly influence his or her decisions.
   d. the price increase that firms use to cover the cost of advertising.

3. The cap-and-trade system designed by economists to limit the overall production of CO_2 emissions is an example of:
   a. mechanism design.
   b. an incentive compatibility problem.
   c. a shadow price.
   d. an "information and encouragement" nudge.

4. Who would agree with the statement, "Even assuming no externalities, voluntary trade might not necessarily make people better off."
   a. Traditional economists.
   b. Behavioral economists.
   c. Both.
   d. Neither.

5. Nudges:
   a. always make consumers better off.
   b. are often suggested by traditional economists as a way to guide individuals to make better choices than they would on their own.
   c. aren't controversial because they meet the libertarian paternalistic criterion.
   d. are sometimes used by firms to guide their customers to make choices that benefit the firm.

6. Structuring a health care program with a default option of automatic enrollment, is an example of:
   a. using choice architecture to influence people's choices.
   b. a policy that is neither libertarian nor paternalistic.
   c. a policy that will lead most people to not choose a health care plan.
   d. a policy that would likely be supported by traditional economists more than behavioral economists.

7. In which of the following cases would consumers be least likely to benefit from a nudge?
   a. Choices in which benefits and costs are separated by time.
   b. Complicated choices with many dimensions.
   c. Choices where the marginal costs and benefits are clear.
   d. Infrequent choices.

8. An advocacy group mailing out flyers with big pictures of melting ice and flooded areas, as well as a list of ways families can cut down on energy usage in order to help slow global warming is an example of:
   a. an advantageous default option nudge.
   b. an infrequent choice nudge.
   c. an information and encouragement nudge.
   d. a push policy.

9. When the government uses a regulatory or tax policy to get firms or individuals to use "appropriate" nudges, it is called a:
   a. nudge policy.
   b. traditional economic policy.
   c. push policy.
   d. default option policy.

10. According to behavioral economists:
   a. conspicuous consumption goods lead to long-term increases in measured satisfaction.
   b. certain types of material goods don't matter much to our well being and often crowd out those goods that do matter.
   c. if people work more so as to buy more, society will be better off.
   d. the government should never try to change the way in which income is distributed.

11. Which of the following is NOT a misgiving expressed by traditional economists about behavioral economic policies?
   a. The only nudges that help society are those by private firms.
   b. Very few policies meet the criterion of libertarian paternalism.
   c. It isn't clear that government knows better than individuals in most cases.
   d. Government policies may make the situation worse, rather than better.

● POTENTIAL ESSAY QUESTIONS

You may also see essay questions similar to the "Problems & Applications" and "A Brain Teaser" exercises.

1. Late pick-ups can be a big problem for day care centers. To solve the problem some centers followed the traditional economic solution: they imposed a fine for parents who picked up the kids late. Use the concept of shadow prices to discuss why this policy made the problem of late pick-ups even worse.

2. Traditional economists assume that individuals are rational and pursue their self-interest at all times. How do the concepts of choice architecture and economic engineering challenge these assumptions? Does this mean that the traditional economic models need to be rethought?

3. In your opinion, should the government pursue nudge policies? What are the benefits and risks of such policy?

ANSWERS

SHORT-ANSWER QUESTIONS

1. Modern economists use their insights about incentive compatibility problems to design mechanisms that align incentives with desired ends. The process of mechanism design involves identifying a goal and then designing a mechanism such as a market, social system or contract, to achieve that goal. (508-509)

2. No, an economist would be highly unlikely to impose such rigid regulations that do not take incentives into account. A potentially more efficient policy (that uses economic reasoning) would be to give companies permits allowing them to produce 1,000 tons of trash and then allow companies to buy and sell permits. This solution (similarly to the cap-and-trade program for CO_2 emissions) is an example of mechanism design because it creates a market to achieve the goal of trash reduction. (508-511)

3. In nudge policy, government structures choices facing people so that they are free to choose what they want, but also more likely to choose what is "best" for them. For example, employees having to check a box to opt-out of a health insurance plan, rather than check a box to opt-into the plan. (512-513)

4. According to behavioral economists, people are predictably irrational and often make choices that are not in their own best interests in the long run. By influencing people's choices via specifically designed choice architecture, nudges can help people behave in predictably positive ways. In other words, nudges help people make choices that are better for themselves in the long run. (510-511)

5. Yes, this is an example of an advantageous default option nudge. Studies show that if the employee was faced with the choice of checking a box in order to opt-in to the health insurance plan, she would be more likely to end up choosing to not have the health insurance. (514)

6. Making employees opt-out of health insurance (or savings) plans is libertarian because no one is making them take part in the plan. They are still free to opt-out, but it requires them to take a specific action to do so. Such policies are paternalistic because they are designed to further what government sees as the employee's best long-run interest. (512-514)

7. Three types of choices where nudges can be useful are choices in which benefits and costs are separated by time, complicated choices with many dimensions, and infrequent choices. Whether to exercise or watch TV is a choice where benefits and costs are separated by time because the benefits of exercising are long-term. What type of student loan to take out is an example of a complicated choice with many dimensions. Choosing a mortgage is an infrequent and complicated decision. People could potentially be helped to make better choices if they were nudged in each of these examples. (513-514)

8. Two types of nudge policies are advantageous default option nudges and information and encouragement nudges. Making an employee check a box to opt out of a savings plan is an example of an advantageous default option nudge. Sending people information about how much energy they use, the effects of high energy use, and how to reduce their energy consumption is an example of an information and encouragement nudge. (514-515)

9. This is an example of a push policy. A push policy is any regulatory tax policy put in place by the government to get firms or individuals to use "appropriate" nudges. (516-517)

10. It depends. Viewed from the perspective of the government and the consumer, it is a type of nudge policy. But when one takes the cigarette company into account, it is a push policy rather than a nudge policy. Cigarette companies do not put such warnings on their boxes by free choice or for the good of the customer; government requires that cigarette companies put the health warnings on their products. This is a case of the government using regulation to get firms to use what it considers an appropriate nudge. (516-517)

11. Traditional economists have expressed serious misgivings about behavioral economic policies. First, they say that very few nudge policies meet the criterion of libertarian paternalism. Second, designing helpful policies is complicated. Third, traditional economists argue that it isn't clear that government knows better than individuals, even if individuals are sometimes irrational. Finally, they believe that government policies often make the situation worse because its policies may be inefficient and may have unintended consequences. (518-520)

ANSWERS

MATCHING

1-a; 2-g; 3-c; 4-b; 5-e; 6-j; 7-f; 8-h; 9-i; 10-k; 11-d.

ANSWERS

PROBLEMS AND APPLICATIONS

1. a. Paternalistic, but not libertarian. The school is trying to help students make healthier choices (paternalistic), but is doing so by restricting their freedom to choose what to eat (not libertarian). (512-513)
   b. Libertarian, but not paternalistic. Customers still have the freedom to purchase whatever they want (libertarian), but the grocery store has its own interests at heart, not the interests of its customers (not paternalistic). (512-513)
   c. Both libertarian and paternalistic. Employees have the freedom to save or to not save (libertarian), but the company uses a nudge to increase the likelihood that they will choose to save (paternalistic). (512-513)

2. a. Yes, a nudge could be useful in this scenario because the benefits and costs are separated by time. In other words, the benefits of exercising aren't enjoyed until well into the future. (513-514)
   b. Yes, a nudge could help in this scenario because the student faces a complicated choice with many dimensions. (513-514)
   c. No, this is not a scenario that could be resolved with a nudge. (513-514)

   d. Yes, a nudge could help in this scenario because the couple is faced with an infrequent and complicated decision. (513-514)

3. a. "A nudge but not one of the two specific types." Firms use advertising to nudge consumers, but this is not one of the types of nudge policies to help the consumer make a better long run choice. (514-517)
   b. "A potentially advantageous default nudge." Consumers would be less likely to purchase this highly subsidized insurance if they had to opt-in to the insurance plan. If the subsidy is high enough, then the insurance could be potentially advantageous from the consumer's viewpoint, although from society's viewpoint it is unclear, since the money to provide the subsidy has to come from somewhere. (514-517)
   c. "An information encouragement nudge." By publishing the study, the college administration is seeking to nudge students to drink less by decreasing the pressure many students feel to drink in order to fit in. (514-517)
   d. "Not a nudge." This is a push policy because the government is using regulation to make firms put a label on their product. (514-517)

4. a. A push. Anytime the government enacts a regulatory policy to get firms or individuals to use "appropriate" nudges it is considered a push policy. (514-517)
   b. A nudge. Advertising by firms is a type of nudge, even if the firm doesn't necessarily have the customer's best interests in mind. (514-517)
   c. There is neither a nudge nor a push in this example. (514-517)
   d. A push. Anytime the government enacts a tax policy to get firms or individuals to use "appropriate" nudges it is considered a push policy. (514-517)

5. a. Behavioral economist. Traditional economists say that having more makes you happier. Behavioral economists, on the other hand, argue that people care about relative as well as absolute consumption and income. This proposition has potentially radical implications because it introduces the possibility that government

can improve society's overall welfare by changing the way in which income is distributed. (517-520)

b. Traditional economist. This is one of the main criticisms by traditional economists cite against the idea that government should use more nudge policies. (517-520)

c. Traditional economist. This is another criticism that traditional economists use against the implementation of push policies. (517-520)

d. Behavioral economist. Although many traditional economists recognize that individuals sometimes make irrational choices, they do not agree that such irrationality is predictable or should be used as the basis for government policies. (517-520)

e. Traditional economist. Traditional economists are likely to focus on prices as the main incentive that consumers consider and therefore base their theories on this assumption. (517-520)

ANSWERS

A BRAIN TEASER

1. Behavioral economists believe that relative income and consumption matter more to people than absolute income or consumption. Economist Robert Frank argues that after societies pass a certain threshold level of income, a threshold all western societies have passed, certain types of material goods don't matter a whole lot to our well being, and crowd out those goods that do matter. In other words, left to their own choices, people spend their extra money in ways that don't lead to significant or lasting increases in satisfaction. If this assumption is correct, then government can improve society's overall welfare by changing the way in which income is distributed. Rather than allowing individuals to spend money on consumption for themselves that does not increase society's well being, the government could collect this money in the form of taxes and use it to provide services for the poor or sick. In this way, even though total consumption may drop, the overall welfare of society is increased. (517-520)

ANSWERS

MULTIPLE CHOICE

1. **b** Behavioral economists argue that the assumptions that individuals are rational and always act in their own self interest are flawed. Instead, behavioral economists suggest that individuals are predictably irrational and that economic theory should take these irrationalities into consideration. See pages 509-511.

2. **c** Shadow prices are not a money price on a good or service, but rather the often obscured opportunity costs that influence the demander indirectly. See page 507.

3. **a** The cap-and-trade system is an example of a market designed by economists in order to help achieve a goal as efficiently as possible. In this case the goal was to reduce CO_2 emissions. See pages 508 and 509.

4. **b** Behavioral economists would agree with this statement because they believe that individuals can be irrational. An irrational individual does not necessarily make trades that will benefit themselves even if there are no externalities. See pages 507 and 511.

5. **d** Nudges are not only used by the government to help people make good choices. In fact, nudges have existed almost as long as firms have been in business. The difference is that firms use nudges for their own benefit, rather than for the benefit of their customers. See pages 511 and 512.

6. **a** This type of advantageous default option nudge works because individuals respond differently to different choice architectures. In this case, employees are more likely to participate in the health care plan. See page 514.

7. **c** If the marginal costs and benefits are clear, there is less reason that individuals need a nudge. Individuals facing the other three choices could be helped by a nudge. See pages 513 and 514.

8. c Whenever the government or an advocacy group provides individuals with information about the effects of their choices and ways to alter those choices, it is called "an information and encouragement" nudge. See pages 512-515.

9. c Firms are often opposed to implementing nudges that will help customers because those nudges will lower the profit of the firm. When the government makes firms implement such nudges, it is called a push policy. See pages 515-517.

10. b Behavioral economists believe that relative consumption and income must be taken into account along with absolute consumption and income. Some consumption is conspicuous consumption and does not increase society's welfare in the long run. The resources that go towards conspicuous consumption could be better used to help the poor or those who need health care. See pages 517-518.

11. a Traditional economists focus their criticisms on the fact that it is difficult to implement true nudge policies and that the government often makes the situation worse because it does not know what is best for individuals. They do NOT, however, argue that nudges used by private firms are good for society. See pages 517-520.

━━━━━ ANSWERS ━━━━━

POTENTIAL ESSAY QUESTIONS

The following are annotated answers. They indicate the general idea behind the answer.

1. Using traditional economic thinking, by increasing the cost of picking up the kids late the new policy should have led to a decrease in the number of late pick-ups. In reality, the number of late pick-ups increased because the new cost of picking kids up late, in the form of a fine, was smaller than the previous moral shadow cost of being late. In other words, when there was no fine, parents felt guilty about being late. This guilt was the shadow price that kept most parents from being late. Once a fine was imposed, the moral shadow price was eliminated. This example shows that people are social creatures and that more than simple price incentives must be considered when designing policies to accomplish a specific goal.

2. Traditional economists base their theories on the assumptions that individuals are rational and always pursue their self-interest. Behavioral economists, on the other hand, argue that choice architecture—the context in which decisions are presented—affects the choices that people make. This means that economists, by engineering the choice architecture people face, can encourage them to make a certain choice. For example, when a school lunch service places the healthier foods in easily visible, easy-to-reach locations, while putting the unhealthy foods mostly out of sight, students are more likely to choose a healthier lunch. This shows that choice architecture can be a useful tool for encouraging students to eat more healthfully. If this is one of the goals of society, then designing choice architecture can be a useful tool for achieving its goals.

3. This is an open-ended opinion question, but a good answer must consider the advantages and disadvantages of nudge policies. Behavioral economists believe that society can be made better off through the use of nudge policies. Without curtailing people's freedom, people can be encouraged to make better choices in the long run through simple changes in choice architecture and economic engineering (the libertarian paternalism criterion). When individuals face choices in which benefits and costs are separated by time, complicated choices with many dimensions, or infrequent choices, nudges can help them make better decisions than they otherwise might. Traditional economists, however, focus more on price and add that there are many risks to nudge policies. First of all, very few policies meet the libertarian paternalism criterion. Second, designing helpful nudge policies is complicated. Third, it isn't clear that government knows better than individuals what is good for those individuals. Finally, government policies often make the situation worse due to inefficiencies and unintended consequences.

MICROECONOMIC POLICY, ECONOMIC REASONING, AND BEYOND

23

● CHAPTER AT A GLANCE

This review is based upon the learning objectives that open the chapter.

1. Economists' views on social policy differ widely because: (525-526)

   1. they have different underlying values,
   2. they interpret empirical evidence differently, and
   3. they use different underlying models.

   Analysis should be as objective as possible. Unfortunately, in practice, social goals are seldom neat—they're generally vaguely understood and vaguely expressed.

2. Liberal and conservative economists agree on many policy prescriptions because they use the same models. These models focus on incentives and individual choice. (527)

   There is more agreement among economists than most lay people realize because they all use cost/benefit analysis. Disagreement among economists usually arises because they assess the qualitative benefits and costs (those benefits and costs that cannot be easily measured) differently.

3. Cost/benefit analysis is analysis in which one assigns a cost and benefit to alternatives, and draws a conclusion on the basis of those costs and benefits. (527-532)

   Economists argue that government should keep regulating until the marginal benefits of regulation just equal the marginal costs. Unfortunately, many costs and benefits (especially social and political) cannot be easily quantified.

4. Three separate types of failure of market outcomes include: (532-537)

   1. failures due to distributional issues,
   2. failures due to rationality problems of individuals, and
   3. failures due to violations of inalienable, or at least partially inalienable, rights of individuals.

   Failure of market outcome occurs when even though it is functioning properly the market is not achieving society's goals.

5. Government failure as well as market failure exists. For the government to correct a problem it must: (537-539)

   1. recognize the problem,
   2. have the will to deal with it, and
   3. have the ability to deal with it.

   Government can often not do all three of these well. Often the result is that government action is directed at the wrong problem at the wrong time. And sometimes the government fails to improve a situation (hence the term "government failure.")

   Economics provides the tools, not the rules, for policy. Economics involves the thoughtful use of economic insights and empirical evidence. An economist must carefully consider all views. Subjective moral value judgments can't be ignored.

● SHORT-ANSWER QUESTIONS

1. List three reasons why the statement "If you laid all economists end to end, they still wouldn't reach a conclusion" is partly true with regard to social policy.

2. Although the quotation in Question #1 has some validity, nevertheless liberal and conservative economists often agree in their views on social policy. What is the basis for their agreement?

3. What is *cost/benefit analysis*?

4. When it comes to the actions of politicians regulating our economy, most economists are cynics. Why?

5. What are three types of failure of market outcomes?

6. Why are many economists doubtful that the government can correct failure of market outcomes?

7. Your friend finds you tucked away in a cozy chair in the library studying for an economics exam on policy issues. Your friend says, "Why are you wasting your time? All you have to remember is *supply and demand* and you'll be able to answer any question in economics." How do you respond?

MATCHING THE TERMS
Match the terms to their definitions

___ 1. cost/benefit approach
___ 2. economic efficiency
___ 3. failure of market outcome
___ 4. Marxian (radical) model
___ 5. Pareto optimal policies
___ 6. public choice model
___ 7. rational
___ 8. sin tax

a. Approach in which one assigns a cost and benefit to alternatives, and draws a conclusion on the basis of those costs and benefits.
b. Policies that benefit some people and hurt no one.
c. A model that focuses on equitable distribution of power, rights, and income among social classes.
d. Tax that discourages activities society believes are harmful.
e. A model that focuses on self-interest of politicians.
f. What individuals do is in their own best interest.
g. Achieving a goal at the lowest possible cost.
h. Even though the market is functioning properly, it is not achieving society's goals.

● PROBLEMS AND APPLICATIONS

1. For the following situations, which of the following regulations would you recommend government implement?

   a. A regulation requiring airline mechanics to check whether all bolts are tightened. This decreases the probability of having an accident by .001. The cost of the average crash is estimated at $200 million for the plane and $400 million in lives. The cost of implementing the program is $16 million.

   b. A regulation requiring that all cars have driver-side airbags. This adds $500 to the cost of a car. Having an airbag in a car reduces the chance of dying in a car crash by 1/720. The average individual values his/her life at $500,000.

   c. A regulation stiffening government rules for workplace safety. The cost per worker is $5,000 and the regulations are expected to reduce workplace fatalities by .002. Workers value their lives at an average of $2 million.

   d. What are the problems with using the cost/benefit approach to decide (a), (b), and (c)?

2. Why does it often appear to the lay public that economists never agree on social policy?

3. Assume economists have undertaken cost/benefit analysis of a problem and are unanimously in favor of a particular policy proposal over all other proposals. Why might this policy recommendation not be enacted as policy?

● A BRAIN TEASER

1. Why did former President Harry S. Truman say in jest that he wished he could find a one-armed economist?

● MULTIPLE CHOICE

Circle the one best answer for each of the following questions:

1. Which statement follows from economic theory alone?
   a. The minimum wage should be increased.
   b. The minimum wage should be decreased.
   c. There should be no minimum wage.
   d. No policy prescription follows from economic theory alone.

2. It is important to be familiar with many economic models because:
   a. the models are objective.
   b. the models are subjective.
   c. each model captures different aspects of reality.
   d. the models are Pareto optimal.

3. When an economist states that whether baby seals should be killed depends upon the costs and benefits, according to the text they are being:
   a. coldhearted.
   b. subjective.
   c. objective.
   d. conjective.

4. In an automobile crash, people were killed because an automobile company saved $10 by placing the gas tank in the rear of the car. An economist would:
   a. determine whether this made sense with cost/benefit analysis.
   b. see this as reasonable.
   c. see this as unreasonable.
   d. argue that no amount of money should be spared to save a life.

5. Suppose that filtering your water at home reduces your chances from dying of giardia (an intestinal parasite) by 1/45,000. The filter costs you $400 to install. You have chosen to install the filter. Which dollar value best reflects the minimum value you implicitly place on your life?
   a. $400.
   b. $45,000.
   c. $1,800,000.
   d. $18,000,000.

6. The government is considering requiring auto manufacturers to reinforce the roofs of SUV vehicles to reduce their collapse in roll-over accidents. The reinforcement adds $600 to the cost of an SUV. The probability of a fatality from a collapsed roof is 1/1,000. The average individual values his/her life at $1,000,000. Economists would be:
   a. in favor of the regulation because the marginal benefit of $1,000 exceeds the marginal cost.
   b. in favor of the regulation because the marginal cost of $600 exceeds the marginal benefit.
   c. against the regulation because the marginal cost of $1,000 exceeds the marginal benefit.
   d. against the regulation because the marginal benefits of $600 exceeds the marginal cost.

7. If the equilibrium wage is below the wage necessary for survival:
   a. there is no problem because the market is in equilibrium.
   b. there is a market failure due to informational problems.
   c. there is a market failure due to an externality.
   d. there is a failure of market outcome.

8. Maximizing total producer and consumer
    surplus in a market means that:
    a. the economy is as well off as it can be.
    b. total market output is as large as it can be in
        that market.
    c. income is unfairly distributed.
    d. income is fairly distributed.

9. As economists generally use the term, in a
    society it is *inefficient* to supply medicine to
    those who do not have the income to pay for
    it. This statement is:
    a. correct because economists use the term
        efficiency as a shorthand referring only to
        total output.
    b. wrong because medicine is necessary for
        life.
    c. correct because economists do not care
        about the poor.
    d. wrong because economics does not take
        distribution into account.

10. If a person buys more of a good, that person is:
    a. better off.
    b. worse off.
    c. most likely better off.
    d. most likely worse off.

11. If society establishes a law preventing people
    from selling themselves into slavery:
    a. consumer surplus will be lowered.
    b. consumer surplus will be increased.
    c. economic theory will find that law incorrect.
    d. economic theory will find that law correct.

12. An economist might *not favor* undertaking a
    policy to correct a failure of market outcome
    because economists:
    a. don't recognize failures in market outcomes.
    b. see the possibility of government failure.
    c. are trained to support the market no matter
        what.
    d. see the possibility of market failure offsetting
        the failure in market outcome.

● POTENTIAL ESSAY QUESTIONS

You may also see essay questions similar to the "Problems & Applications" and "A Brain Teaser" exercises.

1. What is cost/benefit analysis? How is this
    related to why economists often find them-
    selves united with one another but at odds with
    the general public?

2. How can the presence of the economic
    (market), social, and political forces in all real-
    world economies, and economists' use of
    benefit/cost analysis help explain the disagree-
    ment among economists concerning what is
    considered "appropriate" social policy? Even
    if economists all agreed upon what is "appro-
    priate" policy, why might that policy never be
    enacted?

━━━━━ ANSWERS ━━━━━

SHORT-ANSWER QUESTIONS

1. The statement is true to the extent that economists sometimes differ in their views on social policy. Three reasons for their differing views are that (1) they have different underlying values, (2) they interpret empirical evidence differently, and (3) they use different underlying models. (525)

2. Liberal and conservative economists often agree in their views on social policy because they use the same models, which focus on incentives and individual choice. (527)

3. *Cost/benefit analysis* is an analysis in which one assigns a cost and benefit to alternatives and draws a conclusion on the basis of those costs and benefits. The optimal amount of any activity is the level at which marginal benefit equals marginal cost. (528)

4. The typical economist views many government regulations as the result of political expediency, and not a reflection of cost/benefit considerations. Most economists believe that decisions should be made on a cost/benefit basis instead of on the basis of political pressure placed on politicians by special interest groups. (531-532)

5. Three separate types of failures of market outcomes include (1) failures due to distributional issues, (2) failures due to rationality problems of individuals, and (3) failures due to violations of inalienable, or at least partially inalienable, rights of individuals. (532-537)

6. For the government to correct a problem it must (1) recognize the problem, (2) have the will to deal with it, and (3) have the ability to deal with it. Government can seldom do all three of these well. (537-539)

7. You tell your friend to remember the admonition in your textbook: "Teaching a parrot the phrase *supply and demand* does not make it an economist." Elaborating, you tell her that economics involves the thoughtful use of economic insights and empirical evidence. Real-world problems are complex and cannot be explained just with simple models. You are right in taking the time to learn the details. (539)

━━━━━ ANSWERS ━━━━━

MATCHING

1-a; 2-g; 3-h; 4-c; 5-b; 6-e; 7-f; 8-d.

━━━━━ ANSWERS ━━━━━

PROBLEMS AND APPLICATIONS

1. For each of these, you calculate the costs and benefits of the regulation. If the cost is higher than the benefit, you would recommend not implementing the program. If the cost is lower than the benefit, you would recommend implementing the program. For each you are assuming you are given all relevant information.

    a. The benefit is saving a plane worth $200 million and saving lives worth $400 million. The regulation reduces the probability of a crash by .001. The marginal benefit is .001 times $600 million = $600,000. The marginal cost is $16 million. Don't implement the program because marginal cost is more than marginal benefit. (527-530)

    b. The benefit is the value of a saved life of $500,000, times the increased probability of living, 1/720 = $694. This is greater than the marginal cost to consumers of $500. Implement the program. (527-530)

    c. The benefit is the value of a saved life of $2 million times the increased probability of not having a fatal accident, $2 million × .002 = $4,000. The marginal cost is $5,000 per worker, which is greater than the marginal benefit. Don't implement the program. (527-530)

    d. The above examples include only quantifiable costs and benefits and involve a huge amount of ambiguity and subjectivity in the calculations. Economists' subjective estimates of the benefit of lives and costs of the program can vary enormously, thus affecting the recommendation enormously. (530-531)

2. Economists often disagree on social policy because of their different underlying subjective value judgments, because of imprecise empirical evidence and because they focus on different aspects of a policy or problem (because their underlying models differ). (525-526)

3. The policymakers (e.g. politicians) may have weighed the non-quantifiable (qualitative) social and political costs and benefits of the policy recommendation differently than the economists have. Equally reasonable people disagree over non-quantifiable costs and benefits. Therefore, what makes sense from a purely economic perspective may not be deemed politically, or socially, acceptable. (531-532)

━━━━   ANSWERS   ━━━━

A BRAIN TEASER

1. Economists are trained to weigh both benefits and costs associated with any policy or course of action. On the one hand, there are the benefits. On the other hand, there are the costs. Usually, like Harry Truman, politicians only want to hear the benefits. But, unfortunately, "there ain't no such thing as a free lunch." (530-532 and 538)

━━━━   ANSWERS   ━━━━

MULTIPLE CHOICE

1. d   Economic theory must be combined with subjective value judgments and empirical evidence to arrive at policy recommendations. See pages 525-527.

2. c   Models are neither objective, subjective, nor Pareto optimal. They simply are a framework for looking at reality. See page 526.

3. c   Economists are trained to look at every decision in reference to costs and benefits as a way of maintaining their objectivity

and keeping their subjective views out of policy. Conjective is not a word. While that may seem coldhearted, the text emphasizes that it seems so only in the short run. See pages 527-530.

4. a   Economists approach all issues with cost/benefit analysis. See pages 527-530.

5. d   You implicitly value your life at $(45,000 \times \$400) = \$18,000,000$. See pages 528-530.

6. a   The marginal benefit is $1,000 ($1,000,000 $\times 1/1,000$). It exceeds the marginal cost of $600. Economists would favor the regulation. See pages 528-530.

7. d   The market is working as it is supposed to but almost all would agree that the result is undesirable; there is a failure of market outcome. See pages 532-534.

8. b   Consumer and producer surplus focus on total output regardless of how it is distributed. See page 533.

9. a   The statement is correct given the shorthand that economists use when referring to efficiency. What is efficient may not be desirable. See pages 533-534.

10. c   While economists generally assume that people will do what is in their best interest, it is still possible that they will not do so. See page 534.

11. a   Since the law involves a restriction of trade, consumer surplus will be lowered. It still is a good law, however. Economic theory does not find laws correct or incorrect. See pages 535-536.

12. b   Economists see government failure as important and sometimes government intervention can make a problem worse, not better. See page 537.

ANSWERS

POTENTIAL ESSAY QUESTIONS

The following are annotated answers. They indicate the general idea behind the answer.

1. Cost/benefit analysis is analysis in which one assigns costs and benefits to alternatives, and draws a conclusion on the basis of those costs and benefits. Note that it is marginal costs and marginal benefits that are relevant. Economists try to quantify those costs and benefits—to use empirical evidence to help reach a conclusion. The general public often does not.

2. Economists do take into consideration the economic, social, and political consequences associated with a policy. However, not all the costs and benefits associated with a particular policy are quantifiable with respect to each of these three forces. This leaves some room for subjective value judgments with respect to what the benefits and costs of a policy are. Moreover, empirical evidence is not exact. There is also some room for focusing on different aspects of a problem. Finally, if the policy is undertaken in a political environment, as is usually the case, then political considerations by policymakers may take precedence over the social and economic considerations.

Pretest
Chapters 19 - 23

Take this test in test conditions, giving yourself a limited amount of time to complete the questions. Ideally, check with your professor to see how much time he or she allows for an average multiple choice question and multiply this by 23. This is the time limit you should set for yourself for this pretest. If you do not know how much time your teacher would allow, we suggest 1 minute per question, or about 23 minutes.

1. The irony of any need-based program is that it:
   a. increases the number of needy.
   b. decreases the number of needy.
   c. creates other needs.
   d. destroys needs.

2. The term "derived demand" refers to:
   a. demand by consumers for advertised products.
   b. the demand for luxury goods that is derived from cultural phenomena such as fashion.
   c. the demand for factors of production by firms.
   d. the demand for derivatives.

3. As a factor becomes more important in the production process, the:
   a. firm's derived demand for the factor becomes less elastic.
   b. firm's derived demand for the factor becomes more elastic.
   c. firm's derived demand will not be affected.
   d. elasticity of the derived demand could become either higher or lower.

4. A firm has just changed from being a competitive firm to being a monopolist. Its derived demand for labor:
   a. will increase.
   b. will decrease.
   c. might increase or might decrease.
   d. is unaffected because whether the firm is a competitive firm or a monopolist has no effect on the firm's derived demand for labor.

5. Compared to a competitive labor market, a monopsonist hires:
   a. fewer workers and pays them a higher wage.
   b. fewer workers and pays them a lower wage.
   c. more workers and pays them a higher wage.
   d. more workers and pays them a lower wage.

6. The Lorenz curve is:
   a. a type of supply curve.
   b. a type of demand curve.
   c. a geometric representation of the share distribution of income.
   d. a geometric representation of the socioeconomic distribution of income.

7. If the government increases the amount of food stamps and housing assistance it gives out, the level of poverty in the United States, as officially defined:
   a. will be reduced.
   b. will be increased.
   c. will remain unchanged.
   d. cannot be determined from the information.

8. Refer to the graph below. The Gini coefficient is shown by which area?
   a. A/B.
   b. A/(A + B).
   c. B/A.
   d. B/(A + B).

9. Imposing a tax of 40 percent on high income workers in order to give the revenue to low income workers may not be especially effective in redistributing income if the tax:
   a. has large incentive effects.
   b. has no incentive effects.
   c. is seen as a sin tax.
   d. is not seen as a sin tax.

10. An externality is:
   a. the effect of a decision on a third party not taken into account by a decision maker.
   b. another name for exports.
   c. an event that is external to the economy.
   d. the external effect of a government policy.

11. Refer to the graph below. The S curve represents the marginal private cost of production, and the D curve represents the marginal private benefit to consumers of the good. If there is a negative externality of production, and one wants to adjust the curves so that the equilibrium demonstrates the appropriate marginal social costs, either the:

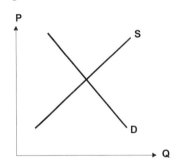

   a. S curve should be shifted in to the left or the D curve should be shifted out to the right.
   b. S curve should be shifted out to the right or the D curve should be shifted in to the left.
   c. S curve should be shifted out to the right or the D curve should be shifted out to the right.
   d. S curve should be shifted in to the left or the D curve should be shifted in to the left.

12. Refer to the graph below. If the government were attempting to set an effluent fee, the amount of that effluent fee should be:
   a. P_1.
   b. P_2.
   c. $P_1 - P_2$.
   d. $P_1 - P_3$.

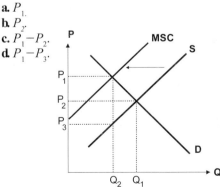

13. A public good is:
   a. any good traded in markets.
   b. a good that is nonexclusive and nonrival.
   c. a good provided only to those who pay for it.
   d. rarely provided by government.

14. Government failure:
   a. always outweighs market failure.
   b. sometimes outweighs market failure.
   c. never outweighs market failure.
   d. is the same as market failure.

15. Which of the following is a key difference between traditional and behavioral economics?
   a. Traditional economics focuses on economic engineering, while behavioral economics is the study of free markets.
   b. Traditional economics bases its analysis on the assumption that individuals are rational and self-interested, while behavioral economics takes into account people's predictably irrational behavior.
   c. Traditional economics emphasizes the positive role that government can have in influencing people's choices, while behavioral economics emphasizes the fact that government does not know what is good for people and is often plagued by inefficiency and failures.
   d. Traditional economics considers the paternalistic component of nudges and pushes to be important, while behavioral economics puts more value on the libertarian basis of free markets.

16. Nudges:
   a. always make consumers better off.
   b. are often suggested by traditional economists as a way to guide individuals to make better choices than they would on their own.
   c. aren't controversial because they meet the libertarian paternalistic criterion.
   d. are often used by firms to guide their customers to make choices that benefit the firm.

17. Structuring a health care program with a default option of automatic enrollment is an example of:
 a. using choice architecture to influence people's choices.
 b. a policy that is neither libertarian nor paternalistic.
 c. a policy that will lead most people to not choose a health care plan.
 d. a policy that would likely be supported by traditional economists more than behavioral economists.

18. When the government uses a regulatory or tax policy to get firms or individuals to use "appropriate" nudges, it is called a:
 a. nudge policy.
 b. traditional economic policy.
 c. push policy.
 d. default option policy.

19. Which of the following is NOT a misgiving expressed by traditional economists about behavioral economic policies?
 a. The only nudges that help society are those by private firms.
 b. Very few policies meet the criterion of libertarian paternalism.
 c. It isn't clear that government knows better than individuals in most cases.
 d. Government policies may make the situation worse, rather than better.

20. Which statement follows from economic theory alone?
 a. The minimum wage should be increased.
 b. The minimum wage should be decreased.
 c. There should be no minimum wage.
 d. No policy prescription follows from economic theory alone.

21. In an automobile crash, people were killed because an automobile company saved $10 by placing the gas tank in the rear of the car. An economist would:
 a. determine whether this made sense with cost/benefit analysis.
 b. see this as reasonable.
 c. see this as unreasonable.
 d. argue that no amount of money should be spared to save a life.

22. Suppose that filtering your water at home reduces your chances from dying of giardia (an intestinal parasite) by 1/45,000. The filter costs you $400 to install. You have chosen to install the filter. Which dollar value best reflects the minimum value you implicitly place on your life?
 a. $400.
 b. $45,000.
 c. $1,800,000.
 d. $18,000,000.

23. If society establishes a law preventing people from selling themselves into slavery:
 a. consumer surplus will be lowered.
 b. consumer surplus will be increased.
 c. economic theory will find that law incorrect.
 d. economic theory will find that law correct.

ANSWERS

1.	a	(19:4)	13.	b	(21:11)
2.	c	(19:7)	14.	b	(21:15)
3.	a	(19:9)	15.	b	(22:1)
4.	b	(19:11)	16.	d	(22:5)
5.	b	(19:13)	17.	a	(22:6)
6.	c	(20:1)	18.	c	(22:9)
7.	c	(20:5)	19.	a	(22:11)
8.	b	(20:8)	20.	d	(23:1)
9.	a	(20:10)	21.	a	(23:4)
10.	a	(21:2)	22.	d	(23:5)
11.	d	(21:3)	23.	a	(23:11)
12.	d	(21:6)			

Key: The figures in parentheses refer to multiple choice question and chapter numbers. For example (1:2) is multiple choice question 2 from chapter 1.

ECONOMIC GROWTH, BUSINESS CYCLES, UNEMPLOYMENT, AND INFLATION

24

● CHAPTER AT A GLANCE

This review is based upon the learning objectives that open the chapter.

1. The long-run framework focuses on supply. The short-run framework focuses on demand. (546-547)

   Issues of growth are considered in a long-run framework. Business cycles are generally considered in a short-run framework. Unemployment and inflation fall within both frameworks.

2a. Growth is usually measured by changes in real GDP. U.S. economic output has grown at an annual rate of 2.5 to 3.5 percent. (547-548)

   Growth is desired because it increases standards of living.

2b. The range of growth rates among countries is wide. (548-549)

   Economies in Africa have consistently grown at below average rates. Japan and Western Europe grew quickly in the last half of the 20th century.

2c. Since 1945 the United States has had 11 recessions. (550-553)

2d. The target rate of unemployment is somewhere around 5 percent. (556)

   The target rate of unemployment has been called the "natural" rate of unemployment.

2e. Since World War II, the U.S. inflation rate has remained positive and relatively stable. (563-561)

3. The four phases of the business cycle are: the peak, the downturn, the trough, and the upturn. (551-552)

   Note!
   - *There is an overall upward secular growth trend of 2.5-3.5% shown by the dotted line.*
   - *We want to smooth out fluctuations because of the problems associated with them.*
   - *Two problems with a downturn (recession) are (a) cyclical unemployment and (b) low growth rate.*
   - *One problem with an upturn (expansion) is demand-pull inflation.*

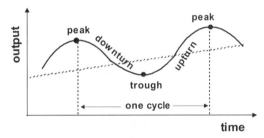

4a. Unemployment rate $= \dfrac{\text{unemployed}}{\text{labor force}} \times 100.$ (554, 559)

   Unemployment measures are imperfect but are still a good gauge of the economy's performance.

4b. Some microeconomic categories of unemployment identified are: reason for unemployment, demographic unemployment, duration of unemployment, and unemployment by industry. (562)

✔ *Remember Okun's rule of thumb:*
   +1 percentage point of unemployment →
   −2 percent change in output

5. Potential output is defined as the output that will be achieved at the target rate of unemployment and the target level of capacity utilization. It is difficult to know precisely where potential output is. (561-562)

   Recession:
   Actual output (income) < Potential output.

   Expansion:
   Actual output (income) > Potential output.

   Target rate of unemployment (about 5%) is the lowest rate of unemployment that policymakers believe is achievable under existing conditions (where inflation is not accelerating). It is the rate of unemployment that exists when the economy is operating at potential.

6a. Inflation is a continual rise in the price level. (563)

   Price indexes are used to measure inflation; The most often used are the Producer Price Index (PPI), GDP deflator, and the Consumer Price Index (CPI).

6b. The "real" amount is the nominal amount adjusted for inflation. Real output is the nominal output divided by the price index multiplied by 100. (564-568)

   Real means "inflation-adjusted."

   $$Real\ Output = \frac{nominal\ output}{price\ index} \times 100$$

   Real interest rate = Nominal interest − Inflation

7. While inflation may not make the nation poorer, it does cause income to be redistributed and can reduce the amount of information that prices are supposed to convey. (569-570)

   Inflation hurts those who cannot or do not raise their prices, but benefits those who can and do raise their prices.

● SHORT-ANSWER QUESTIONS

1. What are the two frameworks economists use to analyze unemployment, inflation, growth, and business cycles? What distinguishes the two frameworks from one another?

2. What is the average growth rate of real output in the United States since 1890 to the present? What are the costs and the benefits of growth?

3. How long has the average expansion since mid-1945 lasted?

4. Since the late 1980s, what has been the target rate of unemployment?

5. What is the difference between pre-World War II and post-World War II (1945) inflation in the United States?

6. Label the four phases of the business cycle in the graph below.

7. How is the unemployment rate calculated?

8. Who in the United States does not work and is nevertheless not counted as unemployed?

9. State two categories of unemployment for which microeconomic policies are appropriate. Why are such categories important to follow?

10. How is the target rate of unemployment related to potential output?

11. Define inflation. If there were no inflation what would happen to the distinction between a real concept and a nominal concept?

12. Suppose the price of a Maserati in 1975 was $75,000 and the price of a Maserati in 2008 was $210,000. Your parents exclaim that the prices of Maseratis have risen by 180%! Wow! You tell them that the price of a Maserati really hasn't risen that much. They are confusing real and nominal concepts. Explain what you mean.

13. What is the difference between expected and unexpected inflation?

14. What are two important costs of inflation?

MATCHING THE TERMS
Match the terms to their definitions

_____ **1.** business cycle

_____ **2.** consumer price index

_____ **3.** cyclical unemployment

_____ **4.** deflation

_____ **5.** frictional unemployment

_____ **6.** GDP deflator

_____ **7.** hyperinflation

_____ **8.** inflation

_____ **9.** labor force participation rate

_____ **10.** Okun's rule of thumb

_____ **11.** potential output

_____ **12.** real output

_____ **13.** recession

_____ **14.** structural unemployment

_____ **15.** target rate of unemployment

_____ **16.** unemployment rate

a. A downturn that persists for more than two consecutive quarters.

b. A continual rise in the price level.

c. A one percentage point change in the unemployment rate will cause output to change in the opposite direction by 2 percent.

d. Lowest sustainable rate of unemployment policymakers believe is achievable under existing conditions.

e. Index of inflation measuring prices of a fixed "basket" of consumer goods, weighted according to each component's share of an average consumer's expenditures.

f. Index of the average price of the components in GDP relative to a base year.

g. Labor force as a percentage of the total population at least 16 years old.

h. Inflation that hits triple digits (100 percent) or more per year.

i. Output that would materialize at the target rate of unemployment and the target rate of capacity utilization.

j. The total amount of goods and services produced, adjusted for price level changes.

k. The upward or downward movement of economic activity that occurs around the growth trend.

l. The percentage of people in the labor force who can't find a job.

m. Unemployment caused by new entrants to the job market and people who have left their jobs to look for and find other jobs.

n. Unemployment resulting from changes in the structure of the economy itself.

o. Unemployment resulting from fluctuations in economic activity.

p. A continual fall in the price level.

● PROBLEMS AND APPLICATIONS

1. State Okun's law (rule of thumb). For each of the following increases in the unemployment rate, state what will likely happen to output in the United States:

   a. Unemployment rate falls 2 percentage points.

   b. Unemployment rate falls 1 percentage point.

   c. Unemployment rate increases 3 percentage points.

2. For each, state whether the unemployment is structural or cyclical.

   a. As the United States becomes a more high-tech producer, labor-intensive factories relocate to low-wage countries. Factory workers lose their jobs and the unemployment rate rises.

   b. As it becomes more acceptable for mothers to work, more women enter the labor market looking for work. The unemployment rate rises.

   c. Foreign economies slow and demand fewer U.S. exports. Unemployment rate rises.

3. Calculate the following given the information about the economy in the table:

Total population	290 million
Noninstitutional population	220 million
Incapable of working	70 million
Not in the labor force	75 million
Employed	135 million
Unemployed	10 million

   a. Labor force.

   b. Unemployment rate.

4. Create a price index for New England Patriots fans using the following basket of goods with 2009 prices as the base year.

Quantities in 2009	Prices 2009	2010
12 packs of Pepsi	$2.50/pck	$2.00/pck
12 fan T-shirts	$15/shirt	$20/shirt
16 football tickets	$25/ticket	$30/ticket

   a. What is the price of the basket of goods in each year? Show how the price index is 100 in the base year 2009.

   b. Using 2009 as the base year, what is the price index in 2010? By how much have prices risen?

   c. What are some potential flaws of this price index?

5. Calculate the following given the following information about the economy in 1985, 1995, and 2006:

	1985	1995	2006
Nominal GDP (in billions of dollars)	4,220.3	____	12,246.6
GDP deflator (index, 2000=100)	69.7	92.1	____
Real GDP (in billions of 2000 dollars)	____	8031.7	11,415.3
Population (in millions)	238	265	300

   a. Nominal GDP in 1995.

   b. Real GDP in 1985.

   c. GDP deflator in 2006.

   d. Rise in the price level from 1985 to 2006.

   e. Growth in real output from 1985 to 2006.

   f. Per capita real GDP in 1985, 1995, 2006. What was the growth in per capita real output from 1985 to 2006?

6. Answer each of the following questions about nominal output, real output, and inflation:
   a. Nominal output increased from $12,445.8 billion in 2005 to $13,246.6 billion in 2006. The GDP deflator rose over that same year by 2.9%. By how much did real output increase?

   b. Real output increased from $9.19 trillion to $9.21 trillion from 2000 to 2001. The GDP deflator rose over that same year by 2.5%. By how much did nominal output increase?

   c. Real output decreased from $6.70 billion in 1990 to $6.67 billion in 1991. Nominal output rose by 3.2%. By how much did the price level rise from 1990 to 1991?

● A BRAIN TEASER

1. How could output and unemployment rise in an economy at the same time?

● MULTIPLE CHOICE

Circle the one best answer for each of the following questions:

1. Inflation and unemployment:
    a. are best studied in the long-run framework.
    b. are best studied in the short-run framework.
    c. fall within both the short- and long-run frameworks.
    d. are not problems of today and therefore are not studied.

2. All of the following are long-run growth policies *except*:
    a. increasing government spending to spur consumer spending.
    b. reducing tax rates to increase incentives to work.
    c. providing funding for research.
    d. following policies to reduce interest rates and increase business investment.

3. If a country of 296 million people has a total income of $12 trillion, its per capita income is:
   a. $32.52.
   b. $35,520.
   c. $40.54.
   d. $40,541.

4. The secular trend growth rate in the United States is approximately:
   a. 1 to 1.5 percent per year.
   b. 2.5 to 3.5 percent per year.
   c. 5 to 5.5 percent per year.
   d. 7 to 7.5 percent per year.

5. Some people have argued that the two goals of (1) environmental protection and (2) economic growth that involves increased material consumption by individuals do not necessarily contradict each other because spending on the environment can create growth and jobs. This argument:
   a. offers great hope for the future.
   b. is incorrect because environmental issues are not as important as material consumption.
   c. is correct because material consumption is not as important as the environment.
   d. is incorrect because the environmental projects will use some of the resources generated from growth, leaving little or nothing for increased personal consumption.

6. From 1950 to 2009, which geographic area or country had the highest per capita growth rate?
   a. China.
   b. Western Europe.
   c. North America.
   d. Latin America.

7. The business cycle characterized by the Great Depression occurred in the early
   a. 1900s.
   b. 1930s.
   c. 1950s.
   d. 1960s.

8. Leading indicators include:
   a. manufacturing and trade sales volume.
   b. number of employees on non-agricultural payrolls.
   c. industrial production.
   d. new orders for goods and materials.

9. A Classical economist is most likely to support government intervention when an economy is:
   a. at a peak.
   b. at a trough.
   c. in a depression.
   d. in an upturn.

10. Under pure capitalism, the main deterrent of unemployment is:
    a. pure government intervention.
    b. pure market intervention.
    c. the fear of hunger.
    d. new immigrants entering the country.

11. Since the 1980s the target rate of unemployment generally has been:
    a. between 2 and 4 percent.
    b. between 3 and 5 percent.
    c. between 4 and 6 percent.
    d. between 7 and 9 percent.

12. Keynesians:
    a. generally favor activist government policies.
    b. generally favor laissez-faire policies.
    c. believe that frictional unemployment does not exist.
    d. believe that all unemployment is cyclical unemployment.

13. Classicals:
    a. generally favor activist government policies.
    b. generally favor laissez-faire policies.
    c. believe that frictional unemployment does not exist.
    d. believe that all unemployment is cyclical unemployment.

14. The level of output that would materialize at the target rate of unemployment and the target rate of capital utilization is called:
    a. nominal output.
    b. actual output.
    c. potential output.
    d. utilized output.

15. The real interest rate is equal to the:
    a. nominal interest rate minus the inflation rate.
    b. nominal interest rate plus the inflation rate.
    c. inflation rate minus the nominal interest rate.
    d. inflation rate plus the nominal interest rate.

16. Okun's rule of thumb states that:
   a. a 1 percentage-point change in the unemployment rate will cause output to change in the same direction by 2 percent.
   b. a 1 percentage-point change in the unemployment rate will cause output to change in the opposite direction by 2 percent.
   c. a 2 percentage-point change in the unemployment rate will cause output to change in the same direction by 1 percent.
   d. a 2 percentage-point change in the unemployment rate will cause output to change in the opposite direction by 1 percent.

17. Using Okun's rule of thumb, if unemployment rises from 5 to 6 percent, one would expect total output of $5 trillion to:
   a. rise by $5 billion.
   b. rise by $100 billion.
   c. fall by $100 billion.
   d. fall by $5 billion.

18. A one-time rise in the price level is:
   a. inflation if that rise is above 5 percent.
   b. inflation if that rise is above 10 percent.
   c. inflation if that rise is above 15 percent.
   d. not inflation.

19. Food and beverages make up about 15 percent of total expenditures. If food and beverage prices rise by 10 percent while the other components of the price index remain constant, approximately by how much will the price index rise?
   a. 1 percent.
   b. 1.5 percent.
   c. 15 percent.
   d. 25 percent.

20. Real output is:
   a. total amount of goods and services produced.
   b. total amount of goods and services produced adjusted for price level changes.
   c. total amount of goods produced, adjusted for services that aren't real.
   d. total amount of goods and services that are really produced as opposed to ones that are resold.

21. If the price level rises by 20 percent and real output remains constant, by how much will nominal output rise?
   a. 1 percent.
   b. 5 percent.
   c. 20 percent.
   d. 40 percent.

22. A cost of inflation is that:
   a. it makes everyone poorer.
   b. it makes the poor poorer but the rich richer.
   c. There are no costs of inflation because inflation does not make the society as a whole poorer.
   d. it reduces the informational content of prices.

23. Unexpected inflation:
   a. makes everyone poorer.
   b. redistributes income from those who raised their prices to those who did not.
   c. redistributes income from those who did not raise their prices to those who did.
   d. is impossible since firms always plan price increases.

● POTENTIAL ESSAY QUESTIONS

You may also see essay questions similar to the "Problems & Applications" and "A Brain Teaser" exercises.

1. Full employment, keeping inflation under control, and economic growth are among the major macroeconomic goals of all societies. Why is economic growth a major macroeconomic goal?

2. What is potential output and how is it related to the target rate of unemployment and the target level of capacity utilization? Which is greater: potential or actual output during a recession? During an economic boom?

3. What are some of the problems with the interpretation of unemployment statistics that can cause unemployment statistics to underestimate and to overestimate the true rate of unemployment? How do Classical and Keynesian economists differ in this regard?

ANSWERS

SHORT-ANSWER QUESTIONS

1. Economists use the long-run framework and the short-run framework to analyze macroeconomic problems. The long-run framework focuses on supply while the short-run framework focuses on demand. (546-547)

2. Real output has grown about 3.5% per year since 1890. In the 1970s and 1980s, the growth rate was more like 2.5 percent. In the late 1990s and early 2000s, it was again 3.5 percent. The benefits of growth are improvements in the standard of living, on average. The costs are pollution, resource exhaustion, and destruction of natural habitat. (547-550)

3. The average expansion since mid-1945 has lasted 57 months. (551-552)

4. Since the late 1980s, the target rate of unemployment has been around 5 percent. (556)

5. The inflation rate in the U.S. before World War II fluctuated and was sometimes positive and sometimes negative. Since World War II the price level has continually risen. (563)

6. The four phases of the business cycle are: the peak, the downturn (recession), the trough, and the upturn. They are labeled in the graph below. (551-552)

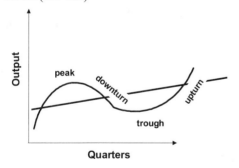

7. The unemployment rate is calculated by dividing the number of unemployed individuals by the number of people in the civilian labor force, and multiplying the result by 100. (559-560)

8. Those who are not in the labor force and those incapable of working are not employed and are not counted as unemployed. They include students, retirees, homemakers, those incapable of working, and those who choose not to participate in the labor force. (559-560)

9. Two microeconomic subcategories of unemployment include the reason for unemployment and demographic unemployment. Others are duration of unemployment and unemployment by industry. These categories are important to follow because policies affect different types of unemployment differently and sometimes macro policies should be supplemented by micro policies. (562)

10. Potential output is that level of output that will be achieved at the target rate of unemployment. (562)

11. Inflation is a continual rise in the price level. If there were no inflation there would be no difference between real and nominal concepts. A real concept is the nominal concept adjusted for inflation. (563, 564-568)

12. Nominally Maseratis have risen by 180% from 1975 to 2008, but all other prices have risen during that time period too, including wages. You must adjust the rise in the aggregate price level to find out how much Maseratis have risen in real terms. From 1975 to 2008, the price level rose by 147%. (We used the *Economic Report of the President* to find this information.) So, the real price of the Maserati rose by approximately 33% from 1975 to 2008. (564-569)

13. Expected inflation is the amount of inflation that people predict. Unexpected inflation is inflation that is a surprise. (568-569)

14. Two important costs of inflation are that it redistributes income from people who cannot or do not raise their prices to people who can or do raise their prices, and it can reduce the amount of information that prices are supposed to convey. (569-570)

■■■ ANSWERS ■■■

MATCHING

1-k; 2-e; 3-o; 4-p; 5-m; 6-f; 7-h; 8-b; 9-g; 10-c;
11-i; 12-j; 13-a; 14-n; 15-d; 16-l.

■■■ ANSWERS ■■■

PROBLEMS AND APPLICATIONS

1. Okun's rule of thumb states that a 1-percent-age point change in the unemployment rate will cause output in the economy to change in the opposite direction by 2 percent.
    a. Output rises 4 percent. (562)
    b. Output rises 2 percent. (562)
    c. Output falls 6 percent. (562)

2. a. Structural because this is a structural change in the economy. (555)
    b. Structural because this is a change in social structure. (555)
    c. Cyclical because this is unemployment due to a change in economic activity. (555)

3. a. Labor force = employed + unemployed = 145 million. (559-560)
    b. Unemployment rate = (unemployed/labor force)×100=6.9%. (559-560)

4. a. The price of the basket in 2009 is $610 and in 2010 is $744. Since 2009 is the base year, the index must be 100. This is calculated as (price of the basket in 2009)/(price of the basket in 2009)=$610/$610 × 100=100. (562-563)
    b. The price index in 2010 is (price of the basket in 2010)/(price of the basket in 2009)=$744/$610 × 100=122. Prices rose by 22%. (562-563)
    c. Some potential flaws are that (1) the basket of goods is small and might not reflect the true basket of goods purchased by Patriots fans, (2) the basket of goods is fixed (since the price of Pepsi fell, fans might be buying more Pepsi and fewer football tickets), (3) the basket does not reflect quality improvements (since the Patriots won the Super Bowl in 2009, the quality of subsequent games in 2010 might

improve, but the tickets are counted as if they were the same as in 2009). (565-566)

5. a. Nominal GDP in 1995 is $7,397.2 billion dollars. Calculate this by multiplying real GDP in 1995 by the GDP deflator and dividing by 100. (564-568)
    b. Real GDP in 2000 dollars in 1985 is $6,055 billion. Calculate this by dividing nominal GDP by the GDP deflator and multiplying by 100. (564-568)
    c. GDP deflator in 2006 is 107.3. Calculate this by solving for GDP deflator in the equation: Real GDP=(nominal GDP/GDP deflator) × 100. (564-568)
    d. The price level rose by 54% from 1985 to 2006. Calculate this by dividing the change in the GDP price deflator and multiplying by 100: (107.3 − 69.7)/69.7 × 100. (564-568)
    e. Real output grew by 89% from 1985 to 2006. Calculate this by dividing the change in real GDP from 1985 to 2006 and multiplying by 100: (11,415.3 − 6,055)/6,055 × 100. (564-568)
    f. Per capita real GDP in 1985 was $25,441; in 1995 it was $30,308; in 2006 it was $38,051. Calculate this by dividing real GDP by the population. Per capita real GDP rose by 50% from 1985 to 2006. (564-568)

6. a. Nominal output increased by 6.4% from 2005 to 2006. Since the GDP deflator rose over that same year, we know that real output increased by less—specifically by 3.5% from 2005 to 2006. Subtract inflation from the change in nominal output to get the change in real output: 6.4% − 2.9% = 3.5%. (564-568)
    b. Real output increased 0.2% from 2000 to 2001. Since the GDP deflator rose 2.5% over that same year, we know that nominal output increased 2.7% from 2000 to 2001. Add inflation to the change in real output to find the change in nominal output: 2.5%+0.2%=2.7%. (564-568)
    c. Real output fell 0.45% from 1990 to 1991. Since nominal output rose by 3.2%, we know the price level rose 3.65% from 1990 to 1991. Subtract the change in real output from the change in nominal output to find the inflation rate: 3.2% − (−0.45%) =3.65%. (564-568)

ANSWERS

A BRAIN TEASER

1. Usually one would expect unemployment to fall as output rises because it takes more workers to produce more output. However, an increase in productivity of workers can cause an increase in output without any reduction in unemployment. Another possibility is that the labor force participation rate could be rising so that the labor force is rising at a faster pace than employment. This would cause unemployment to rise even though output is expanding and the economy is growing. (554-555)

ANSWERS

MULTIPLE CHOICE

1. c   As the text states on page 547, inflation and unemployment are both short- and long-run problems.

2. a   As stated on page 547, the long run focuses on supply issues that increase the incentive to work, create new technologies, and invest in capital.

3. d   Per capita income is calculated by dividing total income by total population as stated on page 548.

4. b   The secular trend is the long-term growth trend. See page 548.

5. d   As more material goods made available by growth are used for antipollution equipment, less is available for personal consumption. The added material goods have already been used. See page 550.

6. a   As seen in the table on page 548, China's per capita growth rate averaged 4.9 percent from 1950 to 2009. Western Europe's per capita growth rate was 2.2 percent, while North America's was 2.1 percent and Latin America's was 2.0 percent.

7. b   The Great Depression of the 1930s was the most severe downturn. See page 550.

8. d   The others are coincident indicators. Even if you didn't remember this, you should be able to figure out that the change in new orders predicts what firms think will be happening in the future, whereas the others tell what is happening now. See page 554.

9. c   Almost all economists believe government should intervene during a depression. See page 551.

10. c   As discussed on page 555, the fear of hunger was the main deterrent to unemployment. A second deterrent would have been emigration, but that would not be as good an answer. Since d says immigration (the flowing in of people), not emigration, d is definitely wrong.

11. c   The target rate of unemployment is around 5 percent. See page 556.

12. a   Keynesians generally favor activist government policies. See page 551.

13. b   Classicals generally favor laissez-faire policies. See page 551.

14. c   As discussed on page 562, the statement that begins the question is the definition of potential output.

15. a   The real interest rate is the nominal interest rate adjusted for inflation. See page 568.

16. b   This is the definition of Okun's rule of thumb. See page 562.

17. c   Total output moves in the opposite direction by 2% times $5 trillion, which equals a fall of $100 billion. See page 562.

18. d   As the text points out on page 563, inflation is a continual rise in the price level, so the use of the term "one-time" should have clued you that d is the answer.

19. b   To determine the price level rise you multiply each component by its price rise. Since only 15% of the total rose, you get 10% times 15% = 1.5%. See pages 563-565.

20. b   See pages 564-568. A reminder: A service is considered just as much a good and a component of real output as is a physical good.

21. c   If real output remains constant, then the nominal output must also rise by 20%, as discussed on page 566.

22. d   Inflation does not make society richer or poorer, and the distributional consequences of inflation differ, eliminating answers a and b. While the second part of c is true, that doesn't mean that there are no costs of inflation and, as discussed on page 569, one of those costs is the reduction in the informational content of prices.

23. c   As discussed on pages 567-569, unexpected inflation is inflation that surprises people. Those people who didn't raise their prices are surprised. Income is redistributed from those people who didn't raise their prices to those who did.

ANSWERS

POTENTIAL ESSAY QUESTIONS

The following are annotated answers. They indicate the general idea behind the answer.

1.   Economic growth is a major macroeconomic goal because it provides more jobs for a growing population. If output increases more than population increases then per capita growth occurs. Assuming there is no change in the distribution of the nation's income then everybody gets a "bigger piece of the pie." In this way economic growth increases the average absolute standard of living for people. *Remember, economic growth is valued by all nations because it raises the standard of living.*

2.   Potential output is the output that would materialize at the target rate of unemployment and the target level of capacity utilization. Potential output grows at the secular (long-term) trend rate of 2.5 to 3.5 percent per year. When the economy is in a recession, actual output is below potential output. When the economy is in a boom, actual output is above potential output.

3.   The Bureau of Labor Statistics (BLS) estimates the rate of unemployment. Underestimation can occur because discouraged workers are not counted as unemployed. Also, many people may work part-time but would like to work full-time. This "underemployment" is not reflected in unemployment statistics and suggests that the official unemployment statistics underestimate the true problem. Alternatively, some people may be counted as being unemployed when they are working in the underground economy–working for "cash under the table." In this case, the official statistics will overestimate true unemployment. The Classicals and Keynesians differ most when it comes to the number of discouraged workers. Some Keynesians argue that the BLS underestimates unemployment significantly because a great number of discouraged workers are not counted as being unemployed.

MEASURING
THE AGGREGATE ECONOMY

CHAPTER AT A GLANCE

This review is based upon the learning objectives that open the chapter.

1a. Gross domestic product (GDP): Aggregate final output of residents and businesses in an economy in a one-year period. (575)

GDP is total market ($) value of all __final__ goods and services produced in a one-year period.

1b. GDP = C + I + G + (X − M) is an accounting identity because it is defined as true. (575-577)

The above identity is really the expenditures approach, which states:

Total output = Total expenditures;
Total output = GDP;
Total expenditures=C+I+G+(X−M);
By substitution: GDP = C + I + G + (X−M).

✔ *Know what C, I, G, and X−M stand for!*

Also note:
(X − M) = Net exports.
If (X−M) is positive, then X>M→Trade surplus.
If (X−M) is negative, then X<M→Trade deficit.
If (X−M) is zero, then X=M→Trade balance.

2. To avoid double counting, you must eliminate intermediate goods, either by calculating only final output (expenditures approach), or by calculating only final income (income approach) by using the value added approach. (577-580)

✔ *Know what is and what is not included when calculating GDP.*

GDP does not include:
- *intermediate goods (sold for resale or further processing);*
- *second-hand sales;*
- *government transfers, housespouse production, or any other non-market activity;*
- *underground economic activity.*

3a. Net investment is gross investment less depreciation. (581-582)

Depreciation is the wear and tear of machines that happens during production. Some production goes to replacing depreciated machinery and is therefore unavailable for consumption.

3b. National output (GNP) is production by citizens of a country, whether the production happens within the geographic borders of a country or not. Domestic output (GDP) is production that occurs within the geographic borders of a country, whether it is done by citizens of the country or not. (582-583)

GNP = GDP + Net foreign factor income where:

Net foreign factor income is the foreign income of a country's citizens less the income of residents who are not citizens.

Net domestic product = GDP − Depreciation

4. Aggregate income is the sum of compensation of employees, rents, interest, and profit. (583-584)

The largest component of aggregate income is compensation of employees.

5. Aggregate income ≡ Aggregate production. (584-585)

Profit is the key to the equality between aggregate output and aggregate income. It is what remains after all the other firm's income is paid out.

6. Real GDP is nominal GDP adjusted for inflation. (586-587)

GDP is a price times quantity (P×Q) phenomenon. GDP can rise due to an increase in P (price level) and/or an increase in Q (real quantity of output).

Real GDP, in essence, holds prices (P) constant. Hence, real GDP is inflation (or deflation) adjusted.

$$GDP\ deflator = \frac{Nominal\ GDP}{Real\ GDP} \times 100$$

7a. Limitations of national income accounting include: (587-590)

- GDP measures economic activity, not welfare;
- Measurement problems exist;
- Subcategories are often interdependent.

GDP is not and was never intended to be a measure of social well-being.

7b. Using GDP to compare standards of living among countries has its problems. (585)

GDP only measures market activity. In developing countries individuals often produce and trade outside the market.

Market prices often vary considerably among countries making the value of the same income in terms of purchasing power different.

● SHORT-ANSWER QUESTIONS

1. What is GDP?

2. What are the four components of aggregate output?

3. Calculate the contribution of Chex cereal (from seeds to consumer) to GDP, using the following information:

Participants	Cost of materials	Value of Sales
Farmer	0	200
Chex factory	200	500
Distributor	500	800
Grocery store	800	1000

4. What is GNP? How does it differ from GDP?

5. What is the difference between gross investment and net investment?

6. What are the four components of aggregate income?

7. Say the price level rises 10% from an index of 1 to an index of 1.1 and nominal GDP rises from $4 trillion to $4.6 trillion. What is nominal GDP in the second period? What is real GDP in the second period?

8. As pointed out by the quotation that begins the chapter on measuring the aggregate economy, statistics can be misleading. In what way can aggregate economic statistics be misleading? Given your answer, why use them at all?

MATCHING THE TERMS
Match the terms to their definitions

___ 1. depreciation
___ 2. gross domestic product
___ 3. gross national product
___ 4. intermediate products
___ 5. net domestic product
___ 6. net foreign factor income
___ 7. nominal GDP
___ 8. real GDP
___ 9. value added
___ 10. wealth accounts

a. GDP calculated at existing prices.
b. Aggregate final output of residents and businesses in an economy in a one-year period.
c. GDP adjusted to take account of depreciation.
d. Aggregate final output of citizens and businesses of an economy in a one-year period.
e. Income from foreign domestic factor sources minus foreign factor incomes earned domestically.
f. Nominal GDP adjusted for inflation.
g. Products of one firm used as an input in the production of another firm's product.
h. A balance sheet of an economy's stock of assets and liabilities.
i. The increase in value that a firm contributes to a product or service.
j. The decrease in an asset's value.

PROBLEMS AND APPLICATIONS

1. Using the value added or final sales approach to calculate GDP, state how much the action described has added to GDP:

    a. A used car dealer buys a car for $3,000 and resells it for $3,300.

    b. A company sells 1,000 disks for $500 each. Of these, it sells 600 to other companies for production and 400 to individuals.

    c. A PC and software company sells 50 computers at a retail price of $1,000 apiece and 100 software packages at a retail price of $50 apiece to consumers. The same company sells 25 computers at $800 and 50 software packages at $30 apiece to retail companies. These companies then sell the 25 computers at $1,250 apiece and the 50 software packages at $75 apiece to consumers.

    d. Fred purchases 100 stock certificates valued at $5 apiece and pays a 10% commission. When the price declines to $4.50 apiece, Fred decides to sell all 100 certificates, again at a 10% commission.

    e. Your uncle George receives $600 Social Security income each month for one year.

2. Use the following table showing the production of 500 boxes of Wheaties cereal to calculate the contribution to GDP using the value-added approach.

Participants	Cost of materials	Value of sales
Farmer	$0	$150
Mill	$150	$250
Cereal maker	$250	$600
Wholesaler	$600	$800
Grocery store	$800	$1,000

a. Calculate the value added at each stage of production.

b. What is the total value of all sales?

c. What is the total value added?

d. What is the contribution to GDP of the production of those Wheaties?

3. There are three firms in an economy: X, Y, and Z. Firm X buys $200 worth of goods from firm Y and $300 worth of goods from firm Z, and produces 250 units of output at $4 per unit. Firm Y buys $150 worth of goods from firm X, and $250 worth of goods from firm Z, and produces 300 units of output at $6 per unit. Firm Z buys $75 worth of goods from firm X, and $50 worth of goods from firm Y, and produces 300 units at $2 per unit. All other products are sold to consumers. Answer the following:
a. What is GDP?

b. How much government revenue would a value added tax of 10% generate?

c. How much government revenue would an income tax of 10% generate?

d. How much government revenue would a 10% sales tax on final output generate?

4. You have been hired as a research assistant and are given the following data about the economy:
All figures are in billions of dollars.

Net exports	$10
Net foreign factor income	3
Gross investment	200
Government spending	190
Consumption	550
Depreciation	65

You are asked to calculate the following:
a. GDP.

b. GNP.

c. NDP.

5. You have been hired as a research assistant and are given the following data about another economy (profits, wages, rents, and interest are measured nationally):

Profits	$505
Employee compensation	880
Rents	30
Interest	175

Calculate Aggregate income.

6. Use the following table to answer the questions:

	Real output bils. of 2000 $	Nominal output bils. of dollars	GDP deflator 2000=100
2000	9,817.0	9,817	——
2001	9890.7	10,128	——
2002	10,074.8	——	104.1
2003	——	——	106.0
2004	——	11,735	108.2

    a. What is output for 2004 in 2000 dollars?

    b. What is the output in nominal terms in 2002?

    c. What is the GDP deflator in 2000?

    d. Real output grew by 1.9% from 2002 to 2003. By how much did nominal output grow from 2002 to 2003?

● A BRAIN TEASER

1. Why must imports be subtracted in calculating GDP?

● MULTIPLE CHOICE

Circle the one best answer for each of the following questions:

1. GDP is:
    a. the total market value of all final goods and services produced in an economy in a one-year period.
    b. the total market value of all goods and services produced in an economy in a one-year period.
    c. the total market value of all final goods and services produced by a country's citizens in a one-year period.
    d. the sum of all final goods and services produced in an economy in a one-year period.

2. To move from GDP to GNP, one must:
    a. add net foreign factor income.
    b. subtract inflation.
    c. add depreciation.
    d. subtract depreciation.

3. If a firm's cost of materials is $100 and its sales are $500, its value added is:
    a. $100.
    b. $400.
    c. $500.
    d. $600.

4. If you, the owner, sell your old car for $600, how much does GDP increase?
    a. By $600.
    b. By the amount you bought it for, minus the $600.
    c. By zero.
    d. By the $600 you received and the $600 the person you sold it to paid, or $1,200.

5. There are two firms in an economy, Firm A and Firm B. Firm A produces 100 widgets and sells them for $2 apiece. Firm B produces 200 gadgets and sells them for $3 apiece. Firm A sells 30 of its widgets to Firm B and the remainder to consumers. Firm B sells 50 of its gadgets to Firm A and the remainder to consumers. What is GDP in this economy?
    a. $210.
    b. $590.
    c. $600.
    d. $800.

6. If a woman divorces her husband (who has been cleaning the house) and hires him to continue cleaning her house for $20,000 per year, GDP will:
    a. remain constant.
    b. increase by $20,000 per year.
    c. decrease by $20,000 per year.
    d. remain unchanged.

7. The aggregate accounting identity shows that the value of:
    a. aggregate income is equal to the value of final goods plus investment.
    b. aggregate income is equal to the value of final goods plus savings.
    c. aggregate income is equal to the value of final goods sold.
    d. consumption goods is equal to the value of aggregate income.

8. Which of the following correctly lists the components of total expenditures?
   a. consumption, investment, depreciation, exports minus imports.
   b. consumption, investment, government spending, exports minus imports.
   c. rent, profit, interest, wages.
   d. consumption, net foreign factor income, investment, government spending.

9. The largest component of expenditures in GDP is:
   a. consumption.
   b. investment.
   c. net exports.
   d. government spending.

10. The largest component of aggregate income is:
    a. rents.
    b. net interest.
    c. profits.
    d. compensation to employees.

11. Gross investment differs from net investment by:
    a. net exports.
    b. net imports.
    c. depreciation.
    d. transfer payments.

12. While the size of the U.S. federal government budget is approximately $2.7 trillion, the federal government's contribution in the GDP accounts is approximately:
    a. $0.9 trillion.
    b. $2.7 trillion.
    c. $3.9 trillion.
    d. $5.0 trillion.

13. Which of the following factors serves to equate aggregate income and aggregate production?
    a. profit.
    b. depreciation.
    c. net foreign factor income.
    d. value added.

14. Switching from the exchange rate approach to the purchasing power parity approach for calculating GDP generally:
    a. does not make a significant difference for a developing country's GDP relative to a developed country's GDP.

b. increases a developing country's GDP relative to a developed country's GDP.
c. decreases a developing country's GDP relative to a developed country's GDP.
d. changes the relative GDP of developing country's GDP, but not in a predictable fashion.

15. If inflation is 10 percent and nominal GDP goes up 20 percent, real GDP goes up approximately:
    a. 1 percent.
    b. 10 percent.
    c. 20 percent.
    d. 30 percent.

16. Which of the following is the *preferable* measure available to compare changes in standards of living among countries over time?
    a. Changes in nominal income.
    b. Changes in nominal per capita income.
    c. Changes in real income.
    d. Changes in real per capita income.

17. If nominal GDP rises, welfare:
    a. has definitely increased.
    b. has definitely decreased.
    c. may have increased or decreased.
    d. most likely has increased.

18. Estimates of the importance of the underground economy in the United States indicate that it is:
    a. very small—under 1 percent of the total economy.
    b. somewhere between 1.5 percent all the way to 20 percent of the total economy.
    c. somewhere between 1.5 percent all the way to 60 percent of the total economy.
    d. as large as the non-underground economy.

● POTENTIAL ESSAY QUESTIONS

You may also see essay questions similar to the "Problems & Applications" and "A Brain Teaser" exercises.

1. Using the circular flow model, explain why any dollar value of output must give rise to an identical amount of income.

2. How might an economy experience an increase in nominal GDP but experience negative growth at the same time?

SHORT-ANSWER QUESTIONS

1. GDP is the aggregate final output of *residents* and businesses *in* an economy in a one-year period. (575)

2. The four components of gross domestic product are consumption, investment, government spending, and net exports (X − M). (575-577)

3. $1,000. We could use either the value added approach or the final output approach. Summing the value added at each stage of production — the difference between cost of materials and value of sales —we get $1,000. (577-580)

Participants	Cost of materials	Value of Sales	Value Added
Farmer	$0	$200	$200
Chex factory	200	500	300
Distributor	500	800	300
Grocery store	800	1000	200
Sum (total output)			1000

4. GNP is aggregate final output of *citizens* and businesses *of* an economy in a one-year period. GDP is output produced within a country's borders while GNP is output produced by a country's citizens anywhere in the world. Add net foreign factor income to GDP to get GNP. (581-583)

5. Gross investment is expenditures on goods and services used for future production. Net investment is gross investment less expenditures used to replace worn out machinery, also called depreciation. (581-582)

6. The four components that comprise aggregate income are compensation to employees, rents, interest, and profits. (583-584)

7. A real value is a nominal value adjusted for inflation. So, nominal GDP in the second period is $4.6 trillion, but real GDP is $4.6 trillion divided by the price index, 1.1, or $4.18 trillion. (586-587)

8. Aggregate accounting statistics can be misleading. They are subject to measurement error; they are based on samples of data and assumptions about behavior. For example, the measurement of inflation is widely believed to overestimate true inflation. Also, GDP does not include non-market activities such as housework. It measures economic activity, not welfare; output could rise when welfare falls. Its subcategories are often interdependent; that is, arbitrary decisions were made when determining what goes in which subcategory. Nevertheless, aggregate accounting makes it possible to discuss the aggregate economy. It is important to be aware of the limitations of the data in those discussions. (587-590)

MATCHING

1-j; 2-b; 3-d; 4-g; 5-c; 6-e; 7-a; 8-f; 9-i; 10-h.

PROBLEMS AND APPLICATIONS

1. a. $300. Only the value added by the sale would be added to GDP, which in this case is the difference between the purchase price and the sale price. (579-580)

    b. $200,000. Total output produced is 1,000 × $500 = $500,000. The intermediate goods are valued at 600 × $500 = $300,000. So, the company's contribution to GDP is ($500,000−$300,000)=$200,000. (577-580)

    c. Only that amount that is sold to the consumer is counted in GDP. This is 50×1,000 + 100×50 = $55,000 sold by the first company plus the sales of the retailer, which is 25×$1250 + 50×$75 = $35,000. Total contribution to GDP is $90,000. (577-580)

    d. Only the commissions of $50 and $45 are counted in GDP. Together they contribute $95. (577-580)

    e. Nothing has been added to GDP. Government transfers are not included in GDP. (580-581)

2.

Participants	Cost of materials	Value of sales	Value added
Farmer	$0	$150	$150
Mill	$150	$250	$100
Cereal maker	$250	$600	$350
Wholesaler	$600	$800	$200
Grocery store	$800	$1,000	$200

  a. The value added at each stage of production is shown in the table above. (578-580)

  b. The total value of sales is $2,800. Find this by adding the rows of the value of sales column. (578-580)

  c. The total value added is $1,000. Find this by adding the value added at each stage of production. (578-580)

  d. The contribution to GDP of the production of those Wheaties is $1,000. Value added at each stage of production is the contribution to GDP. This avoids double-counting. (578-580)

3. **a.** $2,375: GDP is the sum of the value added by the three firms $= 500 + 1400 + 475$. (578-580)

  b. $237.50: A 10% value added tax would generate $(.10)($2,375) = 237.50 of revenue. (578-580)

  c. $237.50: A 10% income tax would generate the same revenue as a 10% value added tax because value added equals income. (578-580)

  d. $237.50: A 10% sales tax on final output would generate $237.50 of revenue: $(.10)(500+1400+475)$. (578-580)

4. **a.** $950: GDP $= C + I + G + (X - M) = 550 + 200 + 190 + 10 = 950$. (575-577)

  b. $953: GNP $=$ GDP $+$ net foreign factor income $= 953$. (581-583)

  c. $885: NDP $=$ GDP $-$ depreciation $= 950 - 65 = 885$. (581-582)

5. $1,590: Aggregate income $=$ Employee compensation $+$ rent $+$ interest $+$ profits $= 880 + 30 + 175 + 505$. (582-584)

6. **a.** $10,845.7 billion in 2000 dollars: Real output $=$ (Nominal output/deflator) $\times 100 = 11,735.0/108.2 \times 100$. (586-587)

  b. $10,487.9 billion: Nominal output $=$ (real output $\times$ deflator) $/ 100 = (10,074.8 \times 104.1)/100$. (586-587)

  c. 100: Deflator $=$ (Nominal output/real output) $\times 100 = (9,817/9,817) \times 100$. (586-587)

  d. Real output grew by 1.9% and inflation rose by 2.1%, so nominal output grew by 4.0%. (586-587)

━━━━ **ANSWERS** ━━━━

A BRAIN TEASER

1. Government spending, consumption, investment include all expenditures in those categories regardless of where the products were produced. That is, they include products produced in foreign countries. Since GDP measures domestic production, the total value of imports must be subtracted from total expenditures. (576)

━━━━ **ANSWERS** ━━━━

MULTIPLE CHOICE

1. **a** As the text emphasizes on page 575, GDP is the total <u>market value</u> of all <u>final</u> goods and services produced <u>in</u> an economy in a one-year period.

2. **a** Since GNP is a country's total market value of production of a country's citizens anywhere in the world, and GDP is total market value of production within a country, one must add net foreign factor income to GDP to get GNP. See pages 582-583.

3. **b** Value added equals value of sales minus cost of materials. See page 578.

4. **c** As discussed on pages 579-580, sales of used goods do not contribute to GDP except to the degree that they are sold by a second hand dealer. Then the dealer's profit would be the value added.

5. **b** GDP doesn't include purchases made between businesses, only final sales to consumers. To calculate the answer, calculate total sales for Firms A and B ($600 + $200 = $800) and subtract those goods sold between the firms ($60 + $150 = $210) to get final sales ($800 − $210 = $590). See pages 578-580.

6. b   As discussed on pages 580-581, GDP measures market transactions. The divorce-and-hire changes the housecleaning activities from non-market to market and hence increases GDP.

7. c   The aggregate accounting identity shows that all income (value of aggregate income) equals all expenditures (value of goods sold to individuals). See page 584.

8. b   GDP = C + I + G + (X – M). See pages 575-577.

9. a   Consumption makes up the majority of expenditures. See Table 25-1 on page 577.

10. d   As you can see in Table 25-3 on page 584, compensation to employees is the largest percent of aggregate income.

11. c   Net investment equals gross investment less depreciation. See pages 581-582.

12. a   As discussed on page 576 only federal government spending on goods and services is included as part of GDP. The federal government's entire budget also includes transfer payments.

13. a   Profit is what remains after all firms' other income is paid out. Thus, profit is the key to the income/production equality. See page 585.

14. b   In developing countries, living expenses are generally lower than in developed countries. Thus moving towards a purchasing power parity approach generally increases GDP in a developing country. See pages 585-586.

15. b   Subtract inflation from nominal GDP growth to find real GDP growth as a first approximation. See pages 586-587.

16. d   As discussed on pages 586-587 nominal GDP must be adjusted for price level increases before comparisons over time can be made. Dividing total real income by the population is a good indication of relative standards of living.

17. c   Nominal GDP must be adjusted for inflation to arrive at real GDP before one can even start to make welfare comparisons. And even if real GDP increases, it is not clear that welfare has increased, as discussed on pages 587-590.

18. b   On pages 588-589 the text states that the underground economy in the United States is between 1.5 and 20 percent of the total economy.

━━━━ ANSWERS ━━━━

POTENTIAL ESSAY QUESTIONS

The following are annotated answers. They indicate the general idea behind the answer.

1. Whenever the business community produces some dollar value of output, that dollar value reflects costs of production that were incurred in producing that output level. Those costs of production are all paid out to the resource (input) owners as their income. Hence, any dollar output level (GDP) gives rise to an identical amount of aggregate income.

2. The price level could have increased by a greater percentage than the decrease in the real quantity of goods and services produced. This would result in an increase in nominal GDP but a decrease in real GDP (negative growth).

GROWTH, PRODUCTIVITY AND THE WEALTH OF NATIONS

26

CHAPTER AT A GLANCE

This review is based upon the learning objectives that open the chapter.

1. Growth is an increase in the amount of goods and services an economy produces. (596-598)

    Growth can be measured either by increases in real GDP or increases in real GDP per person (per capita growth).

    Remember the Rule of 72: the number of years it takes for income to double equals 72 divided by the annual growth rate of income.

2. Markets create specialization and division of labor and have been empirically highly correlated with growth. The growth rate has increased as the importance of markets has increased. Five important sources of growth are: (598, 601-605)

    *   Institutions with incentives compatible with growth;

        Government policy can help or hinder growth. Regulations have both costs and benefits, but too much regulation definitely hinders growth.

    *   Capital accumulation–investment in productive capacity;

        Can be: (1) Privately owned by business, (2) publicly owned and provided by government–infrastructure, (3) human capital–investment in people, and (4) social capital–institutions and conventions.

        Saving is translated into investment in the loanable funds market. The interest rate equilibrates the supply of loanable funds (saving) with the demand for loanable funds (investment).

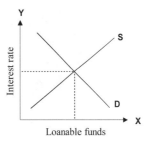

    *   Available resources;

        Technological advances can help overcome any lack of resources.

    *   Technological development;

        Technology not only causes growth, it also changes the entire social and political dimensions of society.

    *   Entrepreneurship.

        This is the ability to get things done. It involves creativity, vision, and an ability to translate that vision into reality.

3. Most growth theories center around the production function: Output = A·f(labor, capital, land). (606-609)

    Returns to scale describe what happens to output when all inputs are increased.

    *   *Constant returns to scale: output rises by the same proportion as the increase in all inputs. (An example: ↑all inputs 10% →↑output by 10%)*

    *   *Increasing returns to scale: output rises by a greater proportion than the increase in all inputs. (An example: ↑ all inputs 10% → ↑output by 15%)*

- *Decreasing returns to scale: output rises by a smaller proportion than the increase in all inputs. (An example:↑all inputs 10% → ↑output by 5%)*

- *Diminishing marginal productivity involves increasing one, not all, inputs. In general, economists assume diminishing marginal productivity—which means the increase in output falls as more of one input is added.*

4a. The convergence hypothesis states that per capita income in countries with similar institutional structures will gravitate toward the same level of income per person. (609-611)

This hypothesis predicts that the U.S. economy will grow more slowly than developing economies because of technology transfers, learning by doing, and the higher marginal productivity of capital in developing countries.

4b. Convergence hasn't occurred because of (1) lack of factor mobility, (2) differing institutional structures, (3) in-comparable factors of production, and (4) technological agglomeration effects. (609-611)

Technology accounts for a significant portion of U.S. growth. If technology continues to advance more quickly in developed countries, rich countries may continue to grow more quickly than developing economies.

5a. The Classical growth model focuses on the role of capital accumulation. Increases in capital lead to growth. (607-609)

It predicts that the rise in output per worker will eventually slow as additional amounts of capital are less productive. It also predicts that capital-poor countries will grow faster than capital-rich countries.

Focuses on diminishing marginal productivity of labor. Increases in the population beyond N* lead to starvation. Below N* the population grows because of the surplus output.

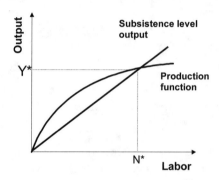

5b. New growth theory focuses on technology. Increasing returns mean growth rates can accelerate over time. (611-615)

Technology and learning by doing often have positive externalities that can accelerate growth.

● SHORT-ANSWER QUESTIONS

1. What are the two ways to measure growth?

2. You've been called in by a political think tank to develop a strategy to improve growth in the U.S. What five things would you recommend they concentrate on to contribute positively to economic growth?

3. Why is a well-functioning financial market essential to growth?

4. Write a production function. Use the production function to explain the difference between diminishing marginal returns and decreasing returns to scale.

5. Which economy does the convergence hypothesis predict will grow faster: Country A with per capita income of $1,000 or Country B with per capita of $10,000? Why might the prediction be wrong?

6. Why did the early Classical model predict that output would gravitate toward a subsistence level?

7. What is the focus of new growth theory?

8. How do the predictions of the Classical growth theory differ from the predictions of the new growth theory?

MATCHING THE TERMS
Match the terms to their definitions

___1.	Classical growth model	a.	Output rises by a greater proportionate increase in all inputs.
___2.	constant returns to scale	b.	Producing more goods and services per person.
___3.	convergence hypothesis	c.	Legal ownership of a technological innovation that gives the owner sole rights to its use and distribution for a limited time.
___4.	decreasing returns to scale	d.	The habitual way of doing things that guides how people approach production.
___5.	human capital	e.	Changes in the way we make goods and supply services and changes in the goods and services we buy.
___6.	increasing returns to scale	f.	Output will rise by the same proportionate increase as all inputs.
___7.	law of diminishing marginal productivity	g.	Model of growth that focuses on the role of capital accumulation in the growth process.
___8.	learning by doing	h.	Output per unit of input.
___9.	new growth theories	i.	Rule in which you divide 72 by the growth rate of income (or any variable) to get the number of years over which income (or any variable) will double.
___10.	patents	j.	Output rises by a smaller proportionate increase than all inputs.
___11.	per capita growth	k.	Positive effects on others not taken into account by the decision-maker.
___12.	positive externalities	l.	The skills that are embodied in workers through experience, education, and on-the-job training.
___13.	productivity	m.	Theories that emphasize the role of technology rather than capital in the growth process.
___14.	Rule of 72	n.	Increasing one input, keeping all others constant, will lead to smaller and smaller gains in output.
___15.	Say's Law	o.	The concentration of individuals on certain aspects of production.
___16.	social capital	p.	Supply creates its own demand.
___17.	specialization	q.	Improving the methods of production through experience.
___18.	technological agglomeration	r.	Tendency of technological advance to spawn further technological advances.
___19.	technology	s.	Per capita income in countries with similar institutional structures will gravitate toward the same level.

● PROBLEMS AND APPLICATIONS

1. According to the Classical growth model how will each of the following events affect a country's growth rate?

   a. An increase in the percent change in population.

   b. An increase in the saving rate.

   c. An improvement in technology.

d. The government passes a law extending the time frame in which the holder of a patent has sole ownership of a technological innovation.

2. State the Rule of 72. Answer each of the following questions:

   a. How many years will it take for income to double if a country's total income grows at 2 percent? 4 percent? 6 percent?

   b. If a country's income doubles in 16 years, at what rate is its income growing?

   c. In 2009 per capita output in the United States was about $40,000. If real income per capita is growing at a 2% annual rate, what will per capita output be in 36 years? In 72 years?

   d. If real income is rising at an annual rate of 4% per year and the population is growing at a rate of 1% per year, how many years will it take for per capita income to double?

3. Calculate per capita income for each of the following countries:

	GDP (in mils. of $)	Population (in millions)
Brazil	773,400	164
Ghana	6,600	18
Croatia	20,700	4
France	1,526,000	59

4. The inputs to an economy are labor and capital only. In each of the following state whether the production function exhibits (a) increasing returns to scale, (b) decreasing returns to scale, (c) constant returns to scale, or (d) diminishing marginal productivity.

   a. Output rises by 16% when both labor and capital rise by 16%.

   b. Output rises by 10% when both labor and capital rise by 16%.

   c. Output rises by 10% when labor rises by 16%. (Capital doesn't change.)

5. What prediction did Thomas Malthus make about growth?

   a. Draw a graph that demonstrates his predictions and explain the predictions using the graph.

b. What law are those predictions based upon?

c. According to Classical economists, why didn't his predictions come true?

6. Country A has per capita income of $10,000 while Country B has per capita income of $20,000.

    a. According to the Classical growth theory, which country is predicted to grow more quickly? Why?

    b. According to the new growth theory, which country is predicted to grow more quickly? Why?

● A BRAIN TEASER

1. How might a country benefit from having misers? How might it be harmed?

● MULTIPLE CHOICE

Circle the one best answer for each of the following questions:

1. Long-run growth analysis focuses primarily:
   a. on demand.
   b. on supply.
   c. on both supply and demand.
   d. on the distribution of output.

2. According to Say's Law:
   a. aggregate supply will exceed aggregate demand.
   b. aggregate demand will exceed aggregate supply.
   c. there will be no relation between aggregate supply and demand.
   d. aggregate demand will equal aggregate supply.

3. If the growth rate is 6%, how many years will it take for output to double?
   a. 4.
   b. 8.
   c. 12.
   d. 16.

4. When earnings are adjusted for inflation, the average worker today earns:
   a. about the same as a worker in 1919.
   b. less than a worker in 1919.
   c. more than a worker in 1919.
   d. more than a worker in 1919 if he/she is unionized, but otherwise less.

5. Suppose output grew at 8% in China and 2% in the United States. Based on this information alone, we can know that:
   a. per capita income grew faster in China.
   b. per capita income grew faster in the U.S.
   c. per capita income could have grown faster in either country. We cannot tell which.
   d. per capita output grew faster in China.

6. Investment relates to capital in the following way:
   a. It is the same thing as capital stock.
   b. It causes a decrease in capital over time.
   c. It causes an increase in capital over time.
   d. It is unrelated to capital.

7. If saving increases from S_0 to S_1:

a. the interest rate will rise, investment will rise, and the economy will grow.

b. the interest rate will fall, investment will rise, and the economy will grow.

c. the interest will rise, investment will fall, and the economy will contract.

d. the interest rate will fall, investment will fall, and the economy will contract.

8. Types of capital discussed in the book do *not* include:
a. human capital.
b. social capital.
c. physical capital.
d. investment capital.

9. Available resources:
a. must always decrease.
b. are always constant because of the entropy law.
c. must always increase.
d. may increase or decrease.

10. A production function:
a. shows the relationship between inputs and outputs.
b. is a type of technological manufacturing.
c. is a type of manufacturing technology.
d. is an important source of growth.

11. If there are increasing returns to scale, as:
a. inputs rise, outputs fall.
b. inputs rise, output rises by a smaller percentage.
c. inputs rise, output rises by a larger percentage.
d. one input rises, output rises by a larger percentage.

12. The law of diminishing marginal productivity states that as:
a. inputs increase by equal percentages, output will increase by less than that percentage.
b. inputs increase by equal percentages, output will eventually increase by less than that percentage.
c. one input increases by a certain percentage, output will increase by less than that percentage.
d. one input increases, output will increase by decreasing percentages.

13. The Classical growth model focuses on:
a. technology.
b. saving and investment.
c. entrepreneurship.
d. available resources.

14. Early predictions of the Classical model of growth were that:
a. the economy would grow without limit.
b. the economy will end because of pollution.
c. wages would be driven to subsistence because of diminishing marginal productivity.
d. wages would be driven to subsistence because of decreasing returns to scale.

15. Which of the following is *not* an explanation for why the growth rates of rich and poor countries have not converged?
a. Human capital has increased in rich countries.
b. Technology has increased in rich countries.
c. The law of diminishing marginal productivity is wrong.
d. Both human capital and technology have increased in rich countries.

16. In empirically explaining per capita growth in the United States, the increase in:
a. physical capital is the most important element.
b. human capital is the most important element.
c. technology is the most important element.
d. the quantity of labor is the most important element.

17. Convergence does not rely on:
    a. Similar institutions.
    b. Equal amounts of capital per person.
    c. Mobile technology.
    d. Comparable factors of production.

18. New growth theories are theories that emphasize:
    a. technology.
    b. human capital.
    c. physical capital.
    d. entrepreneurship.

19. In the new growth theory which of the following may be true?
    a. The law of increasing marginal productivity overwhelms the law of diminishing marginal productivity.
    b. Learning by doing overwhelms the law of diminishing marginal productivity.
    c. The law of technology overwhelms the law of diminishing marginal productivity.
    d. The law of QWERTY overwhelms the law of diminishing marginal productivity.

20. QWERTY is a metaphor for:
    a. the invisible hand.
    b. technological lock-in.
    c. the law of diminishing marginal productivity.
    d. the pollution caused by positive spillovers.

21. Growth usually leads to decreased birth rates because:
    a. men and women are too tired to have kids.
    b. the opportunity cost of having children rises.
    c. pollution reduces the fertility of the population.
    d. immigration crowds out endogenous population growth.

22. Which of the following policies will likely *slow* an economy's growth rate?
    a. Increased trade restrictions.
    b. Increasing the level of education.
    c. Increasing saving.
    d. Protecting property rights.

● POTENTIAL ESSAY QUESTIONS

You may also see essay questions similar to the "Problems & Applications" and "A Brain Teaser" exercises.

1. What does the Classical model predict about the growth rates of poor countries relative to rich countries? What accounts for that prediction?

2. How can two countries with equal population sizes have different levels of output?

SHORT-ANSWER QUESTIONS

1. Growth can be measured either as increases in the amount of goods and services an economy produces (real GDP), or as increases in the amount of goods and services an economy produces per person (per capita real GDP). Increase in per capita output is a better measure of improvements in the standard of living because it tells you how much more income an average person has. (598-601)

2. I would tell them: (1) To promote institutions with incentives compatible with growth. Institutions that encourage hard work will lead to growth. (2) To invest in capital. This would include not only buildings and machines, but also human and social capital. (3) To be creative in recognizing available resources. Growth requires resources and although it may seem that the resources are limited, available resources depend upon existing technology. New technology is a way of overcoming lack of resources. (4) To promote institutions that foster creative thinking and lead to technological development; (5) To encourage entrepreneurship. An economy deficient in the other four areas can still grow if its population can translate vision into reality. Each of these will contribute to growth. (601-605)

3. For saving to contribute to growth it must be translated into investment, which requires a well-functioning financial market. (602-603)

4. A typical production function is: Output = A· f(labor, capital, land), where labor, capital, and land are the only inputs. A is a factor that is used to capture changes in technology. Decreasing returns to scale describes the situation where output rises by a smaller percentage than the increase in all inputs. For example, if labor, capital and land all increase by 20%, but output increases by only 10%, the production function exhibits decreasing returns to scale. Diminishing marginal productivity describes what happens to output when only one input is changed—output rises by a percentage that is smaller than the percentage increase in one input (while all other inputs remain the same). (606-609)

5. The convergence hypothesis predicts that, given the appropriate assumptions, Country A will grow faster because it has less capital and therefore the marginal productivity of additional capital is higher. The prediction is likely wrong because the assumptions are not met. A central assumption is that countries have similar institutional structures. Another is that the factors of production are comparable; they may not be; for example, the workers in Country B might be better educated. Another assumption is that technological advances move from country to country. They may not do so because of agglomeration effects, in which technological advances in one country accelerate growth for that country. Another assumption is that technology and capital are free to move; they may not be. (609-611)

6. The early Classical model predicted that output would gravitate toward a subsistence level because they focused on the law of diminishing marginal productivity of labor. As long as an additional worker could produce more than enough for him or herself, the population would grow. But land was relatively fixed. As more and more workers were added to a fixed amount of land, eventually, additional workers would not be able to produce enough additional output to survive. Workers would starve to death and the population would shrink. The equilibrium number of workers was where output was just enough to survive—no more and no less. (607-609)

7. New growth theory focuses on the role of technology rather than capital in the growth process. New growth theory considers the possibility that there are positive spillover effects associated with technological advance so that growth rates can accelerate. It also focuses on learning by doing. Just the process of producing results in lower costs and technological innovation. (611-615)

8. Classical growth theory predicts that the growth rates of poor countries will be higher than the growth rates of rich countries because the law of diminishing marginal productivity of capital is stronger in rich countries. Eventually the incomes of rich and poor countries will converge. New growth theory, because of the

positive externalities associated with technological advance, is consistent with the possibility that rich countries may grow faster than poor countries because they have more technology. Classical growth theory also predicts that growth rates will slow over time whereas the new growth theory is consistent with an acceleration in growth rates. (607-615)

ANSWERS

MATCHING

1-g; 2-f; 3-s; 4-j; 5-l; 6-a; 7-n; 8-q; 9-m; 10-c; 11-b; 12-k; 13-h; 14-i; 15-p; 16-d; 17-o; 18-r; 19-e.

ANSWERS

PROBLEMS AND APPLICATIONS

1. **a.** An increase in the percent change in population will lead to a reduction in the growth rate per capita because each worker will have less capital to produce with. (607-609)

    b. An increase in the saving rate will lead to an increase in the growth rate per capita because saving results in increased investment and more capital for each worker. Eventually, however, the law of diminishing marginal productivity of capital would set in and per capita income would cease to grow. (607-609)

    c. An improvement in technology will increase the growth rate per capita because each worker will be more productive. This will increase per capita output at the time of the technological improvement, but would not result in a lasting increase in the growth rate per capita. (607-609)

    d. Technological innovation is outside the model. Thus government policies to affect technological innovation would not affect the growth rate of an economy. (607-609)

2. The Rule of 72 is, "the number of years that it takes income (or any variable) to double equals 72 divided by the annual growth rate of income (or that variable)." (597)

a. 36 years if income grows at 2 percent per year; 18 years if income grows at 4 percent per year; 12 years if income grows at 6 percent per year. (597)

b. Its income is growing at 4.5 percent per year. Divide 72 by 16 to find the answer. (597)

c. If real income per capita is growing at 2 percent per year, per capita output will double in 36 years. So, real per capita output will be $80,000 in 36 years and $160,000 in 72 years. (597)

d. Per capita real income is rising at an annual rate of 3% per year (4% - 1%). At 3% per year, real per capita income will double in 24 years (72/3 = 24). (597)

3. Divide GDP by the population to find per capita income: (599-600)

    a. Brazil $4,716
    b. Ghana $367
    c. Croatia $5,175
    d. France $25,864

4. **a.** Since output is rising by the same percentage as the increase in all inputs, the production function exhibits constant returns to scale. (606-607)

    b. Since output is rising by a smaller percentage than the increase in all inputs, the production function exhibits decreasing returns to scale. (606-607)

    c. Since capital is fixed, the correct description involves marginal productivity. Since output rises by less than the percentage increase in labor only, the production function exhibits diminishing marginal productivity. (605-608)

5. Thomas Malthus predicted that since land was relatively fixed, as the population grew, diminishing marginal productivity would set in. The growth in output would not keep pace with the growth in the population and eventually people would starve. (607-608)

a. The graph above demonstrates Malthus'
predictions. The production function is
downward bowed because of diminishing
marginal productivity. Each additional
worker adds less output than the individual
before. At population levels below N*,
there is surplus output (because output per
worker exceeds the subsistence level of
output). Because there is surplus output,
people have more children and the population grows. Once the population grows
beyond N*, per capita output is not
sufficient to feed the population (output per
worker is less than the subsistence level of
output) and some people starve to death.
The population declines to N*. (607-609)

b. The predictions of Thomas Malthus are
based upon the law of diminishing
marginal productivity. (607-609)

c. According to Classical economists, his
predictions didn't come true because some
output produced is used to increase the
amount of capital that workers have to work
with. As capital increases, even if land is
fixed, output can also increase. The economy
can still grow if capital increases at the same
rate that labor increases. (609)

6. a. According to the Classical growth theory,
Country A is expected to grow more
quickly because increases in capital per
worker in Country A are more productive
than in Country B due to the law of
diminishing marginal productivity. (607-609)

b. According to the new growth theory,
income doesn't need to converge. In fact,
new growth theory stresses the possibility
that countries with higher output will grow
faster than poor countries because of
positive externalities associated with
technology and learning by doing.
Increases in technology have significant
positive externalities that can accelerate the
growth rate. Further, as output increases,
the benefits from learning by doing also
increase. Therefore, greater output can lead
to faster growth rates. (611-615)

ANSWERS

A BRAIN TEASER

1. A country might benefit from a miser if the
   miser's saving is translated into investment, and
   therefore productive capital that will help the
   economy grow. In the short-run, however, the
   miser might hurt by not spending, thereby not
   creating demand for goods produced. (602-603)

ANSWERS

MULTIPLE CHOICE

1. b On page 596 it states that in the short run
      economists' analysis focuses on demand;
      in the long run it focuses on supply.

2. d Say's Law states that supply creates its
      own demand. See page 596.

3. c According to the Rule of 72 on page 597,
      divide 72 by the growth rate to determine
      the number of years in which output will
      double.

4. c As discussed in the text on page 599 the
      average worker's wages buy many more
      goods now than in 1919. Whether that
      makes them better off is debatable, but
      they definitely earn more.

5. c Per capita income (output) growth equals
      output growth less population growth.
      Without knowing population growth, we
      do not know for which country per capita
      income (output) growth is greater. See
      pages 598-601.

6. c As defined in the text on page 603 invest-
      ment is the increase in capital over time.

7. b When saving increases from S_0 to S_1,
      there is downward pressure on the interest
      rate. This leads to higher investment
      (demand for loanable funds) and, accord-
      ing to the growth model, growth. See
      pages 602-603.

8. d Investment is the change in capital; it is
      not a description of capital. See page 603.

9. d Available resources depend on technol-
      ogy. That is why they can increase or
      decrease. See pages 603-604.

10. a   The definition given in the text on page 606 is the relationship between inputs and outputs.

11. c   As discussed in the text on page 607 increasing returns to scale refer to the relationship between all inputs and outputs. Increasing returns to scale exist when output increases by a greater percentage than the increase in all inputs.

12. d   The law of diminishing marginal productivity refers to one input, not all, and to what will happen to output as that input continually increases, keeping other inputs constant. It is likely that c is true but it is not the law of diminishing marginal productivity. See page 607.

13. b   The Classical growth model focuses on increases in capital and hence on saving and investment. See pages 607-609.

14. c   In the early Classical model, fixed land and diminishing marginal productivity meant that wages would be driven to subsistence. See page 608.

15. c   Economists continue to believe in the law of diminishing marginal productivity because there are many other explanations for the lack of convergence. See pages 609-611.

16. c   Although increases in technology and increases in the quantity of labor are of almost equal importance in explaining total growth, per capita growth decreases the importance of the quantity of labor. See pages 609-611.

17. b   Convergence depends on similar institutions, mobile technology, and comparable factors of production. The initial amount of capital per person doesn't have to be equal. See pages 609-611.

18. a   New growth theories center their explanation of growth on technology. See page 611.

19. b   Choices a,c, and d name "laws" that aren't laws, aren't mentioned in this chapter, and can't overwhelm anything. See pages 614-615.

20. b   QWERTY stands for the upper left keys on a keyboard. Placing them there is not especially efficient, but once they were placed there, they were locked in. See page 615.

21. b   In industrialized countries, people have chosen to have fewer children in part because the benefits of having children (such as being supported by them in your old age) are reduced. See pages 599-601.

22. a   Economists generally believe that trade increases growth, so increasing trade restrictions would decrease growth. See page 598.

ANSWERS

POTENTIAL ESSAY QUESTIONS

The following are annotated answers. They indicate the general idea behind the answer.

1.   The Classical model predicts that poor countries with little capital will grow at faster rates than rich countries with a lot of capital. The reason for this prediction is the law of diminishing marginal productivity. Capital that is added in poor countries will be much more productive because the law of diminishing marginal productivity is weaker compared to that in rich countries.

2.   Total output in the long run depends upon capital, labor, and land. It could be that the two countries have different levels of capital or natural resources (captured in land). For instance, the United States has many natural resources, but Japan does not. Japan overcomes its lack of natural resources by investing heavily in capital and importing natural resources. If two countries had equal amounts of capital, land, and labor, however, their outputs could still differ if they had different amounts of human capital (the skills that are embodied in workers through experience, education, and on-the-job training) and social capital (the habitual way of doing things that guides people in how they approach production).

THE AGGREGATE DEMAND/ AGGREGATE SUPPLY MODEL

● CHAPTER AT A GLANCE

This review is based upon the learning objectives that open the chapter.

1. Keynesian economics developed as economists debated the cause of the Great Depression. (621-624)

   In the 1930s, the economy was in a Depression with 25 percent unemployment. Classical economists believed that wages would fall and eliminate the unemployment. Keynesian economists believed that the economy could remain in a Depression unless government did something to increase spending.

2a. The slope of the AD curve is determined by the interest rate effect, the international effect, the money wealth effect, and repercussions of these effects. (625-628)

   In principle we would expect the AD curve to be vertical because if all prices changed in the same way, behavior wouldn't change.

   As the price level falls:
   ● *the value of money rises, inducing people to lend more money, which reduces the interest rate and increases investment expenditures (interest rate effect).*
   ● *the price of U.S. goods relative to foreign goods goes down. Assuming the exchange rate doesn't change, U.S. exports increase and U.S. imports decrease (international effect).*
   ● *the cash people hold is worth more, making people richer, so they buy more (money wealth effect).*

   Repercussions of these effects are called multiplier effects (and make the AD curve flatter than otherwise).

   Dynamic feedback effects can overwhelm the standard effects.

2b. Five important initial shift factors of the AD curve are: (628-630)

   ● Changes in foreign income.
   A rise in foreign income leads to an increase in U.S. exports and an increase (outward shift to the right) of the U.S. AD curve.
   ● Changes in exchange rates.
   A decrease in the value of the dollar relative to other currencies shifts the AD curve outward to the right.
   ● Changes in the distribution of income.
   Typically, as the real wage increases, the AD curve shifts out to the right.
   ● Changes in government aggregate demand policy.
   ● Changes in expectations.
   Positive (optimistic) expectations about the future state of the economy shift the AD curve outward to the right.

   Expansionary macro policy (an increase in government spending and/or a decrease in taxes—fiscal policy; or an increase in the money supply—monetary policy) increases the AD curve, shifting it outward to the right.

   Note: Anything that affects the components of aggregate expenditures (AE or "total spending") is a shift factor of AD (aggregate demand). (Recall that AE = C + I + G + X − M). Changes in these components of total spending are multiplied by the multiplier effect.

3a. In the short run, the SAS curve is upward sloping. (631)

   The SAS curve is upward sloping for two reasons: (1) Some firms operate in auction markets where an increase in demand leads to higher prices immediately; (2) Firms tend to increase their markup when demand increases. Along an SAS curve, input prices are constant.

3b. The SAS curve shifts in response to changes in the prices of the factors of production (inputs). (631-633)

Shift factors include change in (1) input prices, (2) productivity, (3) import prices, and (4) excise and sales taxes.

The rule of thumb economists use to predict shifts in the SAS curve is:

% change in the price level = % change in wages − % change in productivity.

4. The *LAS* curve is vertical at potential output. (633-634)

Resources are fully utilized at potential output. The LAS curve shifts when potential output rises or falls.

5a. Equilibrium in the short run is determined by the intersection of the SAS curve and the AD curve. (635-636)

Increases (decreases) in aggregate demand lead to higher (lower) output and a higher (lower) price level.

To find the effect of a shift in aggregate demand, start where the AD curve and the SAS curve intersect. Given a shift of either the AD curve or SAS curve, simply find the new point of intersection. This is the new short-run equilibrium. Remember, initial shifts in the AD curve are magnified because of the multiplier effect.

5b. Equilibrium in the long run is determined by the intersection of the LAS curve and the AD curve. (636-639)

If the economy begins at a long-run equilibrium, increases in aggregate demand will lead to changes in the price level only.

If short-run equilibrium output is below long-run equilibrium output, the economy is in a recessionary gap. The price level will fall and the SAS curve will shift down until output rises to potential. (See the figure below.)

If short-run equilibrium output is above long-run equilibrium output, the economy is in an inflationary gap. The price level will rise and the SAS curve will shift up until output falls to potential. (See the figure below)

6. Macro policy is more complicated than the model makes it look. (642-643)

Fiscal policy is a slow legislative process and is often determined for political, not economic, reasons.

We have no way of precisely determining potential output, making it difficult to know what is the right policy.

7. Dynamic feedback effects can destabilize the economy. (638-639)

A decline in aggregate demand that leads to a drop in the price level may lead to an even larger decrease in aggregate demand, offsetting the effect of a declining price level in bringing the economy back to its potential income.

● SHORT-ANSWER QUESTIONS

1. How does the Keynesian explanation of the Great Depression differ from the Classical explanation?

2. What effects determine the slope of the AD curve?

3. List some of the important shift factors of the AD curve.

4. What is the slope of the SAS curve? Why does it have this shape?

5. What will shift the SAS curve up or down?

6. What is the slope of the LAS curve? Why does it have this shape?

7. Show graphically the effect of increased government purchases on real output when (a) the economy is far below potential output and (b) the economy is at potential output.

8. How can declining prices destabilize an economy?

9. Why is the AS/AD model more complicated than it looks?

MATCHING THE TERMS
Match the terms to their definitions

___ 1. aggregate demand curve

___ 2. countercyclical fiscal policy

___ 3. deflation

___ 4. equilibrium income

___ 5. fiscal policy

___ 6. inflationary gap

___ 7. interest rate effect

___ 8. international effect

___ 9. long-run aggregate supply curve

___ 10. paradox of thrift

___ 11. money wealth effect

___ 12. multiplier effect

___ 13. potential income

___ 14. quantity-adjusting markets

___ 15. recessionary gap

___ 16. short-run aggregate supply curve

a. As the price level falls the interest rate falls, which leads to greater investment expenditures.

b. A curve that shows the amount of goods and services an economy can produce when both labor and capital are fully employed.

c. A curve that shows how a change in the price level will change aggregate quantity of goods demanded.

d. Markets in which firms modify their supply to bring about equilibrium instead of changing prices.

e. A curve that tells us how changes in aggregate demand will be split between real output and the price level.

f. Amount by which equilibrium output is below potential output.

g. As the price level falls, people are richer, so they buy more.

h. As the price level in a country falls the quantity of that country's goods demanded by foreigners and by residents will increase.

i. Amplification of initial changes in expenditures.

j. Amount by which equilibrium output is above potential output.

k. Income toward which the economy gravitates in the short run.

l. Level of income the economy is technically capable of producing without generating accelerating inflation.

m. Deliberate change in either government spending or taxes.

n. Government policy to offset the business cycle.

o. An increase in saving can lead to a decrease in expenditures, decreasing output and causing a recession.

p. A continual decline in the price level.

● PROBLEMS AND APPLICATIONS

1. What will likely happen to the shape or position of the *AD* curve in the following circumstances?

   a. A rise in the price level does not make people feel poorer.

   b. Income is redistributed from poor people to rich people.

   c. The country's currency depreciates.

   d. The exchange rate changes from fixed to flexible.

   e. Expectations of future rises in the price level develop without any current change in the price level.

2. What will happen to the position of the *SAS* curve in the following circumstances?

   a. Productivity rises by 3 percent and wages rise by 3 percent.

b. Productivity rises by 3 percent and wages rise by 5 percent.

c. Productivity rises by 3 percent and wages rise by 1 percent.

3. Graphically demonstrate the effect of each of the following on either the *SAS* curve or the *LAS* curve. Be sure to label all axes.

  a. Businesses find that they are able to produce more output without having to pay more wages or increase their costs of capital.

  b. A severe snow storm paralyzes most of the United States.

  c. The country's currency appreciates dramatically.

4. The government of the UK wants to expand its economy through increased spending. Show the likely effects of an activist policy in the short run and in the long run in the following three cases.

a. The economy is far below potential output.

b. The economy is close to, but still below, potential output.

c. The economy is at potential output.

5. Demonstrate the following two cases using the AS/AD model. What will happen in the long run if the government does nothing?

  a. Inflationary gap.

  b. Recessionary gap.

  c. What could government do with fiscal policy in (a) and (b) to keep the price level constant?

A BRAIN TEASER

1. Suppose the economy has been experiencing a recession for a couple of years with no apparent relief in sight. Currently the unemployment rate is 10%. In response to political pressure "to put America back to work" government policy makers have recently reduced taxes significantly and have dramatically increased government spending on public works projects to rebuild the nation's crumbling infrastructure (roads, bridges, airports...). During a recent press conference the President of the United States remarked that the new government policy of tax cuts and spending programs will be successful in reducing unemployment and there should be no reason to fear inflation either. Because you are a student in an economics course one of your friends has asked you to evaluate the likely success of these recent policy moves. How would you respond?

● MULTIPLE CHOICE

Circle the one best answer for each of the following questions:

1. Classical economists are generally associated with:
   a. laissez faire.
   b. QWERTY.
   c. an activist policy.
   d. their support of low unemployment.

2. Keynesian economics focuses on:
   a. the long run.
   b. the short run.
   c. both the long run and the short run.
   d. neither the long run nor the short run.

3. The term *paradox of thrift* refers to the process by which individuals attempted to save:
   a. less, but in doing so spent less and caused income to decrease, ending up saving even less.
   b. less, but in doing so spent more and caused income to decrease, ending up saving even less.
   c. more, but in doing so spent less and caused income to decrease, ending up saving less.
   d. more, but in doing so spent more and caused income to decrease, ending up saving less.

4. In Keynesian economics equilibrium income:
   a. will be equal to potential income.
   b. will be below potential income.
   c. will be above potential income.
   d. may be different than potential income.

5. In the AS/AD model, the:
   a. price of a good is on the horizontal axis.
   b. price level is on the horizontal axis.
   c. price of a good is on the vertical axis.
   d. price level is on the vertical axis.

6. Which of the following is *not* an explanation of the downward slope of the AD curve?
   a. The money wealth effect.
   b. The interest rate effect.
   c. The consumption effect.
   d. The international effect.

7. If the exchange rate becomes flexible so that changes in the price level have little effect on exports and imports, the:
   a. AD curve will become steeper.
   b. AD curve will become flatter.
   c. AD curve will be unaffected.
   d. SAS curve will become steeper.

8. If the multiplier effect is 2 rather than 3, the:
   a. AD curve will be steeper.
   b. AD curve will be flatter.
   c. AD curve will be unaffected.
   d. SAS curve will be steeper.

9. If there is a rise in foreign income the AD curve will likely:
   a. shift in to the left.
   b. shift out to the right.
   c. become steeper.
   d. become flatter.

10. If there is a rise in a country's exchange rate, the AD curve will likely:
    a. shift in to the left.
    b. shift out to the right.
    c. become steeper.
    d. become flatter.

11. Expansionary monetary policy will likely:
    a. shift the AD curve in to the left.
    b. shift the AD curve out to the right.
    c. make the AD curve steeper.
    d. make the AD curve flatter.

12. If government spending increases by 40, the AD curve will shift to the:
    a. right by 40.
    b. left by 40.
    c. right by more than 40.
    d. right by less than 40.

13. The slope of the SAS curve is determined by:
    a. opportunity cost.
    b. the law of diminishing marginal returns.
    c. institutional realities.
    d. the money wealth effect, the international effect, and the interest rate effect.

14. If productivity rises by 2% and wages rise by 6%, the SAS curve will:
    a. likely shift up (to the left).
    b. likely shift down (to the right).
    c. become flatter.
    d. become steeper.

15. The LAS curve is:
    a. another name for the AD curve.
    b. another name for the SAS curve.
    c. a vertical line.
    d. a horizontal line.

16. Refer to the graph below. The graph demonstrates the expected short-run result if:

    a. productivity increases by less than wages.
    b. the government increases the money supply.
    c. the exchange rate value of a country's currency falls.
    d. there are suddenly expectations of a rising price level.

17. The graph below demonstrates the expected short-run result if:

18. The graph below demonstrates the expected short-run result if:

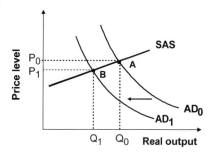

    a. productivity increases by less than wages.
    b. the government increases the money supply.
    c. a country's exchange rate appreciates (gains value).
    d. wages rise by less than the increase in productivity.

18. The graph below demonstrates the expected short-run result if:

    a. productivity increases by less than wages.
    b. the government increases the money supply.
    c. a country's exchange rate appreciates (gains value).
    d. wages rise by less than the increase in productivity.

19. Assume the economy is initially at point B. The graph below correctly demonstrates an economy moving to point C if:

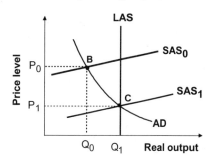

    a. productivity increases by less than the increase in wages.
    b. the government increases the money supply.
    c. a country's exchange rate appreciates (gains value).
    d. wages rise by less than the increase in productivity.

20. Assume the economy is initially at point B. The graph below correctly demonstrates an economy moving to point C if:

a. productivity increases by less than the increase in wages.

b. the government increases the money supply.

c. a country's exchange rate appreciates (gains value).

d. wages rise by less than the increase in productivity.

21. Which of the following distances in the graph below would represent an inflationary gap?

a. A.
b. B.
c. C.
d. D.

22. When the price level in an economy declines,
a. an increase in the quantity of aggregate demand will bring the economy back to potential.
b. a downward shift in the SAS curve will bring the economy back to potential.
c. aggregate expenditures may decline, pushing the economy away from potential.
d. potential output shifts out to the right.

23. An economy with feedback effects that begins at point A and experiences a decline in the price level is most likely to end up at

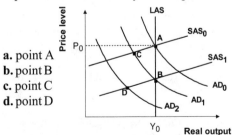

a. point A
b. point B
c. point C
d. point D

24. Expansionary fiscal policy involves:
a. increasing taxes.
b. increasing the money supply.
c. increasing government spending.
d. changing the exchange rate.

25. If the economy has an inflationary gap that it wants to eliminate, the government should use fiscal policy to shift:
a. the LAS curve out.
b. the SAS curve down (to the right).
c. the AD curve out to the right.
d. the AD curve in to the left.

26. If an economy has an inflationary gap and the government does nothing, the macro policy model predicts that:
a. the SAS curve will shift up (to the left) as input prices increase, and output will decline.
b. the SAS curve will shift down (to the right) as input prices decline, and output will rise.
c. the AD curve will shift out to the right as individuals collectively decide to increase expenditures, and output will rise.
d. the AD curve will shift in to the left as individuals collectively decide to reduce expenditures, and output will decline.

27. During World War II:
a. expansionary fiscal policy pushed the economy beyond potential and the price level rose tremendously.
b. expansionary fiscal policy pushed the economy beyond potential, but the price level was controlled by legislation.
c. contractionary monetary policy pushed the economy into a depression.
d. increased taxes to finance the war pushed the economy into recession.

28. If the target rate of unemployment falls, potential income will:
a. first decrease, then increase.
b. increase.
c. decrease.
d. first increase, then decrease.

● POTENTIAL ESSAY QUESTIONS

You may also see essay questions similar to the "Problems & Applications" and "A Brain Teaser" exercises.

1. Why is the AS/AD model more complicated than it looks?

2. What was the Keynesians' main argument against the Classical view that the economy will get itself out of the Depression?

3. What is the paradox of thrift and how does it relate to the AS/AD model?

━━━━━━━━━ ● ANSWERS ━━━━━━━━━

SHORT-ANSWER QUESTIONS

1. Classical economists focused on the real wage. They explained that unemployment would decline if the real wage were allowed to decline. Political and social forces were keeping the real wage too high. Keynesians focused on insufficient aggregate spending that resulted in a downward spiral. The economy was at a below-potential-income equilibrium. (621-623)

2. The interest rate effect, the international effect, the money wealth effect, and the repercussions of these effects (the multiplier effect) determine the slope of the AD curve. (625-628)

3. Five important initial shift factors of the AD curve are changes in: (1) foreign income, (2) exchange rates, (3) distribution of income, (4) expectations, and (5) government aggregate demand policy. (628-630)

4. The SAS curve specifies how a shift in the aggregate demand curve affects the price level and real output. A standard SAS curve is upward sloping. That is, increases in aggregate demand lead to increases in output and the price level. Institutional realities about how firms set prices determine the shape of the SAS curve. Faced with an increase in demand, firms generally respond by increasing production. Some firms will take the opportunity to increase their markup over costs, which will increase the price level also. (631)

5. The SAS curve will shift up or down when input prices rise or fall or if productivity rises or falls. The shift in the SAS curve (and therefore the price level) is determined by the following: % change in price level = % change in wages − % change in productivity. (631-633)

6. The LAS curve is vertical. It has this shape because at potential output, all inputs are fully employed. Changes in the price level do not affect potential output. (633-634)

7. If the economy begins at point A, a well-planned increase in government expenditures (plus the multiplier) shifts the AD out to the right from AD_0 to AD_1. If the economy begins

below potential output, the price level would rise slightly from P_0 to P_1 and real output would increase from Y_0 to Y_1. I've drawn it so that the AD curve shifts out enough so that the economy is in both long-run and short run equilibrium at potential output at point B.

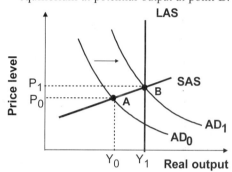

Now suppose the economy begins at point C (graph below) in both short run and long-run equilibrium. In the short-run, when the aggregate demand curve shifts from AD_0 to AD_1, real output rises from Y_0 to Y_1 and the price level rises from P_0 to P_1. Since the economy is now above potential output, however, input prices begin to rise and the SAS curve shifts up. The SAS curve continues to shift up to SAS_1 where the economy returns to a long-run equilibrium at a higher price level, P_2, but the same output level as before, Y_0. (639-640 and Figure 27-9)

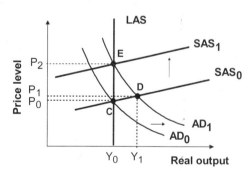

8. A declining price level can lead people to reduce expenditures, shifting the AD curve from AD_0 to AD_1 and pushing the economy to point B. This results in more pressure for the price level to fall. As the SAS curve shifts from SAS_0 to SAS_1 to return the economy to potential output at point C, the AD curve may shift to the left enough to offset the effect of a declining price level on the quantity of aggregate demand. The economy ends up at point D. Further pressure for the price level to

decline pushes the economy even further from potential. (639-641)

9. The AS/AD model is more complicated than it looks because fiscal policy is a slow legislative process and frequently determined by political, not economic, considerations. In addition, we do not know the level of potential output, which is the key to knowing whether contractionary or expansionary policy is needed. Economists have no sure way of estimating potential output. One method is to estimate the unemployment rate where inflation begins to rise. Unfortunately, this is also difficult to predict. Another way is to add a historical growth factor of 3% to previous levels of real output. This can be problematic if the economy is moving to a lower or higher growth rate. Lastly, there are many other possible relationships that the model doesn't take into account. One is that falling asset prices can destablilize the financial system and lead to a cycle of declining demand. (642-643)

━━━━━   ● ANSWERS ●   ━━━━━

MATCHING

1-c; 2-n; 3-p; 4-k; 5-m; 6-j; 7-a; 8-h; 9-b; 10-o, 11-g; 12-i; 13-l; 14-d; 15-f; 16-e.

━━━━━   ● ANSWERS ●   ━━━━━

PROBLEMS AND APPLICATIONS

1. a. This would cause the wealth effect to become inoperative and the AD curve will become steeper. (625-628)
    b. Assuming rich people spend less of an increase in income compared to poor

people, the AD curve will shift in to the left. (629)
    c. As the exchange rate depreciates, exports will rise and imports will fall. This shifts the AD curve out to the right. (626-627)
    d. If the exchange rate was originally fixed and became flexible, increases in the price level will be offset by changes in the exchange rate and the international effect becomes inoperative. The *AD* curve will be steeper. (626-627)
    e. Expectations of future price increases without changes in the current price level will tend to cause the *AD* curve to shift out to the right. (626-627)

2. a. The SAS doesn't shift at all because rises in input prices are completely offset by increases in productivity. (631-633)
    b. The SAS curve shifts up because the rise in input prices exceeds the rise in productivity. (631-633)
    c. The SAS curve shifts down because the rise in input prices is less than the rise in productivity. (631-633)

3. a. The LAS curve shifts to the right as shown below because business people are finding that their productive capacity is larger than they had thought. (634-635)

    b. The potential output curve shifts to the left as shown below because bad weather will hinder production. Because the storm is temporary, however, the shift in the potential output curve is also temporary. (634-635)

c. The short-run aggregate supply curve shown below shifts down from SAS_0 to SAS_1, because businesses will benefit from the declining import prices to the extent that imports are used in production. The fall in input prices is passed through to the goods market. (632)

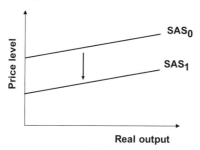

4. a. The economy is far below potential output at point A in the graph below. As the AD curve shifts out, the economy moves to point B—the price level rises slightly to P_1, and output increases to Y_1. As I have drawn the LAS curve, Y_1 is potential output, and point B is both a short-run and a long-run equilibrium. (639-640 and Figure 27-9)

b. The economy is close to potential output at point A in the graph below. The AD curve shifts to AD_1. Real output rises to Y_1 and the price level rises to P_1. Because output is beyond potential, point B is a short-run equilibrium. Input prices begin to rise which shifts the SAS curve up. As the SAS curve shifts up, real output declines and the price level rises even further. The SAS curve will continue to shift up until the economy is at potential output Y_2 and a new price level P_2—point C. Expansionary fiscal policy will be less effective in increasing output when the economy is close to potential. Real output rises by less than in (a) and the economy experiences much more inflation. (639-640)

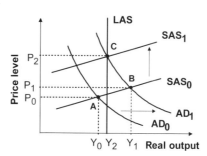

c. The economy is at potential output at point A in the graph below. As the AD curve shifts out, real output rises to Y_1 in the short run and the price level rises to P_1—point B. Since the economy is above potential however, eventually input prices will rise and the SAS curve will shift up. The SAS curve shifts up until real output falls back to potential output—Y_0—and the price level rises even further to P_2 (point C). In the long run, real output remains unchanged at Y_0 and only the price level increases from P_0 to P_2. When the economy is at or above potential, government activism is ineffective in the long run. (639-640 and Figure 27-9)

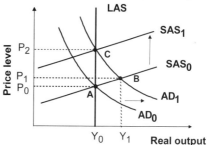

5. a. The graph below demonstrates an inflationary gap—short-run equilibrium output is above potential—point A. If government does nothing, wages will be bid up because there is a shortage of workers. This will shift the SAS curve up to SAS_1. Real output will fall to potential and the price level will rise—to point B. (637)

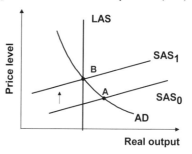

b. The graph below demonstrates a recessionary gap—short-run equilibrium output is below potential—point A. Given the excess supply in the labor market firms will be able to offer workers lower wages. Input prices will fall and the SAS curve will shift down to SAS_1. Real output will rise to potential and the price level will fall—to point B. Generally, government intervenes to increase expenditures (shifting the AD curve) before the price level declines. (637)

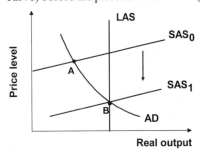

c. To avoid changes in the price level, if the economy is in an inflationary gap, the government can reduce government spending (or raise taxes) to shift the AD curve in to the left. If the economy is in a recessionary gap, it can increase government spending (or lower taxes) to shift the AD curve out to the right. (639-640)

ANSWERS

A BRAIN TEASER

1. My response depends on where I believe the economy is relative to potential output. If we are far below potential output then the President is right—the policy moves will increase the AD curve and the real output (employment) level will rise without creating much inflation. However, if we are close to potential output and the policy pushes the economy beyond potential, then wages will rise pushing the SAS curve up and the price level may rise more. The extent to which wages rise depends on the size of the effect on aggregate demand. It is difficult to predict. Moreover, it is also very difficult to determine how far from potential the economy actually is. (639-641)

ANSWERS

MULTIPLE CHOICE

1. **a**   Laissez faire is the non-activist policy that Classical economists generally support. See page 621.

2. **b**   The essence of Keynesian economics is its focus on the short run. See page 622.

3. **c**   The paradox of thrift is that if individuals increase saving, total income will decline, resulting in lower saving. See page 623.

4. **d**   Because of coordination problems equilibrium income could be different than potential income in Keynesian economics; it could be higher, lower, or equal to it. See page 622.

5. **d**   The AS/AD model is different than the micro supply/demand model. It has price *level* on the vertical axis and *total output* on the horizontal axis. See page 625.

6. **c**   No consumption effect is discussed in the book. See pages 625-628.

7. **a**   This question refers to the international effect; if the international effect is reduced, the change in the price level will have less effect on AD and the AD curve will be steeper. See pages 526-627.

8. **a**   The multiplier effect increases the effect of the other effects and hence a smaller multiplier makes the AD curve steeper. See pages 626-628.

9. **b**   The rise in foreign income will increase demand for exports, shifting the AD curve to the right. See page 628.

10. **a**   The rise in the country's exchange rate will decrease demand for its exports, shifting the AD curve in to the left. See pages 628-629.

11. **b**   Expansionary monetary policy will increase aggregate demand, shifting the AD curve out to the right. See page 630.

12. **c**   The multiplier effect would increase the effect, so the rightward shift would be more than 40. See page 630.

13. c The SAS curve is not a derived curve; it is an empirical curve determined by institutional realities. See page 631.

14. a Because wages are rising by more than productivity, the SAS curve will shift up. See page 633.

15. c The LAS curve shows the amount of goods and services an economy can produce when both labor and capital are fully employed. It is a vertical line since the price level does not affect potential output. See page 633.

16. a The SAS curve shifts upward when wages rise by more than increases in productivity. Real output will decline and the price level will rise. See page 633.

17. b An increase in the money supply will shift the AD curve to the right. In the short run, real output and the price level will rise. See pages 630 and 639-640.

18. c Demand for domestic goods will decline if one's currency appreciates because foreign goods will be less expensive compared to domestic goods. Real output will decline and the price level falls slightly. See pages 628-629.

19. d Since at point B, the economy is below potential, there will be downward pressure on wages. Or at least wages will rise by less than the increase in productivity. The SAS curve will shift down until the economy reaches point C. See pages 635-638.

20. a Since at point B, the economy is above potential, there will be upward pressure on wages. Wages will rise by more than the increase in productivity. The SAS curve will shift up until the economy reaches point C. See pages 635-638.

21. a The inflationary gap occurs when the price level is such that the quantity of aggregate demand exceeds the quantity of potential income. See pages 637-638.

22. c Dynamic feedback effects from a declining price level to aggregate expenditures may create a vicious cycle in which declining prices lead to continual leftward shifts in the AD curve. See pages 638-639.

23. d An economy with feedback effects can end up in a vicious cycle in which a declining price level leads to further shifts in the AD curve to the left. It is possible that the economy may end up even further to the left than point D. See pages 638-639.

24. c Expansionary fiscal policy is the deliberate increase in government expenditures or reduction in taxes. See pages 638-639.

25. d Aggregate demand management policies do not affect SAS, so a and b are out. With an inflationary gap you want to decrease output, so the answer is d. See Figure 27-8 on page 638.

26. a Inflation results in higher input prices, which shift the SAS curve up. See page 638.

27. b During WWII, taxes rose, but spending rose even more so that the net result was expansionary. Although the economy exceeded potential, inflation was avoided by price controls. See pages 641-642.

28. b Potential income varies inversely with unemployment. See pages 633-634.

ANSWERS

POTENTIAL ESSAY QUESTIONS

The following are annotated answers. They indicate the general idea behind the answer.

1. The macro model is more complicated than it appears because we do not know for sure where potential output is and because fiscal policy is more difficult to implement than is portrayed. Because we have no way of precisely determining how close the economy is to potential output, we don't know precisely by how much we should shift the AD curve. In addition, there are a number of other possible interrelationships the model does not take into account, which may destabilize the economy. One example is negative feedback effects of a declining price level on aggregate demand.

2.   The Classical prescription for the Great
     Depression was to do nothing (except remove
     the obstacles that they argued kept wages and
     prices artificially high) and wait for the market
     to work its magic over time.

         Keynes believed that equilibrium income
     was not the same as potential income. He
     disagreed with Say's Law. Supply does *not*
     create its own demand. That is, there is no
     guaranteed equality between savings and
     investment. Savings could exceed investment
     so that aggregate expenditures would not
     purchase all that is produced. Inventories will
     rise, and output, employment, and incomes
     would fall creating a further decline in total
     spending. Keynes doubted whether falling
     prices could stop this downward spiral. So, we
     get stuck in a rut.

         The policy implications are that insuffi-
     cient total spending in the economy could
     result in *an equilibrium* level of output,
     employment, and income *below potential*
     output. Therefore, the Keynesian recommenda-
     tion for a recession: expansionary macro
     policy. That is, increase government spending,
     reduce taxes (fiscal policy), and increase the
     money supply (monetary policy) to stimulate
     aggregate expenditures. (This would shift the
     AD curve to the right and increase real output.)

3.   The paradox of thrift is that when people
     collectively decide to save more and consume
     less, consumption expenditures fall. If that
     saving is not immediately transferred into
     investment, total expenditures fall. Faced with
     excess supply, firms cut production and
     income falls. As people's income falls, con-
     sumption and saving both fall. It is the paradox
     of thrift that leads to the multiplier effect. This
     multiplier effect makes the AD curve flatter
     than it otherwise would have been and
     accounts for the multiplied effect of shift
     factors of aggregate demand.

THE MULTIPLIER MODEL

28

● CHAPTER AT A GLANCE

This review is based upon the learning objectives that open the chapter.

1. Autonomous expenditures are unrelated to income; induced expenditures are directly related to income. (650-651)

   AE_0 (autonomous expenditures) can change (shift the AE curve) if there is an autonomous change in any component of aggregate expenditures (AE).

   Note: $AE_0 = C_0 + I_0 + G_0 + (X_0 - M_0)$.

2. To determine income graphically in the multiplier model, you find the income level at which aggregate expenditures equal aggregate production. (651-655)

3. To determine income using the multiplier equation, determine the multiplier and multiply it by the level of autonomous expenditures (655-657)

   multiplier = $1/(1 - mpe)$.

   Y = (multiplier)(Autonomous expenditures)

   ΔY = (multiplier)(ΔAutonomous expenditures)

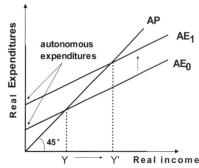

4. The multiplier process works because when expenditures don't equal production, businesspeople change planned production, which changes income, which changes expenditures, which.... (657-661)

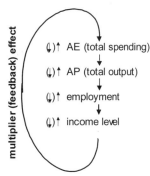

This is the income adjustment process—the multiplier effect on income given a change in spending.

5. Expansionary fiscal policy can eliminate a recessionary gap. It shifts the AE curve up, increasing equilibrium income by a multiple of the shift. (662-665)

If the economy is below potential, at Y_0, in the graph below, expansionary fiscal policy can get the economy out of its recessionary gap by increasing government purchases or decreasing taxes. The AE/AP model assumes the price level is constant, so real output rises by the full amount of the multiplier times the change in autonomous expenditures.

In the model, government knows by how much to increase (decrease) expenditures by dividing the recessionary (inflationary) gap by the multiplier.

The reverse logic explains how contractionary fiscal policy attempts to close an inflationary gap.

6. While the multiplier model is a mechanistic multiplier model, it should be used as a guide to one's common sense. The multiplier model has limitations: (665-667)

- The multiplier is not a complete model of the economy.
  The multiplier is best used as a guide for the direction and rough sizes of shifts in aggregate demand on income.

- Shifts are not as great as intuition suggests.
  Because some saving is brought back into the expenditures flow, a change in autonomous expenditures has less of an effect than the model suggests.

- Fluctuations can be greater than the model suggests.
  The multiplier-accelerator model suggests that changes in investment depend on changes in income. So, a decline in income may result in an even larger decline in investment.

- The price level will often change in response to shifts in demand.
  The multiplier model assumes prices are fixed.

- People's forward-looking expectations make the adjustment process much more complicated.
  Business decisions are forward-looking.

- Shifts in expenditures might reflect desired shifts in supply and demand.

- Expenditures depend on much more than current income.
  People also base their expenditure decisions on future income.

See also, Appendix A: "An Algebraic Presentation of the Expanded Multiplier Model" and Appendix B: "The Multiplier Model and the AS/AD Model."

● SHORT-ANSWER QUESTIONS

1. What is the difference between induced and autonomous expenditures?

2. Draw an AP and an AE curve and show how the level of income is graphically determined in the multiplier model. Describe the forces that are set in motion when income levels are above and below equilibrium.

3. In the multiplier model, if autonomous expenditures are $200 and the *mpe* is 0.75, what is equilibrium income?

4. Explain the process by which the economy reaches a new equilibrium income if autonomous expenditures increase by $100. The marginal propensity to expend is 0.5.

5. How does fiscal policy affect the economy? Demonstrate the appropriate fiscal policy for an economy that has an inflationary gap.

6. True or false: The multiplier model is a complete model of the economy. Explain your answer.

MATCHING THE TERMS
Match the terms to their definitions

___1.	aggregate expenditures	a.	The hypothesis that expenditures are determined by permanent or lifetime income.
___2.	aggregate production curve	b.	Expenditures that change as income changes.
___3.	autonomous expenditures	c.	The theory that fluctuations in the economy reflect real phenomena—simultaneous shifts in supply and demand, not simply supply responses to demand shifts.
___4.	expenditures multiplier		
___5.	induced expenditures		
___6.	marginal propensity to expend	d.	A model that emphasizes the effect of fluctuations on aggregate demand rather than the price level.
___7.	multiplier equation	e.	A number that tells us how much income will change in response to a change in autonomous expenditures.
___8.	multiplier model	f.	$AE = C + I + G + (X - M)$.
___9.	multiplier-accelerator model	g.	In the multiplier model, the 45° line on a graph with real income measured on the horizontal axis and real production on the vertical axis. Alternatively called the aggregate income curve.
___10.	permanent income hypothesis		
___11.	rational expectations model	h.	The ratio of a change in expenditures to a change in income.
		i.	Expenditures that are unaffected by changes in income.
___12.	real business cycle theory	j.	Equation that tells us how much income will change in response to a change in autonomous expenditures.
		k.	Model of the economy in which all decisions are based upon expected equilibrium in the economy.
		l.	A model in which changes in output are accelerated because changes in investment depend on changes in income.

PROBLEMS AND APPLICATIONS

1. Answer the following questions about the aggregate production curve.

   a. Draw an aggregate production curve. Label all axes.

   b. What is the slope of the aggregate production function?

   c. Why is the slope as you have drawn it?

2. You are given the following information about the economy:

Income	Expenditures
0	100
500	500
1,000	900
2,000	1,700
3,000	2,500
4,000	3,300

   a. What is the level of autonomous expenditures?

b. What is the marginal propensity to expend? Explain why it is important.

b. What is the slope of the curve?

c. What expenditures function (an equation) corresponds to the table?

c. What is the vertical axis intercept?

3. Putting expenditures and production together:

d. Add the aggregate production curve to the graph.

a. Graph the expenditures function from question 2 on the aggregate production curve from question 1.

e. What is the multiplier?

b. What is the slope of the expenditures function?

f. What is equilibrium income? Label that point A on the graph.

4. Given the following equation, answer the questions: $AE = C_0 + .6Y + I_0 + G_0 + (X_0 - M_0)$ where $C_0 = 1000, I_0 = 500, G_0 = 300, X_0 = 300, M_0 = 400$.

a. Draw the aggregate expenditures curve.

g. What is the effect of an increase in autonomous consumption of $200 on equilibrium income? Demonstrate your answer graphically.

h. What is the effect on equilibrium income of a change in the *mpe* from .6 to .8? Demonstrate your answer graphically. How does your answer to (g) change with the new *mpe*?

5. Calculate the multiplier in each case.

   a. *mpe* = .7

   b. *mpe* = .6

6. For each of the following, state what will happen to equilibrium income.

   a. The *mpe* is 0.9 and autonomous government expenditures just rose $200 billion. Graph your analysis.

   b. The *mpe* is 0.65 and autonomous investment just fell $70 billion. Graph your analysis.

7. You are hired by the president who believes that the economy is operating at a level $300 billion beyond potential output. You are told that the marginal propensity to consume is 0.5. (Note: assume that the *mpe* = *mpc*.)

   a. The president wants to use taxes to close the gap. What do you advise? Show your answer using the AP/AE model.

   b. The president wants to compare your plan in (a) to a plan using spending to close the inflationary gap. What do you advise? Show your answer graphically using the AP/AE model.

   c. The president's advisers from the council realize that the marginal propensity to consume is 0.75. Recalculate your answer to (b) and show your answer graphically using the AP/AE model.

A1. You've just been appointed chairman of the Council of Economic Advisers in Textland. The *mpc* is .8, and all non-consumption expenditures and taxes are exogenous.

   a. How can the government increase output by $400 through a change in expenditures?

b. Oops! There's been a mistake. Your research assistant tells you that taxes are actually not exogenous, and that there is a marginal tax rate of .1. How can the government change expenditures to increase income by $400?

c. There's more new news which your research assistant just found out. She tells you that not only is there a marginal tax rate of .1; there's also a marginal propensity to import of .2. You have to change your solutions now. How can the government change expenditures to increase income by $400?

B1. What happens to output in the AP/AE model when the AE curve shifts up due to a shift in autonomous expenditures if the economy is at potential output and the price level is flexible?

● A BRAIN TEASER

1. We have all heard about the extent to which local communities go to attract and recruit new businesses, conventions, trade shows, professional meetings, etc., to their area. Sometimes they seem to "give away the farm." They may offer a commitment not to impose property taxes for a particular number of years

or offer land at no charge if a company will build a production facility in the area. Why do local governments offer lucrative tax incentives, etc., to attract new businesses to their area–especially considering that there are only a relatively few number of modestly higher paying jobs created?

● MULTIPLE CHOICE

Circle the one best answer for each of the following questions:

1. In the multiplier model:
   a. production is assumed to be fixed.
   b. planned expenditures are assumed to equal actual production.
   c. the price level is assumed to be fixed.
   d. the price level is assumed to be flexible.

2. Autonomous expenditures are expenditures that:
   a. are automatically created by income.
   b. are unrelated to income.
   c. change as income changes.
   d. automatically change as income changes.

3. The marginal propensity to expend is:
   a. the change in expenditures times the change in income.
   b. the change in expenditures divided by the change in income.
   c. the change in expenditures divided by income.
   d. expenditures divided by the change in income.

4. If the mpe is .8, what is the size of the multiplier in the multiplier model?
   a. .5.
   b. 5.
   c. 1.
   d. 10.

5. As the *mpe* rises, the multiplier:
    a. increases.
    b. decreases.
    c. remains the same.
    d. sometimes rises and sometimes falls.

6. Which of the following is the expenditures
    function depicted in the graph below?

    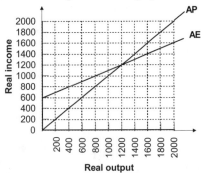

    a. AE=$600+.5Y.
    b. AE=.5Y.
    c. AE=$600.
    d. AE=$600Y/.5.

7. Refer to the graph for Question #6. Planned
    expenditures exceed production at:
    a. income levels above $1,200.
    b. income levels below $1,200.
    c. income level of $1,200.
    d. no income level since planned expenditures
    equals production.

8. If consumer confidence suddenly falls, you
    would expect:
    a. the aggregate production curve to shift
    down.
    b. the aggregate expenditures curve to rotate to
    the right and equilibrium income to fall.
    c. the aggregate expenditures curve to shift up
    and equilibrium income to rise.
    d. the aggregate expenditures curve to shift
    down and equilibrium income to fall.

9. In the multiplier model, if autonomous expendi-
    tures are $5,000 and the *mpe* equals .9, what
    is the level of income in the economy?
    a. $5,000.
    b. $10,000.
    c. $20,000.
    d. $50,000.

10. In the multiplier model, if autonomous exports
    fall by 40 and the *mpe* is .5, what happens to
    equilibrium income?
    a. It rises by 20.
    b. It falls by 20.
    c. It rises by 80.
    d. It falls by 80.

11. In the multiplier model, if autonomous expendi-
    tures increase by 100, income:
    a. will rise by 100.
    b. will rise by more than 100.
    c. will fall by 100.
    d. may rise or fall. We cannot tell without more
    information.

12. In the multiplier model, if autonomous expendi-
    tures increase by 10 and the *mpe* is .8, what
    happens to equilibrium income?
    a. It rises by 8.
    b. It falls by 8.
    c. It rises by 50.
    d. It falls by 50.

13. In the multiplier model, if autonomous exports
    fall by 40 and government spending in-
    creases by 20, and the *mpe* is .8, what
    happens to equilibrium income?
    a. It rises by 300.
    b. It falls by 300.
    c. It rises by 100.
    d. It falls by 100.

14. In the multiplier model, if people begin to
    spend less of the increases in their income:
    a. leakages out of the circular flow will rise and
    equilibrium income will fall.
    b. because leakages from the circular flow will
    still equal injections into the circular flow,
    equilibrium income will not change.
    c. injections into the circular flow will rise and
    equilibrium income will rise.
    d. the flow of income and expenditures will no
    longer be circular.

15. In the graph on the next page, actual income is
    below potential income. The government is
    planning to use expansionary fiscal policy.
    This will:

a. shift the *AP* curve up.
b. shift the *AE* curve up.
c. shift the *AP* curve down.
d. shift the *AE* curve down.

16. The economy has an *mpe* of .5, and a recessionary gap of 240. Using the Keynesian *multiplier model*, an economist would advise government to increase autonomous expenditures by:
    a. 120.
    b. 240.
    c. 480.
    d. 620.

17. The economy has an *mpe* of .8 and an inflationary gap of 500. Assume *mpe = mpc*. Using the multiplier model, an economist would advise government to increase taxes by:
    a. 50.
    b. 75.
    c. 100.
    d. 125.

18. The hypothesis that expenditures are determined by permanent or lifetime income (making the *mpe* close to zero) implies that the AE curve will be close to:
    a. a flat line.
    b. a vertical line.
    c. an upward sloping 45° line.
    d. something economists cannot determine.

19. The interpretative Keynesian macro model differs from the mechanistic Keynesian model in that the interpretative multiplier model:
    a. is essentially a Classical model.
    b. sees the Keynesian model as a guide, not a definitive result.

c. integrates the quantity theory into the *AE/AP* model.
d. integrates the quantity theory into both the Keynesian *AS/AD* and the *AE/AP* models.

20. If there is some price level flexibility, the:
    a. multiplier model is no longer relevant.
    b. results of the multiplier model will be reversed.
    c. results of the multiplier model will be modified but the central point will remain the same.
    d. multiplier model will turn into a Classical model.

21. In the multiplier-accelerator model:
    a. fluctuations are dampened by an mpe that is less than one.
    b. shifts in the AE curve can lead to more shifts in the AE curve.
    c. changes in the price level are destabilizing.
    d. changes in consumption are muted by lifetime income.

22. In the real business cycle theory, business cycles occur because of:
    a. changes in the real price level.
    b. changes in real income.
    c. technological and other natural shocks.
    d. changes in the money supply.

A1. If the marginal tax rate increases, what would happen to the general expenditures multiplier?
    a. It would increase.
    b. It would decrease.
    c. It would remain the same.
    d. One cannot say.

A2. In the multiplier model, if a country has a very large marginal propensity to import:
    a. expansionary fiscal policy would be extremely effective in expanding domestic income.
    b. expansionary fiscal policy would not be very effective in expanding domestic income.
    c. The size of the marginal propensity to import has no effect on the effectiveness of expansionary fiscal policy.
    d. The multiplier model is not relevant to a country with a very large marginal propensity to import.

A3. Assuming the marginal propensity to import is .1, the tax rate is .2, and the marginal propensity to consume is .6, the multiplier will be approximately:
   a. 0.
   b. 1.2.
   c. 1.6.
   d. 2.6.

A4. Assume the marginal propensity to import is .1, the tax rate is .25, the marginal propensity to consume is .8, and that the government wants to increase income by 100. In the multiplier model you would suggest increasing government spending by:
   a. 10.
   b. 35.7.
   c. 50.
   d. 100.

A5. Assume the marginal propensity to import is .3, the tax rate is .2, the marginal propensity to consume is .5, and that the government wants to increase income by 200. In the multiplier model you would suggest increasing government spending by:
   a. 87.5.
   b. 100.
   c. 180.
   d. 200.

B1. When the price level falls:
   a. the aggregate expenditures curve remains constant.
   b. the aggregate expenditures curve shifts down.
   c. the aggregate expenditures curve shifts up.
   d. the slope of the aggregate expenditures curve changes.

B2. To derive the aggregate demand curve from the multiplier model, one must:
   a. relate the initial autonomous shifts caused by price level changes on the *AE* curve to the *AD* curve.
   b. relate the *AE/AP* equilibria at different price levels to the *AD* curve.
   c. relate the *AE/AP* equilibria at different quantity levels to the *AD* curve.
   d. relate the initial autonomous shifts caused by price level changes on the *AP* curve to the *AD* curve.

● POTENTIAL ESSAY QUESTIONS

You may also see essay questions similar to the "Problems & Applications" and "A Brain Teaser" exercises.

1. In the multiplier model, can macroeconomic equilibrium exist below full employment? Why, or why not?

2. Why does the multiplier process exist? What does the multiplier do to the income level given any change in aggregate expenditures?

3. What is the major contribution of the multiplier model to the AS/AD model?

ANSWERS

SHORT-ANSWER QUESTIONS

1. Induced expenditures depend upon the level of income. Autonomous expenditures are independent of income. (650-651)

2. The *AP* curve is a 45-degree line through the origin. At all points on the *AP* curve, output equals income. The *AE* curve is an upward-sloping line with a slope less than one that intersects the expenditures axis at the level of autonomous expenditures. These curves are shown in the graph below. Equilibrium income is where the two curves intersect. At points to the left, aggregate expenditures exceed aggregate production and businesses find their inventories are being depleted. They increase production, which increases income and expenditures, moving income up toward equilibrium. At points to the right, aggregate expenditures are less than aggregate production and businesses see their inventories accumulating. They cut production, which reduces income and expenditures, moving income down toward equilibrium. (651-658)

3. To determine equilibrium income, multiply the sum of all autonomous expenditures by the multiplier. In this case the multiplier is $1/(1-.75) = 4$, so equilibrium income is $800. (655-657)

4. The initial shock is $100. This increase in expenditures causes aggregate production to increase also by $100, which creates an additional $100 in income. Consumers spend $50 of this additional income on additional goods. Once again aggregate production rises by the same amount as aggregate expenditures rose—$50 increase in this case. Subsequent increases in aggregate expenditures and aggregate production are determined in a similar fashion, each time getting smaller and smaller. Equilibrium income is $200 higher at the end of this multiplier process. This is determined by calculating the multiplier, $1/$

$(1 - mpe) = 2$ and multiplying it by the initial rise in aggregate expenditures of $100. (657-658)

5. Fiscal policy affects the economy by changing aggregate expenditures, which changes people's incomes, which changes people's spending even more. Expansionary fiscal policy shifts the aggregate expenditures curve up. Equilibrium income rises by a multiple of the increase in government spending. An economy in an inflationary gap is shown below. To avoid inflation, government can reduce government spending by the inflationary gap divided by the multiplier. A decline in government spending shifts the AE curve down and equilibrium income declines by a multiple of that shift. (662-665)

6. False. The multiplier model is not a complete model of the economy. Although it purports to determine equilibrium from scratch, it doesn't because it does not tell us where those autonomous expenditures come from. The multiplier model is best used as a guide for the direction and rough size of the effects of changes in autonomous expenditures on income. (665-667)

ANSWERS

MATCHING

1-e; 2-g; 3-i; 4-e; 5-b; 6-h; 7-j; 8-d; 9-l; 10-a; 11-k; 12-c.

ANSWERS

PROBLEMS AND APPLICATIONS

1. **a.** The aggregate production curve is a 45-degree line as shown below. Production is on the vertical axis and real income is on the horizontal axis. (649-650)

b. The slope is 1. (649-650)

c. The slope is one because the aggregate production curve represents the identity that aggregate production must equal aggregate income. That can only be represented by a straight line through the origin with a slope of one. (649-650)

2. a. Autonomous expenditures are $100. It is expenditures that are independent of income. (650)

b. The marginal propensity to expend is 0.8: This is calculated as the change in expenditures/change in income = 400/500. It is important because it tells us how much of any additional income is re-spent as the economy expands. It is because of the *mpe* that income changes by a multiple of a change in autonomous expenditures. (651)

c. The expenditures function that corresponds to the table is $AE = 100 + .8Y$. The 100 comes from the level of expenditures when income is zero and the .8 is the *mpe*. (650-651)

3. a. The graphs of the expenditures function from question 2 and the aggregate production from question 1 are shown together on the following graph. (649-651)

b. The slope of the expenditure function is the *mpe,* or 0.8. (650-651)

4. a. The aggregate expenditures curve is drawn below. The slope of the *AE* curve is the *mpe* and the vertical intercept is autonomous expenditures. (650-651)

b. The slope of the curve is .6. It is the *mpe*. (650-651)

c. The vertical axis intercept is 1000+500+300+(300−400)=1700. The vertical axis intercept is the level of autonomous expenditures. (650-651)

d. The aggregate production curve is shown in the graph below. It is a 45-degree line through the origin. (649-650)

e. The multiplier is 2.5. It is 1/(1−*mpe*). (655-657)

f. Equilibrium income is $4,250: autonomous expenditures × multiplier, $1,700×2.5. This is shown as point A on the graph below. (657-658)

g. An increase in autonomous expenditures of $200 will increase equilibrium income by $500. This is calculated by multiplying $200 by the multiplier, 2.5. The new equilibrium income is $4,750. This is shown below as an upward shift in the AE curve by 200. The new equilibrium income is point B on the graph below. (657-658 and Figure 28-7 on page 661)

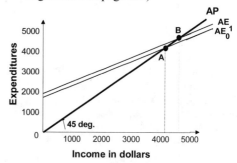

h. The *AE* curve becomes steeper with a slope of .8. The multiplier is now 5 and equilibrium income is now $8,500. This is shown as point C in the graph on the next page. Equilibrium income is calculated by multiplying autonomous expenditures, $1,700, by the multiplier. Since the multiplier is larger, an increase of $200 in autonomous expenditures now increases equilibrium income by $1,000, up to $9,500. (651, Figure 28-5 on page 657, and 655-658)

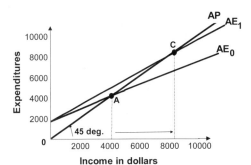

5. **a.** The multiplier is 3.33: $1/(1-.7)$. (657)
    b. The multiplier is 2.5: $1/(1-.6)$. (657)

6. **a.** Income rises by $2 trillion: $200/(1-0.9)$. In this case, the aggregate expenditures curve has a slope of 0.9 as shown in the graph below. The increase in government expenditures shifts the AE curve up from AE_0 to AE_1 and income increases by a multiple of that amount, in this case by a multiple of 10. (657 and Figure 28-7)

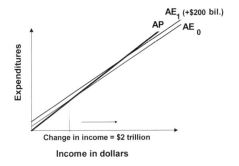

    b. Income falls by $200 billion: $70/.35$. In this case the aggregate expenditures curve has a slope of .65 as shown in the graph below. The decrease in investment shifts the AE curve down from AE_0 to AE_1 and income decreases by a multiple of that amount, in this case by a multiple of 2.86. (657 and Figure 28-7 on page 661)

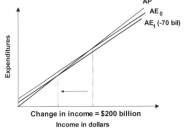

7. **a.** The spending multiplier is 2, $1/(1-.5)$, but only a fraction of the increase in taxes reduces spending. Taxes must be increased by $300 billion to reduce income by $300 billion. We calculate this by solving the following for change in taxes:

change in taxes $\times mpc \times [1/(1-mpe)] = \$300$ billion. The AE curve shifts down by the decrease in consumption spending ($150 billion) as shown below. (665)

    b. The spending multiplier is 2. Spending must be decreased by $150 billion to reduce income by $300 billion. We calculate this by solving the following for change in government spending: change in government spending $\times (1/(1-mpe)) = \$300$ billion. Graphically, the analysis is the same as in part a. (663-664)

    c. The spending multiplier is now 4, $1/(1-.75)$. Government spending must be decreased by $75 billion to reduce income by $300 billion. We calculate this by solving the following for change in government spending: change in government spending $\times 4 = \$300$ billion. This is shown in the graph below. The AE curve is steeper than the AE curve in part b. (663-664)

A1. Given an mpc of .8:
    a. Increase expenditures by $80. The multiplier is $1/(1-mpc)=1/(1-.8)=5$. Therefore, to increase GDP by $400, government spending has to increase $80. (672-674)
    b. Increase expenditures by $112. The multiplier is $1/(1-mpc+t\times mpc)=1/(1-.8+(.1\times.8))=3.57$. Therefore, to increase GDP by $400, government spending has to increase by $112. (672-674)

c. Increase expenditures by $193. The multiplier is $1/(1-mpc+t\times mpc+mpm)=1/(1-.8+.1\times.8+.2)=2.08$. Therefore, to increase GDP by $400, government spending has to increase by $193. (672-674)

B1. In the multiplier model, a change in autonomous expenditures will be offset entirely by a change in the price level that shifts the AE curve in a direction opposite to the initial shift. If the initial shift causes the AE curve to shift up, prices will rise sufficiently to shift the AE curve back to its initial position. (675-676)

ANSWERS

A BRAIN TEASER

1. It may appear that the benefits do not outweigh the costs to the community of "giving away the farm"–especially when one considers that the tax breaks offered to new businesses will likely result in higher property tax rates imposed on other members of the community if the same quantity and quality of local government services are to be provided. However, even though a relatively few number of modestly higher paying jobs are created, because of the multiplier effect, this *can* translate into still more jobs and even more income, etc.–creating "significant growth and opportunities within the community." Next time you read headlines indicating the amount of jobs (or income) created in the city by having the "Pigs are Beautiful" convention in town, you'll know what they mean. (657-658)

ANSWERS

MULTIPLE CHOICE

1. c The multiplier model assumes that the price level remains constant and asks how much aggregate equilibrium income will change when aggregate expenditures change. During the adjustment to equilibrium, planned expenditures will not equal actual production. See pages 657-658.

2. b Autonomous expenditures are expenditures that exist even when income is zero. They do not change as income changes. See pages 650-651.

3. b The marginal propensity to expend is the fraction of additional income that is spent. It can be calculated by dividing the change in expenditures by the change in income. See page 651.

4. b The multiplier equals $1/(1-.8)=1/.2=5$. See page 657.

5. a You can determine this by substituting into the multiplier formula. See page 657.

6. a The graph shows that the y-axis intercept is $600 and the slope is .5. Calculate the slope as rise over run. For example, beginning at the y-intercept, increasing expenditures by 600 means income rises by 1200 (600/1200=.5). Substitute these values in the equation for a straight line: y = (slope)x + (intercept). See page 651.

7. b Planned expenditures exceed production where the AE curve is above the AP curve. This occurs at income levels below $1,200. See pages 651-655.

8. d A drop in consumer confidence would be expected to reduce consumption expenditures. This shifts the AE curve down and leads to a reduction in equilibrium income (output). See pages 661-662.

9. d The multiplier is 10 so the answer is 10 times $5,000. See pages 655-657.

10. d The multiplier is 2 so the answer is $2\times(-40)$. See pages 655-657.

11. b In the multiplier model, a change in autonomous expenditures will lead to a change in income in the same direction that is a multiple of the change in expenditures. See pages 655-657.

12. c The multiplier is 5 so the answer is 5 times 10. See pages 655-657.

13. d The multiplier is 5 so the answer is 5 times $(-40+20)$ or minus 100. See pages 655-657.

14. a If people spend less of their income, the *mpe* will fall. Because more income leaks from the circular flow, less returns in the form of expenditures and equilibrium income falls. See pages 658-659.

15. b Expansionary fiscal policy increases aggregate expenditures, which is shown by a shift up in the AE curve. See Figure 28-9(a) on page 663.

16. a To determine how much to increase expenditures in the *multiplier model* to reach potential income, you divide the recessionary gap of 240 by the multiplier of 2. See pages 663-664.

17. d Since the multiplier is 5, expenditures need to fall by 100. Expenditures will fall by the *mpc* times the rise in taxes, so taxes need to rise by 100 divided by the *mpc*, or 125. See page 665.

18. a The permanent income hypothesis suggests that the *mpe* out of current income would be small so, the AE curve would be quite flat. See page 667.

19. b The interpretative multiplier model views the multiplier model as an aid in understanding. It might integrate the multiplier model with other models but that is not what is distinctive about it. See pages 667-668.

20. c The multiplier model assumes that the price level is constant. If, however, the price level is not constant, the multiplier model is modified. The central point, however, that an increase in expenditures has a multiplied effect on equilibrium output is still relevant. See page 665.

21. b In the multiplier-accelerator model, changes in investment depend on changes in income. So, a change in income can create even greater changes in investment and therefore create even greater changes in income. See page 666.

22. c Real business cycle theory suggests that fluctuations in output are the result of shifting aggregate supply resulting from changes in technology. See page 667.

A1. b This is a hard question since it requires some deduction. The marginal tax rate is one of the components of the marginal propensity to consume. It is a leakage from the circular flow, so it makes the multiplier smaller. See pages 672-674.

A2. b A large marginal propensity to import reduces the size of the multiplier since the marginal propensity to import is one of the components of the marginal propensity to consume. See pages 672-674.

A3. c The multiplier for the full model is $1/(1-c+ct+m)$. Substituting in gives $1/(1-.6+(.6)(.2)+.1)$ or $1/.62$ or a multiplier of about 1.6. See pages 672-674.

A4. c First you determine the multiplier. The multiplier for the full model is $1/(1-c+ct+m)$. Substituting in gives $1/(1-.8+(.8)(.25)+.1)$ or $1/.5$ or a multiplier of 2. Dividing 100 by 2 gives an increase of government spending of 50. See pages 672-674.

A5. c First you determine the multiplier. The multiplier for the full model is $1/(1-c+ct+m)$. Substituting in gives $1/(1-.5+(.5)(.2)+.3)$ or $1/.9$ or a multiplier of about 1.11. Dividing 200 by 1.11 gives an increase of government spending of about 180. The multiplier is very small because the *mpc* is low and the *mpm* is high. See pages 672-674.

B1. c Since a lower price level makes the cash people hold worth more, people feel wealthier, spend more, and the *AE* curve shifts up. See pages 675-676.

B2. b As discussed on pages 675-676, especially Figure B28-1, one considers the effect of different price levels on the *AE* curve to derive an *AD* curve.

━━━━ ANSWERS ━━━━

POTENTIAL ESSAY QUESTIONS

The following are annotated answers. They indicate the general idea behind the answer.

1. Yes, because equilibrium exists *wherever* AE = AP. That is, planned expenditures need not equal production at full employment. If there is inadequate spending then the income adjustment process moves the economy to an equilibrium below full employment.

2. A change in spending changes people's incomes, which changes their spending, which changes people's incomes... Because of the induced effects within the income adjustment process, the multiplier magnifies any changes in spending into much larger changes in income. However, given an increase in expenditures, real income increases by a smaller amount when prices are flexible.

3. The major contribution of the multiplier model to the AS/AD model is that it provides an exact number for the shift in the AD curve when autonomous expenditures change and provides the reasoning behind the multiplier effects needed to derive an AD curve.

THINKING LIKE A
MODERN MACROECONOMIST

CHAPTER AT A GLANCE

This review is based upon the learning objectives that open the chapter.

1. Standard macro models are top-down engineering models of the economy. Examples are the AS/AD and the multiplier models, which are based on historical relationships among variables. They are for policy analysis.

    Modern macro models, such as the DSGE model, are scientific models derived from micro foundations in response to the theoretical weaknesses of the standard macro models. Their primary purpose is to understand how the economy works. (679-684)

    Standard macro models = Engineering models = Keynesian

    Modern macro models = Deductive scientific models = New Classical

2. Classical economists had informal models of the macro economy. The Great Depression led to the development of formal, Keynesian macro models that focused on the fallacy of composition but lacked formal micro foundations.

    In the 1970s new statistical tools raised questions about the aggregate relationships assumed by the standard macro model, which led to New Classical models that downplayed the fallacy of composition and emphasized traditional microeconomic building blocks. (681-684)

    New classical models replaced earlier models because of new economic experiences and the development of new statistical tools.

3. Some advantages of the standard macro models are that they are quickly applicable and provide a reasonable framework for discussing macro problems.

    Some disadvantages of the standard macro models are that they lack formal scientific foundations and are not always internally logical. (680-684)

    Standard macro models are not better or worse than modern macro models. They highlight different aspects of the economy and are used for different purposes.

4. In DSGE models:

    D stands for dynamic, meaning that the model takes time explicitly into account.

    S stands for stochastic, meaning that events happen with a certain probability that can be specified mathematically.

    G and E stand for general equilibrium, meaning that the model is an equilibrium model of all the markets in the economy, not just a single market. (685-686)

    Three policy prescriptions of the DSGE model are (1) policy had better take into account that people are smart, (2) credibility is important, and (3) rules have certain advantages over discretion.

5. Three policy problems that the DSGE model highlights are (1) the Ricardian equivalence problem, (2) the time-inconsistency/credibility problem, and (3) the Lucas Critique problem. (686-688)

    - *The Ricardian equivalence problem is the problem that people respond to government action in ways that offset that action.*

    - *The time-inconsistency/credibility problem is that the best government policy from today's point of view can turn out to be a policy that government wants to change in the future. If the government changes its policies too often, people will begin to anticipate such changes and will no longer see government policy as credible.*

    - *The Lucas critique problem is that historical data can be a misleading predictor of the effect of government action because policies affect behavior.*

6. The complex systems approach sees the macroeconomy as being in constant flux. It assumes that while people don't have perfect foresight, they learn from their mistakes. However, since the economy is in constant flux, there is no one correct learning process. (691)

    Learning procedures are an important part of the complex systems approach.

    The ACE model is an example of a complex systems approach.

● SHORT-ANSWER QUESTIONS

1. What is the standard macro model? How did it develop?

2. What is the modern macro model? How did it develop?

3. What is the fallacy of composition? What role does it have in the standard macro model?

4. List two advantages and two disadvantages of the standard macro model.

5. What does the acronym DSGE stand for? What does each of the terms mean?

6. List two advantages and two disadvantages of the modern DSGE macro model.

7. What are some policy implications of the standard macro model? What are the policy implications of the modern macro (DSGE) model?

8. What is the complex systems approach to macro?

9. What are some difficulties and problems with the DSGE model? How might the agent-based computational economic model help address these difficulties?

MATCHING THE TERMS
Match the terms to their definitions

___ 1. agent-based computational (ACE) model
___ 2. complex systems macro model
___ 3. deductive scientific model
___ 4. dynamic
___ 5. emergent properties
___ 6. engineering model
___ 7. general equilibrium model
___ 8. herd
___ 9. historically based expectations
___ 10. learning procedures
___ 11. Lucas critique problem
___ 12. New Classical macroeconomics
___ 13. rational expectations
___ 14. representative agent
___ 15. Ricardian equivalence problem
___ 16. standard macro models
___ 17. stochastic
___ 18. time inconsistency/ credibility problem

a. The problem that anything the government does to affect the economy will mostly be offset by countervailing actions by private individuals as they optimize over the future.

b. A macro model of the economy that takes into account dynamic interactions of agents in the model, where agents have less than full information and can be less than infinitely rational.

c. The methods by which people learn about the system.

d. A model with loose formal foundations whose primary purpose is to guide thinking about policy.

e. The problem that the best government policy from today's point of view can turn out to be a policy the government wants to change in the future, and that rational individuals can anticipate this.

f. Virtual computer macro economies or rational agents with less than perfect information.

g. An approach to macroeconomics that studies macroeconomic questions using traditional microeconomic building blocks that emphasize rationality.

h. To copy other successful behavior even though that successful behavior may have been just luck.

i. A model with carefully specified formal foundations, whose primary purpose is understanding for the sake of understanding.

j. The problem that because government policies can affect the behavior of individuals, historical data can lead to misleading predictions about the impact of a new policy.

k. Properties of the system that could not have been predicted from a deductive analysis starting from the components of the system.

l. The models (such as the AS/AD and multiplier models and their derivatives) used by most applied macro economists.

m. A model of all the markets in the economy, not just a single market.

n. A single individual that has perfect foresight and is immortal. This single individual is the focus of the DSGE model.

o. Taking "time" explicitly into account.

p. The concept that events happen with a certain probability that can be specified mathematically.

q. Expectations about the future that are based on past events.

r. Expectations that turn out to be correct in reference to the model.

PROBLEMS AND APPLICATIONS

1. What does each of the following models assume about expectations?

   a. The standard macro models.

   b. DSGE macro models.

   c. Complex systems models.

2. State for each of the following models whether it is an example of a standard macro model, a modern macro model, or a complexity model.

   a. The multiplier model.

   b. The Dynamic Stochastic General Equilibrium model.

   c. The Aggregate Demand / Aggregate Supply model.

   d. Agent-based computational economic models.

3. State for each of the following concepts: its definition and whether it is part of standard macro models, modern macro models (read DSGE), or complexity models.

   a. Herding behavior.

   b. A representative agent (single immortal consumer-worker-owner).

   c. Emergent properties.

   d. Historically based expectations.

   e. Perfect foresight and rational expectations.

   f. The fallacy of composition.

4. State for each of the following implications whether they originate from standard macro models, modern macro models (read DSGE), or complexity models.

   a. Since government policies can affect the behavior of individuals, historical data can lead to misleading predictions about the impact of a new policy.

   b. Based on aggregate relationships, government has a significant and active role to play in coordinating the economy.

   c. Anything that the government does to affect the economy will mostly be offset by countervailing actions by private individuals.

   d. Interactive effects among individuals must be taken into account.

   e. Government policy from today's point of view can turn out to be a policy the government wants to change in the future. Rational individuals can anticipate that government will change its policy.

⬤ A BRAIN TEASER

1. Given that advances in analytic capability such as new statistical tools and increased computing power have driven the development of increasingly technical and sophisticated models, what implications does this hold for the future of macroeconomics? Will there ever be a theory or a model that perfectly explains reality?

⬤ MULTIPLE CHOICE

Circle the one best answer for each of the following questions:

1. Modern macroeconomics is:
    a. highly theoretical and mathematical.
    b. based on outdated arguments and theories.
    c. very similar to standard macroeconomics.
    d. used for theoretical and academic purposes rather than to formulate policy.

2. An important reason why students should study modern macro models is that:
    a. they are highly theoretical and mathematical.
    b. they are useful thought-exercises that help develop analytical ability.
    c. they are the correct scientific model.
    d. they are the correct engineering model.

3. Engineering models are:
    a. models with loose formal foundations whose primary purpose is to understand for the sake of understanding.
    b. models with carefully specified formal foundations whose primary purpose is to guide thinking about policy.
    c. models with carefully specified formal foundations whose primary purpose is to understand for the sake of understanding.
    d. models with loose formal foundations whose primary purpose is to guide thinking about policy.

4. Deductive scientific models are:
    a. models with carefully specified formal foundations whose primary purpose is to understand for the sake of understanding.
    b. models with loose formal foundations whose primary purpose is to guide thinking about policy.
    c. models with carefully specified formal foundations whose primary purpose is to guide thinking about policy.
    d. models with loose formal foundations whose primary purpose is to understand for the sake of understanding.

5. Standard macro models focus on:
    a. deductive logic and traditional micro economic building blocks.
    b. quick applicability and providing a reasonable framework for discussing macro problems.
    c. historical relationships and traditional micro economic building blocks.
    d. scientific precision and internal logic.

6. Modern macro models focus on:
    a. how and why the model works as well as its internal logic.
    b. quick applicability and providing a reasonable framework for discussing macro problems.
    c. using inductive logic and traditional micro economic building blocks to provide a rough and ready model for policy analysis.
    d. historical relationships and scientific precision.

7. In the 1940s the informal macro models of Classical economics were replaced by:
    a. the standard macro models of Keynesian economics.
    b. the modern macro models of neo-Classical economics.
    c. the complex macro models of modern macroeconomics.
    d. the modern macro models of Keynesian economics.

8. Keynesian economics and the standard macro model are both loosely based on:
    a. Ricardian equivalence.
    b. perfect foresight.
    c. rational expectations.
    d. the fallacy of composition.

9. The standard macro model:
   a. lacks formal micro foundations.
   b. has formal micro foundations.
   c. is internally logical.
   d. is based on formal relationships among microeconomic variables.

10. DSGE stands for:
    a. Direct Sequential General Equation.
    b. Deductive Simultaneous Geometric Equation.
    c. Differential Stochastic Graphical Equilibrium.
    d. Dynamic Stochastic General Equilibrium.

11. Dynamic refers to:
    a. the fact that the representative individual is making decisions that are meant to guide him through his lifetime.
    b. the fact that the representative individual interacts with other individuals in a dynamic way.
    c. the fact that the representative individual recognizes the tradeoffs in life.
    d. the perfect foresight and rational expectations of the representative individual.

12. Stochastic refers to:
    a. the fact that the representative individual is making decisions that are meant to guide him through his lifetime.
    b. the fact that the representative individual recognizes the tradeoffs in life.
    c. the fact that the representative individual knows the probability that various events will happen.
    d. the fact that the representative individual's decision making process is continually changing over time.

13. The policy implications of the DSGE model are:
    a. Sound finance, strong currency, and the central bank as the lender of last resort.
    b. Ricardian equivalence, time inconsistency/credibility, and the Lucas critique.
    c. interactive effects must be taken into account, Ricardian equivalence, and sound finance.
    d. Government stabilization policies, Lucas critique, and strong currency.

14. The Tacoma Narrows bridge incident is an example of:
    a. positive feedback and the dangers of heavy reliance on formal scientific models.
    b. Ricardian equivalence and the dangers of heavy reliance on informal engineering models.
    c. the Lucas critique and the dangers of heavy reliance on informal engineering models.
    d. the fallacy of composition and the dangers of heavy reliance on formal scientific models.

15. The cobweb model shows that the standard macro models:
    a. rely implicitly on the assumption that people are dumb and don't learn.
    b. result in immediate price adjustments to new equilibriums.
    c. rely implicitly on the assumption that people make rational guesses but don't learn.
    d. rely implicitly on the assumption that people make rational guesses and learn from them.

16. Modern complex systems economists suspect that _____ are central to the expectations process.
    a. historical expectations
    b. perfect foresight and rationality
    c. opportunity costs
    d. learning procedures

17. Herding behavior in a market:
    a. provides fundamental market stability and is therefore important to any modern macro model.
    b. is the result of historical expectations and a hallmark of standard macro theory.
    c. can result in even larger fluctuations away from equilibrium, keeping the market from equilibrium for long periods of time.
    d. is a purely theoretical phenomenon and has not been documented as real-life behavior.

18. Which is the right model for the economy?
    a. The standard macro model.
    b. DSGE.
    c. Agent based computational models.
    d. It depends.

● POTENTIAL ESSAY QUESTIONS

You may also see essay questions similar to the "Problems & Applications" and "A Brain Teaser" exercises.

1. Macroeconomists working on the complexity approach have tentatively found that learning procedures are central to the expectations process, and that people will likely learn from historical data, in highly sophisticated ways. How do the implications of this insight relate to the quote from Keynes on page 695?

2. On pages 691-696, three important insights from the DSGE model and three from the complexity approach are underscored. Examine these six insights. Do any of the six important insights contradict one another?

ANSWERS

SHORT-ANSWER QUESTIONS

1. The standard macro model is a top-down model of the economy based on historical relationships among variables. It is an engineering model suitable for policy. In the early 20th century classical economists had informal, but no formal models of the macro economy. The Great Depression led to development of formal, Keynesian macro models. These standard macro models were top-down models based on aggregate relationships and the fallacy of composition but lacked micro foundations. In the 1960s the early Keynesian models were expanded into complicated multiple-sector models that implicitly assumed micro foundations. (679-681)

2. The modern macro model is a model built from micro foundations. It is a scientific model designed to understand how the economy works. In the 1970s new statistical tools raised questions about the aggregate relationships assumed by the standard macro model. Economist Robert Lucas showed that standard macro models weren't based on micro foundations and therefore were not internally logical. Gradually the old Keynesian models were replaced by New Classical models that discarded the fallacy of composition and emphasized traditional microeconomic building blocks. (681-684)

3. The fallacy of composition is the concept that what is true for the parts is not necessarily true for the aggregate. Keynesian economics as it initially developed was based on the fallacy of composition. Instead of looking at individuals and aggregating up to an entire economy, Keynesian models took an aggregate approach and instead looked at aggregate relationships. (681-682)

4. Two advantages: Standard macro models are quickly applicable and provide a reasonable framework for discussing macro problems. Two disadvantages: Standard macro models are fundamentally unscientific and are not internally logical. The text lists others. (679-684)

5. D stands for dynamic, meaning that the model takes time explicitly into account. The repre-sentative individual makes decisions that will guide him through his entire lifetime rather than decisions for a single point in time.

    S stands for stochastic, meaning that events happen with a certain probability that can be specified mathematically. The representative individual doesn't know what will happen, but he does know the probability that the various events will happen.

    G and E stand for general equilibrium, meaning that the model assumes all markets in the economy are in equilibrium. (685-686)

6. Two advantages: the DSGE model considers that people are not stupid when making their decisions and provides definite insights into the economy. (A third is that it is scientific and internally logical.) Two disadvantages: it makes highly restrictive assumptions that do not hold in the real world; it fails to explain herding behavior or periodic market instability. (685-689)

7. The policy implication of the standard macro model is that the government has a significant role to play in the economy. It justifies government involvement with regard to monetary policy and fiscal policy. Government is capable of guiding and possibly controlling macroeconomic outcomes.

    The overall policy implications of the DSGE model is that government may not be able to guide or control the economy. Some policy prescriptions of the DSGE model are (1) people are smart and policy had better take that into account, (2) credibility is important, and (3) rules have certain advantages over discretion. (690-693)

8. The complex systems approach to macro does not assume that people can predict the future with perfect accuracy (as do modern macro models) nor does it assume that people rely only on historical information (as do the standard macro models). Agents dynamically interact with less than full information and less than infinite rationality. They learn through a complex process of interaction with other agents. (691-696)

9. Periodic market instability is hard to explain with the DSGE model and the concept of

rational choice. Complexity based models that do seem to explain instability are almost always too complex to solve mathematically. Economists use computers to create virtual macro economies called agent-based computational economic models where they experiment with different learning patterns. In this way they can gain insights without having to fully understand the underlying technical complications. (696-697)

ANSWERS

MATCHING

1-f; 2-b; 3-i; 4-o; 5-k; 6-d; 7-m; 8-h; 9-q; 10-c; 11-j; 12-g; 13-r; 14-n; 15-a; 16-l; 17-p; 18-e.

ANSWERS

PROBLEMS AND APPLICATIONS

1. **a.** The standard macro model assumes that people have backward looking expectations. That is, they base their decisions on historical information. (679-680)
    b. In the DSGE model, the representative individual is assumed to take into account all possibilities that might happen and the probability of each and makes decisions perfectly and instantaneously. The representative individual's expectations always turn out to be correct. (685-686)
    c. With complexity, people learn from past mistakes and their learning procedures are central to the expectations process. People use historical data to learn in highly sophisticated ways. (691-694)

2. **a.** The multiplier model is an example of a standard macro model. (679-680)
    b. The Dynamic Stochastic General Equilibrium model is an example of a modern macro model. It is the most widely used modern macro model. (685-686)
    c. The Aggregate Demand / Aggregate Supply model is a standard macro model. (679-680)

d. Agent-based computational economic models are complexity models. (696-697)

3. **a.** Herding behavior refers to when individuals make decisions by copying other successful behavior even though that successful behavior may have been just luck. It is generally incorporated into complexity models. (696)
    b. A representative agent refers to the theoretical focus of the DSGE model, a single immortal consumer-worker-owner who makes decisions in multiple time periods. This specific idea forms part of the theoretical structure of the DSGE model. (685-686)
    c. Emergent properties refer to properties of a system that could not have been predicted from a deductive analysis starting from the components of the system. They are an implication of the complexity models but they also justify the basic macro approach of the standard macro models. (691)
    d. Historically based expectations refer to expectations about the future that are based on past events. They are a component of standard macro models. (679-682)
    e. Perfect foresight and rational expectations refer to how the representative individual is assumed to take into account all possibilities that might happen and their probabilities and makes decisions perfectly and instantaneously. This is a central assumption of the DSGE model. (685-686)
    f. The fallacy of composition refers to how what is true for the parts is not necessarily true for the aggregate. The early standard macro models were based on this idea. (681-682)

4. **a.** This is the Lucas Critique, which is a policy implication that follows from the DSGE model. (687-688)
    b. This is a policy implication that follows from the standard macro models developed during the Keynesian revolution. (679-682)
    c. This implication is the Ricardian equivalence problem that follows from the DSGE model. (686-687)

d.   This implication follows from the complexity approach. (691-696)

e.   This is the time inconsistency/credibility problem that follows from the DSGE model. (687)

━━━━━━ ANSWERS ━━━━━━

A BRAIN TEASER

1.   Predicting the future is a nearly impossible task. Nevertheless there seems to be a historical pattern: economic analysis has become increasingly complex and sophisticated as analytical tools have increased in power and capability. While it is dangerous to extrapolate from historical data, it suggests that future analytical tools will facilitate the development of new and more intricate models and theories. Even so, this does not guarantee that there will ever be a theory or a model that perfectly explains reality. Indeed recent complex models have raised more questions than they have answered. (690-696)

━━━━━━ ANSWERS ━━━━━━

MULTIPLE CHOICE

1.   a   Modern macro is not based on outdated arguments and theories. In addition it is neither similar to standard macroeconomics nor used for only theoretical and academic purposes. Modern macro is considered highly theoretical and mathematical. See pages 679-680.

2.   b   While modern macro models are highly theoretical and mathematical, this is not a reason why an introductory student should study them. They are, however, useful thought-exercises that help one understand forces in the economy. No one model is correct and no macro model predicts what will happen in the economy. Macro hasn't progressed that far. See pages 678-679.

3.   d   Engineering models are models with loose formal foundation whose primary purpose is to guide thinking about policy. See pages 680-681.

4.   a   Deductive scientific models are models with carefully specified formal foundations whose primary purpose is to understand for the sake of understanding. See pages 679-681.

5.   b   The standard macro models do not have micro foundations. The standard macro models aren't internally logical. The standard macro models focus on quick applicability and providing a reasonable framework for discussing macro problems. See page 680.

6.   a   The standard macro models focus on quick applicability and providing a reasonable framework for discussing macro problems. Modern macro models are based explicitly on deductive reasoning. The standard macro model is based on historical relationships. Modern macro models focus on how and why the model works as well as the internal logic of the model. See pages 679-681.

7.   a   The Great Depression challenged Classical economic precepts and led to the development of Keynesian economics and the early standard macro models. See pages 681-682.

8.   d   Ricardian equivalence is an implication of the DSGE model. Both perfect foresight and rational expectations are assumptions of the DSGE model. Keynesian economics and therefore the standard macro model are based on the fallacy of composition. See pages 681-684.

9.   a   The standard macro model is not internally logical. It does not need to be since it is not a deductive model. The standard macro model is based on historical relationships. The standard macro model lacked micro foundations. See pages 682-684.

10. d   DSGE stands for Dynamic Stochastic General Equilibrium. See page 685.

11. a   Dynamic refers to the fact that the representative individual is making decisions that will guide him through his lifetime. While the individual does interact with other individuals, this is not what the word "dynamic" is referring to. See page 685.

12. c   Stochastic refers to the fact that the representative individual knows the probability that various events will happen. See page 686.

13. b   Sound finance, strong currency, and the central bank as the lender of last resort are the policy precepts of classical economics. The policy implications of the DSGE model are Ricardian equivalence, time inconsistency/credibility, and the Lucas critique. See pages 686-688.

14. a   The Tacoma Narrows bridge incident is an example of positive feedback and the dangers of heavy reliance on formal scientific models. See pages 690-691.

15. a   The cobweb model shows that the standard macro models rely implicitly on the assumption that people are dumb and don't learn. See pages 691-692.

16. d   Modern complex systems economists suspect that learning procedures are central to the expectations process. See pages 691-696.

17. c   Herding behavior in a market can result in even larger fluctuations away from equilibrium, keeping the market from equilibrium for long periods of time. See page 696.

18. d   There is no simple answer to this question. Depending on how the model will be used, one would select different models. See pages 697-698.

ANSWERS

POTENTIAL ESSAY QUESTIONS

The following are annotated answers. They indicate the general idea behind the answer.

1. Learning procedures are the methods by which people learn about the system. If it is true that learning procedures are central to the expectations process, people will make rational guesses on the basis of historical data and will learn from their mistakes.

    People will analyze historical data in order to find patterns. If these patterns seem likely to continue, they will base their decisions on these discovered patterns. However, by basing their decisions on the patterns they will often change the pattern. Not to be deterred, people are likely to start looking for patterns in the way that the patterns change when used. If such patterns are found, they will base their decisions on those patterns, changing them, and will again search for a pattern in the change. People will continue with this learning process and will get so caught up in it that they lose all sense of connection with the real economy.

    Keynes' quote on page 695 illustrates the effect of the learning process on expectations, using the example of a beauty contest. Instead of just picking the person who seems prettiest, people wind up trying to guess what the "average opinion" expects the "average opinion" of prettiness to be. Keynes leaves the possibility that there are continually higher degrees of a learning process. Keynes used this example to illustrate how interdependence of expectations can lead to a loss of all sense of connection with the real economy. This opens the possibility of a serious depression because when people realize that their actions no longer relate to fundamental economic realities, the expectations, confidence, and irrational exuberance that drove the market disappear and the bubble pops.

2. Three important insights of the DSGE model are (1) people are smart and policy had better take that into account, (2) credibility is important, and (3) rules have certain advantages over discretion.

Three important insights of the complexity are (1) groups of smart people can act in ways that seem quite irrational, (2) all models leave out elements that can cause complex systems to collapse so it is necessary to pay attention to reality, and (3) there is no solid theory to guide macroeconomists and there are no unchanging rules of macro policy.

While not strictly contradictory, perhaps some of these important insights work at cross purposes. Policy must take the fact that people are smart into account but also take the fact that smart people can act irrationally into account as well. While credibility and rules are important, there are no unchanging rules of macro policy.

Pretest
Chapters 24-29

Take this test in test conditions, giving yourself a limited amount of time to complete the questions. Ideally, check with your professor to see how much time he or she allows for an average multiple choice question and multiply this by 30. This is the time limit you should set for yourself for this pretest. If you do not know how much time your teacher would allow, we suggest 1 minute per question, or 30 minutes.

1. All of the following are long-run growth policies *except*:
   a. increasing government spending to spur consumer spending.
   b. reducing tax rates to increase incentives to work.
   c. providing funding for research.
   d. following policies to reduce interest rates and increase business investment.

2. The secular trend growth rate in the United States is approximately:
   a. 1 to 1.5 percent per year.
   b. 2.5 to 3.5 percent per year.
   c. 5 to 5.5 percent per year.
   d. 7 to 7.5 percent per year.

3. Leading indicators include:
   a. manufacturing and trade sales volume.
   b. number of employees on non-agricultural payrolls.
   c. industrial production.
   d. new orders for goods and materials.

4. Keynesians:
   a. generally favor activist government policies.
   b. generally favor laissez-faire policies.
   c. believe that frictional unemployment does not exist.
   d. believe that all unemployment is cyclical unemployment.

5. The level of output that would materialize at the target rate of unemployment and the target rate of capital utilization is called:
   a. nominal output.
   b. actual output.
   c. potential output.
   d. utilized output.

6. To move from GDP to GNP, one must:
   a. add net foreign factor income.
   b. subtract inflation.
   c. add depreciation.
   d. subtract depreciation.

7. If you, the owner, sell your old car for $600, how much does GDP increase?
   a. By $600.
   b. By the amount you bought it for, minus the $600.
   c. By zero.
   d. By the $600 you received and the $600 the person you sold it to paid, or $1,200.

8. There are two firms in an economy, Firm A and Firm B. Firm A produces 100 widgets and sells them for $2 apiece. Firm B produces 200 gadgets and sells them for $3 apiece. Firm A sells 30 of its widgets to Firm B and the remainder to consumers. Firm B sells 50 of its gadgets to Firm A and the remainder to consumers. What is GDP in this economy?
   a. $210.
   b. $590.
   c. $600.
   d. $800.

9. Gross investment differs from net investment by:
   a. net exports.
   b. net imports.
   c. depreciation.
   d. transfer payments.

10. If inflation is 10 percent and nominal GDP goes up 20 percent, real GDP goes up approximately:
    a. 1 percent.
    b. 10 percent.
    c. 20 percent.
    d. 30 percent.

11. According to Say's Law:
   a. aggregate supply will exceed aggregate demand.
   b. aggregate demand will exceed aggregate supply.
   c. there will be no relation between aggregate supply and demand.
   d. aggregate demand will equal aggregate supply.

12. Suppose output grew at 8% in China and 2% in the United States. Based on this information alone, we can know that:
   a. per capita income grew faster in China.
   b. per capita income grew faster in the U.S.
   c. per capita income could have grown faster in either country. We cannot tell in which.
   d. per capita output grew faster in China.

13. If there are increasing returns to scale, as:
   a. inputs rise, outputs fall.
   b. inputs rise, output rises by a smaller percentage.
   c. inputs rise, output rises by a larger percentage.
   d. one input rises, output rises by a larger percentage.

14. New growth theories are theories that emphasize:
   a. technology.
   b. human capital.
   c. physical capital.
   d. entrepreneurship.

15. QWERTY is a metaphor for:
   a. the invisible hand.
   b. technological lock-in.
   c. the law of diminishing marginal productivity.
   d. the pollution caused by positive spillovers.

16. In Keynesian economics equilibrium income:
   a. will be equal to potential income.
   b. will be below potential income.
   c. will be above potential income.
   d. may be different than potential income.

17. The slope of the SAS curve is determined by:
   a. opportunity cost
   b. the law of diminishing marginal returns.
   c. institutional realities.
   d. the money wealth effect, the international effect, and the interest rate effect.

18. Refer to the graph below. The graph demonstrates the expected short-run result if:

   a. productivity increases by less than wages.
   b. the government increases the money supply.
   c. the exchange rate value of a country's currency falls.
   d. there are suddenly expectations of a rising price level.

19. Assume the economy is initially at point B. The graph below correctly demonstrates an economy moving to point C if:

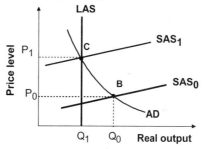

   a. productivity increases by less than the increase in wages.
   b. the government increases the money supply.
   c. a country's exchange rate appreciates (gains value).
   d. wages rise by less than the increase in productivity.

20. If the economy has an inflationary gap that it wants to eliminate, the government should use fiscal policy to shift:
   a. the *LAS* curve out.
   b. the *SAS* curve down (to the right).
   c. the *AD* curve out to the right.
   d. the *AD* curve in to the left.

21. If the mpe is .8, what is the size of the multiplier in the multiplier model?
   a. .5.
   b. 5.
   c. 1.
   d. 10.

22. If consumer confidence suddenly falls, you would expect:
   a. the aggregate production curve to shift down.
   b. the aggregate expenditures curve to rotate to the right and equilibrium income to fall.
   c. the aggregate expenditures curve to shift up and equilibrium income to rise.
   d. the aggregate expenditures curve to shift down and equilibrium income to fall.

23. In the multiplier model if autonomous expenditures increases by 10 and the *mpe* is .8, what happens to equilibrium income?
   a. It rises by 8.
   b. It falls by 8.
   c. It rises by 50.
   d. It falls by 50.

24. The economy has an *mpe* of .5, and a recessionary gap of 240. Using the Keynesian *multiplier model*, an economist would advise government to increase autonomous expenditures by:
   a. 120.
   b. 240.
   c. 480.
   d. 620.

25. If there is some price level flexibility, the:
   a. multiplier model is no longer relevant.
   b. results of the multiplier model will be reversed.
   c. results of the multiplier model will be modified but the central point will remain the same.
   d. multiplier model will turn into a Classical model.

26. Standard macro models focus on:
   a. deductive logic and traditional micro economic building blocks.
   b. quick applicability and providing a reasonable framework for discussing macro problems.
   c. historical relationships and traditional micro economic building blocks.
   d. scientific precision and internal logic.

27. Modern macro models focus on:
   a. how and why the model works as well as its internal logic.
   b. quick applicability and providing a reasonable framework for discussing macro problems.

   c. using inductive logic and traditional micro economic building blocks to provide a rough and ready model for policy analysis.
   d. historical relationships and scientific precision.

28. DSGE stands for:
   a. Direct Sequential General Equation.
   b. Deductive Simultaneous Geometric Equation.
   c. Differential Stochastic Graphical Equilibrium.
   d. Dynamic Stochastic General Equilibrium.

29. The policy implications of the DSGE model are:
   a. Sound finance, strong currency, and the central bank as the lender of last resort.
   b. Ricardian equivalence, time inconsistency/credibility, and the Lucas critique.
   c. interactive effects must be taken into account, Ricardian equivalence, and sound finance.
   d. Government stabilization policies, Lucas critique, and strong currency.

30. Which is the right model for the economy?
   a. The standard macro model.
   b. DSGE.
   c. Agent based computational models.
   d. It depends.

ANSWERS

1.	a	(24:2)	**16.**	d	(27:4)
2.	b	(24:4)	**17.**	c	(27:13)
3.	d	(24:8)	**18.**	a	(27:16)
4.	a	(24:12)	**19.**	a	(27:20)
5.	c	(24:14)	**20.**	d	(27:25)
6.	a	(25:2)	**21.**	b	(28:4)
7.	c	(25:4)	**22.**	d	(28:8)
8.	b	(25:5)	**23.**	c	(28:12)
9.	c	(25:11)	**24.**	a	(28:16)
10.	b	(25:15)	**25.**	c	(28:20)
11.	d	(26:2)	**26.**	b	(29:5)
12.	c	(26:5)	**27.**	a	(29:6)
13.	c	(26:11)	**28.**	d	(29:10)
14.	a	(26:18)	**29.**	b	(29:13)
15.	b	(26:20)	**30.**	d	(29:18)

Key: The figures in parentheses refer to multiple choice question and chapter numbers. For example (1:2) is multiple choice question 2 from chapter 1.

THE FINANCIAL SECTOR AND THE ECONOMY

30

CHAPTER AT A GLANCE

This review is based upon the learning objectives that open the chapter.

1. The financial sector is central to almost all macroeconomic debates because behind every real transaction, there is a financial transaction that mirrors it. (702-704)

    When you buy an apple for 50 cents, the financial transaction is the 50 cents; the real transaction is the transfer of the apple.

2. The long-term interest rate equilibrates the supply for loanable funds (saving) and the demand for loanable funds (investment). See the graph below. (704-705)

    Quantity of loanable funds

    If the interest rate does not perfectly translate saving (flows out of the spending stream) into investment (flows into the spending stream), then the economy will either expand or contract.

3. Money is a highly liquid, financial asset that (1) is generally accepted in exchange for goods and services, (2) is used as a reference in valuing other goods, and (3) can be stored as wealth. (705)

    Money is any financial asset that serves these three functions.

4. The three functions of money are: (706-707)

    *   Medium of exchange;
        As long as people are confident that the purchasing power of the dollar will remain relatively stable over time (by the Fed controlling the money supply) then people will continue to swap real goods, services, and resources for money and vice versa.

    *   Unit of account;
        Money acts as a measuring stick of the relative value (relative prices) of things. Therefore, the value of money itself must remain relatively stable over time.

    *   Store of wealth.
        Money's usefulness as a store of wealth also depends upon how well it maintains its value. The key is for the Fed to keep the purchasing power of money (and therefore prices) relatively stable over time. Inflation can be a problem!

5a. M1 is the component of the money supply that consists of cash in the hands of the public plus checking accounts and traveler's checks. (707-708)

    M1 is the narrowest measure of the money supply. It is also the most liquid.

5b. M2 is the component of the money supply that consists of M1 plus savings deposits, small-denomination time deposits, and money market mutual funds. (708)

    M2 is the measure of the money supply most used by the Fed to measure the money supply in circulation. This is because M2 is most closely correlated with the price level and economic activity.

    Anything that changes M2 changes the money supply!

6.   Banks "create" money because a bank's liabilities are defined as money. So when a bank incurs liabilities it creates money. (711-713)

Banks "create" money (increase the money supply) whenever they make loans. Whenever a person borrows from a bank he/she is swapping a promissory note to repay the loan (the loan is really an IOU; and an individual's IOU is not money because it doesn't meet the criteria of serving the functions of money) in exchange for cash or funds put in his/her checking account. Cash and checking account balances are money! Therefore, the money supply increases.
Also Note: When a loan is repaid, the money supply (M2) decreases.

7a. The money multiplier is the measure of the amount of money ultimately created by the banking system per dollar deposited. When people hold no cash it equals 1/r, where r is the reserve ratio. (713-716)

A single bank is limited in the amount of money it may create. The limit is equal to its excess reserves–the maximum amount of funds that it can legally loan out. However, when considering an entire banking system, where any bank's loans, when spent, may end up being deposited back into that bank or another bank, then the entire banking system ends up being able to increase the money supply by a multiple of its initial excess reserves (the initial maximum amount of funds that can legally be loaned out) because of the money multiplier.

Simple money multiplier = 1/r.

(Initial change in money supply) ×(money multiplier) = change in the money supply

7b. When people hold cash the money multiplier is (1+c)/(r+c). (716)

Money multiplier = (1+c)/(r+c) , where c is the ratio of money people hold in currency to the money held as deposits.

The money multiplier is less than the simple money multiplier because some of the funds loaned out are held as cash and therefore do not return to the banks as deposits.

8.   People demand money for three reaons: (1) transactions motive, (2) precautionary motive, and (3) speculative motive. (717-719)

The transactions motive is the need to carry money to buy things. The precautionary motive is the need to carry money in the event of an emergency. The speculative motive is the desire to hold money instead of another financial asset whose price is falling.

These motives mean people will hold money even if it means forgoing interest payments from holding bonds instead. But, as the interest rate rises, the cost of holding money in terms of lost interest rises, so you hold less money. As the interest rate rises, the quantity of money demanded falls. This explains why the demand for money curve is downward-sloping.

The demand and supply for money in the money market determine the short-term interest rate, as shown in the graph. Notice in the short-term, the supply of money is fixed; that is, the supply of money is independent of the interest rate.

See also, Appendix A: "A Closer Look at Financial Assets and Liabilities"

● SHORT-ANSWER QUESTIONS

1. At lunch you and your friends are arguing about the financial sector. One friend says that real fluctuations are measured by real economic activity in the goods market and therefore the financial sector has nothing to do with the business cycle. You know better and set him straight.

2. What are derivatives and why did financial institutions create them?

3. How does the interest rate regulate the flow of saving into the flow of expenditures during normal times?

4. You are having another stimulating lunchtime conversation, this time about money. Your friend says "I know what money is; it's cash, the dollar bills I carry around." What is your response?

5. You continue the conversation and begin to discuss why we have money. Your friend states that the function of money is to buy things like the lunch he has just bought. Another friend says that because she has money she is able to compare the cost of two types of slacks. Still another offers that she holds money to make sure she can buy lunch next week. What is the function of money that each has described? Are there any others?

6. What are two measures of money? What are the primary components of each?

7. Your friends are curious about money. At another lunchtime discussion, they ask each other two questions: Is all the money deposited in the bank in the bank's vaults? Can banks create money? Since they are stumped, you answer the questions for them.

8. Using the simple money multiplier, what will happen to the money supply if the reserve ratio is 0.2 and the Fed gives a bank $100 in reserves?

9. Using the equation for the money multiplier when people hold cash, what will happen to the money supply if the reserve ratio is 0.2, cash to deposit ratio is 0.3, and the Fed gives a bank $100 in reserves?

10. What is the problem with thinking that only changes in high powered money cause changes in the money supply?

11. Because people don't earn interest on the money they hold in their pockets, why do they hold any money at all? (There are three reasons.)

12. Your study partner listens to your reasons why people hold money, but cautions you that even though people hold money despite the opportunity cost of holding it (lost interest), the interest rate does impact how much people hold. You agree and explain the relationship between the demand for money and the interest rate more fully.

13. At lunch you and your study partner are arguing about what market determines the interest rate. One friend says in the loanable funds market; another says in the money market. You know better than both and set them straight.

MATCHING THE TERMS
Match the terms to their definitions

___	1.	asset management	a.	Cash that a bank keeps on hand that is sufficient to manage the normal cash inflows and outflows.

___ **1.** asset management

___ **2.** excess reserves

___ **3.** Federal Reserve Bank (the Fed)

___ **4.** financial assets

___ **5.** interest rate

___ **6.** liability management

___ **7.** M_1

___ **8.** M_2

___ **9.** money

___ **10.** money multiplier

___ **11.** precautionary motive

___ **12.** reserve ratio

___ **13.** reserves

___ **14.** simple money multiplier

___ **15.** speculative motive

___ **16.** transactions motive

a. Cash that a bank keeps on hand that is sufficient to manage the normal cash inflows and outflows.

b. The need to hold money for spending.

c. Component of the money supply that consists of M_1 plus savings deposits, small-denomination time deposits, and money market mutual fund shares, along with some esoteric relatively liquid assets.

d. Component of the money supply that consists of cash in the hands of the public, checking account balances, and traveler's checks.

e. Assets whose benefit to the owner depends on the issuer of the asset meeting certain obligations.

f. Holding money for unexpected expenses and impulse buying.

g. How a bank attracts deposits and what it pays for them.

h. How a bank handles its loans and other assets.

i. Measure of the amount of money ultimately created by the banking system, per dollar deposited, when cash holdings of individuals and firms are treated the same as reserves of banks. The mathematical expression is $(1+c)/(r+c)$.

j. Measure of the amount of money ultimately created by the banking system per dollar deposited, when people hold no cash. The mathematical expression is $1/r$.

k. Holding cash to avoid holding financial assests whose prices are falling.

l. Ratio of cash or deposits a bank holds at the central bank to deposits a bank keeps as a reserve against withdrawals of cash.

m. Reserves above what banks are required to hold.

n. The U.S. central bank. Its liabilities serve as cash in the United States.

o. A highly liquid financial asset that is generally accepted in exchange for other goods and is used as a reference in valuing other goods and as a store of wealth.

p. Price paid for the use of a financial asset.

● PROBLEMS AND APPLICATIONS

1. In each of the following explain the effect on interest rates. (Note: First choose which interest rate is affected – short or long term rates – and then demonstrate in the appropriate market.)

a. Investment demand rises.

b. People expect bond prices to fall in the near future.

c. People begin to save a greater percent of their income.

2. For each, state whether it is a component of M_1, M_2, both, or neither:

a. Money market mutual funds.

b. Savings deposits.

c. Traveler's checks.

d. Stocks.

e. Twenty-dollar bills.

3. Assuming individuals hold no cash, calculate the simple money multiplier for each of the following reserve requirements:

    a. 15%

    b. 30%

    c. 60%

    d. 80%

    e. 100%

4. Assuming individuals hold 10% of their deposits in the form of cash, recalculate the money multipliers from question 2.

    a. 15%

    b. 30%

    c. 60%

    d. 80%

    e. 100%

5. While Jon is walking to school one morning, a helicopter flying overhead drops $300. Not knowing how to return it, Jon keeps the money and deposits it in his bank. (No one in this economy holds cash.) If the bank keeps only

10 percent of its money in reserves and is fully loaned out, calculate the following:

a. How much money can the bank now lend out?

b. After this initial transaction, by how much has the money in the economy changed?

c. What's the money multiplier?

d. How much money will eventually be created by the banking system from Jon's $300?

6. For each of the following determine if it is an example of the precautionary, transaction, or speculative motive for holding money.

    a. You always carry a $10 bill in your pocket when you go on a date because your mother always said to be prepared for an emergency.

    b. You've lost your ATM card, so you have to carry more money in your pocket for daily purchases.

    c. An entrepreneur who has been "flipping" houses (buying houses, renovating them only to sell them within a short period of time), sees that housing prices are beginning to decline, so he sells his remaining holdings, keeping the proceeds in a money market account.

d It always seems like there is something in the grocery aisle that catches your eye. So you always keep a little extra in your pocket in case you want to buy something.

7. For each of the following, explain the effect on the interest rate in the money market. Demonstrate your answer graphically.

a. The supply of money falls.

b. A national terrorist attack interrupts the banking system. After banks recover, people decide to hold more money in the event of a recurrence and the need for emergency funds.

c. People expect bond prices to rise in the near future and move money out of their money market accounts into bond funds.

A1. Choose which of the following offerings you would prefer having. (Refer to the present value table on page 726.)

a. $1,500 today or $2,000 in 5 years. The interest rate is 4%.

b. $1,500 today or $2,000 in 5 years. The interest rate is 9%.

c. $2,000 today or $10,000 in 10 years. The interest rate is 15%

d. $3,000 today or $10,000 in 15 years. The interest rate is 9%.

A2. A bond has a face value of $5,000 and a coupon rate of 10 percent. (A 10 percent coupon rate means that it pays annual interest of 10 percent of its face value.) It is issued in 2004 and matures in 2009. Using this information, calculate the following:

a. What is the annual payment for that bond?

b. If the bond is currently selling for $6,000, is its yield greater or less than 10 percent?

c. If the bond is currently selling for $4,000, is its yield greater or less than 10 percent?

d. What do your answers to (b) and (c) tell you about what the bond must sell for, relative to its face value, if the interest rate is 10%? Rises above 10%? Falls below 10%?

A3. For each, state whether a financial asset has been created. What gives each financial asset created its value?

    a. Your friend promises to pay you $5 tomorrow and expects nothing in return.

    b. You buy an apple at the grocery store.

    c. The government sells a new bond with a face value of $5,000, a coupon rate of 8%, and a maturity date of 2016.

    d. A firm issues stock.

    e. An existing stock is sold to another person on the stock market.

A BRAIN TEASER

1. Whenever new loans are made the money supply expands. Whenever loans are repaid the money supply decreases. During any given period of time new loans are being made and old loans are being repaid. On balance, what happens to the money supply depends upon the magnitude of these conflicting forces. We also know that making loans is the principle source of profits to banks. Having said this, how can bankers' collective lending decisions (whether to give loans or not to give loans in order to maximize their profits, or to avoid losses) destabilize the business cycle, that is, cause recessions to get worse and upturns to become more pronounced?

MULTIPLE CHOICE

Circle the one best answer for each of the following questions:

1. For every financial asset there is a:
   a. corresponding financial liability.
   b. corresponding financial liability if the financial asset is financed.
   c. real liability.
   d. corresponding real asset.

2. The long-term interest rate is determined in:
   a. the market for loanable funds.
   b. the stock market.
   c. the money market.
   d. the real goods market.

3. If the government runs a deficit and increases its borrowing,
   a. the demand for loanable funds will increase and the interest rate will fall.
   b. the demand for loanable funds will increase and the interest rate will rise.
   c. the supply of loanable funds will increase and the interest rates will rise.
   d. the supply of loanable funds will decrease and the interest rates will rise.

4. Which of the following is not a function of money?
   a. Medium of exchange.
   b. Unit of account.
   c. Store of wealth.
   d. Equity instrument.

5. Which of the following is not included in the M_1 definition of money?
   a. Checking accounts.
   b. Currency.
   c. Traveler's checks.
   d. Savings accounts.

6. Which of the following components is not included in the M_2 definition of money?
   a. M_1.
   b. Savings deposits.
   c. Small-denomination time deposits.
   d. Bonds.

7. In an advertisement for credit cards, the statement is made, "Think of a credit card as smart money." An economist's reaction to this would be that a credit card is:
   a. not money.
   b. dumb money.
   c. simply money.
   d. actually better than money.

8. Using a credit card creates a financial:
   a. liability for the holder and a financial asset for the issuer.
   b. asset for the holder and a financial liability for the issuer.
   c. liability for both the holder and issuer.
   d. asset for both the holder and issuer.

9. Modern bankers:
    a. focus on asset management.
    b. focus on liability management.
    c. focus on both asset management and liability management.
    d. are unconcerned with asset and liability management and instead are concerned with how to make money.

10. Assuming individuals hold no cash, the reserve requirement is 20 percent, and banks keep no excess reserves, an increase in an initial inflow of $100 into the banking system will cause an increase in the money supply of:
    a. $20.
    b. $50.
    c. $100.
    d. $500.

11. Assuming individuals hold no cash, the reserve requirement is 10 percent, and banks keep no excess reserves, an increase in an initial $300 into the banking system will cause an increase in total money of:
    a. $30.
    b. $300.
    c. $3,000.
    d. $30,000.

12. Assuming the ratio of money people hold in cash to the money they hold in deposits is .3, the reserve requirement is 20 percent, and that banks keep no excess reserves, an increase of an initial $100 into the banking system will cause an increase in total money of approximately:
    a. $50.
    b. $100.
    c. $260.
    d. $650.

13. If banks hold excess reserves whereas before they did not, the money multiplier:
    a. will become larger.
    b. will become smaller.
    c. will be unaffected.
    d. might increase or might decrease.

14. The money supply is best described as being:
    a. determined by the size of the money multiplier.
    b. determined by the amount of reserves.
    c. endogenously determined by the monetary system.
    d. fixed, to avoid inflation.

15. If you expect interest rates to rise, you will want to be holding:
    a. more money because bond prices will likely fall.
    b. less money because bond prices will likely rise.
    c. more money because bond prices will likely rise.
    d. less money because bond prices will likely fall.

16. If interest rates fall,
    a. bond prices rise.
    b. bond prices fall.
    c. bond prices do not change.
    d. bond prices could either rise or fall.

17. If housing prices are expected to fall by 10 percent, one could say that the interest rate on housing assets is:
    a. 10 percent.
    b. −10 percent.
    c. nothing –interest rates are on bonds, not on other assets.
    d. the answer depends on what the inflation rate in the economy is.

A1. If the interest rate falls, the value of a fixed rate bond:
    a. rises.
    b. falls.
    c. remains the same.
    d. cannot be determined as to whether it rises or falls.

A2. Two bonds, one a 30-year bond and the other a 1-year bond, have the same interest rate. If the interest rate in the economy falls, the value of the:
    a. long-term bond rises by more than the value of the short-term bond rises.
    b. short-term bond rises by more than the value of the long-term bond rises.
    c. long-term bond falls by more than the value of the short-term bond falls.
    d. short-term bond falls by more than the value of the long-term bond falls.

● POTENTIAL ESSAY QUESTIONS

You may also see essay questions similar to the "Problems & Applications" and "A Brain Teaser" exercises.

1. Why is it important for the macroeconomy that the financial sector operates efficiently?

2. Why aren't credit cards money? What is the difference between money and credit?

ANSWERS

SHORT-ANSWER QUESTIONS

1. The financial sector is important to the business cycle because it facilitates trade and channels the leakage of savings out of the circular flow back into the circular flow either as consumer loans, business loans, or government loans. If the financial sector did not translate enough of the saving out of the spending stream back into the spending stream, output would decline and a recession might result. Likewise, if the financial sector increased flows into the spending stream (loans) that exceeded flows out of the spending stream (saving), an upturn or boom might result and inflation might rise. (702-704)

2. Derivatives are packages of groups of loans. Derivatives spread the risk of default over a larger set of homeowners, geographic areas, and economic conditions. (702-703)

3. Just as price equilibrates quantity supplied and demanded in the real sector, interest rates equilibrate quantity supplied and demanded for saving. The supply of saving comes out of the spending stream. The financial sector transforms those savings back into the spending stream in the form of loans that are then used to purchase consumer or capital goods. (704-705)

4. In one sense your friend is right; cash is money. But money is more than just cash. Money is a highly liquid financial asset that is accepted in exchange for other goods and is used as a reference in valuing other goods. It includes such things as checking account balances and traveler's checks. (705)

5. The first friend has described money as a medium of exchange. The second has described money as a unit of account. And the third has described money as a store of wealth. These are the three functions of money. There are no others. (706-707)

6. Two measures of money are M_1 and M_2. M_1 consists of currency, checking accounts, and traveler's checks. M_2 consists of M_1 plus savings deposits, small-denomination time deposits, and money market mutual funds. (707-708)

7. No, banks do not hold all their deposits in their vaults. They keep a small percentage of it for normal withdrawal needs and lend the remainder out. Banks' maintenance of checking accounts is the essence of how banks create money. You count your deposits as money since you can write checks against them and the money that is lent out from bank deposits is counted as money. Aha! The bank has created money. (711-713)

8. The equation for the simple money multiplier is $(1/r)$ where r is the reserve ratio. Plugging the values into the equation, we see that the money multiplier is 5, so the money supply increases by $500. (713-716)

9. The equation for the money multiplier when people hold cash is $(1+c)/(r+c)$ where r is the reserve ratio and c is the ratio of cash to deposits. Plugging the values into the equation, we see that the money multiplier is 2.6, so the money supply increases by $260. (716)

10. The problem with thinking that only changes in high powered money cause changes in the money supply is that causation is mutual. Changes in money cause changes in reserves and the other way around too. The second reason is that the cash-to-deposit ratio fluctuates which changes the money multiplier. (716)

11. People hold money to buy goods (transactions motive); in the event of an emergency (precautionary motive); and to avoid holding other financial assets whose asset prices are falling (speculative motive). (717-718)

12. Since people lose interest when they hold money, holding money has a cost—lost interest. Just like other goods, when the price of holding money (lost interest) rises, people will hold less of it. In other words, the demand for money and the interest rate are inversely related. (719)

13. Both are right. Even though there are many interest rates in the economy, economists divide them into two types: long-term interest rates and short-term interest rates. Long-term interest rates are determined in markets for long-term financial assets such as mortgages. This is the loanable funds market. Short-term

interest rates are determined in markets for short-term financial assets such as currency and savings deposits. This is the money market. (704-705, 717-719)

![ANSWERS]

MATCHING

1-h; 2-m; 3-n; 4-e; 5-p; 6-g; 7-d; 8-c; 9-o; 10-i; 11-f; 12-l; 13-a; 14-j; 15-k; 16-b.

![ANSWERS]

PROBLEMS AND APPLICATIONS

1. **a.** This would increase the demand for loanable funds and therefore, the long-term interest rate rises. (704-705)
    b. This would increase the demand for money (speculative motive) in the money market and therefore, the short-term interest rate rises. (717-719)
    c. This would increase the supply of loanable funds and therefore, the long-term interest rate falls. (704-705)

2. **a.** M_2. (707-708)
    b. M_2. (707-708)
    c. Both. (707-708)
    d. Neither. (707-708)
    e. Both. (707-708)

3. **a.** 6.67. multiplier = (1/.15). (714)
    b. 3.33. multiplier = (1/.30). (714)
    c. 1.67. multiplier = (1/.6). (714)
    d. 1.25. multiplier = (1/.8). (714)
    e. 1. multiplier = (1/1). (714)

4. **a.** 4.4 = 1.10/(.15+.1). (716)
    b. 2.75 = 1.10/(.3+.1). (716)
    c. 1.57 = 1.10/(.6+.1). (716)
    d. 1.22 = 1.10/(.8+.1). (716)
    e. 1 = 1.1/(1+.1). (716)

5. **a.** $270. (714)
    b. $270: the increase in loans that are then deposited (.9 × 300) represents the change in money. (714)

c. 10: $1/r = 1/.1$. (714)
d. $3,000: money multiplier × initial deposit = 10×300. (713-716)

6. **a.** Precautionary motive. (717)
    b. Transactions motive. (717)
    c. Speculative motive. (717)
    d. Precautionary motive. (717)

7. **a.** A decline in the money supply shifts the supply of money to the left as shown in the graph. Short-term interest rates rise. (717-719)

b. The demand for money shifts to the right as shown in the graph as people hold more cash in the event of an emergency. Short-term rates rise. (717-719)

c. The demand for money shifts to the left as people buy bonds in expectation of their prices rising. Short-term interest rates fall. (717-719)

A1. Using the table to calculate the present value of $1 to be received in the future, we find that the better value is

a. $2,000 in 5 years when the interest rate is 4% is valued today at $1,640. (725-727)

b. $1,500 today. $2,000 in 5 years when the interest rate is 9% is worth only $1,300 today. (725-727)

c. $10,000 in 10 years. $10,000 in 10 years is valued at $2,500 when the interest rate is 15%. (725-727)

d. $3,000 today. $10,000 in 15 years when interest rate is 9% is worth only $2,700 today. (725-727)

A2. a. The annual payment for that bond is $500. (725-727)

b. If the bond is currently selling for $6000, its yield is less than 10 percent. (725-727)

c. If the bond is currently selling for $4,000, its yield is greater than 10 percent. (725-727)

d. My answer to (b) and (c) tell me that the bond must sell for its face value if the interest rate is 10%, less than face value if it rises above 10%, and more than face value if it falls below 10%. (725-727)

A3. a. A financial asset has been created. Your friend's promise to pay you $5 is what gives that asset its value. (725-727)

b. No, a financial asset has not been created, although a financial transaction did occur. (725-727)

c. Yes, a financial asset has been created. The government's promise to pay you $5,000 at maturity and $400 each year until then are what give that asset its value. (725-727)

d. Yes, a financial asset has been created. A claim to future profits is what gives that asset its value. (725-727)

e. No, a financial asset has not been created. The financial asset sold already existed. (725-727)

ANSWERS

A BRAIN TEASER

1. An uncontrolled private banking system (where government is not involved in trying to

control the money supply) is destabilizing to the business cycle. Why? Because during recessions, bankers are reluctant to grant loans due to the greater probability of default on loans (bankers are simply wishing to avoid losses). Fewer loans made during a recession coupled with the concurrent repayment of old loans (most likely given during the previous upturn in the economy) mean that, on balance, the money supply decreases. Less money means less spending. Less spending means the recession gets worse–unemployment rises further and the economy grows even more slowly. Conversely, during an economic expansion, banks make more loans than old loans are being repaid (bankers are happy to make loans when there is a low probability of default–after all, workers are not likely to lose their jobs and businesses' markets and profits are expanding). Therefore, the money supply expands and total spending increases–people spend their loans. The economy expands even more. (711-713)

ANSWERS

MULTIPLE CHOICE

1. a   The very fact that it is a financial asset means that it has a financial liability, so the qualifier in b is unnecessary. See pages 702-704.

2. a   The short-term rate is determined in the money market and the long-term rate is determined in the loanable funds market. See pages 704-705 and 717-719.

3. b   When the government runs a deficit, it must borrow, which means that the demand for loanable funds will increase, which will cause the interest rate to rise. See pages 704-705.

4. d   Money is not a type of stock so it is not an equity instrument. See pages 706-707.

5. d M_2 includes savings accounts. M_1 does not. See pages 707-708 and Figure 30-3 on page 708.

6. d   Bonds are not part of M_2. See pages 707-708 and Figure 30-3.

7. a   A credit card is not money and thus *a* would be the best answer. A credit card replaces money, making the same amount of money able to handle many more transactions. See pages 708-711.

8. a   One is borrowing money when one uses a credit card, thereby incurring a financial liability. See pages 708-711.

9. c   As discussed on page 711, banks are concerned with both asset management and liability management. The second part of answer d is obviously true, but it's through management of assets and liabilities that they make money, so the first part is wrong.

10. d   The simple money multiplier is $1/r=1/.2=5$, which gives an increase in total money of $500. See pages 713-716.

11. c   The simple money multiplier is $1/r=1/.1=10$ which gives an increase of total money of $3,000. See pages 713-716.

12. c   The money multiplier is $(1+c)/(r+c)=1.3/.5=2.6$, which gives an increase in total money of $260. See page 716.

13. b   Holding excess reserves would be the equivalent of increasing the reserve requirement, which would decrease the money multiplier. See pages 713-716.

14. c   The money supply is endogenously determined. Because of this, instead of targeting a specific supply of money, policy makers target an interest rate. From this interest rate, they can calculate the needed money supply, from which they can determine the needed level of reserves. See page 716.

15. a   If interest rates rise, bond prices fall, which means that you prefer to be holding money rather than bonds. See pages 717-719.

16. a   Bond prices move inversely with interest rates. See pages 717-719.

17. b   The expected percentage change in price of an asset is its implicit interest rate. See pages 717-719.

A1. a   The present value formula tells us that the value on any fixed interest rate bond varies inversely with the interest rate in the economy. See pages 725-727.

A2. a   Since bond values vary inversely with interest rate changes, the answer must be a or b. Judging between a and b will be hard for you at this point unless you have studied present value in another course. However, based on the discussion in the text on pages 725-727, you can deduce that since a long-term bond is not paid back for a long time, it will be much more strongly affected by interest rate changes.

ANSWERS

POTENTIAL ESSAY QUESTIONS

The following are annotated answers. They indicate the general idea behind the answer.

1.   Recall that for every real transaction there is a financial transaction that mirrors it. The financial sector's role is to ensure the smooth flow of savings out of the spending stream back into the economy. Whenever the financial sector is not operating efficiently then it is quite possible that the flow of savings out of the spending stream could be greater than the amount of money going through the financial sector and back into the economy. If this happens, we will experience a recession. The opposite would create inflationary (demand-pull inflation) problems.

2.   Money is a financial asset of individuals and a financial liability of banks. Credit card balances cannot be money since they are assets of a bank and a liability of the nonbanking public. In a sense, credit card balances are the opposite of money. Credit is savings made available to be borrowed. Credit is not an asset for the holder of the card. However, ready availability of credit through the use of credit cards does reduce the amount of money people need or wish to hold.

MONETARY POLICY

31

CHAPTER AT A GLANCE

This review is based upon the learning objectives that open the chapter.

1. Monetary policy is a policy that influences the economy through changes in the money supply and available credit. In the AS/AD model, monetary policy works as follows: (731-733)

   Contractionary monetary policy shifts the AD curve to the left:
   $M\downarrow \rightarrow i\uparrow \rightarrow I\downarrow \rightarrow Y\downarrow$

   Used during an upturn in the economy to close an inflationary gap.

   Expansionary monetary policy shifts the AD curve to the right:
   $M\uparrow \rightarrow i\downarrow \rightarrow I\uparrow \rightarrow Y\uparrow$

   Used during a downturn in the economy to close a recessionary gap.

   To increase the money supply (M2), the Fed must first increase banks' excess reserves and therefore bank loans.

2a. The Fed is a semiautonomous organization composed of 12 regional banks. It is run by the Board of Governors. (733-736)

   The Fed (Federal Reserve Bank) is in charge of monetary policy (changing the money supply, credit availability, and interest rates).

   The Federal Open Market Committee (FOMC) decides monetary policy.

2b. Congress gave the Fed six explicit duties. In normal times, the most important is conducting monetary policy. (737)

Six functions of the Fed:
1. *Conducting monetary policy (influencing the supply of money and credit in the economy).*
2. *Supervising and regulating financial institutions.*
3. *Serving as a lender of last resort to financial institutions.*
4. *Providing banking services to the U.S. government.*
5. *Issuing coin and currency.*
6. *Providing financial services (such as check clearing) to commercial banks, savings and loan associations, savings banks, and credit unions.*

In a financial crisis, the most important role is as lender of last resort.

3. The Fed conducts monetary policy by changing the amount of reserves in the banking system. (737-742)

   1. The primary way the Fed changes reserves is through open market operations.
   Open market operations are the Fed's buying and selling of U.S. government securities. This is the most frequently used and most important tool to change the money supply.

   2. Changing the reserve requirement and the discount rate also affect reserves.
   The Fed doesn't use these tools often. The reserve requirement affects (1) banks' excess reserves and (2) the money multiplier.
   The discount rate is the interest rate the Fed charges banks for loans.

   If the economy is in a recession, the Fed could increase the money supply (pursue an expansionary monetary policy) by doing any one or more of the following:

- *Decrease the reserve requirement.*
- *Decrease the discount rate.*
- *Buy government securities.*
- *Use quantative easing tools.*

4. The Federal funds rate is the interest rate banks charge one another for overnight bank reserve loans. The Fed determines whether monetary policy is loose or tight depending upon what's happening to the Fed funds rate. The Fed funds rate is an important intermediate target. (742-743)

    The Fed targets a range for the Fed funds rate. If the Fed funds rate goes above (below) that target range, the Fed buys (sells) bonds. These are "defensive" actions by the Fed.

5. The Taylor rule states: (743-745)
    Set the Fed funds rate at 2 percent plus current inflation if the economy is at desired output and desired inflation and

    - if inflation is higher (lower) than desired, increase (reduce) the Fed funds rate by .5 times the difference between desired and actual inflation.

    - if output is higher (lower) than desired, increase (decrease) the Fed funds rate by .5 times the percentage deviation from potential.

    Formally, the Taylor rule is:

    Fed funds rate = 2 percent + current inflation
    + 0.5 × (actual inflation - desired inflation)
    + 0.5 × (percent deviation of aggregate output
        from potential)

    This rule has described Fed policy since the late 1990s. The Fed deviated from this rule from 2001 to 2006 and again beginning in 2008.

    Because the Fed targets interest rates, it creates a flat effective supply curve for money at the targeted interest rate.

6. The yield curve is a graph of the interest rate of bonds of various maturities, ordered from the shortest to longest term to maturity. (745-746)

    Normally, the yield curve is upward sloping. That is, bonds that mature in a shorter time (for example, 1 year) have lower interest rates than bonds that mature in a longer time (for example 30 years).

    The Fed most directly affects short-term interest rates, but monetary policy affects the economy through its effect on the long-term interest rate. Sometimes when the Fed raises the short-term rate and the long-term rate doesn't change, or even fall, the yield curve becomes inverted (downward sloping). When this happens, the Fed is less effective in impacting the economy than it would like.

● SHORT-ANSWER QUESTIONS

1. You have been asked to speak to the first-year Congresspeople. Your talk is about the Fed. They want to know what monetary policy is. You tell them.

2. Another Congressperson asks how monetary policy can keep the economy from overheating. You reply from the perspective of the AS/AD model.

3. Suppose the economy is below potential output. Now how can monetary policy boost output? You reply again from the perspective of the AS/AD model.

4. To clarify your answer to question 1 you tell them when the Fed was created and what its specific duties are.

5. Another Congressperson asks what monetary policy actions the Fed can take. You answer, mentioning three specific actions.

6. You are asked to elaborate on your answer to question 3. Now that you have told them how the Fed can change the money supply, how does each of the ways to affect reserves work?

7. One Congressperson realizes that the Fed does not have complete control over the money supply. She states that people could demand more cash, which will reduce the money supply. How does the Fed know whether its buying and selling of bonds is having the desired effect? You answer by explaining the Fed's intermediate target.

8. Another Congressperson asks whether there are any rules that they could use to predict what the Fed will do to the Fed's intermediate target. You explain the rule that has described Fed policy since the late 1990s.

9. You take one final question at the conference and it is a difficult one: "It doesn't seem that the Fed is doing a good job. I read in the paper that the Fed has wanted to raise long-term interest rates, but is having difficulty doing so." How do you respond to this concern?

10. If the Fed has exhausted all traditional forms of expanding the money supply, what else can it do?

MATCHING THE TERMS
Match the terms to their definitions

____ 1. central bank

____ 2. contractionary monetary policy

____ 3. discount rate

____ 4. expansionary monetary policy

____ 5. Federal Open Market Committee (FOMC)

____ 6. Federal funds rate

____ 7. inverted yield curve

____ 8. monetary base

____ 9. monetary regime

____ 10. nominal interest rate

____ 11. open market operations

____ 12. quantitative easing tools

____ 13. real interest rate

____ 14. reserve requirement

____ 15. Taylor rule

____ 16. yield curve

a. Interest rate you actually see and pay.

b. Interest rate adjusted for expected inflation.

c. Rate of interest the Fed charges on loans it makes to banks.

d. The Fed's day-to-day buying and selling of government securities.

e. The percentage the Federal Reserve System sets as the minimum amount of reserves a bank must have.

f. A banker's bank; it conducts monetary policy and supervises the financial system.

g. Currency in circulation, vault cash plus reserves that banks have at the Fed.

h. Monetary policy aimed at raising the money supply and raising the level of aggregate demand.

i. Monetary policy aimed at reducing the money supply and reducing the level of aggregate demand.

j. The Fed's chief policy making body.

k. The interest rate banks charge one another for Fed funds.

l. Set the Fed funds rate at 2 plus current inflation plus ½ the difference between actual and target inflation and ½ the deviation of actual output from potential.

m. A predetermined statement of the monetary policy that will be followed in various situations.

n. A curve that shows the relationship between interest rates and bonds' time to maturity.

o. A yield curve in which the short-term rate is higher than the long-term rate.

p. Tools the Fed can use to increase the money supply when the Fed funds rate is already zero.

PROBLEMS AND APPLICATIONS

1. The Fed wants to change the reserve requirement in order to change the money supply (which is currently $3,000). For each situation below, calculate the current reserve requirement and the amount by which the Fed must change the reserve requirement to achieve the desired change in the money supply. Assume no cash holdings.

    a. Money multiplier is 3 and the Fed wants to increase the money supply by $300.

    b. Money multiplier is 2.5 and the Fed wants to increase the money supply by $300.

    c. Money multiplier is 4 and the Fed wants to decrease the money supply by $500.

    d. Money multiplier is 4 and the Fed wants to increase the money supply by $1,000.

2. How do your answers change for 1 (a) - (d) if instead of changing the reserve requirement, the Fed wants to use an open market operation to change the money supply? Assume the reserve requirement remains unchanged. What should the Fed do to achieve the desired change? (The multiplier and desired change in money supply for each are listed.)

    a. Money multiplier is 3 and the Fed wants to increase the money supply by $300.

    b. Money multiplier is 2.5 and the Fed wants to increase the money supply by $300.

    c. Money multiplier is 4 and the Fed wants to decrease the money supply by $500.

    d. Money multiplier is 4 and the Fed wants to increase the money supply by $1000.

3. Instead of changing the reserve requirement or using open market operations, the Fed wants to change the discount rate to achieve the desired change in the money supply. Assume that for each 1 percentage-point fall in the discount rate, banks borrow an additional $20. How do your answers to questions 1 (a) - (d) change? (The multiplier and desired change in money supply for each are listed below.)

    a. Money multiplier is 3 and the Fed wants to increase money supply by $300.

    b. Money multiplier is 2.5 and the Fed wants to increase the money supply by $300.

c. Money multiplier is 4 and the Fed wants to decrease the money supply by $500.

d. Money multiplier is 4 and the Fed wants to increase the money supply by $1,000.

4. Using the Taylor rule, what do you predict will be the Fed's target for the Fed funds rate in the following situations?

    a. Inflation is at the Fed's target of 2 percent, but output is 1 percent below potential.

    b. Output is at potential, but inflation is 5 percent, 2 percentage points above the Fed's target.

    c. Inflation is 4 percent, 1 percentage point above the Fed's target and output is 1 percent above potential.

    d. Inflation is 4 percent, 2 percentage points above the Fed's target and output is 2 percent below potential.

5. Fill in the blanks in the following table:

	Inflation rate	Nominal Interest rate	Real Interest rate
a.	5%	10%	___
b.	___	15%	7%
c.	−3%	___	9%
d.	4%	___	10%

6. Suppose the Fed decides to pursue an expansionary monetary policy. The money supply is currently $1 billion. Assume people hold no cash, the reserve requirement is 10 percent, and there are no excess reserves.

    a. By how much must the Fed change the reserve requirement to increase the money supply by $100 million?

    b. What would the Fed do to increase the money supply by $100,000 through open market operations?

7. The money supply is currently $1 billion. Assume people hold 25 percent of their money in the form of cash balances, the reserve requirement is 25 percent, and there are no excess reserves.

    a. By how much must the Fed change the reserve requirement to increase the money supply by $200 million?

    b. What would the Fed do to increase the money supply by $200 million through open market operations?

8. Given the following yields on Treasury bills and bonds, draw a yield curve.

    a. 3-month 1 year   5 years 10 years 30 years
          2%   3%   5%   5.75%   6.25%

b. 3-month 1 year   5 years 10 years 30 years
        5%   4.5%   3%   2%   1%

    c. Which is a standard and which is an inverted yield curve?

A BRAIN TEASER

1. Assume the economy is currently experiencing a recessionary gap of $1,000. Also assume that the expenditures multiplier is 4, the reserve ratio is 0.1, and the ratio of people's cash-to-deposits is 0.4. Investment changes by $100 for every 1% change in the interest rate. The interest rate changes by 1% for every $50 change in the money supply. Generally, what should the Fed do with its three monetary policy tools? By how much would the Fed have to change banks' excess reserves if it wished to close the recessionary gap? (Assume all excess reserves are loaned out.)

MULTIPLE CHOICE

Circle the one best answer for each of the following questions:

1. In the short run if the Fed undertakes expansionary monetary policy, the effect will be to shift the:
    a. AD curve out to the right.
    b. AD curve in to the left.
    c. SAS curve up.
    d. SAS curve down.

2. In the short run if the Fed undertakes contractionary monetary policy, the effect will be to shift the:
   a. AD curve out to the right.
   b. AD curve in to the left.
   c. SAS curve up.
   d. SAS curve down.

3. Which of the following is the path through which contractionary monetary policy works?
   a. Money down implies interest rate up implies investment down implies income down.
   b. Money down implies interest rate down implies investment down implies income down.
   c. Money down implies interest rate up implies investment up implies income down.
   d. Money down implies interest rate down implies investment up implies income down.

4. The central bank of the United States is:
   a. the Treasury.
   b. the Fed.
   c. the Bank of the United States.
   d. Old Lady of Threadneedle Street.

5. Monetary policy is:
   a. a variation of fiscal policy.
   b. undertaken by the Treasury.
   c. undertaken by the Fed.
   d. the regulation of monetary institutions.

6. There are seven Governors of the Federal Reserve, who are appointed for terms of:
   a. 5 years.
   b. 10 years.
   c. 14 years.
   d. 17 years.

7. Explicit functions of the Fed include all the following *except:*
   a. conducting monetary policy.
   b. conducting fiscal policy.
   c. providing banking services to the U.S. government.
   d. serving as a lender of last resort to financial institutions.

8. FOMC stands for:
   a. Federal Open Money Committee.
   b. Federal Open Market Committee.
   c. Fixed Open Market Commitments.
   d. Federation of Open Monies Committee.

9. The Fed can conduct monetary policy in all the following ways *except:*
   a. changing the reserve requirement.
   b. changing the discount rate.
   c. executing open market operations.
   d. running deficits.

10. If expansionary monetary policy increases real income by 4 percent and nominal income by 6 percent, the price level will rise by:
    a. 2 percent.
    b. 4 percent.
    c. 6 percent.
    d. 10 percent.

11. Assuming $c = .2$ and $r = .1$, the money multiplier would be:
    a. 1.
    b. 2.
    c. 3.
    d. 4.

12. The discount rate refers to the:
    a. lower price large institutions pay for government bonds.
    b. rate of interest the Fed charges for loans to banks.
    c. rate of interest the Fed charges for loans to individuals.
    d. rate of interest the Fed charges for loans to government.

13. The primary way the Fed conducts monetary policy is:
    a. open market operations.
    b. changing the discount rate.
    c. changing the reserve requirement.
    d. imposing credit controls.

14. If the Fed wants to increase the money supply, it should:
    a. buy bonds.
    b. sell bonds.
    c. pass a law that interest rates rise.
    d. pass a law that interest rates fall.

15. When the Fed sells bonds, the money supply:
    a. expands.
    b. contracts.
    c. Selling bonds does not have any effect on the money supply.
    d. sometimes rises and sometimes falls.

16. An open market purchase:
    a. raises bond prices and reduces interest rates.
    b. raises both bond prices and interest rates.
    c. reduces bond prices and raises interest rates.
    d. reduces both bond prices and interest rates.

17. The Federal funds rate is the interest rate:
    a. the government charges banks for Fed funds.
    b. the Fed charges banks for Fed funds.
    c. the banks charge individual investors for Fed funds.
    d. the banks charge each other for Fed funds.

18. Assuming the Fed is following the Taylor Rule, if inflation is 3 percent, target inflation is 2 percent, and output is 1 percent above potential, what would you predict would be the Fed funds rate target?
    a. 4 percent.
    b. 5 percent.
    c. 5.5 percent.
    d. 6 percent.

19. By choosing a monetary rule that targets the short-term interest rate the Fed creates:
    a. an upward sloping yield curve.
    b. a downward sloping yield curve.
    c. an effective supply curve of money that is flat.
    d. an effective supply curve of money that is vertical.

20. Many economists argue that the Fed contributed to the housing bubble by:
    a. passing laws that allowed financial institutions to create credit default swaps.
    b. paying interest on bank reserves.
    c. keeping the Fed funds rate lower than what the Taylor rule predicts.
    d. buying mortgage-backed securities for foreclosed homes.

21. In general, the yield curve:
    a. is flat.
    b. is upward sloping.
    c. is downward sloping.
    d. is shaped like a mountain.

22. If short-term and long-term interest rates are currently equal and the Fed contracts the money supply, the yield curve will most likely:
    a. become downward sloping.
    b. become upward sloping.
    c. become vertical.
    d. be unaffected.

23. If inflation becomes expected, and all other things remain as they were, the yield curve would most likely:
    a. become steeper.
    b. become flatter.
    c. become flat.
    d. become vertical.

● POTENTIAL ESSAY QUESTIONS

You may also see essay questions similar to the "Problems & Applications" and "A Brain Teaser" exercises.

1. According to the AS/AD model, what is considered to be appropriate monetary policy during different phases of the business cycle? What is the cause-effect chain relationship through which a change in the money supply will effect the level of economic activity? How would this cause-effect relationship be reflected graphically?

2. Why do economists keep an eye on the Fed funds rate in determining the state of monetary policy?

3. Explain why the yield curve is important for the implementation of monetary policy.

━━━━ ANSWERS ━━━━

SHORT-ANSWER QUESTIONS

1. Monetary policy is a policy that influences the economy through changes in the money supply and available credit. The Fed conducts U.S. monetary policy. (731, 733-736)

2. The Fed should decrease the money supply by increasing the reserve requirement, increasing the discount rate, and/or selling U.S. government bonds. This contractionary monetary policy in the AS/AD model increases interest rates, and lowers investment. This shifts the AD curve to the left and reduces income. (731-733)

3. The Fed should increase the money supply by decreasing the reserve requirement, decreasing the discount rate, and/or buying U.S. government bonds. This expansionary monetary policy in the AS/AD model decreases interest rates, and raises investment. This shifts the AD curve to the right and increases income. (731-733)

4. The Fed was created in 1913. Its six explicit duties are (1) conducting monetary policy, (2) regulating financial institutions, (3) serving as a lender of last resort, (4) providing banking services to the U.S. government, (5) issuing coin and currency, and (6) providing financial services to financial institutions. (737)

5. The three tools of monetary policy at the disposal of the Fed are (1) changing the reserve requirement, (2) changing the discount rate, and (3) executing open market operations (buying and selling bonds). (737-742)

6. Changing the reserve requirement changes the amount of reserves the banks must hold and thus changes the amount of loans they can make. This changes the money supply. Changing the discount rate changes the willingness of banks to borrow from the Fed to meet reserve requirements, thus changing the amount of loans they are willing to make. This changes the money supply. Open market operations change the reserves banks hold by directly increasing or decreasing cash held by banks and simultaneously decreasing or increasing their holdings of government bonds. This changes the amount of loans banks can make and changes the money supply. (737-742)

7. Economists and policymakers keep a close eye on the Fed funds rate, the rate banks charge one another for loans of reserves, as an intermediate target to determine the effect of an open market operation—whether it indeed was expansionary or contractionary. An expansionary action will lower the Fed funds rate and contractionary action will raise the Fed funds rate. In effect, the Fed chooses a range for the Fed funds rate and buys and sells bonds to keep the Fed funds rate within that range. If the Fed funds rate is below (above) the target, the Fed sells (buys) bonds. (742-743)

8. The Taylor rule has described recent Fed policy relatively well. It states: Set the Fed funds rate at 2% plus the rate of inflation plus one-half the difference between actual and desired inflation and one-half the deviation of actual output from desired output. (743)

9. You tell the Congressperson that conducting monetary policy is difficult. The standard discussion of monetary policy is based on the assumption that when the Fed pushes up (down) the short-term interest rate, the long-term interest rate moves up (down) as well. This is based on the relationship between short and long-term interest rates shown in the yield curve. The yield curve is generally upward sloping. But sometimes the shape of the yield curve changes. That is, when the Fed attempts to contract the money supply, the yield curve can become inverted, or downward sloping. Similarly, if the Fed tries to expand the money supply, the yield curve will generally become steeper. (745-746)

10. It can use quantitative easing tools such as buying short- and long-term bonds. It can also buy corporate bonds and mortgage-backed securities. (746-747)

━━━━━ **ANSWERS** ━━━━━

MATCHING

1-f; 2-i; 3-c; 4-h; 5-j; 6-k; 7-o; 8-g; 9-m; 10-a; 11-d; 12-p; 13-b; 14-e; 15-l; 16-n.

━━━━━ **ANSWERS** ━━━━━

PROBLEMS AND APPLICATIONS

1. **a.** To find the reserve requirement solve $1/r = 3$ for r. $r = 1/3$. These calculations are based on the formula $M = (1/r) \times MB$, where M is the money supply, r is the reserve ratio, and MB is the monetary base (here it equals reserves). We first find out the cash (monetary base) that supports $3,000 money supply with a money multiplier of 3. It is $1,000. We want the money supply to be $3,300. So the multiplier we want is $3,300/1,000 = 3.3. Again solving $1/r = 3.3$ we find r must be 0.3. (740-741)

    b. To find the reserve requirement solve $1/r = 2.5$ for r. $r = .4$. Cash must be $1,200 to support money supply of $3,000. The Fed must reduce the reserve requirement to .3636 to increase the money supply by $300. Use the method described in (a) to find the answer. (740-741)

    c. To find the reserve requirement solve $1/r = 4$ for r. $r = .25$. Cash must be $750 to support money supply of $3,000. The Fed must increase the reserve requirement to .3 to decrease the money supply by $500. Use the method described in (a) to find the answer. (740-741)

    d. To find the reserve requirement solve $1/r = 4$ for r. $r = .25$. Cash must be $750 to support money supply of $3,000. The Fed must reduce the reserve requirement to .1875 to increase the money supply by $1,000. Use the method described in (a) to find the answer. (740-741)

2. These calculations are based on the formula $M = (1/r) \times MB$, where M is the reserve ratio, and MB is the monetary base (here it equals reserves).

    a. The Fed should buy bonds to increase reserves in the system by $100. We find this by dividing the desired increase in the money supply by the money multiplier. (737-740)

    b. The Fed should buy bonds to increase reserves in the system by $120. We find this by dividing the desired increase in the money supply by the money multiplier. (737-740)

    c. The Fed should sell bonds to decrease reserves in the system by $125. We find this by dividing the desired decrease in the money supply by the money multiplier. (737-740)

    d. The Fed should buy bonds to increase reserves in the system by $250. We find this by dividing the desired increase in the money supply by the money multiplier. (737-740)

3. These calculations are based on the formula $M = (1/r) \times MB$, where M is the money supply, r is the reserve ratio, and MB is the monetary base (here it equals reserves). Find out how much reserves must be changed and divide by 20 to find how much the discount rate must be lowered (if reserves are to be raised) or increased (if reserves are to lowered).

    a. To increase reserves in the system by $100, the discount rate should be reduced by 5 percentage points. We find how much reserves must be increased by dividing the desired increase in the money supply by the money multiplier. We find how much the discount rate must be lowered by dividing the desired increase in reserves by 20 (the amount reserves will increase with each percentage point decline in the discount rate). (741-742)

    b. To increase reserves in the system by $120, the discount rate should be reduced by 6 percentage points. See introduction to answer number 3 for how to calculate this. (741-742)

    c. To decrease reserves in the system by $125, the discount rate should be increased by 6.25 percentage points. See introduction to answer number 3 for how to calculate this. (741-742)

    d. To increase reserves in the system by $250, the discount rate should be reduced by 12.5 percentage points. See introduction to answer number 3 for how to calculate this. (741-742)

4. **a.** Begin with 2 + rate of inflation, or 4. Since output is 1 percent below potential, subtract 0.5 to get to 3.5%. (743-745)

    b. Begin with 2 + inflation, or 7. Because inflation is 2 percentage points above target, add 1 percent to get to 8%. (743-745)

    c. Begin with 2 + inflation, or 6. Since inflation is 1 percentage point above its target add 0.5 and since output is 1 percent above potential, add another 0.5 to get 7%. (743-745)

    d. Begin with 2 + inflation, or 6. Since inflation is 2 percentage points above its target, add 1 but since output is 2 percent below potential subtract 1 to get 6%. (743-745)

5.

Inflation rate	**Nominal Interest rate**	**Real Interest rate**
a. 5%	10%	5%

Real rate = nominal - inflation. (746-747)

b. 8%	15%	7%

Inflation = nominal - real rate. (746-747)

c. −3%	6%	9%

Nominal = inflation + real rate. (746-747)

d. 4%	14%	10%

Nominal = inflation + real rate. (746-747)

6. These calculations are based on the formula $M = (1/r) \times MB$, where M is the money supply, r is the reserve ratio, and MB is the monetary base (here it equals reserves).

    a. The money multiplier is $1/r = 10$. Reserves must be $100 million to support a money supply of $1 billion. The reserve ratio to support $1.1 billion money supply with $100 million reserves is about 9.1%. We find this by dividing reserves by the desired money supply. (740-741)

    b. The Fed would buy $10,000 worth of bonds to increase the money supply by $100,000. Calculate this by dividing the desired increase in the money supply by the money multiplier. (737-740)

7. In this case, the money multiplier is $(1+c)/(r+c) = 1.33/(.25+.33) = 2.3$. The cash-to-deposit ratio is .33 since people hold 25% of their money in cash and the remainder, 75%, in deposits.

    a. The reserve requirement must be lowered to about 15%. We find this by first

calculating the monetary base: $1 billion / 2.3 = $435 million (money supply/ multiplier). For the money supply to increase to $1.2 billion, the money multiplier must be $1.2/.435 = 2.76. To find the new reserve ratio solve $(1+c)/(r+c) = 2.76$ for r. We find that $r = .15$. (740-741)

    b. The Fed must buy $86.96 million in bonds to increase the money supply by $200 million. Calculate this by dividing the desired increase in the money supply by the money multiplier: $200 million / 2.3. (737-740)

8. **a.** The graph below shows the yield curve associated with the values given. (745-746)

    b. The graph below shows the yield curve associated with the values given. (745-746)

    c. Yield curve a is a standard yield curve. Yield curve b is an inverted yield curve. (745-746)

━━━━━━ ANSWERS ━━━━━━

A BRAIN TEASER

1. The Fed should undertake expansionary monetary policy: 1) Buy government securities on the open market, 2) decrease the discount rate, and/or 3) decrease required reserves. It

should do any one or more of these things to increase banks' excess reserves by $44.64. This is because to close a recessionary gap of $1,000 when the expenditure multiplier is 4 will require an increase in aggregate expenditures of $250. To accomplish this, investment spending will have to increase by $250. This will require the interest rate to decrease by 2.5%. That will require an increase in the money supply of $125. When the money multiplier equals 2.8, or $[(1+.4)/(.1+.4)]$, excess reserves will only have to increase by $44.64. (737-742)

ANSWERS

MULTIPLE CHOICE

1. a   Expansionary monetary policy reduces interest rates and investment increases. Hence, AD shifts out to the right by a multiple of the increase in investment. See pages 731-733.

2. b   Contractionary monetary policy increases interest rates which reduces investment, a component of aggregate expenditures. The AD curve shifts in to the left by a multiple of the decline in investment. See pages 731-733.

3. a   Contractionary monetary policy increases interest rates which decreases investment, thereby decreasing income by a multiple of that amount. See page 733.

4. b   See page 733.

5. c   The correct answer is "policy undertaken by the Fed." The last answer, d, involves regulation, which is also done by the Fed, but such regulation generally does not go under the name "monetary policy." Given the accuracy of answer c, answer d should be avoided. See pages 733-736.

6. c   See page 735.

7. b   Fiscal policy is definitely not a function of the Fed. See page 737.

8. b   See page 733 and Figure 31-3 on page 735.

9. d   Deficits are a tool of fiscal policy. See pages 737-742.

10. a   The price level rise is the difference between the change in nominal income (6 percent) and real income (4 percent). 6-4=2 percent. See page 432.

11. d   The money multiplier is $(1+c)/(r+c)=1.2/.3=4$. See pages 740-741.

12. b. The Fed makes loans only to other banks, and the discount rate is the rate of interest the Fed charges for these loans. See pages 740-741.

13. a   Open market operations is mostly how the Fed changes the money supply. See page 737.

14. a   The last two answers, c and d, cannot be right, because the Fed does not pass laws. When the Fed buys bonds, it lowers the interest rate but it does not lower interest rates by law. Therefore, only a is correct. See pages 737-740.

15. b   People pay the Fed for those bonds with money—Fed IOUs—so the money supply in private hands is reduced. See pages 739-740.

16. a   As the Fed buys bonds this increases their demand and their prices rise. Since bond prices and interest rates are inversely related, interest rates will fall. See pages 737-740.

17. d   See page 742.

18. d   The Taylor rule states that the Fed targets the Fed funds rate with this formula: 2 + rate of inflation + one-half the difference between actual and desired inflation plus one-half the deviation of output over its target. Thus, it will set a Fed funds target of 6%, (2+3+.5+.5). See pages 743-745.

19. c   When the Fed targets the interest rate, it adjusts the supply of money so that the quantity of money demanded equals the quantity of money supplied at the targeted interest rate. This creates a flat effective supply curve of money. See page 744.

20. c   The Fed kept the Fed fund rates lower than what the Taylor rule predicted from 2001 to 2006. Economists believe this contributed to the housing bubble. See page 744.

21. b   The yield curve is generally upward sloping. Interest rates for short-term

bonds are generally lower than interest rates for long-term bonds because of the risk premium for long-term bonds. See pages 743-746.

22. a If the Fed contracts the money supply, the short-term interest rate will rise. This will tend to make the yield curve inverted, or downward sloping. See pages 744-746.

23. a If expectations of inflation rise, long-term interest rates will likely rise, so other things equal the yield curve will become steeper. See pages 743-746.

ANSWERS

POTENTIAL ESSAY QUESTIONS

The following are annotated answers. They indicate the general idea behind the answer.

1. Use expansionary monetary policy (Fed reduces reserve requirements, reduces the discount rate, and/or buys government securities) during a recession; use contractionary policy during an upturn in the business cycle. Expansionary monetary policy will increase the money supply, which will reduce the interest rate and increase investment spending. This shifts the AD curve out to the right by a multiple of the initial increase in investment spending and brings about a multiple increase in the income level.

2. When the Fed funds rate is above its targeted range many banks have shortages of reserves and therefore money must be tight (credit is tight); and vice versa. The Fed will buy (sell) bonds when the Fed funds rate is above (below) its target and monetary policy is too tight (loose).

3. Economists look at the yield curve because it shows the relationship between short-term and long-term interest rates. It's important to monetary policy because the Fed can only directly impact short-term interest rates. As long as the relationship between short-term and long-term interest rates remains constant, the Fed can also affect long-term interest rates, and therefore investment expenditures, and

ultimately output and the price level. But if the relationship changes, the Fed has less control. One possibility is that the Fed raises short-term interest rates and long-term interest rates fall. This might happen if by raising short-term interest rates inflation expectations fall. But if the Fed wanted long-term interest rates to rise, its raising short-term rates will not be effective.

FINANCIAL CRISES, PANICS, AND MACROECONOMIC POLICY

32

CHAPTER AT A GLANCE

This review is based upon the learning objectives that open the chapter.

1. Economists worry more about the collapse of the financial sector than about the collapse of other sectors because all the other sectors depend on a functioning financial sector. (753-754)

   The collapse of the financial sector would cause all other sectors to collapse.

2. The three stages of a financial crisis are (1) a financial bubble forms, (2) the bubble bursts, and (3) the financial sector melts down. (755)

   A financial bubble occurs when prices of financial assets rise faster than the rise in the true underlying value of those assets. When the bubble bursts a recession usually follows. Whether that leads to a depression depends on the strength of the financial sector.

3. Two central ingredients of a bubble are herding and leveraging. Herding creates a run up in prices. Leveraging increases people's ability to herd; this further increases prices. (757)

   Herding is the human tendency to follow the crowd. Leveraging is borrowing to buy financial assets.

4. When the market experiences a shock that leads to higher prices, extrapolative price expectations can lead to an upward sloping effective demand curve if expectations of price increases become self-fulfilling. (757-758)

   A rise in price causes the demand curve to shift to the right so prices continue to rise, leading to even more shifts in demand.

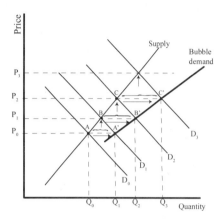

5. Non-systemic risk is a risk caused by one local event. Systemic risk is the risk of an event that affects the entire system. (765-766)

   Systemic risks cannot be insured against because there is nothing to balance the risks against.

6. The three stages of government response to a financial crisis are triage, treatment, and rehabilitation. (766-767)

   (1) Triage: stabilize the economy in the short-run by whatever means necessary.

   (2) Treatment: rehabilitate the economy by using expansionary monetary and fiscal policies to fight the recession/depression.

   (3) Rehabilitation: strengthen the economy through long-run institutional changes.

7. The moral hazard problem, law of diminishing marginal control, and the bad precedent problem make rehabilitating an economy after a financial crisis difficult. (768-771)

   ✔ *Know the definition of each of these terms.*

● SHORT-ANSWER QUESTIONS

1. Why are economists more concerned about the collapse of the financial sector than the collapse of other sectors?

2. What are the three stages of a financial crisis?

3. How can herding and leverage lead to a bubble?

4. How can extrapolative expectations lead to bubbles and depressions?

5. What is securitization? How did it contribute to the 2008 financial crisis?

6. Which can one insure against—a systemic or non-systemic risk? Explain your answer.

7. What are the three stages of government action to get an economy out of a financial crisis?

8. What is moral hazard? What implications does it have for government policy?

9. What is the law of diminishing marginal control? How does it undermine regulations?

10. What are three economic precepts that should be kept in mind when developing regulations?

MATCHING THE TERMS
Match the terms to their definitions

___	**1.**	bad precedent problem	**a.** Risks of one event that are offset by another event elsewhere.
___	**2.**	bubble	**b.** The human tendency to follow the crowd.
___	**3.**	deposit insurance	**c.** A problem that arises when people don't have to bear the
___	**4.**	diversification	negative consequences of their actions.
___	**5.**	extrapolative	
		expectations	**d.** Unsustainable rapidly rising prices of some type of financial
___	**6.**	Glass-Steagall Act	asset.
___	**7.**	herding	**e.** The risks of a problem happening to all parts of the economy
___	**8.**	law of diminishing	simultaneously.
		marginal control	**f.** Whenever a regulatory system is set up, individuals or firms
___	**9.**	leverage	being regulated will figure out ways to circumvent those
___	**10.**	liquidity	regulations.
___	**11.**	liquidity trap	**g.** Buying a financial asset with borrowed money.
___	**12.**	moral hazard problem	**h.** Expectations that a trend will accelerate.
___	**13.**	mortgage backed	**i.** Financial assets whose flow of income comes from a combination
		securities	of mortgages.
___	**14.**	nonsystemic risk	**j.** A system under which the federal government promised to stand
___	**15.**	quantitatiive easing	by individual's bank deposits and thereby help prevent future
___	**16.**	systemic risk	bank runs.

k. The problem that if you give a bailout to one, all want it.

l. One's ability to convert an asset into cash.

m. Nonstandard monetary policy designed to expand credit in the economy.

n. The act of combining different financial instruments, whose prices are not expected to move together, in an effort to reduce risk.

o. A situation where people only want to hold liquid assets, and they would hold them even if they had to pay money to hold them.

p. An act of Congress passed in 1933 that established deposit insurance and implemented a number of banking regulations.

PROBLEMS AND APPLICATIONS

1. How do extrapolative expectations lead to a bubble? Demonstrate your answer with a supply/demand graph.

2. How might the expectational accelerator lead to a depression? Demonstrate your answer using the AS/AD model.

3. Define each of the following and state whether it would best fit in the triage, treatment, or rehabilitation stage.

   a. The Glass-Steagall Act.

   b. The Troubled Asset Relief Program.

   c. The Bank Holiday in 1933.

   d. The New Deal's fiscal policy.

A BRAIN TEASER

1. Bubbles have significant macroeconomic repercussions. Should government actively seek to prevent them? If so, how?

MULTIPLE CHOICE

Circle the one best answer for each of the following questions:

1. What role do economists agree the central bank has in a financial crisis?
   a. Lender of last resort.
   b. Contractionary fiscal policy to reduce leverage.
   c. Expansionary fiscal policy to reduce leverage.
   d. No role.

2. Why weren't economists especially concerned that the 1929 stock crash could cause a depression?
   a. Because only real wealth, not nominal wealth had been destroyed.
   b. Although part of the productive capacity of the economy had been reduced, no nominal wealth had been destroyed.
   c. Because only nominal wealth, not real wealth had been destroyed. The productive capacity of the economy had not changed.
   d. Because they were more concerned with deflation than inflation.

3. In which market did the 1920s bubble form?
   a. Housing.
   b. Gold.
   c. Stock.
   d. Mortgage.

4. In the bubble supply and demand model, extrapolative expectations cause the effective demand curve:
   a. to coincide with the supply curve.
   b. to be horizontal.
   c. to be upward sloping.
   d. to disappear.

5. Which process is most like the money creation process?
   a. Herding.
   b. Leverage
   c. Deposit insurance.
   d. Financial regulation.

6. In which two markets did a bubble form in the early 2000s, leading to a financial crisis in 2008?
   a. Housing and mortgage backed securities.
   b. Housing and technology stocks.
   c. Mortgage backed securities and tulips.
   d. South sea company and tulips.

7. What two advantages did securitization have for local banks?
   a. Herding, leverage.
   b. Reducing non-systemic risk, leverage.
   c. Reducing systemic risk, liquidity.
   d. Diversification, liquidity.

8. Fannie Mae and Freddie Mac buy up and package _____ into derivative securities.
   a. mortgages
   b. non-systemic risk
   c. houses
   d. credit default options/swaps

9. How does the depression model differ from the normal AS/AD model?
   a. The depression model has no money wealth, interest rate or international effects.
   b. In the AS/AD model, the AD curve is fixed.
   c. In the depression model expectations are endogenous.
   d. They are the same model.

10. Risk that can be offset by another event elsewhere is known as:
    a. systemic risk.
    b. non-systemic risk.
    c. herding risk.
    d. leveraging risk.

11. Which of the following is an example of an action taken during the treatment phase of dealing with a financial crisis?
    a. Expansionary monetary and fiscal policy.
    b. Setting a liquidity trap.
    c. Injecting capital into financial institutions.
    d. Establishing institutional structures to prevent recurrence.

12. The creation of the deposit insurance system was an example of:
a. triage policy.
b. treatment policy.
c. rehabilitation policy.
d. non-systemic policy.

13. During 2008 the financial bailout made better sense on economic grounds than a bailout of the automobile industry because:
a. automobile companies are less deserving than financial companies.
b. the automobile industry is smaller than the financial industry.
c. the finance industry is necessary for other industries to function.
d. the automobile industry brought the problems on itself.

14. Moral hazard is a problem that arises when:
a. people are required to bear the negative consequences of their actions.
b. people don't have to bear the negative consequences of their actions.
c. people benefit from the negative actions of others.
d. government discourages companies from taking risks.

15. Given that financial regulations were set up following the problems in the 1930s to prevent panics, why did the problems of 2008 occur?

a. Regulations were gradually removed and regulations lost their effectiveness.
b. Contractionary monetary policy and regulations were gradually removed.
c. Expansionary fiscal policy and regulations gradually lost their effectiveness.
d. Contractionary fiscal policy and regulations were gradually removed.

16. In 2008, the fed purchased bonds from money market mutual funds. This is an example of:
a. standard monetary policy.
b. the paradox of thrift.
c. quantitative easing.
d. systematic policy.

17. What is a paradox of regulation?
a. Regulation lowers growth and profit rates but reduces overall macroeconomic instability.
b. Regulation that protects the majority is undesirable to the minority it regulates.
c. The more one regulates, the less effective that regulation becomes.
d. If regulation is successful, people begin to forget that it was ever necessary.

● POTENTIAL ESSAY QUESTIONS

You may also see essay questions similar to the "Problems & Applications" and "A Brain Teaser" exercises.

1. How did the government respond to the financial crisis in the 1930s?

2. How did the government respond to the financial crisis in 2008?

3. Why is leverage potentially dangerous?

4. Why is monetary policy often ineffective in a financial crisis?

ANSWERS

SHORT-ANSWER QUESTIONS

1. Economists worry more about the collapse of the financial sector than the collapse of other sectors because all the other sectors depend on the financial sector. A working financial market is essential for all other sectors of the economy to function. The collapse of the financial sector would cause all other sectors to collapse. The loss of credit would force many companies to close causing many workers to lose their jobs. The same isn't true for other sectors such as the automobile sector. (753-754)

2. The first stage of a financial crisis is generally a financial bubble. The second stage is the bursting of that bubble, which often causes a recession. The third stage involves the after effects of the bubble on the financial system, which can turn the recession into a depression. (755)

3. Leverage is borrowing for the purpose of making financial investments. Herding is the human tendency to follow the crowd. Leveraging and herding allow people to act on extrapolative expectations, in which people's expectations of price changes become self-fulfilling. Leveraging increases people's ability to herd, which further increases prices. (756-758)

4. Extrapolative expectations are expectations that a trend will continue and even strengthen. When the market experiences a shock that leads to higher prices, extrapolative price expectations can cause expectations of further price increases which increase demand. Expectations of price increases become self-fulfilling, causing a bubble. The more prices rise, the more people want the good, causing shortages to become worse as time progresses. Because demand increases when prices rise, the effective demand curve is upward sloping. (756-759)

5. Securitization is the bundling of several loans together into a new financial instrument (a derivative security) which is then sold. These new securities introduced another layer of leveraging so that when the housing market collapsed, so did the securities market, but at an even faster pace. (759-760)

6. Non-systemic risk is a risk caused by one local event while systemic risk is caused by an event that is more global in nature. One can insure against non-systemic risk because it is offset by an event elsewhere. One cannot insure against systemic risk because there are no offsetting events. (765-766)

7. The three stages of government response to a financial crisis are: (1) Triage: stabilize the economy in the short-run by whatever means necessary. (2) Treatment: rehabilitate the economy by using expansionary monetary and fiscal policies to fight the recession/depression. (3) Rehabilitation: strengthen the economy in the long-run by developing an institutional structure that reduces and changes the incentive structure that leads to crises. (766-767)

8. Moral hazard involves increasing the risk of poor choices by shielding people from the negative consequences of their actions. An example of a moral hazard problem is bailing out the economy. Government must act as though it will never bail out the economy in order to discourage risky behavior. But in the event of a crisis the government must bail out the economy to keep it from collapsing. Such interventions mean that government promises not to intervene are not credible. (769-770)

9. The law of diminishing marginal control states that whenever a regulatory system is set up, individuals or firms being regulated will figure out ways to circumvent those regulations and therefore reduce their effectiveness. Regulation necessarily becomes less effective over time. This law is used to show how financial regulations set up in the aftermath of the Great Depression were undermined over time. (771-772)

10. Three economic precepts to keep in mind are (1) set as few bad precedents as possible, (2) deal with moral hazard, and (3) deal with the law of diminishing marginal control. (771-773)

ANSWERS

MATCHING

1-k; 2- d; 3-j; 4-n; 5-h; 6-p; 7-b; 8-f; 9-g; 10-l; 11-o; 12-c; 13-i; 14-a; 15-m; 16-e.

ANSWERS

PROBLEMS AND APPLICATIONS

1. Demand shifts out from D_0 to D_1. At the original equilibrium price P_0, this new higher demand causes a shortage of Q_1 - Q_0. Because price expectations are extrapolative other things cannot be assumed constant. The rise in prices from P_0 to P_1 leads people to expect further price increases. This shifts the demand out to D_2 and increases the quantity demanded at P_1 to Q_2. There is a shortage represented by the distance B'- B, which is greater than the initial shortage represented by the distance A' - A. The rise in price moved the market further away from equilibrium. Further price adjustments move the market still further away. The larger shortage B' – B causes prices to rise to P_2 which cause demand to shift further out to D_3 and causes even a larger shortage, C' – C.

 Connecting the quantity demanded at each price reveals that the market operates as if the demand curve is upward sloping. This is labeled on the graph as the bubble demand curve. (756-758)

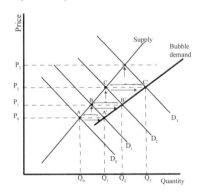

2. The problem starts with a small shift back in the AD curve from AD_0 to AD_1. This causes excess aggregate supply (an aggregate demand shortage) of Y_1 - Y_0. In the standard model, that shortage would be resolved by a fall in the price level to P_1 and a fall in output making the new equilibrium at point B. However, in a depression model, people's expectations about the future changes, which causes them to change their behavior. The fall in the price level leads people to perceive further loss of financial assets. The fall in output leads people to fear an even greater future decline, a fear that reduces investment and consumers' willingness to spend. These changing expectations shift the AD curve back further from AD_1 to AD_2. So at price level P_1 the aggregate demand shortage is now represented by the distance B' – B, which is larger than the initial shortage A' – A. The situation has worsened, and as long as this process continues, the economy will be in freefall. Connecting points A', B' and C' reveals an aggregate demand curve that slopes up instead of down. Whether an equilibrium exists depends on the relative slopes of the AS and effective AD curve. (763-764)

3. a. The Glass-Steagall Act was a financial law passed in the 1930s that established deposit insurance and implemented a number of banking regulations. It was an attempt to address the problem of moral hazard problem. It falls in the rehabilitation stage. (766-768)

 b. The Troubled Asset Relief Program was a law passed in 2008 that permitted the Treasury to use up to $700 billion to buy up distressed assets and recapitalize banks. This was in response to the potential collapse of the financial sector. It is an example of triage. (766-769)

 c. The Bank Holiday of 1933 was the temporary closing of all banks so that no one could withdraw their deposits. It was an attempt to stop the runs on banks that were destroying the financial sector. It is an example of triage. (766-768)

d. Although New Deal fiscal policy was limited, it would best fit in the treatment stage. (766-768)

ANSWERS

A BRAIN TEASER

1. It depends. Bubbles do have significant macroeconomic repercussions. They cause price distortions that call into question the ability of markets to judge value. In addition, bubbles can sometimes lead to market instability, crashes, recessions, and depressions. It would seem to make sense that government should use preventative methods to deflate bubbles before they burst on their own.

    The key problem is that it is hard to determine if rising prices are the result of a bubble or normal market dynamics. Even in hindsight it is somewhat difficult to classify price increases as a bubble. Therefore, despite the dire consequences of bubbles governments have few guaranteed or safe preventative policy recourses.

    Even if government could tell which price increases are bubbles and which are not, government action is still unclear. Artificially bursting a bubble still carries the risk of causing an unnecessary recession or depression. (766-773)

ANSWERS

MULTIPLE CHOICE

1. a   As discussed on pages 753-754, the role of a central bank in a financial crisis is as the lender of last resort. This is a widely accepted role of the central bank.

2. c   As discussed on pages 754-755, economists weren't concerned that the 1929 stock crash could cause a depression because only nominal wealth and not real wealth had been destroyed. The productive capacity of the economy had not changed.

3. c   As discussed on page 755, in the 1920s a bubble formed in the stock market.

4. c   As discussed on pages 755-758, in the bubble supply and demand model, extrapolative expectations cause the effective demand curve to be upward sloping.

5. b   As discussed on pages 757-758, leverage is similar to the money creation process. The difference is that the money multiplier process doesn't create money; it creates credit and financial instruments that serve some of the same functions as money.

6. a   As discussed on pages 759-761, the bubble that caused the 2008 crisis occurred in the housing market and the mortgage backed securities market.

7. d   As discussed on pages 759-760, the two advantages of securitization for local banks were diversification and liquidity.

8. a   As discussed on pages 759-760, Fannie Mae and Freddie Mac are clearinghouses for mortgages.

9. c   As discussed on pages 763-764, in the depression model expectations are endogenous while in the AS/AD model they are not.

10. b   As discussed on pages 765-766, only nonsystemic risk can be insured against.

11. a   As discussed on pages 766-767, injecting capital is an example of triage—stabilizing the economy. Expansionary monetary and fiscal policy are treatment policies. Establishing institutions is part of the rehabilitating stage. The liquidity trap is a problem during recessions, not a treatment.

12. c   As discussed on pages 766-768, deposit insurance is an example of a policy in the rehabilitation stage.

13. c   As discussed on pages 768-769, the automobile industry is not central to the

economy as is the financial sector. If the finance sector fails the automobile sector (and all other sectors) will fail; the reverse is not the case.

14. b   As discussed on pages 769-771, moral hazard is a problem that arises when people don't have to bear the negative consequences of their actions.

15. a   As discussed on pages 771-773, although financial regulations were set up following the problems in the 1930s, the financial problems of 2008 occurred because regulations lost their effectiveness and were gradually removed.

16. c   The fed does not normally purchase bonds from money market mutual funds. It is an example of quantitative easing as discussed in page 768.

17. d   As discussed on pages 771-773, the paradox of regulation is that if it is successful, people begin to forget that it was ever necessary. Therefore the answer is d.

ANSWERS

POTENTIAL ESSAY QUESTIONS

The following are annotated answers. They indicate the general idea behind the answer.

1.   In the 1930s the immediate threat to the economy was the potential collapse of the financial system caused by bank runs. The government declared a national bank holiday to temporarily close all banks and prevent people from withdrawing their deposits. The government then used expansionary monetary policy and limited expansionary fiscal policy to combat the depression. However it took the major fiscal expansion of World War II to fully pull the economy out of recession. The government then set up a regulatory system to prevent future financial panics.

2.   In 2008 the immediate threat to the economy was the collapse of the financial sector. To stop that collapse, government injected capital into failing financial institutions. Foreign governments took similar actions. In addition, the Fed implemented very expansionary monetary policy.

3.   Leverage is what allows a bubble to develop. It is also the cause of the quick bursting of bubbles.

4.   Expansionary monetary policy may not be effective in a financial crisis because while it can provide liquidity it cannot require banks to lend or firms to borrow. No matter how many reserves the central bank puts into the financial system, banks may still not loan the money for fear of losing it.

INFLATION AND THE PHILLIPS CURVE

33

CHAPTER AT A GLANCE

This review is based upon the learning objectives that open the chapter.

1. Inflation redistributes income from those who cannot raise their prices or wages to those who can raise their prices or wages. (776-777)

   For example, if inflation is unexpected, income is redistributed from:

   - *workers to firms if workers have fixed wage contracts but firms raise their prices.*
   - *lenders to borrowers since the real interest rate declines when the nominal interest rate is fixed.*

   On average the winners and losers in an inflation balance out; inflation does not make a nation richer or poorer.

2. Three ways expectations of inflation are formed are: (777-778)

   1. *Rational expectations → expectations that the economists' model predicts.*

   2. *Adaptive expectations → expectations based in some way on the past.*

   3. *Extrapolative expectations → expectations that a trend will continue.*

   Expectations can change the way an economy operates. Expectations play a key role in policy.

   Policymakers use the following equation to determine whether inflation may be coming:

   Inflation = Nominal wage increase – productivity growth.

3. The quantity theory of money basically states that inflation is directly related to the rise in the money supply. It is based upon the equation of exchange: $MV = PQ$. (779-783)

   Three assumptions made in the quantity theory of money:

   1. *Velocity (V) is constant.*
   2. *Real output (Q) is independent of the money supply (M).*
   3. *Causation goes from money (M) to prices (P). That is, an increase (decrease) in M causes an increase (decrease) in P.*
   Note: The price level rises because the money supply rises.

   In the 1990s, the close relationship between money and inflation broke down. Economists debate whether this is temporary or permanent. For large inflations, the connection between money and inflation is still evident.

4. The institutional theory holds that institutional and structural aspects of inflation, as well as increases in the money supply, are important causes of inflation. It sees the causation in the equation of exchange going from right to left. That is, changes in the price level result in changes in the money supply. (783-785)

   Firms find it easier to raise wages, profits, and rents to keep the peace with employees and other owners of the factors of production. To pay for those increases, firms raise prices. Government then raises the money supply to make sure there is sufficient demand to buy the goods at those higher prices.

The "insider" versus "outsider" situation creates imperfect markets. Imperfect markets provide an opportunity for "insiders" to increase their wages and prices even when unemployment and excess capacity exist in the overall economy, thereby creating inflation.

In a nutshell:According to the quantity theory, $MV \rightarrow PQ$

According to the institutionalist theory, $PQ \rightarrow MV$

5a. The long-run Phillips curve is vertical; it takes into account the feedback of inflation on expectations of inflation. (787-789)

In the long run when expectations of inflation are met, changes in the rates of inflation have no effect on the level of unemployment. This is shown as LR in the accompanying graph.

5b. The short-run Phillips curve is downward sloping. Expectations of inflation are constant along the short-run Phillips curve. (785-789)

The short-run Phillips curve reflects the empirically observed trade-off between inflation and unemployment. It is shown as SR in the graph above. Expectations of inflation are constant along the short-run (SR) Phillips curve. Increases (decreases) in inflationary expectations shift the short-run Phillips curve to the right (left).

In the long run we have more time to adjust our expectations to actual inflation. In the short run we may be fooled–we may expect less (more) inflation than actually occurs when inflation is accelerating (decelerating).

6. Quantity theorists believe that inflation undermines long-run growth. Institutionalists are less sure of a negative relationship between inflation and growth. (790-792)

According to the quantity theory, the best policy is a policy that leads to price stability.

Institutionalists believe that low unemployment is an important goal that must be balanced with the risk of inflation.

● SHORT-ANSWER QUESTIONS

1. Your study partner states that inflation is bad because it makes a nation poorer. How do you respond?

2. What are three ways people form expectations of future inflation?

3. If there is a high inflation, most economists are willing to accept that a rough approximation of the quantity theory holds true. Why?

4. What is the quantity theory of money and how does it relate to long-run growth?

5. How does the institutionalist theory of inflation differ from the quantity theory of inflation?

6. Who is more likely to favor a monetary rule: economists who support the quantity theory or economists who support the institutional theory of inflation? Why?

7. Which of the two curves in the graph below is a short-run Phillips curve, and why?

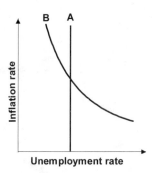

8. Would an economist who supports the quantity theory or one who supports the institutionalist theory of inflation be more likely to see a long-run trade-off between inflation and unemployment? Why?

9. Why does government generally fight deflation?

MATCHING THE TERMS
Match the terms to their definitions

____ 1. adaptive expectations

____ 2. cost-push inflation

____ 3. deflation

____ 4. demand-pull inflation

____ 5. equation of exchange

____ 6. extrapolative expectations

____ 7. inflation tax

____ 8. insider/outsider model

____ 9. long-run Phillips curve

____ 10. quantity theory of money

____ 11. rational expectations

____ 12. short-run Phillips curve

____ 13. stagflation

____ 14. velocity of money

a. Expectations based in some way on the past.
b. An institutionalist story of inflation where insiders bid up wages and outsiders are unemployed.
c. MV=PQ.
d. A curve showing the trade-off between inflation and unemployment when expectations of inflation are constant.
e. A curve showing the trade-off (or complete lack thereof) between inflation and unemployment when expectations of inflation equal actual inflation.
f. The price level varies in response to changes in the quantity of money.
g. Combination of high and accelerating inflation and high unemployment.
h. Expectations that a trend will continue.
i. Inflation that occurs when the economy is at or above potential output.
j. The number of times per year, on average, a dollar goes around to generate a dollar's worth of income.
k. Expectations that the economists' model predicts.
l. An implicit tax on the holders of cash and the holders of any obligations specified in nominal terms.
m. Inflation that occurs when the economy is below potential.
n. A continual fall in the price level.

PROBLEMS AND APPLICATIONS

1. a. What are the three assumptions that translate the equation of exchange into the quantity theory of money?

    b. State the equation of exchange and show how the three assumptions lead to the conclusion that inflation is always and everywhere a monetary phenomenon.

2. With the equation of exchange, answer the following questions:

    a. Nominal GDP is $2,000, the money supply is 200. What is the velocity of money?

    b. The velocity of money is 5.60, the money supply is $1,100 billion. What is nominal output?

    c. Assuming velocity is constant and the money supply increases by 6%, by how much does nominal output rise?

3. Suppose the economy is operating at potential output. Inflation is 3% and expected inflation is 3%. Unemployment is 5.5%.

    a. Draw a long-run Phillips curve and a short-run Phillips curve consistent with these conditions.

    b. The government implements an expansionary monetary policy. As a result, unemployment falls to 4.5% and inflation rises to 6%. Expectations do not adjust. Show where the economy is on the graph you drew for 3(a). What happens to the short-run Phillips curve? Inflation? Unemployment?

    c. Expectations now fully adjust. Show this on the graph drawn for 3(a). What happens to the short-run Phillips curve?

4. Redraw the long-run Phillips curve and the short-run Phillips curve consistent with the conditions of the economy described in question #3 above and explain the effect of the following on inflation and unemployment using the curves you have drawn.

    a. The government implements a contractionary monetary policy. As a result, unemployment rises to 6.5% and inflation falls to 0%. Expectations do not adjust.

    b. Expectations now fully adjust.

5. For each of the following points that represents the economy on the Phillips curve, make a prediction for unemployment and inflation.

    a.

    b.

    c.

6. Suppose inflation is 12%, unemployment is 5.5%, and the natural rate of unemployment is 5.5%. The president believes inflation and unemployment are both too high.

    a. Assume you are a quantity theorist. What policy would you recommend to improve the situation?

    b. Show the short-run effect of this policy on unemployment and inflation using the Phillips curve analysis. Will the president be satisfied? What is your response?

    c. Show the long-run effect of this policy on unemployment and inflation using the Phillips curve analysis. Will the president be satisfied? What is your response? (In that response, discuss the issue of long-run growth.)

● A BRAIN TEASER

1. Why do countries increase the money supply enormously even though they know that doing so will lead to high inflation?

● MULTIPLE CHOICE

Circle the one best answer for each of the following questions:

1. In an expected inflation, lenders will generally:
  a. gain relative to borrowers.
  b. lose relative to borrowers.
  c. neither gain nor lose relative to borrowers.
  d. The effect will be totally random.

2. In an unexpected inflation, lenders will generally:
  a. gain relative to borrowers.
  b. lose relative to borrowers.
  c. neither gain nor lose relative to borrowers.
  d. The effect will be totally random.

3. According to the text if individuals base their expectations on the past we say that their expectations are:
  a. rational.
  b. historical.
  c. adaptive.
  d. extrapolative.

4. If productivity growth is 2 percent and inflation is 5 percent, on average nominal wage increases will be:
  a. 2 percent.
  b. 3 percent.
  c. 5 percent.
  d. 7 percent.

5. If the nominal interest rate is 1 percent and the economy is experiencing deflation of 2 percent, the Fed cannot lower the real interest rate below:
  a. 0 percent.
  b. 1 percent.
  c. 2 percent.
  d. 3 percent.

6. Assuming velocity is relatively constant and real income is relatively stable, an increase in the money supply of 40 percent will be associated with an approximate change in the price level of:
  a. 4 percent.
  b. 40 percent.
  c. 80 percent.
  d. zero percent.

7. According to the quantity theory:
    a. unemployment is everywhere and always a monetary phenomenon.
    b. inflation is everywhere and always a monetary phenomenon.
    c. the equation of exchange does not hold true.
    d. real output is everywhere and always a monetary phenomenon.

8. The quantity theory is most applicable to:
    a. U.S. type economies.
    b. West European type economies.
    c. developing economies.
    d. Japanese type economies.

9. The inflation tax is:
    a. a tax placed by government on inflators.
    b. a tax placed on inflators.
    c. a tax on the holders of cash.
    d. a tax on holders of goods whose price is inflating.

10. Central banks in developing countries such as Zimbabwe do not simply stop increasing the supply of money to slow inflation because:
    a. the economy is producing goods at a greater rate than people can buy them.
    b. they do not believe that rapid money growth causes high inflation.
    c. the central bank must purchase government bonds to avoid an economic collapse.
    d. black markets are so prevalent that currency is disappearing in the market economy.

11. Individuals who hold an institutional theory of inflation argue:
    a. the equation of exchange is incorrect.
    b. the equation of exchange should be read from right to left.
    c. the equation of exchange should be read from left to right.
    d. both the quantity theory and the equation of exchange are incorrect.

12. If an economist focuses on social pressures in his or her discussion of inflation, that economist is likely an advocate of a(n):
    a. quantity theory of inflation.
    b. institutionalist theory of inflation.
    c. insider theory of inflation.
    d. outsider theory of inflation.

13. When there is cost-push inflation, price increases:
    a. tend to lead money supply increases.
    b. tend to lag money supply increases.
    c. tend to have no relationship to money supply increases.
    d. sometimes lead and sometimes lag money supply increases.

14. The Phillips curve represents a relationship between:
    a. inflation and unemployment.
    b. inflation and real income.
    c. money supply and interest rates.
    d. money supply and unemployment.

15. The short-run Phillips curve shifts around because of changes in:
    a. the money supply.
    b. expectations of employment.
    c. expectations of inflation.
    d. expectations of real income.

16. The slope of the long-run Phillips curve is thought by many economists to be:
    a. horizontal.
    b. vertical.
    c. downward sloping.
    d. backward bending.

17. If the economy is at point A in the Phillips curve graph below, what prediction would you make for unemployment?

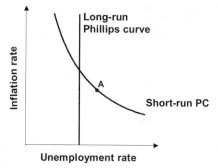

    a. It will increase.
    b. It will decrease.
    c. It will remain constant.
    d. It will explode.

18. If the economy is at Point A in the Phillips curve graph below, what prediction would you make for unemployment?

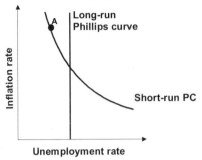

   a. It will increase.
   b. It will decrease.
   c. It will remain constant.
   d. It will immediately fall to zero.

19. Stagflation is:
   a. a combination of low and decelerating inflation and low unemployment.
   b. a combination of low and decelerating inflation and high unemployment.
   c. a combination of high and accelerating inflation and low unemployment.
   d. a combination of high and accelerating inflation and high unemployment.

20. Advocates of the quantity theory are likely to emphasize a trade-off between inflation and:
   a. unemployment.
   b. distribution.
   c. growth.
   d. money.

POTENTIAL ESSAY QUESTIONS

You may also see essay questions similar to the "Problems & Applications" and "A Brain Teaser" exercises.

1. In what way is inflation a tax? Who pays it?

2. What are the differences between the quantity theorists and the institutionalists with respect to unemployment?

3. What role does government play in the Insider/Outsider model?

■■■■■■■ **ANSWERS** ■■■■■■■

SHORT-ANSWER QUESTIONS

1. Inflation does not make a nation poorer. It redistributes income from those who cannot and do not raise their prices to those who can and do raise their prices. On average, the winners and losers average out. An example is lenders and borrowers. Although inflation does not make a nation poorer in the short run, supporters of the quantity theory argue that inflation does make a country poorer in the long run by increasing the costs of doing business and by decreasing the informational value of money. Supporters of the institutional theory disagree and say that long-term inflation does not significantly reduce a nation's growth. (776-777)

2. People formulate expectations in a variety of ways. Three types of expectations are adaptive expectations (expectations based in some way on the past), rational expectations (the expectations that the economists' model predicts), and extrapolative expectations (expectations that a trend will continue). (777-778)

3. The quantity theory is based on the equation of exchange, $MV=PQ$. The quantity theory adds the following assumptions: (1) that velocity is relatively constant; (2) that real output is relatively constant; and (3) that changes in money supply cause changes in prices. In reality, velocity and real output can change sufficiently to make it questionable whether this theory is useful. However, when there is significant inflation—say 100% or more—the relative changes in velocity and real output that are reasonable to assume possible are much smaller than that 100%, leaving a rough correlation between changes in the money supply and changes in the price level.

    The debate between economists does not concern the relationships between money growth and inflation; it concerns the direction of causation. Quantity theorists tend to believe that the causation goes from money to prices, and hence they are willing to accept the existence of a long-run vertical Phillips curve. Institutionalists tend to believe that the causation goes from changes in prices and expectations of prices to changes in the money supply—the government is accommodating the

higher prices. Thus they favor more institutionally-oriented theories of inflation. (779-783)

4. The quantity theory of money is best summarized by the phrase "Inflation is everywhere and always a monetary phenomenon." Essentially, it is that increases in the money supply are the cause of inflation, and all other supposed causes are simply diversions from the key monetary cause. According to the quantity theory there is a long-run inverse relationship between inflation and growth. $MV{\rightarrow}PQ$ (779-783)

5. The institutionalist theory of inflation differs from the quantity theory in that it is more likely to include institutional and social aspects as part of the theory. The insider/outsider model is an institutionalist model of inflation. Another way of stating the difference is that the institutional theory of inflation sees the equation of exchange as being read from right to left, rather than from left to right. $MV{\leftarrow}PQ$ (779-783)

6. Economists who support the quantity theory of money are more likely to favor a monetary rule, because they see the economy gravitating toward a natural (or target) rate of unemployment regardless of monetary policy. Thus expansionary monetary policy can lead only to inflation. A monetary rule will limit the government's attempt to expand the economy with monetary policy and hence will achieve the target rate of unemployment and low inflation. Institutional economists are less likely to see the economy gravitating toward the target rate of unemployment, so they would favor some discretionary policy to improve the operation of the macroeconomy. (783-785)

7. Curve B is the short-run Phillips curve. The short-run Phillips curve represents a trade-off between inflation and unemployment. It is an empirically determined phenomenon, and based on that empirical evidence, economists generally believe that whenever unemployment decreases, inflation increases, and vice versa. They explain that this empirical occurrence is due to slowly adjusting expectations and institutions. In the long run, expectations and institutions can change and hence the reason for the trade-off is eliminated,

making the vertical line represent the long-run Phillips curve—it represents the lack of a trade-off between inflation and unemployment in the long run. (785-789)

8. Institutional economists see institutional and social aspects of the price setting process as more important than do quantity theorists. They also see individuals as having a cost of rationality, so individuals may not notice small amounts of inflation. These aspects of the institutional theory make it more likely that there is a long-run trade-off between inflation and unemployment since, in their absence, we would expect that money is essentially a veil and real forces predominate. (790-793)

9. Governments try to prevent deflation because deflation in goods and services is generally associated with asset price deflation. Asset price deflation creates the illusion of the loss of wealth, which will likely cause a decline in aggregate demand and a recession. (791)

ANSWERS

MATCHING

1-a; 2-m; 3-n; 4-i; 5-c; 6-h; 7-l; 8-b; 9-e; 10-f; 11-k; 12-d; 13-g; 14-j.

ANSWERS

PROBLEMS AND APPLICATIONS

1. a. 1. Velocity is constant, 2. Real output is independent of the money supply, 3. Causation goes from money supply to prices. (782-783)

    b. $MV = PQ$ is the equation of exchange. Since V is constant and Q exogenous, the only remaining variables that change within the system are M and P. Since the causation runs from M to P, to keep the equation balanced, a rise in M must lead to a rise in P (and only P since Q is exogenous). (782-783)

2. a. $V = 10$: $MV = PQ$; $200V = \$2,000$; $V = 10$. (782)

    b. $\$6,160$ billion: $MV = PQ$; $(5.6)(1,100) = \$6,160$ billion. (782)

    c. By 6%. (782-783)

3. a. The long-run Phillips curve is vertical at the rate of unemployment consistent with potential output, here at 5.5%. The short-run Phillips curve is the downward sloping curve shown in the graph below as PC_1. In this case, we drew a short-run Phillips curve where expected inflation equals the 3% actual inflation. It intersects the long-run Phillips curve at 5.5% unemployment and 3% inflation. The economy is at point A. (785-789)

    b. The economy moves along the short-run Phillips curve up and to the left to point B. The short-run Phillips curve does not shift since inflation expectations have not changed. At point B, inflation is 6% and the unemployment rate is 4.5%. (785-789)

    c. Now that expectations fully adjust, the short-run Phillips curve shifts to the right to PC_2 so that it intersects the long-run Phillips curve at an inflation rate of 6%. The unemployment rate returns to 5.5% and inflation remains at the higher 6%. (785-789)

4. a. The economy moves along the short-run Phillips curve down and to the right to point B in the graph below. The short-run Phillips curve does not shift since inflation expectations have not changed. At point B, inflation is 0% and the unemployment rate is 6.5%. (785-789)

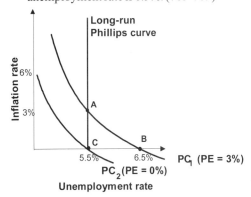

b. Now that expectations fully adjust, the short-run Phillips curve shifts to the left to PC_2 so that it intersects the long-run Phillips curve at inflation rate of 0%. The unemployment rate returns to 5.5% and inflation remains at the lower 0%. (785-789)

5. a. Inflation is below expected inflation and unemployment is higher than the natural rate of unemployment. As expectations adjust, the short-run Phillips curve shifts to the left and unemployment falls. (785-789)

b. Inflation is above expected inflation and unemployment is lower than the natural rate of unemployment. As expectations adjust, the short-run Phillips curve shifts to the right and unemployment rises. (785-789)

c. Inflation equals expected inflation and unemployment equals the target rate of unemployment. Inflation and unemployment will not change. (785-789)

6. a. I would assume that in the long run, only inflation can be improved, so I ignore the rate of unemployment and focus on fighting inflation. A contractionary monetary policy will improve the inflation rate. (779-783)

b. The economy begins at point A in the accompanying graph, where unemployment is 5.5% and inflation is 12%. Inflation expectations equal actual inflation. With contractionary monetary policy, the economy moves along the short-run Phillips curve down and to the right to point B. The short-run Phillips curve does not shift since inflation expectations have not changed. At point B, inflation is lower than 12% and the unemployment rate is higher than 5.5%. The president will be happy that inflation is lower, but disappointed that unemployment is higher. I tell him that in the short run there is a trade-off between the two. Just wait for expectations of inflation to adjust and we will return to 5.5% unemployment. (785-789)

c. Now that expectations fully adjust, the short-run Phillips curve shifts to the left to PC_2 so that it intersects the long-run Phillips curve at inflation rate of below 12% at point C. The unemployment rate returns to 5.5%. The president is now pleased because inflation is lower and unemployment returned to 5.5%. But he wanted the unemployment rate to be below 5.5%. I tell him that 5.5% is the natural rate. If he were to follow an expansionary policy, unemployment would fall in the short run, but would return to 5.5% in the long run and inflation would be higher than it currently is. The higher inflation would undermine the economy's long-term growth. (785-789)

━━━━━━━ ⬤ ANSWERS ━━━━━━━

A BRAIN TEASER

1. The reasons are complicated. If a government does not have the capability of either taxing or borrowing to finance expenditures (and if the central bank is not independent) the government may rely on its ability to print money to finance government expenditures. For some countries the choice is between inflation and allowing an economy and its government to fall apart. (783)

━━━━━━━ ⬤ ANSWERS ━━━━━━━

MULTIPLE CHOICE

1. c   In an unexpected inflation borrowers gain and lenders lose because the money they are paying back will buy less because of the inflation. In an expected inflation the interest rate will have adjusted to compensate lenders for the decrease in the value of money. See pages 776-777.

2. b In an unexpected inflation borrowers gain and lenders lose because the money borrowers are paying back will buy less because of the inflation. See pages 776-777.

3. c Rational expectations are based on models; extrapolative expectations are based on expectations that a trend will continue. Historical expectations are not mentioned in the text. See pages 777-779.

4. d Inflation is the difference between nominal wage increases and productivity growth. See page 779.

5. c One of the problems of deflation is that it sets a floor for the real interest rate. In this case, the real interest rate is 3 percent since the nominal interest rate is 1%. The real interest rate cannot fall below 2 percent. See page 777.

6. b Using the equation of exchange, $MV=PQ$, given these assumptions there is a close relationship between changes in M and changes in P. See pages 779-781.

7. b The quantity theory directly relates money and inflation. See pages 779-781.

8. c The quantity theory is most applicable when there are large increases in the money supply and significant inflation. This is most likely to be the case in developing countries. See page 783.

9. c The inflation tax is a tax on the holders of cash because inflation makes their cash worth less. See page 783.

10. c Central banks in developing countries often must finance the deficit of the government because no one would buy government bonds, and the government would be unable to continue, which would mean that the economy would likely break down. See page 783.

11. b The equation of exchange is a tautology; it cannot be incorrect. Institutionalists see price changes causing money and velocity changes so MV=PQ should be read from right to left. See pages 783-785.

12. b The book describes two general theories of inflation; social pressures definitely fit within the institutionalist theory. One type of institutionalist theory of inflation is the insider/outsider model, but that is not presented as a choice. See pages 783-785.

13. a As the text discusses on page 785, cost-push inflation is associated with the institutionalist theory of inflation that argues that price increases cause money supply increases, and therefore they lead them. The other answers are possible, but a is clearly the best.

14. a The Phillips curve is drawn with inflation on the vertical axis and unemployment on the horizontal axis. See page 787.

15. c The short-run Phillips curve holds expectations of inflation constant. Therefore, it shifts because changes in expectations of inflation cause everybody to build those expectations into their nominal price requests. See pages 784-785.

16. b As discussed in the text, the long-run Phillips curve is vertical. Actually, there is some debate about whether it is downward sloping, but the text focuses on the vertical nature of the curve so that b is the answer that should be given. Remember, one is choosing the best answer relative to what is presented in the text. See page 787.

17. b Since Point A is to the right of the long-run Phillips curve, actual unemployment exceeds the natural rate of unemployment. Therefore we would expect unemployment to decrease. See pages 785-789.

18. a Since Point A is to the left of the long-run Phillips curve, actual unemployment is below the natural rate of unemployment. Therefore, we would expect unemployment to increase. See pages 785-789.

19. d   Stagflation is defined as a combination of high and accelerating inflation and high unemployment. See page 787.

20. c   Quantity theory advocates argue that in the long run a noninflationary environment is conducive to growth and thus there is a long run trade-off between inflation and growth. See pages 790-792.

ANSWERS

POTENTIAL ESSAY QUESTIONS

The following are annotated answers. They indicate the general idea behind the answer.

1.   Inflation can be viewed as a tax because it reduces the value of obligations specified in nominal terms. A simple way to see this is if prices rose at a rate of 5 percent a day, a dollar today will buy only 95 cents worth of goods tomorrow. The holder of the dollar (or any obligation specified in nominal terms) pays the tax.

2.   Quantity theorists see a competitive labor market guaranteeing full employment. Institutionalists see an imperfectly competitive labor market. Institutionalists also envision a potential lack of demand for workers because of a lack of aggregate demand for the goods they produce. To institutionalists, this can create some unemployment at any wage.

3.   Inflation is a result of *im*perfectly competitive markets. This allows workers and firms (especially "insiders") to raise their nominal wages and prices even during periods of high unemployment and excess production. Other groups, feeling relatively worse off, will push for higher wages and prices too. The government can either ratify this inflation by increasing the money supply or it can refuse to ratify it, causing unemployment (especially for the "outsiders").

DEFICITS AND DEBT

CHAPTER AT A GLANCE

This review is based upon the learning objectives that open the chapter.

1a. A deficit is a shortfall of revenues under payments. A surplus is an excess of revenues over payments. (Surpluses are negative deficits and vice versa.) (798-799)

Surpluses and deficits are flow concepts; all deficits must be financed.

1b. Surpluses and deficits are simply summary measures of the financial health of the economy. To understand that summary you must understand the methods that were used to calculate it. (799)

Different accounting procedures yield different figures for surpluses and deficits.

2. A structural deficit or surplus is that part of a budget deficit or surplus that would exist even if the economy were at its potential level of income. A passive (also called cyclical) surplus or deficit is that part that exists because the economy is operating below or above its potential income. (799-800)

Passive deficit = Tax rate (Potential output −Actual output.)

Passive (cyclical) deficits or surpluses are largely due to the automatic stabilizers.

3. The real deficit is the nominal deficit adjusted for inflation. (801-802)

Real deficit = Nominal deficit − (Inflation × Total debt.)

Inflation wipes out debt. Inflation also causes the real deficit to be less than the nominal deficit. However, inflation means a higher

percentage of the deficit (or spending) will be devoted to debt service (paying interest on the debt). Moreover, creditors who do not anticipate the inflation pay the cost of eliminating the debt through inflation.

4a. Debt is accumulated deficits minus accumulated surpluses. It is a <u>stock</u> concept. (802-805)

Debt is a summary measure of a country's financial situation.

GDP serves the same function for government as income does for an individual. The greater the GDP (income) the greater the ability to handle debt. However, government debt is different from an individual's debt. Government is ongoing; it can pay off the debt by printing money; and much of its is internal— owed to its citizens.

4b. Since in a growing economy a continual deficit is consistent with a constant ratio of debt to GDP, and since GDP serves as a measure of the government's ability to pay off the debt, a country can run a continual deficit. (805-807)

The more you earn, the more debt you can handle.

5. Since World War II, until recently, the U.S. government ran almost continual deficits. From 1998 to 2001, the government ran surpluses, but returned to deficits in 2002. (807-809)

But we still have debt.

See Also, Appendix A: " Social Security, Medicare, and Lockboxes."

● SHORT-ANSWER QUESTIONS

1. How much importance do most economists give to the budget deficit or surplus?

2. If the U.S. economy is below potential and the surplus is $40 billion, is the structural surplus greater or less than $40 billion?

3. If the nominal interest rate is 6%, the inflation rate is 4%, the nominal deficit is $100 billion, and the debt of the country is $2 trillion, what is the real deficit?

4. If the nominal interest rate is 5%, the inflation rate is 5%, the real deficit is $100 billion, and the debt of the country is $1 trillion, what is the nominal deficit?

5. In an expanding economy a government should run a continual deficit. True or false? Why?

6. If a politician presents you with a plan that will reduce the nominal budget deficit by $40 billion, but will not hurt anyone, how would you in your capacity as an economist likely respond?

7. Are current budget deficits likely to persist?

A1. In what way is the trust fund not a real solution to the Social Security problem?

MATCHING THE TERMS
Match the terms to their definitions

___ 1. deficit	a. A partially unfunded pension system of the U.S.
___ 2. external debt	b. A shortfall per year of incoming revenue under outgoing payments.
___ 3. internal debt	c. An excess of revenues over payments.
___ 4. nominal deficit or surplus	d. Government debt owed to individuals in foreign countries.
___ 5. passive deficit or surplus	e. That portion of the deficit or surplus that results from fluctuations in the economy.
___ 6. real deficit	f. The deficit or surplus determined by looking at the difference between expenditures and receipts.
___ 7. Social Security system	g. Government debt owed to its own citizens.
___ 8. structural deficit	h. The deficit that would remain when the cyclical or passive elements have been netted out.
___ 9. surplus	i. The nominal deficit adjusted for inflation's effect on the debt.

PROBLEMS AND APPLICATIONS

1. Calculate the debt and deficit in each of the following:

   a. Your income has been $30,000 per year for the last five years. Your expenditures, including interest payments, have been $35,000 per year for the last five years.

   b. This year your income is $50,000; $15,000 of your $65,000 expenditures are for the purchase of the rights to an invention.

   c. Your wage income is $20,000 per year. You have a bond valued at $100,000, which pays $10,000 per year. The market value of that bond rises to $110,000. Expenses are $35,000 per year. Use the opportunity cost approach in your calculations.

2. For each of the following calculate the real deficit:

   a. Inflation is 5%. Debt is $2 trillion. Nominal deficit is $100 billion.

   b. Inflation is −3%. Debt is $500 billion. Nominal deficit is $20 billion.

   c. Inflation is 10%. Debt is $3 trillion. Nominal deficit is $100 billion.

   d. Inflation is 8%. Debt is $20 billion. Nominal deficit is $5 billion.

3. Assume a country's nominal GDP is $7 trillion, government expenditures less debt service are $1.5 trillion, and revenue is $1.3 trillion. The nominal debt is $4.9 trillion. Inflation is 2% and real interest rates are 5%. Expected inflation is fully adjusted.

    a. Calculate debt service payments.

    b. Calculate the nominal deficit.

    c. Calculate the real deficit.

    d. Suppose inflation rose to 4%. Again, expected inflation is fully adjusted. Recalculate (a) - (c).

4. Potential income is $8 billion. The income in the economy is $7.2 billion. Revenues do not vary with income, but taxes do; they increase by 20% of the change in income. The current deficit is $400 million.

    a. What is the economy's structural deficit?

    b. What is the economy's passive deficit?

A BRAIN TEASER

1. How could deficit spending actually reduce the debt burden of future generations?

MULTIPLE CHOICE

Circle the one best answer for each of the following questions:

1. A deficit is:
   a. the total amount of money that a country owes.
   b. the shortfall of payments under revenues in a particular time period.
   c. the shortfall of revenues under payments in a particular time period.
   d. accumulated debt.

2. If the U.S. government raised the retirement age to 72 starting in 2020, the current budget deficit would be:
   a. reduced.
   b. increased.
   c. unaffected.
   d. eliminated.

3. The nominal deficit is $100 billion; inflation is 4 percent; total debt is $2 trillion. The real deficit is:
   a. zero.
   b. $20 billion.
   c. $80 billion.
   d. $100 billion.

4. If the nominal surplus is $200 billion, inflation is 10 percent, and total debt is $2 trillion:
   a. the real surplus is zero.
   b. the real deficit is $100 billion.
   c. the real surplus is $400 billion.
   d. the real surplus is $2.2 trillion.

5. The real deficit is $100 billion; inflation is 4 percent; total debt is $2 trillion. The nominal deficit is:
   a. zero.
   b. $120 billion.
   c. $180 billion.
   d. $200 billion.

6. If creditors are able to forecast inflation perfectly and there are no institutional constraints on interest rates:
    a. the government will not have to make interest payments.
    b. interest payments will rise by the amount that the real debt is reduced by inflation.
    c. the real deficit will equal the nominal deficit.
    d. the government will be unable to finance the debt.

7. Country A has a debt of $10 trillion. Country B has a debt of $5 trillion.
    a. Country A is in a better position than Country B.
    b. Country B is in a better position than Country A.
    c. One cannot say what relative position the countries are in.
    d. Countries A and B are in equal positions.

8. As a percentage of GDP, since World War II:
    a. debt in the United States has been rising.
    b. debt in the United States has been falling.
    c. debt in the United States has been sometimes rising and sometimes falling.
    d. the U.S. government has had no debt.

9. The portion of the budget deficit or surplus that would exist even if the economy were at its potential level of income is called the:
    a. structural deficit or surplus.
    b. passive deficit or surplus.
    c. primary deficit or surplus.
    d. secondary deficit or surplus.

10. If an economy is $100 billion below potential, the tax rate is 20 percent, and the deficit is $180 billion, the passive deficit is:
    a. $20 billion.
    b. $160 billion.
    c. $180 billion.
    d. $200 billion.

11. One of the reasons government debt is different from individual debt is:
    a. government does not pay interest on its debt.
    b. government never really needs to pay back its debt.
    c. all government debt is owed to other government agencies or to its own citizens.
    d. the ability of a government to pay off its debt is unrelated to income.

12. If there is growth and a country with a debt of $1 trillion has decided it wants to keep its ratio of debt-to-GDP constant:
    a. it should run a deficit.
    b. it should run a surplus.
    c. it should run a balanced budget.
    d. the deficit has no effect on debt.

A1. Payroll taxes for Social Security:
    a. reduce the reported deficit and increase the reported surplus.
    b. increase the reported deficit and reduce the reported surplus.
    c. do not affect the budget since it is an off-budget item.
    d. are offset by future obligations in the budget.

A2. The "real" problem of Social Security in 2020 could be solved by:
    a. locking up the Social Security Trust Fund to pay for Social Security benefits only.
    b. raising the eligibility age for Social Security so fewer people are collecting Social Security in 2020, raising taxes on workers, reducing Social Security benefits, or a combination of all three.
    c. allowing current workers to divert some of their payroll taxes into private savings accounts to be withdrawn at retirement.
    d. a rise in the value of the stock market that would raise the value of the Social Security Trust fund so that it remains solvent for longer.

● POTENTIAL ESSAY QUESTIONS

You may also see essay questions similar to the "Problems & Applications" and "A Brain Teaser" exercises.

1. What are three reasons why government debt is different from individual debt?

2. How can a growing economy reduce the concern over deficits and the debt?

━━━━━ ANSWERS ━━━━━

SHORT-ANSWER QUESTIONS

1. While there are differences of opinion, most economists are hesitant to attach too much importance to a deficit or a surplus. The reason is that the deficit or surplus depends on the accounting procedures used, and these can vary widely. Only with much more additional information will an economist attribute importance to a surplus or deficit. It is financial health—the ability to cover costs over the long term—of the economy that concerns most economists. (799)

2. Since the economy is below potential, the structural surplus is larger than the nominal surplus. (799-800)

3. To calculate the real deficit, you multiply inflation times the total debt (4% × $2 trillion), giving $80 billion; then subtract that from the nominal deficit of $100 billion. So in this example the real deficit equals $20 billion. The interest rate does not enter into the calculations. (799-802)

4. To calculate the nominal deficit, you multiply inflation times the total debt (5% × $1 trillion), giving $50 billion, and add that to the real deficit of $100 billion. So in this example the nominal deficit equals $150 billion. The interest rate does not enter into the calculation. (799-802)

5. It depends. In an expanding economy with no deficits, the ratio of debt to GDP will be falling; if the government wants to hold the debt-to-GDP constant it will need to run a continual deficit. If it wants to reduce that ratio, then it need not run a continual deficit. (805-806)

6. TANSTAAFL. I would check to see what accounting gimmick the politician was proposing and what the plan would do to the long-run financial health of the country. (799-802)

7. The Congressional Budget Office predicted in 2009 that the federal government budget will continue to be in deficit for the indefinite future. Much of the increase in the deficit will be the result of increases in Medicare, Medicaid, and Social Sucurity. (806-807)

A1. Ultimately, real expenditures must equal real output in each period. The trust fund provides a financial solution to the Social Security problem, but it does not directly see to it that real expenditures will equal real output in the future. (813-816)

━━━━━ ANSWERS ━━━━━

MATCHING

1-b; 2-d; 3-g; 4-f; 5-e; 6-i; 7-a; 8-h; 9-c.

━━━━━ ANSWERS ━━━━━

PROBLEMS AND APPLICATIONS

1. a. Deficit is $5,000 per year; debt is $25,000. On page 798, deficit is defined as income less expenditures and on page 735 debt is defined as accumulated deficits minus accumulated surpluses. For each of the past 5 years, you have incurred an annual deficit of $5,000. Total debt is $5,000 times five years, or $25,000. (798, 802)
    b. Deficit is $15,000; debt is $15,000. If you count the purchase of the rights to the invention as a current expenditure, the deficit is $15,000. If you had no previous debt, debt is also $15,000. If, however, you count the purchase of the invention as an investment and include it in your capital budget, then your expenses are only $50,000 and your budget will be in balance. (799, 802)
    c. Surplus of $5,000. Using an opportunity cost approach, a person holding bonds should count the rise in the bonds' market value as revenue. Here, wage income is $20,000 per year, interest income is 10,000, and the bond's value has increased by $10,000. Total income is $40,000. Income of $40,000 less expenses of $35,000 per year yields a budget surplus of $5,000. Unless there was a previous debt, there is no debt. (799)

2. As discussed on pages 801-802, the real deficit is the nominal deficit adjusted for inflation's effect on the debt. The definition of real deficit states: Real deficit = Nominal deficit − (Inflation × Total debt).

   a. $0: $100 billion − .05 × $2 trillion. (800-801)

   b. $35 billion: $20 billion − (−.03) × $500. (800-801)

   c. Surplus of $200 billion: $100 billion − .10 × $3 trillion. (800-801)

   d. $3.4 billion: $5 billion − .08 × $20 billion. (800-801)

3. **a.** $343 billion: Debt service payment = nominal interest rate × nominal debt. The nominal interest rate when expected inflation is fully adjusted is the real interest rate plus inflation (5+2). Debt service payment = .07 × $4.9 trillion. (801-802)

   b. $543 billion deficit: The nominal deficit is revenues less government expenditures (including debt service), $1.3 trillion − ($1.5 trillion + $.343 trillion). (801-802)

   c. $445 billion deficit: The real deficit = Nominal deficit − (Inflation × Total debt) = $.543 trillion − (.02 × $4.9 trillion). (801-802)

   d. Since bondholders must be compensated for the loss in the value of their bonds, they demand a nominal interest rate of 9% (5 + 4). Debt service payment is now $441 billion (.09 × $4.9 trillion). The nominal deficit is higher at $641 billion. ($1.3 trillion − ($1.5 trillion + $.441 trillion)). The real deficit has not changed. It is still $445 billion (The real deficit = Nominal deficit − (Inflation × Total debt) = $.641 trillion − (.04 × $4.9 trillion)). (801-802)

4. **a.** If the economy were at potential, government would collect $160 million more in taxes, reducing the deficit by that amount. There would be a structural deficit of $400 − $160 = $240 million. (799-800)

   b. The passive deficit is the deficit that occurs because the economy is below potential. The passive deficit is $800 million × 20 percent, or $160 million. (799-800)

━━━━━ ANSWERS ━━━━━

A BRAIN TEASER

1. If the deficit spending is used to increase the productivity of the nation, enabling the nation to experience much higher rates of economic growth, the income of the nation could expand faster than its debt. If this happens, the debt-to-GDP ratio gets smaller, the interest expense is less burdensome, and the debt will be easier to pay off. (805-806)

━━━━━ ANSWERS ━━━━━

MULTIPLE CHOICE

1. c A country has a budget deficit if it does not collect sufficient revenue to cover expenditures during the year. See page 798.

2. c The U.S. uses a cash flow accounting method, so changes affecting the future are not seen in the current budget. See page 808.

3. b Real deficit = nominal deficit −(inflation × total debt). See pages 800-801.

4. c Real surplus = nominal surplus + (inflation × total debt). See page 802.

5. c Real deficit = nominal deficit −(inflation × total debt). See pages 800-801.

6. b If creditors can forecast inflation perfectly, the interest rate will rise when inflation rises and the subsequent increase in interest payments will match the decline in the real debt due to higher inflation. See page 802.

7. c Debt must be judged relative to assets and to total GDP. See pages 802-803.

8. c See Figure 34-2 on page 806.

9. a The passive deficit or surplus is the deficit or surplus that exists because the economy is below or above potential. The structural deficit or surplus is the deficit or surplus that exists even when the economy is at potential. The text doesn't define primary or secondary deficits or surpluses. See pages 799-800.

10. a The passive deficit is the deficit that exists because the economy is below potential. The government would collect $20 billion more in revenue if the economy were at potential, so the passive deficit is $20 billion. See pages 799-800.

11. b Because government goes on forever it doesn't ever need to pay back its debt. Only about 75 percent of government debt is owed to other government agencies or to its own citizens. The other government debt is owed to foreign individuals. Government is better able to pay off debt when income rises. Both government and individuals pay interest on debt. See pages 804-805.

12. a Real growth will reduce the ratio of existing debt to GDP, so to hold the ratio constant a continual deficit is necessary. See page 805.

A1. a While payroll taxes for Social Security represent future obligations by government to pay social security benefits, they are counted as current revenue today and reduce the reported deficit (increase the reported surplus). See page 813-816.

A2. b The real problem is the mismatch between real demand and real supply of goods as the baby boomers retire and the demand for goods and services by retirees outstrips the supply produced by workers in 2020. Real solutions must address this problem and must either reduce benefits to seniors or reduce consumption by workers in 2020. The other solutions address the financial problem only. See pages 813-816.

━━━━━ ANSWERS ━━━━━

POTENTIAL ESSAY QUESTIONS

The following are annotated answers. They indicate the general idea behind the answer.

1. First, the government's life is unlimited and therefore it never has to settle its accounts. Second, it can pay off debt by creating money (which is not recommended, however). Third, much of the government's debt is internally held and therefore, on average as a group, people are neither richer nor poorer because of the debt (even though it may redistribute income from lower-income individuals to upper-income individuals).

2. When a society experiences real growth (growth adjusted for inflation), it becomes richer, and, being richer, it can handle more debt. Moreover, since in a growing economy a continual deficit is consistent with a constant ratio of debt to GDP, and since GDP serves as a measure of the government's ability to pay off debt, a country can run a continual deficit. Deficits should be viewed relative to GDP to determine their importance.

THE MODERN FISCAL POLICY DILEMMA

● CHAPTER AT A GLANCE

This review is based upon the learning objectives that open the chapter.

1. Ricardian equivalence is the theoretical proposition that deficits do not affect the level of output in the economy because individuals increase their savings to account for expected future tax payments to repay the deficit. (819)

   Basically, the Ricardian equivalence theorem says that increases in government spending are offset by equal declines in private spending. Although this argument is logical, it isn't the reason why economists before the 1930s didn't support activist fiscal policy. They didn't support it for political reasons.

2a. The precept of sound finance is that the government budget should always be balanced except in wartime. (818-820)

   This precept was driven less by economic logic and more by a tradition of believing the government should not direct the economy. During the Depression economists modified this precept to support government involvement under extreme conditions.

2b. Functional finance is the theoretical proposition that government should make spending and taxing decisions based on their effect on the economy, not on moralistic grounds that budgets should be balanced. (820-827)

   In this view, fiscal policy provides government with a steering wheel with which to direct the economy.

3. Economists began to recognize assumptions of the *AS/AD* and multiplier models that could lead to problems with fiscal policy as they applied functional finance precepts. (822-827)

   a. Financing the deficit doesn't have any offsetting effects.

      In reality, it often does. A particular problem is crowding out, which is the offsetting effect on private expenditures caused by the government's sale of bonds to finance expansionary fiscal policy.

   b. The government knows what the situation is.

      In reality the government must estimate what the situation is.

   c. The government knows the economy's potential income.

      In reality the government may not know what this level is.

   d. The government has flexibility in terms of spending and taxes.

      In reality, the government cannot change them quickly.

   e. The size of the government debt doesn't matter.

      In reality, the size of the debt often does matter.

   f. Fiscal policy doesn't negatively affect other government goals.

      In reality, it often does.

4.   An automatic stabilizer is any government
program or policy that will counteract the
business cycle without any new government
action. (827-829)

Automatic stabilizers include:
* *welfare payments*
* *unemployment insurance, and*
* *income tax system.*

*In a recession, government expenditures
automatically rise (because of increased
welfare payments and unemployment claims).
Taxes automatically decrease (because fewer
people are earning income). The budget
deficit increases and AE (total spending)
increases. The opposite occurs during an
upturn in the business cycle. Automatic
stabilizers help smooth out the business cycle.*

● SHORT-ANSWER QUESTIONS

1. What is the Ricardian equivalence theorem?

2. How could Classical economists believe in both sound finance and the Ricardian equivalence theorem?

3. How does sound finance differ from functional finance?

4. How do the six problems of fiscal policy limit its usefulness?

5. Some economists argue that crowding out totally undermines the activist view of fiscal policy. Explain their argument.

6. A country has just discontinued its unemployment insurance program and is experiencing a recession. How will this recession differ from earlier recessions?

7. In the short-run model, you want to lower interest rates and increase income. Would you propose expansionary monetary or fiscal policy? What concerns would you voice about this policy?

8. Suppose you are the featured speaker at a primer for the first-year Congresspeople. You have been asked to speak about fiscal policy. A Congressperson asks what fiscal policy tools Congress has to affect the economy, and what effect they have on the level of output. You tell her.

MATCHING THE TERMS
Match the terms to their definitions

___ **1.** automatic stabilizer

___ **2.** crowding out

___ **3.** functional finance

___ **4.** procyclical fiscal policy

___ **5.** Ricardian equivalence theorem

___ **6.** sound finance

a. A theoretical proposition that governments should make spending and taxation decisions on the basis of their affect on the economy, not on the basis of some moralistic principle that budgets should be balanced.

b. A view of public finance and fiscal policy that the government budget should always be balanced except in wartime.

c. The theoretical proposition that deficits do not affect the level of output in the economy because individuals increase their savings to account for expected future tax payments to repay the deficit.

d. Any government program or policy that will counteract the business cycle without any new government action.

e. The offsetting effect on private expenditures caused by the government's sale of bonds to finance expansionary fiscal policy.

f. Changes in government spending and taxes that increase the cyclical fluctuations in the economy instead of reducing them.

● PROBLEMS AND APPLICATIONS

1. Demonstrate your answers to the following questions both in words and with graphs:

   a. How does a government deficit affect the long-term interest rate in the loanable funds market?

   b. How does the change in interest rates in *a* impact the effectiveness of fiscal policy in the *AS/AD* model?

2. What fiscal policy did the United States adopt in 2009?

   a. Demonstrate your answer using the AS/AD model.

   b. Did most economists think this was the correct policy choice? Why or why not?

● A BRAIN TEASER

1. If someone believed that the Ricardian equivalence theorem was applicable to the real world, could that individual also accept the rules of functional finance?

● MULTIPLE CHOICE

Circle the one best answer for each of the following questions:

1. Fiscal policy is:
    a. the changing of the money supply to affect the economy.
    b. the changing of the money supply to stop any effect of government spending on the economy.
    c. the changing of taxes and spending to affect the level of output in the economy.
    d. a policy of maintaining a balanced budget except in wartime.

2. Sound finance holds that:
    a. government spending is directed toward sound investments.
    b. the government budget should always be balanced except in wartime.
    c. the government budget should be judged by its effect on the economy.
    d. government should always borrow money in a sound fashion when it runs a deficit.

3. The Ricardian equivalence theorem holds that:
    a. government spending is equivalent to private spending.
    b. financing a deficit by bonds will have the same effect as financing it through taxes.
    c. imposing taxes is the equivalent to confiscation of property by government.
    d. all spending in the economy is equivalent.

4. Economists who held that theoretically the Ricardian equivalence theorem was true:
    a. would not support sound finance.
    b. would not support functional finance.
    c. could support sound finance and/or functional finance.
    d. could support either sound finance or functional finance but not both.

5. Functional finance holds that:
    a. budgets should always deal with functional issues.
    b. government should make monetary policy decisions on the basis of their effect on the economy.
    c. government should make fiscal policy decisions on the basis of their effect on the economy.
    d. government's budgets should be balanced.

6. Crowding out is caused by:
    a. government running a deficit and selling bonds to finance that deficit.
    b. government printing money.
    c. government running a surplus and selling bonds and the people who buy those bonds selling their older bonds to the government.
    d. the tendency for new workers to replace more expensive older workers.

7. Automatic stabilizers:
    a. are government programs to employ workers during recessions.
    b. create government budget surpluses during economic recessions.
    c. are designed to reduce the price level directly.
    d. counteract both recessions and expansions through changes in spending without government action.

8. A state constitutional provision to maintain a balanced budget is an example of:
    a. an automatic stabilizer.
    b. monetary policy.
    c. procyclical policy.
    d. countercyclical policy.

9. If the government borrows money in the loanable funds market, the interest rate will likely:
    a. fall.
    b. rise.
    c. remain unchanged.
    d. rise and then fall.

● POTENTIAL ESSAY QUESTIONS

You may also see essay questions similar to the "Problems & Applications" and "A Brain Teaser" exercises.

1. How do the automatic stabilizers add stability to the business cycle? Are there any time lag (delay) problems associated with the use of the automatic stabilizers?

2. What is the crowding-out effect? What impact does this have on the effectiveness of fiscal policy in stimulating the economy during a recession? How large is the crowding-out effect, according to activist economists? Laissez-faire economists? What does the empirical evidence suggest about the size of the crowding-out effect?

3. Say you are a policy adviser to the government of a country that is growing at 6%, has inflation of 1%, and unemployment of 2%. You are hired by the government to advise them how they can improve the economy. What advice would you give?

ANSWERS

SHORT-ANSWER QUESTIONS

1. It is a theoretical proposition that deficits do not affect the level of output in the economy because individuals increase their savings to account for expected future tax payments to repay the deficit. (819)

2. They supported sound finance on the basis of politics; they supported the Ricardian equivalence theorem as a logical proposition that had only limited relevance to the real world. (818-820)

3. Sound finance holds that the budget should be balanced at all times; functional finance holds that spending and taxing decisions should be made on the basis of their effect on the economy. (818-822)

4. The six problems with fiscal policy limit its usefulness in the following ways: (1) Financing the deficit might have offsetting effects, reducing the net effect. (2) The government doesn't always know the current state of the economy and where it is headed, meaning these must be forecast; if you don't know the state of the economy you don't know what fiscal policy to use. (3) The government doesn't know what potential income is, meaning it must be estimated; if you estimated it wrong, you get the wrong fiscal policy. (4) The government cannot implement policy easily; if you can't implement it you can't use it. (5) The size of the debt might matter and since deficits create debt, you might not want to use it. Finally, (6) fiscal policy often negatively affects other government goals; if it does you might not use the policy even though it would change the economy in the direction you want. The bottom line is: In extreme cases, the appropriate fiscal policy is clear, but in most cases, the situation is not extreme. (822-827)

5. If crowding out is so strong that the reduced investment totally offsets the expansionary effect of fiscal spending, the net effect of fiscal policy can be zero. (823)

6. Unemployment insurance is an automatic stabilizer, a government program that counteracts the business cycle without any new government action. If income falls, automatic stabilizers will increase aggregate expenditures to counteract that decline. Likewise with increases in income: when income increases, automatic stabilizers decrease the size of the deficit. Eliminating unemployment insurance will eliminate this stabilization aspect of the policy and will contribute to making the recession more severe than it otherwise would have been. However, it would also make people more likely to accept lower wages and search harder for a job, thereby reducing the amount of unemployment. As usual, the answer depends. (827-828)

7. I would propose expansionary monetary policy. Expansionary fiscal policy would raise interest rates. I would emphasize that while the effect on income may be expansionary in the short run, in the long run, the expansionary monetary policy may simply lead to inflation. (822-823)

8. The tools of fiscal policy are changing taxes and changing government spending. Increasing taxes and lowering spending contract the economy; decreasing taxes and increasing spending expand the economy. (818, 827)

ANSWERS

MATCHING

1-d; 2-e; 3-a; 4-f; 5-c; 6-b.

ANSWERS

PROBLEMS AND APPLICATIONS

1. a. A government deficit increases the demand for loanable funds. The following graph shows this as a shift in the demand curve from D_0 to D_1. An increase in the demand for loanable funds increases the long-term interest rate, in the graph, from i_0 to i_1. (822-823)

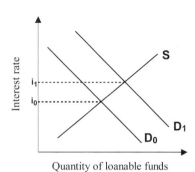

Quantity of loanable funds

b. An increase in the deficit (caused by increased government spending or a reduction in taxes) shifts the AD curve to the right, this is illustrated in the graph below as a shift in the AD curve to the right from AD_0 to AD_1. The increase in the interest rate increases the cost of borrowing for investment, which reduces investment expenditures causing the AD curve to shift to the left by a multiple of the decrease in investment expenditures. This offsets the impact of fiscal policy on the economy somewhat and is shown in the graph as a shift in the AD curve from AD_1 to AD_2 (822-823)

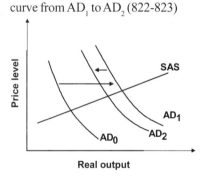

Real output

2. The U.S. adopted expansionary fiscal policy.
   a. Expansionary fiscal policy will shift the AD curve to the right (AD_0 to AD_1), increasing income and the price level. The expansionary fiscal policy will likely result in some crowding out of private investment, meaning it will shift back to the left slightly (AD_1 to AD_2). See the graph in the next column. (830-831)
   b. Most economists agreed that expansionary fiscal policy was necessary to help get the U.S. out of the severe recession. In general, if the economy is headed towards a depression, most economists support functional finance in the form of expansionary fiscal policy. (830-831)

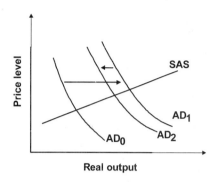

Real output

A BRAIN TEASER

1. Since the rules of functional finance state that government should make taxing and spending decisions on the basis of their effect on the economy, and the Ricardian equivalence theory states that methods of financing make no difference to the real economy, they could accept the rules of functional finance. But, the functional finance policy they would agree with would not be what is normally considered functional financial policy, which is based on the Keyesian model being the true model. (818-822)

MULTIPLE CHOICE

1. c   See how fiscal policy is defined on pages 818-819.

2. b   Sound finance holds the moral stance that government should stay out of the economy, that is, the government budget should always be balanced. See pages 818-819.

3. b   According to the Ricardian equivalence theorem people will save the money needed to repay bonds that will come due in the future, so that financing by bonds will have the same effect as financing through taxes. See pages 819-820.

4. c   The Ricardian equivalence theorem states that it doesn't matter if spending is financed by taxes or by bonds. The effect

will be the same — none. Sound finance doesn't depend on the Ricardian equivalence theorem, it is a moral position. Functional finance just says that government should make the decision whether to run a deficit based on how it will affect the economy. Someone who holds the Ricardian equivalence theorem to be true would recommend a sound finance of no deficit. See pages 818-822.

5. c   Functional finance rejects the moralistic position of sound finance and says government should make decisions based on how fiscal policy will affect the economy. See pages 820-822.

6. a   As discussed on page 822 crowding out is the offsetting of a change in government expenditures by a change in private expenditures in the opposite direction. Answer c, if you could follow it, is nonsensical.

7. d   Automatic stabilizers are welfare payments, unemployment insurance, and taxes that raise income during recessions and lower income during expansions. See pages 827-829.

8. c   State balanced budget provisions mean that states cut spending and increase taxes during recessions and raise spending and reduce taxes during expansions. These actions exacerbate the business cycle and are therefore procyclical. See page 828.

9. b   When the government borrows money, the demand for loanable funds rises, leading to a rise in the interest rate. See pages 822-823.

■■■ **ANSWERS** ■■■

POTENTIAL ESSAY QUESTIONS

The following are annotated answers. They indicate the general idea behind the answer.

1.   When the economy is in a recession and total spending is too low, then government spend-

ing automatically rises while tax collections automatically fall (the government automatically incurs a deficit). This helps to stimulate total spending and cushion the downturn in the economy. The opposite is true when the economy is expanding. Note that these changes take place while the income level falls and expands. Therefore, there are no time lag problems accompanying the automatic stabilizers.

2.   The crowding-out effect states that deficit spending financed by borrowing will increase interest rates and therefore crowd out private spending. Any "crowding out" associated with deficit spending renders fiscal policy less effective in stimulating total spending and therefore the economy during a recession. Activist economists argue that the crowding out effect is relatively small. Committed laissez-faire economists argue that there is a total crowding out effect, which renders fiscal policy impotent in stimulating total spending. Some laissez-faire economists have argued that the effect of deficit spending may even be negative on the economy if private spending is more productive than government spending. The empirical evidence on the size of the crowding-out effect is mixed and has not resolved the debate. However, everyone agrees that the closer the economy comes to its potential income level, the greater is the crowding-out effect.

3.   I would start by pointing out that by most western economy standards the economy is going quite well, and that perhaps they should be satisfied with what they have. If they insist on policy actions, I would try to find out more information about the economy. For example, I would be worried that with high growth and low unemployment, inflation may soon become a problem. Thus I would be very hesitant to use any demand-based policy. With growth of 6%, I would assume that supply incentives are working, but I would consider them carefully to see if a technology or pro-savings policy may make sense.

Pretest
Chapters 30-35

VI

Take this test in test conditions, giving yourself a limited amount of time to complete the questions. Ideally, check with your professor to see how much time he or she allows for an average multiple choice question and multiply this by 30. This is the time limit you should set for yourself for this pretest. If you do not know how much time your teacher would allow, we suggest 1 minute per question, or about 30 minutes.

1. For every financial asset there is:
   a. corresponding financial liability.
   b. corresponding financial liability if the financial asset is financed.
   c. a real liability.
   d. a corresponding real asset.

2. Which of the following is not a function of money?
   a. Medium of exchange.
   b. Unit of account.
   c. Store of wealth.
   d. Equity instrument.

3. Which of the following is not included in the M_1 definition of money?
   a. Checking accounts.
   b. Currency.
   c. Traveler's checks.
   d. Savings accounts.

4. Assuming individuals hold no cash, the reserve requirement is 20 percent, and banks keep no excess reserves, an increase in an initial inflow of $100 into the banking system will cause an increase in the money supply of:
   a. $20.
   b. $50.
   c. $100.
   d. $500.

5. If banks hold excess reserves whereas before they did not, the money multiplier:
   a. will become larger.
   b. will become smaller.
   c. will be unaffected.
   d. might increase or might decrease.

6. Which of the following is the path through which contractionary monetary policy works?
   a. Money down implies interest up implies investment down implies income down.
   b. Money down implies interest down implies investment down implies income down.
   c. Money down implies interest up implies investment up implies income down.
   d. Money down implies interest down implies investment up implies income down.

7. Assuming $c = .2$ and $r = .1$, the money multiplier would be:
   a. 1.
   b. 2.
   c. 3.
   d. 4.

8. The primary way the Fed conducts monetary policy is:
   a. open market operations.
   b. changing the discount rate.
   c. changing the reserve requirement.
   d. imposing credit controls.

9. If the Fed wants to increase the money supply, it should:
   a. buy bonds.
   b. sell bonds.
   c. pass a law that interest rates rise.
   d. pass a law that interest rates fall.

10. Assuming the Fed is following the Taylor Rule, if inflation is 3 percent, target inflation is 2 percent, and output is 1 percent above potential, what would you predict would be the Fed funds rate target?
    a. 4 percent.
    b. 5 percent.
    c. 5.5 percent.
    d. 6 percent.

11. What role do economists agree the central bank has in a financial crisis?
    a. Lender of last resort.
    b. Contractionary fiscal policy to reduce leverage.
    c. Expansionary fiscal policy to reduce leverage.
    d. No role.

12. Why weren't economists especially concerned that the 1929 stock crash could cause a depression?
    a. Because only real wealth, not nominal wealth had been destroyed.
    b. Although part of the productive capacity of the economy had been reduced, no nominal wealth had been destroyed.
    c. Because only nominal wealth, not real wealth had been destroyed. The productive capacity of the economy had not changed.
    d. Because they were more concerned with deflation than inflation.

13. How does the depression model differ from the normal AS/AD model?
    a. The depression model has no money wealth, interest rate or international effects.
    b. In the AS/AD model, the AD curve is fixed.
    c. In the depression model expectations are endogenous.
    d. They are the same model.

14. Which of the following is an example of an action taken during the treatment phase of dealing with a financial crisis?
    a. Expansionary monetary and fiscal policy.
    b. Setting a liquidity trap.
    c. Injecting capital into financial institutions.
    d. Establishing institutional structures to prevent recurrence.

15. Moral hazard is a problem that arises when:
    a. people are required to bear the negative consequences of their actions.
    b. people don't have to bear the negative consequences of their actions.
    c. people benefit from the negative actions of others.
    d. government discourages companies from taking risks.

16. If productivity growth is 2 percent and inflation is 5 percent, on average nominal wage increases will be:
    a. 2 percent.
    b. 3 percent.
    c. 5 percent.
    d. 7 percent.

17. Assuming velocity is relatively constant and real income is relatively stable, an increase in the money supply of 40 percent will be associated with an approximate change in the price level of:
    a. 4 percent.
    b. 40 percent.
    c. 80 percent.
    d. zero percent.

18. The inflation tax is:
    a. a tax placed by government on inflators.
    b. a tax placed on inflators.
    c. a tax on the holders of cash.
    d. a tax on holders of goods whose price is inflating.

19. Individuals who hold an institutional theory of inflation argue:
    a. the equation of exchange is incorrect.
    b. the equation of exchange should be read from right to left.
    c. the equation of exchange should be read from left to right.
    d. both the quantity theory and the equation of exchange are incorrect.

20. The short-run Phillips curve shifts around because of changes in:
    a. the money supply.
    b. expectations of employment.
    c. expectations of inflation.
    d. expectations of real income.

21. If the economy is at Point A in the Phillips curve graph below, what prediction would you make for unemployment?

    a. It will increase.
    b. It will decrease.
    c. It will remain constant.
    d. It will immediately fall to zero.

22. A deficit is:
a. the total amount of money that a country owes.
b. the shortfall of payments under revenues in a particular time period.
c. the shortfall of revenues under payments in a particular time period.
d. accumulated debt.

23. If the nominal surplus is $200 billion, inflation is 10 percent, and total debt is $2 trillion:
a. the real surplus is zero.
b. the real deficit is $100 billion.
c. the real surplus is $400 billion.
d. the real surplus is $2.2 trillion.

24. The real deficit is $100 billion; inflation is 4 percent; total debt is $2 trillion. The nominal deficit is:
a. zero.
b. $120 billion.
c. $180 billion.
d. $200 billion.

25. The portion of the budget deficit or surplus that would exist even if the economy were at its potential level of income is called the:
a. structural deficit or surplus.
b. passive deficit or surplus.
c. primary deficit or surplus.
d. secondary deficit or surplus.

26. One of the reasons government debt is different from individual debt is:
a. government does not pay interest on its debt.
b. government never really needs to pay back its debt.
c. all government debt is owed to other government agencies or to its own citizens.
d. the ability of a government to pay off is debt is unrelated to income.

27. Sound finance holds that:
a. government spending is directed toward sound investments.
b. the government budget should always be balanced except in wartime.
c. the government budget should be judged by its effect on the economy.
d. government should always borrow money in a sound fashion when it runs a deficit.

28. The Ricardian equivalence theorem holds that:
a. government spending is equivalent to private spending.
b. financing a deficit by bonds will have the same effect as financing it through taxes.
c. imposing taxes is the equivalent to confiscation of property by government.
d. all spending in the economy is equivalent.

29. Crowding out is caused by:
a. government running a deficit and selling bonds to finance that deficit.
b. government printing money.
c. government running a surplus and selling bonds and the people who buy those bonds selling their older bonds to the government.
d. the tendency for new workers to replace more expensive older workers.

30. Automatic stabilizers:
a. are government programs to employ workers during recessions.
b. create government budget surpluses during economic recessions.
c. are designed to reduce the price level directly.
d. counteract both recessions and expansions through changes in spending without government action.

ANSWERS

1.	a	(30:1)	**16.**	d	(33:4)
2.	d	(30:4)	**17.**	b	(33:6)
3.	d	(30:5)	**18.**	c	(33:9)
4.	d	(30:10)	**19.**	b	(33:11)
5.	b	(30:13)	**20.**	c	(33:15)
6.	a	(31:3)	**21.**	a	(33:18)
7.	d	(31:11)	**22.**	c	(34:1)
8.	a	(31:13)	**23.**	c	(34:4)
9.	a	(31:14)	**24.**	c	(34:5)
10.	d	(31:18)	**25.**	a	(34:9)
11.	a	(32:1)	**26.**	b	(34:11)
12.	c	(32:2)	**27.**	b	(35:2)
13.	c	(32:9)	**28.**	b	(35:3)
14.	a	(32:11)	**29.**	a	(35:6)
15.	b	(32:14)	**30.**	d	(35:7)

Key: The figures in parentheses refer to multiple choice question and chapter numbers. For example (1:2) is multiple choice question 2 from chapter 1.

INTERNATIONAL FINANCIAL POLICY

36

● CHAPTER AT A GLANCE

This review is based upon the learning objectives that open the chapter.

1a. The balance of payments is a country's record of all transactions between its residents and the residents of all foreign countries. (836-838)

It is broken down into the current account and the financial and capital account.

Remember: If it is a minus (plus) sign, money is going out (coming in). Moreover, if foreigners are buying our goods, services, or assets, that represents a demand for the dollar (an inflow) in international exchange rate markets. If we buy foreign goods, services, or assets, that represents a supply of dollars (an outflow).

1b. The balance of trade is the difference between the value of goods and services a nation exports and the value of goods and services it imports. (838)

The balance of merchandise trade is often discussed in the popular press as a summary of how the U.S. is doing in international markets. However, it only includes goods exported and imported—not services. Trade in services is just as important as trade in merchandise, so economists pay more attention to the balance of trade, which is combined balance on goods and services.

1c. Since the balance of payments consists of both the financial and capital account and the current account, if the financial and capital account is in surplus and the current account is in deficit, there can still be a balance of payments surplus. (838-840)

The financial and capital account measures the flows of payments between countries for assets such as stocks, bonds, and real estate. The current (or trade) account measures the flows of payments for goods and services.

1d. A deficit in the balance of payments means that the private quantity supplied of a currency exceeds the private quantity demanded. A surplus in the balance of payments means the opposite. (840-842)

Whenever the exchange rate is above equilibrium (below equilibrium), the country will experience a balance of payments deficit (surplus).

2. Four fundamental determinants of exchange rates are prices, interest rates, income, and trade policy. (842-843)

A decrease in the value of a currency can be caused by:

● *An increase in the nation's inflation rate.*
● *A decrease in the nation's interest rates.*
● *An increase in the nation's income.*
● *A decrease in the nation's import restrictions.*

3a. Monetary policy affects exchange rates through the interest rate path, the income path, and the price-level path, as shown in the diagram on page 845. (843-846)

Expansionary monetary policy (increasing the money supply) lowers exchange rates. It decreases the relative price of a country's currency. Contractionary monetary policy has the opposite effect.

3b. Fiscal policy affects exchange rates through the interest rate path, the income path, and the price-level path, as shown in the diagram on page 847. (846-847)

The net effect of fiscal policy on exchange rates is ambiguous.

✔ *Be able to explain why!*

4. A country fixes the exchange rate by standing ready to buy and sell its currency any time at the fixed exchange rate. (847-850)

It is easier for a country to maintain a fixed exchange rate below equilibrium. All it has to do is print and sell enough domestic currency to hold the value down.

However, if a country wants to maintain a fixed exchange rate above long-run equilibrium, it can do so only as long as it has the foreign currency (official) reserves to buy up its currency. Once it runs out of official reserves, it will be unable to intervene, and must either borrow, use indirect methods (domestic fiscal and monetary policies), ask other countries to buy its currency (to sell their currency), or devalue its currency.

In reality, because a country has a limited amount of official reserves, it only uses strategic currency stabilization (not a fixed exchange rate policy).

5a. Purchasing power parity is a method of calculating exchange rates so that various currencies will each buy an equal basket of goods and services. (850-851)

The PPP (Purchasing Power Parity) is one method of estimating long-run exchange rates.

5b. A real exchange rate is an exchange rate adjusted for differential inflation in countries. (851-852)

%Δ real exchange rate = %Δ nominal exchange rate + (domestic inflation − foreign inflation).

6a. Three exchange rate régimes are:
- *Fixed exchange rate*: The government chooses an exchange rate and offers to buy and sell currencies at that rate.
- *Flexible exchange rate*: Determination of exchange rates is left totally up to the market.
- *Partially flexible exchange rate*: The government sometimes affects the exchange rate and sometimes leaves it to the market. (852-854)

Which is best is debatable.

6b. Fixed exchange rates provide international monetary stability and force governments to make adjustments to meet their international problems. (This is *also* a disadvantage.) If they become unfixed, they create monetary instability. (852-853)

✔ *Know these advantages and disadvantages!*

6c. Flexible exchange rate régimes provide for orderly incremental adjustment of exchange rates rather than large sudden jumps, and allow governments to be flexible in conducting domestic monetary and fiscal policy. (This is *also* a disadvantage.) They are, however, susceptible to private speculation. (853-854)

✔ *Know these advantages and disadvantages!*

6d. Partially flexible exchange rate régimes combine the advantages and disadvantages of fixed and flexible exchange rates. (854)

Most countries have opted for this policy. However, if the market exchange rate is below the rate the government desires, and the government does not have sufficient official reserves (to buy and increase the demand for its currency), then it must undertake policies that will either increase the private demand for its currency or decrease the private supply. Doing so either involves using traditional macro policy—fiscal and monetary policy—to influence the economy, or using trade policy to affect the level of exports and imports.

7. The advantages of a common currency:
- creates strong political ties
- reduces the cost of trade
- facilitates price comparisons
- creates a larger single market.

The disadvantages of a common currency:
- eliminates independent monetary policy.
- loss of a national currency. (855-856)

✔ *Know the advantages and disadvantages of a common currency.*

The most important disadvantage is loss of independent monetary policy. A country loses the ability to increase the money supply by itself in order to fight a recession.

See also, Appendix A: "History of Exchange Rate Systems."

● SHORT-ANSWER QUESTIONS

1. Distinguish between the balance of payments and the balance of trade.

2. How can a country simultaneously have a balance of payments deficit and a balance of trade surplus?

3. How does each part of the balance of payments relate to the supply and demand for currencies?

4. What are the four fundamental determinants of exchange rates?

5. If a country runs expansionary monetary policy, what will likely happen to the exchange rate?

6. If a country runs expansionary fiscal policy, what will likely happen to the exchange rate?

7. If the demand and supply for a country's currency depends upon demand for imports and exports, and demand for foreign and domestic assets, how can a country fix its exchange rate?

8. How do market exchange rates differ from exchange rates using the purchasing power parity concept?

9. How do inflation rate differentials affect the real exchange rate?

10. Differentiate among fixed, flexible, and partially flexible exchange rates.

11. Which are preferable, fixed or flexible exchange rates?

12. You are advising Great Britain about whether it should join the European Monetary Union. What arguments can you give in support of joining? What arguments can you give against joining?

MATCHING THE TERMS
Match the terms to their definitions

___ **1.** balance of merchandise trade	**a.**	A method of calculating exchange rates that attempts to value currencies at a rate such that each will buy an equal basket of goods.
___ **2.** balance of payments	**b.**	A country's record of all transactions between its residents and the residents of all foreign countries.
___ **3.** balance of trade	**c.**	A regime in which government sometimes affects the exchange rate and sometimes leaves it to the market.
___ **4.** currency stabilization	**d.**	A regime in which a government chooses an exchange rate and offers to buy and sell currencies at that rate.
___ **5.** currency support	**e.**	A regime in which the determination of the value of a currency is left up to the market.
___ **6.** current account	**f.**	The buying of a currency by a government to maintain its value above its long-run equilibrium.
___ **7.** financial and capital account	**g.**	The difference between the value of goods and services a nation exports and the value of goods and services it imports.
___ **8.** fixed exchange rate	**h.**	Government holdings of foreign currencies.
___ **9.** flexible exchange rate	**i.**	The part of the balance of payments account that lists all long-term flows of payments.
___ **10.** forex market	**j.**	The part of the balance of payments account that lists all short-term flows of payments.
___ **11.** official reserves	**k.**	The difference between the value of the goods exported and the value of the goods imported.
___ **12.** partially flexible exchange rate	**l.**	Foreign exchange market.
___ **13.** purchasing power parity	**m.**	Buying and selling of a currency by the government to offset temporary fluctuations.
___ **14.** real exchange rate	**n.**	Exchange rate adjusted for inflation differentials.

● PROBLEMS AND APPLICATIONS

1. State for each whether the transaction shows up on the balance of payments current account, the balance of payments financial and capital account, or neither.

   a. An American buys 100 shares of stock of Mercedes Benz, a German company.

   b. A Japanese businessperson buys Ameritec, an American bank.

   c. An American auto manufacturer buys $20 million in auto parts from a Japanese company.

   d. An American buys 100 shares of IBM stock.

   e. Saturn exports 10,000 cars to Germany.

   f. Toyota Motor Corporation, a Japanese firm, makes a $1 million profit from its plant in Kentucky, USA.

2. For each of the following, state who is demanding and who is supplying what currency:

   a. A French person buys a set of china from a U.S. firm.

   b. A U.S. tourist in Japan buys a Japanese kimono from a department store.

   c. An Italian exchange rate trader believes that the exchange rate value of the dollar will rise.

   d. A Chinese investor invests in Germany.

3. Draw supply and demand curves for British pounds, showing equilibrium quantity and price. Price is shown by price of pounds in dollars.

   a. What is the demand for dollars in this case?

   b. Explain a movement up along the supply curve.

   c. Explain a movement down along the demand curve.

   d. What would be the effect on the price of pounds if there were an increase in demand for pounds by Americans? Show this graphically.

   e. What would be the effect on the price of pounds if there were an increase in demand for dollars by the British? Show this graphically.

4. For each of the following, show graphically what would happen to the market for British pounds. Assume there are only two countries, the United States and Britain.

   a. Income in Britain rises.

b. Income in the United States rises.

c. The prices of goods in the United States increase.

d. Interest rates rise in Britain.

e. The value of the pound is expected to fall.

5. State what will happen to the real exchange rate of the dollar in the following instances:

a. U.S. inflation is 2 percent, Japan's inflation is 5 percent, the U.S. dollar rises 3 percent.

b. U.S. inflation is 4 percent, Japan's inflation is 1 percent, the U.S. dollar rises 2 percent.

c. U.S. deflation is 1 percent, Japan's inflation is 1 percent, the U.S. dollar falls 4 percent.

d. U.S. inflation is 5 percent, Japan's inflation is 2 percent, the U.S. dollar falls 1 percent.

● A BRAIN TEASER

1. What could cause the United States to temporarily experience an increase in its balance of payments deficit even though there is downward movement in the exchange rate value of the dollar? (Hint: Think in terms of demand and supply analysis.)

● MULTIPLE CHOICE

Circle the one best answer for each of the following questions:

1. An exchange rate is the:
   a. rate the Fed charges commercial banks for loans.
   b. rate the Fed charges individuals for loans.
   c. rate at which one country's currency can be exchanged for another country's currency.
   d. speed at which exchange occurs.

2. If a country has perfectly flexible exchange rates and is running a current account deficit, it is running:
   a. a financial and capital account surplus.
   b. a financial and capital account deficit.
   c. a government financial account surplus.
   d. a government financial account deficit.

3. In the balance of payments accounts, net investment income shows up in:
   a. the current account.
   b. the financial and capital account.
   c. the government financial account.
   d. Net investment income is not an entry in the balance of payments.

4. If the government financial account is significantly in surplus, the country is likely:
   a. trying to hold up its exchange rate.
   b. trying to push down its exchange rate.
   c. trying to have no effect on its exchange rate.
   d. sometimes trying to increase and sometimes trying to decrease its exchange rate.

5. In recent years, the United States has:
   a. generally run a balance of trade surplus.
   b. generally run a balance of trade deficit.
   c. sometimes run a balance of trade surplus and sometimes run a balance of trade deficit.
   d. generally run a balance of trade equality.

6. In recent years, the United States has:
   a. generally run a financial and capital account surplus.
   b. generally run a financial and capital account deficit.
   c. sometimes run a financial and capital account surplus and sometimes run a financial and capital account deficit.
   d. generally run a financial and capital account equality.

7. If there is a black market for a currency, the
    country probably has a:
    a. nonconvertible currency.
    b. fixed exchange rate currency.
    c. flexible exchange rate currency.
    d. partially flexible exchange rate currency.

8. Assuming flexible exchange rates, if the
    European demand for U.S. imports in-
    creases, one would expect the price of euros
    in terms of dollars to:
    a. rise.
    b. fall.
    c. remain unchanged.
    d. sometimes rise and sometimes fall.

9. Assuming flexible exchange rates, if the U.S.
    demand for European imports increases, one
    would expect the price of euros in terms of
    dollars to:
    a. rise.
    b. fall.
    c. remain unchanged.
    d. sometimes rise and sometimes fall.

    Use the following graph of the foreign
    exchange market to answer Questions 10 – 12:

Quantity of euros

10. If U.S. income increases the:
    a. supply curve will shift out to the right.
    b. supply curve will shift in to the left.
    c. demand curve will shift out to the right.
    d. demand curve will shift in to the left.

11. If European interest rates increase relative to
    world interest rates:
    a. only the supply curve will shift out to the
       right.
    b. only the demand curve will shift in to the left.
    c. the supply curve will shift in to the left and
       the demand curve will shift out to the right.
    d. the supply curve will shift out to the right
       and the demand curve will shift in to the left.

12. If European inflation increases relative to world
    inflation:
    a. only the supply curve will shift out to the
       right.
    b. only the demand curve will shift in to the
       left.
    c. the supply curve will shift in to the left and
       the demand curve will shift out to the right.
    d. the supply curve will shift out to the right
       and the demand curve will shift in to the left.

13. If a country with flexible exchange rates runs
    expansionary monetary policy, in the short
    run one would expect the value of its
    exchange rate to:
    a. rise.
    b. fall.
    c. be unaffected.
    d. sometimes rise and sometimes fall.

14. Expansionary monetary policy has a tendency
    to:
    a. push interest rates up and exchange rates
       down.
    b. push interest rates down and exchange rates
       down.
    c. push income down and exchange rates
       down.
    d. push imports down and exchange rates
       down.

15. Contractionary monetary policy has a ten-
    dency to:
    a. push interest rates up and exchange rates
       down.
    b. push interest rates down and exchange rates
       down.
    c. push income down and imports down.
    d. push imports down and exchange rates
       down.

16. Refer to the graph below. If the U.S. govern-
    ment wants to fix its convertible currency at
    exchange rate P_1, it will have to:

Quantity of U.S. dollars

a. supply official reserves in exchange for dollars.

b. supply dollars in exchange for official reserves.

c. disallow currency conversion except at the official rate P_1.

d. supply both official reserves and dollars because excess supply of dollars is so large.

17. Say the Bangladeshi taka is valued at 42 taka to $1. Also say that you can buy the same basket of goods for 10 taka that you can buy for $1. In terms of dollars the purchasing power parity of the taka is:

a. overvalued.

b. undervalued.

c. not distorted.

d. nonconvertible.

18. Suppose inflation in the United States is 3 percent and inflation in Europe is 4 percent. If the U.S. dollar exchange rate falls by 5 percent relative to the euro, the real exchange rate of the dollar relative to the euro has:

a. risen 2 percent.

b. risen 6 percent.

c. fallen 2 percent.

d. fallen 6 percent.

19. If a country has fixed exchange rates:

a. the government need not worry about the exchange rate.

b. governments are committed to buying and selling currencies at a fixed rate.

c. the exchange rate is set by law.

d. the exchange rate has a fixed component and a flexible component.

20. If a country has a flexible exchange rate, the exchange rate:

a. is determined by flexible government policy.

b. is determined by market forces.

c. fluctuates continually, changing by at least 1 percent per year.

d. fluctuates continually, changing by at least 10 percent per year.

21. Compared to a fixed exchange rate system, a flexible exchange rate system:

a. allows countries more flexibility in their monetary policies.

b. allows countries less flexibility in their monetary policies.

c. has no effect on monetary policies.

d. allows countries more flexibility in their industrial policies.

22. A reason why a country might choose to join a currency union is:

a. so that its central bank can monetize the country's debt.

b. to broaden the marketplace by reducing costs of trade.

c. to reduce the demand for the common currency as a reserve currency.

d. to increase its sense of nationalism.

A1. The gold standard is a type of:

a. fixed exchange rate.

b. partially flexible exchange rate.

c. flexible exchange rate.

d. nonconvertible exchange rate.

A2. The gold specie flow mechanism works primarily by flows of:

a. money from one country to another.

b. services from one country to another.

c. merchandise from one country to another.

d. exchange rates from one country to another.

A3. Under the gold standard, if a country has a balance of payments deficit:

a. gold would flow out of the country.

b. gold would flow into the country.

c. the country's exchange rate would rise.

d. the country's exchange rate would fall.

A4. SDRs refers to:

a. Specie Draft Rights.

b. Specie Drawing Rights.

c. Special Drawing Rights.

d. Special Draft Rights.

● POTENTIAL ESSAY QUESTIONS

You may also see essay questions similar to the "Problems & Applications" and "A Brain Teaser" exercises.

1. How are a government's exchange rate policy and the government financial and capital account in the balance of payments related? Is it easier for a government to push the value of its currency up or down? Why?

2. Explain how fixed, flexible (or floating), and partially flexible exchange rates are determined. What are the advantages and the disadvantages of each? Why do most nations have a partially flexible exchange rate policy?

ANSWERS

SHORT-ANSWER QUESTIONS

1. The balance of payments is a country's record of all transactions between its residents and the residents of all foreign nations. It is divided into the current account and the financial and capital account. The balance of trade is one part of the balance of payments— specifically that part dealing with the exchange of goods and services. (836-838)

2. As discussed in question 1, the balance of trade is one part of the balance of payments. Thus, if other parts of the international payments—for example, the financial and capital account—are in deficit, the balance of trade could still be in surplus. (839-840)

3. The balance of payments records the flow of a currency in and out of a country (1) in order to buy and sell goods and services in the current account, (2) in order to buy and sell assets along with payments resulting from previous purchases of assets in the financial and capital account, and (3) in order to affect the value of a country's currency in government transactions account. To buy foreign goods and assets one must supply domestic currency and demand foreign currency. Therefore, the balance of payments records the demand and supply of a country's currency during a given period of time. (840-842)

4. Four fundamental determinants of the value of a country's exchange rate are (1) domestic income, (2) domestic price level, (3) domestic interest rates, and (4) trade restrictions. (842-843)

5. Expansionary monetary policy tends to push income and prices up and interest rates down. All these phenomena tend to push the exchange rate down. (843-846)

6. Expansionary fiscal policy tends to push income, prices, and interest rates up. Higher income and higher prices increase imports and put downward pressure on exchange rates. Higher interest rates push exchange rates in the opposite direction, so the net effect of expansionary fiscal policy on exchange rates is unclear. (846-847)

7. The current account and financial and capital account reflect private demand and supply of a country's currency. If the domestic government financial account were zero, then the currency's value is market-determined. If a country wants to fix the value of its currency to maintain its value at the fixed value, the government must buy and sell its currency using official reserves. Buying (selling) one's own currency shows up as a positive (negative) in the U.S. government financial account. (847-849)

8. Market exchange rates are determined by the demand and supply of a country's currency. Since not all goods, services, and assets produced in a country can be traded internationally, the value of an exchange rate may not reflect the relative prices in each country. The purchasing power parity concept adjusts the value of a country's currency by determining the rate at which equivalent baskets of goods can be purchased in each country. (850-851)

9. If inflation is higher in a foreign country compared to the domestic country, and the nominal exchange rate doesn't change, the real exchange rate for the domestic country will fall. This is because the domestic currency will not be able to purchase as many foreign goods as before the foreign inflation. (851-852)

10. A fixed exchange rate is an exchange rate that the government chooses and then holds, by standing ready to buy and sell at that rate. Flexible exchange rates are exchange rates that are determined by the market without any government intervention. Partially flexible exchange rates are exchange rates that are determined by the market but are sometimes also affected by government intervention. (852)

11. It depends. Each has its advantages and disadvantages. Flexible exchange rates give a country more control over domestic policy, but can also cause large fluctuations in the value of the country's currency, hurting trade. With fixed exchange rates, such fluctuations can be avoided. (852-854)

12. The disadvantages of joining the European Monetary Union are that Great Britain would

have to give up the pound as its currency, a source of national pride, and it would have to give up independent monetary policy. The advantages are that if the euro becomes an important reserve currency, Britain will enjoy lower interest rates and its producers and consumers will have greater access to a larger market. (855-856)

——— **ANSWERS** ———

MATCHING

1-k; 2-b; 3-g; 4-m; 5-f; 6-j; 7-i; 8-d; 9-e; 10-l; 11-h; 12-c; 13-a; 14-n.

——— **ANSWERS** ———

PROBLEMS AND APPLICATIONS

1. a. Financial and capital account. This is a long-term outflow. (839-840)
    b. Financial and capital account. This is a long-term inflow. (839-840)
    c. Current account. These are merchandise imports, a short-term flow. (838)
    d. Neither. It is a domestic transaction. (836-838)
    e. Current account. These are merchandise exports, a short-term flow. (838)
    f. Current account. This is net investment income. (838)

2. a. The French person supplies euros and demands dollars because the French person must sell euros to get U.S. dollars to purchase the china. (840-842)
    b. The U.S. tourist supplies dollars and demands Japanese yen because the tourist has to sell dollars to get yen. (840-842)
    c. The Italian trader will supply euros and demand U.S. dollars because he/she wants to purchase the currency that is believed to rise, the dollar. The trader must sell euros to get the dollars. (840-842)
    d. The Chinese investor will supply yuan and demand euros because the Chinese investor needs euros to invest in Germany. (840-842)

3. A market for British pounds is shown below. Price of pounds in U.S. dollars is on the vertical axis and quantity of pounds is on the horizontal axis. Equilibrium price and quantity are determined by where they intersect. (See Figure 36-1 on page 840)

    a. If only two countries exist, the United States and Britain, the demand for dollars is the supply of pounds. (840-842)
    b. As the dollar value of the pound rises, individuals will supply more pounds. (840-842)
    c. As the dollar value of the pound declines, individuals will demand more pounds. (840-842)
    d. An increase in the demand for pounds by Americans would shift the demand for pounds as shown in the graph below. The price of pounds in dollars would rise. (840-842)

    e. An increase in the demand for dollars by the British is equivalent to an increase in the supply of pounds. The supply curve for pounds would shift to the right as shown in the graph below. The price of pounds in dollars would fall. (840-842)

4. a. Demand for imports by the British rises; hence demand for dollars (supply of pounds) rises. This is shown in the graph below. (840-842)

    b. Demand for imports by Americans rises; hence demand for pounds rises. This is shown in the graph below. (840-842)

    c. Demand for imports by the British falls; hence demand for dollars (supply of pounds) falls. This is shown in the graph below. (840-842)

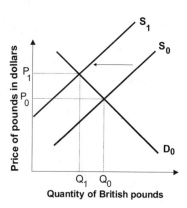

    d. Demand for British assets will rise; hence the demand for the pound rises. This is shown in the graph below. (840-842)

    e. The demand for the pound falls. This is shown in the graph below. (840-842)

5. a. Remains the same $[3+(2-5)]$. (851-852)
    b. Rises 5 percent $[2+(4-1)]$. (851-852)
    c. Falls 6 percent $[-4+(-1-1)]$. (851-852)
    d. Rises 2 percent $[-1+(5-2)]$. (851-852)

======== **ANSWERS** ========

A BRAIN TEASER

1. A decrease in the demand for the dollar and/or an increase in the supply of the dollar in international exchange rate markets will create a temporary balance of payments deficit (because the quantity of dollars supplied will exceed the quantity demanded—imports will exceed exports). The balance of payments deficit will also put downward pressure on the exchange rate value of the dollar. (840-842)

======== **ANSWERS** ========

MULTIPLE CHOICE

1. c   An exchange rate is the rate at which one country's currency can be exchanged for another country's currency. See page 840.

2. a   With perfectly flexible exchange rates the balance of payments must sum to zero; thus the financial and capital account must be in surplus if the current account is in deficit. The government financial account could not be negative because if there are perfectly flexible exchange rates, there are no net government transactions. See pages 836-840 and 853-854.

3. a   Although net investment income might seem to many people as if it goes in the financial and capital account, it is a return for a service and is considered part of the current account, as is discussed on page 838.

4. a   A surplus in the government financial account means the balance of payments would otherwise be in deficit. The country is buying up its own currency. This means it is trying to hold up its exchange rate. See pages 847-849.

5. b   See pages 839-840.

6. a   Running a financial and capital account surplus is the other side of the balance

sheet from the trade deficit. See pages 839-840.

7. a   All the others allow free exchange of currency and hence would not generate a black market. See page 828.

8. b   To purchase greater amounts of U.S. products, the European Union must increase the supply of euros, pushing down the value of the euro relative to the dollar. See pages 840-842.

9. a   To purchase greater amounts of European products, U.S. citizens must increase the supply of their currency, pushing down its value relative to the euro. That means that the value of the euro rises relative to the dollar. See pages 840-842.

10. c   If U.S. income increases, the U.S. demand for European imports will increase, shifting the demand for euros out to the right. See pages 840-842.

11. c   An increase in European interest rates will increase the demand for European assets. As a result, the demand for euros will shift out to the right. In addition, Europeans will substitute domestic assets for foreign assets, shifting the supply of euros to the left. See pages 840-842.

12. d   An increase in European inflation will reduce the demand for European goods. Foreigners will demand fewer euros with which to buy European goods and Europeans will supply more euros as they exchange euros for other currencies to buy cheaper goods abroad. See pages 840-842.

13. b   Expansionary monetary policy decreases interest rates and thereby tends to decrease the exchange rate in the short run. See pages 843-846.

14. b   See the diagram on page 845.

15. c   See the diagram on page 845.

16. a   At P_1, there is an excess supply of dollars. To keep the value of the dollar from falling, the U.S. will have to buy up that excess using official reserves of foreign currencies. Disallowing conversion except at an official rate would make the dollar a nonconvertible currency. See pages 847-849.

17. b   Since the purchasing power parity exchange rate is lower than the actual exchange rate, the taka is undervalued. See pages 850-851.

18. d   The real exchange rate has fallen 6 percent: $[-5+(3-4)]$. See pages 851-852.

19. b   To keep the exchange rate at the stated amount, governments must be willing to buy and sell currencies so that the quantity supplied and quantity demanded are always equal at the fixed rate. See pages 852-853.

20. b   There are no predetermined levels of change with a flexible exchange rate. See pages 853-855.

21. a   Under a fixed exchange rate system, countries must use their monetary policies to meet international commitments. Thus flexible exchange rate policies allow them more flexibility in their monetary policies. Flexible exchange rates *may* allow them more flexibility in their industrial policies, but flexible exchange rates *definitely* do allow them more flexibility in their monetary policy, so a is the preferred answer. See pages 853-855.

22. b   A common currency reduces barriers to trade among member nations, thereby broadening the potential marketplace for domestic producers. See pages 855-856.

A1. a.   See pages 861-863.

A2. a.   When there is an imbalance of trade in the gold system, gold—which is money—flows from the deficit country to the surplus country, pushing the price level down in the deficit country and up in the surplus country. This process brings about a trade balance equilibrium, eventually. See pages 861-863.

A3. a   See pages 861-863 about the flow of gold. The last two answers could be eliminated since the gold standard involves fixed exchange rates.

A4. c   As discussed on page 863, SDRs refers to Special Drawing Rights.

━━━━━ ANSWERS ━━━━━

POTENTIAL ESSAY QUESTIONS

The following are annotated answers. They indicate the general idea behind the answer.

1.   If a country is experiencing a balance of payments deficit (the quantity supplied of its currency exceeds the quantity demanded at the current exchange rate), then its currency will fall in value over time. A country's government could prevent its currency from falling (depreciating) by buying its own currency in exchange rate markets. If it does, then this shows up in the government financial account as a plus sign and we say that the government is supporting the value of its currency. The opposite is also true. Because a country can create and then sell its own currency, it is easier for a country to push the value of its currency down than up.

2.   Notice the "margin list" on page 768. Most nations have opted for a partially flexible exchange rate policy in order to try to get the advantages of both a fixed and a flexible exchange rate.

MACRO POLICY IN A GLOBAL SETTING

37

CHAPTER AT A GLANCE

This review is based upon the learning objectives that open the chapter.

1a. There is significant debate about what U.S. international goals should be because exchange rates have conflicting effects and, depending on the state of the economy, there are arguments for high and low exchange rates. (864-867)

A high exchange rate (strong value of the $) helps hold down the prices of imports and therefore inflation. However, it creates a trade deficit that has a depressing effect on aggregate demand and therefore the income level.

1b. Running a trade deficit is good in the short run but presents problems in the long run; thus there is debate about whether we should worry about a trade deficit or not. (865-866)

Trade deficit→ imports > exports.

Short-run benefit: We are able to consume more than we would otherwise be able to.

Long-run cost: We have to sell off U.S. assets because we are consuming more than we are producing. All the future interest and profits on those assets will thus go to foreigners, not U.S. citizens.

A country with fixed exchange rates must give up any attempt to target domestic interest rates to achieve domestic goals.

2. Monetary policy affects the trade balance primarily through the income path as shown in the diagram on page 868. (868)

Expansionary monetary policy makes a trade deficit larger.

Contractionary monetary policy makes a trade deficit smaller.

✔ *Be able to explain why!*

3. Fiscal policy affects the trade deficit primarily though the income path as shown in the diagram on page 869. (868-869)

Expansionary fiscal policy increases a trade deficit.

Contractionary fiscal policy decreases a trade deficit.

✔ *Be able to explain why!*

4. Governments try to coordinate their monetary and fiscal policies with other governments because their economies are interdependent. (869-871)

Each country will likely do what's best for the world economy as long as it is also best for itself.

5. While internationalizing a country's debt may help in the short run, in the long run it presents potential problems, since foreign ownership of a country's debts means the country must pay interest to those foreign countries and that debt may come due. (871)

The United States has been internationalizing its debt since the early 1980s, which means that it must, at some point in the future, export more than it imports (consume less than it produces) to pay for this.

6. Macro policy must be conducted within the setting of a country's overall competitiveness. (872-874)

In recent years the U.S. comparative advantage has been in assets, not produced goods. When foreigners cease wanting to purchase dollars or U.S. assets, the U.S. dollar will depreciate.

● SHORT-ANSWER QUESTIONS

1. What should U.S. international goals be?

2. Why can a country achieve an interest rate target or an exchange rate target, but generally cannot achieve both at the same time?

3. Which dominates for a country: domestic or international goals? Why?

4. If a country runs contractionary monetary policy, what will likely happen to the trade balance?

5. If a country runs contractionary fiscal policy, what will likely happen to the trade balance?

6. Given the difficulty of doing so, why do countries try to coordinate their monetary and fiscal policies with other countries?

7. The United States in recent years has run a large current account deficit and has become the world's largest debtor nation. What are some of the potential problems that this presents?

8. If foreigners began to demand fewer U.S. assets, why might U.S. policy makers be forced to consider contractionary monetary and fiscal policy?

9. What would happen to U.S. comparative advantage in production of goods if the U.S. dollar fell?

● PROBLEMS AND APPLICATIONS

1. You observe that over the past decade, a country's competitiveness has improved, reducing its trade deficit.

    a. What monetary or fiscal policies might have led to such results? Why?

b. You also observe that interest rates have steadily fallen along with a fall in the exchange rate. What monetary or fiscal policies might have led to such results?

2. You have been hired as an adviser to Fantasyland, a country with perfectly flexible exchange rates. State what monetary and fiscal policies you might suggest in each of the following situations. Explain your answers.

a. You want to increase domestic income and to reduce the exchange rate.

b. You want to reduce interest rates, reduce inflation, and reduce the trade deficit.

c. You want lower unemployment, lower interest rates, a lower exchange rate, and a lower trade deficit.

● A BRAIN TEASER

1. Suppose a country has been running a significant expansionary fiscal policy for many years. Monetary policy has been neutral. What can you expect to have happened to this country's trade balance? What are the benefits and costs of this trade imbalance? If this country wishes to correct for its trade imbalance, what fiscal and monetary policies would you suggest this country pursue now? Will your recommended polices coincide or conflict with any of the country's domestic goals? If so, which goals?

● MULTIPLE CHOICE

Circle the one best answer for each of the following questions:

1. Countries prefer:
   a. a high exchange rate.
   b. a low exchange rate.
   c. sometimes a low and sometimes a high exchange rate.
   d. a fixed exchange rate.

2. Countries prefer:
   a. a trade deficit.
   b. a trade surplus.
   c. sometimes a trade deficit and sometimes a trade surplus.
   d. a trade equilibrium.

3. If a country wants to maintain a fixed exchange rate above equilibrium, but does not have the necessary official reserves, it can:
   a. increase demand for its currency by running contractionary monetary policy.
   b. reduce the supply of its currency by running expansionary monetary policy.
   c. increase demand for its currency by running contractionary fiscal policy.
   d. increase supply of its currency by running expansionary fiscal policy.

4. If the trade deficit has gone up, it is most likely that the government ran:
   a. an expansionary monetary policy.
   b. a contractionary monetary policy.
   c. a contractionary fiscal policy.
   d. an expansionary monetary policy and a contractionary fiscal policy.

5. Expansionary monetary policy tends to push income:
   a. down and the trade deficit down.
   b. down and the trade deficit up.
   c. up and the trade deficit down.
   d. up and the trade deficit up.

6. Contractionary fiscal policy tends to push:
   a. income down and imports up.
   b. income down and the trade deficit up.
   c. income down and the trade deficit down.
   d. prices down and imports up.

7. Assume the United States would like to raise
    its exchange rate and lower its trade deficit. It
    would pressure Japan to run:
    a. contractionary monetary policy.
    b. contractionary fiscal policy.
    c. expansionary monetary policy.
    d. expansionary fiscal policy.

8. According to the textbook, generally, when
    international goals and domestic goals
    conflict:
    a. the international goals win out.
    b. the domestic goals win out.
    c. sometimes it's a toss-up which will win out.
    d. international monetary goals win out but
       international fiscal goals lose out.

9. When a country runs a large trade deficit, the
    amount of crowding out that occurs because
    of fiscal policy is:
    a. increased.
    b. decreased.
    c. unaffected.
    d. sometimes increased and sometimes
       decreased.

10. A country has the greatest domestic policy
    flexibility with:
    a. fixed exchange rates.
    b. flexible exchange rates.
    c. a trade deficit.
    d. a trade surplus.

11. A sudden fall in the price of the dollar in terms
    of other countries' currencies will most likely
    make policy makers face the possibility of
    implementing:
    a. capital inflow controls.
    b. import subsidies.
    c. contractionary macro policy.
    d. expansionary macro policy.

● POTENTIAL ESSAY QUESTIONS

*You may also see essay questions similar to the "Problems
& Applications" and "A Brain Teaser" exercises.*

1. If there was initially a trade balance, what kind
    of trade imbalance would be created by an
    increase in the exchange rate value of the dollar
    (a stronger dollar)? Why?

2. What are the benefits and costs to the United
    States of having a strong dollar–a high
    exchange rate value of the dollar?

3. Why do domestic economic goals usually
    dominate international economic goals?

ANSWERS

SHORT-ANSWER QUESTIONS

1. By "international goals" economists usually mean the exchange rate and the trade balance that policy makers should shoot for. There is significant debate in the United States about what our international goals should be, and there are arguments for both high and low exchange rates, and for both trade deficits and trade surpluses. The argument for a high exchange rate is that it lowers the cost of imports; the argument against it is that it raises the price of exports, making U.S. goods less competitive. The argument in favor of a trade deficit is that it allows a country to consume more than it produces; the argument against is that a trade deficit will have to be paid off at some point. (864-867)

2. Because monetary policy affects the value of one's currency, a country cannot target both interest rates and exchange rates simultaneously. Suppose one's currency is at its desired level, but interest rates are too high. Expansionary monetary policy would lower the interest rate, but a lower interest rate reduces foreign demand for the country's interest-bearing assets. The demand for one's currency will shift in to the left and its exchange rate will fall. Likewise, citizens of the country will invest elsewhere and the supply of one's currency will shift out to the right. The value of one's currency will be lower than its target. (864-865, 868)

3. Generally, domestic goals dominate for two reasons: (1) International goals are often ambiguous, as discussed in answer 1 above, and (2) international goals affect a country's population indirectly and, in politics, indirect effects take a back seat. (869-870)

4. Contractionary monetary policy tends to push income down. Lower income means lower imports, lowering the trade deficit. (868-869)

5. Contractionary fiscal policy pushes income down. This tends to decrease imports and decrease a trade deficit. (868-869)

6. The policies of one country affect the economy of another. So it is only natural that the two countries try to coordinate their policies. It is also only natural that since voters are concerned with their own countries, coordination is difficult to achieve unless it is in the interest of both countries. (869-871)

7. While internationalizing a country's debt may help in the short run, in the long run it presents potential problems, since foreign ownership of a country's debts means the debtor country must pay interest to the foreign countries, and also, that debt may come due. (871)

8. If foreigners begin to demand fewer U.S. assets, the financial and capital account surplus would fall and there would be downward pressure on the price of the U.S dollar. A dramatic decline in the price of the dollar would cause inflation to rise. If that happened policy makers would likely consider contractionary monetary and fiscal policy to stem the decline in the dollar and the acceleration of inflation. (872-874)

9. If the U.S. dollar fell, U.S. goods would be less expensive to foreigners, improving the U.S. comparative advantage in a number of produced goods. (872-874)

ANSWERS

PROBLEMS AND APPLICATIONS

1. a. An increase in competitiveness and a decrease in the trade deficit are probably due to contractionary fiscal policy. Contractionary fiscal policy reduces inflation, improves competitiveness, and decreases income, which reduces imports. Improved competitiveness and decreased income both work to reduce the trade deficit. Contractionary monetary policy would also reduce the trade deficit, but its effect on competitiveness is ambiguous. (868-870)

   b. If interest rates have also fallen, it is likely that fiscal policy has been very contractionary because contractionary monetary policy would have led to higher interest rates and a higher exchange rate value of the dollar. (868-870)

2. **a.** Expansionary monetary policy will reduce the exchange rate through its effect on interest rates and will increase domestic income. Expansionary fiscal policy will increase domestic income. The increase in income will increase imports, which will tend to decrease the exchange rate, but higher interest rates will tend to lead to a higher exchange rate. The effect of expansionary fiscal policy on exchange rates is therefore ambiguous. (868-870)

b. Contractionary fiscal policy will tend to reduce inflation and interest rates. The reduction in inflation will improve competitiveness and a reduction in income will reduce imports. Both work to reduce the trade deficit. (868-870)

c. Expansionary monetary policy will reduce unemployment and reduce interest rates. Lower interest rates will tend to make exchange rates fall. Expansionary monetary policy, however, will make the trade deficit higher. Expansionary fiscal policy will also reduce unemployment. Interest rates, however, will rise and so will the trade deficit. This mix of goals is difficult to attain. (868-870)

ANSWERS

A BRAIN TEASER

1. Because of the expansionary fiscal policy, this country will have moved in the direction of a trade deficit. The benefit of the trade deficit is that the country has been able to consume more than it has produced. The cost, however, is that it has had to sell off some of its assets. All the future interest and profits on these assets will now go to foreigners, not the country's citizens.

To reduce the trade deficit the country should pursue contractionary fiscal and monetary policies. This will reduce imports and increase exports and increase the country's competitiveness in the global economy. That's good. However, even though fewer imports and greater exports should help stimulate aggregate expenditures, the effects of the

contractionary fiscal and monetary policies are also simultaneously at play. Aggregate demand may fall on balance. If it does, then you may have created a recession. That's bad. Sometimes, countries can find themselves "in a pickle." (There could be other effects associated with the prescribed contractionary policies.) (865-866, 868-870, 872-874)

ANSWERS

MULTIPLE CHOICE

1. c   The answer is "sometimes a low and sometimes a high exchange rate" because, as discussed on pages 864-865, there are rationales for both.

2. c   The domestic economy's needs change over time and as they do, so does the country's preferred trade situation. Both a deficit and a surplus have their advantages and disadvantages. See pages 865-866.

3. a   Contractionary monetary policy will increase the demand for one's currency and increase its value. Contractionary fiscal policy will reduce the supply of one's currency and increase its value. Contractionary monetary and fiscal policy are two ways to fix one's exchange rate without intervening in the exchange market. See pages 868-869.

4. a   Both expansionary monetary policy and expansionary fiscal policy increase the trade deficit. Thus, only a fits. See the discussion and charts on pages 868-869.

5. d   See the discussion and diagram on pages 868-869.

6. c   See diagram on page 869 and the discussion on pages 868-869.

7. c   The effect of fiscal policy on the exchange rate is ambiguous, so the only sure option is c. See the box on page 870.

8. b As discussed in the text on pages 869-871, usually, because of political considerations, domestic goals win out.

9. b Since the trade deficit means capital is flowing into the country, the capital usually ends up buying some government debt, which reduces crowding out, as discussed on page 871.

10. b When exchange rates are left to the market (flexible), the government does not have to change its domestic policy to meet its international goal for its exchange rate. Therefore, it is freer to follow domestic policy when exchange rates are flexible. See page 868.

11. c If the price of the dollar falls significantly in the forex market, policy makers will likely be under pressure to slow the fall and prevent inflation, which means that they will have to face the possibility of implementing contractionary policy to keep the dollar from falling too much. The other options are not ones associated with a falling price of the dollar. See pages 864 and 868.

■ ANSWERS ■

POTENTIAL ESSAY QUESTIONS

The following are annotated answers. They indicate the general idea behind the answer.

1. A stronger dollar means that a single dollar will now buy more units of a foreign currency. This makes foreign products cheaper to Americans. The United States would import more. At the same time, a stronger dollar means it will now take more units of a foreign currency to buy a single dollar. This will cause U.S. goods to become more expensive to foreigners. The United States would export less. The combined effects of more U.S. imports and fewer U.S. exports mean a trade deficit will be created or will get larger in the United States.

2. A strong dollar holds down the price of imports and therefore inflation. However, the cost is a trade deficit that would have a depressing effect on total spending and therefore on the nation's income level (there would be an especially depressing effect on the nation's exporting industries).

3. First, there is more agreement on domestic goals. Second, domestic goals affect people within one's country more directly. Finally, pursuing domestic goals is politically more appealing.

MACRO POLICIES IN DEVELOPING COUNTRIES

38

● CHAPTER AT A GLANCE

This review is based upon the learning objectives that open the chapter.

1. Seventy-five percent of the world's population lives in developing countries, with average per capita income of under $500 per year. (877-879)

    Be careful in judging a society by its income alone. Some developing countries may have cultures preferable to ours. Ideally, growth would occur without destroying the culture.

2. There are differences in normative goals between developing and developed countries because their wealth differs. Developing countries face basic economic needs whereas developed countries' economic needs are considered by most people to be normatively less pressing. (880-881)

    The main focus of macro policy in developing countries is on how to increase growth through development to fulfill people's basic needs.

3. Economies at different stages of development have different institutional needs because the problems they face are different. Institutions that can be assumed in developed countries cannot necessarily be assumed to exist in developing countries. (881-882)

    Developed nations have stable governments and market structures, which are often lacking in developing countries.

4. "The dual economy" refers to the existence of the two sectors in most developing countries: a traditional sector and an internationally-oriented modern market sector. (882)

    Often, the largest percentage of the population participates in the traditional sector. Tradition often resists change.

5. A régime change is a change in the entire atmosphere within which the government and the economy interrelate; a policy change is a change in one aspect of government's actions. (883)

    A régime change and macro institutional policies designed to fit the cultural and social dimensions of developing economics are what developing economies need.

6. Central banks recognize that printing too much money causes inflation, but often feel compelled to do so for political reasons. Debate about inflation in developing countries generally concerns those political reasons, not the relationship between money and inflation. (884-886)

    Governments in developing economies risk being thrown out of office unless they run deficits and issue too much money.

7. Full convertibility means one can exchange one's currency for whatever legal purpose one wants. Convertibility on the current account limits those exchanges for the purpose of buying goods and services. (886-887)

    Very few developing countries allow full convertibility.

8. Seven obstacles facing developing countries are: (888-897)
    1. Political instability.
    2. Corruption.
    3. Lack of appropriate institutions.
    4. Lack of investment.
    5. Inappropriate education.
    6. Overpopulation.
    7. Health and disease

    ✔ *Know why these are problems!*
    ✔ *The opposite constitutes the ingredients for growth. Remember them!*

● SHORT-ANSWER QUESTIONS

1. What percentage of the population of the world lives in developing countries?

2. What is the average per capita income in developing nations?

3. Why is there often a difference in the normative goals of developed and developing countries?

4. Why do economies at different stages of development often have different institutional needs? Explain.

5. What is the dual economy?

6. What is the difference between a regime change and a policy change?

7. Inflation is simply a problem of central banks in developing countries issuing too much money. Is this true or false? Why?

8. What are two types of convertibility?

9. Economists can't tell developing countries, "Here's what you have to do to grow." But they can identify seven obstacles facing developing countries. What are they?

MATCHING THE TERMS
Match the terms to their definitions

___ 1.	balance of payments constraint	a.	A change in one aspect of a government's actions.
___ 2.	brain drain	b.	A change in the entire atmosphere within which the government and economy interrelate.
___ 3.	conditionality	c.	A stage when the development process becomes self-sustaining.
___ 4.	convertibility on the current account	d.	A system that allows people to exchange currencies for whatever legal purpose they want.
___ 5.	credentialism	e.	A system that allows people to exchange currencies for the purpose of buying goods and services only.
___ 6.	dual economy	f.	A system that places some limitation on people's ability to exchange currencies to buy assets.
___ 7.	economic takeoff	g.	Changing the underlying economic institutions.
___ 8.	foreign aid	h.	Funds that developed countries lend or give to developing countries.
___ 9.	full convertibility	i.	Investment in the underlying structure of the economy.
___ 10.	infrastructure investment	j.	Limitations on expansionary domestic macroeconomic policy due to a shortage of international reserves.
___ 11.	limited capital account convertibility	k.	Method of comparing income by looking at the domestic purchasing power of money in different countries.
___ 12.	policy change	l.	Outflow of the best and brightest students from developing countries to developed countries.
___ 13.	purchasing power parity	m.	The degrees become more important than the knowledge learned.
___ 14.	regime change	n.	The existence of two sectors: a traditional sector and an internationally-oriented modern market sector.
___ 15.	restructuring	o.	The making of loans that are subject to specific conditions.

● A BRAIN TEASER

1. You are the chief economic adviser to a developing country that is politically stable and possesses a culture you believe to be conducive to growth. What economic policies would you recommend to the developing country to enhance its growth and development?

● MULTIPLE CHOICE

Circle the one best answer for each of the following questions:

1. Annual GDP per capita is about ____ in developing countries and ____ in developed countries.
    a. $50; $20,000.
    b. $500; $40,000.
    c. $50; $10,000.
    d. $4,000; $20,000.

2. Two methods of comparing income among countries are the purchasing power parity method and the exchange rate method. Of these:
    a. the exchange rate method generally gives a higher relative measure of the income in developing countries.
    b. the purchasing power parity method generally gives a higher relative measure of the income in developing countries.
    c. the purchasing power parity and exchange rate methods generally give approximately equal measures of the income in developing countries.
    d. sometimes one gives a higher relative measure of income in developing countries, and sometimes the other gives a higher relative measure.

3. The concept "dual economy" refers to:
    a. the tendency of developed countries to have a traditional sector and an internationally-oriented sector.
    b. the tendency of both developed and developing countries to have a traditional sector and an internationally-oriented sector.
    c. the tendency of developing countries to have a traditional sector and an internationally-oriented sector.
    d. the fight, or dual, between developed and undeveloped countries.

4. If a country changes its entire approach to policy, that is called:
    a. a major policy change.
    b. a policy change.
    c. a regime change.
    d. a constitutional change.

5. The inflation tax is:
    a. a tax on those individuals who cause inflation.
    b. a tax on firms who cause inflation.
    c. a tax on both individuals and firms who cause inflation.
    d. a tax on holders of cash and any obligations specified in nominal terms.

6. The "revenue" of an inflation tax:
    a. goes only to government.
    b. goes only to private individuals.
    c. goes to both private individuals and government.
    d. is a meaningless term because there is no revenue from an inflation tax.

7. If you hold a fixed interest rate debt denominated in domestic currency and inflation rises more than expected, you will:
    a. likely lose.
    b. likely gain.
    c. likely experience no effect from the large inflation.
    d. find that the large inflation could cause you either to gain or to lose.

8. If you hold a fixed interest rate debt denominated in a foreign currency and the exchange rate remains constant, and there is a large domestic inflation, you will:
    a. likely lose some.
    b. likely gain some.
    c. likely lose all your debt.
    d. likely experience little direct effect from the large inflation.

9. Conditionality refers to:
    a. the U.S. government's policy of only making loans to countries who will repay loans.
    b. the IMF's policy of making loans to countries subject to specific conditions.
    c. central banks' policies of making loans to firms only under certain conditions.
    d. the conditions under which inter-firm credit is allowed in transitional economies.

10. Foreign aid is:
    a. the primary source of income of the poorest developing countries.
    b. one of the top three sources of income of the poorest developing countries.
    c. one of the top three sources of income of developing countries who have ties to the United States.
    d. a minor source of income for developing countries.

11. The nickname for economics as "the dismal science" caught on because
   a. the law of diminishing marginal productivity predicted famine.
   b. the law of diseconomies of scale predicted famine.
   c. learning supply and demand economic models is dismal.
   d. it predicted that economic takeoff would seldom be reached.

12. If population grows geometrically, the amount of land is fixed, and there is diminishing marginal productivity, then:
   a. famine is in the future.
   b. income per person will decrease but there will not necessarily be famine.
   c. famine is not in the future if there is technological development.
   d. famine may or may not be in the future.

13. Which of the following best represents the textbook author's view of development?
   a. Optimal strategies for growth are country-specific.
   b. A country's development strategy should include as much education as possible.
   c. Countries should focus on infrastructure investment.
   d. Countries should follow a policy of laissez-faire.

● POTENTIAL ESSAY QUESTIONS

You may also see essay questions similar to the "Problems & Applications" and "A Brain Teaser" exercises.

1. What is the difference between economic development and economic growth?

2. What are some institutional differences between developed and developing countries that make it difficult for developing countries to develop?

3. Why is it that no developing country allows full convertibility?

ANSWERS

SHORT-ANSWER QUESTIONS

1. 75 percent of the population of the world lives in developing countries. (877)

2. The average per capita income in developing countries is about $500 per year. (877)

3. Developing countries face true economic needs. Their concern is with basic needs such as adequate clothing, food, and shelter. Developed countries' needs are considered less pressing. For example, will everyone have access to a DVD player? (880-881)

4. Economies at different stages of development have different institutional needs because the problems they face are different. Institutions that can be assumed in developed countries cannot necessarily be assumed to exist in developing countries. For example, developing countries often lack the institutional structure that markets require. (881--883)

5. Dual economy refers to the existence of the two distinct sectors in most developing countries: a traditional sector and an internationally-oriented modern market sector. (882)

6. A regime change is a change in the entire atmosphere within which the government and the economy interrelate; a policy change is a change in one aspect of government's actions. A regime change affects underlying expectations about what the government will do in the future; a policy change does not. (883)

7. Any simple statement is generally false, and this one is no exception. The reason why this one is false is that while it is true that inflation is closely tied to the developing country's central bank issuing too much money, the underlying problem behind the central bank's actions is often large government deficits that cannot be financed unless the central bank issues debt and then buys the bonds, which requires an increase in the money supply (printing money to pay for the bonds). (884-886)

8. Two types of convertibility are full convertibility and current account convertibility. Full convertibility means you can change your money into another currency with no restrictions. Current account convertibility allows exchange of currency to buy goods but not to invest outside the country. Many developing countries have current account convertibility, but not full convertibility. (886-887)

9. Seven problems facing developing countries are (1) governments in developing countries are often unstable, (2) governments in developing countries are often corrupt, (3) developing countries often lack appropriate institutions to promote growth, (4) developing countries often lack the domestic savings to fund investment for growth, (5) developing countries tend to have too much of the wrong education, (6) developing countries are often overpopulated so that raising per capita income is difficult, and (7) people in developing countries have limited access to healthcare and face greater incidence of disease. (888-897)

ANSWERS

MATCHING

1-j; 2-l; 3-o; 4-e; 5-m; 6-n; 7-c; 8-h; 9-d; 10-i; 11-f; 12-a; 13-k; 14-b; 15-g.

ANSWERS

A BRAIN TEASER

1. Macro institutional policies—those designed to change the underlying macro institutions, and thereby increase output—are what is necessary for development. Although there is some debate about exactly what constitutes the right set of policies for development, all economists agree that developing countries need to get the infrastructure right. That is, they must create a climate within which individual initiative is directed toward production. (888-897)

ANSWERS

MULTIPLE CHOICE

1. b   As stated on page 877, b is the closest.

2. b   As discussed on page 879, the purchasing power parity method of comparing income

cuts income differences among countries in half.

3. c See page 882 for the definition of dual economy. Choice d was put in to throw you off. When the word means "a fight" it is, of course, spelled "duel."

4. c See page 883.

5. d. The answer has to be d, as discussed on page 885. The individuals and firms who cause the inflation are gaining from the inflation; they pay no inflation tax.

6. c The only answer that makes any sense is c. The "revenue" goes from holders of fixed nominal interest rate debt to those who owe that debt. Those who owe the debt include both private individuals and government. See page 885.

7. a Unexpected inflation wipes out the value of fixed interest rate debt. See page 885.

8. d Because the debt is denominated in a foreign currency and exchange rates remain constant, what happens to the domestic price level does not directly affect you. There could be indirect effects, but d specifies direct effects. See pages 885-888.

9. b See page 887.

10. d Total foreign aid comes to less than $14 per person for developing countries. While this does not preclude b or c, it makes it very difficult for them to be true, and in fact, they are not true. See pages 890-893.

11. a The nickname "the dismal science" was used by Thomas Carlyle in an attack on economists for their views against slavery. It became a popular description of economics however largely because of the writings of Thomas Malthus, whose model of population focused on the law of diminishing marginal productivity and led to the prediction that society's prospects were dismal because population tends to outrun the means of subsistence. See pages 896-897.

12. d As discussed on pages 895-897, the Malthusian doctrine predicted famine

based on the elements of this question. That doctrine did not, however, take into account technological development. Technological growth can offset the tendencies for famine. But technological growth does not necessarily have to offset those tendencies; thus c is wrong, and d is the only correct answer.

13. a As discussed on pages 895-897, the author believes the problems of economic development are intertwined with cultural and social issues and hence are country-specific. The other answers do not necessarily fail to reflect the author's viewpoint, but he presented arguments on both sides when discussing them. Thus, a is the best answer.

■ **ANSWERS** ■

POTENTIAL ESSAY QUESTIONS

The following are annotated answers. They indicate the general idea behind the answer.

1. Growth occurs because of an increase in inputs, given a production function. Development occurs through a change in the production function. Development involves more fundamental changes in the institutional structure than does growth.

2. First, developing nations often lack stable, socially-minded governments with which to undertake policy. Second, developing economies often have a dual economy, that is, a traditional and an international sector. This can create some policy dilemmas. A third difference is the way in which fiscal policy is run. Collecting taxes can be very difficult in developing countries. Expenditures are often mandated by political survival.

3. One reason is that they want to force their residents to keep their savings, and to do their investing, in their home country, not abroad. (Remember that saving is necessary for investment, and investment is necessary for growth.) These citizens usually don't want to do this because of the risks of leaving their money in their own countries; a new government takeover could possibly take it all away.

Pretest
Chapters 36-38

Take this test in test conditions, giving yourself a limited amount of time to complete the questions. Ideally, check with your professor to see how much time he or she allows for an average multiple choice question and multiply this by 17. This is the time limit you should set for yourself for this pretest. If you do not know how much time your teacher would allow, we suggest 1 minute per question, or about 20 minutes.

1. If a country has perfectly flexible exchange rates and is running a current account deficit, it is running:
   a. a financial and capital account surplus.
   b. a financial and capital account deficit.
   c. a government financial account surplus.
   d. a government financial account deficit.

2. In recent years, the United States has:
   a. generally run a balance of trade surplus.
   b. generally run a balance of trade deficit.
   c. sometimes run a balance of trade surplus and sometimes run a balance of trade deficit.
   d. generally run a balance of trade equality.

3. Assuming flexible exchange rates, if the European demand for U.S. imports increases, one would expect the price of euros in terms of dollars to:
   a. rise.
   b. fall.
   c. remain unchanged.
   d. sometimes rise and sometimes fall.

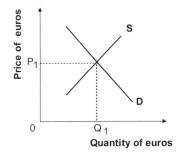

4. Refer to the graph of the foreign exchange market above. If U.S. income increases the:
   a. supply curve will shift out to the right.
   b. supply curve will shift in to the left.
   c. demand curve will shift out to the right.
   d. demand curve will shift in to the left.

5. If a country with flexible exchange rates runs expansionary monetary policy, in the short run one would expect the value of its exchange rate to:
   a. rise.
   b. fall.
   c. be unaffected.
   d. sometimes rise and sometimes fall.

6. Suppose inflation in the United States is 3 percent and inflation in Europe is 4 percent. If the U.S. dollar exchange rate falls by 5 percent relative to the euro, the real exchange rate of the dollar relative to the euro has:
   a. risen 2 percent.
   b. risen 6 percent.
   c. fallen 2 percent.
   d. fallen 6 percent.

7. If a country has a flexible exchange rate, the exchange rate:
   a. is determined by flexible government policy.
   b. is determined by market forces.
   c. fluctuates continually, changing by at least 1 percent per year.
   d. fluctuates continually, changing by at least 10 percent per year.

8. Compared to a fixed exchange rate system, a flexible exchange rate system:
   a. allows countries more flexibility in their monetary policies.
   b. allows countries less flexibility in their monetary policies.
   c. has no effect on monetary policies.
   d. allows countries more flexibility in their industrial policies.

9. If a country wants to maintain a fixed exchange rate above equilibrium, but does not have the necessary official reserves, it can:
    a. increase demand for its currency by running contractionary monetary policy.
    b. reduce the supply of its currency by running expansionary monetary policy.
    c. increase demand for its currency by running contractionary fiscal policy.
    d. increase supply of its currency by running expansionary fiscal policy.

10. If the trade deficit has gone up, it is most likely that the government ran:
    a. an expansionary monetary policy.
    b. a contractionary monetary policy.
    c. a contractionary fiscal policy.
    d. an expansionary monetary policy and a contractionary fiscal policy.

11. Expansionary monetary policy tends to push income:
    a. down and the trade deficit down.
    b. down and the trade deficit up.
    c. up and the trade deficit down.
    d. up and the trade deficit up.

12. Assume the United States would like to raise its exchange rate and lower its trade deficit. It would pressure Japan to run:
    a. contractionary monetary policy.
    b. contractionary fiscal policy.
    c. expansionary monetary policy.
    d. expansionary fiscal policy.

13. A country has the greatest domestic policy flexibility with:
    a. fixed exchange rates.
    b. flexible exchange rates.
    c. a trade deficit.
    d. a trade surplus.

14. Two methods of comparing income among countries are the purchasing power parity method and the exchange rate method. Of these:
    a. the exchange rate method generally gives a higher relative measure of the income in developing countries.
    b. the purchasing power parity method generally gives a higher relative measure of the income in developing countries.

    c. the purchasing power parity and exchange rate methods generally give approximately equal measures of the income in developing countries.
    d. sometimes one gives a higher relative measure of income in developing countries, and sometimes the other gives a higher relative measure.

15. The "revenue" of an inflation tax:
    a. goes only to government.
    b. goes only to private individuals.
    c. goes to both private individuals and government.
    d. is a meaningless term because there is no revenue from an inflation tax.

16. Conditionality refers to:
    a. the U.S. government's policy of only making loans to countries who will repay loans.
    b. the IMF's policy of making loans to countries subject to specific conditions.
    c. central banks' policies of making loans to firms only under certain conditions.
    d. the conditions under which inter-firm credit is allowed in transitional economies.

17. If population grows geometrically, the amount of land is fixed, and there is diminishing marginal productivity, then:
    a. famine is in the future.
    b. income per person will decrease but there will not necessarily be famine.
    c. famine is not in the future if there is technological development.
    d. famine may or may not be in the future.

ANSWERS

1.	a	(36:2)	10.	a	(37:4)
2.	b	(36:5)	11.	d	(37:5)
3.	b	(36:8)	12.	c	(37:7)
4.	c	(36:10)	13.	b	(37:10)
5.	b	(36:13)	14.	b	(38:2)
6.	d	(36:18)	15.	c	(38:6)
7.	b	(36:20)	16.	b	(38:9)
8.	a	(36:21)	17.	d	(38:12)
9.	a	(37:3)			

Key: The figures in parentheses refer to multiple choice question and chapter numbers. For example (1:2) is multiple choice question 2 from chapter 1.